NEW YORK TIMES BESTSELLER

MARK

P9-DBR-307

AUTHOR *of* PICTURES AT A REVOLUTION

FIVE CAME BACK

A STORY OF HOLLYWOOD AND THE SECOND WORLD WAR

NOW A
NETFLIX ORIGINAL
DOCUMENTARY SERIES

NETFLIX

"HARRIS HAS A HUGE STORY TO TELL, AND HE DOES SO BRILLIANTLY." —THE WALL STREET JOURNAL

| JOHN | GEORGE | JOHN | WILLIAM | FRANK |
| FORD | STEVENS | HUSTON | WYLER | CAPRA |

"In *Five Came Back*, Mark Harris's can't-put-it-down history of World War II propaganda films, he . . . shows how the war changed the filmmakers and how the filmmakers changed the cinematic language and content of Hollywood movies."

—*San Francisco Chronicle*

"Harris is handling the broad sweep of history and the themes are rich: Hollywood's fractious relationship with Washington; the ethics of propaganda; real footage versus reenactment; and, most significantly, the impact of the decision to go to war . . . on five influential filmmakers. . . . Harris is a lively commentator, and master weaver of multifarious threads. *Five Came Back* . . . [is] compelling."   —*Empire*

"A fascinating narrative . . . insightful and propulsive . . . Mark Harris has done a superb job winding the separate narratives of five of America's greatest directors together, and his poise in tackling so vast an epoch is a joy to read."   —*A.V. Club*

"Harris is an essential film writer . . . nearly unmatched in relating how people's artistic achievements relate to the times, and he's also a pleasure to read."

—*Flavorwire*

"Harris surpasses previous scholarship on the directors who are the focus here. . . . This well-researched book is essential for both film enthusiasts and World War II aficionados."   —*Library Journal*

"It's hardly news that the movies affect and are affected by the broader canvas of popular culture and world history, but Harris—perhaps more successfully than any other writer, past or present—manages to find in that symbiotic relationship the stuff of great stories. Every chapter contains small, priceless nuggets of movie history, and nearly every page offers an example of Harris's ability to capture the essence of a person or an event in a few, perfectly chosen words. Narrative nonfiction that is as gloriously readable as it is unfailingly informative."

—*Booklist* (starred review)

"A comprehensive, clear-eyed look at the careers of five legendary directors who put their Hollywood lives on freeze-frame while they went off to fight in the only ways they knew how. As riveting and revealing as a film by an Oscar winner."

—*Kirkus Reviews* (starred review)

"Insightful. Harris pens superb exegeses of the ideological currents coursing through this most political of cinematic eras, and in the arcs of his vividly drawn protagonists . . . we see Hollywood abandoning sentimental make-believe to confront the starkest realities."   —*Publishers Weekly* (starred review)

MARK HARRIS

FIVE CAME BACK

A STORY OF HOLLYWOOD
AND THE SECOND WORLD WAR

— ■ —

PENGUIN BOOKS

WILLIAMSBURG REGIONAL LIBRARY
7770 CROAKER ROAD
WILLIAMSBURG, VA 23188

PENGUIN BOOKS
Published by the Penguin Group
Penguin Group (USA) LLC
375 Hudson Street
New York, New York 10014

USA | Canada | UK | Ireland | Australia
New Zealand | India | South Africa | China
penguin.com
A Penguin Random House Company

First published in the United States of America
by The Penguin Press, a member of Penguin Group (USA) LLC, 2014
Published in Penguin Books 2015

Copyright © 2014 by Mark Harris
Penguin supports copyright. Copyright fuels creativity, encourages diverse voices,
promotes free speech, and creates a vibrant culture. Thank you for buying an authorized
edition of this book and for complying with copyright laws by not reproducing, scanning,
or distributing any part of it in any form without permission. You are supporting writers
and allowing Penguin to continue to publish books for every reader.

Photograph credits appear on page 495.

THE LIBRARY OF CONGRESS HAS CATALOGED THE HARDCOVER EDITION AS FOLLOWS:
Harris, Mark, 1963–
Five came back : a story of Hollywood and the Second World War / Mark Harris.
pages   cm.
Includes bibliographical references and index.
ISBN 978-1-59420-430-2 (hc.)
ISBN 978-0-14-312683-6 (pbk.)
1. Motion picture industry—California—Los Angeles—History.
2. Motion pictures—United States—History.
3. World War, 1939–1945—Motion pictures and the war.   I. Title.
PN1993.5.U65H373   2008
791.4302'33092279494—dc23   2013039983

Printed in the United States of America
5   7   9   10   8   6

DESIGNED BY AMANDA DEWEY

WILLIAMSBURG REGIONAL LIBRARY
7770 CROAKER ROAD
WILLIAMSBURG, VA 23188

For my brother

CONTENTS

Prologue: Pearl Harbor 1

PART ONE

1. "The Only Way I Could Survive" *15*
   HOLLYWOOD, MARCH 1938–APRIL 1939

2. "The Dictates of My Heart and Blood" *37*
   HOLLYWOOD AND WASHINGTON, APRIL 1939–MAY 1940

3. "You Must Not Realize that There Is
   a War Going On" *58*
   HOLLYWOOD, JUNE–SEPTEMBER 1940

4. "What's the Good of a Message?" *69*
   HOLLYWOOD, EARLY 1941

5. "The Most Dangerous Fifth Column
   in Our Country" *83*
   HOLLYWOOD AND WASHINGTON, JULY–DECEMBER 1941

PART TWO

— · —

6. "Do I Have to Wait for Orders?" *101*
   HOLLYWOOD, WASHINGTON, AND HAWAII, DECEMBER 1941–APRIL 1942

7. "I've Only Got One German" *117*
   HOLLYWOOD, DECEMBER 1941–APRIL 1942

8. "It's Going to Be a Problem and a Battle" *130*
   WASHINGTON, MARCH–JUNE 1942

9. "All I Know Is That I'm Not Courageous" *145*
   MIDWAY AND WASHINGTON, JUNE–AUGUST 1942

10. "Can You Use Me?" *160*
    WASHINGTON AND HOLLYWOOD, AUGUST–SEPTEMBER 1942

11. "A Good Partner to Have in Times of Trouble" *172*
    ENGLAND, NORTH AFRICA, AND HOLLYWOOD,
    SEPTEMBER 1942–JANUARY 1943

12. "You Might as Well Run into It as Away from It" *186*
    THE ALEUTIAN ISLANDS, HOLLYWOOD, WASHINGTON,
    AND NORTH AFRICA, SEPTEMBER 1942–MAY 1943

13. "Just Enough to Make It Seem Less Than Real" *199*
    ENGLAND, HOLLYWOOD, AND WASHINGTON, JANUARY–MAY 1943

14. "Coming Along with Us Just for Pictures?" *213*
    WASHINGTON, ENGLAND, AND NEW YORK, MARCH–JULY 1943

PART THREE

— —

15. "How to Live in the Army" *231*
    NORTH AFRICA, HOLLYWOOD, FLORIDA, AND WASHINGTON, SUMMER 1943

16. "I'm the Wrong Man for That Stuff" *244*
    WASHINGTON, HOLLYWOOD, AND ENGLAND, JUNE–DECEMBER 1943

17. "I Have to Do a Good Job" *257*
    ENGLAND AND ITALY, OCTOBER 1943–JANUARY 1944

18. "We Really Don't Know What Goes
    On Beneath the Surface" *271*
    WASHINGTON, THE CHINA-BURMA-INDIA THEATER, ITALY,
    AND NEW YORK, SEPTEMBER 1943–MARCH 1944

19. "If You Believe This, We Thank You" *286*
    HOLLYWOOD AND ENGLAND, MARCH–MAY 1944

20. "A Sporadic Raid of Sorts on the Continent" *299*
    HOLLYWOOD, WASHINGTON, AND NEW YORK, MARCH–MAY 1944

21. "If You See It, Shoot It" *310*
    FRANCE, JUNE–JULY 1944

22. "If Hitler Can Hold Out, So Can I" *324*
    HOLLYWOOD AND WASHINGTON, JULY–DECEMBER 1944

23. "Time and Us Marches On" *338*
    FRANCE, BELGIUM, LUXEMBOURG, GERMANY,
    AND ENGLAND, JULY 1944–JANUARY 1945

24. "Who You Working For—Yourself?" *352*

   HOLLYWOOD, FLORIDA, ITALY, AND NEW YORK, FEBRUARY–MAY 1945

25. "Where I Learned About Life" *366*

   GERMANY, MARCH–AUGUST 1945

26. "What's This Picture For?" *378*

   WASHINGTON AND HOLLYWOOD, SUMMER 1945

27. "An Angry Past Commingled with
   the Future in a Storm" *391*

   HOLLYWOOD, NEW YORK, AND GERMANY, 1945

28. "A Straight Face and a Painfully Maturing Mind" *405*

   HOLLYWOOD, NEW YORK, AND WASHINGTON,
   DECEMBER 1945–MARCH 1946

29. "Closer to What Is Going On in the World" *419*

   HOLLYWOOD, MAY 1946–FEBRUARY 1947

Epilogue *439*

Note on Sources and Acknowledgments *445*
Notes *449*
Bibliography *489*
Credits *495*
Index *497*

FIVE CAME BACK

FIVE GAME BACK

Prologue:
Pearl Harbor

John Ford was the first of the five to go. By the time the Imperial Japanese Navy attacked the U.S. military base at Pearl Harbor, he was already three thousand miles from Hollywood and had been in uniform for three months. When news of the bombing came, Ford, now a lieutenant commander in the navy, and his wife, Mary, were guests at a Sunday luncheon at the home of Rear Admiral Andrew Pickens in Alexandria, Virginia. A maid nervously entered the room holding a telephone. "It's the War Department, animal," she said, stumbling over her employer's rank. The visitors braced themselves as the admiral left his table to take the call. He returned to the party and announced, "Gentlemen, Pearl Harbor has just been attacked by the Japanese. We are now at war." As the guests dispersed, the admiral's wife tried to save the afternoon. "It's no use getting excited. This is the seventh war that's been announced in this dining room," she said. She showed the Fords a bullet hole in the wall left by a musket ball during the American Revolution. "I never let them plaster over that," she told them.

Mary Ford later remembered that for "everybody at that table, their lives changed that minute." But Ford had already changed his life, drastically and unexpectedly. By late 1941, most people in the movie industry, like most people in the country, believed that it was only a matter of time before the

United States entered World War II. But what many of his colleagues viewed
as a vague shadow spreading across the distant horizon, Ford accepted as a
certainty that would require, and reward, advance preparation. For months
before he left Hollywood for Washington, D.C., that September, he had been
spending his nights and weekends overseeing the creation of a group he
called the Naval Volunteer Photographic Unit, training camera operators,
sound technicians, and editors to do their jobs under wartime conditions in
close quarters; he even used gimbaled platforms in order to simulate attempts to develop film on ships while they pitched and listed. If war was
inevitable, he believed the effort to record that war would be essential, and
its planning could not be left to amateurs or to the bungling of War Department bureaucrats.

Still, Ford was an unlikely candidate to lead Hollywood's march toward
battle. He was old enough to be the father of a typical draftee; at forty-six, he
was just a couple of years from welcoming his first grandchild. And although
he had done his part in Hollywood over the years on several of the industry's
various committees—toiling among the interventionists, the fervent anti-Nazi
campaigners, the leaders of ad hoc groups trying to provide aid in the Spanish Civil War—he hadn't been on the front lines of those battles recently.
Since 1939, he had spent most of his time and energy directing a string of
movies—among them *Stagecoach, Young Mr. Lincoln,* and *The Grapes of
Wrath*—that had turned him into Hollywood's most respected filmmaker.

What moved Ford, just three weeks after completing production on *How
Green Was My Valley,* the picture that would win him his third Best Director
Academy Award in seven years, to step away from his thriving career and
request a transfer from the Naval Reserve to active duty? Was it lingering
shame at having failed the entrance exam for the Naval Academy at An-
napolis as a high school student a quarter of a century earlier? Was it embarrassment about having missed America's entry into the First World War in
1917, when he was busy trying to break into the movie business as a stunt-
man, actor, and fledgling director? Ford's motivation was an enigma even to
those closest to him—his wife, the colleagues with whom he made movies,
and the drinking buddies at his favorite haunt, the Hollywood Athletic Club.
"Is the ace director . . . tired of the tinsel of Hollywood?" one news story

queried. Ford seemed to delight in withholding any explanation at all, burnishing his public image as a taciturn and cryptic man by accepting an invitation to be interviewed about his decision and then declining to offer anything more expansive than, "I think it's the thing to do at this time."

It may have been that simple—a sense of duty, combined with a fear of how he might feel if he shirked it. That September, he had boarded a train for Washington, D.C., predicting misery and remorse for the able-bodied men in Hollywood who were still waiting, wondering what the war would mean and hoping the draft might leave them untouched. "They don't count," he wrote. "The blow will hit them hard next year." He checked into the Carlton Hotel, hung his uniform in the closet, and installed himself in his modest room with its single window of old, runny glass, stacking a couple of books on the bureau along with his pipes and cigars and living out of an open wardrobe trunk. He had the air, wrote a reporter who visited him, "of a man who might set out to sea with an hour's notice." In fact, that was just what he was thinking and even hoping; as Ford awaited orders from his mentor, intelligence chief "Wild" Bill Donovan, his mind was only on what was to come. "Things are moving apace here," he wrote to Mary, admonishing her to avoid the needless expense of late-night long-distance calls to him whenever she felt lonely or sad or angry, and telling her of the "hum of preparation and excitement" that the city was experiencing. "It would take volumes to say what I think of your unselfish courageous attitude in this present emergency," he added as he awaited her arrival in the capital. "Words literally fail me. I am very proud of you."

When Mary finally joined her husband in Washington, Ford gave his wife of twenty-one years something she had always wanted, a proper Catholic wedding ceremony. It was a preparatory gesture, a gift before what they both knew might be a long separation. And when the moment finally came, Ford and the men he trained, who had been streaming into Washington in the last few weeks, could barely contain their enthusiasm. Just hours after the news of Pearl Harbor broke, his Photo Unit recruits began showing up at the Carlton, knocking on the Fords' door, wanting to know what was going to happen next. The drinks started to flow, and as dusk fell on December 7, Ford and his men welcomed America into the war with cocktails.

The sense of urgency that had led Ford to upend his life was not shared by most of his colleagues in Hollywood until that December Sunday. William Wyler was at home in Bel Air the morning of Pearl Harbor, playing tennis with his friend John Huston. Wyler was a few weeks into shooting *Mrs. Miniver,* a drama about the gallantry of one middle-class British family and the inspiring home-front unity of their traditional village in the face of what, until that day, Americans still felt comfortable referring to as "the war in Europe." Huston, who was Wyler's junior and in many ways his protégé, was riding a wave of acclaim as his breakthrough directorial debut, *The Maltese Falcon,* was opening around the country. During their match, the two friends talked about an idea they had cooked up for a celebratory men-only trip they hoped to take later that winter, once Wyler completed *Mrs. Miniver.* That afternoon, they planned to join another friend, director Anatole Litvak, and meet with a travel agent about a visit to the Far East. "Willy and I wanted to get out of Hollywood for a while. I suggested it would be great to go on a proper trip to China," said Huston. "We wanted to see a bit of the outer world."

When Wyler's wife, Talli, who was pregnant with their second child, received a call telling her that Hawaii had been attacked, she ran out of the house and onto the tennis court, telling her husband and Huston to stop playing. The outer world was now at their doorstep. Later that day, the two men drove to Litvak's Malibu beach house, their prospective jaunt abroad already forgotten, and started making plans: How soon could they wrap up their professional commitments? How quickly could they walk away from the Hollywood work that now seemed to them like a silly game?

Wyler, who was thirty-nine, was exempt from military service because of his age. At thirty-five, Huston was a year under the cutoff and therefore eligible for the draft according to the Selective Service and Training Act of 1940, but the aftereffects of a childhood defined by frail health would probably have gotten him an easy 4-F exemption. However, there was no hesitation or second-guessing for either man. Wyler was a Jewish immigrant whose first sight of Americans had been the troops who liberated his hometown in Alsace at the end of World War I. He had relatives trapped in Europe. Eleven days after Pearl Harbor, he was awaiting his first assignment from the Signal Corps, the army's communications unit. Huston's attitude was more devil-may-care; he had been making up for lost time since his bedbound youth—he had ridden with the Mexican cavalry as an adolescent—and he was sure the war would offer more opportunity to reinvent himself as a man of action. Less than a month after Wyler, he accepted his own Signal Corps commission—"a distinct loss to the Warner studios," noted the *New York Times*, "where he is the directorial find of the year." When he had saddled up in Mexico, Huston said, "I was only a kid . . . I was more interested in going horseback riding than learning how to fight. This time it's different."

The men were seeking adventure, but more than that, they were reaching for relevance in a world that had become rougher and more frightening than anything their studio bosses would allow them to depict on film. Hollywood's best moviemakers shared a growing concern that they were fiddling while Europe burned, using their talents to beguile the American public with diversions—means of escape from the churn and horror of the headlines—rather than striving to bring the world into focus. Hollywood had never been interested in anticipating the news or leading public opinion, but recently its ability to react to changing circumstances had felt agonizingly slow. Wyler had intended *Mrs. Miniver,* a paean to the British national spirit, to galvanize American support for its closest ally; now that the United States itself was at war, he fretted that what he had once intended as a bold statement would seem embarrassingly behind the times. And Huston had spent much of that autumn working with his friend Howard Koch on the script for a Broadway play called *In Time to Come,* about Woodrow Wilson's vision for the League of Nations after World War I. When their drama opened three weeks after Pearl Harbor and, despite good reviews, closed a month later, Huston wasn't surprised. It "seemed dated," he wrote.

Suddenly, Hollywood's most skilled filmmakers faced the possibility that their movies would be of significantly less interest to audiences than the newsreels that preceded them. At MGM, George Stevens was busy making *Woman of the Year,* the comedy that initiated what would become one of the screen's most beloved sparring partnerships by teaming Katharine Hepburn with Spencer Tracy. Over the last several years, Stevens had demonstrated an extraordinary knack for creating light-spirited movies that nonetheless seemed to take place in the here and now; he knew how to use the economic grind of the Depression and the buzz of modern urban life as context for deft romances that delighted moviegoers. His new film would be no exception—his heroine, Tess Harding, was a journalist, a staunch anti-Hitler interventionist whose must-read opinion pieces had themes like "Democracies Must Stand Together or Collapse." (One ad for her columns shouted, "Hitler Will Lose, Says Tess Harding.") The tone of *Woman of the Year* was perfect for a country engaged by world events but not yet ensnared in them. As the script had it, Tess's professional passion was merely a distraction on the way to her real destiny; her meetings with Churchill and Roosevelt would ultimately be exposed as busywork for a woman who was uneasily attempting to avoid a more meaningful future as a wife and mother.

But the picture wasn't working. The weekend of Pearl Harbor, Stevens was coming off a disappointing test screening of *Woman of the Year*. His producer at MGM, Joseph L. Mankiewicz, had told him that audiences had rejected the movie's last scene, in which Hepburn and Tracy reconciled while covering a prizefight. They wanted to see Hepburn brought low, humiliated for her careerism. Reluctantly, he was preparing to shoot a new ending, in which Tess was to be shamed by her inability to find her way around a kitchen and cook a simple breakfast. Stevens had shot some of Laurel and Hardy's funniest short comedies when he was coming up in the 1920s, and he knew how to execute the pratfalls the scene required, but not how to refute Hepburn's bluntly stated conviction that the new ending was "the worst bunch of shit I've ever read." He and Hepburn both went through with the reshoot, but by the time *Woman of the Year* was in theaters two months later, Stevens was already thinking about turning his cameras on the war. That winter, he had sat alone in a Los Angeles screening room and watched, with horror and enthrallment, Leni Riefenstahl's documentary tribute to Aryan invincibility, *Triumph of the Will*. After that, he knew he could not make another movie that could possibly be used to divert anyone's attention from the war. Stevens often said that he decided to enlist that night, but what he saw stirred more than just his patriotic desire to beat the Germans. Watching the movie, he said years later, he realized that "all film," including his own, "is propaganda."

It was no longer a dirty word, although it had been until recently. In the fall, a group of isolationist senators had responded to a simmering combination of antiwar passion, anti-Hollywood rhetoric, and no small amount of anti-Semitism by summoning the movie industry's studio heads to Washington for hearings on whether a small handful of the hundreds of movies they produced every year were barely concealed agitprop, dramas designed to exacerbate paranoia or spark a public appetite for militarism. Now, propaganda—documentaries, dramas, comedies, features, shorts, movies for public consumption, and movies for servicemen only—was being discussed in both Hollywood and Washington as a matter of strategic necessity. Sometimes the projects were given the less tarnished label "morale films," but there was no longer any argument about the rectitude of their purpose.

For Frank Capra, the shift in public sentiment brought about by Pearl Harbor confirmed the wisdom of a move he had been planning to make for months. Capra, already a three-time Academy Award winner, was Hollywood's most successful director, and its richest. At forty-four, he was, virtually alone in his profession, a millionaire, and he had gotten there via a series of comedies—*Mr. Deeds Goes to Town, You Can't Take It With You*, and the more dramatic *Mr. Smith Goes to Washington*—that were expert at rousing a kind of generic populist high-spiritedness in moviegoers without ever getting too specific about their politics, which were as hard to parse as Capra's own.

In the summer of 1941, the columnist Stewart Alsop had written a piece for *Atlantic Monthly* called "Wanted: A Faith to Fight For," that caught the eye of General George Marshall. In the essay, Alsop warned, "To fight the war we will be sooner or later called upon to fight we need a crusading faith, the kind that inspired the soldiers of 1917, setting forth the war to make the world safe for democracy. We haven't got it; certainly the men who will do the fighting haven't got it." Marshall believed that movies could help to instill that crusading faith in both civilian audiences and new enlistees. Given Capra's résumé, which included terms running both the Academy of Motion Picture Arts and Sciences and the Screen Directors Guild in their formative years, he was perhaps more qualified than any other director in Hollywood to draw on the varied resources of an industry that he believed would be indispensable to the coming war effort. Like Ford, Capra had missed serving in World War I, although not for lack of trying; after the death of his father in a farming accident in 1917, he had concluded that his family would no longer be able to bear the burden of his college tuition, and he began ROTC training with the intention of joining the army. Shortly after enlisting, he contracted the flu; by the time he recovered, armistice had been declared. Unlike Ford, the son of first-generation Irish Americans who had settled in Maine, Capra himself was an immigrant, the youngest child of working-class Sicilians who had moved him and three of his siblings to California when he was five. Not until the army tried to process him did Capra learn that he had never been naturalized, and more than twenty years later he still had not fully shaken off the immigrant's desire to do right by his adopted country. ("That was his politics: 'Pleased to be here,'" said Hepburn after they worked together.)

So as the war approached, Capra started planning his departure from Hollywood. He made a lucrative deal with Warner Bros. to direct Cary Grant in an adaptation of the Broadway hit *Arsenic and Old Lace*. "I thought, 'Well, if I go into the Army, I'd like to have something going for my family while I'm there,'" he wrote later. "Perhaps I can find a picture that I can make fast and get a percentage of the profits. That will keep them going." He was a week from finishing the movie when war broke out. Five days later, he agreed to join the Signal Corps as a major.

Decades later, Capra wrote of his decision to enter the army. "Patriotism? Possibly. But the real reason was that in the game of motion pictures, I had climbed the mountain, planted my flag, and heard the world applaud. And now I was bored." If his characteristically self-mythologizing explanation doesn't ring completely true, the grandiosity—and the sense of competition that lay just beneath it—were very real. In a matter of months, the war would reshape Hollywood from the top down, just as it reshaped the rest of America: Fully one-third of the studios' male workforce—more than seven thousand men—would eventually enlist or be drafted. But few of them would enter the war as these directors did, with the sense that in impending middle age, they had found themselves with a new world to conquer, a task that would test their abilities to help win the hearts and minds of the American people under the hardest imaginable circumstances, with the greatest possible stakes.

The War Department's decision to enlist the movie industry's help after Pearl Harbor was not inevitable. The Signal Corps had used movies to train soldiers since 1929, just as the studios were making the transition from silent pictures to talkies, and in the 1930s, Roosevelt and his team had come to understand the power of short films and newsreels to sell the New Deal. But for much of the decade before Pearl Harbor, Hollywood and Washington had remained, in a way, competing principalities, each impressed by and distrustful of the clout held by the other. Hollywood feared the near-constant threat of censure, investigation, and regulation from the capital; Washington watched the growth of a medium that had become unrivaled in capturing the attention of the American people and, by degrees, learned to acknowledge, if sometimes unhappily, its power. But the beginning of the war marked the government's first attempt at a sustained program of filmed propaganda, and its use of Hollywood filmmakers to explain its objectives, tout its successes, and shape the war as a narrative for both civilians and soldiers constituted a remarkable, even radical experiment.

Given how central the movies became to the way the nation perceived the Second World War, it is striking how little forethought or planning went into the War Department's use of Hollywood. It began in an ad hoc way, the brainchild of a few senior officers—Marshall chief among them—who believed that the country, and the armed forces, had something to gain by the deployment of people who knew how to tell stories with cameras. The use of men like Ford and Capra came about in part because they were not only willing to serve, but eager to invent a program where none existed; they brought expertise and initiative to the table in an area that career military officers had neither the time nor the interest to master. In the immediate wake of the attack, there was no possibility of sitting down and calmly planning a cohesive approach to creating a filmed record of the war, or to let the half-dozen different government agencies and offices that shared a role in the dissemination of information sort out the lines of authority among themselves.

Nor was there any opportunity to discuss the complicated ethics involved.

On December 6, 1941, nobody anticipated there might be a need for such deliberation; a day later, the opportunity had already passed. A serious, extended discussion of the problems that might occur when a documentarian's duty to report the war with precision and accuracy conflicted with a propagandist's mission to sell the war to Americans whatever it took, or about the suitability of Hollywood filmmakers for either role, would, without question, have been divisive. It never happened. Some in the armed forces were astounded, and affronted, that directors who had until recently been guiding Fred Astaire and Ginger Rogers across a dance floor or teaching John Wayne to look heroic on a horse would now be entrusted with educating servicemen, inspiring civilians, and, armed with guns and cameras, standing shoulder to shoulder on the battlefield with real soldiers. Hollywood directors could, after all, be put to use in Hollywood; indeed, many of them were quickly deployed on their home turf, studio backlots, where by the end of 1943 they would infuse more than three hundred movies with spirit-building messages that were often handpicked from a list of government-approved suggestions and sewn into scripts on the fly.

Some in the armed forces believed that the prospect of filmmakers without any knowledge of "the army way" wearing officers' bars on their shoulders was an invitation to chaos. The producers of newsreels would have been more natural choices to film the war than a group of fiction makers from California; they had proven experience in getting their crews to far-flung locations, and they knew how to communicate information with energetic, punchy economy to the audiences who saw their work in movie houses every week. But they were journalists, and thus untouchable; the only control over them that the War Department could exert was to keep them supplied with footage advancing the army point of view, and that footage would have to be too compelling for them to resist.

So the decision was left to those in Hollywood who wanted to be of service and who saw a chance to reshape the reputation of their industry in doing so, and to those in Washington who understood their value. The army needed Hollywood—its manpower, its know-how, its equipment, its salesmanship, its experience, and the ideas of its most skilled directors. Movies brought tens of millions of Americans out of their homes every week and stirred them to laughter, tears, anger, and, increasingly, patriotism. Film-makers could not win the war, but Capra, Ford, Huston, Stevens, and Wyler had already shown that they could win the people. That was more than enough to secure the five men—the most influential and innovative American film directors to volunteer for service—a place of critical importance in the war effort.

The men reported for duty with as much naiveté as excitement, almost as if they were novice actors freshly cast in starring roles. They had bid farewell to their families and pried themselves loose from the comfort of their careers, and they began their time in the armed forces ready to serve, though not necessarily to take command. Their first questions were almost childlike: *When do I change into my uniform? Where should I work? What is a salute supposed to look like? How do I get supplies? What do you want me to do first?* The war had begun, but the words Ford had used to describe what was happening back in October—"the present emergency"—felt somehow more appropriate in the early days after Pearl Harbor, before the Allies had mounted a counteroffensive and troops started to ship out. Everything felt temporary, unplanned, contingent.

The directors were ready to pitch in, but none of them, on the day they had enthusiastically received their commissions, had anticipated that they were walking away from their lives not for weeks or months, but years. They were men of vast ability and, in most cases, with egos to match—new officers with the experience of privates and, at least outwardly, the confidence of generals. And as genuine as their desire to make a contribution was, they had more personal reasons for volunteering: They saw their time in the military as the next chapter in the success stories they had all become—a testing ground and a proving ground. Huston imagined that the war might finally slake his thirst for risk and danger. For Ford, naval service represented the last chance to live the seafaring life he had always dreamed of, and a long-deferred opportunity to discover and measure his own bravery. Capra, the immigrant made good who still saw himself as an outsider, responded to the call to duty as a chance to define himself as the most American of Americans and win the respect he still felt eluded him. Wyler—the only Jew among the men, and the only one of the five with an imperiled family in Europe—wanted the chance to fight the Germans that he had never had as a boy. And Stevens, a skilled manufacturer of gentle diversions, hoped to trade in fantasy for truth, to use his camera, for the first time, to record the world as it really was.

Over the next four years, the war would give each man exactly what he wanted, but those wishes would come true at a cost greater than any of them could have imagined. They would go to London and France, to the Pacific theater and the North African front, to ruined Italian cities and German death camps; they would film the war from land, sea, and air in ways that shaped, then and for generations after, America's perception of what it looked and sounded like to fight for the fate of the free world. They would honor their country, risk their lives, and create a new visual vocabulary for fictional and factual war movies; some of them would also blur the lines between the two, compromising themselves in ways they would spend the rest of their days trying to understand, or justify, or forget. By the time they came home, the idea they had once held that the war would be an adventure lingered only as a distant memory of their guileless incomprehension. They returned to Hollywood changed forever as men and as filmmakers.

Decades later, at the end of their lives, they were garlanded with honors and lifetime achievement awards for their enduring contributions to art and entertainment. But privately, they would still count among their most meaningful accomplishments a body of work that most of their admirers had long forgotten or never seen at all. As long as they lived, the war lived in them.

PART ONE

——

PART ONE

ONE

"The Only Way I Could Survive"

HOLLYWOOD, MARCH 1938–APRIL 1939

I n the spring of 1938, Jack Warner hosted an industry dinner for the exiled novelist Thomas Mann. A Nobel laureate whose outspoken opposition to Hitler and his policies had led to the revocation of his German citizenship, Mann was then Germany's leading anti-Nazi voice in the United States. His presence at a Hollywood event was, if not a call to arms, at least a call to wallets. It was also a political coming-out of sorts for Warner and his older brother Harry, who, just three weeks after the Anschluss, were ready to commit themselves—and, more significantly, the company they and their brothers Albert and Sam had founded in 1923—to the fight against the Nazis. The day before the dinner, the studio had shut down its offices in Austria. It had stopped working with Germany four years earlier.

The fact that Warner Bros. was at the time the only studio to take such a step suggests the extreme uneasiness that characterized the behavior of the men, almost all of them Jewish, who ran Hollywood's biggest companies. Freewheeling and entrepreneurial within the confines of the industry they had helped to create, they approached politics only haltingly and after agonized deliberation. While bottom-line imperatives were unquestionably a part of their calculus, their trepidation also emanated from an accurate understanding of their fragile place in American culture; to confront any national or international issue that might turn the spotlight on their religion was to risk animosity and even censure. The motion-picture business was still just thirty years old; most of the people who had built it were first- or second-generation Americans who were still viewed warily by the large portion of the country's political power structure—to say nothing of the press and public—that had in common a tacit and sometimes overt anti-Semitism. The moguls knew they were perceived as arrivistes and aliens whose loyalties might be divided between the adoptive nation that was making them wealthy and their roots in their old homelands.

As Hitler consolidated his power in the 1930s, studio chiefs tended to express their Jewish identity in personal, one-on-one appeals and in the quiet writing of checks to good causes, not in speeches or statements, and certainly not in the movies they oversaw. Mostly, they stayed quiet; the decorous country-club discretion of MGM's Louis B. Mayer was much more the norm than the recent behavior of the Warners (real name: Wonskolaser), Jewish immigrants from Poland who didn't tiptoe around their hatred of Fascism and of Hitler and were increasingly unafraid to go public and to use their position to influence others. The Warners were ardently pro-Roosevelt (unlike most of the other studio czars, who were business-minded antilabor Republicans), and Harry, who was the eldest and very much the voice of his studio, had recently urged all of his employees to join the Hollywood Anti-Nazi League for the Defense of American Democracy, the movie industry's first and strongest anti-Hitler rallying and fund-raising organization.

Warner's rivals were so timid on the subject that his endorsement of anti-Nazi activism was in itself controversial enough to make headlines. The Anti-Nazi League was not at the time openly backed by any other studio heads, nor did it have the support of Joseph I. Breen, the head of the Production Code and one of the most prominent Catholic watchdogs of Hollywood morality. It was also viewed with suspicion by many Washington politicians, among them Martin Dies, the Texas congressman who in 1938 created the first version of what would become the House Un-American Activities Committee with the intention of investigating Communism in Hollywood studios, unions, and political organizations. Warner's dinner for Mann was such a startling break with tradition that the industry newspaper *Variety* was moved to suggest (approvingly) that he was positioning himself at the forefront of a nascent "militant anti-Hitler campaign in Hollywood," and the columnist Walter Winchell cited Harry as "the leader of the fight to get the other major companies to discontinue doing business with" the Nazis. But the "fight" stopped well short of the Warners confronting their competitors at other studios; there wasn't much that Harry and Jack could do except to lead by example and hope that their rivals would start to feel pressure from their own rank and file.

Even as most studios maintained a strong financial interest in the German market and continued to do business with Hitler and his deputies, the issue of how to fight Hitler's rise to power was becoming a subject of discussion, and discomfort, in their boardrooms and executive suites. But in 1938, all of Hollywood's major moviemaking companies—Warners included—were adamant on one point: Whatever they thought about the Nazis, they would not allow their feelings, or anyone else's, about what was happening in Germany to play out onscreen. On rare occasions, a veiled or allusive argument against Fascism or tyranny would make its way into a motion picture, but it was then unthinkable that studios could use their own movies to sway public opinion about Hitler without sparking instant accusations that they were acting as propagandists for foreign—meaning Jewish—interests. Much of Hollywood's creative class—directors, writers, actors, independent producers—was becoming far more forthright about making its political sympathies known at rallies and in aid organizations, but for the most part, the noise they were making stopped when they passed through the gates and reported for work every morning. The studios didn't particularly care who among their "talent" was for or against Roosevelt, a Communist or a Fascist sympathizer, a Jew or a Gentile, but that tolerant indifference stemmed from a steely certainty that nobody's beliefs, whatever they might be, would seep onto the screen.

The stern eye of the Production Code as well as the studios' collective fear of giving offense meant that controversial material was systematically weeded out of scripts before the cameras ever rolled. It also meant that even the most highly praised and successful studio directors were treated as star employees rather than as artists entitled to shape their own creative visions. When a filmmaker's work reliably struck a chord with audiences, he was rewarded with larger budgets, access to the best of his studio's contract stars, and a greater, though not unchecked, ability to pick and choose from among those properties that his bosses wanted to turn into movies. But there were limits, and political self-expression was one of them; no movie under the banner of a studio would ever reach American theaters unless the head of that studio was comfortable defending every frame and every line—and ideally, not a frame or line would need defending in the first place.

Sooner or later, every working director in Hollywood would find himself on the losing end of an argument about the content of one of his movies, fighting against a litany of often self-imposed restrictions about what couldn't or shouldn't or mustn't be said. In 1938, none of them was powerful enough to override the caution of the motion picture industry's leaders—certainly not John Huston, who was still trying to break into the business, or George Stevens and William Wyler, who were still working their way up. Even Frank Capra and John Ford, who were already near the top of their field, knew that on this subject, the men in charge were immovable. Over the course of a career at Fox that had begun well before the dawn of the sound era, Ford had earned the trust and respect of his bosses, most recently Darryl F. Zanuck, who had overseen all production for the studio since its 1935 merger with a rival company called Twentieth Century Pictures. Ford's public identity as a director had not yet been fully formed—the remarkable run that would firmly establish his reputation not just within Hollywood but with the American public would begin at the end of 1938 with the shooting of *Stagecoach*. Thus far, the reputation he had built steadily over the last fifteen years rested most firmly on a film that Fox and most other studios in Hollywood had declined to make because of its politics. In 1935, he had gone to RKO to shoot *The Informer,* a dark, unusually atmospheric melodrama about a man who sells out his friend to the police during the Irish rebellion. The film was close to Ford's heart—he had gone to Ireland as a young man in 1921 to visit relatives and support the IRA—and, although it was not a major hit, it greatly elevated Ford's status with critics and within the industry, winning him his first Academy Award for Best Director.

But if Ford imagined that the acclaim he had received would somehow result in greater clout or creative freedom back at Fox, he was soon disillusioned. Three years after *The Informer* was released, he saw Jean Renoir's *Grand Illusion*, one of the first French-language films to win widespread attention in the United States. He was astonished by the power and the frankness of Renoir's drama, which portrayed officers, including one explicitly identified as Jewish, who were being held as prisoners during the First World War. Ford was moved by its portrayal of personal nobility in the face of a catastrophic clash of nations. It was, he said, "one of the best things I have ever seen." But when he tried early in 1938 to get Zanuck interested in an American remake, he was rebuffed so firmly that he was dissuaded from pressing his case further. The idea of pursuing a more socially or politically committed cinema, was, he felt, futile; no film with a strong political perspective would be able to surmount the studios' fear of being labeled interventionists, or the antipathy of the censors and what he disdainfully called the "financial wizards" to making waves. "If you're thinking of a general run of social pictures, or even just plain honest ones," he complained, "it's almost hopeless."

In 1938, Ford began to do offscreen what he was not permitted to do in his movies, and walked onto the stage of Los Angeles's Shrine Auditorium to speak at an Anti-Nazi League rally for the first time. He was not going out on a limb alone. The league was only two years old, but its membership already included hundreds, soon to be thousands, of actors, directors, screenwriters, and public intellectuals, a broad mix of Democrats, Socialists, and Communists. But Ford was particularly fearless about speaking out. "May I express my wholehearted desire to cooperate to [my] utmost ability with the Hollywood Anti-Nazi League," he said that fall, when Dies's new congressional committee started to go on the attack. "If this be Communism, count me in."

That rhetorical flourish spoke more of Ford's long-standing detestation of bullies like Dies than of his own political sympathies. A lifelong Catholic, he had little in common with the Popular Front leftists—many of them Jewish, many of them Communists—who were among Hollywood's most active anti-Nazi leaders. In a letter to his nephew, he had recently written of his conviction that "Communism to my mind is not the remedy this sick world is seeking." Although he didn't identify his politics publicly, in the same letter he described himself as "a definite socialistic democrat—always left," and that was, at the time, accurate.

Ford was a deeply divided personality. On sets, he could be a sadist, often singling out a cast or crew member for abuse or humiliation. But in the public sphere, he would frequently become affronted at an unfair or lopsided fight and take a stand, always preferring David to Goliath. In 1936, incensed at the studios' antiunion policies and firm in his belief (which was tinged with some unseemly precepts about Jews and money) that "the picture racket is controlled from Wall Street," he urged his colleagues to make common cause with Hollywood's trade unions, and became one of the founding members of the Screen Directors Guild. A year later, he joined the SDG's first negotiating committee. And as the Spanish Civil War pricked Hollywood's conscience, Ford helped found organizations like the Motion Picture Artists' Committee to Aid Spain, which eventually boasted a membership of fifteen thousand; he also served as vice chairman of the Motion Picture Democratic Committee, an anti-Fascist, pro-Roosevelt group that was heavily involved in California state politics.

At the Shrine Auditorium on the day Ford spoke, the subject was Hitler, although Dorothy Parker, who presided over the rally, refused to use his name, referring to him only as "that certain man." The theme of the day was twofold: the evil of Fascism abroad, and the possible menace of Nazi cells within the United States. An audience of four thousand listened as the Anti-Nazi League's special guest speaker, a former U.S. ambassador to Germany, warned via audio hookup from Carnegie Hall that "America is not free from . . . Nazi activity," which was then a common it-can-happen-here refrain in newspapers and radio broadcasts. For many in Hollywood, fighting Hitler was a good cause, but not yet a crisis. For Ford, though, the rally's message was resonant, and the threat felt immediate. It was not premature to imagine a day when the United States would have to defend itself.

Over the last ten years, Hollywood had not made many war movies, and even those that showcased the excitement of combat or of aerial derring-do tended to emphasize above all the grave human cost of military conflict. "War itself is so ugly and so terrible," said the French writer André Maurois that year, "that I do not believe it is possible to see a representation of such life without wishing never to live it. The difficulty is not to give a war film the character of a great adventure—a characteristic which modern war does not have." The trauma of what was then still called the Great War was still fresh, and the loss of more than 100,000 American soldiers in just a year had left the United States deeply averse to the idea of military involvement a continent away. The First World War had been a subject for movies as early as armistice, and in 1928, Ford had made it the backdrop of one of his most moving silent films, *Four Sons,* about brothers from Bavaria who end up fighting on opposite sides. But no movie had defined World War I for American audiences more than Lewis Milestone's 1930 masterpiece *All Quiet on the Western Front,* an adaptation of Erich Maria Remarque's widely read novel. The film had affirmed and reinforced the public's perception of the war as a descent into carnage that had robbed every nation that fought in it of a generation of young men, all for a tenuous peace that few believed would last. Almost ten years later, it remained for many in the industry Hollywood's last and best word on the subject.

George Stevens had been thirteen when the United States entered the war in 1917; as a child, he had read daily reports of the deaths of American boys just a few years older than he was. Twenty years later, he shuddered at the prospect of another costly war—and like many Americans, the conflict in Europe felt remote to him. Stevens had no old-country roots anywhere; he had grown up in California, his parents were stage actors, he had cut his teeth directing slapstick shorts when he was barely out of his teens, and show business was the only life he had ever known. Though he was, at thirty-four, a laconic and introverted man who was sometimes teased on his sets about the expression of impenetrable, stone-faced preoccupation that he tended to wear like a mask, most of the dozen features he had directed for RKO were loose, energetic, and joyful. Under contract to the studio, he had distinguished himself as one of Hollywood's most adroit up-and-coming directors, a filmmaker who had a confident light touch and a gift for bringing out strong work in his actors. He'd made a critically praised literary adaptation, *Alice Adams,* and a hit musical, *Swing Time,* and he was a particular favorite of actresses, including Katharine Hepburn, Barbara Stanwyck (with whom he

had made *Annie Oakley*), and RKO's most important female star, Ginger
Rogers, whom he had just directed in the sparkling comedy *Vivacious Lady*.

As he watched Ford and many of his fellow directors begin to immerse
themselves in a kind of activism that might eventually lead to American intervention in Europe, Stevens felt his own consciousness begin to stir with a
growing sense of alarm. As a filmmaker he believed, for the first time, that
he had a duty to make a movie that engaged with the world's dangerous realities, and he thought the hits he had delivered for RKO had earned him the
right to make a passion project. In 1938, he had one in mind: an adaptation
of Humphrey Cobb's novel *Paths of Glory*, the bleak and harrowing story of
three French soldiers during World War I who face a court-martial and death
sentence for cowardice when they refuse orders from their superiors to advance in an attack that they know amounts to a suicide mission. Like *All
Quiet on the Western Front*, Cobb's novel was a mostly apolitical indictment
of the brutality of war, which it depicted as a vicious game in which vain old
men with little at personal risk heedlessly send young soldiers to their deaths.

Stevens later said that his own position regarding the possibility of another war was vague and uninformed; like many Americans who were old
enough to remember doughboys being gassed in the trenches, he imagined at
the time that an American move against Hitler's reinvigorated Germany
could lead to unimaginable loss, and that the United States would do better
to turn away from the nightmare that Europe was becoming. He thought
Paths of Glory could serve as both a reminder and a warning. But his pitch
to make the movie was rejected repeatedly by RKO's production chief Pandro
Berman. "He [said], 'You can't make that picture,'" Stevens recalled. "And I
said, 'Why the hell can't we?'" When Stevens pressed him, Berman first said
that his resistance was not ideological but financial: Foreign markets were
extremely important to the studios, and he believed that France would not
only refuse to show *Paths of Glory* but might boycott all RKO product in re-
taliation. "Well, don't run it in France," Stevens replied. "This is a picture
for the rest of the world." But another delegation from the studio then approached Stevens and said flatly, "It's an anti-war picture."

"Yes, it's true," Stevens said. "It's an argument against war."

"Well, this is no time to be making an anti-war picture," they replied. "War is in the offing."

"I said, 'What better time for an anti-war picture?'" Stevens remembered decades later. "And they said, 'What about Hitler? If somebody doesn't fight Hitler, what will happen?' . . . It was another eight years before I [understood] that. I got all the way to Dachau before I could say that we should've fought Hitler three years before the development . . . that brought [us] into it."

At the time, though, Stevens didn't recognize what he later viewed as his own naiveté; he just felt thwarted.* And more than that, manhandled, especially when RKO swiftly steered him toward the property it had decided should be his next film: *Gunga Din*. Stevens was given a budget of nearly $2 million—the largest the studio had ever approved—to film Rudyard Kipling's rousing story of the glory and the valor of the British Empire in India, and the film proved to be tremendously successful with audiences, who loved seeing Cary Grant in uniform and Sam Jaffe play an Indian. The movie, which was released in early 1939, raised its young director's profile considerably, and was mostly well received by critics. Stevens gave little thought to its pro-war subtext while he was making it. But decades later, his verdict on *Gunga Din* was close to that of the critic for the Bombay publication *FilmIndia*, which called the movie "Imperialist propaganda." "The film is delightfully evil in the fascist sense," said Stevens. "It celebrates the rumble of the drums and the waving of the flags. . . . I really got that film done just before it would have been too late. Another year . . . and I would have been too smart to do it."

At the same time that RKO was steering Stevens away from *Paths of Glory*, a far more powerful filmmaker found himself in a battle with his bosses over a war movie. It was not a position to which Frank Capra was accustomed. By 1938, Capra was the most important director on the Columbia Pictures lot, and nobody else even came close. Columbia was not a powerhouse, not one of the studios that were then referred to in the industry as the "big five" (Warner Bros., 20th Century Fox, RKO, MGM, and Paramount).

---

* *Paths of Glory* was eventually made in 1957, by Stanley Kubrick.

Like Universal, it was considered a second-tier company with more modest financial underpinnings and a far less impressive stable of talent. Capra was the exception; his 1934 comedy *It Happened One Night* had swept the Academy Awards, *Mr. Deeds Goes to Town* had won him his second Best Director Oscar two years later, and the fall of 1938 brought an adaptation of the Broadway hit *You Can't Take It With You* that would win the Best Picture Oscar and bring Capra his third Best Director trophy in five years.

In the public eye, Capra was the first brand-name director of the sound era; his latest movie had landed him on the cover of *Time* magazine with the headline "Columbia's Gem." The article praised his understated on-set style, explaining that he "works without mannerisms [and] confers quietly with his actors and technical crew before each take." It also enthusiastically advanced the rags-to-riches autobiography that Capra had, even at the outset of his career, actively promoted, taking him from his humble beginnings as an immigrant boy from Sicily selling newspapers on California street corners to his present $350,000-per-annum salary and his and his wife Lucille's lifestyle as "two of the community's most dazzling celebrities. . . . [They] spend most of the year in a vacation cottage in Malibu Beach and send two of their three children to the U.C.L.A. nursery school."

Columbia president Harry Cohn had such confidence in Capra that he had not hesitated to pay $200,000 to buy him the screen rights to *You Can't Take It With You*. But he also knew how to say no, and, just two months after the *Time* story, when Capra came to him with an idea for a new movie, Cohn turned his most valuable employee down flat. For several years, Capra had wanted to film an adaptation of Maxwell Anderson's play *Valley Forge*, a drama about the conditions endured by American fighters in the Revolutionary War during the punishing winter of 1778. The *New York Times* had praised the play as a chance to "worship at the shrine of an inspiring figure," George Washington, but in fact, Anderson's play was perfectly suited to Capra; it was a veneration not so much of General Washington as of the common soldier whose fighting spirit convinced him not to surrender.

Cohn had already turned up his nose at *Valley Forge* when Capra first pitched it three years earlier, just after the success of *It Happened One Night*. Now Capra returned to make his case with considerably more clout as well as the inducement of casting Gary Cooper as Washington—and Cohn told him the answer was still no. The reason was something Capra hadn't anticipated: Cohn said he couldn't bring himself to finance a movie in which audiences would be encouraged to root against British soldiers at a moment when England was under an ever greater threat from Germany. Capra didn't put up much of a fight; he got the point. He hadn't even considered the potential public relations peril of appearing to take the wrong side.

It was not the first time Cohn had saved Capra from himself. Over the last few years, the director's naïve and inconsistent political instincts had sometimes led him close to disaster. In 1935, after he visited Italy and expressed his admiration for Benito Mussolini, Il Duce—a big fan of Capra's movies—offered Columbia $1 million if Capra would direct a film biography based on his life, with Mussolini himself writing the screenplay. Capra, who was said to have a picture of the dictator on his bedroom wall, may have been interested, but Cohn, after briefly considering it, scotched the idea, saying, "After all, I'm a Jew. He's mixed up with Hitler and I don't want no part of it." Cohn was blunt, coarse, and abrasive—most filmmakers couldn't stand him—but he was also hard-nosed and shrewdly protective of his assets, Capra chief among them, and he believed that as an outsider, the director could not afford to dabble in global politics without having his loyalty questioned. Hollywood was already seen by too much of the rest of America as a nest of perversion and subversion, and the industry's growing population of foreign-born filmmakers, writers, and actors had to walk an especially careful line. Even in 1938, Capra's foreign origins made him such an easy target for casual distaste that a *Collier's* magazine profile could lightly refer to him as a "little wop."

Capra's infatuation with Mussolini soon subsided, but his sympathies remained maddeningly difficult to track, even for those who knew him. He supported Franco during the Spanish Civil War while most of his Hollywood colleagues were raising funds for the Loyalists. And when it came to domestic affairs, his politics were described as "reactionary" by Edward Bernds, a sound engineer who worked with him several times and who wrote in his diary in 1936 that Capra was a "bitter Roosevelt hater" who couldn't stop complaining about the income tax.

At any given moment, Capra's passions could be inflamed by populism or by distrust of the working class, by loathing for Communists or contempt for capitalists, by economic self-protection or New Deal generosity. Throughout the 1930s, his politics had been defined more by his quick temper than by any ideological consistency. His conflicting impulses were manifest in *Mr. Deeds Goes to Town,* a comedy about an eccentric young New England poet who inherits $20 million and learns what it's like to have the whole world reach into his pockets. Capra's left-wing screenwriter Robert Riskin brought an unmistakable progressivism to the film, especially in an episode in which a farmer is driven to madness by his inability to feed and clothe his family in the Depression; his plight moves Deeds to a quasi-socialistic resolve to spread the wealth. But the movie's ideas, and its ideals, are highly mutable. In one scene, *Deeds* can sound like a people's cry against the greed of entrenched financial barons; in the next, it turns into a near-Fascist rant against big-city sophistication, with both positions expressed in a kind of one-size-fits-all anger ("Salesmen, politicians, moochers—they all want something!" Deeds complains). Still, few in *Deeds*'s audience would have guessed that its director was an Alf Landon supporter who shunned practically every Hollywood organization as a potential hotbed of Communism. While Ford and many of Capra's other colleagues worked to found the Screen Directors Guild in 1936, Capra refused to join for eighteen months. When he did, it was only because his growing interest in the fight for directors' rights finally overtook his deep scorn for unions.

In 1937, Capra took a trip to Russia with Riskin; he was treated as royalty by apparatchiks who were convinced that his movies were anticapitalist, and he was said to have reciprocated their hospitality by expressing great enthusiasm for Stalinism and contempt for "the bosses of cinema" in America. But he also made his antiwar views plain; when he was invited to watch a military parade in Red Square, he asked to be excused, saying, "I can't stand the sight of so much war paraphernalia. . . . Just imagine what will happen when all these tanks, guns and rifles begin to shoot. No, I definitely don't want to see this. We Americans are a peaceful nation. We don't intend to fight."

All of his contradictory perspectives were even more apparent in *You*

Can't Take It With You, which he started shooting in early 1938. George S. Kaufman and Moss Hart's comedy about the eccentricities of a large and chaotic New York family whose elderly patriarch has for years refused to pay any income tax allowed Capra (with Riskin's considerable help) to combine his various economic and social hobbyhorses into something approaching a unified semiphilosophy. In the film, the grandfather opposes the tax system in part because of his belief that the money he would pay is likely to be spent on armament. One of the movie's villains is a rapacious millionaire who serves as a mouthpiece for the then-popular contention that profit-obsessed tycoons would eventually manipulate the United States into entering a war: "With the world going crazy," he practically cackles, "the next big move is munitions, and [we] are going to cash in on it! . . . There won't be a bullet, gun, or cannon made in this country without us." Kaufman and Hart's play had also included some pointed jabs at anti-Communist paranoia, but those lines may have hit too close to home for Capra; the movie stripped them away and replaced them with a virtually indecipherable monologue that begins, "Communism, fascism, voodooism—everybody's got 'ism' these days! . . . When things go a little bad . . . go out and get yourself an 'ism' and you're in business!" The speech then goes on to praise (but not define) "Americanism," and concludes, "Lincoln said, 'With malice toward none and charity to all.' Nowadays they say, 'Think the way I do, or I'll bomb the daylights out of you.'"

Critics and the public loved the madcap homilizing of *You Can't Take It With You*—at least in America. Overseas, there was considerable dissent, much of it along the lines of Graham Greene's assertion that Capra "emerges as a rather muddled and sentimental idealist who feels—vaguely—that something is wrong with the social system" but cannot come up with a better solution than for Wall Street magnates to "throw everything up and play the harmonica."

As the opening of his movie approached, Capra was rocked by a personal tragedy. While he was at the first Los Angeles press screening of *You Can't Take It With You,* he received an emergency call summoning him to the hospital, where he learned that his severely disabled three-year-old son John had died after what was supposed to be a routine tonsillectomy. As he and Lucille grieved, he again turned his attention outward and quickly returned to work. In late 1938, after Cohn told him he couldn't make *Valley Forge*, Capra visited Washington, D.C., with the notion of making a sequel to *Deeds*. He had in mind a film, wrote one reporter, "with a political theme. He wants to show one of his honest people—say, a cowboy Senator in the guise of Gary Cooper—against the artificial background of the two august bodies of government we know as the houses of Congress."

Capra's original notion for the new movie, which he was then calling *Mr. Deeds Goes to Washington*, won Cohn's approval, which meant that almost alone among his peers, he would have the chance to make a film that commented directly on contemporary American politics—whether or not he could figure out exactly what he wanted to say. In a 1938 interview, he tried, for the first time, to explain where he stood on various issues, but what emerged was an awkward laundry list of tenets from a man who saw himself as an embattled patriot surrounded by enemies even within his own industry. "Capra likes American institutions," the sympathetic reporter wrote, clearly paraphrasing him. "He doesn't regard the men who made the country as a lot of fools. He is against dictatorship. He believes in things like freedom of the press. All this makes him a marked man in Hollywood, where so many of the intellectuals are sound, orthodox American-haters."

Capra had long been a pacifist, but on a trip to Washington to research his new movie, that began to change. He had always been susceptible to the charisma of powerful men, and when he met President Roosevelt for the first time, he was surprised to find himself dazzled; the president's "awesome aura" made his "heart skip." Capra, who had twice voted against Roosevelt, couldn't quite come around to supporting him for a third term, but soon after his visit east, he broke with many of his fellow Republicans by becoming a publicly committed interventionist. He returned to Los Angeles, and on November 18, 1938, he attended an Anti-Nazi League rally titled "Quarantine Hitler" at the Philharmonic Auditorium. Before an audience of thirty-five hundred, he stepped to the microphone and spoke in support of a trade boycott, endorsing a statement that "capitulation to Hitler means barbarism and terror." Capra never looked back. Like Ford, he was about to become one of the movie industry's strongest advocates for America's involvement in what he now believed was a rapidly approaching world war.

The "Quarantine Hitler" rally was held a week after the rampage of *Kristallnacht*, which had made most studios realize with dismay that their days of releasing movies in Germany were probably numbered; in the wake of so much destruction, many in the Hollywood community (though by no means everyone) also came to grips with the fact that complacent silence was no longer a moral option. The beating of Jews and the burning and looting of thousands of synagogues and Jewish-owned businesses in Germany and Austria might have galvanized the nation and moved Washington to action more quickly if Americans had been able to see the mayhem and cruelty unfold on movie screens. But the producers of newsreels were dependent on footage they received from overseas, and all they had to present to movie-goers were some photographs of the aftermath. The inability to show Americans an unfiltered version of what was happening overseas was of great enough concern to spur an unusual summit meeting the day of the rally among the five major producers of newsreels (which included Fox, Paramount, and Universal) to discuss pooling their resources in order to better educate the public about Nazi atrocities.

For the many émigré Jews in Hollywood's creative class, *Kristallnacht* marked the moment when the oppression they or their families had fled Europe to avoid could no longer be forgotten or ignored. William Wyler had not been back to his hometown of Mulhouse on the French-German border since 1930, when he had traveled there during a vacation. At the time, he had described Berlin as "the most interesting and most pathetic city in Europe . . . torn by groups of radicals and reactionaries, each fighting for a different government. . . . The people . . . seem to be hopeless in all this chaos." In the decade since, he hadn't gone home again, nor did he do much to identify publicly with his Jewish or his European roots. Jewish filmmakers in the 1930s were easy targets—for anti-Semites, for anti-Communists, for xenophobes. Wyler, whose English was impeccable but unmistakably accented, had worked hard to become an American; as the situation in Germany worsened, he had shown little interest in activist engagement. When Jack Warner would press the point in a letter, he would write a hundred-dollar check to the Hollywood Anti-Nazi League; when the Motion Picture Artists' Committee— whose rallying cry was, "Watch for the Ambulance from Hollywood to

Spain!"—would nudge him, he would donate two hundred dollars to a relief
fund. But more than anything, he simply wanted to be left alone to make
pictures, preferably without having to infuse them with any topicality or political resonance.

By 1938, Wyler was so fully assimilated that it almost came as a surprise
when his background became a subject for discussion—which it did a month
before *Kristallnacht,* when he married. The future Talli Wyler was a tall,
attractive Texan with a calm and gracious demeanor, a graduate of Southern
Methodist University who had come to Hollywood with some minor acting
ambitions, which she would quickly abandon after her marriage. She met
Wyler that September; they married a month later. Not until that December
did he meet Talli's concerned parents, who had come from Dallas to Hollywood to spend Christmas with their daughter and the man she had impul-
sively wed. By then, Talli was pregnant (they would name the baby girl Cathy,
after the heroine of the new movie Wyler had just started directing, *Wuthering Heights*). Talli had told her mother and father that Wyler was Jewish, and
she remembered later that they arrived for the holidays worried about what
their daughter's new life would be like "because of all the terrible things
happening in Europe." Wyler, as a new husband and expectant father, shared
their distress. As a private citizen, an emigrant, and a Jew, he was profoundly
troubled by the news he was reading and determined to do what he could to
fight back. But as an artist, he was relieved to report for work every morning
freed from the burdens he carried in the rest of his life. On the set, he could
be a director; not having to be anything else for those hours was a kind of
luxury.

One of the few men in Hollywood who was close enough to Wyler to understand how hard he had worked to forge a new identity for himself was John
Huston. When Wyler decided to marry, he and Talli had resolved that the
ceremony would be private; he called Huston, who arranged for the wedding
to take place at the home of his father, the actor Walter Huston. Aside from
Wyler's brother, lawyer, agent, and his aged parents (whom he had helped
emigrate from Alsace and installed in a house near his), the only guests
Wyler invited to the wedding were John and his wife, Lesley, who provided
the cake. The friendship between Wyler and Huston, one of the deepest and

most enduring bonds between two directors in Hollywood history, was in some ways a marriage of opposites. Huston was tall, brash, sybaritic, and reckless; Wyler was a compact five foot eight, quiet, and so meticulous that he earned his lifelong nickname ("Forty-Take Wyler" or "Fifty-Take Wyler," depending on who was doing the complaining) before he had directed even a single major success. Huston's romantic dalliances, which included but were not limited to five marriages, were wild, public, sometimes simultaneous, and almost always impulsive. Wyler, after a stormy early marriage to Margaret Sullavan and a serious affair with his most famous leading lady, Bette Davis, married Margaret Tallichet, the woman he called "Talli," in 1938, and at thirty-six settled into a life of contented domesticity that lasted until his death more than forty years later. Huston, thirty-two when he helped his best friend plan his wedding, was just beginning to get past what had amounted to a destructive and anarchic adolescence that had seemed to stretch through his twenties.

But the two men were more alike than they appeared to be. Wyler, despite the buttoned-down reticence that would lead one columnist, just a few years later, to call him "an iron gray man in a gray flannel suit," was, under the surface, something of a thrill seeker who loved downhill skiing and outdoor adventure; before he married Talli, he could often be seen at the end of a shooting day tearing through the studio gates on his Harley-Davidson, frequently with an actress holding on for dear life. And Huston, a last-call bon vivant who liked to present himself as a disheveled renegade (the *New York Times* called him "The Great Unpressed"), was painstaking and focused when it came to his work, a quality he deeply admired in Wyler and sought to emulate.

Both men were among the first filmmakers who could legitimately be called second-generation Hollywood. Huston was the son of the highly regarded actor Walter Huston, and Wyler was a distant cousin of the man *Time* magazine labeled "Famed Nepotist Carl Laemmle," the head of Universal whose propensity for hiring relatives led Ogden Nash to quip, "Uncle Carl Laemmle has a very large faemmle." It was Laemmle who had paid for Wyler's emigration from Alsace to America and had given him his first apprenticeship as a studio shipping clerk in 1920.

A decade later, it was Wyler who gave Huston his first job on a movie, rewriting dialogue for one of his earliest talkies, a loose adaptation of Eugene O'Neill's *Desire Under the Elms* called *A House Divided*. Wyler hired him to please Huston's father, the film's star, and he never regretted it. "Willy was certainly my best friend in the industry," said Huston. "We seemed instantly to have many things in common. . . . Willy liked the things that I liked. We'd go down to Mexico. We'd go up in the mountains. We'd gamble." Wyler was the teasing older brother/mentor who would mock Huston as a "long-legged, lobster-nosed, shark-livered, mutton-fisted, pernivorous Presbyterian land-lubber"; Huston was the devil on his shoulder, his barstool comrade, and his eager pupil in the ways of the movie business.

After *A House Divided* was finished, Wyler and Huston cemented their comradeship by taking an unlikely road trip together, dressing as hobos and sleeping in boxcars, all in the name of research for a movie they didn't end up making. It may have been a lark for Wyler, but for Huston it was one more symptom of a life that was careening out of control. His first marriage, to an alcoholic he had wed when he was just twenty, had fallen apart. In 1933, he was involved in a drunk-driving accident in which a starlet was injured. Soon after that, a young actress was killed when she stepped in front of a car Huston was driving on Sunset Boulevard. Huston, who insisted he had not been drinking, was cleared of any wrongdoing by a grand jury, but the case generated harsh headlines across the country ("Why Should Auto Murderers Go Free?" asked a *Los Angeles Herald Examiner* editorial) and he was branded a spoiled, irresponsible wreck. "The experience seemed to bring my whole miserable existence to a head," he said. Almost broke, he exiled himself to Europe. "Whatever I turned my hand to, nothing seemed to work," he recalled. "I'd pull myself out halfway and slide back in again."

When Huston returned to the United States in 1935, he had done little to change the perception that, as James Agee wrote, he would "never amount to more than an awfully nice guy to get drunk with." He was, said producer Henry Blanke, "hopelessly immature. You'd see him at every party, wearing bangs, with a monkey on his shoulder. Charming. Very talented, but without an ounce of discipline in his makeup."

It was Wyler who rescued Huston, giving him a writing job and, more important, the chance to reinvent himself. He saw a kindred spirit in Huston—"we were both young and adventurous and we did a lot of things together, everything, from girls to skiing, God knows what," he said—but he also saw nascent talent. "He was a good writer," he said. "Otherwise, we wouldn't have lasted together."

While Huston had been away, Wyler's stock had soared thanks to well-received adaptations of Lillian Hellman's Broadway play *The Children's Hour* and Sidney Kingsley's *Dead End.* He had also stayed close to Walter Huston, directing him in *Dodsworth* and winning his first Best Director Academy Award nomination for the movie in 1937. Now Wyler was behind the camera again, working with Bette Davis in the Civil War melodrama *Jezebel,* Warner Bros.' attempt to jump in front of *Gone with the Wind,* and he was unhappy with the screenplay. A week into production, he urged the studio to hire Huston not only to do rewrites but, in Blanke's words, "to sort of represent him in preparing the last half of the script." Blanke told Warner production head Hal Wallis that Wyler "apparently knows Huston personally, spends a great deal of time with him and will see him at night, and he maintains that Huston knows exactly his feelings and thoughts about the script. . . . Huston apparently will be a sort of a go-between operating between the writers, and you, and himself. . . . [I] told Wyler we would try it out." Wyler's faith was repaid when *Jezebel,* which was released in early 1938, became a hit and won Davis her second Oscar. Warner rewarded Huston by hiring him as a full-time contract writer who would move from one project to another depending upon where he was needed.

With Europe still fresh in his experience, Huston had a keen interest in the brewing war and its political roots, and soon after *Jezebel,* the studio gave him a writing assignment that would fuel that passion and consume him for a year: *Juárez,* an expensive, overscaled nineteenth-century historical drama about the emperor Maximilian, installed by France as Mexico's monarch, his mad wife Carlotta, and Benito Juárez, the country's president. Huston would work with two other writers, Wolfgang Reinhardt and Aeneas MacKenzie, and all three men shared Reinhardt's vision that "the dialogue, as far as it is political and ideological, must consist of phrases from today's newspapers; every child must be able to recognize that Napoleon in his Mexican intervention is none other than Mussolini plus Hitler in their Spanish adventure."

Huston was enthralled by the lengthy process and the three-way writing effort, which he said was "by way of being dialectic" given Reinhardt's historical knowledge of Europe, MacKenzie's love of "the monarchical system," and his own status as "a Jeffersonian Democrat espousing ideas similar to those of Benito Juárez." And he knew the film was lucky to have a home at Warners, the first studio that seemed willing to champion a strong anti-Hitler allegory. Throughout 1938, as Germany's threat to Czechoslovakia became ever greater, the three writers redrafted their script to make the parallels even more explicit. At one point the screenplay ran to 230 pages, a blueprint for what would have been a four-hour movie. With each new draft, Huston in particular would embroider, adding lines like "Our task is to fight the tyrant . . . fight . . . fight . . . to keep the cause of democracy alive."

It's not clear that Huston's preferred version of the screenplay would ever have been filmable, but when *Juárez* finally foundered, what undid months of his work wasn't corporate trepidation but movie-star egotism. Warner Bros. had given the title role to Paul Muni, at the time the studio's most prestigious male star. In the last few years, Muni had made a specialty out of transformative historical roles in costume dramas, having played Louis Pasteur and Emile Zola. Though still held in critical esteem, he was a vain and humorless man who was beginning to panic about his waning box-office strength and would do anything to get his own way. When he read the script and saw that his character was written with aphoristic minimalism while his costars Brian Aherne and Bette Davis got all of the big emotional scenes as Maximilian and Carlotta, he brought his brother-in-law onto the production and had him rewrite the entire screenplay to amplify his role, while the director, William Dieterle, stood by haplessly. "The first thing Muni wanted was more dialogue. . . . He just tore the script apart and ruined it," said Huston.

At the end of 1938, a few months before *Juárez* was released, Wyler helped Huston bounce back from his disappointment by hiring him to do a final polish of Ben Hecht and Charles MacArthur's script for *Wuthering Heights*, which he was about to start for his boss, the independent producer

Samuel Goldwyn. Huston gratefully took the job but declined credit, saying, "Hecht and MacArthur had written a beautiful screenplay but it was almost in treatment form, so I put it into a screenplay. . . . For me to have intruded my name would have been vulgar."

Wuthering Heights and *Juárez* had their premieres within days of each other in April 1939. Wyler's movie was rapturously received, and despite Goldwyn's infamous remark that "*I* made *Wuthering Heights*—William Wyler only directed it," the film—lushly mounted, extravagantly romantic, and perfectly suited for audiences who sought refuge from the troubles of the modern world—did a great deal to burnish Wyler's growing reputation; in what later came to be seen as an epochal year for American movies, it won the New York Film Critics Circle Award for best picture, edging *Gone with the Wind*. *Juárez* ended up as little more than an unhappy footnote; the version that was first tested before audiences was received so poorly that Warner Bros. immediately cut twenty-five minutes out of it. The parallels to Hitler and Mussolini that Huston had worked so hard to instill remained thunderously clear, starting with the opening titles, which refer to a "dictator" building a "war machine," and the first scenes, in which Napoleon III (Claude Rains) intones, "Let the world know that the conquest of Mexico is only the beginning of the fulfillment of our holy mission." Reviewing the movie in the *New York Times*, Frank S. Nugent took notice that Hollywood finally seemed to be shaking off its studious neutrality about Europe; he wrote approvingly that "in the contest between dictator and democrat the Warners have owned their uncompromising allegiance to the latter. . . . With pardonable opportunism, they have written between the lines . . . the text of a liberal's scorn for fascism and Nazism." But other critics were chillier; the movie, which was still long and ungainly, was a costly box-office flop, and the experience left Huston determined not to have his work undercut again. "I knew that if I'd been the director instead of William Dieterle, this wouldn't have happened," he said. "So I knew I was going to have to be responsible for the things I wrote" by becoming a director. "That was the only way I could survive."

Juárez failed in part because its elliptical, propaganda-as-historical-allegory approach felt quaint to an audience that had been watching goose-stepping German soldiers in newsreels every week and was now primed for tougher, more direct attacks on Hitler from Hollywood. The week Huston's movie opened, it was overshadowed by the premiere of an energetic Warner Bros. crime drama that marked the first time any studio had allowed a movie to take as its subject the perceived German threat within U.S. borders. The challenge built into the new film's ad campaign took aim not only at the pusillanimous self-interest of other studios but at the evolving taste of moviegoers. Finally, Warners announced in its slogan, the public would have a chance to see something that had been too long kept off screens: "The Picture That Calls A Swastika A Swastika!"

TWO

"The Dictates of My Heart and Blood"

HOLLYWOOD AND WASHINGTON,
APRIL 1939–MAY 1940

Confessions of a Nazi Spy opened in New York City on April 28, 1939, the day Hitler gave a speech at the Reichstag in which he made it clear that he considered Poland to be his for the taking. Its title alone was shocking: The word "Nazi" had never before appeared in the name of a major studio movie, and this one had been the subject of controversy from the moment Warners had acquired the movie rights a year earlier. *Confessions* was directed by Wyler and Huston's close friend Anatole Litvak, a Ukrainian-born Jew who had fled Germany as the Nazis rose in the early 1930s. The story was based on a former FBI agent's account of the infiltration of a ring of Nazis within the German-American Bund in New York City. Other companies had openly opposed Warners' intention to make the film; the head of Paramount's internal censorship department warned that if *Confessions* was "in any way uncomplimentary to Germany, as it must be if it is to be sincerely produced, then Warners will have on their hands the blood of a great many Jews in Germany." Some within the Production Code office, which had never been particularly sympathetic to the industry's Jewish leaders, argued that the movie courted disaster by failing to depict Hitler's "unchallenged political and social achievements" and would be "one of the most lamentable mistakes ever made by the industry." Others feared that it would inflame anti-Semitic accusations that Hollywood was clannishly advancing a Jewish interventionist agenda. As *Confessions* sped toward production, Warner Bros. assumed that it would inevitably be banned in many European countries (which it was) and might also face serious opposition from state and municipal censorship boards (which it did not). But the studio stood by its conviction that the country was ready for the movie, and was aided considerably by its star, Edward G. Robinson (born Emanuel Goldenberg), who lobbied hard to play the FBI agent Robinson, telling Hal Wallis, "I want to do that for my people," and who proved to be an articulate and compelling spokesman for its themes. "The world is faced with the menace of gangsters who are much more dangerous than we have ever known," Robinson told a reporter. "And there's no reason why the motion pictures shouldn't be used to combat them."

Opinions about the movie's quality varied, but it had arrived at the perfect moment—one in which Warners' delivery of exactly the blunt-force drama promised by all the advance publicity looked not simply shrewd, but bold and prescient. "Hitler's pledge of non-aggression toward the Americas reached the Warners too late yesterday," wrote one reviewer. "They had formally declared war on the Nazis at 8:15 A.M. with the first showing of their *Confessions of a Nazi Spy* at the Strand. Hitler won't like it; neither will Goebbels." *Variety* wondered about its "bearing on German-American relations" and worriedly described it as "a wartime propaganda picture in flavor and essence." And a few weeks after the movie opened, *Time* called it "as matter-of-fact and unmincing as a newsreel, undiplomatic as an artillery bombardment" and reported that other studios, noticing the long lines outside theaters, were dusting off "productions calculated to please haters of Hitler & Co." Among the filmmakers mentioned was Charlie Chaplin, who was working on a comedy about der Führer and a lookalike that he had tentatively titled *The Dictator*.

For Hollywood, there was no going back, and so, a year after he had failed to get RKO to greenlight *Paths of Glory*, George Stevens thought it was time to try again with a new project. *Gunga Din*'s success had made him even more valuable to the studio, and recent headlines had shaken him out of his antiwar stance. Now, rather than directing another comedy or musical, he wanted to take on the Nazi threat. Stevens was an avid reader who, when he wasn't shooting a movie, could happily spend a day in an armchair paging through one book after another, and in late 1938 he had come across two newly published novels that he thought were ideal for adaptation. One of them, *Address Unknown*, told the story of a Jewish bookseller in the United States and his business partner, a Gentile German American who returns to the homeland and becomes enraptured by the Third Reich, then destroyed by it when he is mistaken for a Jew. The other, *The Mortal Storm*, was set entirely in contemporary Germany and traced the professional and personal disintegration of an anti-Hitler professor and his family as the Nazis rose to power. Both novels were brutal, vividly anti-Fascist tracts with appropriately unhappy endings.

George Schaeffer, RKO's president, was one of the few studio chiefs who was not Jewish; he was also arguably the most risk-averse of all his colleagues. When Stevens urged Schaeffer's lieutenant Pandro Berman to acquire movie rights to the novels, Berman warned him that Schaeffer was "definitely afraid [to] commit . . . to any picture that is propaganda against anything. . . . He has every wish that we make a picture with regard to Americanism or democracy but [is] opposed to any specific movement against any other force." *Address Unknown* was immediately ruled out as a possibility; Berman cabled Stevens that "after serious thought [I] believe if [RKO] would be willing to proceed with a picture that might be classed as anti-Nazi propaganda that we would do better to consider *Mortal Storm*." But Stevens barely had a moment to hold on to that hope. Later the same day, Berman cabled him again, gently but firmly pushing him toward more benign material, an adaptation of a melodramatic novel about the sins and sacrifices of a pair of British nurses called *The Sisters*, which the studio felt would make a fine "women's picture" and put Stevens back on familiar turf.

Stevens was furious. At times of distress or adversity, he tended to turn inward, becoming withdrawn rather than combative. So it was characteristic that rather than confronting Berman or Schaeffer, he drafted a long letter to himself in which he railed against RKO, complaining that he had worked tirelessly for the studio, that he had been given just four weeks off in the last four years, that he had never been thanked for delivering *Gunga Din*, and that the company's heavy hand was making it impossible for him to "do first-rate pictures" that were "comparable in quality to those of the first-rate directors." Stevens was in the middle of a contract renegotiation with RKO, and in the spring of 1939 he reluctantly re-signed with the company and agreed to make *The Sisters* (which was retitled *Vigil in the Night*) as his next film that fall. Other directors would make the movies he had proposed; almost immediately, the rights to *The Mortal Storm* were sold to MGM, Columbia acquired *Address Unknown*, and before he had shot even a foot of film under his new contract, Stevens began to feel certain that he was at the wrong studio.

In the spring of 1939, Frank Capra was at the height of his power in the film industry. He had just tested his authority in a remarkable game of brinksmanship between the Screen Directors Guild, which was petitioning the National Labor Relations Board for certification as a union, and the Academy of Motion Picture Arts and Sciences, which was in the late 1930s the primary representative of the interests of studios and which fiercely opposed unionization. Capra, who had been president of the Academy since 1935, had recently overcome his initial reluctance to join the SDG and had become its president as well. He thus had the power to turn himself into a kind of Trojan horse who could undermine either institution from within— that is, once he chose a side. He could have gone either way, but ultimately he chose to cast his lot with directors and, although he disliked them, unions. Capra threatened to resign from the Academy—the strong implication being that the creative community of Hollywood, which gave the organization whatever credibility it had, would quickly follow—unless antiunion producers agreed to leave the Academy altogether. It didn't come to that, but the producers did agree that the Academy would no longer play any role in labor negotiations. In one bold stroke, Capra had permanently altered the Academy's role in Hollywood, and had helped strengthen the SDG. Then, perhaps even more impressively, he managed to broker a peace between the SDG and the Association of Motion Picture Producers. In February, when the Academy presented him with a surprise third Best Director Oscar for *You Can't*

Take It With You and President Roosevelt's son James, an aspiring producer, showed up at Los Angeles's Biltmore Hotel to give the film the Academy Award for Best Picture, the honors were widely seen as a recognition not just of Capra's artistry but of his service to the industry.

It was a surprising moment for Capra to decide to make *Mr. Smith Goes to Washington.* Hollywood was beset not only by labor unrest, but by racketeering charges, the stain of organized crime in its largest trade union, and accusations that it was rife with Communists. In addition, a serious antitrust case was being pursued by the Justice Department; as one columnist would soon write, "it is probable that the industry has never faced blacker days." The studios were trying to curry favor in the nation's capital, not alienate it, which meant that the timing was spectacularly bad for a script that painted the entire political establishment as a swamp of crooks and cronies. Moreover, *Mr. Smith*'s screenwriter, Sidney Buchman, *was* actually a Communist. (Like many in Hollywood at the time, he was attracted by the party's committed opposition to Fascism.)

Buchman, who became a victim of the blacklist two decades later when he refused to name names to the House Un-American Activities Committee, said that Capra was "terribly suspicious" about the possibility that his screenplay for *Mr. Smith Goes to Washington* might contain a "hidden message" that would not be apparent to him until it was too late. But what seems most remarkable about the dialogue and storyline of the finished film is that, while replete with the quasi-populist anger that Capra had first dramatized in *Mr. Deeds Goes to Town,* its politics are completely nonspecific. The idea of making the movie as a sequel to *Mr. Deeds Goes to Town* was dropped when Sam Goldwyn refused to loan Gary Cooper to Columbia. But Jefferson Smith (Jimmy Stewart) is very much a cousin to the pugnacious innocent that Cooper played; he's an overgrown child, the head of the Boy Rangers and publisher of a kiddie newspaper, who is appointed to fill a Senate vacancy. He has no experience, little knowledge, and very few concrete ideas; his primary virtue, according to love interest Jean Arthur, resides in his "plain, decent, everyday common rightness. And this country could use some of that. Yeah. So could the whole cockeyed world." Capra's definition of the "cockeyed world"—a favorite locution that he would go on to use in both private letters and subsequent movies—was broad enough to encompass the entire U.S. Senate, which is steeped in corruption and pork-barrel politics, as well as most reporters, several of whom Smith beats up after they write stories noting, correctly, that he is a stooge who doesn't understand how he's being used. Nobody in *Mr. Smith Goes to Washington* belongs to any party or espouses any recognizable cause—Smith's only big idea is a "national boys' club," and the closest he comes to stating an ideology is his argument that "lost causes are the only ones worth fighting for" and his climactic plea to "love thy neighbor."

The contradictions—a veneration of the little guy but a deep distrust of a bunch of little guys once they coalesce into a mob, a pronounced contempt for the intellectual elite intermingled with a hyperpatriotic montage of monuments to great political thinkers—were pure Capra. "He was a very simplistic man," said Buchman. "His view of the world came down to that of a fairy tale. . . . For him a politician or a capitalist were [*sic*] always marionettes representing good or evil. . . . I really believe that he never knew what Mr. Smith actually was saying."

Even Capra's closest associates were confounded by the chasm between the man and his movie. At one point during the shooting of *Mr. Smith*, Buchman tried to draw Capra out about some of the ideas that mattered to him in the film, particularly that of the importance of maintaining vigilance in a democracy. "Go get fucked with your *theme*!" Capra snapped, arguing that his only obligation was to entertain the public. "Are you a Communist?"

"Are you a Fascist?" Buchman shot back. He wasn't the only one who wondered. In July 1939, as Capra neared the end of production in Los Angeles, Edward Bernds witnessed him explode when he couldn't get a large group of extras to pay attention. "*These* are the people, the fellows you want to do things for!" Capra sneered, baiting his pro-union colleague. The tantrum led Bernds to speculate in his diary that Capra's real credo was that "the mob is so lazy, so stupid, so wrong-headed that only harsh leadership of energetic, able men (fascism) is practical. Sure F.C. feels something like it."

If war was on Capra's mind, there is little evidence of it in *Mr. Smith Goes to Washington*. When Smith makes an ardent plea to "get boys out of crowded cities"—a favorite target of Capra's scorn—"and stuffy basements for a couple of months of the year" so they can "build their bodies and minds for a man-sized job," it's not the job that many were speculating was imminent; Smith quickly explains that "those boys are going to be behind these desks" sometime soon. During the making of the film, Capra almost willed himself to ignore the front pages; for all its rhetoric, *Mr. Smith Goes to Washington* makes almost no mention of international events at all. Capra was locked away in an editing room on a September Friday working on a cut he was planning to test a few weeks later in New York City when he learned that Germany had invaded Poland. By the time he returned to work on Monday morning, *Time* had given a name to what had begun. The magazine, using its own coinage, was calling it "World War II."

Capra still had a movie to promote, and he had no intention of allowing Mr. Smith to arrive quietly. On October 16, 1939, he presided over an invitation-only preview at Washington, D.C.'s four-thousand-seat Constitution Hall with a guest list that included 250 congressmen and about half of the ninety-six senators who were so pointedly lampooned in the film as thieves, boobs, and ineffectual fogies. In his autobiography, Capra, relishing every embellishment, recounts the story of how that evening unfolded as an inexorably mounting fiasco of tragicomic proportions, with cries of "Insult!" and "Outrage!" reverberating in the auditorium and a handful of walkouts eventually turning into a stampede that left more than a thousand seats empty. Capra claimed that the press corps, which was in attendance cheek by jowl with cabinet secretaries, Supreme Court justices, and elected officials, had turned on the movie because journalists "envied and feared film as a rival opinion maker" and were offended at being depicted as alcoholic layabouts; they "berated, scorned, vilified and ripped me open" after the movie ended, he wrote. Their contempt, in his telling, was rivaled only by that of the senators, who were affronted by the film's suggestion that "graft could rear its ugly head in the august Senate chamber."

The reality was less dramatic—newspaper reports at the time mentioned only minimal walkouts, no catcalls, and a polite though not effusive reception that included a round of applause at the end. But there was no disputing that *Mr. Smith* had made Capra some powerful enemies that evening. Kentucky senator Alben Barkley, the Democratic majority leader and a dead

ringer for the Senate president played in the film by the veteran character actor Harry Carey, was particularly vocal, denouncing Capra's work to
the *New York Times* as "silly and stupid" and complaining that it "makes the
Senate look like a bunch of crooks." Republican senator Henry Cabot Lodge
Jr. dismissed the movie as "ridiculous—just something from Hollywood,"
and Senator George Norris, an independent from Nebraska, remarked, "I've
been in Congress 36 years, but I've never seen a member as dumb as that
boy." "Not all Senators are sons of bitches," complained another.

With some congressmen punitively suggesting to the press that it might
be an ideal moment to advance anti–block booking legislation—a series
of laws intended to loosen the studios' collective chokehold on theater
owners—Washington's hostility to the movie industry was threatening to
reach another of its now-frequent boiling points. Joseph P. Kennedy, then
serving a brief term as U.S. ambassador to the United Kingdom, weighed in
as well, telling Will Hays, head of the Motion Picture Producers and Distributors of America, that he considered the film "one of the most disgraceful
things I have ever seen done to our country," and warning Columbia's Harry
Cohn that "to show this film in foreign countries will do inestimable harm to
American prestige all over the world."

Capra wasted no time in launching a counteroffensive. Days after the
Washington preview, he told reporters, "With all those things they've got to
do down there, with the neutrality bill, and social legislation, with war breaking loose in Europe . . . the whole majesty of the United States Senate has to
move against one moving picture. It's amazing!" As soon as it opened,
Mr. Smith Goes to Washington found all the defenders it needed; the *New York
Times* spoke for most critics when its reviewer commented that the picture
was protected by "that unwritten clause in the Bill of Rights entitling every
voting citizen to at least one free swing at the Senate. Mr. Capra's swing is
from the floor and in the best of humor; if it fails to rock that august body to
its heels—from laughter as much as injured dignity—it won't be his fault
but the Senate's and we should really begin to worry about the upper
house." Even those who belittled the movie's plot as "eyewash," as the sharp-
minded, sharp-tongued Otis Ferguson did in the *New Republic,* argued that

"the Senate and the machinery of how it may be used to advantage is shown better than it ever has been."

Although *Mr. Smith* was only a middling box-office hit at the time of its release, the movie's warm critical reception reaffirmed Capra's status as, in the words of the *New Yorker*, "the surest director in Hollywood" and "professionally, at least, a consistent champion of people in the lower income groups." In interviews, Capra was becoming increasingly prone to lofty self-aggrandizement, and in early 1940, as the film opened around the country, he was moved to announce that "the underlying value of my movies is actually the Sermon on the Mount" and to reveal his desire to make a film in which "Mussolini . . . or the Prince of Wales . . . goes down to a bordello, and then a little trollop like Mary Magdalen tells him . . . to throw away your guns, throw away every goddamn cannon in the ocean, open up your borders."

But in private, Capra was generally more modest and temperate. Even as he started making plans for his next film, he was deeply troubled by first-hand news of the war in Europe. For the last several years, he had corresponded with Lionel Robinson, a bookseller in London whose help he had enlisted when he decided he wanted to furnish his Brentwood home with more than $100,000 of rare and antique volumes and first editions. "My dear Frank," Robinson wrote just weeks after England declared war on Germany. "I think you might like to know what is happening to us in London now that this dreadful war has been forced upon us. So far the expected has not happened and instead of being regularly bombed by enemy aircraft we have been subject only to an uneasy anticipation of them. . . . We shall of course remain in Pall Mall as long as we can but if, and when, the position becomes really dangerous we have arranged for temporary accommodation in Oxford . . . God willing . . . whatever happens the world of books will carry on." Within a month Robinson and his family were forced to evacuate. "I am glad your wife and children are at least out of the center of things," Capra wrote back. "Somehow, we feel over here this terrible thing will end without too much destruction. Maybe it is just . . . hope."

His encouraging words notwithstanding, Capra was coming to believe that the war would not be a short one. And he was among the first of his colleagues to realize that film and filmmakers would have a crucial role to play. "I never cease to thrill at an audience seeing a picture," he said in February 1940. "For two hours you've got 'em. Hitler can't keep 'em that long. You eventually reach even more people than Roosevelt does on the radio." After four years as Academy president, Capra had recently decided to hand the reins over to the outspoken liberal producer Walter Wanger, but he planned to stay active in the organization, and in the spring, he and the Academy's Research Council met with James Roosevelt and began to formalize plans to oversee the production of a series of new training films for the Signal Corps. The meeting, and Roosevelt's presence at it, helped to quiet some of the anti-studio bluster coming from the capital, and would mark the war's first official alliance between Hollywood and Washington.

Soon after *Mr. Smith Goes to Washington* opened, Capra made a career decision that would prove pivotal: He left Columbia Pictures, the studio that he had helped put on the map over the past decade, to become an independent producer-director. At first, he considered taking his new company, Frank Capra Productions, to United Artists, which at the time functioned as what would now be considered an independent distributor, bringing strong producers like David O. Selznick, Samuel Goldwyn, and Alexander Korda into the fold, then sharing costs and profits with them while letting them make virtually all the creative decisions on their movies. But when a deal with UA failed to materialize, Capra decided he would remain itinerant. He assumed, correctly, that any studio in town would be happy to have his next movie, and it took little time for him to get Warner Bros. to agree to cofinance the film he wanted to make, *Meet John Doe*.

Capra's departure left Columbia with a huge void, and created an opportunity for George Stevens. When war broke out in Europe, Stevens was just ten days from beginning production on *Vigil in the Night*, the melodrama RKO had insisted he direct instead of *The Mortal Storm*. *Vigil* was based on a novel by A. J. Cronin, a Scottish physician turned writer whose best seller *The Citadel* had been the basis for an extremely popular MGM movie two years earlier. His new story, about a young British nurse who lets her sister take the fall after her carelessness causes the death of a child, was contrived and soapy. Three writers had worked on the screenplay, but none of them could do much to fix the scene in which an elderly gossip who threatens to expose the young woman conveniently goes over a cliff in a bus, or a preposterous last act that punishes the guilty sister by having the 1918 flu epidemic sweep through London.

Stevens never felt engaged by the material, but the start of war offered him an opportunity to make it relevant. Suddenly, stories of British grit and determination under fire had an immediacy that RKO hadn't anticipated six months earlier; throughout 1940 and 1941, stories of English patriotism would become a staple of pro-intervention Hollywood filmmaking. With almost no time to overhaul the script, Stevens did whatever he could to bring it up to date once his cameras were rolling. He had already abandoned the World War I setting and reset *Vigil* in present-day London. Now he made sure that the street scenes were dressed with army recruiting posters. He had background extras appear in military uniforms. He even managed to insert a few lines that acknowledged present-day realities—"Do you realize we're as close to war as we'll ever be?" says a hospital administrator arguing for the conservation of resources. And in *Vigil*'s final scene, he planned to make the presence of war explicit: As the climax played out, the main characters would hear the speech that Prime Minister Neville Chamberlain had delivered just weeks earlier, on September 3, 1939, in which he announced over the radio that the British government had warned Berlin that "unless we heard from them by eleven o'clock that they were prepared at once to withdraw their troops from Poland, a state of war would exist between us. I have to tell you that no such undertaking has been received, and that consequently this country is at war with Germany. You can imagine what a bitter blow it is to me that all my long struggle to win peace has failed."

Over the next several years, directors, writers, and producers would become accustomed to revising their war movies on the fly, sometimes frantically adding or rewriting scenes just weeks before production ended or even scheduling last-minute reshoots to keep their work as reflective as possible of the latest breaking news. Since Hollywood pictures could reach theaters as little as six weeks after shooting was finished, timeliness, especially in the hundreds of movies that would be made about the war while it was still taking place, would quickly become of paramount dramatic (and box-office) value. By the middle of 1940, Walter Wanger and Alfred Hitchcock wouldn't think twice about scrapping the ending of a movie they had already completed, *Foreign Correspondent*, and shooting a new final scene that acknowledged the bombing of Britain with an impassioned plea that the United States remain engaged and alert. ("It feels as if the lights were all out everywhere, except in America . . . It's a big story and you're part of it . . . Hello, America! Hang on to your lights! They're the only lights left in the world!" the reporter played by Joel McCrea shouts over the radio.) With his hasty addition to the ending of *Vigil in the Night*, Stevens may have been the first American director after the start of the war to try to bring some of the immediacy of a newsreel to a Hollywood drama.

But audiences never got the chance to see Stevens's finale. RKO head George Schaeffer flew from New York to Los Angeles to order the director to cut the scene in which the characters listened to Chamberlain's speech. "In the film," said Stevens, "the great irritation of the war overcomes the lesser irritation of their mundane activities, which is something I was really aiming for. . . . They wanted the [scene] cut on the basis that we brought up the idea of war, and America [was] not in war, and people would be so disturbed by the picture they wouldn't go and see it. . . . It ruined the picture."

Stevens later said he wished that *Vigil in the Night*, which was ignored by audiences and rejected by critics ("heavy and stolid" was one of the kinder verdicts), had never been released. In its promotional materials, RKO made no mention of the war at all, selling the movie, which opened in February 1940 as a soap opera, with the slogan "The world's most famous doctor rips the veil from the hidden lives of those bitter women who know men too well!" Stevens may have felt all the more mistreated because the day *Vigil* had its first preview for the press, the movie he had really wanted to make, *The Mortal Storm*, began production at MGM with Frank Borzage directing.*

* Although MGM had softened *The Mortal Storm* considerably, insisting that the screenplay not even identify Germany as the country in which it took place, the German government was nonetheless livid that it was being made at all and, according to Scott Eyman's *Lion of Hollywood*, dispatched an emissary from the Swiss consulate to the Los Angeles set to warn Borzage and his cast that their treachery would not be forgotten after the war. By mid-1940, Germany would ban the exhibition of all Hollywood movies within its borders.

This time, he did not keep his feelings to himself. In March, the *New York Times* reported that "after several weeks of friction that started when George Stevens was assigned the megaphone at RKO for *Vigil in the Night*, the director and the studio parted company today." Within a month, Stevens had signed a two-picture deal with Columbia, which was so eager to replenish its roster of talent after Capra's departure that it agreed to an unusual proviso: Stevens, wary of any further interference from studio chiefs, stipulated that the company's notoriously meddlesome president Harry Cohn would not be allowed to visit his sets during production. Cohn, surprisingly, agreed, promising, "You make a picture here, and I'll never speak to you." But looking to the future, Cohn insisted on a new contractual rider of his own, one which, with some variations, would soon become an industry standard: If a war or national emergency resulted in the closing of American movie houses for more than a week, all contracts with talent would be null and void.

William and Talli Wyler were in Tijuana on a brief vacation with two of their closest friends, Wyler's agent Paul Kohner and his wife, Lupita, when they heard the war had started. For the Wylers, the Labor Day weekend getaway was an attempt at a brief respite after a summer of upheaval. Wyler's father had died in July 1939, shortly before Talli had given birth. Carl Laemmle, the grudging early mentor who had helped Wyler come to America and then seen him grow into the family's greatest success, was gravely ill with heart disease and just weeks from death. Wyler had been working nonstop— he and Talli hadn't even had time for a real honeymoon during their first year of marriage, and as soon as they returned to Los Angeles, Talli would have to begin preparing for their move to a new home in Bel Air while Wyler started preproduction on *The Westerner*, Sam Goldwyn's attempt to capitalize on the surprising success of John Ford's *Stagecoach*. It was pure happenstance that the Wylers were out of the country when the news broke—they had been staying in San Diego and had just crossed into Mexico for a day trip to see a bullfight—but for Wyler it was a reminder that the border represented for so many not just a formality but a terribly significant barrier. While in Tijuana, they ran into Franz Planer, a respected cinematographer in Europe who had fled Austria and was now, like many refugees, watching weeks stretch into months while he was stuck in the no-man's-land of a Mexican hotel, waiting for permission to enter the United States legally and hoping to obtain employment in the American movie industry.

As he returned to Hollywood, Wyler felt the war was closing in on him, but he shared his feelings with colleagues only when the pressure became too great to bear. When he declined repeatedly to contribute to Harry Warner's pet cause, the Hollywood Community Chest, Warner gave him a private scolding. "I don't know of anything that will breed more discontent . . . more resentment among those unfortunates who must be helped, than the knowledge that people with heaven blessed incomes refuse to extend a helping hand," Warner told Wyler. "It is of such stuff that Communism is born. And brother, I'm sure neither of us want that in America. This is a pretty stiff letter to write, especially by one who is appealing for charity . . . but I'd rather thrash this out between ourselves than have the public learn that the 'fantastically wealthy' movie people are too self centered and too selfish to give a thought to their unfortunate neighbors." The subtext, from one "brother" naturalized American to another, would have been easily understood by Wyler: Successful Jews in Hollywood had a special obligation to practice nondenominational good-neighbor philanthropy as an inoculation against the increasingly loud charge that the industry was, as one anti-Semitic senator would soon claim, "swarming with refugees" who were only "interested in foreign causes."

Warner was serious about going public if Wyler didn't comply; he had already planted an item with the syndicated Hollywood gossip columnist Jimmie Fidler in which he threatened to take out newspaper advertisements listing the names of all showbiz luminaries who had failed to make donations. Wyler sent Warner a check for a hundred dollars, acknowledging that it wasn't the "real generous contribution" he had requested, but explaining in almost pleading terms that he had to put his money to "more vital" use. "Due to the fact that my original home and all branches of my family are abroad, and the political situation as it is today, I have had to distribute my charities according to the dictates of my heart and blood, and I ask you to believe me when I say that my quota has been more than commensurate with my income." Wyler went on to tell the studio chief that he had spent so much money that he had even been forced to renege on a pledge to the United Jewish Welfare Fund. Warner softened his tone and did not make good on his threat, but his reply was still stern: "I know your heart has been disturbed by what has been going on in this turbulent world," he wrote back, "but the fact remains that we do have hundreds of thousands of people living right here in our community and we must all extend ourselves to help them."

As a director, Wyler was well compensated—a few months after he finished *The Westerner*, Warner would borrow him from Goldwyn to direct Bette Davis in an adaptation of W. Somerset Maugham's stage melodrama *The Letter* at a salary of $6,250 a week. But he had not exaggerated the severe financial strain he was under. Since 1936, he had been in ongoing correspondence with the State Department, trying to sponsor two dozen distant relatives and family friends, including the man who had been his parents' personal physician, all of whom wanted to emigrate from Mulhouse to America. In each of the cases in which Wyler petitioned the government, he had to pay the application fees and agree to serve as the guarantor not just of their travel expenses but of their financial security if they were permitted to come to the United States. As the situation for Jews in Europe grew more dire, the tone of the letters he received became desperate. "Mein Lieber Willy, we will eternally thank you for this with all our hearts," read one. "Please do not let me and my child go under," read another. "Give me the chance to pull ourselves through."

In those months, Wyler seemed to want nothing more than to escape, either by throwing himself into work or by leaving the country. But there was little refuge to be found. In early 1940, he and Talli decided to plan their long-postponed honeymoon, driving from Lake Placid to Montreal and then planning a visit to a ski lodge in Quebec. When they attempted to make reservations, they were rebuffed by a hotel clerk, who told them, "I'm terribly sorry. Jews are not allowed." The Wylers were welcome to ski and dine, but not to stay overnight. "We were stunned," Talli said. "We had never run into anything like that. . . . It was so bald it was shocking." After a few days at a smaller resort, the Wylers decided to end their ski vacation and take a cruise down to Cuba instead. The liner they boarded was painted with the Dutch flag—a sign of neutrality in case Hitler's U-boats were in the vicin-

ity. After a couple of weeks, the Wylers cut that trip short as well and returned home.

At the end of February, Wyler attended the Academy Awards banquet at
the Coconut Grove in Los Angeles. He had received a nomination for Best
Director—his second—for *Wuthering Heights,* which was also up for Best
Picture. His competition included Capra, who was in contention for *Mr.
Smith Goes to Washington,* and Ford, who was nominated for *Stagecoach.* To
nobody's surprise, they were all beaten by Victor Fleming, whose *Gone with
the Wind* swept the awards. But in some ways the night also belonged to Ford,
who had been on an unprecedented run during the last twelve months that
had ended with three of his movies up for Oscars and a fourth opening just
past that year's voting deadline and bringing him the highest praise of his
career.

A year earlier, Ford's *Stagecoach* had arrived in theaters to reviews that
were not only positive but openly surprised. Westerns had long been an essential part of Hollywood's output; as many as 20 percent of the movies
produced every year were cowboy films, but most of them were ultra-low-
budget "programmers," generally running under an hour and used to fill out
double bills in rural theater chains. *Stagecoach,* which Ford had made for
Walter Wanger at United Artists, was something different: an "A" picture
with a top-notch cast, a strong screenplay by Dudley Nichols (who had won
an Oscar for writing Ford's *The Informer*), and an unabashedly adult story
that tested the limits of the Production Code by including the apparent endorsement of a revenge killing and sympathetic depictions of a prostitute and
an alcoholic. Ford won considerable credit from critics for turning a lesser
genre into something respectable and even challenging, and also for his work
with the hitherto unremarkable John Wayne. Ford had known Wayne for
years before casting him as the movie's hero, the Ringo Kid; he thought the
actor was able but lazy, and he upbraided him mercilessly on the set ("Why
are you moving your mouth so much? Don't you know that you don't act with
your mouth in pictures? You act with your eyes!"), but *Stagecoach* helped
make Wayne a star and turned Ford into a first-rank director.

Wanger, a committed progressive and interventionist with a sharp eye for
publicity opportunities, used the opening of the movie to initiate an attack on

the Production Code in particular and industry timidity in general, proclaiming at a press conference that Hollywood was America's best hope against European totalitarianism and that "democracy depends on the easy and prompt dissemination of ideas and opinions," which should not be "hobbled or haltered" by censorship. Wanger would have been happy to enlist his director to the cause, and Ford did use *Stagecoach* to score his own political points, making one of the movie's villains a rapacious banker, a Hoover/Coolidge surrogate prone to rhetoric like "America for Americans!" and "The government must not interfere with business . . . what this country needs is a businessman for president."

But Ford wasn't much interested in joining Wanger's war of words. By the time *Stagecoach* opened in March, he was already back at 20th Century Fox directing *Young Mr. Lincoln* with Henry Fonda. The film, which was shot quickly and opened that June, didn't make much of an impression with moviegoers, but Ford's gentle, elegiac treatment of Lincoln confirmed for many critics that he was now, as Graham Greene wrote, "one of the best directors of the day." Ford spent the summer of 1939 making *Drums Along the Mohawk*, a drama about the Revolutionary War that marked his first foray into Technicolor; although less elegantly wrought and finely shaded than *Young Mr. Lincoln*, the vivid, crowd-pleasing picture also offered history without politics, and high-spirited Americana with no attempt at contemporary allegory.

Ford was preparing to shoot his fourth movie in a year when the war started; this time, the politics would be so overt that there would be no chance of avoiding controversy. When Fox's Darryl Zanuck bought the rights to John Steinbeck's just-published novel *The Grapes of Wrath*, Ford told Zanuck he would "leap at the chance" to make it, but some in Hollywood assumed he had acquired an unfilmable property. Even apart from a climactic scene in which a young woman whose child has died offers her breast milk to a starving man, the story of the Joad family's agonizing displacement was an unremitting portrait of the plight of migrant workers amid Dust Bowl poverty that depicted exactly the kind of suffering most Hollywood movies were designed to help audiences forget. Zanuck and Ford planned to shoot the film in stark black and white, using many outdoor locations and working quickly—production lasted just six weeks in October and November. Fearful of leaks to the press, they kept Nunnally Johnson's script under lock and key.

Zanuck worried about attacks from the California Chamber of Commerce and the Associated Farmers of California, which were shown treating migrant workers as animals, and he kept the identities of those groups murky in the film, but there was no missing the fact that *The Grapes of Wrath* was domestic agitprop on a scale that Hollywood had almost never dared.

In the movie's most direct political statement, Tom Joad (Henry Fonda) is in a work camp when someone reads him a headline about vigilantes running "Red agitators" out of the county. "Listen, what is these 'Reds' anyway?" Tom asks. "Every time you turn around, somebody's callin' somebody else a Red." In Ford's hands, the gentle, almost throwaway moment is hardly pro-Communist; it's more an expression of contempt for the mob idiocy that Ford felt anti-Communist paranoia was fueling. But that, plus the movie's implicit suggestion that a kind of benevolent, self-sustaining socialism emerged naturally from the work camps, was enough for some on the right to call Ford a Communist sympathizer. (It probably didn't help that in the *Daily Worker,* Woody Guthrie announced that Ford had made "the best cussed pitcher I ever seen.") The Catholic-run *Motion Picture Daily* huffed, "If the conditions which the picture tends to present as typical are proportionately true, then the Revolution has been too long delayed. If, on the other hand, the picture depicts an extraordinary, isolated, and non-usual condition . . . then no small libel against the good name of the Republic has been committed." And *Time* magazine, its editorial pages all firmly in the grip of the fanatical anti-Communist Henry Luce, sneered, "Pinkos who did not bat an eye when the Soviet Government exterminated 3,000,000 peasants by famine will go for a good cry over the hardships of the Okies."

When *The Grapes of Wrath* opened in January 1940, those dissents were soon drowned out. *New York Times* critic Frank Nugent—who after World War II would change professions and become Ford's most prolific screenwriter—praised its "resoluteness of approach to a dangerous topic. . . . If it were any better, we just wouldn't believe our eyes." *Variety,* rarely moved to praise topicality in its bottom-line, give-the-people-what-they-want reviews, called it "a shocking visualization of a state of affairs demanding generous humanitarian attention. . . . It took courage, a pile of money, and John Ford" to tell the story. The *New Republic* wrote with astonishment, "There is no country in the world where such a film of truth could be made today . . . and the public is *going* to this picture." And even *Time* grudgingly conceded that "*The Grapes of Wrath* is possibly the best picture ever made from a so-so book." Ford didn't do many interviews to promote the movie, allowing only that he was moved by the story's similarity to the Irish potato famine, "when they threw the people off the land and left them wandering on the roads to starve. That may have had something to do with it . . . part of my Irish tradition."

Suddenly, Ford was threatening to unseat Capra as the populist conscience of the movie business, a role he couldn't have been less interested in taking on. As *The Grapes of Wrath* continued to open around the country in the spring of 1940, his mind was not on Hollywood at all. Back in 1934, Ford had attempted to rekindle his twenty-year-old dream of joining the navy by buying a 106-foot boat he named the *Araner*, as a tribute to his Irish mother's Aran Islands heritage. The ketch was a perfect fit for Ford's romantic conception of himself as a roving seaman always ready to light out; it fit right in with his founding of what he first called the "Young Men's Purity, Total Abstinence, and Snooker Pool Club" and then the "Emerald Bay Yacht Club," a dues-paying members-only group of high-powered Hollywood friends who would meet to drink and talk and take steambaths and sometimes go out on the water, and whose mission was, Ford said, "to promulgate the cause of alcoholism." His jocularity wasn't far from the truth: Ford was a blackout drunk whose long, brutal, self-obliterating benders, which always occurred when he was between movies, could last for days or weeks and sometimes ended with friends rescuing him from soiled sheets in hotel bedrooms. By that time, he would often be gaunt, malnourished, and sometimes ill enough to require hospitalization. "Drinking," said John Wayne, "was one way Jack could really relax and shut off his mind." But the *Araner* was another means of escape, and the navy commission Ford had secured for himself in 1934 meant a great deal to him.

After *The Grapes of Wrath* finished production, Ford and some friends, including Wayne, had boarded the *Araner* and sailed down from San Pedro to Guaymas harbor, a Mexican port sheltered from the open sea by Baja and the Gulf of California. While there, Ford did some semiofficial reconnaissance for the navy, looking for Japanese trawlers off the coast and filing, with almost boyish eagerness, a report to the navy's chief intelligence officer in San Diego. "The Japanese shrimp fleet was lying at anchor," Ford wrote. "The most striking point concerning the fleet is its personnel. This has me completely baffled. The crew came ashore for liberty in well-tailored flannels, worsteds and tweed suits. All carry themselves with military carriage. . . . For want of a better word I would call them the Samurai or military caste. . . . During three trips to Japan I have studied this type very closely. I am positive they are Naval men. . . . They constitute a real menace. Although I am not a trained Intelligence Officer, still my profession is to observe and make distinctions. . . . I will stake my professional reputation that these young men are not professional fishermen." The pro forma letter of commendation Ford received from the navy seemed to mean more to him than any movie could. In March 1940, when Ford learned that his Emerald Bay Yacht Club pal Merian C. Cooper was leaving his job as an executive at RKO to help form the Flying Tigers, a fleet of American pilots who would work with the Chinese air force to help defend China against Japanese attacks, he was, wrote his grandson Dan Ford, "green with envy."

That April, Ford decided to devote a greater part of his life to the navy. He had been moved by letters from friends in England predicting "heavy bloodshed if the [Germans] start air raiding" and testifying to the "great unity of purpose" in England and France. As he began production on the seafaring drama *The Long Voyage Home*, he worked with Merian Cooper and Frank "Spig" Wead, a World War I navy pilot who had become a successful screenwriter, to draft an official proposal for a new "Naval Photographic Organization." Ford did not entertain any fantasies of further spy missions or glamorous postings abroad; he knew that most of the men in what came to be known as Field Photo would be, as his wife, Mary, unsentimentally put it, "over-age and rich, people who could never have been drafted." Instead, his proposal emphasized the potential value of Hollywood professionals in creating propaganda that would show "the Navy's weight, prowess, power, high morale, and striking force." Ford had been impressed by the success of German propaganda and wanted to "show that a Democracy can and must create a greater fighting machine . . . than a dictator power."

The armed forces did not yet have any cohesive plan to assemble an organized unit of filmmakers that could be widely deployed during a coming war; nobody in the navy imagined at that time that a group of middle-aged civilian filmmakers would ever find themselves anywhere near a battlefront. Ford's proposal simply seemed like a good way to boost the navy's image through public relations, and with surprisingly little bureaucratic impediment, he quickly won approval from the 11th Naval District Command in San Diego to oversee photographic personnel for the Naval Reserve and was told to recruit up to two hundred volunteers along with his *Grapes of Wrath* cinematographer Gregg Toland and sound engineer Edmund Hansen, each of whom were to bring in specialists in their own areas of expertise. They combed lists of employees at studios and processing labs, looking for electricians, film developers, publicity photographers, assistant cameramen, lab technicians, and cutters, contacting anyone with valuable experience, and many who had little more to offer than enthusiasm. The men would meet on Tuesday nights on the Fox lot, often training with props and using costume uniforms. It was, wrote Dan Ford, "a ragtag little band that looked more yacht club than navy. . . . From the very outset, John loved the theatrical side of the military . . . and if nothing else, everyone in the [unit] learned all the drills." One early recruit recalled Ford's decision that "all the officers were going to wear swords. . . . I was always afraid that he was going to kill someone the way he waved his sword around." (Ford, who had an arthritic thumb, would often need help with the resheathing.)

Ford was serious about his passion for the navy, but initially Field Photo was a part-time indulgence—little more than an extension of the director's love of pageantry, his fondness for uniforms, and his desire to spend as much time as possible in the company of like-minded men in a sort of fraternity where he could indulge a vision of himself as an admiral manqué. That changed on May 10, 1940, just weeks after Field Photo was approved, when Germany invaded France. The unit was no longer a wealthy man's unpaid hobby. Ford was now in charge of a part of the Naval Reserve that was just eighteen months from being called up for active duty.

THREE

"You Must Not Realize That
There Is a War Going On"

HOLLYWOOD, JUNE–SEPTEMBER 1940

I n 1940, 60 million Americans—more than half of the adult population of the United States—went to movie theaters every week. What they got, for the price of a twenty-five-cent ticket, was usually a double feature, a cartoon or two, a historical or musical short, and ten or twenty minutes of newsreels—narrated weekly reports from Fox or Hearst or Pathé or The March of Time that served as one of the primary means by which Americans saw and heard their news before and during the war. Theaters in the 1940s were more likely to advertise what time they opened their doors—and, far more crucially, the fact that they had air-conditioning—than the actual starting time of the main feature. People would straggle in, take their seats in the middle of a picture, and watch until a full cycle had been completed. The programs were often seamless, without long breaks or sharp dividing lines between information and entertainment, documentary, reenactment, and fiction. For some, theaters were a place to shelter from the troubles of the world, but they were also where most Americans were first confronted by vivid images of the troubles themselves, brought home in footage that was more immediate and overwhelming than newspapers or radio broadcasts could ever be.

The fall of France in June 1940 was a shock that millions of Americans took in as a collective experience at movie houses, where footage of Nazi soldiers on the march and Parisians weeping in the streets made the war feel closer and more frightening. To many moviegoers, Poland and Czechoslovakia were foreign countries with foreign cultures, points on a map somewhere far away. France was closer, more real: It was the country of Charles Boyer and Jean Gabin, of romance and sex comedy and sophistication. Just a year earlier, Americans had watched Paris thaw Greta Garbo's icy exterior in *Ninotchka* and turn Claudette Colbert from an ordinary girl into a pretend baroness in *Midnight*. Now, in the space of just six weeks, moviegoers across the country saw Winston Churchill take over from Neville Chamberlain as prime minister; they filled theaters as newsreels competed to present the best footage of the successful evacuation of Dunkirk; they heard Churchill's thunderous "We shall fight on the beaches . . . we shall never surrender" speech to the House of Commons; and they witnessed the occupation of Paris by the Wehrmacht.

The so-called phony war was over, and Hollywood responded with a combination of economic apprehension—it was now apparent that much of the lucrative European market for its movies was going to shrivel away in a matter of months—and fervent activism. The interventionist Committee to Defend America by Aiding the Allies, which opposed any further enforcement of the Neutrality Act that Congress had passed the previous fall, had formed in May, with a strong outpost in Hollywood that was funded by, among others, Zanuck, Wanger, Goldwyn, and the Warners. Weeks later, writer Philip Dunne, an instrumental early organizer of the Screen Writers Guild, helped found the Motion Picture Committee Co-operating for Defense, the first official Hollywood group committed to making films that would support any future war effort. That summer, the committee, which had been formed by all eight studio heads with the tacit approval of Roosevelt and his inner circle, kept its activities quiet, hoping not to spark any new antitrust charges or inflammatory accusations from isolationists. Its members scrupulously avoided using the word "propaganda." But the group stood ready to produce movies if ever the administration made an official request; among those who served on its production committee was Capra, who was there to represent the Directors Guild and had agreed to make a short himself if necessary.

That summer, the Warners again made their voices heard first and loudest. The day after Churchill's speech, Harry Warner summoned more than three thousand of his employees (as well as several members of the Hollywood press) to a vacant soundstage on the Warner lot and made a speech denouncing, in parallel terms, Nazism and Communism, all totalitarian governments, American anti-Semitism and racism, isolationists, and appeasers. His language was sometimes more impassioned than coherent, but it won considerable attention and national news coverage. In case his point had been missed by other studios—many of which, unlike Warner Bros., were still attempting to hold on to their businesses in countries that Germany had invaded—Warner promptly had his speech printed as a pamphlet he titled "United We Survive, Divided We Fall!" and made sure it was mailed not just to his colleagues and rivals but to columnists, congressmen, cabinet members, and Roosevelt.

In June, Warner Bros. had brought William Wyler back into the fold, convincing Goldwyn to loan them the director so that he could reteam with his *Jezebel* star Bette Davis, who was becoming so instrumental to the studio's fortunes that she was jokingly referred to as "the fifth Warner brother." (In the typically elaborate and personalized system of talent trading that was common at the time, a year later Jack Warner would loan Davis to Goldwyn so that Wyler could direct her again in *The Little Foxes;* in exchange, Goldwyn would loan Warner Gary Cooper and forgive Jack part of a $425,000 gambling debt.)

Wyler's affair with Davis had, by all accounts, ended with his marriage to Talli, but the two were eager to work together again. *The Letter*, the story of a married woman on a Malayan rubber plantation charged with murdering her lover, would be the greatest of their three collaborations; it stands as one of the most psychologically acute melodramas of the era, with deep, fine-grained work by both director and star. But the shoot was, from the beginning, fraught with misery. Davis discovered she was pregnant during the first week of filming; uncertain who the father was, she kept it a secret and had an abortion, her third, the following week, telling friends later, "I should have married Willy." She and Wyler fought several times over her interpretation of the role, and at one point she walked off the set. In the end, she said,

"I did it his way. . . . Yes, I lost a battle, but I lost it to a genius. . . . So many directors were such weak sisters that I would have to take over. Uncreative, unsure of themselves, frightened to fight back, they offered me none of the security that this tyrant did." Davis loved Wyler's intensity, the way he braced for battle on the set, the "Who do you hate today?" attitude that she said they shared. Nor did she mind his request for repeated takes of scene after scene; she felt it mirrored her own perfectionism.

Jack Warner, however, was not so forgiving. His studio was a factory; second and third takes were permissible if something went wrong with the first one, but he had little patience for more. After he received a daily production report on *The Letter* showing that Wyler had used sixty-two takes to complete nine scenes, he was furious. "You are a very good director and no one can tell me you can't make a scene in 2 to 4 takes tops and print the one you really know is right. . . . I am not going to let any one man put us out of business," he wrote. "You must not realize that there is a war going on and that the film industry is in a very bad condition. . . . I will not stand for this practice and you must discontinue it immediately."

Warner's jab about the war must have particularly stung Wyler, whose attempts to help get his relatives out of France through promises of sponsorship were giving way to more direct, and probably hopeless, gestures; he had started to send packets of cash abroad with the intention that the money be used to bribe Vichy officials to protect his family. It took him a couple of false starts before he was able to compose his polite, cool response. "Please be assured that I have no intention of putting your company out of business," he replied. "Quite the contrary. If I found it necessary to make fourteen takes of one scene there must have been a very good reason. I . . . have made a particular effort toward speed and economy in the production of this picture (even at occasional sacrifices of quality). . . . I would consider it a favor if you would . . . at least give me the benefit of the doubt." Wyler kept his temper and got his way; Warner did not interfere again, and *The Letter* came in at $665,000, $35,000 under budget. Wyler never learned whether the money he had sent to France had reached its intended recipients, or if it had done any good.

Harry Warner's public equation of Communism with Nazism may have been calculated to cool the tempers of politicians who were taking every opportunity to attack the movie industry as the epicenter of the "Red menace," but it didn't work. For the last two years, Martin Dies had rarely missed an opportunity to rail against what he saw as the potentially treasonous politics of Hollywood and the men who ran it. Dies was a blustery, none-too-bright conservative Democratic congressman from an at-large district in Texas. In 1938, he had run the House's first version of the Un-American Activities Committee, sometimes chairing hearings alongside like-minded colleagues, but often serving as a committee of one. That year, he had become the target of widespread national mockery, including from the Roosevelt administration, when he had released testimony about a list of Hollywood stars believed to have Communist sympathies; the list included Shirley Temple, who was then eleven years old. Dies had quickly retreated onto safer ground, restricting his purview to inquiries about Nazi and Ku Klux Klan cadres. But in July 1940, a month after Warner's speech, he reared up again, this time with a witness—a onetime Communist Party functionary and hanger-on named (exquisitely) John Leech—who, during closed one-on-one testimony, had furnished him with the names of forty-two Hollywood luminaries whom he claimed gathered regularly at the Malibu home of Paramount production chief B. P. Schulberg to "read the doctrines of Karl Marx." Leech testified that the Communist Party was using the movie colony's fear of Nazis and of anti-Semites to build loyalty. Among the biggest names on his list were Philip Dunne, Fredric March, James Cagney, and Humphrey Bogart.

As the names were leaked and reported nationally, Dies announced that he intended to hold hearings, swept into Los Angeles, installed himself at the Biltmore Hotel, and summoned his first witness. When Bogart arrived in the company of his lawyer, he was surprised to find that the only other person at the hotel conference table was Dies himself. There was no committee, nor was his accuser Leech anywhere to be seen. Bogart told Dies he was not a Communist and didn't know of any. Asked to name names, he replied that he could not call anyone a Communist unless he saw a party membership card. Dies kept pressing; Bogart remained nonchalant and calm, and offered him nothing. The testimony ended quickly, and as the press began to turn on the congressman, calling his tactics "repugnant," Dies hastily announced that he had found no evidence to support his witness's charges against anyone. Within a couple of days, he gaveled his own hearings closed and fled Los Angeles.

The episode, which had been designed to throw a scare into Hollywood's interventionists, instead emboldened them by its very ineptitude. John Ford appeared not to be shaken in the slightest. The charges that his adaptation of *The Grapes of Wrath* was a veiled pro-Communist tract had failed to stick, and as the movie continued to attract large audiences, he started a production company that would, for the first time, allow him a degree of independence in the films he made. His newest project would combine two of his current passions, his love of the sea and his hatred of the Nazis. *The Long Voyage Home,* an adaptation of four short Eugene O'Neill plays set aboard a merchant marine ship, marked a reunion between Ford and several of his closest recent collaborators: *Stagecoach* producer Walter Wanger and its stars John Wayne and Thomas Mitchell, *Informer* screenwriter Dudley Nichols, and, perhaps most important, Gregg Toland, who had shot *The Grapes of Wrath.* On *The Long Voyage Home,* Ford considered Toland's expressionist compositions so important that director and cinematographer shared their credits on a single title card.

O'Neill and Ford were born five years apart—O'Neill in 1888 and Ford in 1893—and had much in common: They were the children of Irish immigrant fathers who had attained middle-class respectability in America, they were raised in New England, and Ford, whose real name was Sean Aloysius O'Feeney and whose father had run a saloon, shared with O'Neill a fondness for barrooms and the whiskey-enriched storytelling of the sailors who always seemed to be around when he was growing up. O'Neill had written his quartet of one-acts, known as the Glencairn plays, between 1914 and 1918, and they acknowledged the Great War only tangentially. But Ford and Nichols, who had told a reporter in 1939 that they had been looking "for years" for a film project that would allow them to make a statement against Fascism, quickly made the decision, with Wanger's enthusiastic endorsement, to update the story to the present.

Nichols wove the plays into an ensemble piece portraying, with a melancholy romanticism that deeply appealed to Ford, the salt-of-the-earth crew of alcoholics, dreamers, and bums aboard a tramp steamer carrying a cargo of dynamite to England. Life aboard the ship feels timeless; the movie begins with a title card that states, "With their hates and desires men are changing the face of the earth—but they cannot change the Sea," and throughout, Ford remains committed to the idea of a ship as a comradely haven of close-quarters rue and bonhomie, even as the map of the world is being redrawn. News soon seeps in over the ship's radio through a haze of static, as word comes that "another ship exploded under the fire of German anti-tank guns." A sailor named Driscoll (Mitchell) gets into a brawl with local policemen when one calls him a "neutral"; he exclaims, outraged, "I never was a neutral in all my life!" Later, when the *Glencairn* docks in England, Driscoll and his mates walk through the black, foggy night and are attracted by the warmth and music pouring out of a service club, only to be told, "Sorry, you civilians can't go in there—that's for these lads going off to war . . . Move along . . . Get inside somewhere. Best place to be during a blackout." In one shot on a London street, we see a newsboy's placard announcing Germany's invasion of Norway—news that had broken just eight days before the movie began production.

Nichols and Ford were immensely proud of *The Long Voyage Home*. ("You're a thorny guy," Nichols told him, "but a grand thorny guy—the O'Neill of the picture makers.") The film is not suffused with the gung-ho patriotism that would soon characterize the majority of Hollywood war films, but its clear statement that the world was now in the grip of a conflict between good and evil was a distinct step away from the Great War sensibility of O'Neill's original plays, which depicted war as a largely abstract horror. The movie's tone is plaintive and sorrowing, not belligerent; the theme is fully expressed in Driscoll's plea, "Everywhere, people stumbling in the dark. Is there to be no light in the world?"* Still, *The Long Voyage Home*'s impassioned bluntness about the Nazi threat startled many who did not expect to see Hollywood movies confronting world events so forthrightly after years of expressing little more than the kind of generalized pacifism that *All*

---

* The line was closely echoed—"It feels as if the lights were all out everywhere"—in Wanger's production of *Foreign Correspondent*, which was shooting at the same time.

Quiet on the Western Front had epitomized. If one of the country's leading directors had become so bold and unconcerned about a possible backlash, others would surely follow his lead. "With their foreign market already lost," wrote one critic, "the movies are getting pretty reckless. They say 'Nazi' and 'Fascist' and 'Ribbentrop' as easily as if they were the names of cocktails." Another remarked on Ford's staging of the film's climactic sequence, in which the *Glencairn*'s crew comes under assault from German machine guns and Stuka dive bombers. Ford, he wrote, had reached "the highest pitch of realism."

Frank Capra was also eager to make a "statement" movie; he just didn't know what the statement should be. In many ways, *Meet John Doe,* which he shot during the summer and fall of 1940, would serve to conclude a thematic trilogy that had begun with *Mr. Deeds Goes to Town* and continued in *Mr. Smith Goes to Washington.* The film brought Capra back together with his Mr. Deeds (and his first choice to play Mr. Smith), Gary Cooper, as well as with *Deeds* screenwriter Robert Riskin, with whom he'd worked on and off for a decade. Their new project, initially titled *The Life and Death of John Doe,* would tell yet another story of a little guy steeped in the unschooled wisdom of the common people who puts his plainspoken ideals up against the cynical interests of entrenched power. The picture would be the first made by Capra's new company, and in order to cofinance it with Warner Bros., he borrowed $750,000—a third of which was for his own salary—from the Bank of America, where he had a friendly relationship (the bank had for years been the primary financer of Capra's former home Columbia Pictures).

Looking back at the making of *Meet John Doe* decades later, Capra admitted that for the first time in his career, he had felt he had something to prove. Even after three Oscars, he bristled at his standing among reviewers who had treated his films as likable diversions but didn't imagine him capable of the kind of uncompromising social treatise for which Ford had recently become known. "An ego like mine needed—nay, required—the plaudits of sophisticated criticism," he wrote. "The 'Capra-corn' barbs had pierced [my] outer blubber. And so *Meet John Doe . . .* was *aimed* at winning critical praises." To that end, Capra and Riskin contrived a story so convoluted in its determination to take on everything from the power of the press to the corruption of state and city governments to the possibility of a Fascist movement arising within the United States to the manipulation of presidential politics that nobody, including the two of them, could ever figure out exactly whom they wanted to confront or what argument they intended to advance.

Meet John Doe begins with the slogan of a venerable newspaper—"A free press for a free people"—being chiseled off the cornerstone of a building as a new corporate owner takes over and initiates massive layoffs. It's an image that swiftly establishes the film's central if vague thematic through-line, which is that standards are declining, American freedoms are in danger, and even foundational principles are (literally, in the opening shot) being ground to dust. Among the reporters fired is a columnist played by Barbara Stanwyck, who, in a last-ditch effort to save her job, fakes a letter from an outraged everyman who complains that "the whole world's going to pot" because of "slimy politics" and threatens to jump off the roof of city hall unless things change. Stanwyck parlays that into a regular feature, "I Protest, by John Doe," in which Doe angrily albeit generically complains about "all the evils of the world! Man's inhumanity to man!" All she needs is a trainable stooge— "a typical American who can keep his mouth shut"—to be the face of the column. Enter Cooper, a down-on-his-luck former baseball player named Willoughby—"human flotsam . . . devoid of ideals," said Capra—who needs a job and agrees to play Doe.

The overelaborate farrago that follows finds Capra swinging at many targets with a kind of easy yahooism—the Democratic and Republican parties (which he depicts as collusive), corporations that put people out of work, and the news media, which is portrayed in true Capraesque fashion as either a bunch of savvy skeptics or an easily swayed mob, depending on the demands of the narrative at any given moment. As the plot thickens (and thickens), thousands of John Doe Clubs spring up, inspired by Cooper's credo ("Be a Better Neighbor"—"the one thing capable of saving this cockeyed world," he says, echoing a line from *Mr. Smith*). Soon enough, the John Doe Party is formed, and a viable third-party run for president threatens to undermine the status quo.

Whether this is a good or a bad thing is something about which *Meet*

John Doe consistently hedges. "Hitler's strong-arm success against democracy was catching," wrote Capra. "Little 'fuhrers' were springing up in America . . . the 'new wave' was Blood Power! Riskin and I would astonish the critics with contemporary realities: The ugly face of hate; the power of uniformed bigots in red, white, and blue shirts; the agony of disillusionment; and the wild dark passions of mobs." But Capra had never quite let go of his veneration of Mussolini, and in the film, he and Riskin career from exalting ordinary people in theory to expressing shock at how easily a would-be dictator—in this case, a press baron—can hypnotize them; the film winds up suggesting, inadvertently, that any populace that pliable probably shouldn't be trusted. And "Doe" himself comes off as what the critic Andrew Sarris, writing in the 1960s, called "a barefoot fascist, suspicious of all ideas and doctrines, but believing in the innate conformism of the common man."

Meet John Doe is less a narrative than a snapshot of Capra's own overheated and erratic political impulses at the time he shot it. Somewhat ominously, he conflated the gullible average Americans in the story with his movie's potential audience, calling them "my John Does." But he didn't need the public's verdict; he knew he was in trouble even before he began production. "The first two acts were solid; the third act was a wet sock," he wrote. "Our story problem was self-inflicted: To convince important critics that not every Capra film was written by Pollyanna, Riskin and I had written ourselves into a corner." Or, more specifically, onto a roof: Capra and Riskin knew that the movie would have to end with "John Doe" ready to make good on his promise to jump off a building, but neither man had any idea how to get him out of it. At one point, Capra called in Jules Furthman, a veteran screenwriter whose credits dated back to 1915, and asked him to consider doing a rewrite. Furthman declined. "You guys can't find an ending to your story," he told the director, "because you got no story in the first place."

Capra's uncertainty about his own storytelling couldn't have come at a worse time. As he shot *Meet John Doe* in the summer and fall, American movie theaters were suddenly filled with pictures that knew exactly what they wanted to say and how they wanted to say it. Charlie Chaplin's *The Great Dictator* became the first major Hollywood movie to lampoon Hitler on screen. *The Mortal Storm* finally opened, and despite MGM's unwillingness to identify Germany and Hitler in the script by name, *Variety* called it "the most effective film expose to date of the totalitarian idea . . . a combination of entertainment and democratic preachment," and the *New Yorker* identified it as the first movie "that can be considered of any major consequence" to take on Hitler. United Artists imported an uncompromising British drama called *Pastor Hall*, about a peace-loving minister imprisoned in a concentration camp after he resists the storm troopers who overrun his small village; theaters ran it with a filmed introduction by Eleanor Roosevelt. And on the day the United States began peacetime conscription for men between the ages of twenty-one and thirty-one, Paramount released *Arise, My Love*—a romantic drama about a European war correspondent (Claudette Colbert) and a soldier of fortune (Ray Milland); Billy Wilder's script for the movie overtly identified American apathy about the rise of Hitler as a moral evil. Paramount had cautiously insisted on shooting "protection takes" that would soften the film's extensive and explicit anti-Hitler dialogue for release abroad, but with the studios' business in Europe now at an end, Hollywood no longer had anything to lose. The rougher version of the movie was widely released and audiences could hear Milland say of Hitler and Germany, "We'll get another crack at those big boys. War is coming, and I can smell it." The film's last line urged Americans directly to "be strong, so you can stand up straight and say to anyone under God's heaven, 'All right—whose way of life shall it be, yours or ours?'"

"Themes which had been skittishly skirted or avoided altogether in less perilous times have lately been advanced upon the screen with exceptional fervor and frankness," reported the *New York Times*. "Films are fast assuming the role predestined for them in time of crisis." The week Capra finished shooting *Meet John Doe*, the bombing of London began. He still didn't know how the movie would end.

FOUR

"What's the Good of a Message?"

HOLLYWOOD, EARLY 1941

At a packed black-tie banquet at the Biltmore Hotel, William Wyler stood on stage, waiting patiently to be humiliated. It was February 27, 1941, the night of the 13th Academy Awards, and for the third time in five years, he was a nominee. His film *The Letter* had opened in November to general acclaim, especially for Wyler and Bette Davis, who was also nominated. But as he and Talli drove to the ceremonies that evening, they were both at peace with the fact that it probably wasn't going to be his night. What they didn't realize until Frank Capra walked out to the podium and began to speak was that an unanticipated and particularly stinging public embarrassment was in store. Capra was hard at work in the editing room on *Meet John Doe*, and he may have been too preoccupied to consider the gracelessness of what he was about to do. When the time came to announce the winner of the award for Best Director, he decided to break form and, instead of reading the list of nominees, called them all to the stage and instructed them to shake one another's hands in front of the audience.

Wyler left his wife's side and grimly walked away from his table to join his competitors—first-time nominee Alfred Hitchcock, who was up for *Rebecca*, the veteran Sam Wood, who had directed Ginger Rogers in *Kitty Foyle*, and George Cukor, who was in contention for *The Philadelphia Story*.

As the four men shuffled in place and muttered pleasantries, Capra opened the envelope and revealed that the winner was the only nominee who had announced in advance that he had no intention of showing up: John Ford, for *The Grapes of Wrath*. Ford, who had already finished his next picture for 20th Century Fox, an adaptation of the long-running Broadway play *Tobacco Road*, had told everyone that win or lose, he planned to be in Mexico on a sailing trip with another of that year's nominees, his *Grapes of Wrath* star Henry Fonda, "for as long as the fish are biting," and he was as good as his word. As Darryl Zanuck stepped to the stage to collect the statuette for him, Wyler and his fellow losers awkwardly made their way down the steps and, recalled Talli, "all had to slink back to their tables."

When a colleague of Ford's sent him a congratulatory telegram about his second Oscar, the director sternly replied, "Awards are a trivial thing to be concerned with at times like these." That was largely posturing; in practice, Ford had almost as great an appetite for recognition and honors as Capra did, and was at least as zealous about curating his reputation. (Right around the time of the ceremony, he approved a Fox press release in the guise of a written and reported story headlined, "John Ford's Pictures Win Acclaim and Money"; many small-circulation papers ran the release as news, which was then a routine practice.) His reasons for staying away that year probably had as much to do with the widespread (and, it turned out, correct) assumption in industry circles that *Rebecca* was going to beat *The Grapes of Wrath* for Best Picture as with any concern about the propriety of participating in a ritual of collective self-celebration while Europe was being torn apart. It's likely that he was also happy to be out of the country given that *Tobacco Road* had just opened to withering reviews. Ford himself had little use for the movie, a grotesque story of southern sharecroppers that seemed as tin-eared about regional poverty and family struggle as *The Grapes of Wrath* had been acute, and it's unclear why he took it on in the first place or made such a rushed and sloppy job of it.

Distraction may have been part of the problem. Even as Ford shot the picture, he was devoting more of his time and energy than ever to preparation for war. In that, he had a willing partner in Zanuck, his longtime boss, who now preferred to be known as "Colonel." That January, Zanuck had accepted a commission as a reserve lieutenant colonel in the Signal Corps, and as chair of the Academy Research Council, he had recently agreed to oversee the making of four training films. Zanuck stood just five foot two, which could make the fits of energetic excitability to which he was prone appear comical; Ford sometimes referred to him as "Darryl F. Panic." For his part, Zanuck would make fun of the director for the nervous habit he had of chewing on a sodden, ragged handkerchief while he worked. But the two men shared a sense that America's involvement in the war was coming sooner and on a greater scale than most of their colleagues anticipated, and Ford didn't hesitate to say yes when Zanuck asked him to supervise production of a short Signal Corps instructional movie.

He could not have matched Ford with a less likely subject. Official Training Film 8-154, a coproduction of the corps, the Academy, and the Surgeon General's office, was called *Sex Hygiene;* it was an explicit, for-inductees-only documentary about what young servicemen should do if they're exposed to syphilis or gonorrhea, replete with frontal nudity and excruciating close-ups of penile chancroids. Ford's sensibilities in this area were prim, almost chaste; he had been married to the same woman for twenty years, and despite the occasional romantic crush on a leading lady, his weakness was widely known to be alcohol, not women. But whatever distaste he had for the subject, he either overcame it or translated it into gruff man-to-man language: *Sex Hygiene* is full of talk, infused with the sternness of Ford's Catholic upbringing, about the dangers of coming in contact with a "contaminated woman," the importance of using condoms (and of testing them for leaks), and the consequences men face in exchange "for the satisfaction of their sexual impulses," including the remarkable assertion that any woman who makes herself sexually available to a soldier "probably" carries a disease.[*]

Although the twenty-six-minute *Sex Hygiene* gets its message across with straightforward candor, Ford's hand can be discerned in the film's relatively sophisticated structure—it's framed as the story of a group of soldiers who go see a sex-hygiene training film, and Ford moves seamlessly between the main narrative and the movie within the movie. He turns his camera on his

---

[*] *Sex Hygiene* remained in use until well into the Vietnam War.

audience of soldiers, tracking in on a dozen different faces in sequential close-ups as each young man takes in the harsh reality of what he's being told about his body, something "most men know less about . . . than they do about their automobiles," according to the unsmiling lecturer. And Ford's heart seems to be in the sharp warning that ends the movie, when a doctor tells the boys that nothing is more likely to endanger the health of a soldier than a bad decision made when he's drunk. "Zanuck . . . said to me, 'These kids have got to be taught about these things . . . do you mind doing it?'" Ford told Peter Bogdanovich. "It was easy to make. We did it in two or three days. It really was horrible, not being for general release. We could do anything—we had guys out there with VD and everything else. I think it made its point and helped a lot of young kids. I looked at it and threw up."

Ford was also approaching his duties as head of the Field Photo Unit more seriously, amassing camera and sound equipment from the studios, dividing the photographers, editors, and sound men whom he had spent months recruiting into nine discrete units, and arranging training sessions for the men at the Naval Reserve Armory in Los Angeles. In January, he drew up a budget proposal for Field Photo that recommended the navy allot $5 million for the first year, $3 million for the second, and $2 million for year three of what he believed would be a long engagement. In addition, he urged that funds be set aside for the development of new cameras that would be designed to withstand the battering that they would undoubtedly take during daily use in sea combat. Ford also got his somewhat starstruck navy superiors in San Diego to authorize another quasi-spy mission for the *Araner* along the Mazatlán coast, a three-week mission that does not appear to have been a matter of urgent national security but did dovetail nicely with his desire to go fishing during the Oscars.

For Wyler, losing the Academy Award to Ford was the bitter anticlimax of a fall and winter that he had spent working on projects that had come to nothing. He was now in his sixth year under contract to Goldwyn. After his first twelve months working for the stubborn, mercurial producer, Wyler had written to him begging that his contract be severed since they were both so unhappy. Since then, their tense, testy relationship had, if not mellowed, at least deepened into a kind of mutual respect and understanding about the value each man had to the other. Goldwyn had the bankroll and the willingness to buy great dramatic properties for his best director, and didn't force him to make three films a year like a studio workhorse, and Wyler had great sway with him as, in his friend Lillian Hellman's words, one of "the only . . . people in the Goldwyn asylum who [wasn't] completely loony."

In 1940, Wyler was eager to get to work on an adaptation of Hellman's Broadway play *The Little Foxes*, for which Goldwyn had managed to pry Bette Davis loose from Warner Bros. But by September, Hellman's adaptation of her script still wasn't ready, and while he was idle, Wyler found himself a pawn in a complicated set of deals that Goldwyn was engineering with two different studios. In order to obtain Davis, the producer had agreed to loan Wyler and Gary Cooper to Warner Bros. for *Sergeant York*, the story of a pacifist who became one of World War I's bravest heroes; it had all the makings of a biopic that Harry and Jack Warner believed would serve as a rousing interventionist reminder of the glories of fighting for your country. Cooper was a perfect fit for York; Wyler, who had previously evinced little flair for action films and had no taste for jingoism, was not. As soon as he got the assignment and realized the screenplay was months away from being shootable—his friend John Huston was about to be brought aboard for a rewrite—he begged off. Goldwyn didn't waste a week before loaning him out again, this time to 20th Century Fox, where Zanuck offered Wyler $85,000 to direct *How Green Was My Valley*.

This time, Wyler was enthusiastic: Richard Llewellyn's just-published novel about life in a Welsh coal-mining town, and Zanuck's ambitions for it, were much closer to his heart than *Sergeant York* had been. The record-shattering success that David O. Selznick had achieved with *Gone with the Wind*, which was still the most popular movie in U.S. theaters nine months after its opening, had emboldened every studio head to take chances on a grander scale, and initially Wyler and Zanuck seemed to share a vision for a big-budget, four-hour Technicolor adaptation that could rival anything from Selznick in its scope. But even before Wyler came aboard, Zanuck was having problems with the proposed film: He was determined to oppose any attempts to turn the novel into a polemic for workers' rights, despite the fact that the most exciting and dramatic sequence in Llewellyn's episodic, lei-

surely five-hundred-page best seller was built around a miners' strike over
unsafe conditions. In the summer, Fox had rejected a draft of the script by a
writer named Ernest Pascal who had highlighted the unrest among the town's
workers. Zanuck may have been worried about presenting English mine owners as villains at a moment when American sympathies for the British were
at their highest, but he also complained that Pascal's script had turned the
novel "into a labor story and a sociological problem story instead of being
a great, warm, human story. . . . The labor issue should serve only as a
background. . . . This is far from a crusade picture."

Bizarrely, Zanuck decided to implement those changes by replacing
Pascal with Philip Dunne, a founder of the Screen Writers Guild, an active
member of Hollywood's progressive left, and perhaps the most vigorous pro-
labor writer in the industry. For the last three months of 1940, Dunne and
Wyler collaborated in a daily struggle to wrestle a story that took place over
sixty years into a shootable script. While Dunne wrote and rewrote, Wyler
went through a hardcover copy of the novel, page by page, jotting down dialogue, props, gestures, and even colors that he wanted to include in the
finished film. With production scheduled to begin early in 1941, he also
concentrated on casting. For each role, he worked from a long list of possibilities, considering everyone from Laurence Olivier and Henry Fonda to
Merle Oberon, Geraldine Fitzgerald, and Ida Lupino. Only for the role of
Huw, the young boy at the center of the story, did he make up his mind early.
Fox's Lew Schreiber wrote to him that a twelve-year-old "boy by the name of
Roddy McDowall" had recently fled England with his family and made a
screen test. Wyler saw the footage, and under the name "Huw" in his casting
notes, he simply wrote, "The little English refugee."

McDowall's casting would prove to be one of the essential elements in the
success of *How Green Was My Valley*, but in other areas, Zanuck opposed
Dunne and Wyler at every turn. With the economic constriction of the world-
wide movie market that the war had caused, Zanuck now wanted to back
away from his original plans for a lengthy epic and was horrified when Dunne
turned in a 260-page first draft. And Zanuck and Wyler clashed constantly,
an inevitability since Wyler had always struggled with his own lack of screenwriting experience ("Willy couldn't write a line, but he knew what *you* could

do," said Dunne), while Zanuck fancied himself a story-structure savant. For weeks, he pummeled Wyler with one objection after another: He and Dunne weren't narrowing down and focusing the narrative sufficiently; labor unrest was still too much a part of the story; their vision for the movie was unfilmably long and expensive; the tender, modest qualities of the book were being lost.

Even as Wyler pared Dunne's screenplay into a more shapely form, he felt besieged. "It is going to be a very simple job to bring this script down to a proper length," Zanuck told him, "and I believe my judgment at the present moment is much closer to the judgment of an audience than is your judgment." At the same time, Wyler's own assistant argued to him that his streamlining was resulting in a narrative that was "smooth—even—and dull. . . . The people who are now left in our story are . . . unexciting and colorless characters." Dunne revised the draft again, and a note came back saying, "The lack of suspense is still felt. Each sequence is interesting in itself but . . . the story never reaches a climax." In December, Zanuck lowered the boom, telling Dunne and Wyler that they had "so far failed to achieve that which you set out to do many weeks ago . . . you are never going to achieve it unless you get some help. . . . You have been given every possible chance and even you must admit that the net result has been unsatisfactory. . . . I think it is high time that I step out of my role as a non-belligerent observer and become active creatively. . . . it is the only way I know how to produce."

That was enough for Wyler, who wrote back, "I must ask that in matters of taste, you limit your interference. I am frightened of your attack on this script since you of course have the last word . . . but you and I have entirely different styles of telling a story and I honestly think that for this one mine is better. Before I started to work for you I was greatly encouraged by your apparent eagerness to get for the picture all that I could possibly give it. [But] I am not a good director in the sense that I could direct scenes as instructed."

Wyler was never told that he had been fired; one day while he was on the lot, he ran into an executive who informed him that the picture had been canceled. He was stunned, since he felt the screenplay was finally in good shape, but he returned to Goldwyn to resume work on *The Little Foxes*. Soon after the Academy Awards, he heard that Zanuck had decided to go ahead with *How Green Was My Valley* after all; John Ford would be directing it. Philip Dunne was called into a meeting at which Ford, "chewing on his handkerchief," told him his screenplay was terrible. He went on to film it with virtually no further changes.

Talk of war pervaded that Oscar night at the Biltmore, and for the first time, Hollywood was ready for the discussion. The honorees represented a commitment to engagement, not escape. The evening had begun with a radio address to the Academy by President Roosevelt, who praised the industry for its social responsibility and leadership in defense fund-raising—a welcome endorsement for a business that had recently endured a barrage of attacks— and then urged everyone to support the Lend-Lease Act. When the incendiary *Arise, My Love*, with its stentorian plea that America pay attention and get involved, was awarded Best Original Story, one of its two honorees, Benjamin Glazer, announced from the podium that his cowriter John Toldy could not be present because he had done his work under a pseudonym; he was actually an Austro-Hungarian Jew named Hans Szekely who was presently in hiding from the Nazis. A special Oscar was awarded to Nathan Levinson, a sound engineer, for his work in marshaling the resources of Hollywood to assist in the making of army training films. And expressions of Anglo-American solidarity were everywhere—in the short-film nominee about Britain under siege, *London Can Take It*, in the Best Picture award to *Rebecca*, and in the three Oscars—the most for any film that year—that were given to producer Alexander Korda's *The Thief of Bagdad*. The visually spectacular Technicolor fantasy-adventure had begun production in England but was forced to shut down and relocate to Hollywood when the Blitz began. Its young star, John Justin, had just entered the RAF as a flying instructor.

By the time Frank Capra summoned the nominees to the stage for the presentation of Best Director, he was already beginning to fear that the still unfinished *Meet John Doe*, the movie he had hoped would be the next *Grapes of Wrath*, was instead poised to become, in his words, "The Great American Letdown." He and Riskin had finished production more than four months earlier, but they had never been able to crack the ending. Riskin had argued that the main character played by Gary Cooper should go through with his threat to commit suicide, a final scene that Capra dismissed out of hand as too bleak, saying, "You just don't kill Gary Cooper." Instead, they tried an ending that stopped just short of that, with a scene in which Cooper's microphone is cut off during his attempt at a stirring final speech and the crowd turns against him. In that version, *Meet John Doe* ends on a sympathetic newspaper editor's sardonic line, "Well, boys, you can chalk another one up to the Pontius Pilates." Preview audiences hated it.

Capra had more at stake than his self-esteem. He had mortgaged his new home to collateralize the loan for his company's debut movie and he complained, not for the first time, that he was nearly broke because the government had taken 80 percent of the $300,000 he had earned last year for income tax. He couldn't afford to have *Meet John Doe* fail, so in January 1941, he called his cast back in front of the cameras and shot a new ending in which the movie's chief villain, the fascistic publisher with designs on the White House, sees the error of his ways and recants. It was Capra's return to an old trick—an uncomfortably close rewrite of the breakdown of the corrupt senator played by Claude Rains at the end of *Mr. Smith Goes to Washington*. It was also exactly the kind of last-minute sentimental reversal that Capra thought gave his critics permission not to take him seriously. On Oscar night, that version of the movie was just days from its first press preview.

To the end of his life, Capra insisted publicly that *Meet John Doe* had in the end won him the respect he had long sought. It was not the case. The film had the phenomenal misfortune to go before critics who had just gotten their first look at Orson Welles's *Citizen Kane*. Capra's depiction of a newspaper tycoon with a rotting soul could not help but look sketchy by comparison. But aside from the poor timing, Capra's filmmaking and his thinking took a beating even from those who liked aspects of the movie. For the first time, *Variety* wrote, "the director is more zealot than showman . . . the synthetic fabric of the story is the foundation[al] weakness of the production." The *New Republic* shrugged it off as "holy hokum" that "talks too much to no purpose" and marked an unwelcome return to "Capra's familiar and favorite American type, the easy shambling young man . . . a loveable innocent but don't tread on him." The *New York Times* approved of the film's anti-Fascist message but called it "overwritten." *Time* thought the picture threatened to "topple artistically from sheer pompous top-heaviness." And critics hated the new ending almost as unanimously as test audiences had hated the old one.

Capra still thought the movie could be saved, and took an extraordinary step to save it: Nine days after it opened at two theaters in New York City, he shot yet another new ending. This time, Doe would be heartened by some kind words from one of the lads in a local John Doe Club who tells him that he's sorry that he and the other boys "acted like a mob." The new, generically cheerful last line of *Meet John Doe* would be "There you are . . . The people! Try and lick that!" a brazen pilfering of Ma Joad's "They can't lick us, 'cause we're the people!" speech from *The Grapes of Wrath*. Capra had the new ending spliced onto all prints of *Meet John Doe* before the movie's national release, and withstood a good deal of public mockery; one columnist ran an item that joked, "Do you know why today is so refreshing? . . . This is the day Capra isn't shooting a new ending for Doe." But the latest fix did nothing to clarify the film's muddled arguments; *Doe* was a failure with the public, and Capra's first attempt at an independent production company was soon out of business.

On March 23, 1941, the day after shooting the new scene, Capra made an appearance on the radio show *I'm an American!*, a program in which every week a different immigrant would express his or her patriotism. The Justice Department, which oversaw the series, had asked Capra to "give a defense of Hollywood and its people, showing their strong sense of Americanism and loyalty to democratic ideals," and Capra complied. Despite his wealth and success, he knew that his status as an immigrant made him a second-class citizen to millions of Americans. Just that week, *Ladies' Home Journal* had published a profile of him in which the writer remarked that he looked "like any youngish, likable Italian who might beam at you across a fruit stand." Given the prevalence of that kind of stereotype, it is unsurprising that Capra felt that the invitation to speak on the air was a thinly veiled request for a public loyalty oath. In a carefully prepared script, he equivocated about war, calling it "abhorrent" but warning that it might be inevitable, and he declined to make the case for message movies, saying, "Personally, I refuse to believe the American public needs educating in democracy."

Until recently, Capra had toyed with plans to make a sequel to *Meet John Doe*. Now he had to abandon them; the making and reception of the movie had been so disheartening that, just a year after his statement to the *New Yorker* that films could become even more powerful than Hitler and Roosevelt, he seemed ready to give up on using the medium to say anything at all. In an interview that April, he told a journalist that he had recently decided against directing a drama about a mobster tasked with assassinating Hitler. "Can you make a million people sit still while you editorialize at them in pictures? I don't think so," he said. "With the world in its present state, what's the good of a message?"

On May 19, a couple of months after the Oscars, Capra relinquished the presidency of the Screen Directors Guild after several terms during which he had increased the group's bargaining power so effectively that he probably could have continued to hold the post indefinitely had he wanted it. Instead, he accepted the tribute of an honorary lifetime membership—a proposal made by Wyler—and handed the reins over to George Stevens. It was an apt passing of the torch since, a year earlier, Stevens had essentially replaced Capra at Columbia, and his ascension in the SDG's leadership was, in a way, official recognition that he was now a major filmmaker.

The week Stevens began his yearlong term as the SDG's president also brought the opening of his new movie, the first he had made since signing with Harry Cohn. Stevens had not adjusted easily to life at Columbia, where he had discovered upon his arrival that his new bosses were no more interested in having him make a political movie than RKO had been.

Capra later took credit for Stevens's arrival at Columbia, claiming that "because my way had produced five home runs in a row, other committee-hating directors were attracted to the studio." But in fact, Columbia interfered with Stevens almost from the moment he started there, first asking him to develop a romantic comedy titled *This Thing Called Love* and then abruptly taking it away from him and moving him onto a bigger project. The studio had bought the rights to a piece of short fiction from *McCall*'s magazine titled "The Story of a Happy Marriage," which it saw as a property that could reunite two major stars, Cary Grant and Irene Dunne, who had already proved irresistible to audiences as a romantic couple in the comedy *The*

Awful Truth (1937) and in the recently released hit *My Favorite Wife.* Stevens's new picture, which he retitled *Penny Serenade,* would be a departure for both actors—a shamelessly manipulative tearjerker in which Grant and Dunne would play a husband and wife who learn they can no longer have children after she miscarries during an earthquake. They then adopt a little girl, only to lose her as well.

The story strained credibility, and its framing device—each memory of the marriage was triggered by a different song—threatened to make it even more contrived. Stevens himself later admitted that he may have been attracted to *Penny Serenade* as an overreaction to the "light, frothy comedy" that had been his stock-in-trade. "I guess I was in a mood by this time, and so these poor [actors] became involved in my indulging myself," he said. "But they became wholeheartedly engaged in it." So did Stevens; as filming proceeded through the fall and into the winter of 1940, Cohn became alarmed at the amount of footage his director was shooting. But Stevens kept him at bay, holding him to his promise to stay away from the set while he strove to find a tone that would somehow keep the story from becoming too mawkish.

On his sets, Stevens was famously unreadable, "taciturn, always grave-looking, even when he was cracking jokes," his friend Irwin Shaw said later. When he was trying to solve a storytelling problem or figure out a scene, he would walk back and forth endlessly, meeting nobody's gaze. He liked to tell people he had Indian lineage, and "he looked very much like an Indian chief," said Joseph L. Mankiewicz. "Stoic. He couldn't talk. Suddenly, he *wouldn't* talk. His remoteness! He'd sit there and listen, with that look, and you could go mad." His friends referred to it as "the chill." On *Vigil in the Night,* his frustrated star Carole Lombard finally called her agent in the middle of the night and told him, "I just [realized] what that pacing and thoughtful look of Stevens' means—not a goddamn thing." But Stevens was also capable of intimate and precise communication with his actors, and on *Penny Serenade,* he encouraged his two stars to dig deeper than they had before. "I have often humbled actors, creating stories that will bring a kind of humility out of them, rather than letting them come forth on the screen in their established aura," he said. That was his goal this time, especially for

Grant; the actor had begged to be let out of a part that he was sure was too serious for him, but Stevens had directed him in *Gunga Din* and believed that he was capable of more than the affable romantic charm that had become his signature. He also felt that audiences would be all the more moved to see a star who was usually all smiles experience anger, grief, and loss.

The *Penny Serenade* shoot lasted for four months—a long schedule for any studio, but especially the brisk and budget-conscious Columbia. In January 1941, Stevens was just days from wrapping when tragedy struck. Grant was working on a soundstage on the lot when he received news that the Luftwaffe had bombed Bristol, the hometown he had left twenty years earlier. Five members of his family had been killed: his aunt and uncle, their daughter and son-in-law, and their grandchild. Grant was still a British citizen; when England had declared war, he had thought of going home and enlisting, but his stock in Hollywood was rising, and he had decided to stay in the United States, donating half his salary for some movies to British War Relief. When he learned of the deaths, he was shattered, but he refused to let the studio cancel a day of filming.

Stevens finished *Penny Serenade* in the spring, test-screened it, cut it from 165 minutes to just under two hours, and won some of the best notices of his career. His work with Grant paid off with the actor's first Academy Award nomination as well as with praise for the restraint Stevens brought to a story that, as one critic wrote, "employs not one but six or seven of the recognized sob-story tricks . . . take along a couple of blotters and a sponge . . . you might even take along a washtub."

Stevens moved on quickly, agreeing to extend his deal with Columbia from two pictures to three if the studio would consent to loan him to MGM, where he planned to reteam with his *Alice Adams* star Katharine Hepburn for *Woman of the Year*. His desire to make movies about war had been thwarted so many times that it seemed, finally, to have abated altogether; the Hepburn movie would mark a return to the safer ground of romantic comedy, the genre in which he had most frequently distinguished himself. That spring, the rest of the industry seemed to be in retreat as well. The day Stevens took over the Screen Directors Guild, the *New York Times* published a widely discussed story that essentially reiterated Frank Capra's recent dismissal of message movies, contending that propaganda movies had "proved to be a costly mistake. . . . Not one of the several films devoted to arousing America against Germany has been more than a casual success." Citing the modest box-office returns for movies like *Confessions of a Nazi Spy* and *The Mortal Storm,* both of which had initially looked like hits only to peter out quickly, the *Times* concluded that "audiences were convinced of the depravity of the Nazis and were bored by the constant reiteration on the screen . . . the necessarily hopeless endings [are] depressing and . . . there [is] no money in preaching."

That verdict, reinforced by any number of anxious producers and bottom-line executives, had in the spring of 1941 become the newest article of faith for an industry whose brief flirtation with boldness appeared to be ending. As interventionist as many of Hollywood's leaders were in their private lives or their philanthropic efforts, they were convinced that if they ever allowed their politics to spill onto the screen, audiences would inevitably turn away. But just a few weeks later, Warner Bros. released a movie made by John Huston and Howard Hawks that completely upended that conventional wisdom. The resulting showdown would change the balance of power between Hollywood and Washington for the duration of the war.

FIVE

"The Most Dangerous
Fifth Column in Our Country"

*HOLLYWOOD AND WASHINGTON,
JULY–DECEMBER 1941*

A lvin C. York was, at least in theory, ideal movie material. For twenty years, Americans had known of him as an exemplar of personal bravery during World War I, a simple, religious, dirt-poor Tennessee mountain man who read the Bible, loved his country, and prayed for peace on earth. York had entered the war only because his status as a conscientious objector did not exempt him from military service. He had gone on to defend himself and his troops by killing two dozen German soldiers and capturing 132 others; reverent home-front newspapers nicknamed him "the one-man army." When he returned to the United States, he refused to profit from his battlefield heroism. Instead, he traveled the country giving lectures in which he advocated nonmilitary solutions to world problems, and then returned home to Tennessee, where he used his renown to champion the construction and funding of an agricultural school. Even when he went broke and had to mortgage his farm, he declined offers to sell his life story to the movies.

When producer Jesse Lasky flew to Nashville to try to get York to change his mind, he knew that what he was attempting to purchase was not the narrative of York's life but rather his consent to be used in the service of a case for war, and then, ideally, to be quiet about it. By 1940, the fifty-three-year-old York had become a somewhat problematic figure. At 275 pounds, he was no longer the image of a lean, strapping American warrior, and although he had turned into a polished public speaker after years working the national lecture circuit, on home turf he could easily slide into unreconstructed racism (he liked to say that Negroes never stayed in his farm's county for long because the field work was too hard for them). Lasky, one of the founders of Paramount Pictures, was a wily and persistent veteran of the trade, and a man not easily rattled. He didn't flinch for a moment when York, who soon took to referring to him as a "fat little Jew," told him the language in his proposed contract was too fancy, insisted on a stipulation that he be played by Gary Cooper, and, to cap off the negotiations, announced, "I don't like war pictures." Fifty thousand dollars later, they had a deal.

Cooper also took some persuading. Warners' Hal Wallis had decided to partner with Lasky after one of the studio's deputies convinced him that the story of Sergeant York could be adapted into a variation on one of the actor's biggest hits; on the lot, they were already calling it "Mr. Deeds Goes to War." But at forty, Cooper felt he was too old to be believable in the scenes that depicted York's backcountry youth; besides, he said, "I don't think I can do justice to him. He's too big for me . . . he covers too much territory." In one sense, Cooper was right. The character of York, and his story, were being asked to do double duty—the movie, which Howard Hawks was to direct, was conceived not only as an inspiring tale of how one man's personal code served him before, during, and after combat, but as a recruiting poster for the next war. *Sergeant York* was a film with an unconcealed ideological purpose: It was intended to persuade the tens of millions of Americans who detested war, and who held what was still a majority opinion that the United States never should have entered World War I, that supporting American intervention against Hitler did not mean that they had to abandon their convictions.

And in spreading the message that pacifism need not equal isolationism, Warners found a surprising ally in York himself. The sergeant had been a frequent speaker for the Emergency Peace Campaign, and as late as the summer of 1939, in a speech at the World's Fair in New York City, he had argued that America should concentrate on problems within its borders, not overseas. But the start of the war in Europe had changed his mind, and by early 1941, as the film neared production, York had become a fervent and public interventionist, making headlines with his declaration that "Hitler can, will, and must be beaten."

The first two screenwriters on the project had titled their treatment "The Amazing Story of Sergeant York." But what had begun as pure inspirational drama now needed a different, more forcefully dogmatic approach. For that, Warner turned to John Huston, who had in the two years since the *Juárez* debacle become one of the studio's most proficient and successful screen-writers. Huston's interest in world politics remained as keen as it had been in 1939, and his command of Hollywood politics had improved considerably since the days when he watched Paul Muni run roughshod over his script. After *Juárez*, Warner had put Huston to work rewriting a screenplay about the biologist who had discovered the first effective treatment for syphilis. Huston thought the original script "was shit," and that the director assigned to the film, William Dieterle, would be no more capable of standing up for himself on the set than he had been during *Juárez*. But this time, Huston won the allegiance of the movie's leading man, Edward G. Robinson; he skillfully turned the picture from a romance into a scientific detective story, and won a bitter arbitration battle to protect his screenwriting credit.

The movie, *Dr. Ehrlich's Magic Bullet*, was accorded a reception strong enough to win Huston a more high-profile assignment—the screenplay for Raoul Walsh's gangster melodrama *High Sierra*, an adaptation of W. R. Burnett's crime novel about the last heist of a gangster who has just been released from prison. Huston loved the book and pitched himself to Warner hard, telling Hal Wallis that he knew exactly how to capture the novel's special early-noir quality, which he identified as "the strange sense of inevitability that comes with our deepening understanding of the characters and the forces that motivate them." The only problem was that Warner had offered the leading role to Huston's old nemesis Muni. The actor, who had little use for writers in general and still less for Huston, resisted his hiring, demanded that Burnett be brought in as a cowriter, and then fatally overplayed his hand by rejecting the draft Burnett and Huston handed in. Warner, aware of his diminished box-office allure and tired of his petulance, fired Muni from the picture that day. After George Raft also dismissed the script as unworthy of his talents, the studio gave the leading role to a contract player who had never quite managed to find a niche. "I want you to give the utmost attention to the building of Humphrey Bogart," read an internal studio memo written on July 17, 1940, the day Muni's contract with Warner Bros. ended. "Let us see if within the next two or three months we cannot have the country flooded with Bogart art and column breaks . . . predicting great success for him as a star."

By December, Huston was headed toward a screenwriting Oscar nomination, his first, for *Dr. Ehrlich,* and *High Sierra* had turned out so well that he was able to convince the studio to put him back together with Bogart and give him his first chance to direct. Warner liked Huston's idea—a remake of a property that had already been filmed twice, *The Maltese Falcon*—but Wallis asked him to take on the rewrite of *Sergeant York* first. Huston was brimming with confidence when he accepted the assignment; after ten years of false starts and personal crises, his career was finally taking off. Initially, Warner put him together with a cowriter, his old friend Howard Koch. But, said Huston, "I took that picture over. I worked alone on it." After meeting with Alvin York a couple of times, Huston proceeded with the studio's mandate to make the film "not a success story, as virtually all screen biographies have been," but the "story of a hell-raising mountaineer who is a conscientious objector but goes to war anyhow and becomes a hero."

Huston's work on *Sergeant York* was not subtle. He added battle scenes, he deemphasized York's postwar life as a progressive education reformer, he amplified York's heroism to such preposterous proportions that three dozen of his former platoon mates had to be paid off by Warner to keep quiet about it, and he infused the scenes of York's rural life with so much hayseed comedy that Abem Finkel, one of the screenwriters he had replaced, wrote an outraged memo to Wallis deploring the new script's "blundering stupidities" and predicting that Warner was in for a "helluva mess" if the movie went forward.

In later years, Huston would sound faintly embarrassed about his work on *Sergeant York.* In his expansive autobiography *An Open Book,* he devotes only three lines to the movie, and he told Howard Hawks's biographer, the

critic Todd McCarthy, "I don't believe that the film delivers a terribly profound and relevant message. . . . We weren't trying to make *All Quiet on the
Western Front*. That was a film which set out to show the First World War in
all its horror, all the better to shock the viewer so that he won't repeat it." In
fact, Huston understood precisely the ideological force of what he was being
asked to do, and proved himself a willing instrument in the creation of the
boldest piece of pro-intervention propaganda that had yet emerged from a
Hollywood studio. In *Sergeant York,* he and Hawks consciously tried to replace *All Quiet on the Western Front*'s version of World War I with a new
piece of mythmaking in which the Great War was indeed great—not pointless but noble—and the sacrifice it entailed was not senseless but heroic.* "I
ain't a-goin'-a war. War is killin'! And the Book's agin killin'! So war is agin
the Book!" says York in the movie. After going into battle and becoming a
hero, he explains his change of heart: "I'm as much agin killing as ever . . .
but I figured them guns was killing hundreds, maybe thousands." "You
mean you did it to *save* lives?" says his commanding officer incredulously.
"Yes, sir—that was why."

The declarative bluntness of much of Huston's dialogue was matched by
the publicity campaign that led up to *Sergeant York*'s opening. Ads announced that the movie was made as "a result of World War II's menacing
threat to democracy," and on July 2, 1941—just ten days after Germany had
invaded Russia and one day after America's second prewar wave of draft
registration had begun—Warner Bros. staged a New York City premiere at
the Astor Theater that looked more like a full-dress military parade than like
the debut of a Hollywood movie. The studio corralled as many World War I
veterans, including members of York's old platoon, as it could accommodate,
and invited dozens of active-duty officers up from Washington as well. The
list of opening-night attendees included Eleanor Roosevelt and Wendell

---

* In 1939, *All Quiet on the Western Front* itself was the victim of revisionism. Universal decided not only to rerelease
the film, but to recut it; footage that was sympathetic to German soldiers was removed and a voice-over was added,
interrupting the film a dozen times to describe war atrocities and emphasize Germany's plan for world domination,
specifically mentioning Hitler. The *New York Times* described the new version as "stupid vandalism" that deliberately undercut the original film's antiwar message, but with the disingenuous billing "The Uncensored Version," it
did business well into 1940.

Willkie. York, the guest of honor, was greeted personally by Mayor Fiorello La Guardia, and Warner arranged for Gary Cooper to receive a "Distinguished Citizenship Medal" from the Veterans of Foreign Wars.

The point that *Sergeant York* was a look both backward and forward was almost impossible to miss, and while few critics claimed that the movie was an artistic masterpiece, most hailed it as an exceptionally effective means of delivering a message. "The suggestion of deliberate propaganda is readily detected here," wrote *New York Times* critic Bosley Crowther, calling it "a little naïve" but "good native drama." The *New Republic* referred to it as a "stunt picture . . . about the army and arming in a time when people damn well *have* to think about the army," *Time* called it "Hollywood's first solid contribution to national defense," and *Variety* praised it as "a clarion film that reaches the public at a moment when its stirring and patriotic message is probably most needed. It is as timely as a White House fireside chat." Warner had planned a gradual release for *Sergeant York,* but the movie turned into a national phenomenon almost immediately, becoming the highest-grossing film in the country while it was still playing in just a few cities, and demolishing the recently minted Hollywood axiom that audiences weren't interested in war-related pictures.

But the movie's success was also the last straw for a cadre of isolationist politicians. Throughout the first half of 1941, Burton K. Wheeler, a Democratic senator from Montana, had been nursing his anger at President Roosevelt's support for greater involvement in the war, predicting that Hitler "would plough under every fourth American boy." When newsreel producers declined to give equal time to his speeches despite his petitioning, he took it personally and warned Hollywood that if it did not pull back its commitment to producing "propaganda for war," he would propose legislation designed to mandate "a more impartial attitude."

Wheeler had a strong, though unofficial, ideological ally in Joseph Breen, a virulently anti-Semitic Catholic who had until recently run the Production Code Administration and had privately referred to Jews as "dirty lice"; these days, Breen was especially affronted by the Hollywood Anti-Nazi League, an organization he contended was "conducted and financed almost entirely by Jews." As the threat of war grew more imminent, Hollywood's Jewish leadership had become less fearful about attacks from those who questioned their loyalties. In April, an urgent invitation to a dinner for elderly Zionist leader Chaim Weizmann was sent to "all important members of Jewish faith within motion picture and allied industries"; it was signed by either the Jewish heads or the senior Jewish executives of all eight studios, a collective assertion of identity that would have been taboo in the industry even a year earlier. (William Wyler was among those who attended.) The counterreaction was fierce. Wheeler and his fellow isolationists decided to make common cause with anti-Semites (there was already plenty of overlap between the two groups) and stepped up their rhetoric to include ever more pointed references to the ethnicity and religion of the men who ran the movie business.

A confrontation that Hollywood had long been hoping to avoid was finally ignited on August 1, when Gerald P. Nye, a Republican senator from North Dakota, made an invective-laden speech to the isolationist group America First in which he directly attacked the "foreigners" who ran Hollywood, especially those with "non-Nordic" last names. He accused the industry of promoting the war in "at least 20 pictures . . . produced within the last year—all designed to drug the reason of the American people, set aflame their emotions, turn their hatred into a blaze, fill them with fear that Hitler will come over here and capture them, [and] rouse them to a war hysteria." Among the films he cited were *Sergeant York* and Charlie Chaplin's *The Great Dictator*. He went on to address the motives behind the films, deploying analogies of disease and infection that had become ominously familiar. "In each of these companies there are a number of production directors, many of whom have come from Russia, Hungary, Germany and the Baltic countries . . . these men . . . can address 80,000,000 people a week, cunningly and persistently inoculating them with the virus of war. Why do they do this? Well, they are interested in foreign causes. . . . Go to Hollywood. It is a raging volcano of war fever. The place swarms with refugees." Nye reminded his listeners, who included a national radio audience, that it had taken "the great Christian churches" to purge Hollywood of indecency a few years earlier, when the Production Code had been instituted, and he concluded by asking, "Are the movie moguls doing this because they like to do it, or has the government of the United States forced them to become . . .

propaganda agencies? . . . Are you ready to send your boys to bleed and die in Europe to make the world safe for Barney Balaban and Adolph Zukor and Joseph Schenck?"*

Nye's message was incoherent—he was at once accusing Jews of leading a propagandistic conspiracy and claiming that they were acting on orders from the government. He did not even attempt to encode or couch his beliefs in "acceptable" language, and his tone drew sharp responses from both the film industry (one trade publication said he had spoken "in the best storm trooper fashion") and from newspaper editorial writers on the left, who called him an anti-Semite. But his speech reflected the reality of a divided American populace; as war grew likelier, polls showed that fully half of all Americans believed that Jews had too much power in the United States. Perhaps emboldened by the rise of America First, which even had a small membership in Hollywood, Nye was prepared to back up his incendiary language with action. The day he gave the speech, he and Senator Bennett Clark of Missouri introduced a resolution to hold Senate hearings to investigate the origins of "propaganda [that] reaches weekly the eyes and ears of one hundred million people and is in the hands of groups interested in involving the United States in war." For good measure, the resolution threw in a charge of monopoly, predicated on the argument that Hollywood studios were in collusion not only with the Roosevelt administration but with one another. Hearings were set to begin September 9. The movie industry was about to go on trial.

Although the accusation that the studios were propagandists dominated press coverage, the monopoly issue was potentially more serious for many reasons, including the fact that any number of independent theater owners could testify to it; that charge reflected a provable concern that had been expressed by Roosevelt's own Justice Department. But since the committee itself was clearly treating the issue of monopoly as something of an afterthought, the studio chiefs gambled that they could ignore it and concentrate instead on rebuffing the attack on their movies and their motives. To build

* Balaban and Zukor were the president and cofounder of Paramount; Schenck, the chairman of 20th Century Fox, had recently been convicted of income tax evasion.

their case, they obtained the support of an unlikely high-profile ally when the industry's official lobbying group, the Motion Picture Producers and Distributors of America, hired Wendell Willkie to represent it at the hearings. Willkie, who received $100,000 for his services, had been the Republican nominee for president a year earlier, but after his loss to Roosevelt he had become something of an outcast in his own party for his support of the Lend-Lease Act and of the president's war policies. In the spring of 1941, after publicly debating Charles Lindbergh in the pages of *Collier's* magazine, he became the most prominent Republican politician in the country to take a firmly pro-intervention stance.

The studios could not have picked an advocate who was better immunized against charges of being a stooge either for Hollywood or for the administration. Roosevelt himself was already deeply invested in strengthening the ties between Hollywood and Washington that war would necessitate, and was keeping a close eye on Willkie's involvement with the impending hearings. He had recently appointed Lowell Mellett, a former newspaperman, to serve as a liaison between the movie industry and the War Department; two weeks before the hearings began, Mellett wrote to the president that under Willkie's tutelage "the best men in the industry are ready to go into these hearings fighting. They say they'll proclaim they are doing everything they know how to make America conscious of the national peril; that they won't apologize— just the reverse."

Privately, some in Hollywood thought appeasement would be a wiser strategy. As the hearings approached, the Hays Office rushed to gather statistics demonstrating that only a handful of 1940's features had been war-related, and hoped to reassure Washington that "the essential service of motion pictures is entertainment." But Willkie, who relished a good fight, rejected any strategy that smacked of apology, and he was instrumental in convincing the industry to go on the offensive. In a series of late-night meetings with the studio chiefs, he encouraged them to speak forthrightly about their lives, their patriotism, even their Jewish identities. He had the backing of Hollywood's trade unions—just before the hearings, the Screen Writers Guild fired off a telegram questioning their constitutionality—and of its trade papers, including the *Hollywood Reporter,* which scorned and rebuked the senators almost daily. Some accidents of timing helped Willkie as well; the first anniversary of the Blitz, widely noted in newspapers and newsreels, drove home the danger that the world faced from Hitler just two days before the hearings started. That was also the day the president's mother died, creating a wave of public sympathy and muting the possibility that what was known as "the Nye Committee" would be able to come out of the gate on day one with a barrage of anti-Roosevelt invective.

Nye was not actually part of the five-man committee, which had been stacked four-to-one with isolationists, but he was granted the opportunity to give testimony as the first day's only witness. Before Nye spoke, Willkie opened strongly, saying he could save the committee plenty of time since he was willing to admit up front that the studios "make no pretense of friendliness to Nazi Germany nor to the objectives and goals of this ruthless dictatorship. We abhor everything that Hitler represents." Of eleven hundred Hollywood movies produced since the start of the war in Europe, he claimed only fifty had war-related themes (the reality was closer to 140); however, he stood behind all of them and dismissed the charge that Roosevelt was pressuring Hollywood to make interventionist pictures, by saying, "Frankly, the motion-picture industry would be ashamed if it were not doing voluntarily what it is now doing in this patriotic cause."

With Willkie already threatening to dominate the proceedings, the committee shut him down by telling him that he would not be allowed to question their witnesses. (Democratic senator Ernest McFarland—the panel's only interventionist—objected in disgusted dissent.) They then gave Nye the floor for the rest of the day. The senator began by woundedly refuting the now-public charges of anti-Semitism against him ("I have splendid Jewish friends in and out of the moving-picture business") and then called the heads of Hollywood's movie studios "the most potent and dangerous 'fifth column' in our country." He inveighed against a spate of movies that had recently portrayed the British "as a nation of people suffering and standing courageously . . . against the violent bombardment by a hideous enemy," explaining that "the people of Germany or of Italy . . . are also suffering . . . their blood is red too." He cited a Wall Street study of Hollywood's profits abroad to suggest that the studios were supporting England only to protect a major foreign market for their product. And he attacked Fox chief Darryl Zanuck for urging his employees to attend an anti-Nazi rally.

Then Willkie saw an opening. Nye listed a dozen films he wanted investigated, and despite the rules barring him from engaging with a witness, Willkie jumped in to ask Nye if he had seen any of them—*Convoy* or *Flight Command* or *That Hamilton Woman* or *Man Hunt* or *The Great Dictator* or *Sergeant York*. Nye hedged, eventually admitting that he hadn't seen "all of them." Willkie offered to set up screenings for the committee at their convenience.

After Nye finished his testimony, some journalists who were present wrote pieces mocking the hearings as a show trial that was designed only to give the isolationists a chance to score points against Hollywood, not to elicit new information or launch any kind of serious-minded investigation. Day two only confirmed their suspicions; it was devoted entirely to the testimony of Senator Bennett Clark. Clark complained that "the motion-picture industry is . . . controlled by half a dozen men, and . . . most of those men are . . . determined, in order to wreak vengeance on Adolf Hitler, a ferocious beast, to plunge this nation into war on behalf of another ferocious beast" (meaning Stalin). He attacked "20th Century Fox, of which Mr. Joseph Schenck was chairman until he was sent to the penitentiary, and of which Mr. Darryl Zanuck is now head," and also went after producer Alexander Korda and Charlie Chaplin, "who has lived in this country for thirty years and never thought well enough of the United States to become a citizen." And he said darkly that "if the industry does not end this propaganda for war and return to its normal function of entertainment, I shall do everything in my power to bring about at once and forever the utter destruction of the monopolistic grasp of this little handful of men on the screen."

By the following evening, momentum began to turn decisively against the isolationists. That was in part due to a day of testimony that descended, or perhaps ascended, into farce. The day's star witness was John C. Flynn, a journalist who was then serving as chairman of America First. By this point, Senator McFarland had grown so weary of the proceedings that he suggested they just cancel all further testimony and screen *Sergeant York* instead. When he mentioned the movie, Senator Charles Tobey, a New Hampshire

Republican who had remained almost completely silent for three days, suddenly stirred with interest. "It was a good picture!" he exclaimed.

Willkie jumped in. "Let's discontinue the bunk and look at the pictures! . . . The old monopoly humbug is being dragged out again to divert momentarily attention from the real object of the investigation—the sabotage of the country's foreign policy."

Undeterred, Flynn spent the day waging an uphill battle to build a case against Jack Warner by suggesting sinister intent behind Warner's 1939 comment that films could be used to promote "Americanism." Flynn offered up his own list of forty-nine movies he thought were propaganda; unlike the first two witnesses, he had actually seen many of them and was able to quote lines that sounded to him like "a regular 1941 war speech." He wasn't wrong about the pro-war message of the movies, but just as Nye and Clark had been, he was hopelessly ensnared by the certainty that the studios had been taking their orders from Roosevelt.

Then McFarland began to question him. If Washington had so much authority over Hollywood's output, he asked, how could a film as unflattering to elected officials as Frank Capra's *Mr. Smith Goes to Washington* ever have been made? "After all," said McFarland, "don't you think that people recognize propaganda when they see it?"

"Certainly not, Senator," Flynn replied.

"You think you have a great deal more ability than the average person to recognize it?" McFarland said.

"I have been a newspaperman all my life," Flynn said, "and I have been looking at propaganda in eruption and I have read books on propaganda. Senator, you better look out, if you don't think you should protect yourself against it. Look out. Somebody is going to sell you something some day."

McFarland didn't miss a beat. "I have been listening to you here for several hours trying to sell me something," he said.

The room exploded in laughter.

The next morning, many papers reprinted that exchange, but the headlines were dominated by something far more shocking. While that day's hearings had unfolded, Charles Lindbergh had made a speech at an America

First rally in Des Moines at which he denounced three groups of "war agitators"—"the British, the Jewish, and the Roosevelt administration." He was especially incensed about one of those groups, and in the inflammatory climax of his remarks, he warned that American Jews who advocated for military intervention "will be among the first to feel its consequences." Citing the "danger to our country . . . in their large ownership and influence in our motion pictures, our press, our radio, and our government," he concluded that Jews, "for reasons which are not American, wish to involve us in the war. . . . We cannot allow the natural passions and prejudices of other peoples to lead our country to destruction."

Over the last year, as he had become more outspoken, Lindbergh had turned himself into a hero of the isolationist movement—crowds at America First rallies would sometimes greet him with shouts of "Our next president!" But his advocacy of racial purity, his open awe at the size and strength of Hitler's army, and his chilly lack of sympathy for Jews had alienated much of the rest of the country; in April, he had resigned his air force commission in anger after Roosevelt publicly compared him to a Civil War "copperhead." After Lindbergh's wife, Anne, who had urged him to use more restrained language, listened to his speech on the radio, she wrote in her diary that she felt "black gloom. . . . No matter what his intentions were, he has lit the match. I would prefer to see this country at war than shaken by violent anti-Semitism."

Those were among the kindest words the speech provoked. Even Lindbergh's natural allies turned on him: The isolationist and anti-Roosevelt Hearst newspapers ran a national front-page editorial denouncing him as "un-American" and "unpatriotic." The condemnation was so unanimous and devastating that it all but ended the isolationist movement in America overnight; America First even considered disbanding, realizing that their shining light had become, in his own wife's words, "the symbol of anti-Semitism in this country."

Two days later, Alvin York stepped into the fray with a speech of his own in which he became the first public figure to yoke Lindbergh and Nye together. The two men, he said, "ought to be shut up by throwing them square in jail—today, not tomorrow. . . . They're either looking at the world through rose-colored glasses or they're downright Nazi-inclined, and one is about as dangerous as the other.

"I'm anti-Nazi and proud of it," York continued. "And I'll be glad to tell that to the Senate committee investigating what they call 'war propaganda' in Hollywood."

Suddenly the hearings seemed less urgent—including to the senators who had demanded them. After several postponements, the Nye Committee reconvened in late September to hear testimony for the defense from some of the movie industry's top executives. The day began with an elegant rebuke from California's Democratic senator Sheridan Downey, who told his colleagues, "If propaganda be stretched, as it all too often is, to mean the strong expression of one's views, with the hope of convincing one's fellows, then we are all guilty of it 10 times a day." Downey then asked, "Should we expect Hollywood to turn its back upon the reality of our world and plunge into an unrelieved mist of fantasy? Should it ignore the chaos and the strife and the tragedy of the world we now live in, and devote itself exclusively to musical comedy, boy-meets-girl plots, and horse operas? Heaven knows that is a sufficiently prevalent tendency not to need encouragement from the United States Senate. . . . Frankly, gentlemen, it strikes me that the subcommittee is focusing its inquiry in the wrong direction. The world is on fire, and because a few pale shadows of its conflagration flicker for a moment or two on the screen . . . you seek to throw cold water on California. You pursue an illusion. The blaze is in Europe and Asia, not in my state; the propaganda you seek for is history itself."

Over the next week, Hollywood rewrote its reputation in each day's dispatches from the hearings. Men who had been dismissed as outsiders, immigrants, and agitators were now before the committee as patriots; it was the loyalty and integrity of the isolationists that suddenly seemed to be on trial. Harry Warner, who had carefully prepared his testimony in advance after consulting with his studio's lawyers, now felt confident enough to tell the senators, "I am ready to give myself and all my personal resources to aid in the defeat of the Nazi menace to the American people," and added, "I have always been in accord with President Roosevelt's foreign policy. . . . I am unequivocally in favor of giving England and her allies all supplies which our country can spare. . . . In truth, the only sin of which Warner Bros. is guilty is that of accurately recording on the screen the world as it is or as it has been." Point by point, he took on the committee's charges, explaining that Warner Bros. scrupulously researched its movies and had been "producing pictures for over 20 years. . . . Our present policies are no different than before there was a Hitler menace." And he refuted the charge that propaganda films were being produced even in the face of public indifference by pointing to *Sergeant York,* "which I believe will gross more money for our company than any picture we have made in recent years." (He was right; by the end of its run two years later, the movie was the most profitable in the studio's history.)

The senators didn't give up without a fight, but they sounded more cornered with every exchange. That afternoon, Warner got into a testy exchange with Idaho isolationist senator D. Worth Clark, who accused him of wanting to make pictures that "inflame the American mind to hatred for Germany."

"I say it will not incite you," Warner replied. "It will only portray to you what actually exists. You will see, for one thing, what you have kind of missed, my dear Senator."

"I am asking questions," snapped Clark. "I will take care of what I missed. . . . I am asking you whether when the ordinary American family goes in the evening to [the movies] the tendency would be to come out . . . hating the German people and wanting to go to war with them."

"I can't talk for the rest of the world," said Warner. "I think in America, we have our own minds and we use them."

The applause that broke out might have ended the hearings, but they continued for one more day, with testimony from Darryl F. Zanuck that helped reposition Hollywood, for so long condemned by moral watchdogs as a repository of subversive anti-Americanism, as the country's most reliable bastion of patriotic values. Introducing himself to the committee, with sly and charming self-deprecation, as a Methodist, a midwesterner with roots in Nebraska, and a World War I veteran who never made it past private first class, Zanuck started by saying, "When I first read and heard of this proposed investigation or inquiry I was deeply resentful, naturally. After a while, in thinking it over, my anger cooled a bit. It gives me an opportunity to say what I am going to say now. I am proud to be a part of the moving picture business."

He then took the senators on a warmly nostalgic tour through thirty years of movie history, shrewdly citing the films that were then held in high esteem as classics—*The Birth of a Nation, The Big Parade, The Jazz Singer, Disraeli*, and his own recent success, Ford's *The Grapes of Wrath*, whose "We're the people" speech he took the opportunity to recite to the assembled senators. "I look back and recall picture after picture, pictures so strong and powerful that they sold the American way of life not only to America but to the entire world. They sold it so strongly that when dictators took over Italy and Germany, what did Hitler and his flunky Mussolini do? The first thing they did was to ban our pictures, throw us out. They wanted no part of the American way of life."

When Zanuck was done speaking, Senator McFarland told him he wished his statement could "go throughout the world. . . . I think it . . . is one of the best I've ever heard." And even Worth Clark conceded the battle. "You are not only a creative artist, Mr. Zanuck," he said. "You are a rather skilled salesman. Maybe I will see those pictures!"

Even the senators knew that, as Senator McFarland put it, if they brought any of these issues before the full Senate, they "would not get 18 votes." (The issue of monopoly, a potential economic catastrophe for the studios, had been all but abandoned, and would not be successfully reapproached until 1948.) With McFarland now threatening an investigation of his own to ferret out who was responsible for the lie that the U.S. government controlled the content of Hollywood pictures, the committee hastily adjourned. Several dates to reconvene were set, then postponed. In late October, a new schedule for the resumption of hearings was announced: January 1942.

The committee never met again. It disbanded on Monday, December 8, 1941.

PART TWO

——

PART TWO

SIX

"Do I Have to Wait for Orders?"

HOLLYWOOD, WASHINGTON, AND HAWAII,
DECEMBER 1941–APRIL 1942

On the morning of December 7, 1941, Catholic churches across the United States resounded with a denunciation of the Greta Garbo comedy *Two-Faced Woman*. Thanks to an organized campaign by the National Legion of Decency, the church's censorious watchdog group, stern condemnations of the movie's depravity rang from every pulpit. Even by the standards of the time, MGM's light romance was hardly scandalous—it contained nothing more risqué than the line "I like older men; they're so grateful"—but parishioners were warned to shun the picture and to tell their friends and families to do the same.

It was the last moment of its kind for quite some time. While Pearl Harbor's initial effect on Hollywood was by no means uniform or even unifying, news of the bombing did have at least one immediate consequence for Hollywood: The war temporarily halted a cultural crusade led by guardians of morality who had long regarded movies as easy targets. The abortive campaign against *Two-Faced Woman* came to stand as a symbol not of an uprising against big-screen smut but of misdirected hysteria; those who once made news by vilifying a movie now risked looking like silly scolds with little more to contribute to a serious moment than irrelevant finger-wagging. For the moment, no politician, demagogue, columnist, or church had anything to gain by railing against the putative "indecency" of the movie business. Overnight, the denigration of Hollywood as a subculture of filth had lost its currency. Instead, the film business would swiftly come to be viewed as the country's chief exponent and manufacturer of what Jack Warner had called Americanism, a nebulously defined product that many in both Hollywood and Washington nonetheless hoped could materially contribute to an Allied victory.

Within the industry itself, the reaction to Pearl Harbor was an uneasy combination of ardent patriotism, head-in-the-sand solipsism, and bottom-line pragmatism. The morning after the attack, studio chiefs awoke to a banner headline in the *Hollywood Reporter* that read "War Wallops Boxoffice." Sunday's gloomy revenue reports had already been cabled to the studios from around the country, and movie attendance was down between 15 and 50 percent, with the worst numbers coming from the West Coast, where the populace was in a near panic about air raids. Industry reporters fretted that Americans would continue to stay home, glued to what was then Hollywood's only real rival for entertainment consumers, the radio. It was with a palpable sense of relief that three weeks later, the paper announced that ticket sales had bounced back over the Christmas holiday. Just a week after the end of America's first extended engagement of the war, the brutal and unsuccessful battle against Japan for control of the North Pacific atoll Wake Island, the public was apparently ready to go to the movies again in order to "forget jitters" and "seek joy."

"Hollywood! Jump Out of It!" barked a front-page *Reporter* editorial. "Stir yourself out of your depression. The making of motion pictures is just as important in the conduct of this war as is the production of ammunition, planes or boats. . . . Our warring nation must be entertained." But what that entertainment should be, and how much Hollywood's "war effort" should be reflected in the movies it made, was still an open question. Some pushed for a business-as-usual approach that would have required no greater effort than encouraging the sale of defense bonds in movie theaters, but they were soon outnumbered by those who advocated a new emphasis on "morale movies"— the very propaganda that had just a few months earlier placed the studios under suspicion.

In the wake of Pearl Harbor, most in Hollywood came to believe that even comedies, fantasies, and romances could contribute some passing commentary about democracy, freedom, shared sacrifice, or the "American way of life." But at first the studios were still skittish—in those early weeks, they canceled the release of a couple of already completed military farces out of concern that the movies might be construed as mocking the armed forces. It was the wrong call. Over the past year, a series of cheap service comedies had turned a pair of radio comedians named Bud Abbott and Lou Costello into the highest-grossing stars in the movie business and transformed Universal Pictures into an impressive box-office force. It soon became evident that the start of the war had only increased the public's appetite to see men in uniform onscreen in every possible genre. That hungry audience included children; in a December 1941 survey of underage moviegoers, kids revealed that their favorite picture of the last year had been *Sergeant York.*

Any trepidation the studios felt about making war movies vanished within weeks. During the congressional hearings, York had made a speech in which he said, "It's just as much the duty of the people in Hollywood to tell us the truth about Hitler's outfit as it is [of] the newspapers." The studios agreed with him, and ordered their New York story editors to scout appropriate material—"morale-building stories, biographies of Naval and American war heroes. Anti-Nazi, but especially anti-Italian works; and pro-Chinese anti-Jap tales." But there were serious obstacles to translating that enthusiasm into production. The draft was going to create a major labor shortage at the studios, and hours for their thirty thousand employees would be shortened. Night shoots were now impossible; working days would, for the foreseeable future, end at 5 p.m., a cutoff mandated by the evening blackouts all along the California coast. The thriving nightlife of Los Angeles was curtailed, and nighttime movie attendance was sparse; the week after Pearl Harbor, one columnist noted that "about the only places that were lit up . . . were the Strip night spots that had equipped themselves with blackout protection."

Perhaps because the Nye Committee hearings were still so fresh in their minds, nobody who ran a studio—not even Harry or Jack Warner—was particularly eager to take charge, or to suggest a course of action unilaterally; what most of the moguls wanted was a cooperative emissary from the government, someone whose presence would formalize the fact that despite the recent acrimony, everyone was now on the same side. As one trade reporter wrote on December 11, "Hollywood wants to know to whom or what office it must answer." Within two weeks, a plan began to take shape: President Roosevelt would ask Lowell Mellett, his recently appointed Hollywood-Washington liaison, to relocate to California and establish a bureau to deal with the content of motion pictures under the aegis of the Office for Emergency Management. Darryl Zanuck, now on active duty as a lieutenant colonel, would essentially serve as Mellett's mirror image, traveling once a month to Washington to meet with War Department and national defense officials and serve as the industry's first de facto lobbyist.

Although Mellett's purview was technically limited to the movies Hollywood would produce for government agencies, there was a widespread, and accurate, sense that he was going to weigh in about entertainment films as well. The industry was reassured when, just before Christmas, Roosevelt declared unequivocally, "I want no censorship of the motion picture. I want no restrictions . . . which will impair the usefulness of the film other than those very necessary restrictions which the dictates of safety make imperative." But the studios were not entirely comfortable taking marching orders from Mellett, a former Washington, D.C., newspaper editor who had had only a few months of experience dealing with the film business. *Variety* suggested that someone who already commanded respect from Hollywood would have been a smarter choice, and argued that Roosevelt should have appointed John Ford.

But Ford had no interest in riding a desk, even in a prestigious position, and he possessed little skill or instinct for shuttle diplomacy. Although he had a respect bordering on reverence for the trappings of military hierarchy, he wasn't especially interested in answering to anyone within it. Back on September 9, "Wild" Bill Donovan, soon to become the head of the newly formed Office of Strategic Services, had made a formal request to Navy Secretary Frank Knox that the director be placed on active duty. Two days later, while Lindbergh was making his controversial speech, Ford was aboard the Union Pacific en route from Los Angeles to Washington, D.C., where he would undergo a physical, receive a waiver for the vision problems that had plagued him for years, and be inducted into the navy. ("Congratulations,"

Zanuck cabled him, "but you still have to salute me as I outdate you.") According to his biographer Joseph McBride, Ford's initial fitness report rated him above average in initiative, intelligence, leadership, attention to duty, and aptitude for success. His marks were less impressive in the areas of military bearing, tact, and cooperation.

Ford had shot *How Green Was My Valley* over the summer, using the Philip Dunne script that William Wyler had supervised, and retaining Wyler's pick Roddy McDowall in the starring role. Before production, Fox remained nervous about the movie, particularly about any possible anti-British language in its depiction of the miners' strike. "Inopportune to make this film now," one producer on the lot wrote to Zanuck before production started. "Shouldn't throw stones at England. Postpone until after hostilities are over." Zanuck didn't listen, and Ford, in one of his few textual revisions to the screenplay, actually played up the strike, paraphrasing some of Roosevelt's pro-union language in the miners' dialogue. In his hands, the Welsh clan at the heart of the film became, in spirit, more like his own Irish family—Ford later said that character actress Sara Allgood, who played the movie's matriarch, "looked like my mother, and I made her act like my mother." Any worry that Fox might have had vanished when Zanuck saw that, even in black and white and with a much more modest budget than originally intended, Ford had made a lushly emotional and affecting family saga. "Picture went over marvelously. Everybody crazy about it," he cabled Ford as the director's train neared Washington. "If this is not one of the best pictures ever made, then I will eat a film can." The reviews were almost as warm; although many critics noted that—as almost everyone involved in the film already knew—the anecdotal, rambling nature of the book's narrative hadn't been given sufficient shape, they were impressed by its pictorial craftsmanship. Audiences found it irresistible as well.

Throughout the fall, Ford had lived in a kind of limbo, away from his wife Mary, his son Patrick, and his teenage daughter Barbara, alone in a Washington hotel room four blocks from the War Department, ready to serve in a war that America had not yet entered but uncertain about what to do until then. (On his official entrance report, under "Experience Since Leaving School," he wrote, "Motion picture industry entirely," and under "Work for

Which Best Qualified," he wrote, "Anything pertaining to photography . . . propaganda films . . . documentary, training, etc.") In the capital, he was treated as something of a visiting dignitary from a profession that could still turn politicians and naval officers into wide-eyed fans. In late October, he traveled to New York City for *How Green Was My Valley*'s premiere; the next night, he was back in Washington dining at the White House as a guest of the first family. The navy brass viewed Ford as a man of talent and importance. But in the absence of a war, he had no real function, and his usefulness was still in question. Although he had successfully prepared a team of 150 men to begin work in the new Field Photo Unit, neither they nor he had any navy experience or battle testing, and some still weren't sure that Ford's desire to serve would endure once he experienced the unglamorous life of a naval officer in Washington. "It is beyond my comprehension," wrote one senior navy commander—a friend of Ford—to another, "why a man earning in excess of a quarter of a million dollars a year would be not only willing but anxious to throw that overboard in order to accept active duty and do a job for the navy in this emergency."

Donovan, a powerful figure who had Roosevelt's trust, liked Ford and was inclined to grant him a good deal of unsupervised freedom, but that only made the director's role more uncertain: Could a man who had stepped into the title of commander without a day's military experience actually command? And did he even want to? When he was interviewed in November 1941, Ford said that his greatest desire while in Washington was to visit an art gallery. The story called him "strange," noting that he had little to say about Hollywood and still less about the navy; he preferred to speak of Ireland. It did not inspire confidence.

Ford was not a dilettante, but he knew that people thought he was eccentric and that his own behavior didn't always help his case. He was sloppy, he was curt, and he didn't care that the dark glasses he wore to protect his weak eyes made him look intimidating and remote. During the shooting of a movie, he could be warmly sentimental one moment and caustic the next. The combination was appealing to some of his recruits—Robert Parrish, a twenty-five-year-old film editor turned second-class petty officer who soon became one of Ford's most reliable deputies in Field Photo, loved his brashness and autocracy, treating him with what Parrish's wife, Kathleen, called "respect, awe, and a little bit, 'That old son of a bitch . . .'" But others who had worked with him in Hollywood stayed away. When Philip Dunne was approached about joining Field Photo, he pointedly declined, saying, "I don't know that [I'd] like very much being a lieutenant (jg) when Ford is the commander." Ford explained himself years later by saying that on movie sets, "I'm very courteous to my equals, more than courteous to my inferiors . . . and I'm horribly rude to my superiors. So-called." He was half joking, half bragging.

Ford was prepared at least to attempt to toe the line when it came to military conduct, but the navy still viewed him as something of a wild card. His first two assignments in the weeks after Pearl Harbor were low-stakes, short-term jobs that kept him far from the action. Donovan sent him to Reykjavik to film a report on Iceland's viability as a future hub for Allied landings and transports, and then to Panama, where he was to prepare a one-reel (ten-minute) study of the security of the canal. Both movies were for military use only, and neither would require the deployment of a full Field Photo crew; they were tests of Ford's ability to carry out an order efficiently, and he almost certainly knew it.

The results, including Ford's extensive written reports, impressed Donovan enough to give Ford something more important to do. In early 1942, he was ordered to oversee the War Department's first significant piece of filmed propaganda. Within just a few weeks of the attack on Pearl Harbor, the navy decided to make a documentary that would reassure Americans about the fleet's preparedness, focusing on the speedy rebuilding of the ships and planes that had been Japan's targets. In fact, the bombing had done a staggering amount of damage; although it had spared American aircraft carriers, two-thirds of the naval air fleet on the ground was destroyed or damaged, and four of eight battleships were sunk, capsized, or blown up. The movie Ford was to produce for the navy, which had the working title *The Story of Pearl Harbor: An Epic in American History,* was not intended to tally the damage or to provide an honest assessment of whether the navy had been adequately prepared for an attack, which was already a subject of intense public debate. The movie was simply meant to relay to the American public the news that the fleet was well on its way back to fighting strength. And the navy wanted it made quickly.

Gregg Toland, who had been instrumental in helping Ford organize the cinematographers in Field Photo, had been yearning for an opportunity to direct, and Ford gave him the assignment, sending him to Honolulu at the beginning of January along with Lieutenant Samuel Engel, a journeyman writer-producer whose Hollywood experience consisted mostly of movies like *Charlie Chan in Rio* and *Viva Cisco Kid;* Ford wanted him to help Toland prepare a script. Six weeks later, when Ford had not heard from either man or been sent a single can of footage, Donovan told him to go to Hawaii and find out what the hell was going on.

In Ford's official naval oral history, he reported that when he arrived in Honolulu, he found the army and navy "all in good shape, everything taken care of, patrols going out regularly, everybody in high spirit. . . . Everybody had learned their lesson from Pearl Harbor." But even the idea that a lesson had been necessary was controversial, and Ford discovered with some alarm that the free hand he had given Toland and Engel was threatening to result in a movie that was less a can-do rallying cry than an indictment of American apathy and inattention before the attack. Left to his own devices, Toland had decided to turn the Pearl Harbor project into his unofficial feature directorial debut; instead of a twenty- or thirty-minute documentary that could run in theaters before the main feature, he had mapped out a full-length scripted drama that would include extensive recreations of the Pearl Harbor attack. The execution of Toland's idea would also require a long shoot on the Fox lot in Los Angeles, where he had gotten Walter Huston to agree to play "Uncle Sam" (depicted in the script as a neglectful old man taking a long nap in a hilltop getaway), character actor Harry Davenport to play the embodiment of Sam's stricken conscience, and a newcomer named Dana Andrews to play the ghost of an American soldier who had been killed in the attack.

As Toland acted out scenes from the film he was imagining, Ford said little, but he was unsettled by the scale of its vision. He didn't pull the plug on the movie, but soon after he landed in Hawaii he decided to take over some of the filmmaking himself, shooting basic, newsreel-style footage of ships and planes being rebuilt, of storehouses of munitions being refurbished, of masses of enlisted men working together with energetic aplomb. He didn't tell Toland and Engel to scrap their approach to the movie, but he did warn them to be circumspect, the clear implication being that the less the navy knew about actors, special effects, and reenactments, the better; all that work could be done back in Hollywood, away from prying eyes. But Toland still felt he had Ford's confidence, writing in a letter to Samuel Goldwyn that he and Engel were "doing a great job of our assignment."

Ford stayed on in Hawaii to oversee production of the movie, which would now be called *December 7th,* until early April. During the days, he and his team worked with a briskness that was dictated by necessity; in Honolulu, all cars had to be off the streets by 7:30 p.m. and curfews were so strictly enforced that anyone who found himself at a friend's house at 9 p.m. was expected to stay there for the night. That seems to have led to some drunken evenings, but Ford stayed focused; he wrote Mary that while he missed her terribly, he hadn't felt so well in years. He was happy to be in Hawaii doing "terrifically vital" work, telling her, "Naturally one can't write a great deal of what is happening here, but somehow I like this place better now than ever." He joked with her about colleagues who suddenly wanted to be a part of Field Photo ("I love that request for Frank Borzage—'Couldn't he get a commission because he's drinking something awful!' I'm afraid, honey, he's got to get a better reason than that.") He kidded about his contempt for the actors Ward Bond and John Wayne, whom he imagined were scanning the Southern California skies for possible air raids while they still collected studio paychecks. ("Ah well—such heroism shall not go unrewarded," he wrote, "it will live in the annals of time.") After several weeks, Ford finally lost his temper when an admiral started suggesting shots. "Sir, do you ever direct complete movies," Ford snapped, "or do you just kibitz when you have nothing better to do?" Turning away from the admiral, he barked at his cameraman, a young sailor named Jack Mackenzie, "Put the camera on a tripod. Let's stop wasting time. We've got a lot of work to do today."

The next morning, when Ford received orders to leave Honolulu immediately, Robert Parrish assumed it was as punishment for having mouthed off to a superior. In fact, Ford's work in Hawaii had only bolstered the navy's confidence in him; he was now being placed aboard the aircraft carrier USS *Hornet* to film one of the first secret missions of the war, the Doolittle raid on April 18. The raid was the first Allied airstrike over Japan, and was planned not as a major tactical advance but as a confidence-builder engineered in part because, in the words of General James Doolittle, "Americans badly needed a morale boost." The film Ford shot was not action-packed—it consisted mostly of footage of the sixteen B-25 bombers used in the raid taking off from and returning to the carrier landing deck.* But Ford, who took exceptional care to capture images of male camaraderie throughout the war, interspersed the aerial shots with scenes of African American sailors on the deck waving and smiling at the pilots, a reminder that the armed forces included them even though individual units were segregated. The brief series of shots, which was recut—sometimes excluding the African Americans— and used in newsreels, was the closest American cameras had yet gotten to combat.

If Roosevelt had wanted to name a coordinating chief from within Hollywood, Capra would have been the obvious choice, not Ford. Having run both the Academy and the Screen Directors Guild, he knew his way around bureaucracies, he had become an expert negotiator and, any lingering hurt feelings about *Mr. Smith Goes to Washington* in the capital notwithstanding, he commanded respect in both Washington and Hollywood. Capra already had the trust that Lowell Mellett would never quite manage to earn, and he didn't share the distaste for authority that rendered Ford and so many other directors unsuitable for the job. But he was a foreigner from a country with which the United States was now at war; right after Pearl Harbor, his older sister, Ann, who had never been naturalized, was briefly listed as an "enemy alien." His appointment to such a prominent position would have been freighted with unwelcome controversy.

Capra was nonetheless ready to serve. Conscious that his entry into the army would mean a greatly reduced salary, he had spent the fall of 1941

---

* In 1944, director Mervyn LeRoy incorporated Ford's footage into an MGM drama about the raid, *Thirty Seconds over Tokyo.*

shooting *Arsenic and Old Lace* for Warner Bros. as a kind of insurance policy
for his family; the $125,000 fee he received would tide his wife and children
over for a while, and more money would arrive when the movie was released
and his percentage of the profits started to roll in. (In an unusual arrangement that would eventually put a great financial strain on Capra, Warner had
signed a contract pledging not to release the movie until the play on which it
was based had closed on Broadway, never guessing that it would continue to
run well into 1944.) As he shot the comedy in October and November, Capra
seemed to be planning for two different futures simultaneously, playing Warner Bros. and 20th Century Fox against each other in an attempt to secure a
new contract that would pay him $250,000 per movie, and at the same time
making plans that would allow him to walk away from Hollywood at a moment's notice. In the army, his yearly salary would top out at $4,000.

Days after Pearl Harbor, Capra was back on the Warner lot filming the
last few scenes of *Arsenic and Old Lace* when he was visited by Sy Bartlett
and Richard Schlossberg, who had come to Hollywood as a kind of good cop/
bad cop team in an attempt to induce some of the industry's biggest names to
join up. Bartlett, a screenwriter who was now an army captain, believed
strongly that the army could benefit from men of Capra's skill; he also knew
how to talk to directors and producers who wanted to serve but were not, in
their professional lives, used to being so low in the chain of command. "I
know only too well the standards by which you live and the necessity for giving your creative urge lots of elbow room," he told Capra, promising him "an
assignment . . . worthy of your excellent talents." Schlossberg, a lieutenant
colonel who was Bartlett's commanding officer, was impatient with the cock-
iness and inexperience of movie people, but he understood their potential
usefulness. The two men had reached out to Capra earlier in the fall, and the
combination of Bartlett's reassurance and flattery and Schlossberg's all-
business call to duty was every bit as effective as they intended it to be.
When they returned, Capra didn't need much more convincing. At the end of
the conversation, he filled out an application to join the army.

Bartlett and Schlossberg returned to Washington with a plan to carve out
a special role for Capra. They took his application to General Frederick Osborn, a charming, patrician New Yorker from an old-money family who

headed the army's Morale Branch, which was then charged with overseeing all films intended either as propaganda for civilians or as training for new inductees. Osborn, who would become Capra's patron and most powerful ally in the War Department, enthusiastically endorsed the idea of tailoring a position for Capra. "Since General Osborn is reputed to be such a swell guy," Bartlett wrote to Capra, "I think you would be happy. . . . I would suggest a hurried trip to Washington. . . . General Osborn is anxious to know when you could report for active service." A cable from Osborn himself promising that "you will at all times have free access to me and I will work closely with you" sealed the deal. Capra formalized his enlistment in early January, asking for and receiving a thirty-day deferral before he reported to Washington so that he could finish postproduction on *Arsenic and Old Lace.* Even as he edited, previewed, and reedited the movie, he was undergoing his army physical and preparing to report for duty as a major.

Capra later wrote, "I suppose it was in my blood to resent arbitrary authority," and claimed that on February 11, 1942, when Lucille drove him to the train station, her parting words to him were, "Darling, now please! Don't go trying to direct the Army! Promise?" But in reality, he was eager to please and exceptionally worried about living up to the expectations of the men who had recruited him. "Do I have to wait for orders or can I come without them?" he cabled Schlossberg. "Should I or should I not come in uniform?" When Osborn met him, his first impression was that Capra "has a sincerity of purpose and a loyal simplicity of character which have enabled him to get the help of innumerable people in Government and in the army and in Hollywood; and he has an indomitable energy and belief in the cause."

Schlossberg, though, was still a skeptic, and soon became Capra's first nemesis in the army hierarchy. Capra thought the lieutenant colonel "had the charm of a bag of cement," and Schlossberg, who resented the mere presence of movie people on his terrain, returned the sentiment, telling him, "You Hollywood big shots are all alike, a pain in the ass. If you can't get what you want, you cry. One Darryl Zanuck around here is enough." The hidebound, bureaucratic Signal Corps, which was Schlossberg's domain, had been in charge of army filmmaking since 1929; he told Capra that he simply "wouldn't fit in with the Army way of producing films" and instructed him to await further orders.

It took the intervention of General George Marshall to move Capra out from under Schlossberg and over to Osborn's Morale Branch. More than any other senior official in the Roosevelt administration, Marshall had a vivid if still unformed vision of the critical role filmmaking could play in the war. He saw it as a medium that could help the army win the ardent confidence not just of civilians but of its own recruits. A decade earlier, as a leader of Roosevelt's Civilian Conservation Corps program, Marshall had projected movies on the sides of trucks for laborers, and he knew that they were a cost-effective and efficient way to motivate and inspire working men. Moreover, he was willing to deputize professional filmmakers, Capra first among them, to make almost every major decision regarding a program of war propaganda.

In February, Marshall met with Capra and gave him his first assignment— a job that eventually resulted in a set of movies collectively known as *Why We Fight,* the single most important filmed propaganda of the war. In the fall before Pearl Harbor, the army had begun a program to educate new draftees and volunteers in a series of fifteen lectures that covered, in sequence, world military history from just after the end of World War I up through 1939. The lectures were intended not only as a crash course in recent history but as an inspiring assertion of the principles of democracy that were at stake. Only a few months after the lectures had gone into use, it was apparent that they were complete failures. Inductees were doodling, talking, even falling asleep. And the wildly outdated Signal Corps films with which the lectures were supplemented were even worse; they were frequently greeted with hooting and Bronx cheers.

Within the Signal Corps, there was stiff resistance to any movie that would use plot or character, humor, animation techniques, or even nonmilitary music to drive home its point. One lieutenant within the corps spoke for many senior officers when he complained that anything that smacked of a night out at a Hollywood movie would be "a gross abuse of the principle of a training film. . . . There is no obligation on the part of a textbook to be amusing or ingratiating." Marshall overrode the complaints. He wanted the lecture series and the old films scrapped and replaced by short movies that would be energetic and exciting enough to capture and hold the attention of young men. The general had seen the army films made by documentarians and, according to Capra, "didn't like them. He didn't think they were professional enough. They didn't carry the kind of sock he wanted. . . . and so he said, 'If I'm sick I go to a doctor. If I want a film made, why don't I go to the guys who make films?'"

Marshall told Capra he "wanted a series of films made which would show the man in uniform why he was fighting, the objectives and the aims of why America had gone into the war, the nature and type of our enemies, and in general what were the reasons and causes of this war and why were 11 million men in uniform and why must they win this at all costs." And he wanted them made with a level of Hollywood professionalism rather than no-frills efficiency, even if that meant bringing in studio crews and screenwriters. Capra was elated, and ready to roll up his sleeves. Marshall and Osborn placed him under the supervision of a young, dynamic, and likable colonel named Lyman T. Munson, and when Munson asked him if he wanted a couple of weeks to get his bearings, Capra replied that in a couple of weeks he expected to have half a dozen scripts written. He promptly started cabling Hollywood's studio chiefs to tell them they were going to have to prepare to loan out some of their best writers for the month.

As Capra began his new life in Washington, his enthusiasm in those first weeks was unbridled; he fired off proposals, budgets, idea memos, and letters urging his colleagues in Hollywood to join him. He reached out to Lowell Mellett with a proposition that President Roosevelt film a short speech that could be used to welcome all new inductees, and he wrote the draft himself. "I come to you with no salute, no goose-step, no clap-trap," he had Roosevelt say. "No, I come to you man-to-man. . . . As other free men have done before you in time of danger, you have had to lay down your tools, your plows and your pens and take up guns, because our country and our people are in danger! . . . Whatever the reason, the great test has come. The chips are down. We either win this war or Hitler and the Japs meet in the White House to decide for us which manner of slavery will best satisfy their sadistic im-

pulses." The speech ended, "Go to it, men! Show these self-appointed supermen that free men are not only the happiest and most prosperous, but also
that we are the strongest." Capra modestly noted that he was sure the president or his speechwriters could do a better job, but he was thrilled to begin
his war work not just by selling a war message, but by essentially scripting
policy that was to be put in the president's hands. Mellett liked his work
enough to explain to Roosevelt that Capra was "one of our greatest movie
directors" and that he thought his idea would be successful. Roosevelt, whose
admiration for movies and moviemakers would keep the war filmmaking
project alive for the duration, wrote back the next day calling it "a good idea"
and telling Mellett to have the speech cut to four minutes and vetted for content by some younger army officers.

As he got to work, Capra started to see himself, and describe himself, as
the lead character in one of his own movies, a determined outsider ready to
go up against any number of government cynics. When the columnist Drew
Pearson invited him to a stag party one night, he walked into a house full of
"generals, senators, cabinet members, J. Edgar Hoover and Brazilian ambas-
sadors and lots more." The talk was pessimistic and anxious; the prevailing
sentiment was one of uncertainty about whether the Pacific fleet could rebuild in time to prevent another attack or major loss. "I couldn't stand it any
longer," he wrote to Lucille, "so I made a speech in which I told them as
leaders they certainly stunk, and it was about time for the people to take over
because they seemed to have sold out. . . . I told them America was much
bigger than they knew. . . . Well, a major in uniform telling them that certainly surprised them. . . . As a matter of fact I forgot all about the uniform
and was just talking to a lot of scared old men. When I got out I thought
maybe I had gone too far. . . . I may end up in the brig or out on my tail. . . .
But . . . I'm getting things done."

As he set up an office, he told Lucille that he was looking for a four-
bedroom house in the D.C. suburbs and that she should prepare to move east
for an extended stay: "This is beginning to look like a day and night job, but
it's new and interesting. Don't talk to anybody about what I'm doing as it's all
supposed to be undercover right now.

"I've presented enough propositions to keep making pictures for a year," he told her. "I've got six writers coming from Hollywood right now. I've got a project for each one of them. I'm up to my ears in professors, psychologists and experts who want to give their views, but I'm not interested in anything but action. . . . The Japs won't wait while we debate. . . . Please kiss the kids for me darling and the next letter will be a lot different. I'll talk about nothing but us."

SEVEN

"I've Only Got One German"

HOLLYWOOD, DECEMBER 1941–APRIL 1942

The Academy Awards ceremony that was held on February 26, 1942—the "austerity Oscars," some called it—was Hollywood's first collective attempt to recreate its own public image to befit a country at war. Two months earlier, some on the Board of Governors had talked seriously of canceling the evening altogether. After Pearl Harbor, a bitter divide had opened between those who protested the unseemliness of staging a lavish banquet while bombs were dropping and American servicemen were risking their lives, and those who believed that the show must go on as grandly and noisily as possible as proof of national resiliency. The Academy's newly elected president, Bette Davis, came up with an intriguing compromise: She proposed that the annual celebration be turned into a fund-raiser for war relief and, for the first time, opened to the ticket-buying public. Her idea was met with vehement opposition from industry columnists and from several senior members of the Academy's board. When Davis's plan was shot down, the actress, who was then at her most exhausted and volatile, told the Academy she had no intention of serving as a figurehead president and angrily resigned her post just weeks after taking it. The traditionalists had won the round: The Oscars would still be the Oscars, although there would be no dancing, formal wear was discouraged, and guests were asked to give money to the Red Cross in lieu of spending it on lavish accoutrements.

That night, the industry audience at the Biltmore participated in an odd mixture of festivity and solemnity; the room was at once gung-ho about the war and haunted by it. A week earlier, many of the attendees had gone to the Los Angeles premiere of *To Be or Not to Be*, Ernst Lubitsch's biting satire about a troupe of Polish theater actors outsmarting the Nazis. The movie's reception had been subdued; its star Carole Lombard, one of the country's most popular actresses, had been killed along with fifteen army flyers in January when the plane that was bringing them back to Los Angeles from an Indiana war bond rally crashed into a mountain. Watching her final performance, critics and audiences found themselves trying to shape new rules about what was permissible and what was tasteless. Lombard was, in some ways, the first famous casualty of World War II, and her loss cast a pall over Oscar night. The show, like all of Hollywood, was caught in a struggle to sound the right note; it alternated uneasily between Bob Hope's throwaway gags and the robust declamations of the industry's new hero Wendell Willkie, who lauded the assembled studio chiefs for being in the vanguard of attempts to expose "the vicious character of Nazi plotting and violence" to the public.

The Wylers and the Hustons had decided to attend together. Wyler's adaptation of *The Little Foxes*, Lillian Hellman's southern gothic about a greedy family on its last legs fighting over a dwindling fortune, was nominated for Best Picture; he was also up for Best Director and had, for the third time, steered Davis to a Best Actress nomination. But making the movie had been miserable for both of them and marked the last collaboration of their careers. Davis had seen Tallulah Bankhead play the part of Regina Giddens on Broadway as a smiling demon who relished watching her husband collapse and die before her eyes; Wyler looked for every opportunity to humanize and complexify the character. The rapport that had sparked their romantic involvement and energized their collaborations on *Jezebel* and *The Letter* disintegrated within days of the start of filming, and their interaction on the set was so acrid that they could not even bother to hide it from visiting journalists. Wyler complained that Davis "was playing Regina with no shading"; Davis, spiraling into a nervous breakdown, walked off the set for three weeks while Wyler shot scenes with other actors. When she returned to work, noth-ing had been resolved between them. A *New York Times* reporter witnessed their tense rapprochement and wrote that "Miss Davis seemed intent . . . on interpreting her role with gayety and daring; Wyler wanted subtle repression. . . . Miss Davis was icy in deferring to his wishes, and each was monstrously patient with the other. When one scene reached its eighth or ninth take, Mr. Wyler told Miss Davis she was rattling off her lines. Her re-sponse was cool enough to make the set suitable for a Sonja Henie skating spectacle. She said she found his statement remarkable because it wasn't her habit to waste film. Their careful politeness never varied."

Davis finished *The Little Foxes* certain that she had given one of her worst performances, and when Wyler went public with his veiled critique of her mannered acting style in an interview with the *New York World-Telegram* ("Are you thinking what the character is thinking," he asked, speculatively discussing her approach, "or are you wondering, 'Shall I give them a bit of the old profile?' or 'Shall I wave my arm a little?'"), she swore they would never work together again. Her affection for him was gone, but her respect was not. When Wyler moved on to his next film, *Mrs. Miniver*, his star, the thirty-seven-year-old British actress Greer Garson, bridled at his character-istic desire for multiple takes and vainly insisted that she looked far too young to play a woman in her forties; surely she would have to wear padding and gray her hair in order to be believable as the film's title character. When she sought counsel about how to bend Wyler to her will, Davis warned her to stop complaining and follow her director's instructions to the letter, telling Garson, "You will give the great performance of your career under Wyler's direction."

Wyler started shooting *Mrs. Miniver* on November 11, 1941. Unlike Capra and Ford, he had not yet considered going into military service; that would change immediately after Pearl Harbor. But he did see *Mrs. Miniver* as a welcome chance to step away from period pieces and into a story that felt contemporary and relevant. The *Miniver* script was based on a series of Brit-ish newspaper columns—brief, breezy, anecdotal glimpses into the life of what was meant to represent a typical English family during wartime. In 1940, the columns had been gathered into a book that was acquired by

MGM, which enlisted half a dozen writers to shape what was little more than a loose series of vignettes into a story. Draft by draft, they managed to turn the screenplay into a narrative of sacrifice. The first half of *Mrs. Miniver* establishes the fundamental, complacent comfort of a secure family living in upper-middle-class ease in an English village that is made to look like any small, prosperous American town. An opening title tells the audience that they're about to meet "a happy, careless people who worked and played, reared their children and tended their gardens in that happy, easy-going England that was so soon to be fighting desperately for her way of life." The second half brings the war home to them, robbing the Minivers of peace of mind, safety, food, family members, and even the roof over their heads. The Minivers and their fellow villagers respond by growing in character and courage, meeting the Nazi threat by forgetting their own petty squabbles and abandoning the class distinctions that had defined their world. War ennobles them, and the unity of a family and a town in the face of grave peril and loss becomes symbolically the unity of a country under siege.

"I jumped at it because it was an out-and-out propaganda film and [in the fall of 1941] you were not supposed to make propaganda pictures," Wyler said. "This was an opportunity to, in a small way, make a small contribution to the war effort." *Miniver* was also a perfect fit for MGM, always the most cautious and decorous of the major studios. Louis B. Mayer had stayed far away from the Nye Committee hearings that fall, and had winced when isolationists included MGM movies like *The Mortal Storm* and *Escape* on the list of propaganda films they brandished. Although the hearings had ended with a resounding win for the studios, Mayer was still squeamish about making any movies that could ignite charges of bias. This particular project was safe, he explained to Wyler, because it was about British heroism. "It's very sympathetic to them—but it's not directed against the Germans," he told Wyler. "We're not at war with anybody. We don't hate anybody." With that in mind, Mayer instructed Wyler to tone down a scene in which Mrs. Miniver is trapped in her home by a wounded German flyer, warning the director not to make the soldier a "self-righteous, fiendish" slogan-spouting proponent of Hitler's policies.

Wyler was incredulous. "Mr. Mayer," he said, "if I had several Germans in this picture, I wouldn't mind having one who was a decent young fellow. But I've only got one German. And if I make this picture, this one German is going to be a typical Nazi son of a bitch. He's not going to be a friendly little pilot but one of Goering's monsters."

"Well, we'll look at the scene when it's finished," replied Mayer. "Just remember what I told you." The day after Pearl Harbor, he called the director. "I've been thinking about that scene," Mayer told him. "You do it the way you want."

Wyler loved that story, and both his defiance and Mayer's timidity grew with every retelling, but there was no question that, of all the movies whose productions were interrupted by Pearl Harbor, *Mrs. Miniver* changed the most dramatically as a result. Wyler had always wanted the screenplay to incorporate the specifics of the war, and the events the Minivers experience over the year during which the film unfolds would have been familiar markers to any American. The family learns of the outbreak of war in September 1939, Mr. Miniver (played by Walter Pidgeon) captains one of the hundreds of small boats used to help 300,000 British and French soldiers evacuate Dunkirk in what was known as the "miracle of the little ships" in May 1940, and the devastating effects of the Nazi bombardment of Britain throughout that summer and fall form the movie's climax. But the entry of America into the war dramatically transformed the way the Minivers would be perceived; they were no longer merely sympathetic foreigners but examples of fortitude that Americans could follow. Before Pearl Harbor, U.S. audiences would have heard the music used throughout the film as "God Save the King"; now they were likelier to identify it as "My Country 'Tis of Thee." The window onto those "happy, careless people" now seemed more like a mirror.

Talk of war was pervasive on the *Miniver* soundstage at MGM. Dame May Whitty, the seventy-six-year-old actress who was playing the town's snobbish grande dame, spent her time between takes knitting scarves for the Red Cross and reminiscing about her days as the head of England's Women's Emergency Corps during the last war. And soon after December 7, actor Henry Wilcoxon told Wyler he was joining the navy. Wilcoxon was playing the village vicar, and in the film's last scene, as the Minivers mourn the loss of their daughter-in-law and several neighbors, his character was to deliver a eulogy in a bombed church—a church "with a damaged roof, but one through which the sun now shines as it never could before." In the shooting script that Wyler had approved in October 1941, the sermon was to end with the 91st Psalm:

> I will say of the Lord, He is my refuge and my fortress; My God; in
>   him will I trust. . . .
> Thou shalt not be afraid for the terror by night; nor for the sorrow
>   that flieth by day;
> Nor for the pestilence that walketh in darkness; nor for the
>   destruction that wasteth at noonday.
> He shall cover thee with his feathers, and under His wings shalt
>   thou trust.

By the time Wyler was ready to film the scene, Wilcoxon was already on active duty and had to request two days' leave to return to the MGM lot to complete his role. The night before shooting, he and Wyler rewrote the sermon. Following the psalm, the vicar would now make a more secular speech that explicitly echoed Roosevelt and Churchill in its assertion that "this is not only a war of soldiers in uniform, it is a war of the people—of all the people—and it must be fought not only on the battlefield, but in the cities and in the villages, in the factories and on the farms, in the home and in the heart of every man, woman and child who loves freedom! . . . We have buried our dead but we shall not forget them. Instead, they will inspire us with an unbreakable determination to free ourselves and those who come after us from the tyranny and terror that threatens to strike us down! Fight it, then! Fight it with all that is in us! And may God defend the right." The final version of *Mrs. Miniver* would now end with "Onward Christian Soldiers, marching as to war" as Wyler panned dramatically up to the hole torn in the church roof—through which thirty Allied planes are seen taking the fight to the Nazis. With a final title urging Americans to "Buy Defense Bonds And Stamps Every Pay Day," Wyler had finally made a war movie—one more immediate and impactful than he had ever imagined it would be.

With *Mrs. Miniver* almost finished and the reality of war sinking in, MGM

granted Wyler permission to shut down production for three weeks in February and March. Greer Garson had agreed to go on a tour to help sell war
bonds, and Wyler, who had submitted his application to join the Signal Corps
on December 18, was, his wife recalled, "wild to get involved . . . and get to
Europe. He was violently anti-Hitler. He wanted to be a part of the struggle.
And also, by his nature, he wasn't about to miss all that." Like Capra, Wyler
had been recruited by Bartlett and Schlossberg, and he was still awaiting his
commission. The day after he halted work on *Mrs. Miniver,* he cabled Schlossberg to let him know that he wasn't going to wait any longer for his orders; he
would come to Washington, D.C., right after the Academy Awards to learn
more "about my status and what action has been taken." Wyler was thirty-
nine and his second child was about to be born, but "if he had qualms, he
didn't reveal them," recalled John Huston. "I doubt he had any. Willy was a
fearless man."

Oscar night felt like something of a leavetaking for Wyler—the last special occasion that he and Talli would enjoy together for quite some time—
and they were sharing it with close friends whose marriage was crumbling
before their eyes. John and Lesley Huston had been married for five years,
but Huston's infidelities had started almost immediately and were now in-
sultingly indiscreet. During the making of *The Maltese Falcon* in the summer of 1941, he had had an affair with his leading lady, Mary Astor; he had
since moved on to a new picture, *In This Our Life,* a new leading lady, Olivia
de Havilland, and a romance so unconcealed that, as Huston sat next to his
wife, he and de Havilland blew kisses at each other across the empty dance
floor in a manner that Talli Wyler found "uncomfortably obvious."

Huston was never more reckless than when he was riding high, and his
work on two different films had made him the season's most celebrated young
director except for Orson Welles. *The Maltese Falcon* had been nominated
for Best Picture, and Huston was a double nominee in the writing categories,
for both his *Falcon* script and his rewrite of *Sergeant York.* As a neophyte
director, he was still earning only a tiny fraction of what his more established
colleagues were paid—his salary for *The Maltese Falcon* was just $1,250 a
week and the five-year contract he had recently signed with Warner Bros.
would, by its end, pay him only about a third of what Wyler was making.

Warner Bros. had had only the most modest hopes for *The Maltese Falcon* when Huston started production; the studio budgeted the film at less than $375,000, and George Raft, who had been assigned to play Dashiell Hammett's detective Sam Spade, quit the project in a huff, writing to Jack Warner, "As you know, I strongly feel that *The Maltese Falcon* . . . is not an important picture." Just as with *High Sierra*, Humphrey Bogart, who got the role of Spade just four days before shooting started, became the beneficiary of Raft's narcissism and bad judgment.

Huston had a knack for instilling an us-against-the-world team spirit in his casts; the filmmakers who had unsuccessfully adapted *The Maltese Falcon* for Warner Bros. in 1931 and again in 1936 were, he said, "idiots" and "assholes," and this time they were going to do it right. "We had an odd, childlike territorial imperative about our set," said Astor, "a sneaky feeling that we were doing something different and exciting." They were the bad kids—especially Bogart, the star who was never the studio's first choice, and Huston, for whom Bogart chose an affectionate, and appropriate, nickname. "The Monster is stimulating," he said. "Offbeat kind of mind. Off center. He's brilliant and unpredictable. Never dull." (After visiting the set, a *Look* magazine reporter described Huston as "a First Class Character with a busted nose, cadaverous frame, stooped shoulder, rubber face and berserk hair—all adding up to his nickname 'Double Ugly.'") Initially, Warners' Hal Wallis monitored Huston's work closely, telling him that the tempo of his scenes was "too slow and deliberate, a little labored"; Huston, who had learned from Wyler how to soothe nervous producers, reassured him that he was "shrinking all the pauses and speeding all the action" but also told him that he was pacing each scene "with the whole picture in mind." Wallis liked the results, but Warner Bros. kept its expectations low, opening the movie with little fanfare in October 1941.

The praise was unanimous. "The Warners have been strangely bashful about their new mystery film . . . and about the young man, John Huston, whose first directorial job it is," said the *New York Times* in a rave review. "Maybe . . . they wanted to give everyone a nice surprise . . . for *The Maltese Falcon* . . . turns out to be the best mystery thriller of the year, and young Mr. Huston gives promise of becoming one of the smartest directors in the field. . . . He has worked out his own style, which is brisk and supremely hardboiled." James Agee called it "frighteningly good evidence that the British (Alfred Hitchcock, Carol Reed, et. al.) have no monopoly on the technique of making mystery films. . . . It is rich raw beef right off the U.S. range," and the *New York Herald Tribune* labeled the movie "a classic in its field," adding, "it is hard to say whether Huston the adapter or Huston the fledgling director is most responsible for this triumph."

Warner Bros. responded by giving Huston what he thought amounted to a promotion, assigning him to an adaptation of a recent Pulitzer Prize–winning novel that was to star the studio's two most important actresses, Davis and de Havilland. "I felt rather ashamed of the way I got into *In This Our Life*," he later said. "Ambition stepped in. . . . I thought, oh, boy, I've arrived. . . . I did it because it was good for my career." Huston was disdainful of the material, which offered little more than an excuse to cast Davis in a by then stereotypical role as the savage center of a troubled family; during production, he devoted most of his attention to courting de Havilland. "Anyone could see that . . . it was Valentine's Day on the set," Jack Warner said. "When I saw the rushes I said to myself, 'Oh-oh, Bette has the lines, but Livvy is getting the best camera shots." Huston kept Davis calm by letting her do whatever she wanted on camera. "There is something elemental about Bette—a demon within her which threatens to break out and eat everybody, beginning with their ears," he wrote. "I let the demon go." Davis, who preferred to fight to get her own way rather than have a director surrender to her, thought the resulting movie was "one of the worst films made in the history of the world," and critics were not much kinder, comparing it unfavorably to *The Little Foxes*. Huston didn't much care; home movies from the time show him and de Havilland engaging in romantic clowning as he pushes her into a swimming pool and then jumps in after her; she throws her arms around his neck and climbs on his back.

The Wylers were sympathetic to Huston's wife, and Huston's flirtation at the Oscar ceremony (from which both men went home empty-handed) made a difficult evening more unpleasant. By this time, Wyler, a four-time nominee, had taken to joking that he was going to bring an empty carrying bag to the Academy Awards just in case the voters finally felt like putting some-

thing in it, but it was not to be. For the second year running, he lost the Best
Director Oscar to Ford, who was in Hawaii working on *December 7th* and
unable to pick up his prize for *How Green Was My Valley*. Darryl Zanuck accepted on his behalf as Wyler sat and watched the film he had spent months
developing take the statuette for Best Picture as well. ("Have you put your
new Oscar on the mantle [*sic*] yet?" Ford wrote to Mary when he got the news.
"The Navy is very proud of me. It's made a tremendous impression. Admirals, generals, etc. have called to congratulate me. Strange!")

Wyler quickly shrugged off his disappointment. *The Little Foxes* already
seemed like a distant memory; days after the ceremony, he traveled to Washington, where he implored Schlossberg to finalize his commission and give
him a job. Schlossberg was no more welcoming to him than he had been to
Capra, calling him a "pain in the ass." With nothing to do but wait, Wyler
decided to plan a movie on his own. While in the capital, he met with Lillian
Hellman, with whom he had remained close since the making of *The Little
Foxes*, and the two hatched an idea to make a documentary about the Soviet Union's struggle against the Nazis. Hellman got approval from the Soviet
embassy for the two of them to travel to Russia to make the movie, but although the project was known to have the blessing of President Roosevelt,
Wyler and Hellman would still have to find a Hollywood producer to finance
it. They flew to New York to meet with Sam Goldwyn, who enthusiastically
agreed to send them on a scouting mission to Moscow. But the conversation
foundered when Wyler mentioned that he wanted his salary sent to Talli in
monthly installments. Goldwyn blanched. "You say you love America, you
are patriots you tell everybody. . . . Now it turns out you want *money* from
me?" he spluttered. "Sam," Hellman replied, "your problem is that you think
you're a country—and that all of the people around you are supposed to risk
their lives for you!"

The notion of a documentary ended there, although Goldwyn did agree to
pay Hellman to write a fictional treatment of the Soviet struggle.* With his
commission still stalled, Wyler returned to Los Angeles in March to shoot

---

* The movie Hellman wrote, *The North Star*, a drama about a Ukrainian village shattered by the Nazi invasion in the
summer of 1941, was directed by *All Quiet on the Western Front*'s Lewis Milestone and released in 1943; it was one
of the few examples of pro-Soviet propaganda to emerge from Hollywood during the war.

some final scenes for *Mrs. Miniver* and to consider whether there might be
any way to circumvent Schlossberg and get into uniform.

Huston was in somewhat less of a hurry to get out of Hollywood. Earlier
in the year, Bartlett and Schlossberg had recruited him for the Signal Corps,
and the possibility of a war adventure excited him, but so did his suddenly
vital career. After years of toil as a screenwriter for Warner Bros., he had
become, in the space of just a few months, one of the studio's most valued
directors. Hal Wallis was working to secure him the rights to B. Traven's
novel *The Treasure of the Sierra Madre*, which Huston wanted to write and
direct as soon as possible, and the success of *The Maltese Falcon* had so
impressed Jack Warner that in early 1942 he demanded a sequel. When
Warner, to his disappointment, learned that novelist Dashiell Hammett had
retained all rights to his characters, he simply transferred the idea to another
movie and decided to reunite Huston, Bogart, Astor, and Sydney Greenstreet
in a light thriller called *Across the Pacific*. The studio had picked up the
rights to a prescient *Saturday Evening Post* serial by Robert Carson called
"Aloha Means Goodbye," published in the summer of 1941, about an undercover government agent aboard a freighter who foils a plot by Japanese spies
to blow up two warships at Pearl Harbor. After the war started, many scripts
and story treatments involving espionage or foreign intrigue were rewritten
to increase their timeliness and relevance; *Across the Pacific* was one of the
few that was refocused *away* from the war. It was much too soon for Pearl
Harbor to be used as the backdrop for an essentially fanciful and unserious
entertainment, so Wallis had the Japanese target changed to the Panama
Canal. Despite the movie's title, the freighter never made it into, let alone
across, the Pacific.

Huston started shooting the movie that March, in a Hollywood that was
rapidly changing. Japanese villains were being written into dozens of pictures, often as grotesque stereotypes baring their buck teeth in phony smiles
and feigning exaggerated politeness behind bottle-thick glasses; more than
one screenplay referred to them as a race of monkeys or dogs. The number of
Japanese American actors working in Hollywood was low, and under a presidential order issued on February 19, most of them were among the 100,000
U.S. citizens facing extended confinement in internment camps. To replace

them, studios often used Chinese American performers or white actors in preposterous makeup. Huston had notably avoided racial stereotypes in his earlier movies (the sole praise *In This Our Life* received was for a rare and exceptionally progressive portrayal of a black character). But he does not seem to have thought twice about the use of anti-Japanese caricatures; he was more invested in keeping the mood bright and energetic. The first draft of the script, submitted in January, had ended with an explicit and unsettling acknowledgment of the damage done to Pearl Harbor. As Bogart's character stares up at "an immense armada of Japanese planes," he says "grimly," "This is it. We're too late. We've <u>all</u> been too late. . . . The Japs are like a little squirt picking on a great big guy. The little guy picks up a bottle. That may work, except that when he swings it, he'd better swing it good. If he misses, the big guy finally picks him up and tosses him out the window."

After a "terrific salvo of explosions," the film's heroine replies, "It looks to me like the little guy isn't missing."

Huston was not yet in uniform, but he treated *Across the Pacific* as his first propaganda assignment. He discarded that last scene and replaced it with a simpler and more optimistic denouement. His version of the film ends on December 6, 1941; the Japanese, at least within this particular story, are soundly defeated, with the collaborator played by Greenstreet attempting to commit hara-kiri, and Bogart telling the enemy, "You guys have been looking for a war, haven't you? . . . You may have started it, but we'll finish it."

If much of *Across the Pacific* feels slapdash and hurried, that may be because Huston already had one foot out the door while he was shooting it. The army had granted him a sixty-day deferral to make the picture, but even on a tight shooting schedule, he didn't have time to finish. When his orders to report for duty arrived, Huston had tossed them away thinking they were junk mail, only to discover late that he was expected in Washington to begin service as a lieutenant on April 29. When it was clear that he wasn't going to be available to shoot the movie's climactic action sequence, the studio drafted one of its most reliable second-tier directors, Vincent Sherman, for the last ten days of filming. Huston liked to say that he left Bogart's character tied to a chair and surrounded by enemy agents and told Sherman, "You figure it out," but Sherman recalled an orderly transition with more complicated reasons behind it. "I can't believe the Army would not allow him to finish the film," he told Jack Warner, who replied, "The poor guy is having other troubles. His wife comes in one door as Olivia de Havilland is walking out the other, and sometimes he doesn't know what he's doing. . . . Take over in the morning." In Sherman's view, Huston knew that the hasty revisions made after December 7 had resulted in a subpar script, and "under emotional pressure from his romantic entanglement, he used the Army as an excuse to get away." When his active duty began, perhaps suspecting that his marriage was coming to an end, Huston listed his father, not his wife, as next of kin.

As he saw his friend off, Wyler felt more out of the action than ever. Schlossberg was continuing to tell him that the Signal Corps had no room for him. An increasing number of his colleagues were now in uniform in Washington, and even those who stayed in Hollywood were contributing to the war effort by working in a new, post–Pearl Harbor style that suddenly threatened to make *Mrs. Miniver* irrelevant before it even opened. Fox had just released the Marine Corps recruitment drama *To the Shores of Tripoli*, Paramount had begun production on *Wake Island*, the first movie that would depict American soldiers in combat against the Japanese, and Warner Bros. was developing Howard Hawks's *Air Force*, one of the earliest portrait-of-a-platoon movies. Wyler could wait no longer. When Frank Capra reached out to him with an idea for a documentary, he jumped at it. The assignment would get him out from under Schlossberg's thumb, and he wouldn't have to wait for a commission to get started. He said goodbye to Talli and, four days after his second daughter was born, packed his bags for Washington.

EIGHT

"It's Going to Be a Problem and a Battle"

WASHINGTON, MARCH–JUNE 1942

The seven men who had been asked to wait for Frank Capra in a make-shift office in Washington, D.C.'s Archives Building didn't know exactly why they had been summoned. Capra had cabled them and their studios with something between a request and an order: They would be needed in the capital for a month of work. They dropped everything and came. For Julius Epstein and his brother Philip, it meant temporarily walking away from their screenplay for *Casablanca*, much to the disgruntlement of Jack Warner. The studio "was quite mad at us," Julius said later. "But we certainly felt we had to go." The others were doing less momentous work and were happy to abandon it—what was the point of toiling on *Tombstone: The Town Too Tough to Die* or *Butch Minds the Baby* when you could be, if not on the front lines, as close to them as a middle-aged screenwriter was likely to get? Nobody turned Capra down. They didn't even complain that their only compensation for the next four weeks would be free housing and twenty dollars a day.

"You've all heard what they say of me in Hollywood," Capra told the men, none of whom had ever worked with him before. "'He can't tell you what he wants, but he'll know it when he sees it.' That's pretty much the truth." Capra cited one of his most famous scenes—the dialogue-free moment in *It Hap-*

pened One Night when Claudette Colbert gives Clark Gable a lesson in how
to attract a ride by hiking up her skirt, adjusting her stocking, and flashing
some leg. "That," he said, "is the kind of thing I want you to give me when
you turn these lectures into training films. I want you to turn words into
pictures."

Capra made it clear to the men that he would supervise every aspect of
the series of historical-lecture films that General Marshall had commissioned; when a writer jokingly said, "So we're necessary evils?" Capra replied that that's exactly what they were. He would require twenty-page scripts
within a week or ten days, each of them based on a different moment that,
when run in sequence, would guide new soldiers chronologically from Japan's invasion of Manchuria in 1931 up through Pearl Harbor. When the
writers finished, they would be expected to read Capra the scripts out loud,
the only way he could satisfy himself that the narratives were clear enough
for a child to understand. The perspective he wanted the movies to take was
simple: Americans were fighting for a free world, Hirohito and Hitler were
fighting for a slave world. The GI he pictured sitting in a mess hall watching
the movie projected on a bedsheet "was 18 years old when they took him and
put a uniform on him, was so uninformed," Capra said later. A plain black-
and-white version of history was, he believed, "the only way you could reach
that guy at that moment. You give him a lot of 'On the other hand's and you
confuse him completely."

At that meeting, Capra asked the men to volunteer for different
segments—the Sino-Japanese War, the Anschluss, the Battle of Britain, the
fall of France. When a writer named Julian Shapiro who had changed his
name to John Sanford to get work in the movies said he was interested in
writing a segment about the Russian front, Capra dismissed the other men
and kept him back. "Is there anything," he asked Sanford warily, "that would
prevent you from taking the Oath of Allegiance?" Sanford told him there was
not, and Capra gave him the assignment.

There may have been a degree of old-fashioned tribalism in Capra's concern. The screenwriters he had recruited were almost all Jewish, and all
were committed leftists whose politics had been diametrically opposed to
Capra's since the days of the Spanish Civil War. "He was a big Francoite,

and he always felt we were for the radicals," Leonard Spigelgass, one of the recruits, remembered. "That was what was killing him." But Capra was also trying to impress upon the men the seriousness of their mission, which he believed would be integral to the early war effort. His fervor was contagious; the writers got to work immediately. With no official offices yet designated for his project, Capra commandeered a few small unoccupied warrens in the Library of Congress for his team, and he made himself available almost around the clock seven days a week to talk through an approach, a sticking point, or an issue of history. On many evenings he would summon his team to a group dinner so they could give him progress reports.

The urgency Capra felt was real; in those first months of the war, he, like many Americans, believed that there was no time to lose since an attack on the West Coast might be imminent. Even as he told Lucille that he would soon "start thinking seriously about whether you should come out here or not," he warned her about air raids, telling her, "If anything happens, put all the kids in the cars and head for San Bernardino, and then to Arizona or Reno." Nevertheless, his mood overseeing the writers was initially one of irrepressible exhilaration. "I call them my seven little dwarfs," Capra exulted. "I've sent them up a Chinese stenographer I call the Slant-Eyed Snow White. They're still working like mad. . . . One of these days I'm going to get purposely sick so I can sleep until eight or so."

The good cheer ended a couple of weeks later, when Capra saw the screenplays. "I was aghast," he wrote in his autobiography, *The Name Above the Title*. "The unexpected and unfunny happened . . . the outlines were larded with Communist propaganda." Based on the few surviving early drafts of the scripts, this seems largely to have been a figment of Capra's imagination. It was more likely the case that the series of spirited late-night political discussions he had been having with a group of writers who weren't shy about their ideological leanings reawakened the same fear that he had expressed on the set of *Mr. Smith Goes to Washington*—that his own lack of political sophistication would allow a writer to sneak pro-Communist language into a screenplay without his knowing it. ("Frank thought *everything* was full of Communist propaganda," Spigelgass later complained.) In any case, there was no arguing with Capra; he immediately sent all but one of the men back to Hollywood, telling them that while he personally didn't have a problem with their work, he feared that the Dies Committee would use any evidence of Red sympathy to defund his whole enterprise before it even got started. He jettisoned their screenplays and began negotiating with the studios for a new set of writers.

Capra later recalled that those first drafts "murdered our confidence," but memos from the period show that he treated the episode not as a setback but as impetus to create an even grander plan. In early March, under General Osborn's supervision, he started drafting a comprehensive proposal for a set of propaganda pictures—fifty-two of them to be produced by the end of 1943. In addition to the adaptations that would replace the GI lectures, the list of what he called "orientation films" included two other ongoing series, *Know Your Allies* and *Know Your Enemies*, a program of training films for officer candidates, a project to photograph all lectures given by the Bureau of Public Relations, and a biweekly armed forces information reel intended to "keep our troops informed on world events." He asked for money not only to import more writers from Hollywood, but directors, editors, and production assistants as well. When his request that the army find him office space became snarled in War Department paperwork, he simply bypassed his bosses and made a deal with the Department of the Interior to use empty space in a cooling tower in one of their buildings.

Capra convinced Osborn to ask for an initial appropriation of $400,000—then about the cost of a single modestly budgeted Hollywood feature—to finance the entire series of movies that would "tell the Armed Forces the whys and wherefores of this war," noting that Marshall had "emphasized the need for speed in telling the troops who we are fighting and why." The scope of Capra's plan, which he conceived almost entirely on his own, was immense. His competitive instincts had been spurred by the indifference with which Schlossberg had treated him when he first arrived in Washington, and now that he was operating under Marshall and Osborn's directives rather than under the authority of the Signal Corps, he felt he had something to prove. "I've got budget troubles. You have no idea what it takes to get permission to spend one dollar," he told Lucille. "I have presented them with some staggering plans. . . . If I can get the program I've got in mind to go, then it'll really be something. Zanuck and the Signal Corps will be eclipsed and they know it, so it's going to be a problem and a battle."

One of Capra's most significant ideas was earmarked for William Wyler—a documentary described in Osborn's overall proposal as "a 'Negro War Effort' film to show . . . Negro contributions to this war, to show the Negro that this is his war, and not a 'white man's war,' to prove that this is not a 'race war.'" Osborn added that "the necessity for judicious handling of this problem is obvious," and Capra thought Wyler was the right man for the job. At a time when Hollywood movies still routinely trafficked in shamelessly racist clichés, depicting black characters only as servile, inept, "sassy," lazy, or childlike comic relief, he was one of the few major directors who consistently avoided those stereotypes. Even when his films featured black servants, as *The Little Foxes* did, he won approval for finding what the *New Republic* called "that rare balance of humor and dignity that so many pictures and plays . . . strive for without achieving more than a Tom-show."

Capra and Osborn knew that a well-received documentary about Negroes in the military could have salutary effects on both black and white moviegoers. In Hollywood, Lowell Mellett would soon begin a sustained campaign on the government's behalf to convince studios to increase the visibility of black people in their movies; he urged filmmakers to put them in crowd scenes, in the stands of ball games, in stores, restaurants, and hotels, and on sidewalks as background presences whenever possible. The Office of War Information believed that as more and more young men joined up, Hollywood could help white Americans get used to seeing black men in jobs that hadn't until now been open to them. But Osborn also knew that given the oppressive racism black people faced daily in America, they needed to be won over by a direct appeal. In a survey conducted in Harlem at the start of the war, half of the African Americans polled said they didn't imagine they would be any worse off if Japan won, and in the South, paranoid chatter about the potential of a "Japanese-Negro alliance" was becoming more common.

In early April, right after he finished editing *Mrs. Miniver*, Wyler heard Capra's idea and enthusiastically agreed to make the movie. He was left to his own devices—so far, the army had had virtually no experience commissioning anything but training films from Hollywood, and Capra didn't have the time or the focus to offer him much guidance. Wyler's first instinct was to try collaborating on the script with Lillian Hellman. But the treatment she came up with was more incendiary than what the army had in mind: a colloquy between a thirteen-year-old black newsboy and a black soldier named John, set on the night of a heavyweight championship fight featuring "Private Joe Louis." Hellman's idea was timely—Louis had been a national hero and a symbol of anti-Nazi strength since beating the German Max Schmeling in 1938, and in January 1942, after a charity bout for the Navy Relief Society, he had enlisted, saying, "Let us at them Japs." His induction was featured in every newsreel and his face adorned recruiting posters in cities with large black populations. It was Hellman's notion to have the young boy complain that by turning over part of his championship purse to military families, Louis was helping a country that didn't particularly care about the fate of people who looked like him. Hellman then had the soldier explain to the boy that Louis was able to "rise above bitterness" and was joining up to fight not for "what's bad, [but] for what's good now, and what'll maybe get better." "What's bad" in America was made explicit in her script, which included graphics of newspaper headlines like "White Neighbors Refuse Occupancy to Negro Tenants."

Hellman hoped that Paul Robeson would agree to play the soldier, but she and Wyler had never conferred on the approach the movie should take, and when he told her that he was interested in filming a documentary rather than a dramatization, Hellman dropped out. Looking for a treatment of the subject that felt more authentic to him, Wyler then recruited a black writer named Carlton Moss to collaborate with him and playwright Marc Connelly (whose Pulitzer Prize–winning play *The Green Pastures* had featured one of the first all-black casts on Broadway) on a new approach.

In May, Capra gave Wyler clearance to take his two writers on a research tour of army bases in the Midwest and South; they would travel to Kansas City; New Orleans; Alexandria, Louisiana; Montgomery and Tuskegee, Alabama; Fort Benning, Georgia; and finally Fort Bragg, North Carolina, before arriving in Washington. The trip was disheartening for Wyler, who found that he hated the South. The virulence of American racism was brought home to him every time they were told that Moss had to ride in a different train compartment or find a room in a "colored-only" hotel. When they met with a group of black Army Air Force flyers in Georgia, the pilots told Wyler that the locals hated them and considered it "uppity" of black men to fly planes; they said they lived in constant fear of attacks from the local chapter of the Ku Klux Klan.

Wyler was starting to have misgivings about making the movie, and once he arrived in the capital in June, he lost his taste for it altogether. Capra told him that *The Negro Soldier* was still a "top priority," but he seemed less interested in commissioning an honest documentary from Wyler than in avoiding cataclysmic mistakes or potentially divisive depictions. At Capra's directive, army researchers had created a set of guidelines for the movie that would make any director feel as if he were tiptoeing across a minefield; they ranged from the embarrassingly obvious ("Avoid stereotypes such as the Negroes' alleged affinity for watermelon or pork"), to the politically expedient ("Show colored officers in command of troops, but don't play them up too much"), to the manifestly offensive ("Play down colored soldiers most Negroid in appearance" and omit all references to "Lincoln, emancipation, or any race leaders or friends of the Negro"). As recently as 1937, a study of black soldiers conducted by the U.S. Army War College had referred to the typical black GI as "docile, tractable, light hearted, care free [*sic*] and good natured" but also "careless, shiftless, irresponsible and secretive. . . . He is unmoral, untruthful and his sense of right doing is relatively inferior. . . . He has a musical nature and a marked sense of rhythm." Wyler said he had no interest in helping a government that was so clearly part of the problem paint a rosy picture of the life of black enlistees—who would number almost 300,000 by the end of 1942—when his trip across America had provided such a grim education in the isolation, suspicion, and prejudice they had to endure. Capra reluctantly reassigned the film to another director.

Wyler was still glad to be in Washington; he felt he would stand a better chance of convincing the army to expedite his entry into service in person than by plaintive cable sent from Los Angeles. His friend George Stevens was still in Hollywood, unable to join up until he finished working off his contract for Columbia, but most of his other close colleagues had come east. Capra and Ford were fully occupied running competing fiefdoms, one in the army, one in the navy, Tola Litvak had just arrived to start working under Capra for the Morale Branch, and Huston, whose commission, unlike Wyler's, had gone through without a hitch, had arrived in D.C. a month earlier and had already been given oversight of a short movie.

Wyler must have envied the fact that his protégé had received an assignment so swiftly, but in fact, Huston was desperately bored and already chafing under the army's authority. His trip to Washington had started out in high spirits: In April, Olivia de Havilland had joined director Mark Sandrich's Hollywood Victory Caravan, a traveling ensemble of star fund-raisers for army and navy relief who had volunteered for a three-week whistle-stop tour of cities between Los Angeles and Washington. After she finished performing alongside the likes of Laurel and Hardy, Charles Boyer, Bert Lahr, Jimmy Cagney, and Groucho Marx, and the Caravan was received at the White House, she and Huston planned to have a romantic rendezvous in the capital. But when the time came, de Havilland had to rejoin the tour and leave for San Francisco right away, and Huston, who had thought the army would immediately put him behind a camera, instead found himself alone, poring over charts and protocols in an itchy uniform in a sweltering office.

"I spent weeks and weeks doing nothing," he said. "Christ, it was hot. I begged to be sent where the action was—China, India, England. I pulled strings to no avail. It looked as though I was going to see the war out from behind a desk." When Huston had received his commission, the inducting officer noted that he was "forceful, capable, intelligent" but warned that he was also "self-centered" with an "odd personality." The War Department now seemed determined to bring him to heel; the only thing the army seemed to care about was that Huston keep his jacket on at all times. He was almost in tears when he told Litvak how miserable he was. Capra sent him back to Hollywood for a brief trip to oversee the making of a short about the building of a B-25 bomber—"a propaganda film," said Huston, "to make people give their services and go and make airplanes, and . . . to let them know that what they were doing was a great thing." It may have lifted their spirits, but it did nothing for Huston's, especially when he realized that Capra had essentially contrived the job as busywork.

Wyler's arrival in the capital, however, turned out to be perfectly timed. His expectations for the reception of *Mrs. Miniver* were modest; when Lillian Hellman emerged from a screening wiping tears from her eyes and Wyler asked her why she was crying, she sobbed, "Because it's such a piece of junk, Willy! You ought to be ashamed of yourself! It's so below you." But when the movie opened on June 5, its impact was seismic. The *New York Times* called it "the finest film yet made about the war" and the first to "crystallize [its] cruel effect . . . upon a civilized people," and wondered if it was "too soon to call this one of the greatest motion pictures ever made." *Time* called the film "that almost impossible feat, a great war picture that photographs the inner meaning, instead of the outward realism of World War II," and gave full credit to the "perseverance and talent" of its "softspoken, chunky, wire-haired" director, deploring the fact that he had not yet won an Oscar. The tone struck by the *New York Post*, which claimed the movie was "so rightly done that it glows with an inner light which is truly inspired," reflected the near reverence with which it was received not just as a film, but as what *Variety* called "one of the strongest pieces of propaganda against complacency" yet made.

Mrs. Miniver became almost instantly a part of the narrative America told itself about the war. Some critics complained of its sentimentality and manipulation—James Agee was so repelled by the still photographs from the movie that MGM sent him that he flatly refused to go see it for more than a year—but they were soon drowned out. More than one national magazine reprinted the entire text of the vicar's climactic sermon, and President Roosevelt asked the Voice of America to broadcast it abroad as a speech. Nelson Poynter, Mellett's right-hand man in the Office of War Information's Hollywood bureau, gave his first major address to the studios the week after the movie opened and, urging them to make more pictures about America's foreign allies, pleaded with them to "give us a *Mrs. Miniver* of China or Russia." And Joseph Goebbels somehow got hold of a print; he called the movie "an exemplary propaganda film for [the] German industry to copy."

Roosevelt urged MGM to release *Miniver* as quickly and widely as possible; after playing for a record ten weeks at Radio City Music Hall, it opened around the country and became the year's highest-grossing picture. The studio launched a major campaign in which various film luminaries, including Capra, declared the movie to be one of the ten best films ever made. And for once, Wyler, not his leading lady, was treated as the star—*Time* published a lengthy story about his background as a young boy growing up in Alsace-Lorraine, "wondering whether he was French or German" during World War I, and the reviewer for the *Catholic World* wrote that it was a shame that it had not "been some Catholic's privilege to have directed *Mrs. Miniver.* Perhaps it was God's retort to anti-Semitism to have chosen William Wyler."

The acclaim for *Mrs. Miniver* gave Wyler a card to play. In Washington, he was suddenly a figure of national stature, a symbol of Hollywood's power to transform the public's understanding of the war, and his name landed on every guest list. One evening, Sy Bartlett invited him to a going-away party for Major General Carl Spaatz, who was about to travel to Europe, where he would become commander of the Eighth Air Force and head of the Army Air Force's European Theater of Operations. "When I spoke to him," said Wyler, "I said, 'General, I don't know where you're going'—which wasn't true—'or what you're going to do, but somebody ought to make a picture about it.'" Spaatz called another general over and told him to take care of Wyler. "What do you want? Do you want to be a major?" he asked Wyler. "I thought he was kidding," the director recalled. "I said yes, he says okay, next minute I was a major." Wyler was rushed through his physical the next morning; the army doctors agreed to overlook his potbelly, his false teeth, and the fact that he was days from turning forty. "I'd never even been told how to salute," he said. "I went and bought myself a uniform and I was in the Air Force."

Wyler's literally overnight transformation was the rare exception in a bureaucracy that, six months after Pearl Harbor, had all but halted the movement to integrate Hollywood filmmakers into the armed forces and to bring their work either to soldiers or to the moviegoing public. "I was anxious to serve and give my talent to this war," Capra wrote to Lucille in May, "and I found a tremendous organization dead set against my functioning." By mid-1942, jurisdictional confusion was endemic: Were filmmakers supposed to

answer to Mellett and the Office of Government Reports, or the Office of
Civilian Defense, which was overseen by Fiorello La Guardia, or the Office
of Facts and Figures, an information agency overseen by poet Archibald
MacLeish, who ran the Library of Congress? Did the Division of Information
within the Office for Emergency Management outrank the Office of the Coordinator of Information? Would the Signal Corps or the Morale Branch oversee the making of propaganda? Ironically, even as territorial squabbling
paralyzed filmmakers in Washington, it gave the studios a measure of freedom they had never anticipated at the start of the war. With nobody telling
them what to do, they simply started developing and greenlighting wartime
romances, spy thrillers, combat movies, service comedies, and home-front
melodramas; they retooled and updated franchises, turning Sherlock Holmes
and the Invisible Man into anti-Nazi crimefighters; and each production
head approved scripts based on his own instincts about what felt entertain-
ing, patriotic, or both. By the time Roosevelt consolidated authority within
the Bureau of Motion Pictures of the OWI, many of the three hundred war-
themed movies that the studios would release in 1942 and 1943 were in development or production, and despite the midsummer announcement of a set
of guidelines the films should follow, the bureau would never quite manage
to keep pace with Hollywood's production schedule.

But in Washington, Capra found himself caught in a tussle between Osborn's Special Services division and the Signal Corps, which had let him go
and now wanted him back. "It's almost a dime novel," he told Lucille. "They
thought they had all the picturemaking in the Army sewed up. Well . . . I
started buying and stealing and collecting film, using my name and my bluff
to get it. I started to hire writers and write scripts. I got [editors] and went to
work. . . . When they finally woke up to the fact that I was making pictures
all alone, they blew up, and made a demand that I turn over to them all my
organization of 18 people, all my millions of feet of film that I had ferreted
out, and all my cutting rooms and equipment. I was to go back to my desk
again and merely become an advisor. . . . No Sir."

Capra had written to executives at Warner Bros. and Paramount asking
them to free up some new writers for the job, which they did. ("Frankly and
sincerely," the head of Warners' publicity department wrote him back, "we

consider our whole Warner Bros. setup as another agency of the government. . . . We all want to do more than our share to win this fight.") Other studios were more cautious, beginning a dispute that would have far-reaching consequences after the war by warning Capra that any time their writers spent away from Hollywood in his service would have to be tagged on to the end of their contracts. But Capra got his men, and began work on a new approach to the lecture adaptations.

As early as March 15, Capra had leaked to the press that he was working on a series of movies intended to show Americans "why they are fighting." But it was during a research trip to New York in April that his idea for how to make them began to come into focus. Over the last few years, the Museum of Modern Art had amassed an extensive collection of pro-Nazi propaganda films and newsreels. They weren't hard to find. Well into 1941, at least one theater in the heavily German American Manhattan neighborhood known as Yorkville would draw large crowds of Nazi sympathizers for pro-Hitler documentaries like *Campaign for Poland* and *Victory in the West;* the films, made under Goebbels's supervision, were intended to advance the Third Reich's position that Germany "has been forced to defend itself over and over again" through the centuries and that the Treaty of Versailles represented "the rape of Germany." Through private acquisitions from Germans who were willing to sell their prints, the museum had pulled together enough footage to give Capra a clear picture of what the other side was seeing.

Among those movies was *Triumph of the Will,* of which the museum owned one of only two copies then known to exist in the United States. Many of Capra's fellow directors had seen it in the 1930s, when Leni Riefenstahl had visited Hollywood, but Capra had not, and by 1942 her work was considered so incendiary that he needed to obtain special clearance from the Signal Corps to view it. When he and Litvak emerged from the screening onto West 53rd Street, Capra was shattered: "The first time I saw that picture, I said, 'We're dead. We're gone. We can't win this war.'"

Capra's gloom reflected a moment when American optimism about the eventual outcome of the war was at its nadir. The Philippines had just fallen in the battle of Bataan, a three-month engagement that had resulted in ten thousand Allied deaths; fifteen thousand Americans had been taken as prisoners of war. Corregidor, the last point of resistance in the islands, would fall within weeks. Both in the Pacific and in Europe, the enemy seemed, to many, invincible. Watching Riefenstahl's movie, "I could see where the kids of Germany would go any place, die for this guy," said Capra. "They knew what they were doing—they understood how to reach the mind. 'Surrender or you're dead'—that was what the film was saying to you. So how do we counter that? How do I reach the American kid down the street?" It was a serious question, since even if Capra and Osborn were granted the budget they had requested, they would still have to make all the movies they planned at a minuscule average cost of under $20,000 per picture.

Then Capra had an idea that would give the *Why We Fight* series much of its power; he would save money and drive his point home by incorporating as much Axis propaganda footage as possible, but with new narration that underscored the horror of what was being shown. "Let our boys hear the Nazis and the Japs shout their own claims of master-race crud," he said, "and our fighting men will know why they're in uniform." Capra's notion wasn't entirely new; two years earlier, a well-regarded documentary called *The Ramparts We Watch*, produced by the newsreel company The March of Time, had made similar use of a pro-Nazi film called *Feuertaufe (Baptism of Fire)*. But Capra was energized by what he saw as an opportunity to turn Nazi filmmaking against itself. And his new strategy would also allow him to exploit what Osborn called a "gold mine" of Japanese, German, and Italian footage that had been impounded by the Treasury Department.

Capra found perhaps his most valued right-hand man in one of the new recruits to his unit. Eric Knight was an unlikely propagandist; he was a British émigré who until recently had been toiling as a film critic for a small newspaper in Philadelphia and, less successfully, as a contract screenwriter at 20th Century Fox. In 1941, he had written a novel called *This Above All*, a moving, Miniveresque story of British wartime courage that caught Capra's attention. He cabled Knight with a concise request: "Producing important series information films for armed services. Your experience & talent would be invaluable to us. Please phone me collect War Department 6700 Extension 5208 or can arrange meet you in Washington or New York."

It was, Capra later said, "love at first sight. Knight had all the talents that could be compressed into a single writer: Wit, compassion, sensitiveness, an intriguing style, and a great, great love for human beings." Although he was exactly Capra's age—forty-four—he seemed to carry with him an extra generation or two of knowledge and wisdom; he had been an army captain in the 1920s and was already a grandfather. And unlike some in Capra's unit, Knight had no trepidation about telling the director exactly what he thought. When Capra asked him to go over the attempts his new team of writers had made at revising the discarded screenplays, he responded with an impassioned letter that ran eight single-spaced pages. "You asked me to read the scripts and I've been at them all night," he began. "What I have to say of them I know you can take. This isn't Hollywood and you're one of the least Hollywood guys in the game. . . . Anyway, it's what I see as truth and it's the only way I know how to write, and that's why I sat eight months at Fox in hell. The scripts are very good. And man, that's the goddamdest thing a man could say of anything in this world. Because the films are going to be seen by an army that can't be 'very good.' It's got to be the best goddamed fighting army in this war. And you aren't a 'very good' producer and director. You're the best bloody film man standing on this green earth at this moment of existence. And these films have to be the finest ever made."

Knight felt the screenplays were dry, factual, and numbingly informational, and that they desperately lacked fiery rhetoric and a cohesive theme. A writer who took them on, he said, would need "to pull them all into a strong unity" in which the goal is "to make every soldier in the army sure right down to his boot-tips that this is a <u>JUST</u> war . . . The same angle must be pounded, pounded, pounded. I'm sorry if I sound hot, but . . . we're fighting a bloody war for existence, and by god we've got to fight with films. . . . The scripts I read don't have that unity. . . . It often sounds to me as if the men who wrote them were writing cold facts, and didn't care very much one way or another how the film-watcher received those facts. Dammit, that's not good enough." He went on to give page-by-page notes on all the scripts before ending, "To hell with it. I'm tired. I hope you don't think me a presumptious [*sic*] bastard. . . . It was swell meeting you. You're a grand guy, as I always knew you had to be to make films like you have."

Capra had assigned Knight to try his hand drafting a script for a *Why We*

Fight movie about the Battle of Britain, but he was so impressed by the passion and detail of his notes that after Knight's letter he made the Englishman the de facto supervising writer for the entire series. Capra had hoped to get the first movie, *Prelude to War,* in front of audiences by May, a deadline that had come and gone. But he now had a clear set of goals for the series that he could propose to Mellett: He told him the movies would be devoted to "making clear the enemies' ruthless objectives, promoting confidence in the ability of our armed forces to win, showing clearly that we are fighting for the existence of our country and all our freedoms, showing clearly how we would lose our freedom if we lost the war, [and] making clear we carry the torch of freedom."

After that statement of primary principles, Capra listed some additional objectives that were eventually deemed inessential; they included exposing the "economic evils" of the Third Reich and promoting "better understanding between nations and peoples." But Mellett approved his plan, and on June 6, 1942, a directive was issued creating the 834th Signal Service Photographic Detachment, Special Services Division, Film Production Section. Capra had eight officers (including Wyler, who was just getting his commission) and thirty-five enlisted men in his charge; by the end of 1943 he would oversee 150 men. He was at that moment the most powerful American propagandist of the war. But he was about to be overshadowed by a longtime rival. The day the directive came through, John Ford was six thousand miles away on a navy ship, recovering from shrapnel wounds he had received the day before. He had just filmed the Battle of Midway.

NINE

"All I Know Is That I'm Not Courageous"

MIDWAY AND WASHINGTON, JUNE–AUGUST 1942

I t wasn't the navy's idea to send John Ford to Midway. In late May, Admiral Chester Nimitz called the director to tell him that several Field Photo cameramen would soon be needed to document a mission in the Pacific that he called "dangerous" but did not describe in detail; he asked Ford to identify and select a few good men for the job. Ford's work on the Doolittle raid had pleased the navy, but he had been commissioned to serve primarily as a high-level administrator, not a roving combat cinematographer. Just two weeks earlier, Bill Donovan had sent him an official letter charging him to "exercise full responsibility" for Field Photo in Washington, D.C., giving him authority to oversee the payroll, secure office space and supplies, and approve any travel he deemed necessary. Ford's unit already numbered more than a hundred men and was granted an annual operating budget of $1 million—more than twice the money that Capra had to spend. And where Capra complained repeatedly that he often needed as many as two dozen different departments and agencies to sign off on a single request, Ford answered almost exclusively to Donovan, who gave him a free hand.

When Nimitz made his request, Ford immediately volunteered himself for the mission without knowing where or what it was. Nimitz told him to pack

a bag and get to Pearl Harbor, where he boarded a speedboat that took him
to a westbound destroyer. A couple of days and five hundred miles later, they
were joined by a flotilla of PTs, the inexpensive, wood-hulled, torpedo-armed
vessels that were so fast and effective that the Japanese came to call them
"devil boats." As the destroyer resupplied them and they continued farther
west, Ford began to wonder if something much more significant than the
provocation of the Doolittle raid might be in the offing.

Midway Atoll was one of a cluster of tiny islands under American control
located in the North Pacific about halfway between the California coast and
Tokyo. Its strategic importance was evident in its name. Since Pearl Harbor,
the navy had known that the United States could not hope to win the war in
the Pacific without continuing to control the islands as a refueling stop for
flyers. Aware that a Japanese attack on Midway was inevitable, the navy had
been readying itself for a large-scale battle since April, something that neither Ford nor most of the men on the ship knew. When the destroyer reached
Midway, Ford, assuming the navy wanted him to make a documentary about
life at a remote outpost, started photographing the sandy, desolate island and
its gulls and albatrosses, as well as the naval base, the PT boats, and their
squadrons of laughing, joshing men, making what he called "a pictorial history of Midway" and not worrying about whatever was to come. "Up here for
a short visit," he wrote to Mary just days before the attack. "This is some
place. Really fascinating . . . the food is delicious, best I've had in the Navy.

"I think at the time there was some report of some action impending," he
recalled. "But . . . I didn't think it was going to touch us. So I . . . spent about
12 hours a day in work, had a good time up there."

Ford finally learned what was in store two nights before the battle began.
On the evening of June 2, Captain Cyril Simard, commanding officer of the
Midway air station, told him that they had received intelligence that a major
offensive by "Zeroes"—the long-range Japanese fighter planes that the Imperial Navy had deployed over Pearl Harbor—was planned for June 4, and
that the men of Midway were ready to fight back with planes, PT boats, destroyers, and marines on the ground.

Simard suggested that on the morning of the attack, Ford position himself
on the roof of the main island's power station. Ford agreed, telling him, "It's

William Wyler with his three-time star Bette Davis and Henry Fonda during production of *Jezebel*: "Yes, I lost a battle," Davis said of their later creative tussles, "but I lost it to a genius." (*Photofest*)

George Stevens. "He'd sit there and listen with that look," Joseph Mankiewicz said, "and you could go mad trying to convince him of something." (*Photofest*)

Ford (*left*) with Henry Fonda on 1940's *The Grapes of Wrath*, which won him his second of four Academy Awards for directing. (*Photofest*)

Frank Capra studies the script on the set of 1939's *Mr. Smith Goes to Washington.*
He was Hollywood's highest-paid director at the time. (*Everett Collection*)

Ford aboard his ketch, the *Araner*. During the war, he leased it to the U.S. Navy, which used it to patrol the Pacific coast. (*AP Photo*)

"Yes. This really happened." Ford's documentary *The Battle of Midway* was the first film to bring combat footage to moviegoers on the home front.

Ford with some of the men of Field Photo. Well before Pearl Harbor, he trained them to serve in the navy's film unit. (*Mary Evans/Ronald Grant/Everett Collection*)

Ford (*center*) on the set of *They Were Expendable*, with Robert Montgomery and Richard Barthelmess. (*ZumaPress.com*)

(*From left*) Anthony Veiller, Huston, Maj. Hugh Stewart of the British Army Film Unit and Capra, after the American team was sent to London with faked footage of the North African campaign. (*Bettmann/CORBIS*)

Capra at his desk at the War Department in March 1942. Upon his arrival in Washington, he promised to have *Why We Fight* scripts finished in weeks. (*AP Photo*)

In England, Capra (*right*) confers with Capt. Roy Boulting of the British Army Film Unit on footage for *Tunisian Victory*. (*Ministry of Information Photo Division Photographer/IWM via Getty Images*)

With little money available from the army, Capra fleshed out
the *Why We Fight* films with footage from Axis propaganda movies.

Capra in London. "Tough people, these English," he wrote. "Soft cover and hard cores—each layer getting harder and harder." (*AP Photo*)

Wyler and actor Henry Wilcoxon (*center*) rewrote the vicar's climactic sermon in *Mrs. Miniver* as a stirring Churchillian call to duty after the war began. (*Everett Collection*)

Wyler (*right*) with Lt. W. J. Stangel and Capt. Thomas Wallace (the husband of actress Carole Landis) after Wyler was posted to a British air base. (*Hulton Archives/Fox Photos/Getty Images*)

Gen. George Marshall, chief proponent of the filmed propaganda program, meets Lucille Ball. (*Thomas D. McAvoy/Time & Life Pictures/Getty Images*)

Texas Congressman Martin Dies was one of the first politicians to seek—and win— publicity by claiming that Hollywood was overrun with Communists.
(*Thomas D. McAvoy/Time & Life Pictures/ Getty Images*)

The war at home: Long Island doubles for the Pacific jungle in an army training film shot near the Signal Corps Center in Astoria, New York, in 1943. (*Photoquest/Getty Images*)

The soundtrack for *The Memphis Belle* was created in a Hollywood studio, but all of the aerial footage was shot during combat by Wyler and his men.

a good place to take pictures." To his surprise, Simard had no interest in Ford's plans for filming; what mattered to him was that the power station roof had working telephones. "Forget the pictures as much as you can," he told Ford. "I want a good accurate account of the bombing. We expect to be attacked."

Ford tested his equipment that night. The next day, a close friend, Captain Francis Massie Hughes, took him out on an aerial recon mission, drawling, "Well, it looks like there's going to be a little trouble out there," and muttering to Ford, "You and I are too damned old for this war anyway." The quiet, businesslike, almost casual demeanor of both the officers and the young sailors and flyers in the days before the attack impressed Ford and moved him deeply. There was little bluster or bravado, he said; in fact, "they were the calmest people I have ever seen." As he and Hughes flew through the cloudy skies, they spotted a couple of Japanese planes at a distance and reported their position to Nimitz. "I was amazed at the lackadaisical air everyone took," said Ford, "as though they had been living through this sort of thing all their lives."

At about 6:30 a.m. on June 4, Ford and his men hunkered down on the concrete roof. They were equipped with Eyemo and Bell & Howell 16-millimeter cameras and hundreds of feet of Kodachrome color film. Ford had assigned a young lieutenant named Kenneth Pier to the nearby aircraft carrier USS *Hornet*, but to work with him on the island, he had handpicked twenty-four-year-old Jack Mackenzie Jr., who had been an apprentice cameraman at RKO and had helped Ford on Gregg Toland's *December 7th* project in Honolulu. Ford was fond of Mackenzie, who was about the same age as his own son; when it looked like he was about to be transferred to Wake Island, the director stepped in to keep him under his wing. The young man was eager for action; as he climbed the ladder to the top of the power station tower, he felt the only protection he needed was the rabbit's foot he kept in his pocket. The tower, he said, was "the highest spot I could work from. . . . I could view the entire island unobstructed and far out to sea. . . . I had every advantage to get the pictures I wanted."

Ford and his team started shooting film as soon as the first formation of what would eventually number more than one hundred Zeroes approached.

"I estimated that I saw . . . from 56 to 62 planes" in total, he reported. While Ford filmed, he stayed on the telephone, relaying the news to officers in the power house fifty feet below whenever he saw a bomb fall or a plane get shot down. The marines, positioned in readiness on the island and in PT boats, started to fire back. Ford saw them take down three planes. Zeroes flew low to bomb the Midway airfield, at first concentrating on a decoy plane that the navy had positioned next to an empty oil tank as a distraction that was designed to waste Japanese effort and ammunition. (The actual planes had been camouflaged off the sides of the runway.) Then "hell started to break loose . . . the attack had started in earnest."

"The planes started falling—some of ours, a lot of Jap planes," Ford said. "One [Zero] dove, dropped a bomb and tried to pull out, and crashed into the ground." Ford saw the Zeroes "dive bombing at objectives like water towers. . . . [The Japanese planes] got the hangar right away." Ford had his camera trained on the building as "a Zero flew about fifty feet over it and dropped a bomb and . . . the whole thing went up. The place that I was manning, the power house, they evidently tried to get that. I think we counted 18 bombs."

The last of those bombs tore a corner off the power station roof and blew Ford off his feet with his camera still running—its impact is visible on the film. "I was knocked unconscious," he said. "Just knocked me goofy for a bit." When he came to a minute or two later, a couple of young enlistees were telling him that he had a shrapnel wound in his arm; they wanted to get him off the roof to less exposed ground. "They came in and bandaged me up and said, 'Don't go near that Navy doctor, we will take care of you . . .' Talking right under fire like that, it was very interesting."

Mackenzie had also been knocked over by a bomb that had exploded within twenty feet of the power station, although before that happened, he said, "I got a swell shot of a Jap formation coming in straight toward me." After that close call, he scrambled down the ladder and ran around to the front of the tower "to photograph the rest of the battle action. . . . The hospital . . . was smashed and on fire, and the commissary was all busted up and burning something fierce." Meanwhile, Lieutenant Pier was inside an American plane that had taken off from the *Hornet,* photographing as much of the sea-to-air combat as his position would allow.

Ford had not been precisely at the center of the action, much of which was dispersed over miles of ocean. The power station roof was more a gateway, and although he had an ideal vantage point from which to witness the approach of the Zeroes, much of the most intense fighting on the atoll itself took place behind him, and the battle's critical engagements were far out at sea, well beyond the visibility of anyone stationed on the island. But, first among all directors who went to war, Ford had, without question, been in the right place at the right time. Most of the fighting at Midway happened that day, and when the last fires were put out and the skirmishes ended three days later, the United States had won what would turn out to be the war's most important battle in the Pacific. For months before Midway, the story that had been brought home to Americans in papers, radio broadcasts, and newsreels was one of noble defeat—of young American fighting men holding out as long as they possibly could at Wake Island or Bataan or Corregidor, trying to buy the navy some desperately needed time to rebuild its fleet after Pearl Harbor. Their valor was measured in the number of days or weeks they could stand their ground before the Japanese navy inevitably outmanned and outgunned them, and their stories would soon be told in almost a dozen Hollywood movies. Midway brought America welcome news not just of a victory, but of a turning of the tide. The navy had lost 150 planes and more than three hundred men, but Japanese casualties numbered in the thousands, and the United States had destroyed four of Japan's six aircraft carriers, a deficit from which the Imperial Navy never recovered.

The significance of Midway would become clear within the week, but in the immediate aftermath of the battle's first day, Ford was shaken to his core. He had seen an American flyer bail out of his plane only to be shot out of his parachute harness by a Japanese gunner. "The kid hit the water and the Jap went up and down strafing the water where he had landed, even sunk the parachute," he said. "I only prayed to God that I could have gotten a picture out of it." Mackenzie, who had not been injured, spent the days after the battle "photographing records of the destruction, interrupted only as each rescue squad with wounded and fatigued men who had been adrift in little rubber boats were brought in."

News of the victory they had achieved came to the men at Midway fitfully; at that moment, the American losses felt much more immediate and real on the island. Ford watched the young men who had seemed so unconcerned and laconically confident just a day or two earlier being loaded onto stretchers and into body bags. In the run-up to Midway, Ken Pier had spent some time with one group in particular, filming the men—mostly inexperienced, some barely out of their teens—in Torpedo Squadron 8. Cameras had captured them singly and in pairs, horsing around, mugging, posing proudly in front of their planes aboard the *Hornet*, drawing faces or warnings to the Japanese on their torpedoes with chalk. On the day of the battle, they had been the first to approach Japan's aircraft carriers, and had done so without any cover. The Japanese shot them all down within minutes. Of the thirty men in the squadron, twenty-nine were now missing or dead. The sole survivor, a young ensign named George Gay, watched his comrades perish as he hid under his plane's seat cushion in the sea with only his nose and mouth above water, hoping that the Japanese would mistake him for debris.*

"I am really a coward," Ford said later. "Courage is something that, I don't know, it's pretty hard to find . . . All I know is that I'm not courageous. Oh, you go ahead and do a thing, but after it's over, your knees start shaking." The bravery of the boys he had watched go into battle, most of whom he had met just days before the end of their lives, humbled him. "They were kids," he said, "having a swell time. None of them were alarmed. I mean, [a bomb] would drop . . . they would laugh and say, 'My God, that was close.' . . . I was really amazed. I thought that some kids, one or two, would get scared, but no, they were having the time of their lives. . . . I have never seen a greater exhibition of courage. . . . I figured, 'Well, when this war is over, at least we are going to win it if we have kids like that.'"

As navy medics tended to what the official medical report described as a three-inch surface laceration on his left arm, Ford had little time to sort

---

* The story of Torpedo Squadron 8 was made into a feature film, *Wing and a Prayer*, that 20th Century Fox released in 1944.

through his own sense of loss within victory, or his conflicting feelings about his own courage compared to that of the men he had watched fight that day. The war was a narrative; he had been sent to Midway not simply to record a conflict but to turn it into a story that could be told to the American people. Ford's first words about the battle were simple: "OK. LOVE, JOHN FORD," he cabled his wife days later. The press did the rest. By the time Ford got back to the United States, he was a hero; all he had to do was agree to play the part. His injury in the line of duty had made national headlines; the gossip columnist Louella Parsons described his arm as "rendered almost useless" by shrapnel (in fact, his wound was categorized by the navy as nonincapacitating). Parsons also caught Mary Ford off guard, securing a one-sentence "interview" that she managed to spin into a portrait of *Mrs. Miniver*–like home-front stoicism. "Mary is a wise Navy wife who never talks," she wrote knowingly. "All I could get her to say about John's bravery in filming the Battle of Midway . . . was 'I hope we can see all the pictures.' . . . But you won't get her to say that she fought the Battle of Midway from her chair, or that she burns the midnight oil thinking of her husband filming movies right where the shelling and the bombing are the thickest."

Ford was being recommended for medals and honors and heralded by his colleagues ("We were thrilled at account of Midway action and congratulate you on the splendid part you played in it," George Stevens cabled him on behalf of the Directors Guild), and his relationship to the official narrative of his heroism moved by degrees beyond mere tacit consent and into enthusiastic reiteration. As time passed, the work of other cameramen at Midway went largely unmentioned. ("I did all of it," he told Peter Bogdanovich decades later. "We only had one camera.") Ford started to tell stories about how one Japanese pilot had gotten so close to him that he could see his sinister smile, and he described his working relationship with his Field Photo cameramen in brazenly self-flattering terms: "I had one boy with me, but I said, 'You're too young to get killed,' and I hid him away, I thought in a safe place. I just kept reporting," he said. "I was wounded pretty badly there . . . however I managed to come to long enough to finish the job." By 1944, Mackenzie had been excluded from the story of Midway so thoroughly that he felt compelled to set the record straight in a first-person account of the battle for the magazine *American Cinematographer* in which he wrote specifically about what he and Kenneth Pier had filmed, mentioning Ford respectfully, but only once. Pier's footage, said Mackenzie, "had a lot to do with the success of the picture that was released to the public."

Ford returned to Los Angeles in mid-June with four hours of silent film—about five hard-won minutes of which showed explicit combat—and his instincts as a director soon overrode any concern he may have had about observing navy protocol. He was, not without justification, zealous about guarding his footage and slightly paranoid. He knew that what he and his men had captured was unlike anything American moviegoers had seen before, not just in its up-close view of war and its toll, but in the fact that they had chosen to shoot in color, which audiences in 1942 viewed as less "real" than the black and white of newsreels. Studios at the time reserved Technicolor for fantasies, musicals, spectacles, and travelogues, and Ford himself had only made one color picture, *Drums Along the Mohawk.*

Ford knew that once the navy took possession of his footage, he would lose control of it; the best shots would be indiscriminately parceled out to newsreel companies by a War Department that was more eager to share visual evidence of an American triumph as quickly as possible than to wait for the polished movie that he believed could have exponentially greater impact. In Hollywood, Ford had all of the footage printed; then he returned to Washington and showed it to his Field Photo recruit Robert Parrish, who had assisted him during the editing of *How Green Was My Valley.* Using the authority Donovan had given him a month earlier, Ford gave Parrish the footage and ordered him to take it back to Los Angeles that day. "Never mind the [travel] orders, I'll send them on to you later," he told Parrish. "And don't bother to change your clothes. Just pick up the film and get out to the airport. The navy censor will be around here looking for our film. I want to be able to tell him I don't have any film." Ford feared that the navy would immediately assign "associate producers and public relations officers" to oversee the project. "The four services will start bickering over it and the goddamn thing will get so bogged down in red tape that we'll never get it released. . . . Get in your mother's house [in Los Angeles] and hide until you hear from me."

Parrish did as he was told. He found a small film lab and editing facility in the San Fernando Valley, away from prying eyes, and began to organize the footage and cut some sequences together. Ford told him not to worry about navy men "snooping around," assuring him, "There'll be no problem. They'd never expect an enlisted man with no orders to be working on a classified project." Since some of what Field Photo had captured was grisly and far more graphic than anything that had ever gotten past army censors, Parrish asked Ford whether he intended to make the movie as an intelligence document to be shown only to senior officials within the War Department, the White House, and the newly formed Office of Strategic Services, or was it to be a propaganda picture intended for public consumption?

Ford, who detested the word "propaganda," told Parrish never to use it again. "This is a film for the mothers of America," he said. "It's to let them know that we're in a war, and that we've been getting the shit kicked out of us for five months, and now we're starting to hit back." In fact, Ford had already thought through exactly what he wanted *The Battle of Midway* to be: He envisioned the film as running eighteen minutes—a length that would allow it to play across the country in hundreds of theaters simultaneously since it could be booked to run before any number of main features.

Ford soon joined Parrish on the West Coast, where they and a sound effects editor named Phil Scott began the work of turning *The Battle of Midway* not just into a movie, but into a John Ford movie—a short whose dialogue, music, profound sentiment, and emphasis on loss, duty, and sacrifice would be unmistakably of a piece with *The Grapes of Wrath* and *How Green Was My Valley.* An entire soundtrack—music, narration, dialogue, and the sound effects of soaring planes, ocean waves, PT boat motors, gunfire, and falling and exploding bombs—had to be created, and as each layer was added, the simple and straightforward footage, the vast majority of which had not been shot by Ford, bore his signature more strongly. Knowing that a great deal of music and overdubbed language would be necessary to compensate for the lack of synchronized natural sound, Ford asked two men, *Stagecoach* writer Dudley Nichols and an MGM screenwriter named James Kevin McGuinness, to prepare separate short scripts. He discarded McGuinness's and used some of Nichols's, but for the most part chose to rely on his own instincts to create an innovative amalgam of four voices—a baritone, newsreel-like narrator; a second narrator, more hushed and ministerial, who takes over during moments of particular solemnity; and the voices of an elderly mother and a well-informed, enthusiastic young man. The last two would serve as unseen audience surrogates who seem to be watching and commenting on the footage as it unspools, each reflecting what Ford thought an ordinary viewer's stream of consciousness might sound like.

To provide those voices, Ford turned to a quartet of actors whom he knew would awaken emotional associations in moviegoers on an almost unconscious level. The opening narration would be spoken by Donald Crisp, the patriarch of *How Green Was My Valley*. The gentler narration was to be read by director Irving Pichel, whom Ford had used as *Valley*'s narrator. And to play the mother and the young man—the voices of America—Ford recruited his *Grapes of Wrath* stars Jane Darwell and Henry Fonda, who were given an afternoon off from shooting William Wellman's *The Ox-Bow Incident* to record his two-page script. Ford further reinforced the connections to those films by asking Alfred Newman, the 20th Century Fox musical director who had overseen *The Grapes of Wrath*, to create a dense score that, according to Ford's specifications, had to include "Red River Valley," which had been used as a prominent, evocative recurring theme in *Grapes*.

Ford worked with extraordinary speed and decisiveness. Six days after he arrived in Hollywood, the soundtrack and first cut of *The Battle of Midway* were finished. Parrish challenged the director on some of his choices, particularly the insertion, over footage of wounded sailors, of an overdubbed exclamation from Darwell—"Get those boys to the hospital!" she implores as "Onward, Christian Soldiers" plays. "Please do, quickly! Get them to clean cots and cool sheets! Get them doctors and medicine, a nurse's soft hands! . . . Hurry, please!" Parrish felt it was mawkish and manipulative; Ford kept it in. Concerned that he might encounter bureaucratic objections if any branch of the service was underrepresented, he also had Parrish clock their relative screen time, cutting in one place and filling in another until nobody could complain of being slighted. Just when Parrish thought the movie was done, Ford handed him a small spool of film, amounting to just over three seconds, and told him to splice it into the last third of the picture during a sequence that showed a memorial service at Midway for soldiers killed in action. It was a close-up of the president's son, James, now a major in the Marine Corps, looking solemn. The shot did not match the others; Roosevelt was looking up, not down, and the light suggested either a different time of day or different weather. Parrish said that he didn't recall hearing that Major Roosevelt was at Midway. Ford replied that perhaps he had been there without official orders, and told him to stop asking questions.

At Ford's order, the completed print of the movie was taken in turn to each studio chief for private screenings. While the film played, Parrish and Jack Bolton, a lieutenant commander and early Field Photo recruit, stood by, waiting to bicycle the print to the next Hollywood lot. Bolton told Ford that, with the exception of Columbia's Harry Cohn, who urged the director to use recreations and miniatures to make the battle scenes more vivid, the reception was "wonderful." There would be no recreations, Ford said. The picture was finished.

Ford returned to Washington and left the print with Parrish, telling him to arrange one more screening before bringing the movie to the capital. Gregg Toland and Sam Engel had returned from Hawaii and were now working on *December 7th* on the 20th Century Fox lot, filming the scripted scenes that they hoped would allow them to expand what they had already shot into a full-length feature. Ford wanted his movie screened for them and instructed Parrish to call him afterward and report their reaction. In Parrish's telling, Toland and Engel watched *The Battle of Midway* silently until, when the movie was almost over, they saw that Ford had scored a burial at sea using "My Country 'Tis of Thee." The moment felt too close to a sequence the two had excitedly described for Ford when he first arrived in Honolulu.

"The son of a bitch stole our scenes," Engel shouted at the screen as an ashen Toland slumped in his seat. "The bastard sabotaged our movie— everything we've been working on for six months."

When Parrish recounted what he had overheard to Ford, the director simply replied, "Maybe he's right," and shrugged it off, telling him to get on a plane with the movie as soon as possible. The navy was getting impatient; officers were beginning to show up at the San Fernando editing room. Parrish hid the negative under a bed in his mother's house and flew to Washington, where he finally realized why Ford had inserted the shot of James Roosevelt. The first official screening of *The Battle of Midway* would not be for navy brass, but for the president, his wife, and his senior advisers. The Joint Chiefs of Staff would also attend, and Ford knew they would be watching the president as closely as the movie.

What Roosevelt and his men saw that afternoon was perhaps the most personal, idiosyncratic, and directorially shaped movie made by any Hollywood filmmaker under the auspices of the federal government during World War II. *The Battle of Midway* begins with a musical collage—"My Country 'Tis of Thee" giving way to "Anchors Aweigh" and then to "Yankee Doodle Dandy" and "From the Halls of Montezuma" as American soldiers splash into the surf at Midway and bring the flag of the Sixth Marine Defense Battalion to the island. Then Ford cuts to the nature shots he had taken of the atoll before the attack started—the rocks, the low scrub on the horizon, and the waddling birds. "These are the natives of Midway," the narrator drolly remarks over a Looney Tunes–like musical accompaniment. "Tojo has sworn to liberate them." "Red River Valley" plays on accordion as the sun sets on the peculiar, unspoiled landscape and the contemplative men who have arrived there, and then, with an ominous roll of thunder, Crisp explains that an attack is coming.

As soldiers and sailors prepare for battle, Ford introduces the chatter of Fonda and Darwell—"That fella's walk looks familiar! . . . Why, that's young Will Kinney! He's from my hometown of Springfield, Ohio! He's not gonna fly that great big bomber . . . !" "Yes, ma'am. That's his job. He's a skipper!" "Well, Junior Kinney! Good luck! God bless you, son."

When American planes start to take off from the Midway landing strip, Ford used the post-dubbed roar of their engines to eradicate the soundscape of music and voices. For the next several minutes, Roosevelt and his men saw the rawest battle footage American cameras had yet captured. Buildings are set aflame; the smoke appears to turn day into night. A plane on fire spirals toward the sea. Gunfire sprays from a carrier deck; a fighter crashes in the distance. Ford used virtually every frame of actual battle footage he had, and supplemented it with shots of American flyers taking off from the carrier as the crew cheers them on from the deck. And for the first time ever, the impact of a bomb on film was presented in its most literal form; Ford chose to include several "mistakes" in which the camera was rattled so hard by an explosion that the film was jolted loose from its sprockets. All of this, with every yellow fireball and plane in blazing color against a blue sky, was so new that it would be hard for viewers accustomed to black-and-white footage to process it as "news" rather than as the latest manifestation of Hollywood technical wizardry. Ford knew that, which is why, to conclude the film's astonishing combat sequence, he had had Irving Pichel record what would become the movie's best-remembered line of narration. As the U.S. Navy raises the American flag at Midway, he says quietly, "Yes. This really happened."

Those are the only four words heard during the middle section of *The Battle of Midway*. After the conclusion of the combat sequence, in which Ford does not allow narration to compete with what "really happened" for the viewer's attention, the movie recedes by degrees to the more familiar, though still deeply personal, contours of a documentary. The two narrators return—"Men and women of America, here come your neighbors' sons, home from the day's work! . . . There's Jimmy Patch—seven meatballs on his plane." (A "meatball" was a kill, presumably a reference to the Japanese flag.) Fonda and Darwell resume their conversation excitedly, with a sense that they have recovered from their own awestruck silence.

In the last third of the movie, Ford avoids triumphalism or exultation. "The Battle of Midway is over," Crisp says. "Our front yard is safe. But a big job is still to be done." The film's final minutes are notably somber and mournful, a representation of the costs, not the spoils, of war. The audience is informed that planes are still searching for men "who fought through to the last round of ammunition, and through to the last drop of gas, and then crashed into the sea." Exhausted and wounded Americans, smiling but bandaged and bloodied, are seen being carried on stretchers to the bombed Red Cross hospital—"the symbol of mercy the enemy was bound to respect," the narrator says, making the case that was then being drummed into American civilians and servicemen that the Japanese were particularly dangerous because they did not honor the rules of war. The final shots are devoted to a burial of "our heroic dead," a ceremony at which a number of naval officers are identified on camera. The last of them was Major Roosevelt.* His name was the last word spoken in the movie.

The impact of *The Battle of Midway* on its White House audience that day was such that nobody in the room had much time to consider what the film didn't do, or might have done differently. Ford's work was not explanatory or informative—he didn't devote more than a few sentences of narration to reporting how the battle unfolded or what was at stake. The movie completely shrugged off several of the mandates that Lowell Mellett and Frank Capra had outlined; Ford was not interested in making a case about why Americans were fighting, or reiterating democratic principles, or provoking any greater anti-Japanese sentiment than its intended audience already felt. Most strikingly, he had chosen to end an account of America's first great victory of the war on a note of elegy and loss. But such was the film's power that any consideration of a different approach was moot. When the president saw his son onscreen, he turned to the room and said to William Leahy, his chief of staff, "I want every mother in America to see this film." Ford had gotten his wish; the navy would not be allowed to strip *The Battle of Midway* for parts, and the newsreels would be scooped. Five hundred Technicolor prints were struck, and 20th Century Fox, in partnership with Hollywood's War Activities Committee, agreed to distribute the film nationwide in September.

Ford returned to his duties in Washington, awaiting his next posting, but he had one more job to do. The loss of Torpedo Squadron 8 still haunted him. Footage of some of the men who had died had been used to flesh out the central sequence of *The Battle of Midway*—a minor bit of chronological fakery, since the shots of the pilots in front of their planes had actually been filmed a couple of days before the fighting started. But Ford wanted to pay them a greater tribute. In the weeks after *The Battle of Midway* was finished, he assembled all of the film that had been taken of the men of the squadron— about eight minutes in total—into a reel memorializing them. He appended a set of opening titles to the footage in which he praised the men for having "written the most brilliant pages in the glowing history of our Naval Air Forces," and made sure that each man's brief moment on camera was pre-

---

* It has never been determined whether James Roosevelt was actually present at Midway.

ceded by a title with his name and rank. He then had the movie reduced to 8-millimeter film—a size that would allow it to run on inexpensive home-movie projectors—and had copies of *Torpedo Squadron 8* hand-delivered across the country to each of the dead men's families. He rarely spoke of what he had done, and the movie was not shown publicly for almost fifty years.

TEN

"Can You Use Me?"

WASHINGTON AND HOLLYWOOD, AUGUST–SEPTEMBER 1942

Ford's decision to keep the Japanese faceless and undefined in *The Battle of Midway* was less a matter of caution or sensitivity on his part than the reflection of a propaganda policy that by the summer of 1942 was hopelessly muddled and conflicted about what America's enemy should look like on movie screens. Some in the War Department thought military films should take their cues from a new Hollywood genre the press was worriedly calling "hate pictures" and depict the Japanese not just as another race but as a virtually subhuman species of scrawny, simian death-dealers. Others believed, even in the war's darkest days, that an Allied victory was inevitable, and that the reintegration of Japanese Americans into society would soon follow. They pressed filmmakers to pursue an alternative approach that would present the Japanese as a simple, primitive people who had been hypnotized by a spooky, ghost-filled religion—Shintoism—and by megalomaniacal leaders bent on world domination. But even within that faction, a rift opened between those who felt that in War Department propaganda, Emperor Hirohito should serve to embody a nation's evil just as Hitler and Mussolini did for most Americans, and others who contended that since Hirohito would likely remain in power even after the war, it would be wiser to use General Tojo as the face of Japan's lust for conquest. That was met with the counterargument that "Americans . . . will be better haters—and thus better fighters and workers—if they are not beclouded with the false idea that the enemy is a bunch of poor, misguided people who deserve more pity than bullets and bombs."

The conundrum of how to handle Japan was threatening to stop Capra in his tracks just as he was starting work on his new *Know Your Enemy* series. He had proposed three films that would explain to American fighting men the cultural, military, and sociological history of the people and armies of Japan, Germany, and Italy. As his roster of projects grew, he had become frustrated by the fact that the writers and directors he needed were a continent away, and also by the endless negotiation it took to get Hollywood to free them up and the army to pay for them. In July, he convinced General Osborn to let him move his unit from Washington to Los Angeles, where Darryl Zanuck agreed to rent him an unused 20th Century Fox stage on Western Avenue for a dollar a year. Osborn told Capra that "so far as it means we would see you less often, we all regret the necessity for you being out there," but he added warmly, "We know that the films you will bring out will carry a hallmark of quality. . . . If they fall short of what you could do with more time and less difficulties thrown in your way, that is just part of the war and don't let it worry you."

Capra was heartened by the endorsement of his efforts—Osborn promoted him to lieutenant colonel in August—and he was elated to be back home in California, where he could preside over his own, bureaucracy-free kingdom. He rallied his troops on the empty lot that had been nicknamed "Fort Fox," telling them, "Some carping individuals will accuse you of fighting 'the Battle of Hollywood.' Don't argue with them. This is a total war fought with every conceivable weapon. Your weapon is film! Your bombs are ideas! Hollywood is a war plant!"

But if that was the case, the bombs weren't going off, and what the plant was manufacturing was of questionable value. Hollywood no more knew how to depict the Japanese than Washington did, and, left to their own devices, the studios chose approaches that were at best obvious and at worst savagely racist. At Columbia, Harry Cohn took Capra's own 1937 film *Lost Horizon*, cut twenty-five minutes out of it, and rereleased it in an attempt to capitalize on an offhand joke President Roosevelt had made that the American army had built "a secret base at Shangri-La" from which to attack Tokyo. What had been made as a fantasy about a Himalayan utopia was now being resold as propaganda, with a tacked-on prologue explicitly setting it during the Sino-Japanese War. And 20th Century Fox had just completed a low-budget picture called *Little Tokyo, U.S.A.*, that traded on the conviction that a Japanese nest of covert agents had operated in the United States for a decade. The movie portrayed Japanese Americans as part of "a vast army of volunteer spies" whose members posed as flower merchants and friendly, quasi-assimilated citizens while actually operating in robotic allegiance to what one thickly accented character calls "our revered home-rand." As they plot to destroy the Los Angeles water system, they sneer that America's "stupid complacency will aid us greatly," and ominously prognosticate "the end of the white man's domination." The movie's hero, a Los Angeles cop, calls them "an Oriental Bund" numbering twenty-five thousand in Los Angeles alone—"half-pint connivers" who are "getting ready to tear us apart." A voice-over batters away at the point, warning moviegoers that America must not be lulled into a "false sense of security" since it already "slept at the switch once."

Despite a pro forma disclaimer, hastily dubbed into one scene, that "there are many Japanese here in Los Angeles who are loyal to America," the invective in *Little Tokyo, U.S.A.* was so virulent that it spurred Mellett and the Bureau of Motion Pictures to take a more aggressive role in overseeing the content of Hollywood releases. The bureau called the movie "an invitation to a witch hunt" and deplored its "Gestapo tactics," asking, "Did somebody mention that we are presumably fighting for the Bill of Rights?" The U.S. Relocation Authority, which oversaw the Japanese internment camps in America, also objected to the film. At the time, it was considering a social-engineering experiment to scatter internees around the country, presumably to prevent them from clustering and conspiring; administrators worried that the picture's paranoid rhetoric would create resistance to the Japanese in small middle American communities.

Burned by the controversy, the studios agreed to have Mellett's office assess their new pictures at the screenplay stage rather than once they were finished, an immense concession to the idea of government oversight. Mellett urged the studios to consider not just how their films portrayed enemies and allies, but whether they risked "creating a false picture of America"; he also cautioned them against merely "using the war as the basis for a profitable picture" and against including the kind of hyperbole that might give "the young people of today . . . reason to say they were misled by propaganda." His marching orders to the studios came perilously close to state censorship— the codification of matters of taste into a federally mandated production code. Since the BMP was not empowered to enforce its opinions, it was often ignored. But Mellett had one strong card to play: The U.S. government maintained control over what movies could be sent abroad, and for the studios, a "not recommended for export" label from his office represented a serious economic penalty.

As he watched leaders in Hollywood and Washington struggle with these issues and with one another, Capra found it almost impossible to commission a script for *Know Your Enemy—Japan* or to give its writer any useful guidance. He asked Warren Duff, a prolific screenwriter who had written two of James Cagney's most popular recent movies, *Angels with Dirty Faces* and *Each Dawn I Die*, to try his hand at a draft, but what Duff came up with was both bullying and off the point. "We didn't bother about your way of life because it was none of our business," said his narrator, directly addressing the Japanese rather than U.S. servicemen. "But now we're interested, and we're going to bother quite a bit—because you're our enemy. We think we'll surprise you." Capra scrapped the screenplay as soon as he read it, and, seeing no way to fix it, shelved the series until the following spring.

He still had plenty to keep him busy in Los Angeles. His plan for a seven-film *Know Your Ally* series was progressing quickly—he was in touch with the National Film Board of Canada about one segment, and Janet Flanner, the Paris correspondent for the *New Yorker*, would soon start work for him on an installment devoted to "The Fighting French." More important, the first episode of the *Why We Fight* movies was nearing completion. At Eric Knight's urging, Capra had stopped tinkering with the scripts and narrowed the history-lesson plan down considerably. ("We have eliminated the Battle of the Atlantic and the Battle of the Mediterranean and most of the

Balkan campaign," he wrote to a colonel at West Point, "figuring that we would take these up at a later date.") Crews at Disney were busy executing Capra's innovative idea to use animated maps to illustrate Germany's advance through Europe with spills of spreading black ink and the pincers of a crab grabbing at neighboring countries, and demonstrating Japan's ambitions with tentacles into China and across the Pacific. And with Knight's help, Capra had finally conceived a viable overall structure for the series. The first film, *Prelude to War*, would take GIs through Japan's invasion of Manchuria and Italy's push into North Africa. That would flow seamlessly into *The Nazis Strike*, about Germany's conquest of Austria, Czechoslovakia, and Poland, and then *Divide and Conquer*, which would cover the fall of France. The fourth and fifth installments would explore the Battle of Britain and the Russian front, the sixth would analyze Japan's attempt to conquer China, and the seventh, *War Comes to America*, would finish with Pearl Harbor. Each of the chapters was to run about an hour.

By early fall, all seven scripts were far along, and spirits in Capra's unit were high enough so that the writers he and Knight were overseeing could afford to joke about the difficulties they faced. Working on the narration for the sixth segment, *The Battle of Russia*, Leonard Spigelgass—the only one of the original seven writers Capra had kept on—told the director in a letter that it was "as difficult to write as the Versailles Treaty. The Consul and the Soviet Representatives went over every word with a fine tooth comb . . . after breaking my back to try to teach her, we were forced to the conclusion that Lieutenant Pavlinchenko could never learn to speak a word of English even phonetically, but by gargantuan effort, we finally got her to say, 'Fellow soldiers, forward to victory.' . . . I think we can get away with it."

While he was in Hollywood, Capra was finally able to recruit the last major member of his team, and perhaps the most important. According to his own recollection, he was on the Columbia lot having some secondhand desks, chairs, and office equipment loaded onto a truck for use at Fort Fox when George Stevens ambled up to him. "You?" Stevens said. "*You* need an old desk? I thought you were chief of something."

Capra replied that he was. "Can you use me?" Stevens asked. By the end of the conversation, Capra had offered him a commission as a major.

Although the meeting was happenstance, Stevens's decision was not nearly as impulsive as Capra made it sound. The most deliberative of young directors, a man whom *Time* magazine had recently said was best known for "getting over a bad spot [while shooting] a picture [by striding] up & down interminably while everyone waits," Stevens had been thinking about enlisting since Pearl Harbor. *Woman of the Year,* the Hepburn-Tracy romantic comedy he had been shooting at the time of the attack, had opened in February to mostly generous reviews, and although it had become a sizable hit, Stevens knew the movie still bore too many traces of the compromised, timid prewar moment in which it had been conceived. It now seemed ludicrous that Louis B. Mayer had nervously forbidden him to include a scene in which Hepburn's character shows her linguistic fluency by speaking a bit of Yiddish because it might have stirred up anti-Semitism. And a few critics gently noted that the story of an avid globetrotting journalist who needs her priorities corrected by, of all people, a sportswriter seemed to have its own priorities backward. The *New Yorker* suggested that it might have been a better idea to make a movie about a woman who persuades her man "to give up writing stories about games played by other people and take a grown-up interest in the collapse of this planet," whereas *Woman of the Year* has it "just the other way around."

Stevens wasn't defensive about the picture; he was all too aware that it depended on "the audience . . . accepting what in many ways could be questionable." Soon after the movie opened, he received a gently scolding letter from an old friend who was now an editor at *Time* magazine in New York. "*Woman* is a hell of a hit and should do you plenty of good," he said. "[But] I think you should give some thought to making your pictures a bit thicker—not quite so easy to grasp and perhaps a bit more provocative." He also implied that a stint in the military might do Stevens some good as an artist, writing, "You're lucky enough to be young enough to take the war in stride and not be an old man when it's over. I think you've made some swell pictures, but I know they're not a patch on what you'll be making ten years from now.

"I'm full of military secrets, but I can't tell you any of them," the letter concluded. "Get ready for lots of bad headlines and few pleasant surprises for a long time, however. This war is really a toughie. It's the third quarter, and we're about three touchdowns behind. It's going to take a team of All-Americans to pull us out of this one."

The implication that Stevens was choosing to stay on the bench while his colleagues were going off to fight—or at least relocating to Washington to await orders—was not lost on him. He had no shortage of reasons to remain at home. He had a wife and a ten-year-old son, George Jr., whom he adored, and he suffered from asthma that was serious enough to exempt him from any active duty. His responsibilities as president of the Screen Directors Guild were considerable, and he was also under contract to make two more pictures for Columbia, which greeted any sign of wavering on his part by warning him that if he went off to war, his career would stall just when it was on the ascent.

But Stevens felt increasingly consumed by a sense of duty, and resolved to work off his Columbia deal as quickly as he could manage. Immediately after finishing *Woman of the Year,* he began preparing *The Talk of the Town,* a high-minded comedy-drama that was designed to give Columbia exactly the kind of semisophisticated, vaguely political, somewhat romantic crowd-pleaser it had sought since Capra left the studio. Stevens brought a light touch to the story of a prison escapee (Cary Grant) framed for arson and the Supreme Court nominee (Ronald Colman) who attempts to exonerate him. But during production, he retreated into himself more than ever, taking hours between scenes to contemplate each setup and driving his cast and crew half-mad with his impassive mien and stony silences.

Although critics applauded the results—the film became Stevens's first Best Picture nominee—many of them noted that he was working in a vein that had already been well mined by Capra, a similarity that was only under-scored by his use of the costar (Jean Arthur) and screenwriter (Sidney Buchman) of *Mr. Smith Goes to Washington. The Talk of the Town* was Stevens's first attempt to go "a bit thicker"—it makes a political statement, but the statement is about the horror of lynch-mob rule and vigilante hysteria, which had been a favorite Hollywood subject since the mid-1930s and was by 1942 a relatively safe way for a film to be topical. Nelson Poynter, the young, progressive deputy of the BMP, praised *Talk* for dramatizing "one of the basic things we are fighting for—a decent social contract." But Stevens knew that he still hadn't made a picture that belonged in a post–Pearl Harbor America, something that was brought home to him bluntly when he tested two different endings before preview audiences. Unable to decide whether Jean Arthur's character should end up with the firebrand played by Grant or the older, more professorial Colman, he put the question to moviegoers, wondering whether they would prefer a man of action or a man of intellect. The audience chose Grant, but for reasons Stevens hadn't anticipated. "While there are men of draft age on the screen, the girls should marry them," read a typical comment card. "Later on the mature men will have it all to themselves." Another viewer, rooting for Colman, wrote, "Send Grant off to war without Arthur to stay true to life." It was the beginning of the era of the 4-F movie hero—three years during which, if a young man appeared on screen in a contemporary film set in the United States, moviegoers wanted to know why he wasn't in uniform.

The Talk of the Town had just opened when Stevens ran into Capra on the lot, and by then he had made up his mind. His agent, Charles Feldman, tried one last time to scare him out of leaving. "You go in, this war will last seven years, or five years—you're finished as far as the films are concerned, if nothing worse happens to you," he told his client. Stevens was undeterred. He informed a resigned Harry Cohn that his next picture for Columbia, a romantic comedy called *The More the Merrier* in which he planned to reteam Grant and Arthur, would be his last. His active duty would begin just days after he finished work in the editing room. "The war was on . . . I wanted to be in the war," he said later. "It's hard to get a fifty-yard-line seat like that."

World War II was no longer a shock; it was an ongoing fact of life with no end in sight. Any hopes that an American victory would be swift had evaporated with daily headlines about fresh casualties and new combat zones in the Pacific. Over the summer, U.S. planes had flown their first, tentative missions over France, and the army would soon begin Operation Torch, opening a new front with its first major deployment of ground troops in North Africa. As summer turned to fall, nobody in Hollywood was calling the war an "adventure" any longer; there was fearful talk that it could last until 1950. The commitments to service that Hollywood's directors had made were just beginning, and around Labor Day they all came home to Los Angeles for short reunions with their loved ones, followed by a series of farewells that felt sadder and more permanent than when they had first gone off to Washington and uniforms and salutes and protocol were still new.

John Ford had already been away from home for almost a year, and his wife was unhappily getting used to life alone; they had not wanted to uproot their teenaged daughter, Barbara, with a move to Washington. The Fords had a tender and companionable relationship, but not an especially intimate one—they had long slept in separate beds, and Mary looked the other way at his occasional indiscretions, drawing the line only at a passionate romantic attachment to Katharine Hepburn that had persisted through the late 1930s. ("She doesn't like me anymore," Hepburn had said in late 1938. "But I can't blame her for that.") While he was away, Ford had kept in touch with Mary by writing frequent and emotional notes. "Dear Ma," he wrote, using his preferred endearment, "Your letter written Tuesday pleased me—gave me pictures of our beautiful home—the home and family we are fighting to preserve. . . . All my love. Miss you so much. Daddy."

As the summer of 1942 ended, the Fords enjoyed a brief and bittersweet family reunion. Their son Michael Patrick, whom they called Pat, had just married his college sweetheart and graduated from the University of Maine with the hope of joining his father as an officer in the navy, but he was rejected for a commission because his eyes were weak. When he enlisted, Ford tried to get him assigned to duty on his ketch, the *Araner*. ("The kid is really tops," he wrote the commander in charge of the boat. "You would be doing Mrs. Ford and me a great favor.") But Ford's plea failed; instead, his frustrated son would serve out the war at a desk, as an apprentice seaman in the navy's West Coast public relations office, feeling "like a failure" while his father traveled the world. Ford was soon called back to duty. He urged Mary to be brave and keep busy. Bette Davis, John Garfield, and MCA president Jules Stein had just founded the Hollywood Canteen, the nightclub on Cahuenga Boulevard where servicemen of all ranks could dine, dance, and even mingle with stars. Mary intended to take an active role when it opened in October. Ford returned to Washington in late August. It would be well over a year before he would be able to spend another week at home.

William Wyler was in Los Angeles on army business. He had traveled west to convince MGM to donate cameras, editing bays, and sound equipment that could be used in the war. But despite the fact that *Mrs. Miniver* was on its way to becoming a huge hit, the studio held him at arm's length. "I have seldom been so busy or worked so hard and accomplished so little," he fumed to Talli. "It's shameful how we got no cooperation—nothing but evasion when it came to giving up some equipment they could really spare. They all talk big, but when it comes to doing something, the tone changes. Sometimes I feel I should just get on a ship and go. . . . But there's no sense in my going without proper equipment." Louis B. Mayer, ever pragmatic, may have felt he had nothing to gain in helping Wyler, who, after all, was still under contract to another man's company. But while he was in town, Wyler made arrangements through his lawyer to suspend the deal he had recently renewed with Sam Goldwyn for the duration of the war. He had no interest in making another movie in the near future; what he really wanted was to recruit a unit of filmmakers that could serve as his team once his posting to an Army Air Force base in England came through.

Wyler got most of the men on his wish list: Screenwriter Jerome Chodorov (one of the original *Why We Fight* writers whom Capra had fired in his fit of anti-Communist panic), William Clothier, a camera operator whose experience with aerial photography included the 1927 film *Wings,* and Harold Tannenbaum, a sound recorder for RKO. The only man to turn him down was Irwin Shaw, a rising star who had had his first Broadway play, the antiwar drama *Bury the Dead,* produced when he was just twenty-three. Six years later, Shaw, a first-generation American Jew from the Bronx, was a sought-after screenwriter who had just written *The Talk of the Town* for Stevens. He admired Wyler and agreed to meet with him, but he wasn't sure he wanted to serve out the war in a Signal Corps unit. "After sober reflection," he cabled the director, "I've decided that going with you as a private would mean a long succession of frustrations—military, artistic, economic and social. And the war effort would suffer. . . . So I'm going into the regular army this morning at 6:45. I feel I've waited too long as it is." (Shaw's attempt to game the system by volunteering failed; the army, noting his résumé, promptly assigned him to the Signal Corps anyway. Within a year, he would end up serving under Stevens.)

Wyler's parting from Talli was particularly painful. He was leaving her with Cathy, then a toddler, and their new baby, Judy, who was only a month old. He returned to Washington with just one 16-millimeter camera to take overseas. He promised to write home regularly. Like Ford, he would not see his wife and children for a year.

John Huston's departure from Hollywood was of a somewhat different character. His declarations of fidelity were made not to his estranged and humiliated wife Lesley but to Olivia de Havilland, and before he left he sat down with Warner Bros. to do some business, urging them not to assign *The Treasure of the Sierra Madre* to another screenwriter before he could take a crack at it, and also checking in with the studio about a script he had written called *Background to Danger*, based on a spy novel by the British writer Eric Ambler.*

Huston assumed he would be back soon; for him, a return to steady work in Hollywood seemed to be just one wartime assignment away. But he'd waited impatiently to get that assignment, and when it finally came, he saw an opportunity to make a great movie. On June 6, as the Battle of Midway was being fought, the Japanese army launched a separate offensive, landing on and taking Kiska, one of the small "Rat Islands" at the western end of the Aleutians in the Bering Sea between Alaska and Russia. Five hundred Japanese soldiers captured the ten members of the U.S. Navy who constituted the entire population of the remote base; the next day, the Japanese captured the neighboring island of Attu as well. Until that attack—the only ground invasion of U.S. territory during the war—most Americans had no idea where Kiska, Attu, or the Aleutians were. Now their strategic importance had become front-page news, and they would soon be the focus of a major army counteroffensive. The Signal Corps wanted Huston to travel to Adak, a larger island southeast of Kiska that housed a navy air station, and make a documentary, intended to be shown theatrically, about the U.S. fight to take back the two islands.

Huston eagerly accepted the job; he left Hollywood for Alaska in September 1942 and soon after was promoted to captain. His goodbye to de Havil-

---

* Warner Bros. agreed to hold off on *Sierra Madre*, but the studio reassigned the Ambler project to Huston's *High Sierra* collaborator W. R. Burnett. William Faulkner also worked on the screenplay for *Background to Danger*, which was released in 1943.

land was, the actress later said, "very difficult" and "painful." It was also not as private as either of them imagined. For weeks, he had been under surveillance. And as soon as he left, the army began a formal investigation "to determine the discretion, integrity and loyalty of Subject, who is suspected of being a Communist."

ELEVEN

"A Good Partner to Have in Times of Trouble"

ENGLAND, NORTH AFRICA, AND HOLLYWOOD, SEPTEMBER 1942–JANUARY 1943

John Ford was already in England when *The Battle of Midway* opened across the United States on September 14, 1942. Of the many venues in which the short film played—often on a bill with *Mrs. Miniver* or *The Talk of the Town*—the largest was New York's six-thousand-seat Radio City Music Hall, where some patrons were so overwhelmed by what they saw on-screen that they fainted. Ford's name did not appear anywhere in the credits, which simply stated that the "greatest Naval victory of the world to date" had been shot by "U.S. Navy photographers." But every review credited Ford—or, as the *New York Times* now referred to him, "Commander John Ford, U.S.N.R., the former Hollywood film director"—and repeated the story of how "the unsung camera men and Commander Ford, who was wounded while operating a 16mm. hand camera, risked their lives in making this astounding factual film record." People had been waiting three months for color footage from Midway, and most critics cautioned that anyone expecting to see a clear record of the battle would be disappointed. *Newsweek* called it "a hastily assembled job," *Time* faulted Jane Darwell's "corny" narration, and the *New Yorker* warned that the movie offered "nothing . . . that a spy would waste invisible ink on. . . . Things were obviously happening too hot and heavy to be very neatly photographed." Still, they asked, couldn't there have been maps, or an explanation of Japan's strategy, or an analysis of the military objectives behind the battle and the significance of America's victory?

Many reviewers had been expecting something more definitive and less emotional and impressionistic than the movie Ford had made. But they also admitted, almost universally, that none of their reservations mattered. Moviegoers were stunned to see a film that was "so real it jars you," and virtually everyone who wrote about *The Battle of Midway* noted Ford's decision to include "many scenes where the concussion of bombs actually knocked cameras out of the photographers' hands." The juddering, jolting, damaged images captured at Midway had, it turned out, created a new standard for realism in which, for the first time, lack of polish was taken as a benchmark of veracity. The result, James Agee wrote, "is a first-class failure to film the most difficult of all actions—a battle—but a brave attempt to make a record—quick, jerky, vivid, fragmentary, luminous—of a moment of desperate peril to the nation. . . . In the oily blue-blackness of smoke, the strange black flowers and white streamers painted on the sky by planes and bursting ack-ack, the mortal brilliance of blood, Technicolor vindicates the remark made about it at its birth a decade ago that 'Now Hollywood is ready to film the Last Judgment.'"

In his *Time* review, Agee stated that Ford's documentary "should be seen by all Americans," and for once, that oft-invoked wish came remarkably close to being realized. The five hundred prints Technicolor had made were in such heavy demand that by the end of its run *The Battle of Midway* had been booked more than thirteen thousand times, playing in three-quarters of all U.S. theaters. Frequent moviegoers saw it so often, before so many different features, that more than any other single film, Ford's rough-hewn, sentimental, patriotic, and sorrowing version of the battle created a national understanding of what the war in the Pacific looked and felt like.

In August, Donovan had told Ford to pack up and prepare for an extended stay in Europe; he was to travel to London and begin preparations to film the planned British-American invasion of Morocco, Algeria, and Tunisia. But before he left Washington, he managed to squeeze in a crucial bit of campaigning for his movie. Ford, who had skipped the Oscars all three times he won Best Director, nonetheless wanted a fourth trophy, though he liked to cultivate an air of nonchalance about such things. When Walter Wanger, who had produced *Stagecoach* and *The Long Voyage Home* and was now the president of the Academy, came to town, Ford arranged a private showing of *The Battle of Midway* for him and sat in the back of the screening room while the film played.

"It's definitely award material, Jack," Wanger said as the lights came up.

"Oh, for Christ's sakes, Walter," snapped Ford. "I'm not interested in awards. I just want to remind you Hollywood guys that somebody's out there fighting a war."

As Ford lit his pipe, Wanger politely replied that the war had already yielded an extraordinary number of impressive documentaries and that the decision would be particularly difficult this year. By the time he left the screening room, Ford had convinced him to change the Academy's rules. When Wanger announced the 1942 nominations the following February, the list would include *Midway* among an unprecedented twenty-five candidates for Best Documentary—more than half of them produced by U.S. government agencies or branches of the military—and, for the first and only time, the promise of four winners rather than one.

Ford was, more than ever, writing his own rules, and his high-handedness was beginning to make him some enemies. When the Office of War Information sent a request for him to turn over all of the footage he had shot at Midway for their use, he refused on the assumption that a civilian propaganda agency had no justification for requesting any property belonging to the navy. His intractability infuriated Mellett, who wanted the OWI's Bureau of Motion Pictures to have oversight of all filmed material, whether it came out of Hollywood or Washington. Mellett was not one of *The Battle of Midway*'s admirers; he thought the film was off-message and had made his distaste clear to Ford, who had responded that if Mellett wanted the footage, he was going to have to go up the OSS chain of command all the way to Bill Donovan to get it. Mellett, whose taste for turf wars was becoming a serious impediment to his leadership, responded by threatening to prevent the movie from being shown overseas. As Ford flew to London, Sam Spewack, a genial screenwriter who had left Hollywood to serve as one of Mellett's deputies, tried to broker a peace on the plane.

"I had a 36 hour talk with John Ford," he wrote to Mellett. "He finally broke down and said he was for releasing all his Pacific stuff [in Europe]. . . . Incidentally, Ford was very hurt at your criticism of *Midway*. I think personalities are pretty silly at a time like this. He's an extremely able director and a nice fellow, but just why he should be in a position to release or withhold film is beyond this non-government mind." Mellett and Spewack both knew but could not express even in correspondence exactly why Ford was in that position; almost a year into the war, the Roosevelt administration had done nothing to demarcate lines of authority among the various agencies that were producing, vetting, and releasing films designed to aid the war effort. In part, the administration's reluctance stemmed from an aversion to creating any kind of propaganda system that was centralized or formalized enough to arouse the ire of congressional Republicans. But as a result, Mellett, who had been used to getting his own way as a newspaper editor and regarded Hollywood filmmakers with an outsider's suspicion, increasingly found himself outmaneuvered by directors who had years of experience at doing whatever it took to protect their work from interference.

Spewack succeeded in soothing Ford enough to get him to turn his footage over to the BMP, but Ford didn't wait for Mellett's approval to take the movie overseas. He cabled Robert Parrish and instructed him to fly to the UK with a print of *The Battle of Midway* on an OSS mission to show the movie to the British high command. Ford thought the film would help "to prove that we were actually in the war with them"—a sore point among many in England who by the end of 1942 were becoming impatient that the United States was still focusing almost exclusively on the Pacific when sixty thousand Britons had already been killed by bombs. All year, American soldiers and officers had been streaming into London. For the most part, they had behaved well; the War Department had given them all pamphlets with guidelines that included "Don't be a show off," "If you want to join a darts game, let them ask you first," "To say 'I look like a bum' is offensive to their ears," and "You can rub a Britisher the wrong way by telling him, 'We came over and won the last one.'" But Anglo-American tensions were still running

high. "You won't be able to tell the British much about 'taking it,'" the pamphlet read. "They are not particularly interested in taking it any more. They
are far more interested in getting together in solid friendship with us, so that
we can all start dishing it out to Hitler."

To that end, Ford was charged with helping to set up film crews for the
impending Operation Torch under the auspices of the OSS. The navy installed him in Claridge's, the luxury hotel in London's Mayfair district that
was then home to a kind of rotating international gentlemen's club of senior
Allied military officers, exiled European royals, and the ad hoc community
of British and American filmmakers who had volunteered for the war. The
guests when Ford arrived included producer-director Alexander Korda, Darryl Zanuck, who had just begun a leave from 20th Century Fox for full-time
army duty, and the young British director Carol Reed, one of the most talented recruits in the British army's film unit.

Ford also found one of his longtime rivals there. William Wyler had arrived at the Eighth Air Force headquarters and checked into Claridge's a
couple of weeks before him. He had quickly been befriended by Korda and
Reed, and was immersed in mapping out plans for a series of war documentaries while he awaited assignment to an Army Air Force base. Wyler wanted
to make a movie about joint missions flown by the air force and the RAF; he
also had in mind a picture about the Eagle Squadron, the volunteer pilots
who were the first to fly in the war and had been the subject of a drama that
Universal had just released. Two of his other ideas were particularly strong—
a film he wanted to call *Nine Lives*, a group portrait of an American crew on
a bombing mission, and *Phyllis Was a Fortress*, which would track a single
mission over France flown by one of the USAAF's B-17 bombers, known as
Flying Fortresses.

Wyler's slate of documentary proposals reflected the focus and ambition
of a man who now expected to be in the army for a long time and wanted to
contribute as much as possible. But when he got to England, he found himself
sitting at Claridge's with nothing to do but wait. The army still hadn't sent
over the crew he had recruited, and the equipment he needed, other than the
single camera he had brought with him, was on a ship that was making its
agonizingly slow way across the North Atlantic. When Ford arrived in grand

style, "it just drove Willy crazy," said Talli Wyler. "Willy didn't know the Army ways. He couldn't requisition even a typewriter, much less cameras."

"Suddenly, John Ford showed up, eye patch, cigar and all," said Wyler. "He was in the Navy and his equipment was *flown over* by the Navy. I don't know how he did it." He later complained that by the time his own gear finally arrived, "half of it had been sunk by the Germans." The 35-millimeter cameras that Wyler believed would be essential for his planned documentaries never made it across the Atlantic; instead, he would have to rely on whatever 16-millimeter equipment he could beg or borrow in London. And Ford was no help; when Wyler sent word that he needed cameras, Ford abruptly replied that he couldn't spare a thing. "[Ford] didn't like Willy Wyler," said cameraman William Clothier, who knew both men well. "I really don't know [why]."

Wyler's spirits were low. "The trouble with London at the moment is too damn many Americans," he wrote in one of many long letters to Talli. "The British call it 'the invasion.' . . . Dinner invitations are few and far between. Also, whiskey is at a premium, so just being invited for a drink is usually quite a gesture." Whenever he was able to host a guest or two himself, he dolefully referred to his room as "Wyler's Mortuary."

His grim mood changed abruptly when *Mrs. Miniver* started to be shown in London. Wyler was not surprised to hear that British critics cast a dubious eye on an American director's depiction of their country and people. "The picture of England at war suffers from that distortion which seems inevitable whenever Hollywood cameras are trained on it," sniffed the reviewer for the *Times* of London. The *Spectator*, noting that the putatively middle-class Minivers enjoyed a kind of ostentatiously moneyed luxury that bore little resemblance to the lives of the average English family, dismissed the movie as a "defense of bourgeois privilege" and condemned its opening-title description of the British as "a happy, careless people" who were oblivious to the coming war as "unconsciously pro-Fascist propaganda." And Eric Knight, who was still doing part-time duty as a movie critic, called the film "hogwash. . . . Oh, God, those Hollywood men with their funny ideas of what this war is about!"

What Wyler did not suspect was how little the critical verdict would matter. Ordinary British moviegoers, it turned out, loved *Mrs. Miniver* every bit as much as Americans had. Whether or not Winston Churchill actually ever told Louis B. Mayer that it was "propaganda worth many battleships," the prime minister had more important things to do than to refute MGM's widely publicized contention that he had said it, and others were open in their praise to Wyler: Lord Halifax, the British ambassador to the United States, cabled the director that the film "portrays the life that people live in England today in a way that cannot fail to move all that see it. I hope this picture will bring home to the American public that the average Englishman is a good partner to have in times of trouble."

In London, Wyler's newfound celebrity as a visiting American eminence overshadowed even Ford's. Invitations started coming more frequently, and one of them was from Laurence Olivier. The last time Wyler had been in England, in 1938, he was courting the actor to star in *Wuthering Heights*. This time, Olivier was courting Wyler. In May, he had joined the Royal Navy as a pilot—by all accounts, one of the worst in the history of the British military. After weeks of flying lessons that more than once ended in near catastrophe—he is said to have destroyed five planes—the Royal Navy and Olivier came to the mutual conclusion that he could better serve his country on the ground. Olivier was granted a leave from service to aid the war effort by making films. The actor was about to embark on a mediocre dramatic propaganda effort called *Adventure for Two*, in which he was to play a Russian engineer who warms to the British during an extended stay in England. But when he met with Wyler, it was to propose something more ambitious—a filmed adaptation of Shakespeare's *Henry V* that he believed could serve as an inspiring testament to British valor during the war. He felt certain that Wyler, who had recently said that "a propaganda picture doesn't have to be filled with blood and brutality," was the man for the job. "Don't worry," he told the director. "I know Shakespeare, you know how to make pictures."

Wyler declined his offer, explaining that his first obligation was now to his documentary work, and he had the satisfaction of recommending Ford, knowing that however unequal they were in the armed forces, in the movie business the man who had beaten him twice for Best Director was, at least for the moment, a runner-up. Olivier took Wyler's advice and went to Ford a few weeks later. He got another rejection, as Ford laughingly told him he was completely unqualified to direct a Shakespeare play.*

Ford got his orders to move out long before Wyler did. On October 28, 1942, after two months at Claridge's, he traveled to Scotland and boarded a freighter bound for Algiers. For two weeks, the ship made its way south, so uneventfully that Ford said "we might just as well have been on a pleasure cruise." He and the mostly British fighting force spent their days aboard "stripped down and getting tanned" on the deck. He arrived in Algiers with a Field Photo crew of thirty-two men, just four days after American forces had landed and begun their push east toward Tunis, where the most serious fighting would take place.

At Midway, Ford had been the ranking filmmaker. But in Algiers, he discovered he would be answerable to his old boss at 20th Century Fox. Zanuck, whom the members of the 13th Armored Regiment derided behind his back as "the little colonel,"† was presiding over filming operations in North Africa with the bluff and brio of a know-it-all on his first big-game hunt. "Can't I ever get away from you?" Ford said, perhaps not entirely amiably, when they first saw each other. "I'll bet a dollar to a doughnut that if I ever go to heaven you'll be waiting at the door for me under a sign reading 'Produced by Darryl F. Zanuck.'" Ford liked Zanuck, but he wasn't happy that for this campaign, his Field Photo Unit had been moved under the authority of the Signal Corps, and he was not alone in his distaste for the Fox chief's dilettantish behavior. Zanuck had somehow managed to take possession of a private car in which he traveled while everyone else used army or navy transport; he was planning to write a book about his experience in Algiers and Tunis, he kept his own schedule, and he made no secret of the fact that he was less interested in filming the Allied advance for newsreels than in amassing footage for a feature-length documentary he intended to produce himself.

Ford wanted to get his crew to the front, which was near a port city called

---

* After several more rejections, Olivier decided to direct *Henry V* himself, and won an honorary Academy Award for his work on the picture when it was released in the United States after the war.
† The derogation, a reference to his short stature, was also the title of a 1935 Shirley Temple movie.

Bône about three hundred miles east of Algiers, as soon as possible. While Zanuck worked to secure transportation for him and his photographers, Ford strove to be as unobtrusive as possible, getting to know the men of D Company, and taking care that his own demeanor did nothing to fuel the resentment about entitled movie people with unearned officer's commissions that Zanuck's behavior was generating. The Allies were successfully pushing the Germans to retreat, but as they did, Ford recalled, "the Germans were making sporadic [air] raids. . . . Usually about half an hour after we would leave a port, the German planes would come over and blast hell out of the town, evidently looking for us," as Ford's Field Photo Unit moved up the coast, guided by a fishing schooner to which someone had attached a motor.

Ford and his men landed at Bône and then, with the 13th Armored, made their way inland to Tebourba, just twenty miles from Tunis and at the moment they arrived the center of an intense firefight. D Company was under a near-constant barrage from German tanks and dive bombers, and Ford filmed whenever he wasn't forced to take cover. By traveling along the coastline, he had managed to outpace Zanuck, who was genuinely worried by the time he reached the nearby town of Majae al Bab. "All along, I have inquired about Jack Ford and his O.S.S. boys," he wrote in his journal on December 1. "I have been unable to locate them, although I have successfully made contact with several Signal Corps cameramen. . . . I have collected their film and resupplied them. . . . I am sure Ford is somewhere in this area and it worries me not to be able to find him."

Zanuck made it to Tebourba on December 3, after Ford had been there for three days, and on December 6 he ordered Ford and his men to retreat to safer ground and relieved them with Signal Corps photographers. Ford later told James Roosevelt that he had been under fire "twenty-four hours a day for six weeks" with virtually nothing to eat, a pointless exaggeration. But there was no doubt that, just as at Midway, he had put himself in harm's way. This time, however, there would not be a John Ford movie to show for it; before retreating, Ford had to turn over everything he had shot—his footage of the siege of Tebourba, of Bône, of a captured German bomber pilot standing by his downed plane—to Zanuck, who was flying home to make his battlefront documentary. Ford was sent back to the United States by Coast Guard transport ship and didn't get home until two weeks after Zanuck. He celebrated Christmas with a few of his Field Photo cameramen in the middle of the Atlantic, and arrived back in Washington, D.C., just in time for New Year's Eve.

Ford was deeply skeptical about Zanuck's ability to pull together a credible pictorial record of the North African campaign, and so was Capra, who was unimpressed with Zanuck's footage and increasingly frustrated at the weakly made accounts of the war to which American moviegoers were being exposed. While the British were managing to astonish U.S. audiences with documentaries, dramas, and hybrids like the air raid dramatization *Target for Tonight,* Capra felt that the Signal Corps was being stymied by territorial bickering—and particularly by Lowell Mellett. In September, Mellett's pet project *The World at War*—the first movie with the opening title "The United States Government Presents" to receive a major national release—had opened. The film was an Office of War Information documentary that compressed the ten years of history Capra was planning to spread through seven *Why We Fight* scripts into one very brief movie—a cram session that, just as Capra was doing, traced both the history of Japan since the invasion of Manchuria and the rise of Hitler and German expansionism.

Over the past year, Mellett had acted alternately as a moral scourge to studios and a self-styled representative of their interests to Washington. Early in the war, he had attempted to assuage the industry's concerns by assuring them that the OWI and all other propaganda-producing agencies would keep their movies under thirty minutes so that they could run before, rather than instead of, the for-profit entertainment films Hollywood was producing. But with *The World at War,* he violated his own edict; he had his department prepare two different versions of the picture, one running forty minutes and one running sixty-six minutes, and encouraged the wide distribution of the latter as a feature film by providing it free of charge to theaters.

Mellett's standard, newsreel-style documentary received some admiring reviews—the *New York Times* called it "the sort of complacency-shattering picture we should have had six months ago" and praised "the vigor and sweep of its presentation." The picture was a box-office failure, probably because it offered moviegoers no new information about the war itself and relied entirely on archival newsreel footage rather than freshly shot material.

Nevertheless, its appropriation of *Why We Fight*'s approach to historical narrative rankled Capra, who had already spent the summer watching Ford reap praise for *The Battle of Midway* and was becoming increasingly irritated that he was stuck making training films while his colleagues documented the actual war.

Capra had worked on *Why We Fight* for almost a year, and now, the first installment, *Prelude to War,* was ready to be shown. In October, he and Osborn screened the film in Washington for General Marshall. Over the next fifty-three minutes, Marshall watched exactly what he had hoped to see when he first gave Capra his marching orders—an illustrated lecture in which animation, newsreel footage, narration (delivered with calculated folksiness by Walter Huston), and blunt language combined to strike a balance between history lesson and rallying cry. *Prelude to War* took one of Capra's earliest ideas—the notion that the war was a fight between those who wanted freedom and those who wanted slavery—and expanded it into a heartfelt American ideology that was more far-reaching than any that had yet been officially articulated as national policy. The picture began with references to Moses, Muhammad, Confucius, and Christ, moved with bracing rapidity through Washington, Jefferson, Lincoln, Garibaldi, and Kościuszko, and then jumped dramatically to Japan, Italy, and Germany, presenting those countries as having imprinted evil in their national character over centuries—the German "inborn natural love of regimentation and discipline," the Japanese people's "fanatical worship of the God emperor," and—reflecting Capra's long-standing hatred for the common-man mob—the "mass, the human herd" that had led to the rise of Fascism in Italy. The populations of all three nations, the film explains, are "hopped up on the same idea. Their leaders told them they were supermen."

After depicting German godlessness in a montage showing the destruction of churches, labeling Hitler, Mussolini, and Hirohito as "three gangsters," praising the "free people of China and Russia" for fighting alongside America and England, and evoking the nightmare of a "conquering Jap army marching down Pennsylvania Avenue," and showing a Disney-animated radio tower broadcasting the word "LIES," *Prelude to War* sums up its case: "It's us or them," says Huston. "The chips are down. Two worlds stand against each other. One must die and one must live." With little official guidance and not much to go on but his own instincts and Eric Knight's passion for films "as tough and ferocious . . . as a super-bayonet," Capra had made a case for war that felt like a nonfiction rhetorical extension of *Mr. Smith Goes to Washington* and *Meet John Doe.*

When *Prelude to War* was over, Marshall turned around in his chair, scanning the back of the room for Capra. "Superb!" he exclaimed. "Colonel Capra, how did you do it? That is a most wonderful thing."

"Darling—Have so many things to tell you I don't know where to start. . . . Marshall loved it!" the exuberant director wrote his wife. "He calls me over and says, 'Capra, that's a great job. Every soldier and every civilian should see that picture.' We talked about 15 minutes. . . . Next day [Secretary of War] Mr. Stimson! He brought his wife. . . . The picture knocked them cold. This was the tough hurdle. After the picture Mr. Stimson got up and [walked] all the way across the room to shake my hand and say how fine it was. . . . Now the word was around Washington. . . . To top it all, a White House showing is temporarily slated for Tuesday! . . . I'm a little dizzy."

Capra took Marshall's comment about "every civilian" seeing the picture to heart. Although *Prelude to War* had been made expressly for servicemen, he started envisioning a theatrical release, and took a print to Hollywood, where he showed it to movie-business colleagues and started to lobby for a Best Documentary Oscar nomination.

Mellett, feeling challenged, responded angrily. He wrote a note to Roosevelt calling the movie "a bad picture in some respects, possibly even a dangerous picture," and added, "Engendering nervous hysteria in the army or the civil population might help to win the war, although I doubt it. It won't help in the business of making a saner world" after what he called "the armistice." Mellett's use of the World War I term, reflecting a belief that the war might end with a truce rather than an Allied victory, might have been behind his aversion to films that inflamed Americans against Germany or Japan. But his argument was transparently disingenuous since *The World at War* and *Prelude to War* essentially covered the same material in the same tone.

Mellett's real motive may have been reflected in a wire he sent to the Academy of Motion Picture Arts and Sciences shortly after he wrote to FDR.

Responding to the Academy's request to arrange a screening of *Prelude* for
its members, he wrote acridly, "Appreciate desire of Colonel Capra's Academy
friends but suggest in all sincerity that they refrain from embarrassing him
and other able directors who have entered armed services by confusing their
present service as soldiers with their private careers." Mellett was affronted
that Ford had made *The Battle of Midway* with no input from the OWI and
that Zanuck had apparently been given license to shoot his own movie in
North Africa; Capra's circumvention of his authority was the last straw. "This
is the third instance in which a Hollywood director, put in a service uniform
and given the government's money to spend, has come up with a finished
Hollywood product that has evaded scrutiny by the OWI," he complained. "I
hate to have to spend so much of my time trying to outwit these boys." His
remarks infuriated both Capra and General Osborn, who wrote to Mellett
and told him he had impugned the director's character and should apologize.

Osborn also told Capra to keep his temper, admitting, "I don't know what
got into Lowell Mellett." But Mellett wouldn't back down, and in fact even
raised the stakes by playing on the fears expressed by some movie-house
owners that the government might try to control their wartime bookings. In
letters, Mellett darkly alluded to the possibility that if Capra's picture was
permitted to play in theaters, the army would feel free to start forcing them
to run propaganda films regularly. Capra countered by arguing that Mellett
and the OWI shouldn't be making movies at all. "I have no particular objection to them making semi-propaganda and information films, but then we
shouldn't be making them too," he said, adding that Mellett's office was systematically undercutting the propaganda effort by seizing all the best foreign
footage for itself and leaving him to "beg, plead and steal what crumbs we
can. If we don't get a clear definition of duties between us we will be constantly in competition for the same material," Capra warned, "and will certainly be giving . . . uncorrelated viewpoints."

As 1942 drew to a close, the two men were still locked in an angry stale-
mate. Capra had gotten his Academy screening, but Mellett was still block-
ing a nationwide release for the film. However, Capra could take some
satisfaction in the knowledge that *Prelude to War* was now being shown to all
new army recruits, who had been greeting it with rowdy approval since Oc-

tober. And Knight, who had cowritten the film and was largely responsible for its hard-hitting style, was thrilled. He was still working in the makeshift Washington office that Capra had created in the Department of the Interior's cooling tower, finalizing the scripts for several subsequent *Why We Fight* chapters while Capra remained in California. Every time *Prelude to War* screened in the capital, Knight told him that "there is always one instant reaction: 'Everyone in the U.S. should see it.'" Knight did admit, with great good cheer, that after watching the movie, "I'm afraid a soldier will get the idea that he's got to lick every German and Jap in the world to get victory." And he added a surprising postscript to his letter: The Yorkshire-born Canadian army veteran had, at the age of forty-five, become a U.S. citizen. "Did you know I'm an American now?" he wrote. "I can't say, 'There's the White House we burned' anymore. Every night when I go home now, I say, 'There's our White House that those redcoat bastards burned up.'" Citizenship would give Knight security clearances that would make it easier for him to travel on army business. Six weeks later he was on his way to the Casablanca Conference in Morocco, a meeting at which Roosevelt, Churchill, and de Gaulle were to determine an Allied strategy in Europe for the next phase of the war, when his plane crashed, possibly as the result of antiaircraft fire from a German U-boat. All thirty-five passengers aboard were killed.

TWELVE

"You Might as Well Run into It as Away from It"

THE ALEUTIAN ISLANDS, HOLLYWOOD, WASHINGTON, AND NORTH AFRICA, SEPTEMBER 1942–MAY 1943

Nothing in John Huston's experience, let alone in the minimal amount of army training he had received, had prepared him for life in the Aleutians. Huston left for the island of Adak in mid-September 1942, a week after *Across the Pacific*, the Humphrey Bogart espionage thriller he hadn't quite been able to finish before being called up to duty, opened in New York. He approached his first major wartime assignment with the same kind of methodical precision that he brought to his preparation for any feature film. On graph paper and lined sheets, in tiny, clear handwriting, he kept lists of what he would need to make the documentary he was already envisioning ("aerial photos of Kiska," "tactical maps," "get names of men who've been decorated") right alongside lists of what he would need to get through what looked to be a punishing autumn in the Bering Sea—"toilet articles," "liquor," "tobacco," "bullion cubes," and "two sets of heavy underwear per man." A skilled draftsman, he also filled notebooks with pen-and-ink storyboard sketches in black and blue—an overhead shot of officers and flyers standing over a table studying battle plans; another of the same group, this time poring over a map to be filmed through the gap between an officer's torso and the arm he's resting on the map's corner. "Over these shots," Huston wrote in a note to himself, "explain the tactical principals [*sic*] by which the missions are planned."

Huston was, finally, going off to war. But he hadn't counted on the drab, icy desolation that would overwhelm him when he arrived on the island of Adak. As he surveyed his new home, he started to create thorough, imaginative lists of every shot he wanted and roughed out a tentative script with notes about what images he planned to show in conjunction with particular pieces of narration. But the movie he had structured in his head, a sort of American version of the no-nonsense British documentaries he had seen in which crisp voice-overs described efficient strategy sessions and daring raids, had been conceived for a place that bore little resemblance to this barren landscape with its chilly northern light and uncanny quietude. Huston and his crew were five hundred miles from the Japanese-occupied island of Kiska— "nearer to the enemy than any other American territory anyplace in the world," Huston wrote, and yet so far away that during the first weeks of his stay the army officers stationed there were fairly certain that the Japanese had no idea they were even present. What he called the "strange beauty [of] the Aleutians—undulating hills of spongy moss . . . without a tree or anything like a tree for 1500 miles" and sunny skies that could give way to dank, obliterating fog within a minute—was unearthly to him, and nothing could have seemed less like a battlefront.

Everything on Adak felt makeshift. While the senior officers of Bomber Command and Fighter Command stayed in Quonset huts, the prefabricated shells made of corrugated steel and plywood that the navy had been using since the start of the war, the rank and file, including Huston and his five-man crew, lived in canvas tents scattered along the beachfront. The airstrip, such as it was, consisted of interlocking sheets of metal that had been laid down by navy construction battalions (CBs, or "Seabees"), and the low hills on either side were dotted with dugouts for antiaircraft guns. There was loose talk of an aerial offensive to retake Kiska and Attu from the Japanese sometime in October, presumably before Huston's forty-five-day stint was to end, but nobody seemed in any hurry to clarify exactly what those plans were. The constant threat of fog made for what Huston called "literally the worst flying weather in the world," and the planes the army was planning to use, B-24 bombers, had problems; although they could cover the long distances that would be essential to the mission, they tended to break apart during rough landings, and the placement of their heavy fuel tanks made them more likely to catch fire than the B-17 Flying Fortresses that were being used in Europe.

After Huston had been on Adak for a couple of weeks, he began to realize that the subject of his film might be the particular combination of boredom and fear that characterized life at this outpost—the anticipation, the mundane chores, the uneventful afternoons with nothing to do but wait for the sun to set, the lassitude ("Every day is Sunday," he scribbled onto an early draft of the script), all of which could be unexpectedly cut short by orders for the men to abandon their chatter or poker games and head to their planes for a dry-run mission over Kiska or Attu.

Then, one day while walking across the airstrip, Huston heard the roar of an unfamiliar engine. He looked up to see a Zero on reconnaissance five hundred feet overhead. The Japanese now knew the Americans were there. After that, a more accelerated schedule for the fight to retake the islands became necessary, and Huston started to feel acutely aware that his romantic idea of himself as a roving soldier of fortune–cum–war correspondent was about to be tested against a considerably less glamorous reality. For one thing, he was not, either by training or by natural talent, a cinematographer— "nothing I had ever shot personally as a photographer turned out well," he wrote—which meant that he had to rely a great deal on the men on his team. Before he left for Adak, Huston had consulted with the highly regarded cinematographer James Wong Howe about what kind of production crew he would need. Howe had badly wanted to join Ford's Field Photo Unit, but despite forty years in the United States, as a Chinese national he was ineligible. Eager to help, he ended up advising many Hollywood directors on how to shoot in difficult wartime conditions; he told Huston to request three cinematographers and to keep an eye out for "men who can serve as grips, gaffers, electricians and assistant cameramen—a four way threat as it were."

Huston got approval to bring along five men, one of whom was a cameraman named Rey Scott, who in 1941 had written, produced, and shot a feature-length documentary called *"Kukan": The Battle Cry of China,* about Japan's attack on China in 1940. Scott had wangled an assignment from England's *Daily Telegraph* and had made his way from Hong Kong to the city of Chongqing, where he had stood on the roof of the U.S. embassy and filmed as two hundred tons of Japanese bombs rained on the city all around him. His efforts won him an Academy Award certificate for filming "under the most difficult and dangerous conditions." He was now a lieutenant, Huston's right-hand man on Adak, and, the director said with immense admiration, "a bloody, no-good rogue" and a "crazy son of a bitch—a cameraman who loved being shot at." Big, bearded, and often drunk, Scott, said Huston, had "no regard for appearances, and no particular regard for authority." He was also by all accounts completely fearless, at one point flying nine missions in six days.

The conditions for shooting documentary footage could hardly have been worse. The Kodachrome film that Huston had brought with him required a level of bright light that was in short supply in the Aleutians. Aside from that, Huston, for all his taste for adventure, found the work terrifying. He took his role seriously; he believed that the army had essentially asked him to serve not as a propagandist but as a war reporter and that shirking from any chance to obtain information would constitute a dereliction of duty, so he never backed away from an opportunity to fly a mission in a B-24. But he quickly came to believe that his very presence in a plane was a bad omen. "Every time I went with them," he recalled, "shit, something awful happened, and I got to be known as a Jonah. Bombs wouldn't work; people would be shot out from under me."

The first time Huston rode along on a mission, it was aborted. The bomber he was in was late taking off because the crew's tail gunner couldn't be found, and, low on fuel and unable to catch up with the rest of the formation, the plane was ordered to turn back when it was still a hundred miles from Kiska. When it touched down on the airstrip back at Adak during a sky-blackening rainstorm, the brakes froze and the B-24 screamed down the runway, shearing off the wings of two other planes and skidding to a halt in a field, still carrying its full bomb payload. "Christ! We've got to get out of here before the bombs go off!" someone yelled as the crew, trailed by Huston, raced to get out of the plane through its only unjammed door. Huston ran around to the nose, trying to get some footage as a rescue ground crew attempted to extricate the unconscious pilot and copilot from the cockpit. Then, he recalled, "I began to shake uncontrollably. I put the camera down and ran." On his second air mission, Huston was filming a Zero from over the shoulder of a B-24's waist gunner in the center of the plane when the Zero fired back and the soldier fell dead at his feet. On another flight, Huston and his men came back empty-handed because of the simplest of rookie film-making mistakes; after loading the camera, he had forgotten to run out the "leader"—the strip of celluloid that precedes the unexposed film—so no images were captured.

Whenever Rey Scott would get in a plane to shoot a mission, he would calmly leave his watch, his life insurance policy, and a letter of instruction on a piece of plywood near his gear, always assuming that he wouldn't be back. Just as Ford had been at Midway, Huston was awed by the indifference to danger expressed by the men around him. He once listened to Colonel William Eareckson, who led the Aleutian bombing missions from Adak, tell his pilots that if they came under fire from Zeroes, there was little point in trying to take evasive action. "When you get into your run, stay there," he said to the men. "You might as well run into it as away from it. And if someone plucks you by the sleeve and you look around and it's a man with a long white beard, well, your troubles are all over."

As Huston's forty-five days on Adak turned into two months, then three, then a fourth, he found himself "getting into a high state of nerves." One night he and his men were asleep in their tents when they were awakened by a series of explosions followed by three sharp shots—the army signal for "Stand By to Repel Japanese Landing." Convinced that they were about to find themselves in direct combat with the Imperial Navy, they ran for the slit trenches they had dug and waited ninety minutes before the all-clear sounded and they could go back to their tents and try to calm themselves and get some rest. The same jolting alarm was repeated the next night, and the next, and the next. "The thunder of engines makes the earth tremble and the ravens rise," he wrote in his journal as the bombs fell in the distance. "Soon the earth below will blaze with hatred." By late December, Huston felt he had all the footage he could use. Kiska and Attu were still in the hands of the Japanese, but there was no knowing when or if they would be retaken. He asked for and received permission for a thirty-day leave during which he would go home to Hollywood, visit his family, and begin to pull together a documentary. It was with a sense of flooding relief that Huston boarded USS *Grant* and made his way to Kodiak, then Anchorage, then Whitehorse in the Yukon, Prince George, Vancouver, Seattle, and finally Hollywood.

Back at home, he was able to relax. With the Aleutians initiative seemingly stalled, the army was in no special hurry to have him complete his film, and investigators were no longer monitoring his every move. Unbeknownst to Huston, the army's probe into his suspected Communist ties had proceeded straight through his time on Adak, with military investigators questioning his friends, colleagues, and employers at Warner Bros. Along with many others in Hollywood, Huston had been flagged because in the 1930s he had joined the League of American Writers, which had been founded by the CPUSA (Communist Party USA), in order to support Republican Spain; he had also been a sponsor of the National Fund Raising Campaign for Russian Relief. It is unclear who initiated the inquiry, but it came to a dead halt as soon as it reached Huston's immediate superiors in the army. Colonel Schlossberg, though still no fan of Hollywood directors in uniform, exonerated Huston in his final report, writing, "His loyalty and integrity to the United States is unquestioned. . . . Lt. Huston has no Nazi, Fascist, or Communistic ties whatsoever." Although his allegiance to the United States was no longer in doubt, his priorities were. One of his army colleagues described him as "one who cares for nothing else and talked of nothing else but the picture business" and "one who was self-centered." Schlossberg's report recommended that he not be given any assignment that would involve "access to confidential or secret information, and that he be kept under observation" while in the Aleutians. However, with Huston's return from Adak, the army closed its file on him for the duration of the war.

In California, Huston was able to spend some time with his father, who had recently finished playing "Uncle Sam" in Toland's still unreleased *December 7th* project and was also doing a good deal of voice-over work for Capra's office on various propaganda and informational films. John told Walter that he wanted him to narrate *Report from the Aleutians* once he had finished editing it, and he spent a little time working on the film at Capra's Fort Fox facility. But when his thirty-day leave ended, Huston relocated to the East Coast, where the army had leased space for its filmmakers at Astoria Studios in Queens.

Huston was still married to Lesley Black and involved with Olivia de Havilland, but neither circumstance prevented him from pursuing a new romance. In New York, he was instantly smitten with a young, beautiful, and married socialite named Marietta Fitzgerald (later and better known as Marietta Tree), who met him at a dinner at "21" hosted by the playwright Sidney Kingsley and made a lasting impression on Huston by fainting in front of him. Fitzgerald's husband was away at war, and although their involvement initially remained platonic, "it was a very romantic period and he had knockout charm," she told Huston biographer Lawrence Grobel. "John's outlook was so arresting and exciting. Everything he said was an astonishment, and of intense interest. I was overwhelmed by his knowledge. . . . There was nothing thin or superficial about him."

Huston was more than happy to be out of Los Angeles, where the lively party circuit of actors, agents, and executives that had until recently been at the heart of his social life now felt alien to him. "Having just returned from working with authentic heroes," he wrote, "I was in no mood to put up with the screen variety." New York seemed livelier, more heterogeneous, and pleasingly chaotic. On a bar crawl through Manhattan, he found himself alongside H. L. Mencken on one night, Robert Flaherty on another. And the Army Photographic Center in Astoria, where Huston did most of his work on *Report from the Aleutians* as 1943 began, was, he wrote, "colorful, to say the least"—a teeming, loosely managed facility where talents as diverse as William Saroyan, Clifford Odets, and Burgess Meredith were all hard at work on different projects. Huston loved his brief time there, and believed that the level of talent surrounding him exceeded that of "most of the Hollywood professionals" with whom he had worked.

Rey Scott, his fearless Adak cameraman, wound up at the Army Photographic Center as well, and so did Irwin Shaw, now a private first class who was still looking to find his place in a filmmaking unit. Shaw had been sent east by the army, and as a member of Capra's team found himself traveling back and forth between New York and Washington, D.C., on various short-term assignments, but he was just barely managing to stay out of trouble. One night, he was at the entrance of a private dining room in Washington's Statler Hilton, ready to throw a punch at a maître d' who was barring him from entering. Shaw was convinced that he was being kept out of the dining room because of anti-Semitism, and he was on the verge of starting a brawl with a civilian—an infraction that could get a soldier court-martialed—when a major who was out to dinner with his family saw what was happening and rushed over. He calmed Shaw down and explained to him that he wasn't being prevented from entry because he was a Jew but because he was a private: The hotel's restaurant had an officers-only policy.

The major who saved Shaw from serious trouble that night was George Stevens, and his calm, unflustered sense of quiet authority made a strong impression on the hotheaded young author. Shaw was moved to see Stevens in uniform, just as he had been months earlier to see Wyler join up. "These were men who were way past military age who were all rather pacifistic," he recalled. "Not pacifistic when it came to dealing with studio heads . . . but all very liberal men who had grown up with pacifistic ideas. And one and all, they gave up very lucrative and prestigious careers and went right into the Army. And they put themselves at the disposal of the Army even though they knew . . . that the possibility of making great pictures was almost nonexistent, because what the Army wanted from us was propaganda to help win the war, [and] propaganda doesn't make great pictures."

Stevens was probably less concerned with making "great pictures" during his army years than were any of the major Hollywood directors who had preceded him into war; he was simply excited and ready for his service to begin—and still wondering where it would take him. In the fall of 1942, he had shot his last movie, *The More the Merrier*, for Columbia. Cary Grant, his three-time leading man and first choice to star, had become unavailable, so Stevens teamed Joel McCrea with Jean Arthur for what turned out to be one of the most sophisticated and charming home-front romantic comedies of the era. The film drew on wartime headlines in the lightest possible way; it was set in Washington, D.C., where so many young soldiers were billeted that within a few months after Pearl Harbor the district found itself in the middle of a major housing shortage. Against this backdrop—a city full of young "government girls" and rowdy GIs who were just passing through—Stevens created a romantic fairy tale with one foot in contemporary reality. He cast Arthur as Connie, a young woman who rents half of her apartment to a kindly old retiree named Dingle (played by jowly character actor Charles Coburn), who in turn rents half of *his* half to a handsome young guy named Joe (McCrea) who's temporarily stuck in Washington waiting for his rather nebulous orders (he'll "go where they send me—the government").

Stevens had shot *The More the Merrier* with the purposefulness and ease of a man who was finally getting what he wanted, but the picture made almost everyone else involved in its production terribly nervous. They seemed bewildered, if not downright frightened, by its combination of farcical shenanigans and a script so current that it not only acknowledged the housing shortage but recent news about the war in the Pacific ("Oh, Jimmy Doolittle flew over the seas / He wants to nip at the Nipponese," Dingle sings at one point). McCrea, who had recently starred in a pair of comedies for Preston Sturges, asked his agent to get him out of the movie after the first day of rehearsal and had to be talked into returning. Harry Cohn panicked that the movie would make light of people in the service; Stevens had to reassure him that a scene with a group of WACs enjoying themselves in a D.C. bar would not include anyone in uniform. The Breen Office, which administered the Production Code, was convulsed with distress at the opportunity for innuendo created by so many beds in such close quarters and by the film's depiction of Washington's "eight gals to every fella" atmosphere: "We deem it very essential that these beds be a few inches from the thin partition which separates the two rooms," Breen warned. "This is vitally important." In addition, Breen recommended that "'bathroom gags' be minimized and some of them eliminated. . . . It is unacceptable to show Joe merely clad in his BVDs. He should be wearing some sort of bathrobe at all times." The Production Code office also insisted that the script be approved by the FBI, since the bureau was mentioned in dialogue (J. Edgar Hoover signed off on it personally). And Breen asked that the phrase "Damn the torpedoes, full speed ahead!" be deleted, a request so prim that Cohn felt free to ignore it. Cohn didn't even know what to call the movie; at one point Columbia offered a fifty-dollar savings bond to any studio employee who could come up with a title (among the names tested were *Love Is Patriotic Too* and *Come One, Come All*).

None of the anxiety touched Stevens. He worked with care and grace, particularly to shape the tender, adult, and erotically charged relationship between McCrea and Arthur, but he did so without subjecting the cast and crew to his characteristic delays and silences, and he didn't linger. In January 1943 he put together a cut of the film, tested it twice in front of preview audiences, and packed his bags without giving it another look; to Cohn's evident distress, his contract was fulfilled. Cohn still wasn't ready to let go: "George Stevens is leaving at the end of the week to enter the Service of his Country," he wrote in a memo that seemed to express equal parts admiration and despair. He added, hopefully, "Anyone to whom you assign his office must take it with the understanding that he will vacate it when Mr. Stevens returns."

After Stevens's year of deliberation, his transition from director to major happened so quickly that, in the memory of his son, "One day he came home and told my mother, 'I've joined the Army.'" On Jan. 6, Capra's office sent a letter to Stevens's local draft board in North Hollywood explaining that he would be "sent by the Special Service Division of the War Department on a mission outside the continental limits of the United States for an indefinite period." Stevens received his letter of commission two days later. "I certainly didn't know whether I was ever going to pick up a life with films again," he said. "Everyone said, who knows, that might be the end for you."

More than most other directors, Stevens seemed to be at peace with that possibility. At thirty-eight, he considered himself to be "retired" after a fine career in the movies, and was now moving on to the next phase of his life. In February he packed his uniform and whatever Kodachrome film he could carry, traveled to New York City with his family, and prepared for his departure, taking George Jr. sightseeing and signing over his power of attorney to his wife, Yvonne. He then went to Washington for a quick check-in with Capra, and returned to New York on a TWA flight to say a final goodbye to his wife and son.

The Stevenses were already adjusting to the downsized life of a military family; their room in the Waldorf-Astoria was one of the tiny ones that the hotel had set aside for officers who were paying the five-dollars-per-night rate that the army permitted. Stevens received his immunization shots and was just a day or two from beginning service when he became sick. In January, Stevens had had an appendectomy and was still weak. Soon after arriving in Manhattan, he became so ill with pneumonia, made worse by his chronic asthma, that he had to be hospitalized at Fort Jay on Governors Island in New York Harbor, where it took him weeks to recover. Through March, Stevens and his family lingered in a kind of limbo far from their California home—Yonnie and George Jr. in a New York hotel room, Stevens in a hospital bed. It was almost April before he was well enough to be released.

Stevens and his family took the train back to Washington, where he met with his army supervisor, Colonel Lyman Munson, and Darryl Zanuck, who was still working on his documentary, to discuss an assignment that would send him to North Africa. There was time for him to take in the opening day of baseball season with George Jr., but five days later, on Easter Sunday 1943, "separation was really upon us," he wrote in his diary. "Got up early and had breakfast with my two dear ones. We all felt pretty blue. . . . I had a hard time to keep my eyes dry when I kissed my dear little boy and my dear little wife good-by. I'm so happy when I'm with those two. They are both so fine. I'm a very lucky person to have them for my own. I will be very happy when I can come back to them."

The next week was one of the most disorienting Stevens had ever experienced. He was shipping out with only the vaguest orders, and every time he got back into military transport for the next leg of his long journey, he found himself another degree farther from anything he could call familiar. From Washington, he was flown to Miami, then to British Guiana, then to Brazil, and then to Nigeria, where he arrived in the sweltering military garrison in Maiduguri and dropped his gear in a makeshift bunkroom, still not sure what he was supposed to do there. "Almost everyone sick," he wrote. "Slept on the porch of the barracks right by the door." He went to bed pouring sweat under nothing but mosquito netting, then woke up freezing and looking for a blanket. The next morning, he was back on an army puddle-jumper, bound east for Khartoum. He and his men grabbed a brief nap there—they barely knew what time of day it was anymore—and were awakened at 1:15 a.m., given breakfast, and driven to an airstrip. "We flew along in the dark, down the Nile Valley," he wrote. The men bundled up in the blackness against the plane's metal hull, shivering until 5 a.m., when they saw the sun rise. They tried not to vomit as the plane bounced in the choppy air.

They landed in Cairo, where Stevens had an unlikely encounter with Hollywood, which now seemed many worlds away. He was taken to an open-air amphitheater where hundreds of American GIs, starved for entertainment or any taste of home, were treated to a two-year-old 20th Century Fox thriller called *I Wake Up Screaming* that featured Betty Grable, a popular starlet whose pin-up pictures had made her an army favorite. "It was a film you would avoid seeing," said Stevens. "It just wasn't my cup of tea. But I sat there with 20,000 other guys, and I saw the Passion Play! . . . There was a good sister and a bad sister, and a foreign chap, and what do you think—it's the bad sister who's winning all the way. Betty Grable is the good sister, because she's glossy and cute and the G.I.'s dream." Every moment in the movie, Stevens recalled, had "fifty times the weight on each individual" than its makers had intended. Cut off from the simplest experiences of their lives back home—a date, a night out, a soda fountain, a kiss—the men experienced what Stevens called a "catharsis" through exactly the kind of work he had been so eager to leave behind. "I was a little bit more of a person after that," he said.

But he was back on the road the next day, this time headed for Tripoli and then Benghazi, where the only sign of war he saw was the graffiti "Hitler is bastard" that someone had chalked onto a piece of concrete. He knew he was getting closer to the action because he and his men were now accompanied by air escort as they flew into Algeria, first to Constantine and then to Algiers. The day he arrived, more than two weeks after leaving Washington, D.C., *The More the Merrier* was opening four thousand miles away in New York. *Time* magazine called it "a smart, civilized [comedy] about wartime that does credit to Director George Stevens (now an Army major) as his last civilian job."

Stevens was finally where he wanted to be—he was ready to shoot the campaign in North Africa that the Allies had been successfully waging for more than six months, pushing the Axis forces to retreat all the way to Italy. He stepped off the plane into Algiers, the city that had served as the campaign's central base of operations, and was surprised to find himself in an atmosphere of unhurried comradeship and general relaxation. Hitler's army in central Tunisia had been badly beaten and was one day from surrendering. The campaign was over. There was no combat left to film. Stevens had, so far, filled his journals with thoughtful notes and observations. "Life's a journey," he wrote at one point early in his war travels, "and it's always most interesting when you're not sure where you're going." But on the day he learned he had gotten to Algeria too late, he confined his entry to three words: "THIS DAMN WAR."

THIRTEEN

"Just Enough to Make It Seem Less Than Real"

ENGLAND, HOLLYWOOD, AND WASHINGTON, JANUARY-MAY 1943

A s the new year began, William Wyler was starting to wonder if he was fated to sit out the war in a London hotel room without ever shooting a frame of film. He rang in 1943 at Claridge's drinking bad scotch with William Clothier and Harold Tannenbaum, both members of his crew—although they could scarcely be called a crew since all they did was show up regularly at Army Air Force headquarters on Grosvenor Square and ask if any orders had come through. It had been more than four months since Wyler had been instructed to "organize and operate the activities of the Eighth Air Force Technical Training film unit," but, as his supervisor wrote in a sympathetic memo, those orders "did not state with 'what' he was to organize and operate it, nor where or how he would get the 'what.'"

In the fall, Wyler had asked Major General Ira Eaker, the head of the Eighth Air Force, if there was anything he could do to help him get to an airbase. Wyler had already requested flight training that would allow him and his small team to be aboard the B-17s as they went on their bombing missions; without that training, they would be limited to serving as a ground crew, trying to teach gunners how to operate cameras when they weren't shooting at the enemy, and then watching the planes take off and hoping that young men who had never even held cameras before would return with usable footage. Eaker responded with a memo in which he ordered that Wyler be granted "the necessary directives . . . funds . . . and authority" to start making a documentary about "the U.S. Army Air Force carrying the air war to the enemy." He also gave Wyler a new on-site boss who was sympathetic to his frustration: Lieutenant Colonel Beirne Lay, who had written the screenplay for a popular 1941 drama about the Air Corps called *I Wanted Wings* and who was instructed to get Wyler what he needed and then light a fire under him.

When Lay first met Wyler at Claridge's, "Willy had this brand-new uniform and his military experience consisted of that—a change of wardrobe," he told Wyler biographer Axel Madsen. "I was immediately struck by his warmth, his intelligence, and his enormous inferiority complex. . . . He had been a general on Hollywood sets, and here, he was completely lost." Lay soon realized that Wyler had no idea how to negotiate army bureaucracy and was instead spending most of his time bogging down in internecine disputes. He wasn't getting along with his handpicked writer Jerome Chodorov, who was urging Wyler to use reenactments to make his documentaries rather than to insist on actual flight footage. In addition, producer Hal Roach, who had committed his independent film company to making war documentaries and was now in London, had been overseeing him with a heavy and obstructive hand. Lay reassigned both of them and became Wyler's champion just as the army was about to write the director off as ineffectual and out of his depth.

Wyler still had only one piece of equipment—the camera he had brought with him—and his unit was "only partially functioning," Lay wrote in a stinging army memo. Tannenbaum, who had been brought over to record sound, was now training as a cameraman, since nobody believed that the sound equipment he needed would ever cross the Atlantic. "Supply agencies have appeared to be mystified by the existence of a Film Unit," Lay wrote, since the general who had given Wyler his assignment at a Washington, D.C., party back in June had never followed up with any official orders. As a result, "one of the most talented directors in the world, with tremendous prestige in British film circles, was dispatched to England without funds, without a qualified Army officer assistant, without a written directive from Washington and without an organization, and was instructed on arrival to make pictures. Major Wyler attempted this task, starting out minus an office, a car, or even a typewriter, and with no knowledge of Army procedures." Lay concluded his report by stating his "considered belief that the highest credit is reflected on Major Wyler by the patience, initiative, humbleness and loyalty to duty he has displayed under the most discouraging circumstances."

Lay was able to do what Wyler couldn't; his stern report thrashed through army red tape, and in early February, Wyler and his men finally received approval to attend gunnery school for four days. During the long wait, Wyler had merged his two best ideas for documentaries into one—he now wanted to make a film that portrayed the crew of a B-17 bomber as it flew a single mission. But before he would be permitted to fly, he needed a quick education in aerial combat photography. "We had to learn aircraft recognition, so we would shoot at enemy planes and not our own," he said. In addition, Wyler and his men would need to learn how to "take a machine gun apart and put it back in 60-degree-below-zero weather" and how to operate their equipment behind heavy masks that were attached to oxygen bottles, since the B-17s were uninsulated, unpressurized, and so cold that frostbite was taking a substantial number of flyers out of the action.

Wyler's mission was almost cut short before he ever got off the ground when a 50-millimeter cannon exploded near his face as he was learning how to fire it. He dashed off a letter to Talli assuring her that the headlines the incident had made back in the States ("Director Escapes Injury") had exaggerated the danger he had been in, although, he added, "I was also glad to see I wasn't forgotten."

A few weeks later, in the middle of the night, he was awakened and driven along blacked-out roads to Bassingbourn Air Field, twenty miles north of London, where he arrived at 4 a.m. for his first mission, which would be aboard a B-17 nicknamed the *Jersey Bounce*. The bomber's captain, Robert Morgan, was a twenty-four-year-old from South Carolina; he had been piloting another plane since November, but on its most recent mission a week earlier, the *Memphis Belle* had sustained serious damage and was temporarily out of commission. Only a dozen B-17s would go out that day; the 91st Bomb Group, known as the "Ragged Irregulars," had been flying first over occupied France and then over Germany itself, and by the time Wyler got there almost half of its fleet of thirty-six planes had either been shot down or grounded for repairs.

The bombing missions that the 91st undertook were high-risk even before the planes reached enemy territory. The B-17s would typically fly northeast over the North Sea with ten-man crews, and their necessarily rapid ascent from six thousand to twenty-six thousand feet would often cause engine or fuel-pressure problems. On February 26, 1943, just before dawn, the plan was to bomb Bremen in northwest Germany. Wyler was worried enough to write another short letter to Talli before taking off: "All my thoughts are with you and the children—just in case—But I'll be back. Love darling, Willy."

The mission that day was not a success. "Nothing happened as it should," wrote Clarence Winchell, the *Jersey Bounce*'s waist gunner, in his diary. A navigation miscalculation put the plane on a course far south of Bremen, which brought it directly into the line of German fire. Over the North Sea, "the flak was terrific," Wyler recalled. "We'd fly through entire belts of it, so thick that . . . the blue sky looked like a punctured sieve." With Bremen under heavy cloud cover, the Allied planes were redirected sixty miles northwest to the coastal town of Wilhelmshaven, which housed a German naval base.

As they flew, Wyler moved up and down the plane's catwalk, trying to get a shot through one of the gun openings on the plane's sides and in its tail. Because everyone wore oxygen masks and the roar of the plane's four engines obliterated every sound but gunfire, the only possible communication was over the open speakers the crew shared. The gunners and navigators weren't sure what to make of the slightly rotund, bespectacled, vaguely foreign-sounding man almost twice their age who had no fixed position and was manning not a gun but a camera. "We could hear him cuss over the intercom," said Vincent Evans, the crew's twenty-two-year-old bombardier. "By the time he'd swung his camera over to a flak burst, it was lost. Then he'd see another burst, try to get it, miss, see another, try that, miss, try, miss. Then we'd hear him over the intercom, asking the pilot if he couldn't possibly get the plane closer to the flak."

The *Bounce* ended up dropping its bomb payload into the harbor short of

Wilhelmshaven. Wyler tried to film from the nose of the plane, but in the 60-degree-below conditions, his camera had frozen. By the time the plane returned to Bassingbourn that afternoon, it was clear that the American losses had been terrible. Seven B-17s had gone down, and dozens of men were dead, missing, injured, or hypothermic, a toll that resounded all the more loudly because the 91st had decided to use that mission as the first-ever fly-along opportunity for half a dozen Allied journalists, each in a different plane. One of them was twenty-six-year-old Walter Cronkite, who called the time in his plane "a hell 26,000 feet above the earth" and described "Fortresses and [B-24] Liberators plucked out of the formations around us" and plummeting into the sea. But Cronkite also wrote of the extraordinary excitement of seeing bombs with inscriptions like "Nuts to Hitler—Love, Mabel" hit their targets. His impassioned account of the heroism of the bombardiers ("Talk about concentration!"), navigators, pilots, and gunners ("Kids in their early 20s who are now old-timers in air warfare") helped to create a new breed of war hero as America's focus started to shift from the Pacific to Europe, and Hollywood pictures like Howard Hawks's *Air Force* began to capture their imaginations.

Wyler couldn't wait to go up again; he was finally where he wanted to be. A week after he flew his first mission, the Academy Awards were held at the Coconut Grove in Los Angeles's Ambassador Hotel. *Mrs. Miniver* led the field with twelve nominations and was heavily favored to win, but when Wyler thought of the movie at all these days, it was with a combination of pride in its reception and embarrassment. Just before he went to Bassingbourn, Beirne Lay had arranged a showing of the film for high-ranking British officers. Before the first hour was over, they were audibly affected by what they were watching. "It was a handkerchief job," said Lay. "You could hear people sobbing and sniffing all over the room." Wyler, sitting in the back, felt more than slightly embarrassed. "I made this picture and I didn't know what I was doing," he told Lay beforehand, in a futile attempt to beg off of attending the screening. "Now, with an audience like this . . . !" After the film ended, Wyler's cheeks were also wet, but he dismissed his own work by saying, "Christ, what a tearjerker!"

The months Wyler had spent watching Londoners deal with the strains of the blackout and the Blitz, trying to go about their daily lives even as those lives were threatened, made him feel that he had sold the public a sentimental, glamorized version of life during wartime. "As soon as I went to England," he said shortly after the war, "I began to see all the mistakes I had made [in *Mrs. Miniver*], small errors of emphasis, little details unimportant in themselves, but just enough to make it seem less than real." By Oscar night, every one of those mistakes had become a mortification for him. "I was handicapped by dealing with places, periods I knew nothing about," he said. "I had Greer Garson running out on an airfield in Britain to wave her son tearfully goodbye as he flew off in a Spitfire. Ridiculous!"

Wyler didn't go home for the Oscars: Talli attended in his place. By now, it was no longer a novelty that the ceremony was filled with talk of the war and designed as a conspicuous demonstration of patriotism: Jeanette MacDonald opened by singing the national anthem, Tyrone Power and Alan Ladd appeared in uniform, carrying the flag, and Bob Hope cracked jokes about how the day was nigh when every last leading man would join up and romantic parts would have to be played by senior citizens. As the evening began, Walter Wanger read out a letter from President Roosevelt to an uncomfortably crowded audience. "It is a matter of deep satisfaction to me, as it must be to you, that we have succeeded in turning the tremendous power of the motion picture into an effective war instrument without the slightest resort to the totalitarian methods of our enemies," Roosevelt had written. He went on to warn the audience that "in the months to come, war conditions may [require] the motion picture industry to play an even larger part in the war against Axis tyranny. . . . I know that you will not fail the American people and the cause of democracy."

The Oscars that night unfolded so tediously, with so many long speeches and presentations, that they finally wrapped up five hours after the guests had sat down to dinner. Academy cofounder Mary Pickford told reporters that she didn't know who to blame for such a fiasco because "no one person could arrange anything this boring." But in the end, *Mrs. Miniver* emerged triumphant with six awards; Wyler, on his fifth try, had finally won a Best Director Oscar. "I wish he could be here," said Talli, who accepted the award from Frank Capra. "He's wanted an Oscar for a long time. I know it would thrill him a lot, almost as much as that flight over Wilhelmshaven."

A few hours later, a writer for the army paper *Stars and Stripes* arrived at Bassingbourn to interview Wyler. "Have you got a photograph of yourself?" the reporter asked.

"I don't know," he said. "What do you want one for?"

"You won the Academy Award," the reporter told him.

Wyler smiled and said, "Well, I'll be damned."

As congratulatory telegrams poured into air force headquarters and MGM took out trade ads congratulating "Major William Wyler" on what the *Los Angeles Herald Express* called "a clean sweep, almost like the year *Gone With The Wind* grabbed most of the honors," Wyler allowed himself a moment to savor his victory. Sam Goldwyn told him it was "the most popular award ever made." "Will, you bridesmaid!" joked Huston. And Talli wrote, "My darling, how I missed you tonight, but I love collecting Oscars. We must do it more often."

"Darling terribly thrilled family enlarged by Oscar," Wyler cabled back. "Must make postwar plans to build trophy room. . . . All my love and don't let Cathy play with my new doll."

"Now I feel I can win the war," Wyler told his publicist Mack Millar. "Only hope it won't take as long."

Ford and Capra also emerged from the Academy Awards that night able to claim victory. Both men saw their skilled manipulation of the system pay off as two of the four Oscars for Best Documentary were awarded to *The Battle of Midway* and—although it still had not received permission for a theatrical release—*Prelude to War.** But those awards came at a cost: Ford and Capra had each run afoul of Mellett, whose insistence on exerting his authority both in and out of Hollywood was rapidly making him one of the industry's least popular figures. Mellett's clout with the studios was undeniable; it was almost mandatory that he be invited to speak at the Oscar cere-

---

* The other two winners were also war documentaries—the Australian News Information Bureau's *Kokoda Front Line* and Russia's *Moscow Strikes Back*.

mony that evening, but his remarks and reassurances struck many of the guests at the Coconut Grove as hollow. "If the assembled industry people expected to hear anything new from Mr. Mellett, they were doomed to disappointment," wrote the *Hollywood Reporter* the next day, "for he merely reiterated in his speech . . . the same things he has been saying right along—that the government has no desire or intention of telling the industry how to make pictures."

The exception was, of course, pictures that were being made by or for the government, and even as Ford was reaping acclaim for *The Battle of Midway*, Mellett was causing him and the entire Field Photo Unit some serious embarrassment over *December 7th*. A year after being assigned to Hawaii, Gregg Toland had finally finished his first cut, and when Mellett was given an advance look at the resulting picture, he was horrified—and not only at its eighty-five-minute length or at Toland's free use of reenactments to depict the Pearl Harbor attack (only a few moments of which had been captured by any cameras that day). The picture's virulent and lengthy invective against Japanese Americans took the very ugliness the Bureau of Motion Pictures had tried to countermand after *Little Tokyo, U.S.A.* and reiterated it; any moviegoer who saw it would assume that racist hypervigilance against suspected domestic treachery had now become official government policy. Toland had used his film to excoriate the U.S. government and in particular the navy for its lack of preparedness before the Pearl Harbor attack, and also to suggest that the large immigrant population of Hawaii was rife with enemy agents.

December 7th went further than the most exploitative Hollywood picture in suggesting that every bilingual sign in a shop represented a threat to national security. Hawaii's 150,000 residents of Japanese origin were, according to the movie's narration, a grave menace: "Inch by inch, their sons and grandsons . . . began to penetrate into the industrial life of the islands. And all the time, their numbers kept growing. Yep, there are a lot of 'em." In the fanciful, paranoid dialogue that the filmmakers had fashioned between Walter Huston's Uncle Sam and Harry Davenport's "Mr. C"—his conscience—Sam asserts that all Japanese immigrants live in "an American spirit," and Mr. C snaps back, "A *hyphenated* spirit." A long montage follows in which white people are seen chatting heedlessly about national security matters in front of placid Japanese barbers and gardeners who wear expressions of ste-reotypical inscrutability, the implication being that the walls have ears and every bystander is a spy. The Japanese in Hawaii even have access to a tele-phone book "published for them," warns the narrator. "In *Japanese*."

Mellett had suspected that *December 7th* would be unreleasable as soon as he was shown Toland's completed script. At the end of 1942, he wrote to Undersecretary of the Navy James Forrestal that "this project, as a picture for public exhibition, should be stopped . . . not merely because it seems certain to be a very, very bad picture per se, but because the whole approach is, in my opinion, unwise from the government's standpoint. It is a fictional treatment of a very real fact, the tragic disaster at Pearl Harbor, and I do not believe the government should engage in fiction."

The completed film only confirmed Mellett's worst fears. Ford and Toland had been loaned the very limited amount of footage shot during the attack, which included the bombing and explosion of USS *Arizona*, on which 1,177 officers and seamen were killed. But they had used it as a visual reference to create a version of the bombing of Pearl Harbor that employed model-plane Zeroes built by 20th Century Fox's special effects department and Hollywood-style close-ups of American soldiers and sailors—some filmed in Hawaii, some on the Fox lot—firing back as the enemy strafed the harbor.

Mellett was the first prominent government official to raise his voice about issues of accuracy, policies of disclosure, and the ethics of reenact-ment in filmed propaganda. More than a year after Pearl Harbor, the War Department still had not formalized any policies for films that were made or released under its imprimatur. After he saw the film, Mellett took his com-plaints up the chain of command. While he believed the public should have the opportunity to view the documentary footage that Ford and Toland had overseen of the reconstruction of the Pacific fleet, it would have to be ex-tracted from *December 7th* and shown in another form. Mellett marshaled the support of his boss Elmer Davis, who ran the Office of War Information and agreed with his assessment that "presentation of fictional propaganda . . . would seem to be an improper activity for the U.S. government."

Ford was, for the first time since the war had begun, in the doghouse, and even the protection of Bill Donovan was an insufficient shield. *December 7th* had from the beginning been a project of special interest to Roosevelt, who saw news of the rebuilding of naval strength in the Pacific as vital to national morale. Now the film had come in long, late, and so inadequate that Secretary of War Henry L. Stimson agreed it could not be released. In the spring of 1943, Roosevelt issued a directive that in the future, all movies produced by Field Photo would be subject to censorship by the War Department. Toland, who had nursed hopes of using the movie to make the jump from cinematography to direction once he got back to Hollywood, was shattered; although he was still a part of Field Photo, he requested reassignment to South America, and he and Ford never worked together again.

As the film historian Tag Gallagher has noted, the strongly anti-Japanese tone of Toland's cut may have been, rather than a reflection of personal bias or conviction, an attempt to justify Roosevelt's internment policy. As it stood, the picture reflected the War Department and the administration's conflicted instincts about how to depict Japan, Japanese nationals, and immigrants—the same problem that was continuing to bedevil Capra as he worked on the *Know Your Enemy* series. Ford had been concerned about the direction Toland was taking from the time he first arrived in Honolulu, but it remains unclear whether he distanced himself from *December 7th* only after the negative reaction or whether, absorbed in his own work after Midway, he had failed to give Toland much attention and was taken by surprise at how far off track he had gone. But there was no doubt that he was expected to shoulder a share of the blame for the movie's failure.

Ford was returned to his office in Washington, D.C., and unofficially grounded there for the foreseeable future. With Toland gone, he and Robert Parrish worked to save face by attempting to reshape *December 7th* into something that could be shown publicly, and they wasted little time or sentimentality in doing so. Two of his most trusted writers, Frank Wead and James Kevin McGuinness, started to work on a revised narration script for the film, and McGuinness advised Ford to take out anything that smacked of editorializing or fictionalizing: "Crowd in every interesting foot of the salvage operations . . . and finish off with a burst of glory when the battle wagons put to sea again." Ford discarded Toland's first forty minutes almost completely. He left in a brief appearance by Huston as a sleeping giant but removed an exchange in which Mr. C chided Uncle Sam by saying, "You've done a lot of vacationing this year." Toland's montage of Hawaii store signs with ominous Japanese lettering and his race-baiting history of the Japanese in Hawaii were also swept away. And Ford discarded the movie's final act—a long scene set in heaven in which a soldier (Dana Andrews) who died at Pearl Harbor reminisces with other veterans of American wars and uses a particularly tortured metaphor to discuss the eventual outcome of World War II. "I'm puttin' my dough on a ball slugger called reason," says Andrews, "on a pitcher called common sense, on an outfield called decency, faith, brotherhood, religion. Teams like that are warming up all over the globe. They're in spring training now. But when the season starts, they're gonna be all out there, slugging, pitching, feeling their way to a World Series pennant called peace."

By the time Ford and Parrish were finished, *December 7th* had been shortened from eighty-five to thirty-four minutes and remade as a more sentimental, straightforward, and unmistakably Fordian film—a less visually dramatic cousin to *The Battle of Midway*. As he had done in the earlier movie, Ford started with a vision of a quiet and unspoiled island that was soon to be marred by the sounds and sights of war. He filled the soundtrack with favorite songs, several of which, including "My Country 'Tis of Thee" and "Anchors Aweigh," had been used in *Midway*. And he interrupted the picture's newsreel-style narration for a sequence in which viewers meet some of the American sailors who died—an idea that had probably been his all along. "Who were these young Americans? Let us pause for a few minutes at their hallowed graves and ask them to make themselves known," says the narrator. "Who are you boys? Come on, speak up, some of you!" The "boys" pointedly represent an ethnically diverse group—an Irishman from Ohio, a German from Iowa, a Jew named Rosenthal from Brooklyn, a black man from North Carolina, a Mexican American from just outside Albuquerque. In each case, we see pictures of the men and then footage of their parents, who are sometimes shown holding or sitting by a picture of their lost son. The mother of the black sailor (he is the only man not shown to have a father) is seen alone, hanging laundry on a line.

Ford replaced Toland's racial provocation with a few lines indicating that the majority of Japanese Americans were loyal to the United States—one young man is shown after the attack replacing his "Banzai Café" sign with a new one reading "Keep 'Em Flying Café"*—and he had the narrator lecture "Mr. Tojo" that Pearl Harbor only "served to further complicate the already complex life of the Japanese in Hawaii." And instead of Toland's eviscerating depiction of the navy as being asleep at the helm, he inserted a reference to "the Axis style of war—a stab in the back on a Sunday morning." The War Department still didn't want the movie shown publicly—thirty-four minutes was an awkward length for exhibitors, and the picture was by then considered damaged goods—but Ford's changes were sufficient to win *December 7th* approval for exhibition to servicemen and munitions workers later in 1943. Although Mellett had succeeded in thwarting the general release of the movie, his overriding point about the ethics of using staged war scenes in a film that purported to be a documentary went unaddressed. As for Ford, he was back in the good graces of the navy, but he was still stuck at a desk. As spring gave way to summer, he wondered when, if ever, he would get another chance to be at the center of the action.

Mellett had managed to keep his fight against *December 7th* out of the papers, but his battle with Capra over *Prelude to War* soon made its way into the press. After Pearl Harbor, the isolationists in the House and Senate had retreated into embarrassed silence for a time, but they were now resurfacing in opposition not to the war itself but to Roosevelt, accusing him of stoking fear and fury among Americans in order to keep himself in power—and of using war propaganda to do it. In February, Senator Rufus Holman, an Oregon Republican, denounced *Prelude to War* as "personal political propaganda" that was intended only to secure a fourth term for the president. In doing so, he brought the War Department's whole filmmaking strategy into question and won sympathetic attention from many who felt that in a time of national belt-tightening, government moviemaking was a profligate use of limited resources that resulted in self-indulgent nonsense. "I want our generals to put their time in winning battles rather than fighting psychological

---

* *Keep 'Em Flying* was the title of a huge recent movie hit, a 1941 service comedy that starred Abbott and Costello.

warfare," he fumed. "Does the administration have the nerve to say that our fighting men don't know why they're fighting the war?"

A strain of yahooism that had temporarily been quieted after Pearl Harbor was now reasserting itself with a vigor that caught many in Hollywood off guard. And despite the fact that the Bureau of Motion Pictures had only recently released its own version of a "why we fight" movie, Mellett shocked the filmmaking community when he chose to make common cause with Holman publicly. In an interview with the *Hollywood Reporter,* Mellett aired his conviction that *Prelude to War* should be shown only to servicemen since it "played too many notes of hate for general audiences"; he also said that he welcomed Holman's push for congressional hearings on the question of government propaganda. The contretemps marked the first time since the start of the war that the Office of War Information and the War Department had openly opposed each other over the question of filmed propaganda, and even after *Prelude to War* was nominated for the Academy Award, Mellett had shown no signs of budging from his position.

Suddenly, the entire program that had brought so many filmmakers into military service was being called into question. An informal coalition of former isolationists, skeptics about the ethics of propaganda, anti-Hollywood rhetoricians, and members of the entertainment press who wanted the movie industry to resume business as usual combined in an unlikely drive to stop virtually all government-sponsored film documentation of the war. The directors who had suspended their careers and only months earlier had been characterized as patriots for doing so were now being dismissed as dilettantes and thrill seekers who were selfishly shirking their real duty, which was to entertain the public. The Roosevelt administration "should see to it that the best workers, the great artists of the movies, are kept right where they belong" in Hollywood, wrote critic Leo Mishkin in the *New York Morning Telegraph.* "John Ford is doing his own essential industry no good by sailing around the world with the Navy. Frank Capra and William Wyler haven't been heard from in the movies since *Meet John Doe* and *Mrs. Miniver.* Darryl Zanuck is now editing what, stripped of all verbiage and hullabaloo, is essentially only a newsreel of the invasion of Africa. . . . But none of them is making movies for the American people."

They would now be called to account. In early 1943, for the first time since the Nye Committee hearings before Pearl Harbor, Congress decided to summon some of Hollywood's biggest names to Washington, where they would be expected to defend exactly what they were doing in the war and why they were doing it.

FOURTEEN

"Coming Along with Us Just for Pictures?"

WASHINGTON, ENGLAND, AND NEW YORK, MARCH–JULY 1943

When *Time* magazine put Harry Truman on its cover in March 1943, it referred to the Missouri senator as America's "billion-dollar watchdog" and stated that the bipartisan committee he chaired represented "the closest thing yet to a domestic high command." Truman's task force—everyone called it the Truman Committee, although it was officially the Senate Committee Investigating National Defense—was charged with overseeing all expenditures related to the war, and its chairman's sharp eye for waste, sloppiness, and corruption had, in the fifteen months since Pearl Harbor, turned the previously low-profile fifty-eight-year-old into one of the country's most popular politicians. "The goal of every man on the committee is to promote the war effort to the limit of efficiency and exertion," he said—but it was also to throw a harsh spotlight on all areas in which those qualities were lacking. "It doesn't do any good to go around digging up dead horses after the war is over, like the last time," Truman told journalists. "The thing to do is dig this stuff up now, and correct it."

When Truman turned his attention to Hollywood, the industry knew he wouldn't be vulnerable to counterattack, shaming, or mockery, as Dies, Nye, and the isolationists had been a couple of years earlier. And in truth, nobody

in Hollywood or Washington was entirely sure what the best defense of the
war's various propaganda programs might be. America wanted accurate pictures of and about the war, but the reputation of filmmakers in uniform was
still fragile and subject to quick and temperamental revision: Headlines
would characterize them as selfless heroes one week and preening nuisances
the next.

Darryl Zanuck had not helped matters. Since his return from Tunisia, he
had devoted most of his energy to transforming his assignment in North Africa
into a one-man show. Early in 1943, he published a book about his experiences, *Tunis Expedition;* although Zanuck donated his royalties to Army
Emergency Relief, eyebrows shot up at the introduction he had commissioned
from Damon Runyon, who vowed that "no man alive takes his duty to flag and
country more seriously than Colonel Darryl Zanuck. . . . Were [he] a newspaperman he would probably be one of the greatest war correspondents of this
generation." Such florid claims were more than the wide-eyed diary-like rem-
iniscence that followed could sustain. ("All of Algeria reminds me of California" and "I still can't seem to understand that this is really a battle and I am
in it," were typical Zanuck *aperçus.*) *Tunis Expedition*'s alternating tones of
gee-whiz boy's-book innocence and self-aggrandizement were too much for
many critics to stomach. "One would like . . . to have heard something more
between Colonel Zanuck's hour-by-hour adventures about the men who were
taking the pictures, and what they thought and felt, and what their problems
were," wrote the reviewer for the *New York Times* in one of the gentler cri-
tiques of the book.

Zanuck had only himself to blame for the degree to which the press
turned on him. In his years running 20th Century Fox, he had always fancied himself a writer, but he was also a sentimentalist who brought some of
the unfortunate tropes of his studio movies to a book that purported to be
journalism. His account of his conversation with a black deckhand in the
merchant marine ("Ah been goin' to sea steady foh the las' ten yeahs, an' no
little to'pedo trouble is gonna make me quit") turned the sailor into—in Zanuck's own delighted assessment—"a perfect double for Stepin Fetchit." And
his assessment of the Germans ("Hell, you want to kill them all in cold
blood, smother the entire bloody race. . . . No sir, there is no alternative")

was, even by the standards of the time, tone-deaf. It was one thing to vilify Hitler and another to appropriate his fantasies of racial annihilation.

During his time in North Africa, Zanuck had not made a good impression tooling around in his blue Chevrolet, toting boxes of cigars and an expensive sleeping bag, and insisting on visiting his studio's abandoned headquarters in Algiers, where, as the staff sergeant who accompanied him recalled, he "strolled about his fief with all the sureness of the sovereign in his own bit of extraterritoriality in a foreign land." At times he seemed unable to distinguish between war and a war movie—"I feel like a character in an Edward G. Robinson epic," he wrote—and in the middle of one air raid, he insisted on being allowed to fire off a tommy gun. The ill will Zanuck generated during his time in Algiers made its way back to the United States, and by the time he released his documentary, *At the Front in North Africa*, the press was downright derisive, referring to the film as "Darryl Zanuck's War." To many who saw it, the picture seemed padded; it was light on actual combat footage and filled out with what one review dismissed as "arty shots of tank treads, dawns, sunsets, [and] many another ill-placed frippery. . . . It has all the Zanuck fingerprints: It is flamboyant, melodramatic, sometimes corny, sometimes hysterical." Zanuck's team of more than forty Signal Corps and Field Photo cameramen had in fact captured some strong images of air and tank combat in the siege of Tebourba, but he couldn't resist putting himself at the film's center; he can be seen in *At the Front in North Africa* looking authoritative, serious, and supervisory, and brandishing a cigar.

When the Truman Committee decided to take aim, Zanuck was the easiest, and certainly the biggest, target. In a series of hearings, the committee questioned whether he was using his positions as the head of the Academy Research Council and the Army Training Film program to push military contracts for movies toward 20th Century Fox, whether he had sufficiently separated himself from Fox by placing his stock in the studio in a blind trust (he had not), whether drawing an army salary while he was still being paid by Fox represented a double dip at the expense of the American taxpayer, and whether the officer's commissions that he and other filmmakers had received after Pearl Harbor were given because of merit or fame. Zanuck was furious and humiliated, telling the committee that he thought it was "a dirty, lousy outrage to do such a thing to a patriotic American. . . . I am to blame for being a sucker and trying to help my country. . . . They will never catch me . . . ever doing anything again for anybody." Zanuck indignantly offered to resign his commission, but his manifestation of high dudgeon was met with scorn. "I think he is an officer in the Army and he ought to stay there," Truman replied. "The Army has spent a lot of money training him. . . . Why don't you send him to school and make a *real* officer out of him? I cannot understand how an officer would want to quit. . . . I don't believe in these fellows backing out."

The committee publicly cleared Zanuck of any malfeasance, but the office of the army inspector general, which had initiated a separate, private investigation into his financial relationship with Fox, did not, and Zanuck did in fact agree to resign his commission that spring to avoid further bad publicity. His experience felt like a cautionary tale to both Ford and Capra, whose names were thrown around in the hearings as well. Ford had kept scrupulous records of his own time in North Africa and he made sure that almost all of Field Photo's work was labeled as classified; in the wake of the *December 7th* imbroglio, he stopped bragging to journalists about having been in high-risk combat and kept a low profile in Washington. When the committee, casting a wide net, requested information on his stock holdings and on the income he had received from movie profits during his two years in the navy, he had Bill Donovan respond with a letter assuring them that his record was clean. Capra was similarly called to account for the monies he had received for *Meet John Doe* and the still-unreleased *Arsenic and Old Lace,* but like Ford, he had no apparent conflicts of interest, and once it became clear to the senators that no directors were drawing full-time salaries from studios while cashing army paychecks, they lost interest.

But the Truman Committee had made its point by using Zanuck to raise questions about the complicated power-sharing arrangements between the War Department and the movie industry. After the hearings concluded, lines of authority were simplified; the Academy Research Council, which had served as an important liaison between the War Department and the studios since before Pearl Harbor, was now marginalized, and the Signal Corps, rather than General Osborn's looser and more filmmaker-friendly Morale

Branch, would henceforth have authority over just about everyone in uniform who was making pictures for the army.

While the hearings cast light on the danger of financial impropriety when studio executives kept a hand in the movie business after they received commissions, larger questions about the creation of propaganda and the oversight of army filmmakers continued to fester. Truman had made it clear that he thought it was a mistake to put directors in uniform in the first place; he believed they would better serve their country as consultants rather than as officers. But it was far too late to undo a policy to which the Roosevelt administration and the War Department were already committed.

George Marshall had brushed off Senator Holman's accusations that *Prelude to War* was a government-financed advertisement for Roosevelt's reelection, but Capra and Mellett remained in a standoff over whether it would receive a theatrical release. After the film won an Oscar, Capra got Undersecretary of War Robert Patterson to argue that the movie should be shown nationwide; at the same time, Mellett persuaded the War Activities Committee, the Hollywood board that acted as a kind of sponsor for war-related documentaries seeking theatrical release, to support him in opposition.

It was Mellett who finally overplayed his hand, defying even his own boss, OWI head Elmer Davis, who had told him to back down. "That goddamned Lowell Mellett!" sputtered Patterson a couple of weeks after the Oscars. "I talked to Elmer Davis . . . and he told me that by all that was holy [the *Why We Fight* films] would be shown and there'd be no more fooling about it and now there is more fooling about it!" Finally, on April 22, Mellett gave in. "Torrid conference today," Colonel Stanley Grogan cabled General Alexander Surles, who ran the army's Bureau of Public Relations and wanted *Prelude to War* in theaters as soon as possible. "Industry took stand pictures are not worth showing and will not draw audiences, lacking entertainment value, etc. . . . Elmer Davis very helpful, Lowell Mellett not at all helpful. . . . Army is to use *Prelude to War* as a test picture. . . . [Radio City] Music Hall, NY will be furnished with one print by OWI for showing one week in May. . . . Only way out of an impasse since industry and war department plus Lowell Mellett cannot agree."

Capra's victory was pyrrhic. By the time *Prelude to War* opened, it was, in every sense, old news, a late-arriving history lesson that reached the general public at a moment when moviegoers were much more interested in what happened last week than they were in troop movements in 1931 Ethiopia. Reviewing the film for the *New York Times,* Bosley Crowther said he hoped Americans would find it "inspirational" but admitted that "its effectiveness with the public . . . is questionable. Its generalizations are vague and it leans heavily on patriotic symbolism. . . . It leaves many obvious 'why' questions completely unanswered." And while James Agee felt that the script that the late Eric Knight had overseen and redrafted was "respectably written," he wasn't convinced that *Prelude to War* was anything more than exactly what Marshall had originally requested—an effective illustrated lecture "the broad contents of [which] are wearily familiar to many."

The War Activities Committee had struck 250 prints of *Prelude to War* and had agreed to make the film available for no charge to any exhibitor who wanted to show it; any profits from ticket sales would go to war relief. (The sales pitch to theaters read, "Brother, can you spare 55 minutes of screen time?") But even with a lurid ad campaign touting it as "the greatest gangster movie ever filmed. . . . More vicious . . . more diabolical . . . more horrible than any horror movie you ever saw!" *Prelude to War* was a dismal failure in theaters, and a film that soured exhibitors on giving over their screens to feature-length propaganda for the duration of the war. Swept up by his desire to outmaneuver Mellett, Capra hadn't considered that a moviegoing public that was being offered two or three new war-related pictures every week would have no interest in paying for a crash course in the not very recent history of Fascism. Mellett's fears that average Americans would be alarmed and terrified by the information in the *Why We Fight* series had proved to be unfounded, but their indifference was at least as disappointing to Capra. The final insult came from General Surles, who was bitterly convinced that Mellett's office had somehow sabotaged the film by poor-mouthing it to theater owners. After all, Surles insisted, movie theaters had ways of drawing "large audiences to lousy pictures when[ever] they felt like it!"

With the war well into its second year, generic sops to patriotism and adroit use of newsreel footage were no longer enough to stir a jaded public or to make a war documentary worth showing in theaters. Moviegoers didn't

want the story behind the war—they wanted the war, brought home in pictures they couldn't see anywhere else. When William Wyler had insisted that
recreations of dogfights and bombings could be no substitute for the real
thing, he had already been away from home for six months, but his understanding of changing American tastes would prove prescient, and his stub-
bornness was now paying off with a degree of firsthand war experience that
not even John Ford could claim. After his mission over Wilhelmshaven, Wyler
stayed on with the 91st Bomb Group at Bassingbourn, getting to know the
crews, figuring out how to prevent his equipment from freezing at high alti-
tudes again, and waiting for another opportunity to fly. It came when the
newly repaired *Memphis Belle* was brought back into the rotation of active
B-17s. Robert Morgan, who had piloted the *Jersey Bounce* with Wyler aboard,
returned to the *Belle*, and as Wyler spent more time with the *Belle*'s young
navigators and gunners, its radioman and its copilot, his almost paternal feelings toward the men convinced him he had found the subject of a great film.

The crew of the *Belle*, in turn, came to admire Wyler's bravery and lack
of pretense; if he was never quite one of them, he was at least welcomed into
their ranks with generosity and respect. "I knew he was this great Hollywood
director," navigator Charles Leighton told Wyler biographer Jan Herman.
"But I liked the way he worked. He wasn't bossy or offensive. What amazed
me was why a guy like him would do something he didn't have to. I remember
thinking, 'What a way to make a living. Coming along with us just for pictures?' The guy had guts." In the name of getting a good shot, Wyler was
willing to take risks that even the most cocksure young flyers thought were
foolhardy. Morgan and the men were shocked when Wyler and Bill Clothier
insisted on lying flat along the belly of the B-17 so that they could shoot footage through the ball turret, the position on the plane's underside that allowed
a gunner to fire in all directions. Wyler wanted to use the vantage point to
capture a wheel's-eye view of the *Memphis Belle*'s takeoff and descent, a
decision that could have gotten him killed if the plane had had to make the
kind of rough, runway-scraping landing that had put more than one B-17 out
of commission. He got his footage, but some of the men thought he was crazy
to have tried in the first place.

Wyler flew his first mission in the *Memphis Belle*, a bombing run over

U-boat bases at Brest and Lorient, on April 16, 1943. Shooting conditions were, as always, almost impossibly difficult. "It was all done with these 16-millimeter cameras you had to wind," he said. "If you wanted to change the film you had to take off your glove, but if you took it off for more than one or two minutes you would lose fingers from frostbite. Being on oxygen, your efficiency was at a minimum. Taking three steps was like walking a mile. If you filmed out of one side—the windows were open because the machine guns were sticking out—the exposure would be different than from the other side. By the time you looked through the camera the fighter plane coming at you was gone. If you took time to look through, by the time you were ready to shoot you were over a target."

Twenty-one Flying Fortresses and Liberators went out that day, and not until the *Belle* returned to Bassingbourn did Wyler learn that he had lost one of the small handful of men he had personally recruited. Harold Tannenbaum had died when the B-24 in which he had been filming was shot down. He was forty-six years old. It would be Wyler's task, as the head of his unit, to write a letter of condolence to his widow. "I'd seen a good many go over and not come back," he wrote to Talli. "But it makes a difference when it's one of your own men, and you got him into the army and sent him on the particular job." Wyler was shaken, but a month later he was back in the air over Lorient, "hanging out the window with a camera in [his] hand" as dozens of German fighters buzzed around the formation of B-17s.

By that point, General Eaker had become concerned about what might happen if Wyler were to be captured by the Germans. He was far and away the most prominent Jewish filmmaker in the army and was now internationally known for *Mrs. Miniver*, and after Wilhelmshaven it was no longer a secret that he was flying missions over Germany and occupied France. A celebrity on an active air force base was a ripe target and a potential threat to everyone's safety; when the king and queen of England made an official visit to Bassingbourn in the interest of raising morale and strengthening Anglo-American relations, even they wanted to meet Wyler. "Talked with Queen about 5 minutes while King and generals waited," Wyler, who filmed the visit, wrote in his journal. "Spoke of *Mrs. M*, going on missions, RAF, etc. . . . she was charming, interested—loved *Mrs. Miniver*."

Around that time, Beirne Lay told Wyler he was grounded, but he ignored the orders and went out on a fourth mission, this time in a plane nicknamed the *Our Gang*, after Hal Roach's popular series of Little Rascals shorts. His decision almost proved fatal. The *Our Gang* was part of a mission over the port city of Kiel in northern Germany that was the target of the largest airstrike Wyler had witnessed so far; at one point he looked out of the plane's ball turret and counted 160 B-17s in perfect formation. Kiel was about 550 miles north of Mulhouse, where Wyler had grown up, and when he was a boy and his town was under German control for long stretches of the First World War, he had been taught about the city's strategic importance in school. As the *Our Gang*, which was leading the formation, approached Kiel, Wyler crawled around the belly of the plane, getting good aerial shots but using his film sparingly, intending to save most of it for the beginning of combat. It escaped his notice that the tube of his oxygen bottle had come loose, and he blacked out. "Bad show," he wrote in his diary. "Good thing I came to—so dopey I thought I was dead—strange feeling—don't think I like it. Thought of Talli and Cathy naturally and what a fool I was to go." It took all of the effort and concentration Wyler could muster to crawl, then climb the few feet to the nose of the plane, where he could reattach his breathing tube, a task that felt like "a 5-mile run." Wyler and the crew returned safely. Just three days later, the *Our Gang* was shot down.

By the time Wyler, again in defiance of orders, flew his fifth and final mission on May 29—an extremely dangerous raid on Saint-Nazaire in which more than a dozen Flying Fortresses were shot down—he knew he had everything he needed to make the movie he had come to England to make. Although the documentary he had in mind would use all of the good footage that he and Bill Clothier had shot on many different flights in many different planes over the last few months, it would tell the story of only one B-17, the *Memphis Belle*, which had just flown its twenty-fifth mission, a benchmark that rendered its entire crew eligible for home leave. Wyler was awarded the Air Medal, a decoration that had been established a year earlier for any serviceman or officer in Europe who had flown five sorties, and Eaker and Lay told him to return to the United States and take the next ninety days to turn the footage he had amassed into a movie. "Suggest brushing up Cathy on use of word Daddy and prepare Judy for an early introduction," he cabled Talli. Almost a year after he had said goodbye to his wife and two small children, Wyler was going home.

A few days before he arrived in New York City, his friend John Huston's *Report from the Aleutians* received its first public showing at the Museum of Modern Art. The screening was a hard-won victory for Huston, who had re-turned from Adak almost six months earlier. The Signal Corps had not really known what to do with him once he was back in the United States. In the early part of the year, there had been some talk of plans for a propaganda film about China and Burma that he would oversee alongside James Wong Howe and some members of Ford's Field Photo Unit. Huston had expected orders to come through that would have sent him to Asia in March, but the plan was scuttled with no explanation, and he was left to wonder if superior officers had something against him.

Huston had spent the first months of 1943 fashioning a singular and personal film that, in its final form, played as a clear compromise between the movie about the Aleutians that he wanted to make and the movie he thought the army expected from him. The first scenes of *Report from the Aleutians* are intended to immerse moviegoers in the fogbound, forbidding natural landscape that had so awed him when he arrived there. The camera lingers on mountains, ice floes, volcanoes, and what appear to be near-constant cyclones and windstorms. Huston took a page from Ford's *Battle of Midway* in presenting war as the despoliation of nature; narrating the foot-age himself in an extravagantly written voice-over that almost never lets up, he informs audiences about "bird life on the island—scavenger ravens," the only natural residents of a place that he tells us is "as remote as the moon and hardly more fertile . . . next to worthless in terms of human existence." Always attentive to the play of fading light on the barren horizon, Huston then introduces the men and their mission, working to create the sense of dislocation and slowed-down time that he had experienced on Adak during his months there. As his camera seeks out oddity and unlikely beauty (a soldier carrying a guitar, a rainbow shimmering as a fighter plane touches down on the runway), *Report from the Aleutians* brings those who see it to a part of the World War II front unlike any that had been featured in gung-ho newsreels—a quiet, distant world in which "customary military formality is relaxed with plain civil necessity taking its place." Letters from home arrive, but they're already out of date. Food shipments reach the men, but never any vegetables. USO shows and outdoor movies may provide relief for American troops somewhere overseas, but they never get all the way to Adak. While Huston nods to the melting-pot unity of "down-eastern accents . . . Texas drawls and low-Western twangs and Brooklynese, bookkeepers, grocery clerks, college men and dirt farmers," all of whose differences are swept away by the job at hand, he turns the first twenty minutes of *Report from the Aleutians* into a melancholy, almost poetic portrayal of waiting and watchfulness, of the lonely languor of the American fighting man who has no one to fight.

At the film's midpoint, Huston's tone and style change so abruptly that what follows feels like a different movie, almost as if, having explored his own interests, he had now decided to deliver the required assignment. The second half of *Report from the Aleutians* is about risk and accomplishment, and looks remarkably like the early storyboards he had drawn. Reconnaissance experts study aerial photographs and pick their targets. Bombs are hoisted into bays as the narration provides information about their size and power and the preparedness of American troops. Pilots and bombardiers— corn-fed hotshots in leather helmets and goggles—grin at the camera. And then, at the film's climax, moviegoers are taken on a bombing run. The conclusion of Huston's film is efficient, energetic, and somewhat impersonal— even the narration changes, as Huston's own distinctive, bluff cadences give way to the more reassuring and authoritative voice of his father, who had done so many Signal Corps voice-overs by this point that for most of America his was the default voice of inspirational army documentaries.

Huston had ended *Report from the Aleutians* on an irresolute note— necessarily so, since the mission to retake Kiska and Attu from the Japanese was no closer to being completed when he left Adak than it had been when he arrived there. But in May, after he finished the movie, U.S. forces engaged in a fierce and protracted battle to drive the Imperial Army off the islands. Five hundred American soldiers died, as did twenty-five hundred Japanese, but when it was over three weeks later, the Allies had retaken Attu.

All month, Americans had been reading daily dispatches from the Aleutian battlefront in newspapers and eagerly following the progress of their troops. Suddenly, Huston's film, which had been all but forgotten by the Signal Corps and the OWI, represented the most exciting "morale picture" that the War Department had had to offer exhibitors and audiences since *The Battle of Midway*. And once again, Mellett got involved. One week into the battle for Attu, he saw Huston's movie and reported to his bosses that "it is a picture the people will want to see and have a right to see without delay— it is actual news of the war." But Mellett also felt that at forty-four minutes, the film was much too long to gain any traction with exhibitors, who had made it clear after *Prelude to War* that they weren't interested in showing anything from the Signal Corps that was longer than two reels—roughly twenty minutes.

Mellett was pleased to see footage that showed the "bombardment of Kiska" (actually a composite of several small-scale missions that had taken place months before the battle had begun in earnest) as well as the "construction job on the American island base," but he found *Report from the Aleutians* "excessively theatrical" and called it, not inaccurately, "a hybrid Hollywood-Army product." Moreover, he didn't believe that Huston was capable of cutting his own picture down to size. Mellett took it upon himself to ask Zanuck to edit the movie, and Zanuck promised to try, but, bogged down in the Truman Committee hearings and his own impending departure from active duty, he had been "unable to accomplish the reduction." Mellett then turned to his own deputy Sam Spewack and asked him to take Huston's film and turn it into a short that could be released to theaters immediately. By June, he had Spewack's sixteen-minute version of *Report from the Aleutians* in hand, and he asked General Surles for permission to release it to the War Activities Committee for distribution right away, telling him that "it is certain to be more successful in the theaters than the 44-minute version could be." Surles would have none of it; Huston, knowing his movie was threatened, had moved quickly to arrange screenings of the full-length cut for major critics in New York City, and Surles told Mellett that reaction among reviewers was "universally favorable" and that "it is our view that the complete version is essential to the telling of the story."

Huston hadn't simply shown critics the movie; he had made sure they understood that it was in jeopardy, and they lost little time in rallying to his side. "The U.S. Army, which has consistently trailed its British allies in the making of war documentaries, moves up a peg," said *Variety* in an influential piece that was the first review to be published; the paper's reviewer expressed concern that the film would "suffer from the severe shaving demanded by the WAC. It hardly can be expected in that length to retain the fine, friendly, human quality which, contrasted against that bleak background, is its strength."

As the weeks dragged on, the Bureau of Motion Pictures became the subject of furious attacks in the press for its interference and obstruction. In the *New York Times,* Theodore Strauss, who had been shown Huston's cut, called the delay "deplorable" and lamented the fact that *Report from the Aleutians* had not been shown "when it would have been most timely. . . . The public has been badly served. For two months at least a fine war document has been withheld . . . because of a disagreement which should have been resolved in a very brief time." The press was especially prickly because the reports from the actual battle of Kiska and Attu had been heavily censored. "This is not the time or place to discuss the merits of that," Strauss wrote, but he and many others argued that both Huston, "one of the finest of Hollywood's younger directorial talents," and cameraman Rey Scott, whose bravery in flying nine missions Huston had also shared with the press corps, were being as ill-treated as the public. "Men with honesty and talent can bring close to us the realities of the war," he concluded. "It is frustrating when their efforts are ensnarled in red tape and wasteful argument back home."

The clash over *Report from the Aleutians* was Lowell Mellett's last fight. He had expended all of his political capital and had run out of allies. The War Department saw him as an obstructionist. Exhibitors had tired of his hollow reassurances and found him to be an ineffective guardian of their interests. And to the studios, he was a power-hungry autocrat with an ungovernable appetite to control the content of their movies and the shape and scale of their businesses. They had never quite forgiven him for his suggestion that they conserve resources by halving their output and abolishing double features—an argument that Mellett had been typically unwilling to let drop until long after it became clear that it was falling on deaf ears.

For all his pettiness and clumsiness, Mellett had used his office as a powerful and influential force in steering dozens of Hollywood scripts toward a slightly more progressive and internationalist view of the world. With good intentions that he often undercut with heavy-handed tactics, he had spent the year and a half since he agreed to run the bureau imploring filmmakers for Hollywood and the War Department alike to avoid jingoism, cautioning against films that would fuel race hatred among moviegoers, and warning directors, to almost no avail, about the ethical dangers of reenactment. But by the summer of 1943, the Office of War Information had become the scapegoat for anyone who was suspicious of official propaganda efforts, and even as Mellett was engaging in a test of wills with Huston, his influence was collapsing. When it came time for Congress to approve a budget for the 1943–44 fiscal year, the Bureau of Motion Pictures fell victim to a coalition of House Republicans and southern Democrats. Some congressmen were convinced that Roosevelt was overreaching and using his network of information agencies to create a permanent presidency for himself; others were certain that the OWI was filled with Communists who had insinuated their ideology into everything they touched. By a two-to-one margin, the House voted to slash the OWI's budget drastically and to defund the Bureau of Motion Pictures completely.

Even as he packed up his office in July and prepared to leave his unsalaried job and return to Washington as one of the president's administrative aides, Mellett attempted, one last time, to take care of what he called "unfinished business" on the day he resigned, reminding his boss Elmer Davis that *Report from the Aleutians* "could have been completed back in April" and that the War Department's insistence on releasing the film at its full length would mean that only "a limited number" of moviegoers would see it. He was right: Despite generous praise for Huston's work, it was not a success when it finally opened theatrically in August on a double bill with a "B" melodrama called *Bomber's Moon*, almost three months after the battle for Kiska and Attu had last been in the headlines. Once again, the American public, so hungry for war footage in newsreels, had shown little interest in paying to see it.

Although the OWI managed to retain a presence in Hollywood, it would no longer have much to do with directors who worked for the Signal Corps. With Mellett's departure, the World War II propaganda effort lost the closest thing it had to a watchdog and ombudsman. For the next two years, filmmakers would be on their own. The question Mellett had often said was more important than any other—"Will this picture help us win the war?"—would be all but forgotten, and the propaganda effort would enter its darkest and most troubling days.

PART THREE

——

PART THREE

FIFTEEN

"How to Live in the Army"

NORTH AFRICA, HOLLYWOOD, FLORIDA, AND WASHINGTON, SUMMER 1943

T he sorriest and most shameful episode in the history of army propaganda efforts during World War II—a misbegotten project that ended up consuming and compromising three directors on three continents—began with a single piece of bad luck. In November 1942, when Darryl Zanuck went to Algeria to oversee the army's attempt to film the North African campaign, he decided to maximize his chances of obtaining good footage by breaking the photographers under his command into several small crews and sending each to a different city. Other than Ford, the most experienced Hollywood director Zanuck had working for him was Anatole Litvak, and so it was Litvak who got one of the mission's plum assignments: He was the first filmmaker sent into Casablanca, where General Patton led thirty-five thousand American troops in the landing that initiated Operation Torch and the battle in which the Allies successfully took control of the port city from the occupying Vichy forces. For the documentary Zanuck intended to produce, the fight for Casablanca was important not only as the opening gambit in the campaign to retake Morocco, Algeria, and Tunisia, but also as the most spectacular show of Allied military force since the start of the war. Patton and his men would provide the first real chance for army filmmakers to show moviegoers at home the strength of American ground troops on the offensive.

Although Zanuck was later criticized for his decision to assign only a couple of men to a site as important as Casablanca, he had done his best with relatively limited filmmaking resources; at the same moment that Patton's forces were arriving, seventy thousand more ground troops, Ranger battalions, and parachutists were coming ashore at four different points in Algeria, all of which were several hundred miles east. Zanuck didn't want any major deployment to go unphotographed, and that day, Casablanca happened to be the location where the most vivid images were captured. Litvak, like the other men under Zanuck, had filmed with a handheld 16-millimeter camera equipped with a Kodachrome magazine clip; it was light, easy to use, and ideal for capturing long stretches of battle and sudden firefights since it could be reloaded quickly. As soon as the city had been taken and the Allies started moving east, Litvak packed up all of the reels he and his co-cameraman had shot and put them aboard a navy transport vessel bound for Europe. Shortly after Litvak stepped off the ship to return to shore, it was hit by a German torpedo and sunk. All of his film was lost.

In later years, several people involved with what would become a large and carefully coordinated effort to reenact the North African campaign for use in army propaganda claimed that they made the decision to fake it because the army was afraid to admit to Roosevelt that only two men had been assigned to Casablanca. But it seems unlikely that there was any large-scale attempt to keep the truth from the White House: Zanuck bluntly reported the loss of Litvak's footage in his book *Tunis Expedition*, which was published in April 1943, and the fact that he had no footage of Patton's landing in Morocco was also apparent in his indifferently received documentary *At the Front in North Africa*. The deficiency of the Signal Corps' overall effort was underscored by the U.S. release, just a few weeks earlier, of *Desert Victory*, a documentary that had been produced by the Army Film Unit of Britain's version of the OWI, the Ministry of Information. When they got their first look at the British film, critics and audiences were astonished; they had seen nothing so action-packed or immediate from any American moviemakers since the war began. *Time* called *Desert Victory*, which depicted the push toward Tunisia with an understandable emphasis on British fighting forces, "the finest film of actual combat that has come out of this war," and the magazine's critic James Agee reiterated his praise in *The Nation,* writing that "there is hardly a shot which by any sort of dramatizing, prearrangement or sentimentalization gets in the way of . . . magnificence." The movie, he wrote, amounted to "a stunning textbook on how to make a nonfiction war film," the clear implication being that America's wartime filmmakers should take it as an opportunity to learn from their betters.

The acclaim *Desert Victory* received extended to the British not only as filmmakers but as warriors. "The casualties they suffered in its production," wrote David Lardner in the *New Yorker,* "can perhaps be justified by the confidence it will instill in their allies. . . . It demonstrates, at least to the layman, that, given equipment and time for solid preparation, this particular United Nation can wage one nifty campaign." So exciting was the picture that most reviews were willing to overlook the fact that it had made some judicious use of reenactments to depict key moments in the drive to retake Tobruk in Libya. "The captious will certainly find room for criticism of a film sold as 100% McCoy battle footage, for some of it, to anyone familiar with picture-making, is obviously not that," wrote *Variety*'s reviewer. "It's the overall effect, however, that counts."

To the men in charge of filmmaking for the army, that effect was twofold: The success of *Desert Victory,* with its deafening nighttime gun battles, lines of soldiers advancing through the dust and sand, and terrifying Luftwaffe bomb strikes, provided further evidence that the British were continuing to outstrip the Americans in the quality and impact of their war filmmaking. More ominously, it suggested that if the army didn't improve its pictures, American moviegoers might be left with the impression that the British were leading the Allied effort to win the war. The proudly Anglocentric *Desert Victory* placed great emphasis on the second battle of El Alamein in Egypt, which had ended in an Allied victory in November 1942 before the Americans had even arrived; by contrast, Zanuck's film had failed to make any kind of case for the leadership of U.S. forces in the region. As far as the War Department was concerned, the propaganda campaign could not be allowed to rest there. A second film would have to be made—and not by Zanuck—that depicted the U.S. Army leading the Allies to victory in Tunisia.

For that, the Signal Corps turned to Capra, who by the time Zanuck's movie opened was yearning for the kind of public validation that he now understood he would not be likely to achieve with the *Why We Fight* series. In some ways, Capra's division had never been stronger. Although his hopes that all of the *Why We Fight* installments would be released theatrically had died with the box-office failure of *Prelude to War,* the next three chapters were now finished and being shown to all new army recruits. In addition, to a remarkable extent given his shoestring budget, Capra was making good on the overall plans he had mapped out a year earlier. He had assigned a fresh team of writers and directors to come up with new approaches for two of the stalled projects about which he cared most deeply, *The Negro Soldier* and *Know Your Enemy—Japan.* He had also begun production of a newsreel, at first titled *The War* and soon renamed *Army-Navy Screen Magazine,* that would keep GIs around the world up to date on military events and international news every two weeks for the next two years, until the end of the war in Europe.

And almost on a whim, Capra had conceived and commissioned what would turn out to be by far the most popular series of training films made for servicemen during the war. Soon after he had arrived in Washington, he had commissioned one of the writers in his charge to draft a lighthearted script for a short called *Hey, Soldier!* in which a complaining private would be made to understand the importance of various army rules and regulations. The movie was never made, but, inspired by the way draftees were responding to the use of animation in the *Why We Fight* films, Capra reconceived *Hey, Soldier!* as a series of cartoons. He came up with a character called "Private SNAFU," a grumbling, naïve, incompetent GI who would be featured in an ongoing run of short black-and-white cartoons in which—usually by catastrophically negative example that more than once ended with him being blown to bits—he would inform young enlistees about issues like the importance of keeping secrets and the need for mail censorship, as well as the hazards of malaria, venereal disease, laziness, gossip, booby traps, and poison gas.

To oversee the writing and production of the shorts, Capra recruited an editorial cartoonist from New York City who had been doing caustic satirical work for the left-wing newspaper *PM.* Theodor S. Geisel—later famous as Dr.

Seuss—had first gotten Capra's attention in early 1942, when he had depicted isolationist Senator Gerald Nye, one of his favorite targets, as a literal horse's ass. Geisel was a strongly pro-Roosevelt German American who, in his single-panel sketches, had demonstrated an unerring ability to draw blood and get laughs at the same time. With a few strokes of his remorseless pen, Hitler became a tantrum-throwing infant and isolationism was reduced to a scrawny bird being blown to kingdom come after Pearl Harbor. In several memorable drawings, Charles Lindbergh was transmuted into an ostrich with his head in the sand and his butt—sometimes emblazoned with a disparaging message—waving in the breeze.

Capra sent one of his army writers, Leonard Spigelgass, to New York to recruit Geisel, and Spigelgass sent word back to his boss that "he has a remarkably good brain, and seems to me useful infinitely beyond a cartoonist." Geisel, who had no animation or filmmaking experience, was sworn in as a captain in New York and brought west to Fort Fox, where Capra walked him through the animation studios. They ended up at the editing bays. "He gave me the tour," Geisel said, "and the last thing he said was, 'Here, Captain, are the Moviolas.' I said, 'What is a Moviola?' He looked at me rather suddenly and said, 'You will learn.'"

Disney and Warner Bros. had both put in bids to produce the SNAFU shorts, but Disney had insisted on retaining rights to the characters and images; Warners did not, and won. In a historically felicitous pairing, Capra teamed Geisel with a thirty-year-old animator named Chuck Jones. For the last couple of years, Jones had been developing a new character named Elmer Fudd in a handful of Merrie Melodies shorts. He had been refining Elmer's appearance with each new cartoon, and had experimented with giving him different voices. Working with Geisel, he took some early character sketches and turned Fudd into Private SNAFU.

With Mel Blanc providing voices for the characters, Geisel writing the early scripts, and a team of animation directors that included not only Jones but Friz Freleng, Frank Tashlin, and Bob Clampett, the "Private SNAFU" shorts—twenty-six in all would be produced over the next eighteen months—were the funniest, most original, and unquestionably the raunchiest movies ever produced for the Signal Corps. Munro Leaf, a pacifist whose popular illustrated children's story about Ferdinand the Bull had been widely viewed as an antiwar parable, also worked on the series, and Geisel and Jones took his great contribution—the advice that if they wanted GIs to pay attention, they should "make it racy"—and ran with it. That approach began with the explanation of the title in the very first cartoon—"SNAFU means Situation Normal All . . . *Fouled* Up," says the narrator, inserting a droll pause before "fouled" that never would have passed muster with either the Production Code or Lowell Mellett. Geisel and Jones used the fact that the only audience for the cartoons would be adult men as a permission slip to break every barrier in the movies, and Capra gave them his blessing. The first SNAFU shorts, which introduced the main character—the private who was always wishing for things to be different and his fairy godfather, "Technical Fairy, First Class"—were made for about $2,500 each. Unfolding with proto-Seussian rhyming narration that played like an early draft of *How the Grinch Stole Christmas*, they included words like "hell" and "damn," fleeting cartoon nudity, burlesque jokes, toilet humor, and sometimes lines that even its creators couldn't believe they were getting away with. "It's so cold it would freeze the nuts off a jeep!" wrote Geisel as a dare to Jones, who promptly storyboarded a cutaway to lug nuts falling off a shivering army vehicle.

Capra was on a winning streak—the SNAFU shorts were a hit with GIs around the world as soon as they made their first appearance in the biweekly newsreels his team was producing—but it seemed more and more likely to him that his war output would be limited to films that were seen only by men in uniform. Then he received a letter from Bob Heller, who had contributed to a couple of *Why We Fight* scripts and was now working at the army post-production facility in Astoria. "I imagine you have seen *Desert Victory*," Heller wrote. "Perhaps you'll agree with us that this is the finest documentary that has come out of the war. . . . If we in America can evolve a use of combat film as effectively as this, we shall have done more than render our best services." The crisis over the lost Casablanca footage and the Signal Corps' increasing competiveness with England represented an opportunity for Capra. He took Heller's words as a challenge to make a major, feature-length documentary for public release, and he decided that if the Signal

Corps didn't have great combat material from the now-completed North African campaign, they would simply have to falsify it.

He recruited two of his best men for the job. George Stevens was still in Algiers, wondering why he had traveled so far from home to film a battle that was already over. There and in Egypt, he had shot what little there was to shoot—home-movie-style scenes of his men going swimming, postcard images of striking landscapes, caves and carvings, and newsreel-ready records of the occasional color guard, dress inspection, or medal presentation. But over the last few weeks, he had had little to do but observe the differing operational styles of the U.S. and British forces, and he wasn't alone in feeling that the English seemed to understand the terrain better than the Americans did. "Our . . . uniforms look like outing clothes the Wichita Kiwanis Club would use. . . . Nothing about them is functionally good," he wrote in his journal. "We could be so much more sensibly garbed if we took some things from the British." Idle and directionless, Stevens wrote letters home and planned drinking parties with his men. "Purchased 4 pints Mumm's Champagne and one pint Courvoisier brandy at seven dollars for the brandy. Very expensive but I have been spending very little money—and the boys want to have a party Thursday night and the [champagne] will be my contribution. The brandy I will save for 'medicinal purposes.'"

On June 4, Stevens was in the senior officers' mess when orders from Capra's office came through from his colonel. "He wants me to get our group together and shoot some re-enactment scenes to round out the film taken on the African Tunis campaign," Stevens wrote. In fact, there was almost no good material from the campaign to "round out"—the best of it had already been used in Zanuck's film—and the restaging would require a large-scale appropriation of troops and materiel. "We are going to use some infantry and five tanks," Stevens wrote, "some motorized 75 mm artillery on half-trucks, scout cars, jeeps and the other vehicles necessary to simulate actual battle condition[s]. We are using an area along the water so that the shell fire can drop into the sea."

Over the next week, Stevens organized his ideas for what the staged battle scenes should look like into different shots and scenes, filming them and

noting each day's work in his journal. In Algiers, he had sought out cameraman William Mellor, an ace Hollywood cinematographer who was being un-
derused in the army—"they didn't know whether to send him into the MP or
the KP or what," said Stevens. (Mellor would go on to win two Academy
Awards for his Hollywood films with the director after the war.) Working to
get Capra the action scenes he wanted, the two men filmed "already blown-
up villages being blown up more, and tanks going in" to Algerian towns. The
local residents "would always scream when you went through the villages in
jeeps," he recalled. "It was as good after the campaign as it was [during
combat]." Stevens didn't simply recreate the advance through Algeria; he
transposed some of what the British had done into American accomplishment. "We took tanks and ran them through the water like they did when the
British Seventh Armored Division cut off the Germans [who had built road-
blocks designed to prevent the tanks from moving over land] by taking their
tanks out into the water," Stevens recalled, adding that doing so was a lesson
in the realpolitik of competing propaganda efforts. "We . . . learned a little
bit about how to live in the Army."

Stevens made no effort to disguise the fact that he was staging the combat
scenes, something that would have been evident to anyone with moviemaking
experience at the time, as well as to sharp-eyed general audiences. His work
is perfectly framed, with the cameramen often seeming to have advanced
through a combat zone well before the actual soldiers, who are seen moving
carefully across the frame from right to left, painstakingly working to seize a
position the camera has already achieved. When there are explosions, the
camera is positioned to catch them perfectly, and the image doesn't jolt because the cameraman isn't startled. (Sometimes even the advancing troops
forget to react.) Most of the recreated scenes were filmed by Stevens and
Mellor simultaneously from different angles, and in some of the shots the
other camera is visible.

Stevens spent two weeks shooting for Capra, but not with great enthusiasm. In Algiers, he clashed with his superior officer, Colonel Melvin Gillette,
a fifteen-year veteran of the Signal Corps whom Stevens thought was untrust-
worthy and unintelligent. Stevens badly wanted autonomy over his own group
of combat cinematographers—a position akin to what Ford had in the navy—

and he was unsuccessfully lobbying General Osborn in notes to Washington. He believed the overcautious Gillette was forcing the need for reenactments by keeping him and other Signal Corpsmen away from actual combat until it was over. "Although Gillette had agreed that I was to handle show my way," Stevens wrote in his diary, "I did not trust him." The corps, he added, "would give us everything we wanted (except freedom)." Stevens patiently explained to Gillette that letting him get closer to actual frontline fighting would not only provide the army with better material, lowering the odds that they would have to restage battles later, but also allow him to create more authentic re-enactments if they were eventually found to be necessary. "We could make [the] greatest war picture by going through the action with troops, then coming back and simulating action with the next wave. Later I wished I hadn't told him this great trick," Stevens admitted in his diary, "but he's probably too dumb to know its value."

Stevens sent Capra all of the film he shot, but he couldn't wait for his unhappy time in North Africa to end. When orders came through for him to move on to Iran, he was elated. "25th Day—Escape From Algiers," he wrote. It took him two weeks of ground travel to reach his next posting in An-imeshk, a town near the Iran-Iraq border that had for the last two years been used as a way station for refugee Poles, most of them women, who had fled their country and were now awaiting safe passage to India or South Africa. In Animeshk, the lucky ones were able to pick up a little money by working as washerwomen or mess hall servants. The unlucky ones worked as prosti-tutes. Venereal disease was widespread. It had been half a year since Ste-vens left the United States to begin his service, but this was his first look at the human consequences of war, and he was unnerved and repelled. He wrote of entering "a foul, filthy little village where the children follow you and with great persistence cry for baksheesh and old crones claw at you as you pass through . . . one tries desperately to avoid their touch because of the typhus lice they both carry."

Animeshk served as a kind of Allied crossroads where U.S. and UK forces would go about their business, barely interacting with either the vil-lagers or the Russians whose military supply convoys would frequently pass through. Nothing Stevens saw there felt particularly coordinated or effective to him. "The trucks have just been assembled and on the door in chalk is marked the things that the inspector found out of order," he wrote. "One item on [the] door just read 'Fucked up.' The adjective of two armies. The British and American." There were ways to pass the time—at night, the officers would drink and occasionally join the GIs to watch late-arriving movies like *Wake Island* and *How Green Was My Valley*—but for Stevens, whose only real assignment in the war thus far had been to fake it for Capra, the sense of aimlessness in this new Persian outpost only exacerbated his frustration.

"Alright," he wrote in his journal, "I have been [in the army] for six months now. . . . Needed that experience to discover what difficulties might be encountered in getting my job done under conditions new to me. . . . Now, starting all over again." In notes to himself that July, for the first time, he enumerated his goals. One was to show home-front moviegoers exactly what the army was doing—"If you have bought a two bit war stamp this is our show. This is what you are getting for your money." More than most other directors, Stevens also believed that part of his duty was to ready Americans for a time after combat. The Signal Corps, he felt, should "prepare the civil-ians, by sharing the soldiers' experiences, for resuming relationship with men who have been away" and "make the casualties easier to bare [*sic*] for those who have suffered bereavement." But he believed those goals were achievable only if the reality of battle was brought to movie screens as soon as possible. "Construct a celluloid monument to those who have been the ones to go," he wrote in a set of instructions to himself. "*Show the war.*"

Stevens was more and more certain that nobody based in Washington, including Capra, had the knowledge it took to make good decisions about what needed to be filmed on the ground; his experience staging battles and faking advances had led him to the conviction that the Signal Corps was badly misusing the men it had recruited from Hollywood. "Gave up my per-sonal film projects to make films for the war dept of the highest possible caliber," he wrote in a draft of a letter intended for General Osborn. In his early days working on silent westerns, he reminded the general, he had been "a cameraman on the most formidable outdoor projects. . . . Twenty-five years getting ready for—this job. Now I am ready." He told Capra's boss Lyman

Munson that the Signal Corps was a disorganized shambles: "We should have gone to [Pantelleria, in Sicily] and filmed destruction of guns and gun emplacements—showing greater damage done by our firepower." Instead, "we wait for someone higher up to tell us what to do. We are never told because no one higher up presumes to know what to tell us. The great American ability to make movies," he concluded, is "lost in our war effort."

His complaints were ignored. In Washington, Capra was still hell-bent on turning the Allied victory in Tunisia into a feature film, and Stevens's work had gotten him only halfway there. For the next phase of his project, he turned to John Huston, who was passing the summer in New York doing little other than carrying on a public flirtation with Marietta Fitzgerald and fighting for the theatrical release of *Report from the Aleutians*. Capra told him it was time to get back to work, and summoned him to Washington along with Lieutenant Colonel Jack Chennault, a cameraman who had been with Huston in Adak.* The men were told that their new job was to restage the rest of the Allied operation in Tunisia without ever leaving the United States.

Huston and Chennault were first flown to the Mojave Desert in Southern California, the closest visual match for Tunisia that Capra could find. They were ordered to "'manufacture' a North African film and be quick about it," Huston wrote. With Capra traveling alongside them and supervising them every step of the way, they went to an army base called the Desert Training Center, where many American soldiers assigned to North Africa were sent before going overseas in order to become accustomed to desert conditions; the army also used the center to field-test equipment and dry-run tactical operations. Huston was given a large cast of "extras"—GIs who had not yet shipped out—and told to start filming. "We had troops moving up and down hills under fake artillery concentrations," he said; "the worst kind of fabrication." While Huston focused on shooting ground troops, Chennault was given command of several P-39s, low-altitude single-engine fighter planes that he sent into the air and then had bomb and strafe the desert as the cameras

---

* Chennault was the son of USAAF major general Claire Chennault, who had become something of an American hero as the leader of the Flying Tigers and was widely recognized for shooting down four Japanese planes soon after Pearl Harbor in the first direct U.S. hit against the Japanese army.

rolled. The army gave Huston some dummy tanks—metal frames with painted canvas stretched over them—and he shot from a distance as Chennault's planes bombed the empty shells.

Capra and Huston then went back to New York to do some editing work on the movie. Huston, who felt at home in the city, had been enjoying a playboy's schedule that was barely distinguishable from the life he would have led had he never left Hollywood; he spent his days seeing friends or, on rare occasions, checking in at the army HQ in Astoria, his evenings in nightclubs, and his nights either at the St. Regis or at the Park Avenue apartment of wealthy friends. Capra, out of his element, was anxious for the movie to be completed swiftly. "The work is getting more complicated," he wrote to Lucille. "It just seems we keep standing still . . . in this hot weather you never seem to get anything done. . . . The women have discovered John Huston's place. They will have to move out [in order for him] to do any work. They simply barge in and take charge. . . . I hate this place and all the people."

After a week, Capra dispatched Huston to shoot the most elaborately staged combat sequences he had yet commissioned. This time his destination was Orlando, Florida, where he and Bill Mellor, who had returned from Algeria, were to simulate the heavy bombardment of Axis fortifications in North Africa as well as aerial combat between Allied and German planes. "I set it up so that the fighters—which were supposed to be German planes—would dive so close to the bombers from which we were filming that you couldn't possibly identify them," Huston wrote later. "There were no casualties, thank God! . . . The bomber crews were sweating blood, and on several occasions were all for knocking down the attack planes. My camera crew was utterly bewildered by it all. I remember shouting to my first cameraman, 'They're coming in at two o'clock!' and seeing him look at his watch."

Huston knew that what he was shooting was "trash" and approached it as something of a joke. "Looking back on it, it was absurd, and I was also aware of its absurdity at the time, I'm afraid. But Frank was undertaking in all seriousness to make a proper picture out of it, and . . . he was very skillful at concealing his deceit."

In August, with postproduction work on *Tunisian Victory* almost completed in New York, Capra and Huston were called back to Washington for a meeting with the War Department and General Surles of the army's Bureau of Public Relations. "We all met and looked at the material, which was just disgraceful," said Huston. And then he and Capra were given the bad news: The film they had shot would now be employed not only to deceive the moviegoing public, but to bully America's closest ally as well. The army had gotten word that the English were in the final stages of creating a documentary sequel to their own *Desert Victory* called *Africa Freed!*, with which *Tunisian Victory* would surely suffer in comparison. Surles told Huston and Capra that their next assignment was to convince the British to abandon their own picture in favor of a collaborative enterprise with the United States. As bait, they were told to use what they had just shot in California and Florida to demonstrate the high quality of the contribution that the Signal Corps could make. "The English were told that we had North African material," said Huston. "And since we were allies and so on, wouldn't it be a great gesture of friendship, making the bonds even stronger, if this was a joint English-American production?" In early August 1943, Capra was asked to step back from his full-time responsibilities running the 834th Signal Service Photographic Detachment and concentrate full-time on this mission. He turned his administrative job over to Anatole Litvak and prepared to leave Washington. A few days later, orders came through dispatching him and Huston to London, footage in hand, to make their case to the British Army Film Unit.

SIXTEEN

"I'm the Wrong
Man for That Stuff"

WASHINGTON, HOLLYWOOD, AND ENGLAND,
JUNE–DECEMBER 1943

The crew of the *Memphis Belle* beat William Wyler back to the United States by ten days. Their arrival in Washington, D.C., on June 16, 1943, felt like a movie; in fact, it had been scripted like one. The army planned to herald the *Belle*'s unblemished twenty-five-mission record as a symbol of success through perseverance, which, deep into the second year of America's involvement in the war, had replaced readiness as the most important idea that army propagandists could promote. "With a new wing and a patched-up tail, a Flying Fortress glided down before a cheering crowd at National Airport today," reported the Associated Press. "She is the first combat bomber to fly home from the European theatre under her own power." Newsreel cinematographers were present to record the landing, and H. H. Arnold, the general in charge of the air force, greeted the ten men personally and told reporters that "the grandest thing of all is that . . . only one man, the tail gunner, was wounded." With that, Captain Robert Morgan, the bomber's pilot, was whisked off for a very public reunion in Tennessee with Margaret Polk, the young woman who had inspired him to give the plane its name; at the navy's behest, the couple obligingly told the reporters who were swarming them that they would wed in August. (Once they were out of the spotlight, their relationship ended almost immediately, and by August, Morgan was engaged to another woman.) The air force had a great story to sell and ten young war heroes to help sell it; from Memphis, the crew and the *Belle* itself embarked on a six-week morale-building tour of factories, flying schools, and airbases that would take them across the country before they returned to the capital.

Wyler's homecoming was quieter. The journey across the Atlantic, via military cargo transports that stopped in Iceland, Greenland, and Nova Scotia, had been fitful and almost dreamlike; Wyler was alone for much of the time, sleeping when he could, staring at the aurora borealis in awe from his airplane window and feeling slightly disoriented, after months on a British airbase, by the lightheartedness and comfort of the celebrity life to which he was, by degrees, returning. In Reykjavik he stayed in officers' quarters that had once been a flophouse for homeless men. In Newfoundland, he had a meal with Irving Berlin, who was visiting Canada. And when he finally arrived in New York around midnight a week after he left London, he barely had time to sleep and shave before Sam Goldwyn was taking him to lunch, Elsa Maxwell was buttonholing him for a conversation, and he was expected at a dinner given by Wendell Willkie to honor Walter Lippmann. "DEAD (tired)," he wrote in his daybook after that night's gala. "Long speeches & shows to get money from all the rich for the war. It's depressing to think that's the only way they can get it, with a big dinner show and lots of glamour."

Talli had made her way to New York, and finally the two were reunited in a tender moment that both of them experienced in almost cinematic terms. "I was standing in the door of a room at the Plaza Hotel at the end of a long hall," she said, and suddenly there in the distance was her husband emerging from the elevator bank, confused. "I got the room number," he recalled. "I couldn't find it at first. Finally, I saw Talli. . . . It was a little unusual. We had to run to each other."

The Wylers went to Washington, where he was to be interviewed for the radio broadcast *Army Hour*, about what it was like to fly missions over France and Germany. "Fear," he told the reporter. "Just plain, honest-to-God fear. Afraid to die, a feeling you realize you've never had before if you've never been shot at. But there's another feeling that is also strong—and it helps a lot. As you look around and see a sky full of Fortresses—as you look down and see the enemy coast—you'd rather be where you are than down there. . . . This fear comes in spells—and never when you are busy. First, it grips you just after briefing—in those minutes before take-off. When you get into the plane, you are full of confidence, in the ship, in the crew, in yourself. Then there are minutes, which seem like hours, and hours, which seem like days—before you reach the target, and after you've left it, on the way home."

As Wyler started to think about what he wanted the documentary he was tentatively calling *25 Missions* to convey, he hoped to reproduce that combination of adrenaline, terror, and exhilaration, as well as the complicated and intense bond of the *Belle*'s crew. In the air, he said, "you're inclined to worship the skipper, adore the ship, and look on all the other men on board as brothers. They depend on each other. They save each other's lives every day. They're human, naturally, and they make mistakes, but they'd rather get killed than let each other down. I heard a waist-gunner say, 'I've got a whole new family. . . . There's ten of us, and I know 'em better than I know my own brothers and sisters, and it's just as tough to lose one.'"

Wyler was determined to use only the footage that he, Bill Clothier, and the late Harold Tannenbaum had shot on their missions with the 91st Bomb Group; there would be no backlot recreations or miniatures in his movie. But it would be necessary to create a complete soundtrack from scratch, since the bone-shaking roar of a B-17's four engines made audio recording in the air impossible. Even so, Wyler strove for verisimilitude, and in July he convinced the air force that after the *Belle*'s publicity tour was over, the crew should be flown to Los Angeles, where they themselves would record the comments and instructions they had spoken to one other over the bomber intercom. Wyler wrote an extremely simple script, in keeping with his memories of the terse communications used aboard the plane—"Fire at 1030 coming round," "Got 'em," "Upper or lower"; he also stayed true to the language the men used ("Come on, you son of a bitch!"). He would supervise the dialogue recording himself to keep the men sounding unforced and natural.

Wyler and the Signal Corps had originally envisioned *25 Missions* as a twenty-minute short, but as he began to piece together the sixteen thousand feet of 16-millimeter film he had brought back from Europe, he became excited enough to start planning a longer picture of forty or fifty minutes. He cabled Beirne Lay, advising him that the footage's "complete authenticity and [the] fact that Morgan and crew have become national heroes" (they were now doing aerial acrobatic shows in the South and Midwest as part of their victory tour) were ample justification for a more substantial film. And before he left Washington to work on the movie at home in California, he met with Capra and showed him the best of the footage he had compiled. Capra loved it—"very exciting air stuff," he reported to his wife, who was still living in Los Angeles with their three young children.

As Wyler prepared for ninety days in California that would give him time he badly wanted with Talli, Cathy, and Judy, Capra packed to leave for England, uncertain of how long his mission to strong-arm the British into collaborating on *Tunisian Victory* would keep him there. The time he spent away from home was beginning to tug at his conscience; he had been largely absent for almost two years, and he had barely seen his youngest child, two-year-old Tommy, since his first birthday. "Just a last-minute note," he wrote to Lucille, "to tell you that the happiest moment of my life will be to get back to you and the children. Dear Tommy," he added, "even though you can't read I know you can feel how much your daddy loves you." But as he explained, there could be no turning back. The Tunisian project, he wrote, "is a tough job—we didn't have much film. . . . It's up to me. I'm to make a deal for all future joint [British-American] operations. . . . This looks like the opportunity, and Surles has given me the power to make any kind of a deal I want to make. . . . It looks like I've finally got a free hand."

Capra, Huston, and Anthony Veiller, a half-British, half-American screenwriter in the Signal Corps whose presence was intended to help ease tensions and smooth over cultural differences, arrived in London at a moment when English tensions were running especially high. "Politically, the war is going stale," wrote George Stevens, who was also in London briefly on his way back from Iran for a sixty-day leave in the United States. "People . . . are more and more turning their thoughts toward the resumption of normal peacetime activities." In London, some politicians were urging a relaxation of air raid precautions and even advocating an end to nighttime blackouts. But the prevailing atmosphere was still one of vigilance. Hundreds of sixty-foot long "barrage balloons"—a network of stationary blimps designed to thwart low-flying German bombers—hung in the skies over the city, a constant reminder that London was now beginning its fifth year in peril. Goebbels had promised a relentless bombing campaign in reaction to RAF airstrikes on Germany, and there was fearful talk in the streets and the newspaper columns about rumors of a new Axis "secret weapon."

The American filmmaking delegation was prepared for the British to be resolute and knew they would resent U.S. interference with a movie they had already completed, but Capra and his men had not crossed the Atlantic with a particularly well-organized master plan about how to present themselves. "I didn't even have time to buy a razor," said Huston. "Everything in the Army was always done in a rush—same psychology prevails as [in] the movies." And their English hosts were already braced to resist any American complaints that the United States had been treated unfairly in their new movie. A month earlier, the British Army Film Unit had preemptively rebutted any possible charge of "intentional bias" by warning OWI liaison Sam Spewack that their film *Africa Freed!* would have almost no "representation . . . of the part played by the Americans in the Tunisian campaign . . . due entirely to [the] lack of satisfactory film material of American troops in action." Spewack told Capra that the British had agreed to emphasize American valor in their film's narration, but he sent an urgent cable saying that the Signal Corps would have to step in immediately to stop the picture from giving an "inadequate impression of [the] joint operation. . . . British most anxious to release this month and will do so unless Capra appears soonest."

Capra and Huston had barely checked into Claridge's when things started to go sour. At his first meeting with the British, over dinner at the hotel to discuss the joint venture, Capra got into a heated argument with James Hodson, the writer of *Africa Freed!* Hodson made no secret of the fact that he believed the Americans were there to co-opt a British success story. Nor did he share Capra's comfort with the use of extensive reenactments in documentaries. The next day, Capra and Huston were invited to see *Africa Freed!* They "said it was a swell picture and I think they were sincere in that," wrote Hodson. "But they think we ought to have a joint film."

The movie was "very good, but American representation nil," Capra wrote in his diary that night. "Said so. British claim we gave them no film. Very true." In response, Capra had tried to go on the offensive, suggesting that the British had their own footage of American troops that they had not only kept out of *Africa Freed!* but had withheld from the United States in order to weaken the American film *Tunisian Victory,* something for which no evidence existed, but which he seems to have talked himself into believing. The British denied it. "Something screwy here," Capra wrote.

Over the next few days, Capra bickered with the British over the fate of their movie. "Dialectics," he wrote. "They want to talk of future instead of this picture. We threaten to leave. Finally British have big meeting with MoI [the Ministry of Information]. Joint picture on. MoI and some American agency to have final approval" (authority over army propaganda was, by late summer, so convoluted that even Capra couldn't guess what division of the War Department would eventually sign off on the film). In his journal, he spared a moment of sympathy for the makers of *Africa Freed!,* whose work would now be completely shelved so that the United States could save face. "[British] film boys heartbroken," he wrote, "as they feel they have [a] fine picture which will now be . . . taken over by Americans."

Huston had sat through the week of contentious meetings glumly, and was acutely aware that his own side had acted in bad faith. He thought that *Africa Freed!* was a strong movie full of "good, authentic material" and he hated his part in its dismantling. "I must say I didn't have much heart for any of this," he recalled. "They had a picture quite ready to show, and it was delayed for us." As soon and as often as he could, Huston left Pinewood Studios, where the British and American filmmaking teams were now attempting to work together, and escaped into London. "England was just wonderful during the war," he wrote. "You always wanted to stay up all night. You never wanted to go to sleep." Quickly, he fell into a mad romance with a married twenty-year-old starlet named Leni Lynn, chasing her through London showbiz society, dazzling her with notes, flowers, and promises, then leaving her with a parting gift of diamonds. At the same time, he slept with a Canadian journalist who turned out to be a vicious anti-Semite, "the blackest bitch I've ever encountered," and a possible Nazi agent; she left him with a parting gift of gonorrhea. And as much as possible, he avoided any further work on *Tunisian Victory* and tried to forget his contribution to it.

When it became clear that Capra, Huston, and Veiller were going to be in London for months rather than weeks, they moved out of Claridge's and into a set of flats in a house on Hill Street near Berkeley Square. But they were rarely home at the same time; Huston spent his nights out while his boss worked late into the evening at Pinewood. In England, Capra was all business; even on the rare occasions he partook in London's social life, he ended up feeling alienated and homesick. "Party at John Mills' house," he wrote. "Bob Hope, Frances Langford and others there. Much food and vodka. I got claustrophobic and walked home in blackout. Got lost and fell down. Impossible [to] get cabs after 9 p.m. . . . Just realizing how far away I am from home."

As Capra began weeks of collaboration with his British counterparts on ideas for a new version of their film, he kept his guard up. Every time he thought a deal for an Anglo-American coproduction was firm, he would learn that it was subject to the approval of yet another layer of British army bureaucracy. More than once, he lost his temper. "Shock of my life," he wrote at the end of August. "The British haven't decided on joint picture yet. Some bloke called Tritton [General Surles's counterpart, the head of public relations in the British War Office] demands to see the film. . . . We bring over [our] film, show it, then they decide. . . . I blew up." Aware of the appalling quality of the American reenactments, Capra insisted that the British make a deal without seeing his footage. "I will show no film to anyone until I know joint picture was on or off."

Remarkably, even within the privacy of his own diary, Capra was able to make himself believe that he was holding out as a matter of principle rather than of strategy. "Now convinced we're right," he wrote. "Our point is cooperation whether either side had any film or not, not only when it suits. . . . British annoyed at not being able to have their way. Their idea of co-operation is to do it their way. I'm the wrong man for that stuff."

Eventually, a new and final deal was reached; the British and American film units would make all of their footage available to each other. England's footage of the actual campaign and Capra's staged reenactments would be pooled into a new coproduction, and once a rough cut had been completed, both countries would have the option to request changes or even cancel the project entirely. The arrangement satisfied Capra, who was happy to roll up his sleeves and devote himself to an actual movie instead of another bargaining session; he soon relaxed and his initial pugnacity gave way to open admiration. "Tough people, these English," he wrote to Lucille. "It's certainly not the same country we used to know. The people are just grand the way they put up with everything without any complaint. In fact they all go out of the way to be nicer and more pleasant." In his diary, he added, "[I] never cease marveling at British people. They are like golf balls. Soft cover and hard cores—each layer getting harder and harder."

In early September, Capra called Huston back to Pinewood for two weeks during which they, Veiller, and Hodson would attempt to write a fresh script. Hodson, outnumbered and outtalked, found himself "doing a little fighting to prevent our picture . . . becoming disbalanced in favour of America—after all, we did most of the dirty work and had twice as many casualties." He also complained that the screenplay the three Americans were drafting was "so long that . . . if we took *War and Peace* and *Gone with the Wind* and this script, we'd have a great trilogy." But he came to like Capra and his team. "The generosity of the Americans when we write something that tickles them is unbounded," he wrote. "We had some blunt talk over who did the fighting in Tunisia and a day or two later Frank Capra came down to Pinewood with the suggestion that we ought not to be worrying who did the fighting, but we should make a film whose real theme is the unity of the Allies and the need for carrying on that unity into the days of peace. He wasn't sure we should agree, but we're 100% for that."

Capra's notion to emphasize future cooperation in a postwar world, was, everyone agreed, the ideal solution for the last third of the script. He was now happy with the progress of the film, but also terribly lonely; he wrote to Lucille almost daily. Mail traveled slowly and unreliably, so personal wartime communication, except for the rare cable, was a jagged, fragmentary affair in which responses to letters often arrived late or out of order. "Please," he wrote to Lucille on September 16, their daughter's sixth birthday, "cable me once in a while just to tell me you are alright. There are moments when I get panicky about you." Capra, Huston, and Veiller were all in their rented flats on Hill Street that night when, for the first time since their arrival in London, they heard the piercing rise and fall of air raid sirens, and then gunfire. "This is the real thing," he wrote in his journal. "Bombs drop in the distance. Hyde Park guns shake the building. Tony and John go outside like most newcomers. Old ladies and children cower in the hallways. Maids and valets talk reassuring to them. . . . I was scared but I was more sick at the thought of these dear old ladies and little girls being mangled. How far has man gone mad? Will we never learn to get along better than to drop bombs on each other? Surely God didn't mean that to happen? Please God put love and understanding into the hearts of men." Thirty years later, Capra said that that night, as he shivered on the street, "war lost its glamour for me."

By the beginning of October, with the Americans and British both working around the clock at Pinewood, the new picture was almost finished, but the mood of all involved had darkened considerably. Veiller was, according to Capra, "unhappy" with the compromised documentary they had produced, Capra found himself "unmoved and not very excited about anything—we've done our work well so what the hell," and an exhausted Huston asked Capra for permission to take a few days off and travel north.

Capra himself was "really weary both physically and mentally" by October 7, when, in the middle of "a bright [moonlit] night, cold as hell," he was caught in a second air raid. "The searchlights are frantic," he wrote. "They get a German once in a while and hold him while the ack-ack keeps popping . . . it all seemed so inefficient to me. Thousands of shells going off but never seeming to hit anything. . . . I wonder how much longer the common people of the world are going to stand for this. I suppose [it will continue] till the German people realize the futility of war. . . . What a crime."

The next morning, Capra screened *Tunisian Victory* to see whether the Ministry of Information would approve it. He was in no mood to be judged. "British big wigs . . . All frozen faced and tight assed gents who try to make you feel like a burglar," he wrote. "What keeps me from telling them all to go to hell I don't know."

While Capra awaited their verdict, he came up with a new assignment that he felt would reinvigorate Huston, and would also remove him from what had become a distracting web of personal entanglements. "Between his genius and his social life," Capra told Lucille, "he's pretty much of a disorganized man." During his time in London, Huston had met with Eric Ambler, a young, hard-nosed British spy novelist whose work he much admired. Ambler was only thirty-three, but he had already published half a dozen best sellers that used contemporary political events as the backdrop for cloak-and-dagger adventure, and his work had drawn the attention of Hollywood. Orson Welles had just cowritten and produced an adaptation of *Journey into Fear*, and Huston himself had done a draft of another Ambler adaptation, *Background to Danger*, for Warner Bros. Ambler was a committed anti-Fascist who had stopped writing and entered the war as a private in 1939; he had since risen to become a high-level assistant in the British Army Film Service.

In London, Huston had approached Ambler about a possible collaboration on a Hollywood film once the war was over, but Capra had something else in mind. Weeks earlier, the Allies had begun Operation Avalanche, the attempt to liberate Italy that had begun with a landing on the country's western coast. They had successfully taken Salerno and were now pushing inland. "The idea, dreamed up . . . by Colonel Frank Capra," wrote Ambler, "was that John Huston and a US Signal Corps film unit should go with the Allied armies to Rome and make [a] picture . . . about civilian Italy under its new conquerors." The Army Pictorial Service unit back at Fort Fox was then deep into preparation for two new training films, "Occupation of Friendly Countries" and "Occupation of Enemy Countries," and Capra believed that it was time for the Signal Corps to expand its propaganda effort from the home front to foreign nations. His plan had the enthusiastic backing of both General Osborn and the Office of War Information. "It was from one of the OWI people that I first heard the bromide, new then, about 'going for the hearts and minds' of a population," Ambler wrote. "There was, however, a snag. It had been agreed at some high-level meeting that all psychological warfare films for propaganda in occupied territories should be joint Anglo-American ventures. John Huston therefore needed a token Britisher." Ambler was surprised, and not particularly pleased, by the assignment, but he had no choice, and the blow was softened by an immediate promotion; the

British army made him a captain so that Huston would not outrank him. He and Huston left London at the end of October on an air force transport plane bound first for Marrakesh, then for Naples.

Capra's time in England was also coming to an end. After some deliberation, the Ministry of Information and the British War Office told him they would approve the release of *Tunisian Victory* as a joint production if the War Department would do the same. They were as polite and gracious to him as they had been when he first arrived, even throwing him a farewell party on November 4, the day he left for Washington. "Well the British have passed the opus calling it much better than theirs," he wrote Lucille. The strain of their long separation was taking a toll on both of them; Lucille had let him know she was unhappy about it. "Please snap out of it, sweetheart," he wrote back. "I'm not away from you because I like to be. This is no picnic. . . . I'm certainly looking forward to seeing you again soon. It will probably be the biggest treat of my life. . . . This thing will be over sometime, but while it's on we've got to stick it. Everyone in the world must carry his particular little share."

The movie Capra was bringing back to Washington was unmistakably his own, but it was also an uncomfortably negotiated hodgepodge of realism and falsification, conflicting styles and voices, and British and American interests. At seventy-five minutes, *Tunisian Victory* is padded not just with the reenactments Stevens and Huston had shot but with overly studied images of British soldiers at work that also have the air of contrivance. The strength of both countries' contributions comes in the film's quieter moments—the soldiers in their off hours, the melancholy Christmas celebrations, the hunkering down in miserable weather. But the tone is inconsistent and the depiction of the operation itself is spotty. One of the great U.S. Army triumphs in the campaign, the climactic "battle of Hill 609"—a brutal, sustained, and ultimately successful attempt by General Omar Bradley to gain control of one of the highest vantage points in Tunisia—is portrayed entirely through American recreations. In many places, narration is used to paper over gaps in the footage—a voice-over explains that "the lights burned all night" when Churchill came to see Roosevelt in Washington as the camera lingers on a long, distant nighttime shot of a lit White House. There are competing stretches of narration, one from an American GI (voiced by Burgess Meredith) and one from an actor playing a British soldier with a Cockney accent, and Capra allows viewers to eavesdrop on their stilted chat. Rarely during the war had the propagandistic intent of a film meant for general audiences been put forth on screen with such little art or attempt to disguise it. Capra's insistence that Hitler's rise was traceable to an intrinsic German appetite for thoughtless regimentation is given lengthy expression. "Suppose somebody said, put that fellow's eyes out, or turn the 'osepipe on that Jew or on that woman," says the Cockney to the Yank. "Would *we* do it? You and me, Joe, we may not always think alike, but we do *think*. You 'n' me and old Alphonse"—the picture briefly cuts to a French soldier with the word "France" superimposed—"and the rest, we certainly think, all right."

"You know, George, I got an idea," replies the American. "Why can't we, after the war—the same work gang, I mean—keep on swinging together? What couldn't we do? . . . Buildin' things up instead of blowin' things up. Like, I dunno, dams in the desert and roads through the jungle." *Tunisian Victory* ends with a montage of hands-across-the-ocean brotherhood. The last line is nothing if not Capraesque. "Boy oh boy, what a job," the GI concludes. "Bringin' back the smiles to kids' faces."

Capra felt that he had fulfilled his mission, but he also expressed an angry certainty that he would take the fall for whatever the movie's inadequacies were judged to be. "I'm the hatchet man," he told Lucille soon after he returned to Washington. "[I'm] trying to raise the efficiency [*sic*] and most of all the prestige of the Army Pictorial Service, which has been hitting a new low, mostly because they're scared to death to move or to argue. . . . I've been trying to tell them they must never lose an argument, right or wrong. The old technique I used to use against the producers."

Capra had won, but his insistence on cementing the special relationship between British and U.S. propaganda forces with shoddy work had left a bitter taste behind. "No war documentary can be made with absolute integrity and truth," Hodson wrote in his diary soon after Capra left. "Some reconstruction is inevitable if the story is to be properly told. . . . There are two schools of thought. The first says, 'Preserve integrity—make it real . . . even if the resultant picture is poor.' . . . The other school says, 'Make a good picture. If the "real" stuff isn't good enough, fake some that's better. The result is all that counts.' The second, as I understand it, is the American view, and [*Tunisian Victory*] pretty well conforms to it."

SEVENTEEN

"I Have to Do a Good Job"

ENGLAND AND ITALY,
OCTOBER 1943–JANUARY 1944

illiam Wyler and George Stevens came back to London at the end of October, just as Huston and Capra were leaving. Wyler's return was tense and urgent—the result of a summons by cable from Eighth Air Force commander General Eaker that read simply, "You come back or I get a replacement." Wyler had spent the summer and early fall at home on the West Coast working on *25 Missions*, but his stubborn, methodical, painstakingly slow progress had not escaped the attention of his commanding officers. Some of the delays were unavoidable: The backlogged processing labs at Technicolor had taken weeks to blow up his film from 16-millimeter to 35-millimeter, essential for a movie that Wyler was now sure he wanted to play in "thousands of theaters all over the country." But the director, upon his return to Hollywood, had also reverted to "Forty-Take Wyler" form, working at his own pace to get exactly what he wanted and worrying little about the prescribed schedule.

In late August, the crew of the *Memphis Belle* had finally ended its national rallying tour and arrived in Los Angeles to work on the picture. Wyler saw their visit as an occasion to honor their achievement, and as a treat, he and Talli threw them a welcoming party at his home, asking each crewman in advance which Hollywood star he most wanted to meet. Nobody turned down his invitation—by then, the ten flyers, the youngest of whom was only nineteen, were celebrities in their own right, and for an evening they happily chatted and flirted with Veronica Lake, Hedy Lamarr, Olivia de Havilland, and Dinah Shore. The next morning, they met with Wyler and his post-production team. Wyler listened to their suggestions, made a few changes in the lines he had planned to have them record, and started rehearsing them. He had to work around their availability—the navy was still putting the crew through its paces with daily appearances at Lockheed and Douglas aircraft plants along the Southern California coast, and by the time Wyler had finished recording their voice-overs and filming some brief insert shots, it was September and he still hadn't written a narration script or gotten close to assembling a rough cut.

Wyler may have been in no hurry to finish the film, but he wasn't lingering in Hollywood because of any eagerness to return to the movie business. When Sam Goldwyn asked him if he was ready to come home yet—studios and producers were increasingly anxious to get their top-tier talent back in the fold—Wyler told him he intended to stay in the war for the duration. Goldwyn then asked him to sign a punitive amendment to his contract which stipulated that he was to resume work in Hollywood within sixty days of his discharge and gave Goldwyn the right to terminate their deal unilaterally if the war didn't end by December 31, 1945.

By October, the army was growing impatient, for both the movie and the resumption of Wyler's service abroad. He had been working on *25 Missions* for more than three months, and it still needed original music, narration, sound effects, and further editing. He cabled Eaker asking for a sixty-day extension, and when he received the general's stern one-sentence threat to remove him from his job, he decided it would be more politic to make his case in person. He got on a C-54 army transport plane and flew to London.

When Wyler walked back into air force HQ in Grosvenor Square, Eaker was soon mollified and reassured, and he gave the director everything he wanted—another two months in Los Angeles, a promotion to lieutenant colonel, and—after several weeks of further long-distance negotiation and cajoling—permission to release the film as a five-reel feature attraction rather than a twenty-minute short. But for the rest of the year, the army would

be watching him more closely; particularly among officers in Los Angeles, a
suspicion that Wyler was dragging his feet had taken hold. In December, he
was accused of showing up two hours late for a sound effects recording session, and received an army reprimand that in some particulars sounded as if
it could have come straight from Hal Wallis or Sam Goldwyn. "The recording crew . . . was given a shooting time of 1900," the memo read. "Please
note that this same crew had been on duty since 0800 the same day. Colonel
Wiler [sic], who is in charge of this job, did not appear until after 2100. . . .
Seventeen (17) takes were made. . . . This appears to me to be an unnecessary expenditure of man hours and material and an unnecessary imposition
on the dispositions of a group of men conscienciously [sic] trying to do a good
job." Wyler wrote a dismissive response denying that he was late and reminding the officers who were monitoring him that the care he was taking
was in the service of "recording sound to go over some of the scenes shot by
Lt [Harold] Tannenbaum, 47-year-old soundman, who . . . lies in a grave on
the Brest peninsula, buried by the enemy . . . [and who] considered no 'imposition on his disposition' too great when his country was at war and a job
had to be done."

Tannenbaum's death weighed heavily on Wyler as he worked on 25 Missions and struggled to find a balance between the triumphalism of a hard-
won air force success story and the lasting ache of losing a comrade in arms.
He found himself shaping a film that was more somber, personal, and
haunted than the one he had sketched out before his first trip to Bassingbourn, and he struggled to find an appropriate tone for it. Late in 1943, he
asked the writer Maxwell Anderson, whose credits included the play What
Price Glory? and the screenplay for All Quiet on the Western Front, to watch
the latest cut of the film and then try his hand at writing narration for it.
Wyler had always planned to end 25 Missions with Captain Morgan and his
men celebrating at the airbase after their final flight, and the voice-over that
Anderson conceived for the scene was intimate and anguished.

"The co-pilot asks the pilot if he's going to 'buzz the field'? Fly 'round it,
that is, to celebrate," Anderson wrote. "The pilot shakes his head. They lost
some ships. Glad as he is to get through and get his rest, he can't celebrate—
not with those fellows in mind he's not likely to see again. . . . It's not all

happiness. . . . That night there is a party, with girls and drinks, and one veteran who hadn't tasted liquor since he entered the air corps went quietly and happily under the table. But in the middle of the hilarity Captain Morgan, who had never been accused of sentimentality, was seen sitting in a corner of the room with tears running down his cheeks. The reason was simple. He had been in charge of allocating men to planes in his squadron. One of the crews he sent out had also only one mission to go—and they had not come back. If he had only given them another plane—or chosen some other pilot! . . . And somehow the girls can't recapture the party after that."

Anderson ended his script on a bleak and uncompromising note: "This war hasn't made many heroes. It's not a war in which heroes stand out. But nothing that great heroes ever had to face in world history has been tougher or sterner than what confronts the crews now flying our Fortresses over Europe. All too few of them complete that last assignment."

Wyler was dazzled by Anderson's work, and sent it to Beirne Lay, asking for his notes and suggestions. Lay also loved it and returned it untouched, with nothing but the handwritten note "How about my polishing up *Hamlet*?" But both men soon realized that the wrenching, sorrowful notes that Anderson had sounded—of alienation during victory, of loss in the middle of celebration, of a bereavement that lingers long after the glow of a successful mission has worn off—were in direct opposition to the reason the army wanted the movie made in the first place. Wyler ended up using chunks of Anderson's script throughout the film, which was now to be called *The Memphis Belle: The Story of a Flying Fortress*. But he reluctantly concluded that Anderson's ending had to be jettisoned entirely. The picture would instead end with the footage Wyler's team had shot of the king and queen's congratulatory visit. And the new words to be spoken in the movie's last minutes, which had been rewritten by a member of Wyler's unit named Lester Koenig, tapped a different vein of sentimentality: "The ground crew were a little self-conscious about being dressed in fatigues," the narrator says. "But the queen thought they were very nice." What follows, perhaps inevitably, is some flattering footage of General Eaker as he gives the *Belle* crew orders for their "twenty-sixth and most important mission—to return to America to train new crews and to tell the people what we're doing here, to thank them for their help and support, and tell them to keep it up so *we* can keep it up! So we can bomb the enemy again and again and again until he has had enough. And then we can all come home." Even the initial grace note in Anderson's draft was cast aside: In the final cut of *Memphis Belle*, Captain Robert Morgan is shown joyously buzzing the field.

When Stevens arrived in London in late October 1943, it was for a considerably longer stay, and with a renewed sense of purpose. His six months in North Africa, Egypt, and Iran had produced nothing but the staged Tunisia footage he had turned over to Capra; he had spent the last few weeks back in the United States, trying to forget the futility of his time away and fill his days with as much fun as possible. At home in California, he took George Jr. to a doubleheader. In New York, he dined with Bennett Cerf, escorted the starlet Ann Shirley to the Wedgwood Room to hear Frank Sinatra sing, and enjoyed a reunion with Bert Wheeler, the vaudevillian had who starred in some of the first comedies he had directed a decade earlier. But Stevens didn't linger; he was ready to return to service provided that this time he had an actual mission. "When I am put on the ground to make a film, I have to do a good job," he wrote in his journal that fall. "These amateurs can stay out on a job indefinitely, no picture comes from their effort and so long as they keep a pleasant social relationship with the local command their job is accepted as well done. . . . [But] I cannot go off on an expedition and not make film."

Stevens's new task—the first of a series of assignments that would keep him in Europe for the next two years—was an important one: Capra had directed him to organize a Special Coverage Unit (SPECOU) of forty-five cameramen and sound recorders to photograph the coming American landing in Europe. The Allies had started mapping out plans for the liberation of France as early as the summer of 1942, when it was code-named Operation Sledgehammer, but their first plan wasn't feasible; it would have relied on the already overstretched British fighting forces with insufficient support from the Americans, who were then pouring all of their manpower into the war in the Pacific. A second iteration of the idea, Operation Roundup, which would have provided considerably more Allied troop strength, was discussed with a target date of April 1943, and also scrapped. But that August, at the Quebec

Conference, the Allied chiefs of staff had begun strategizing in earnest about a third try, Operation Overlord, with a possible landing on the Normandy coast now planned for May 1944.

Stevens, of course, knew only what all of the other officers who were arriving in England that fall knew—that an Allied entry into Europe, either through France or Scandinavia, was coming, and that it would surely be decisive in the war. Just as he reached London, news came that General Dwight D. Eisenhower had been moved over from the Mediterranean Theater of Operations to command the Supreme Headquarters Allied Expeditionary Force (SHAEF); he would be based in the suburban London neighborhood of Teddington. Stevens had met Eisenhower over the summer in Tunis and the two had had a testy exchange when he asked the general if he planned to talk to General Hans-Jürgen von Arnim, Rommel's replacement, who had just been captured. Eisenhower, "to keep me in my place," replied, "'I'm here to kill Germans, not to talk to them.'" Stevens came away disliking him intensely: "What a horse's ass he was . . . I'll never forget it." But that didn't matter: This assignment would put Stevens in the center of the action for the duration of the war.

In London, he began working with the men who would become his squad mates and closest companions on the front—Irwin Shaw, who was now assigned to his unit; Bill Mellor, his cameraman in Tunis; Tony Veiller, who decided to share digs with Stevens the day after his housemate Capra moved out and returned to the United States, and Ivan Moffat, a debonair, witty, and well-connected British-American screenwriter who had grown up in both coutries, enlisted in the Signal Corps, and was now back in the UK under Stevens's authority. The British Army Film Unit had viewed Capra and Wyler as American eminences, but Stevens, despite years of success, was less familiar to them—the British hadn't seen many of his films other than *Gunga Din*. "I didn't really know much about . . . his work or anything else," said Moffat. "There was no particular George Stevens cult in England." Moffat and Stevens would end up working together for the next twenty years, but they didn't connect instantly. "When I first met him, George didn't like *Citizen Kane*!" he recalled. "He had been something of a philistine in his outlook before then, and rather boohooed anything that smacked of too much intellectuality."

Organizing a large unit of men did not come naturally to Stevens, who was not gregarious, made friends slowly, and felt caught between the desire to be their comrade and colleague and the necessity of serving as their commander. Like Wyler, he was flabbergasted by the difficulty of requisitioning supplies and expediting orders; the power struggles over his head seemed so byzantine that it was often unclear to him who could, or would, get SPECOU what it needed. Early in 1944, he reached out to Capra for help, begging him to cut through the red tape. "We have, as you might know, been anxious for clarification of the overall situation here," he wrote. "Many different authorities have been making plans. . . . We have followed the simple procedure here of reminding the policy makers of the job we were sent here to do, and requesting the privilege of doing it."

Capra already knew firsthand of the frustration of working in London while decisions were being made an ocean away but admitted to Stevens that his hands were all but tied. "In some vague way," he wrote from Washington, "I'm supposed to be in charge of all overseas combat photographers," but "as you can well imagine . . . we have no direct communication or control over camera men at the front." He told Stevens to hang in and predicted optimistically, "Don't be surprised if a lot of us come bouncing in on you one day" to provide more support. That day never came; delayed and nonspecific encouragement was all that Stevens would ever get from Washington.

Stevens was far from home when the surprising news came to him that the New York Film Critics Circle had, by a one-vote margin on the seventh ballot, voted him the year's best director for his comedy *The More the Merrier*. It was the first major award he had ever won, and when his friend, *Talk of the Town* screenwriter Sidney Buchman, accepted for him in a nationally broadcast ceremony, he praised Stevens's "special, unique, irreplaceable" quality as a director. Stevens was happy about the win. The gentle, lighthearted sensibility of his movie, in which war was little more than an abstract inconvenience and an impetus for romance, now felt impossibly distant and innocent. "Miss you and my boy more than you can know," he cabled

Yvonne shortly after the awards dinner. "Working endlessly on difficult job, for me much discouragement. . . . The main thing I am looking forward to is for this to end successfully. . . . Wish Hitler was in hell and am glad to help in any way to put him there."

The New York critics also honored Huston and Capra that winter, splitting a special award for documentary filmmaking between *Report from the Aleutians* and the first five *Why We Fight* installments. It was *Why We Fight*'s newest chapter, *The Battle of Russia,* that had convinced reviewers that Capra's series was something much more than a set of history lessons for new GIs; together, the movies had come to constitute a democratic manifesto that encouraged Americans to view the war as a struggle of international allies, not just U.S. soldiers. Back in the spring of 1942, when Eric Knight had gone through the scripts and sent his eviscerating evaluation of them to Capra, he had exempted *The Battle of Russia* from his scorn, calling it the only script that "sounds as if it were written by a guy who had an ache in his gut." Capra agreed, and with Mellett finally out of the way, he mounted an all-out campaign for the American theatrical release of the film while he was still in London, arranging screenings for Academy members and securing national bookings in November.

The Battle of Russia was the first *Why We Fight* picture since *Prelude to War* to be approved for distribution to civilian audiences. It was initially supervised by Capra, written by Veiller, and, while Capra was abroad, completed by Anatole Litvak, who was widely acknowledged as its director. Like the previous films in the series, this one was, as the *New Yorker* put it, a "scissors and paste" production that was cobbled together out of previously shot film—everything from foreign newsreels of anti-Soviet atrocities to silent pictures from twenty-five years earlier and footage from Sergei Eisenstein's 1938 film *Alexander Nevsky* that was used to fill in Russian history. But the Russians, who provided the Signal Corps with extensive footage from their own news films, war reports, and propaganda pictures, had documented their own struggle with skill and power, and Capra and Litvak had a wealth of material about the siege of Leningrad and the sustained and heroic Stalingrad campaign on which to draw. Unlike the first four installments, which each ran about fifty minutes, the eighty-minute *Battle of Russia* was designed to leave its audience, both in and out of uniform, in a fevered state of patriotic militarism. It did so with such effectiveness that James Agee insisted, in an uncharacteristically naïve burst of enthusiasm, that not a moment of it was ever intended "for propaganda, always for the maximum of human and emotional force." It was Agee who a month earlier had urged the War Activities Committee to approve the picture for public release, calling it "the best and most important war film ever assembled in this country." The Russians agreed; the Cinema Section of the USSR Society for Cultural Relations with Foreign Countries met to discuss the impact of the film and admiringly called it "a real super-powered celluloid bomb."

After the end of the war, *The Battle of Russia*'s unblemished version of Russian history and what Agee described as its "figure-skating" around the German-Soviet pact would be used by proto-McCarthyites to tag Capra as soft on Communism. But in late 1943, its portrayal of a people who, according to the opening narration, "for all time shattered the legend of Nazi invincibility" had a profound impact on those who saw it and helped to cement Capra's reputation as first among all the American filmmakers who were contributing to the war effort. The essayist Alfred Kazin, then a young soldier stationed at an army base in Illinois, was shaken and excited by what he saw. This was not "the trustworthy old American movie magic working on us like a liberating storm"; it was "the real thing . . . Russia as my parents had not been allowed to see it." Watching the picture on the base, he said he lost "all separateness, [felt] absolutely at one with the soldiers in the dark theater. It was a physical shock . . . how much I had been worked over, appealed to."

Huston's award for *Report from the Aleutians* was a vindication of his battle with Mellett to have the film released at its full length, but he wasn't in New York to savor the moment. In early November, he and Eric Ambler had arrived in Italy with ambitious plans to make the war's first serious American nonfiction film about the results of an Allied ground campaign. They were joined by Jules Buck, a bright, even-keeled lieutenant in the Signal Corps who had been a mainstay of the small team Huston had brought to the Aleutians. The director described Buck as "my one-man army throughout the war" and had requested him as a right-hand man as soon as Capra had told him to go to Italy.

Naples had been hit by more than a hundred airstrikes from both sides by the time Huston got there, including an August assault by four hundred Allied B-17s from which it had not begun to recover. The city, he wrote, was "like a whore suffering from the beating of a brute. Little boys were offering their sisters and mothers for sale. . . . Rats appeared in packs outside the buildings and simply stood there, looking at you with red eyes, not moving. . . . The souls of the people had been raped." The "unholy" place that Naples had become was at that moment a magnet for Americans who wanted to document war at its most searing and destructive. In his first days there, Huston met Robert Capa, the Hungarian Jewish combat photographer who had been covering the Allied campaign in Sicily and Italy for *Life* magazine. Ernie Pyle, the roving correspondent for the Scripps-Howard newspaper chain whose GI's-eye-view columns had made him one of the most widely read American war reporters, was also on the scene, hoping to accomplish in print something akin to what Huston wanted to do on film.

Ambler was still wary of his American counterpart, whom he found a "bit pretentious"; he couldn't stand Huston's grandiosity, his mannered way of speaking, or his habit of surveying the landscape from behind air force–regulation dark glasses that seemed to give him "a somewhat exaggerated view of [his] own might." He also thought Huston's posturing was intended to conceal his growing awareness that the assignment he had been given seemed silly in the face of the horrifying realities they were now witnessing on every street corner. "He was probably too appalled to say . . . that the idea of a film about the little people of Italy that dear old Frank Capra had dreamed up . . . would be in Naples preposterous." But the two men were stuck working together against a common foe. Colonel Melvin Gillette, the same Signal Corps lifer who had made it so difficult for George Stevens to get anywhere near the action in North Africa, was now in charge of the army photographic section at Caserta, and had little interest in helping Huston realize his ambitions.

Without Gillette's approval for supplies and equipment, there could be no documentary, and he stalled the team for a month. "John set out to make Colonel Gillette believe that a good movie made while we were under his jurisdiction would bring him credit," Ambler wrote. "In the end, I think,

John bored him into giving way." Gillette and Huston struck a deal: If he pleased Gillette's commanding officer by shooting some boilerplate newsreel footage of the U.S. Army joining forces with the Goums, a unit of Moroccan and Algerian fighters that had just arrived in Italy, Gillette would give him everything he needed.

Weeks of waiting had brought Huston, Ambler, and Buck closer together, especially after a hepatitis epidemic turned so many rooms at army headquarters into quarantined convalescent wards that the three of them were forced to bunk in the same room. Ambler came to admire Huston's persistence, if nothing else; Huston conceded that Ambler, "except for his snoring . . . was a good man to have around." By December, according to Ambler, they had formulated a plan to find "a small town immediately after the enemy had left, and then make a film of what happened next to its inhabitants." They had settled on San Pietro, an ancient *comune* forty-three miles northwest of Naples from which the Germans had finally been driven after ten days of heavy bombardment and shelling during which many American soldiers were killed, three-quarters of the Allied tanks in the battle were blown up, and the town itself was destroyed.

Buck secured a jeep, and he, Huston, Ambler, and a three-man Signal Corps camera crew drove to nearby Venafro, where they set up camp in a farmhouse and started planning their first day of shooting. But after an initial scouting expedition, the sergeant in charge of the cameramen returned, clearly rattled. The all-clear that the Signal Corps had given Huston back in Naples had been premature. San Pietro was still spiderwebbed with German mines, booby traps, and tripwires. It was also completely abandoned; no relieved or joyous returning villagers were anywhere in sight.

The roads to San Pietro were open, however, and Huston decided they should venture out on foot with Buck's Eyemo camera and see if they could find anything worth filming. Ambler, whom Huston called "one of the coolest men I've ever seen under fire," was apprehensive, believing that Huston "still had not understood" the degree to which he was putting himself and his team in harm's way. The trip started benignly; they happened upon a group of cheerful soldiers from Texas who were excited to see the camera and thought they might be lucky enough to make it into an American newsreel. Buck shot some footage of them, and then they moved on. When they had almost reached the town, Huston stopped suddenly. He and Ambler turned and saw a GI kneeling by a tree, aiming his rifle. "For an instant he looked alive, but only an instant," Ambler wrote. "A mortar bomb fragment had sheared away the whole of one side of his head."

As they turned to look at the spare, leafless, rocky woods around them, they saw that the way forward was littered with the corpses of American soldiers, and the town of San Pietro, visible a quarter mile away, appeared to be little more than rubble and the charred skeletal shells of what had once been buildings, only a few of which were left standing. The Italian interpreter would go no farther, nor would the sergeant and his cameramen—not for the sake of a movie. Huston and Ambler kept moving forward with Buck, past the dead. As Buck started to film, a mortar shell shrieked past their heads and, with the camera still rolling, they tumbled into a ditch together. They left San Pietro as quickly as possible.

Huston and Ambler angrily reunited with their crew back in Venafro; they were both disgusted that the sergeant and his men had refused to proceed and all but called them deserters. There was tension and uncertainty about what to do next. Ambler had hurt his leg jumping away from the mortar and was having difficulty walking. Faulty Signal Corps intelligence about the safety of the town had endangered all of their lives. But the next morning, Huston was determined to go back. To him, San Pietro felt like the center of the war. Pyle had already made his way there and was seen walking the roads, looking for soldiers to interview. A team from the British Army Film Unit had shown up as well, led by David MacDonald, who had overseen *Desert Victory* and was now perhaps going to do for the reputation of British forces in Italy what he had done for them in Tunisia. Ambler had been in England during *Desert Victory*'s postproduction and, its warm American reception notwithstanding, he knew enough about the film's artifice— "carefully-lit matching close-ups . . . contrived . . . in Pinewood Studios . . . [with] make-up men waiting to dab on artificial sweat"—to take a jaundiced view of any combat documentary that made claims of complete authenticity. But Huston's sense of competitiveness was sparked; he would not be outdone by the Brits this time. He, Ambler, and Buck set out again, this time by jeep in deference to Ambler's injured leg.

They made it all the way to what remained of San Pietro's central piazza, where Huston started planning shots and mapping out a potential opening for the movie. Their work was interrupted by the sound of planes overhead—perhaps Allied, perhaps Axis—and howitzer fire. They raced toward one of the only buildings still intact—the church—and hid in its crypt, where, for the first time, they encountered some of San Pietro's residents: six dirty, cowering villagers, three of them young children, who could have been there for hours or days.

When the shelling stopped, all three men ran for the jeep and got on the road back to Venafro. In the Aleutians, Huston had had a few moments of uncontrolled terror, once when his plane crash-landed, once when a midnight air raid seemed imminent. Now he was just barely holding himself together. As they were crossing a bridge to get out of the town, their jeep's wheels got stuck. They were temporarily frozen in place in an open vehicle, exposed on all sides. Huston exploded at Buck, who was driving. "Filthy little shit!" he shouted. "Dirty Jew bastard!"

That night in Venafro, a livid Ambler asked Huston "whose side we were on in the war—the Allies or the editors of *Der Stürmer*?" Huston, ashamed, apologized to Buck. It was now clear that Capra's idea to document the celebratory liberation of a town with villagers timidly emerging to cheer on the American troops was a fantasy. None of them knew what their next move should be.

Rather than routing his concerns through Colonel Gillette, who would certainly tell him and his men to pull out, Huston decided to try to reach Capra directly and ask for further instructions from Washington. He spent the day writing a letter, and that night they all drove to an airfield near Naples, where Huston had friends in the army who would put his communiqué on the next plane. With little else to do for the rest of the night, Huston, Ambler, and Buck walked into a palazzo that the Fifth Army was now using as its headquarters in Italy. One large, drafty room had been turned into a makeshift bar. A lone couple sat there; they had clearly been drinking for some time. The man turned around. "You still shooting pictures, kid?" said Humphrey Bogart.

The actor and his wife, Mayo Methot, had come to Italy as part of a good-will tour. Huston introduced his colleagues, and they sat down to a long, sour, boozy evening. Methot, a onetime Broadway musical performer, was a serious alcoholic, so combative when under the influence that Bogart had nicknamed her "Sluggy." She and Huston had always disliked each other, and as he ignored her, she turned truculent. The night ended with her barely coherent, slurring the song she had introduced on Broadway fifteen years earlier, "More Than You Know," off-key as someone tried to accompany her on an old piano.

"Whether you're right
Whether you're wrong
Man of my heart
I'll string along"

Huston thought the evening was "embarrassing." As for Ambler, he had found his time in the company of a Hollywood director not only distasteful, but pointless. He had no intention of returning to Venafro or of waiting for Capra's reply; as far as he was concerned, the San Pietro project was unsalvageable. They would have to start again and find a new town that would fit their concept. "We still thought it possible to make that sort of documentary in a forward area without 'reconstruction,' 're-enactment' or other essential falsification," he wrote. "We had not yet understood that for us, with our brief from Washington, nothing but falsification would be of any use, or even possible."

EIGHTEEN

"We Really Don't Know What Goes On Beneath the Surface"

WASHINGTON, THE CHINA-BURMA-INDIA THEATER, ITALY, AND NEW YORK, SEPTEMBER 1943–MARCH 1944

J ohn Ford wondered if the war was over for him. The imbroglio over *December 7th* had not resulted in any kind of reprimand; in fact, Ford had gotten some credit for saving the film. But as his colleagues from Hollywood were shuttling to and from Europe on high-level missions that put them close to the front lines, he was planted in Washington, supervising short informational and training films for Field Photo but shooting nothing himself. An officebound bureaucrat was the last thing Ford had imagined he would become when he left Hollywood for the navy, and despite his extensive responsibilities, it felt like a kind of impotence. Some directors didn't see themselves as actual film shooters; John Huston, for example, remarked that he "didn't take one successful photograph during the whole war. . . . I carried the cameras as a sort of token. . . . The camera separates one from the world." But for Ford, the opposite was true; it was the camera that connected him to the world, and when he wasn't behind one he could feel lost, almost derelict.

He had already served longer than any other director; perhaps it was time to go back to his old life in California, to make a war film rather than film the war itself. MGM was actively urging him to get back to his real job;

Louis B. Mayer had acquired the rights to a nonfiction bestseller called *They Were Expendable,* an account of the brave, doomed attempt of a fleet of American PT boats to defend the Philippines against overwhelming Japanese force in 1942. Mayer saw it as a project for Spencer Tracy, and thought Ford, also a rough-hewn, hard-drinking Irish Catholic, would be a perfect match for him, especially with his firsthand knowledge of the war in the Pacific. Ford liked the idea; as early as the spring of 1943, he knew that he wanted to make it his next film. But when MGM asked Bill Donovan if he would consider taking Ford off active duty so that he could make the picture immediately, Donovan said no. That was fine with Ford—any sign that the navy still believed it had some use for him was encouraging—but the director himself was torn. He was now fifty years old, months away from the birth of his first grandchild, with his twenty-fifth wedding anniversary approaching. And his long separation from Mary seemed to have strengthened his sentimental attachment to her. "I guess we might just as well break down and confess we miss each other—what the hell," he wrote to her. "I pray to God it will soon be over so we can live our life together with our children and grandchildren and our *Araner.* . . . I'm tough to live with—heaven knows and Hollywood didn't help—Irish and genius don't mix well. But you know you're the only woman I've ever loved."

Ford had practical reason to consider requesting an early discharge. He was earning just $4,000 a year from the navy, and although his annual profit checks from the movies he had made before the war were ten times that, his yearly income was still only a small fraction of what it had been in Hollywood. His business manager had recently told him that he was overdrawn and that he and Mary would have to remain on a tight budget for the rest of 1943. But he never seriously considered leaving the navy; it would have felt selfish to him, perhaps even cowardly. Since the war had started, he had watched with increasing contempt as John Wayne had made and broken one vague commitment after another to join up. Wayne's star had risen since his breakthrough in *Stagecoach* and he was now in constant demand in Hollywood; he talked earnestly of going into the army or the navy, but always right after the next movie. In the spring, when Ford point-blank offered Wayne a spot in Field Photo, he had declined, and he declined again when the offer was reiterated in August. At the end of 1943, Wayne, who had four young children, was reclassified from 3-A (a deferment granted to men who had exceptional family obligations) to 1-A (fully eligible). Republic Studios, where he was under contract, jumped in quickly to have him reclassified again as 2-A, a deferment granted to those whom the armed forces deemed should keep their civilian jobs in the national interest. Wayne never would enter the war; he would fulfill his commitment to the armed services by doing a USO tour, getting no closer to combat than the starring role in Republic's *The Fighting Seabees*. Ford found his behavior reprehensible.

In September, Donovan had brought Ford out of limbo with an assignment to travel to the China-Burma-India Theater of Operations as an observer for the OSS. As a trip to the front, it lacked anything like the urgency of Midway; Ford and two Field Photo colleagues were sent to New York and put on a freighter that would take two months to reach its destination, and the mission came with a request that Ford temporarily turn over his duties running the unit he had created to a colleague, Ray Kellogg. But it didn't matter: Ford was happy to be in the field again.

His two months in Burma and China did not result in a major documentary, but it did get him back in the thick of things. He got off to a slightly rocky start because of his overfondness for military dress when he lingered in Calcutta, awaiting some tailored uniforms, and Colonel Carl Eifler, head of the Burmese OSS detachment, told him, "You'd damn well better be here within twelve hours or I'll court-martial your ass!" "You old bastard—who the hell do you think you're talking to?" Ford replied. Eifler, who did not know whom he was talking to, told him he didn't care. But tensions dissolved once the men met and Ford got down to work. It soon became apparent that Donovan had sent him across the Pacific for reasons having more to do with internal Washington politics than with the need for a great director at this particular battlefront. Ford's job was to make a visual case for the usefulness of Donovan's new intelligence agency abroad by shooting footage of officers at work that could, if necessary, be shown to Congress as a pitch for further appropriations to the OSS, and he fulfilled his assignment without complaint. He and his men shot some material for newsreels and shorts, mostly concentrating on cooperative endeavors between the Americans and the Burmese—troops working together, supply planes arriving. He also did some aerial reconnaissance, and even made his first and only parachute jump into the jungle, saying Hail Marys all the way, in order to film the Kachins, an indigenous tribe that had been working with the OSS. And he spent some time training cameramen to use 35-millimeter equipment for geographic surveys from the air as part of the Intelligence Documentary Photographic Project, known within Field Photo as "Ippy Dippy Intelligence." He spent New Year's Eve in China, and left for Washington a couple of weeks later.

The rightward drift of Ford's politics, which began around this time, was fitful and remains difficult to trace. Before the war, he had never allied himself with isolationists, as many conservatives did; unlike Capra, he had always been staunchly anti-Fascist, and he was in sympathy with Roosevelt on many issues. But in early 1944, fervent anti-Communism began to dominate his thinking.

In his biography *Searching for John Ford*, Joseph McBride suggests that Ford's time in Burma, particularly under the hard-right General Albert Wedemeyer, influenced his political retrenchment. He notes Ford's fears that Communist ideology was insidiously pervading American life and his own industry, a suspicion that, in the Ford family, was frequently connected to a degree of hostility toward Jews that set him apart from most of his fellow directors. Nothing that was happening in Germany or Europe seems to have altered a level of anti-Semitism that letters suggest was a kind of lingua franca among the Fords. When he was on his way to Burma, he had written Mary from aboard ship that one of the travelers with whom he was sharing the voyage was a Jewish doctor he called "The Yid." Mary, who was spending much of her time at home volunteering for the Hollywood Canteen, complained to him that the organization was dominated by leftist Jews who hated the Irish, and at around the same time, the Fords' son Patrick expressed disgust that Jews had overrun the navy's public relations department, where he worked. "Yid," "hebe," "mockie," and worse show up in the Fords' letters, but the recurrence of the terms seems to stem less from deep-seated hatred than from a kind of cultural parochialism that probably persisted from their middle-class Irish Catholic upbringing. Ford himself believed that Catholics

and Jews, as outsiders, should make common cause; he had said to his longtime agent Harry Wurtzel at the start of the war that "we've got to win . . .
because Jews like you and Catholics like myself and family, who have no
place in the world, can't let these bastards succeed." And although he dis-
trusted Jews as a group, he was fond of announcing that some of his best
friends, including Wurtzel, were Jews. (One of Ford's letters to Wurtzel begins, cordially, "Dear Christ-Killer," suggesting that Ford, raised to think of
Jews as a historical enemy, often disguised his genuine unease with them as
arm-punching bonhomie.)

In early 1944, Ford, for the first time, cast his lot publicly with a group
of virulently anti-Roosevelt Hollywood colleagues whose anti-Communist
rhetoric helped to set the table for McCarthyism. Their leader was Sam
Wood, a well-known Hollywood director whose credits included *Goodbye,
Mr. Chips; The Pride of the Yankees;* and, most recently, an adaptation of
Ernest Hemingway's *For Whom the Bell Tolls* that had managed to erase all
anti-Fascist and leftist ideology from the screenplay, spreading the thin story
that remained over nearly three hours. Wood's own daughter believed that it
was his failure to win an Academy Award for directing *Mr. Chips* that started
to sour him on Hollywood; he began to mutter incessantly about Communism, listing in a little black notebook the names of colleagues whom he was
sure were subversives, and he soon turned from "a charming man" into "a
snarling, unreasoning brute." Wood's rhetoric won over a number of people
in Hollywood, from Victor Fleming to Gary Cooper to Walt Disney to John
Wayne, and together they formed the Motion Picture Alliance for the Preservation of American Ideals. Among the members of its executive committee
was Ford's friend James McGuinness, who had a couple of years earlier been
one of the writers to whom Ford turned when he needed a voice-over script
for *The Battle of Midway.* Since Ford wasn't in Hollywood for the series of
meetings and discussions that preceded the MPA's public launch in February 1944, it is possible that McGuinness brought him into the fold; in any
case, Ford wrote a forty-dollar check that made him a founding member and
put him at odds with most of his Hollywood associates in the Signal Corps
and Field Photo.

That included Capra, whose own anti-Communism, based largely on the fear that he himself would be the target of red-baiters, did not lead him to join the MPA. Capra, back in the United States after his long stay in London, saw himself as a servant of the army and, by extension, of the Roosevelt administration for as long as he was on active duty; his job was to convey the government's political ideals, not to express his own. It was not always easy for him to decipher what those ideals were. Almost two years after he had conceived the *Know Your Enemy* series, Capra was still struggling with the first installment, about Japan. After an initial false start with a failed treatment that trafficked in overt anti-Asian racism, he had turned to a filmmaker who promised a completely new approach.

Joris Ivens was a Dutch-born socialist documentarian whose pro-Soviet political sympathies had led the FBI to label him a "dangerous Communist." He would have been an unlikely candidate to join Capra's team except for his impeccable reputation as a filmmaker and his international experience: He had shot documentaries in the Netherlands and Russia as well as New Deal–era propaganda shorts for the U.S. Film Service and the National Film Board of Canada, and in 1937 his anti-Fascist documentary about the Spanish Civil War, *The Spanish Earth*, was shown at the White House, after which he had dined with the Roosevelts. Capra had used footage shot by Ivens in at least two of the *Why We Fight* films. When Capra asked him to direct *Know Your Enemy—Japan*, Ivens agreed on the condition that he could pick his own screenwriter—Carl Foreman, a former member of the Communist Party who was then a private in the army.*

Ivens moved to Los Angeles, where he took a job as a steelworker in a shipyard in order to make ends meet while he and Foreman worked on the project for nine months, all the while under FBI surveillance. The twenty-minute film they ultimately created included a sequence animated by the Walt Disney Studios in which Emperor Hirohito was depicted as a kamikaze pilot nosediving toward earth; as he plunged, his ceremonial robes gradually changed into a uniform of the Imperial Army. The narration that Foreman wrote to accompany Ivens's footage bluntly indicted a cabal of Japanese

---

* After the war, Foreman went on to write *High Noon* and many other films; he became one of Hollywood's most famous blacklisted screenwriters after refusing to name names to HUAC.

businessmen and military leaders as "the real rulers of Japan—the power-hungry generals and admirals, the money-made industrialists, the grinning hypocritical politicians [who] want to rule the world."

Ivens and Foreman wanted *Know Your Enemy—Japan* to do more than educate American soldiers and movie audiences; they hoped it could some-how be used to stir the people of Japan into revolting against their own cor-rupt system if the Allies ever occupied the country and could thus expose the Japanese to American propaganda. That idea ran directly into a buzzsaw; when Capra submitted Ivens's completed film at the end of 1943, the army and the administration both summarily rejected it. The picture's unsparing treatment of Hirohito ran counter to the State Department's conviction that since the United States would almost surely have to reestablish some kind of relationship with the emperor after the war, it would be wise to avoid deni-grating him more than necessary. (The same warning was being given to producers of entertainment films; as late as 1945, the OWI cautioned United Artists, which was releasing the anti-Japanese James Cagney picture *Blood on the Sun,* to depict Hirohito "only . . . as a tool of Japanese militarists, not as a personal heavy.") The army also balked at Ivens's suggestion that Hiro-hito should be considered a war criminal; it wanted more blame for the war directed at the Japanese people themselves, even though that approach could easily lead to the kind of racism that Hollywood filmmakers, under Mellett's watchful eye until recently, had been instructed to avoid.

Capra scrapped Ivens's film completely, removed him from his unit, and started again with Foreman and a young aspiring screenwriter and novelist named Irving Wallace who had been working alongside Theodor Geisel at Fort Fox. Wallace claimed that Capra was "totally unsophisticated when it came to political thought. He only knew one thing: America had been good to him, America was beautiful. . . . He came up with a simple foreign policy . . . : The only good Jap is a dead Jap." Wallace hated that approach and argued for a more refined version of the anti-industrialist, antimilitary case that Ivens had made, but he knew that Capra was working in the dark; it was impossible to make a film articulating a policy that had not in fact even been formed by policymakers. "From FDR to General Marshall on down," Wallace said, "no one knew what to tell the troops about who their real enemy was"—Hirohito, Tojo and his army, or the people of Japan, a tempting target at a time when polls showed that half of all GIs believed that Japan's entire population would have to be wiped out in order to guarantee a lasting peace. "There was a policy vacuum," said Wallace, "and in fact Foreman and I were left alone to design what our fighting men's attitudes should be toward the Japanese."

After two years of service, Capra was tired of being stymied by unclear policy, poor lines of communication, and military bureaucracy. After his months in England acting with virtual autonomy to make *Tunisian Victory* happen his way, it had been hard for him to come back to Washington and return to service as a functionary who was stuck, seemingly permanently, somewhere in the middle of the chain of command, always subject to second-guessing. The success of *The Battle of Russia* had emboldened him to speak his mind, and in a letter to General Surles he argued for more authority. In late November 1943, a group of Signal Corps filmmakers who were not under Capra's command had been assigned to the Cairo Conference in Egypt, a war-strategy summit following the defeat of Rommel and the Allied victory in North Africa that had been attended by Roosevelt, Churchill, and Chiang Kai-Shek. When Capra saw the footage they had shot, he told Surles, "I nearly vomited. Out of focus, light flashes, incompetent, inept, and criminally amateurish. It's a disgrace to the profession, a disgrace to the Army, and a disgrace to our country to have such a world shattering conference be recorded by amateurs. . . . I'm supposed to be head of Special Coverage. For the sake of future efforts I sincerely request that I be given the opportunity to assign the right men and equipment to these important jobs."

Capra got a Christmas Day promotion from lieutenant colonel to colonel, but he didn't get the expanded role he wanted. Nor did his new rank hold much sway in Hollywood. Like Ford, he found himself in straitened financial circumstances as America's involvement in the war moved into its third year, and a significant piece of income he had counted on—profits from the release of *Arsenic and Old Lace*—had failed to come through; Warner Bros. had released the Cary Grant comedy for showing to troops stationed overseas, but more than two years after Capra had completed the picture, it still had no U.S. release date and could not contractually be scheduled until the

Broadway play closed. In January, Capra, who had, like Zanuck, made it known that he now liked to be called "Colonel," asked Harry Warner to put the film in theaters. Warner turned him down. The war was becoming an inconvenience for the studios; onscreen it was overexposed and audience fatigue was beginning to show at the box office; offscreen, it continued to be a drain on talent and resources. Warner told Capra he intended to sit on *Arsenic and Old Lace* until the war was over—"and I hope that will be soon," he added, "so that people won't have forgotten you."

On January 10, 1944, Ernie Pyle's report "This One Is Captain Waskow" appeared in newspapers across the country. The account of the death of a twenty-five-year-old American soldier in the battle of San Pietro became one of the most widely read stories of Pyle's career; it helped him win a Pulitzer Prize, inspired a movie the following year called *The Story of G.I. Joe*, and brought the small village of San Pietro and the bravery of Allied soldiers there to the attention of millions of Americans who never would have heard of the battle otherwise. Pyle had gotten to San Pietro four days before John Huston and his team had; he had waited three days for Waskow's corpse to be retrieved, walked alongside the mule that carried the body on its back, and then watched the young survivors of his heavily depleted unit say a shattered goodbye to their captain before burying him.

Pyle's story was the kind of firsthand, unflinching reportage that Huston, who was still in Italy, had hoped to do in San Pietro, and he was not deterred by the fact that by the time the article appeared, the battle was long over. Now there could be no question of finding a new town to serve as the subject of his film; it could only be about the place where Captain Waskow and so many other young Americans had died for their country. Eric Ambler had been reassigned to North Africa by British intelligence, but Huston, Jules Buck, and a Signal Corps crew had remained in Venafro, and for the next six weeks, with the army's full cooperation, he conceived, staged, and shot the film that was released to U.S. movie theaters as the combat documentary *The Battle of San Pietro*.

In his autobiography, Huston did not acknowledge that the film was entirely a reenactment. Instead, he recounted his and his team's first, genuinely dangerous visit to San Pietro—embellishing it to include not only the shelling, the hiding, and the precarious escape in the jeep but the presence of a little Italian orphan whom he considered adopting—and he suggested that the documentary had actually been filmed on the spot over those two days. He took his own terror and displaced it into the character of an unnamed captain alongside him who got the shakes while they were waiting together for the shelling to stop. He recounted his explosion at Buck when the jeep's wheels got stuck, but without the anti-Semitic outburst that Ambler recalled. And he invented a joyous scene after the battle had been won—"What a welcome the people of San Pietro gave us! Whole cheeses and bottles of wine appeared from God knows where." Huston's self-mythologizing about the picture had by then been his practice for decades; soon after the war, he gave a newspaper interview in which he said, "When I made *San Pietro*, I was a wet nurse for the camera crew, trying to save them from mines and booby traps."

None of it was true. *The Battle of San Pietro* was a scripted, acted, and directed movie that contained barely two minutes of actual, unreconstructed documentation. The most "real" shots in the movie are the pictures Jules Buck had taken the very first day they approached the town and run into the smiling, eager Texas soldiers—many of whom had since been killed in other battles—and the crazy, tumbling, unreadable shot from Buck's still-rolling camera as he, Huston, and Ambler had dived for cover to avoid a mortar shell. That shot is distinguishable from the others in the movie because of its sudden, violent, and chaotic movement; it is not an approximation of the terror of coming under fire, but an exact representation of it.

The rest of *San Pietro* is a contrivance, albeit one that Huston pulled off with the considerable assistance of the Signal Corps in Italy, which provided him with time, equipment, a crew, and all the soldiers he needed to play the GIs who had liberated the town. Huston and the army both wanted the picture to be correct in its details; at the end of 1943, he was given access to an extensive and confidential written account of the battle that had been compiled by the 143rd Infantry from army interviews with several of the soldiers who had fought at San Pietro, and he used it to create an accurate timeline of the battle.

With that report as his basis, Huston started to jot down ideas for a shooting script that would follow exactly the narrative line Capra had imagined
when he had come up with the assignment—an explanation of the strategic
importance of a victory, followed by the army's approach to the town, the
battle itself, and then the elated return of the townspeople. Some of Huston's
notes were practical—"Greater clarity needed in the maps," he wrote. "Figures and names are not legible enough." But others indicate clearly just how
far he was willing to go in manufacturing a story that would fit the army's
propaganda needs. Although both German and American planes had bombed
the town, he wrote, "the woman that is dug up from the ruins should be a
casualty caused by German shelling." In addition, "after San Pietro is occupied by Americans—and civilians return—the Germans should shell the
town as they are retreating."

Huston had learned a good deal about battle-scene reconstruction by the
time he shot *San Pietro*. His time in England working on *Tunisian Victory*,
and his access to the more sophisticated recreations the British had staged,
had given him an education in the inadequacy of his own reconstructions. As
he staged the quasi-documentary battle scenes for *San Pietro*, Huston worked
to achieve a kind of ragged-edged verisimilitude that helped to create a general American understanding—one that persisted long after the war was
over—of what "real" war film is supposed to look like. When guns were fired
or shells exploded, he made sure the image jolted as if the ground had shaken
or the cameraman had been taken by surprise. He slowed the action down,
shooting soldiers belly-crawling over rocky terrain under mortar fire or advancing through treacherous passes by halting, jittery fits and starts rather
than at a steady pace. And he even allowed a couple of the soldiers to notice
the camera, just as they would under actual battle circumstances, catching its
"eye" for a split second, then expressionlessly turning back to their business.

By February 22, 1944—more than two months after the battle had
ended—Huston had shot all the film he needed. Fourteen unedited reels of
his work at San Pietro survive in the National Archives, and they provide
ample evidence of the many different techniques he tried, some more successful than others, to recreate the battle. The unused film also reveals that he
systematically discarded any shot that looked too perfectly composed or

overstaged—several images in which the cameraman changes focus, moving from the foreground to the horizon just in time to capture a distant explosion, and other scenes in which the soldiers or the cameramen forget to react to sudden gunfire or shelling. The unused footage provides fascinating glimpses of Huston directing the untrained men in front of his cameras—a smiling GI goes from "alive" to "dead' at his cue, and a team of soldiers proceeds cautiously into an abandoned farmhouse looking for bombs and mines, only to have the camera cut when one of them insouciantly kicks at a misplaced prop grenade. The villagers eventually did return to San Pietro, and Huston made full use of them, cajoling them into enacting the images of relief and good cheer that Capra had craved. Some familiar contrivances did make it into the finished film—a cameraman shooting from inside a trench, with a soldier already in perfect focus jumping in after him, and several shots in which the camera already seems to have advanced comfortably through terrain that the soldiers onscreen are still trying to take while under heavy fire. But for the most part, Huston followed his instinct to include slightly imperfect images—a jumpy rather than smooth camera movement or a momentary loss of focus—as a badge of authenticity, taking a cue from the home-front audience's enthusiastic reaction to the moments in *The Battle of Midway* when John Ford let them see the film come loose from its sprockets.

After four months in Italy, the strain of recreating a bloody battle on location in a country that was still very much in the middle of the war began to take its toll on Huston. The close calls that he had experienced months earlier during his first two days at San Pietro had terrified him; now that the pressure of filming was over, his fear returned and he was unable to shake it off. Italy was still under heavy German bombardment, and Huston became wildly sensitive to unexpected sounds; he would sometimes confuse the screech of jeep wheels with the high-pitched whine of enemy mortars. "I had never before seen dead in numbers," he wrote, "and for someone raised in conventional America . . . it was deeply shocking. I felt I had adjusted. I remember saying to myself one day in Italy that I was really seasoned at last, a proper soldier. That same night I woke up calling out to my mother. We really don't know what goes on beneath the surface."

The army sent Huston home, back to New York's Astoria Studios, to work on his documentary. Although he had never deceived anyone in the Signal Corps about what he had filmed at San Pietro—there would have been no need to, since he had the full endorsement of his superior officers—by early 1944 there was considerable dispute within the armed forces about both the ethics and the usefulness of extensive reenactments. The completed version of *Tunisian Victory* was soon to open theatrically; it had not yet been seen by the press or the public, but the Signal Corps' staged North African footage was making the rounds within the army, and some of the reaction was withering. "The re-enactments in most cases are done so poorly and with no military supervision," wrote Second Lieutenant James Faichney, chief of the army's Film Security section, "that seasoned Army officers who saw it viewed the material with a mixture of laughter and disgust." In his memo, Faichney wrote that he did not dispute the need to recreate a scene or two that would have been impossible to film in actual combat, but he argued that Capra and his men had now gone far beyond that and were "attempting to re-enact the war on a Hollywood scale." In a harsh report at the end of January, just as Huston was starting to shoot in San Pietro, Faichney had urged that filmmakers in Italy not make the same mistakes, recommending that they go "as near to the front lines as possible and not . . . stay behind the lines and 'go on location' as if they were in Indio or Palm Springs."

Faichney's report was met with self-righteous outrage from Huston, who went up the chain of command to demand an apology. The twenty-six-year-old officer was called on the carpet and forced to retract his accusation that the Signal Corps was shooting "a 'phoney' war." After watching Huston's San Pietro footage, Faichney called it "far superior in over-all quality" to previous reenactments done for the Army Pictorial Service, but he would not back down from his eminently reasonable concern that "material of a re-enacted nature is still not being slated or marked in a fashion whereby such material is easily recognizable."

Huston received a promotion to major for his work in San Pietro, but his time in New York that spring was marked by behavior so impulsive and erratic that it would now be called post-traumatic. He pushed his romantic life, always overcrowded, closer to complete self-destruction—although he was still married to Lesley Black, he continued his long-standing relationship with de Havilland and his pursuit of Marietta Fitzgerald while beginning an affair with Doris Lilly, an editor at *Town & Country* who pursued him with unembarrassed avidity. Faichney's report had injured him, and, de Havilland said later, he "couldn't take . . . any kind of rejection without desperately going off and comforting himself with some female conquest. . . . He had no self-discipline. And he didn't have much taste either." De Havilland knew about both Fitzgerald, whom she liked and thought was a good match for Huston, and Lilly, whom she saw as a vulgar climber; Lilly was so smitten with Huston that she didn't care what anyone thought of her, even when their affair made the papers. "He was in a uniform," she said later, "and the idea that there was Italian mud on his boots was just absolutely devastating. He was so divine."

Huston had gone into the war with an appetite for derring-do and a desire to test his fearlessness; now, even as he worked on the movie in New York, he was both witnessing a kind of disintegration in his colleagues he never would have imagined possible and experiencing it himself. Rey Scott, the big, bluff cameraman on *Report from the Aleutians* whose seeming indifference to putting his life at risk had so impressed Huston, was now at Astoria and spiraling rapidly toward a psychotic break. Scott had been in Italy as well, where he was known for his willingness to run toward wherever the guns were firing or the bombs were falling. "But Astoria," Huston wrote, "was not Rey's cup of tea. He had been living in cellars and tents for years and he felt ill at ease in these more civilized surroundings. . . . Finally it got to him." Scott was on guard duty at the film facility in Queens one night when he called the colonel in charge at home and told him there was an emergency, then started firing his .45. Nobody was hurt, but Huston came in to work the next morning to learn that Scott had been arrested and was being held in an army psychiatric ward.

When Huston had gotten back to the United States, Capra had sent him a telegram that read, "Dear John Welcome home what are you doing and why." He no longer knew how to answer those questions. He would work at

Astoria all day, roar around town with one or more women well into the evening, and then return to his room at the St. Regis, where he would lie in bed unable to sleep until he could no longer bear it. Then he would get dressed, load his service revolver, take the elevator downstairs, and walk alone across Fifth Avenue into Central Park. He later said he was hoping to get mugged so that he would have someone to kill.

NINETEEN

"If You Believe This, We Thank You"

HOLLYWOOD AND ENGLAND, MARCH–MAY 1944

I n early 1944, after two years of war, the studios, which had become ever more deeply entangled with Washington, began, first gently and then forcefully, to reclaim their autonomy and to reassert themselves as servants of popular taste rather than of the national interest. In the months after Pearl Harbor, they had been quick to meet the government's request for pictures about battlefield bravery and home-front sacrifice. But more and more, American moviegoers were turning away from war pictures and toward other genres for entertainment—musicals, comedies, religious epics like *The Song of Bernadette*, historical biographies like *Madame Curie*—or to pictures that exploited the war not as their primary subject but as a backdrop, at once topical and exotic, for foreign adventure or intrigue. In March 1944, the Best Picture Oscar went to *Casablanca*, in which the war was used to provide atmosphere and raise the stakes for romance. Some in the industry expressed surprise that a mere piece of genre entertainment could sweep past films that were thought to be either more hard-hitting or more high-minded, but the win for *Casablanca* reflected changing tastes both within the movie business and outside it; films that dealt directly with the realities of combat or global politics went home empty-handed, and were increasingly being ignored by audiences as well.

Some critics decried what they saw as Hollywood's expedient abandonment of responsibility in favor of escapism, and bemoaned the eagerness with which studios were now acceding to the general public's seeming lack of curiosity about what was happening in the rest of the world. "We suffer . . . a unique and constantly intensifying schizophrenia which threatens no other nation involved in this war," James Agee wrote in an essay bitterly titled "So Proudly We Fail" about Hollywood's abrogation of its duty to educate moviegoers and soldiers alike. "Those Americans who are doing the fighting are doing it in parts of the world which seem irrelevant to them; those who are not remain untouched, virginal, prenatal, while every other considerable population on earth comes of age. In every bit of information you can gather about breakdowns of American troops in combat . . . a sense of unutterable dislocation, dereliction, absence of contact, trust, wholeness, and reference . . . clearly works at the root of the disaster."

But moviegoers felt, if anything, overexposed to the war and its ramifications. Aside from the barrage of newsreels and morale-building shorts that preceded practically every main attraction, there were the pictures themselves; at the end of 1943, an Office of War Information report noted that out of 545 feature films currently in production or development, 264 had content that was related, either directly or tangentially, to the war or to the OWI's propaganda objectives. But as the pictures started to falter financially, the studios put the brakes on dozens of war-themed scripts. "Hollywood has finally thrown up its hands in despair at attempting to keep pace with headlines," wrote Mildred Martin in the *Philadelphia Inquirer;* she cited "downright apathy on the part of audiences" and contended that "the imminent invasion of Europe seems to have been the last straw [since] neither writers, producers, nor directors are in any position to forecast on film the real-life drama of that campaign."

The Oscar ceremony held in the spring of 1944 at Grauman's Chinese Theatre in Hollywood paid dutiful tribute to the troops, as it had for several years running: After "The Star-Spangled Banner" played, ten rows of seats were raised by elevator onto the back of the stage; the invited soldiers and sailors who filled them would remain there as guests of honor for the evening. But the show's nod to the war effort was more perfunctory than it had been recently. A year after Lowell Mellett had addressed the room, there would be no renewed call from the OWI for the studios to keep their movies on message, nor were any cables of encouragement from Roosevelt or George Marshall or Wendell Willkie read out at the podium that evening. Hollywood was, in a way, reclaiming ownership of itself, and the filmmakers it chose to honor were, for the most part, those who had stayed home. Although Capra, Stevens, Huston, and Ford were all responsible for nominated movies, the opening of the envelopes mostly brought them disappointment. The only American picture to win a documentary prize that evening was, ironically, one that nobody particularly wanted to claim: Ford's recut version of Gregg Toland's *December 7th* took the statuette for Best Short Subject.

Capra and Ford had walked away as cowinners of the Best Documentary Feature award a year earlier, the beneficiaries of Academy president Walter Wanger's agreement to have twenty-five nominees and four different winners. That largesse was, it turned out, a one-year-only experiment. This year, just five movies were nominated. Huston's *Report from the Aleutians* was in the race, as were Capra's *Why We Fight* installment *The Battle of Russia* and *War Department Report*, an OSS propaganda film produced by Ford's Field Photo Unit with narration by Walter Huston, who announced at its outset, "This is *not* a propaganda film." The word was tainted again—anathema to politicians, studios, and moviegoers. Those three pictures, as well as a fourth armed forces–produced film called *Baptism of Fire*, all lost. The Oscar went to *Desert Victory*, the British film that Capra had tried so hard to outdo.

And with *Tunisian Victory* now just a couple of weeks from opening, critics were already telling him that he had failed. Everyone who wrote about the Anglo-American coproduction that Capra had spent the better part of 1943 overseeing found something different to dislike about it. The *New York Times* thought its account of troop movements was "deficient," "inaccurate," and "dubiously described," and questioned the relevance of a film that was arriving in U.S. theaters a full year after the campaign had ended. The battle action that Capra, Huston, and Stevens had contrived in Tunisia, California, and Orlando was, according to the *New Yorker*, "all a bit too much like other guns and planes and bombs in the movies and not particularly indigenous to the Tunisian campaign." *Time* faulted Capra's unchecked taste for narration, including the "unfortunate . . . off-screen voices of a British and a U.S. soldier philosophizing vaguely about the postwar world." Manny Farber complained that "the continuity has been chopped practically to confetti. The film seems to have been worked by several thousand cooks, each of whom decided to throw in another commentator, some more maps, and some business he found exciting in another documentary." And Agee left little doubt as to what that other documentary was. "The film," he wrote in *The Nation*, "never escapes for more than a few seconds at a time into the sort of pure tragic excitement which *Desert Victory* proved a war film can be. . . . I . . . felt that the people on the screen and in front of it were being unconsciously patronized; and judging by the run of British and American films I have seen, I feel pretty sure whose national disease that is."

Public tastes in war documentaries were changing as quickly as they were in Hollywood features. Oversaturated with booming declarations of patriotism, gung-ho optimism, and arm-twisting voice-overs about the American way of life, moviegoers were now looking for filmed coverage of the war that felt concise, direct, and unsparing. Just as *Tunisian Victory* opened, a Marine Corps short by Louis Hayward* called *With the Marines at Tarawa* also reached theaters. Its account of the November 1943 battle to retake a two-mile piece of a Pacific atoll, a staggeringly bloody four-day siege in which seventeen hundred marines and navy men had been killed, gave audiences a picture of the war they had not seen before in a report that was sober and even at times discouraging. (Two of the fifteen marine cameramen who worked on the short had been killed in action.) For the first time, a picture from the armed forces gave audiences a long, unblinking look at dead bodies—not only ugly piles of Japanese corpses, but young American men splayed across the sandy ground or floating slowly back and forth in the shallow, bloodied surf. "This is the price we have to pay," the terse, pared-down narration concluded, "for a war we didn't want." *Tarawa* was, as the *New York Times* put it,

---

* Hayward, born in South Africa, was a popular actor in Hollywood swashbuckler movies who became an American citizen shortly after Pearl Harbor, then joined the marines as a combat photographer. He won the Bronze Star for his work at Tarawa.

"overpoweringly real," and, combined with the unexpected and startlingly swift box-office failure of *Tunisian Victory,* it marked a turning point in America's nonfiction films about the war.

George Stevens, who was still in London preparing his SPECOU team for the Allied invasion of France, was also up for an Academy Award that night—his first nomination ever—for directing *The More the Merrier.* Yvonne Stevens attended the banquet, ready to pick up the prize for her absent husband just as Talli Wyler had done a year earlier; she brought eleven-year-old George Jr. to the ceremony as her date. Stevens lost to *Casablanca*'s Michael Curtiz, moving young George to write his dad a disappointed letter that read in part, "*Casablanca* stinks, we was gypped."

"I feel like a big loafer letting [you] down like that," Stevens wrote to Yvonne when the results reached him weeks later. "We didn't hear anything about it where I was at the time and I certainly didn't know my darlings were going. I would have felt very blue thinking about their disappointed little faces as they walked out of the theatre. . . . That junk seems so far away and unimportant, that Academy Awards hooey, that I didn't even worry about it. Which I would have done had I been home. Then, all of a sudden, I realize my dear family was there and it made me wish terribly that I had won. I felt bad about disappointing George. . . . I thought probably the disappointment was good for him. But I can assure you it was not very satisfactory philosophy. Then along came his 'we wuz robbed' letter . . . and I didn't worry any more about my boy. I remembered that the black cloud on his face when Babe Herman struck out only lasted an hour or two and then the sun would come out and light up all those freckles of his like neon."

Stevens wrote to his son separately, as he almost always did. "You are all a lot of big shots going to high-powered affairs like that. I bet we darn near won it," he told George Jr., "and I must agree with you on the fact [that] as long as we didn't win it we must have been gypped—dem bums weel moider em! Did you get the two games that I sent you for your birthday? . . . I packed them as well as I could but paper is very scarce."

Stevens was privy to few specifics of the coming invasion; he used the scarce information that was shared with him to make provisional plans for how SPECOU might be best deployed to create a film record of an Allied landing that some thought might happen in May, others in June. While he and his team waited for the call to mobilize, he had little to do but study French (many of his fellow officers were boning up), play poker in a running game that included Irwin Shaw, Bob Capa, and Bill Saroyan, and read and write letters. More than any of the other directors who went to war, Stevens kept up a near-constant correspondence with his family, and his letters to Yvonne and George Jr. from the spring of 1944 reflect a deep longing to be a part of their daily lives. While he was stationed in London, Stevens bound all of the correspondence from his family into a book that he would page through and reread whenever he was lonely or sad, and his responses were long and conversational. "Hello my pal," he wrote to George Jr. "This letter is from a Dad that is missing his boy very much this winter. I think [of] an awful lot of things that we could be doing together. For instance playing ball, seeing a couple of basketball games, perhaps a couple of Hockey games, have a game of golf together, having a trip down to Palm Springs in the Zephyr, . . . 'Ahh oui, c'est la guerre.' But I'm not worrying, my boy, mom and you and I will make up for the lost time after this dreary war is 'terminer.' And [after] I have been home long enough to forget all about the whole miserable affair, and long enough to earn a few bucks to keep us all in shoes and sufficient groceries, I am going to take you and our darling 'mere' on the biggest and most wonderful trip that you or I or anybody has ever been on. . . . There is much that I want to tell you but of course it is impossible to write home about [those] things. . . . Adolph might be listening. P.S. I'm learning a few French words and trying them out on the dog. That's you."

Even from a distance of thousands of miles, Stevens fought to remain engaged and connected as a father. He would joke and conspire with his son, tease him, turn his schoolwork into a battlefront and the war itself into a boy's adventure. Sometimes he would ride George Jr. about his grades ("What's this D in Gym? Flat feet! Well pick them up. I'm not kidding"), congratulate him for his achievements ("Third in his class of many boys. First in his father's regard and affection"), and fill his letters with gentle maxims, caution, and advice: "For Jeep's sake be careful with that thirty pound bow and arrow son," he wrote soon after George Jr.'s twelfth birthday. "Remember people's eyes are the most precious thing they have got. I guess

I'm forgetting that you are a big boy and know how to take care of yourself, but nonetheless we can be unthinking no matter how old we get."

Only in his letters to Yvonne, who was working in an army hospital in California, did Stevens betray the sadness and uncertainty that lowered his spirits and kept him awake at night. "These have been dreary months, these last," he wrote her, "and if it hadn't been for your letters . . ." He wrote "life would have been nothing," then struck it out and replaced it with "there would have been nothing to think cheerfully about." Stevens's army duties often felt pointless to him, a morass of plans, logistics, and paperwork that led to nothing. He had been struggling to secure promotions for Shaw and Bill Mellor, but he felt unheeded and frustrated. "You know that I find much [of] this difficult to believe in fundamentally," he told Yvonne. "The fellows in our work overseas are really the orphans. . . . We never know what is going on in our outfit back home, have to do a large amount of guessing . . . and a thing that really gets our boys goats, they give out all the promotions to the fellows back home answering the telephone. Anyway . . . I have the soldiers privilege of gripeing [sic]. . . . I don't do it with anyone but you."

In England, Stevens took pleasure less in the society of fellow officers than in occasional trips to the theater or long walks alone at twilight. Like Capra, he came to feel a deep admiration for the cheerful toughness of Londoners in wartime. After attending a "panto," one of the many seasonal variety shows that went up on London stages over the winter holidays, he was moved to hear the entire crowd gaily singing the chorus to a comic number about rationing, "When Can I Have a Banana Again?" "How the audience . . . enjoyed this little joke," he wrote in his journal. "No moaning about being blasted from homes, losing hundreds of their people in one blast—they just reduced the war to this simple little inconvenience. . . . If only Goering in 1941, while confidently dispatching his Luftwaffe legions to the destruction of London[,] had been a seer and could have looked ahead to this result, he would have realized the futility of all that blasting total war of his. He succeeded only . . . in depriving Londoners of their bananas and cream for breakfast & gave them a great joke on themselves."

What is strikingly absent from Stevens's letters during this period is any interest at all in Hollywood or thoughts about the resumption of his career after the war. Unlike Ford, who was already actively considering his return to the director's chair, or Huston, who would check in frequently with Warner Bros. throughout the war to make sure the studio was keeping *The Treasure of the Sierra Madre* warm for him, Stevens apparently pushed movies far from his thoughts. In May, his agent Charles Feldman wrote his client a letter trying to turn his mind back to Hollywood and warning him not to be seduced by the idea of making a combat movie. "[They] have been taboo in Hollywood for the past year. The production companies insist that the public does not want war pictures." David O. Selznick put out a feeler to Stevens about signing him, and Warner Bros. and 20th Century Fox expressed their interest as well.

Stevens was indifferent. While overseas, he barely even went to a picture, having been told by a friend that in the absence of many of their brightest talents, the studios were now producing and releasing "the lousiest crap imaginable." But on April 18, he made an exception and arrived at the USAAF screening room for a 6 p.m. showing of a movie by one of his Signal Corps colleagues that had just opened in the United States days earlier— and he loved what he saw. "We ran the first print to come here of the Air Force's film 'Memphis Belle,'" he wrote in his journal, "the film Willie Wyler put together out of the stuff he and Bill Clothier shot with the 8th Air Force last year. It is a very good film, one of the best war films our side has made up until now. Memorable shot: A great Flying Fortress spinning to its end. This is cultivated and played for suspense as the narrator counts the parachutes as they come out and blossom white against the sandy panorama of the distant ground below."

It had been more than a year since Wyler had flown on his first missions over France and Germany, and since then he had done little but work on *Memphis Belle*. After discarding Maxwell Anderson's script, he had struggled to find the tone he wanted, a narrative voice that incorporated some acknowledgment of vulnerability and frailty, even if it was accomplished through humor. At one point, he considered a printed onscreen introduction that, with a wink or two, completely subverted the declamatory, chest-thumping opening titles that were by then a standard feature of war documentaries: "The makers of this film wish to apologize for certain shortcomings in those sequences that depict bombing missions," Wyler's proposed prologue read. "They were photographed under adverse conditions, which is to say, people were shooting at us. This regrettable lack of cooperation robbed us of many of the finer details of camera work, such as intimate views of the destruction wrought by our bombs, or close-ups of enemy pilots plummeting in flames. It will be observed that, in the scenes photographed under combat conditions, the camera sometimes shakes and quivers. This was due to the concussion of flak and gunfire, and not to any unsteadiness on the part of the hand that held the camera. If you believe this, we thank you."

Ultimately, Wyler chose not to start the film that way; *Memphis Belle* begins with a simpler and more conventional title, albeit one that pointedly distinguishes the movie from the reenactment-laden work of many of his colleagues: "All aerial combat film was exposed during air battles over enemy territory." Over shots of the English countryside, the narrator announces, "This is a battlefront. A battlefront like no other in the long history of mankind's wars. This is an air front." If anything was going to sell war-weary audiences on another army documentary, this was it: The air war offered moviegoers a chance to see World War II from a literally new perspective. A year earlier, Howard Hawks had fictionalized the bravery of a wartime flight crew in the combat drama *Air Force*, which had become an immense success for Warner Bros. and heightened public interest in the youngest division of the armed forces. In his film, Wyler would exploit that curiosity with an evocative, detailed, minute-by-minute style of second-person narration that made *Memphis Belle* one of the most effective nonfiction films of the war. He took every opportunity to articulate the sensations and emotions of being in or near aerial combat: "If you're a mechanic you've got your own bomber. You get attached to it. But you know when your ship goes out on a mission you may never see it again." If you're assigned to the actual crew, once you learn your destination, "sometimes your face turns white. . . . Sometimes the feeling that you won't come back tightens your insides."

Wyler then introduces Captain Morgan and his crew by name. As the bombing missions unfold, the narration becomes frank in its anti-German rhetoric, saying that the German people have "twice in one generation . . . flooded the world with suffering . . . in such quantity as the history of the human race has never known." As the aerial footage that serves as the movie's centerpiece begins, the narration drops away for several minutes and is replaced by the emotionless voices of the crew on the intercom that Wyler had recorded in Hollywood; they get louder only when they see one of their planes shot down and spiral toward the ground. "B-17 out of control at 3 o'clock . . . Eight men still in that B-17, come on, guys, get outta there . . . Come on, you son of a bitch!" The last third of *Memphis Belle* takes place back at the airfield after the bombing, and although Anderson's wistful voice-over was never used, Wyler is unstinting about showing the ground crew nervously counting the planes as they come back—"sweating out the mission," the narrator explains—and pulling badly injured men out of the B-17s and onto stretchers. "Our losses were heavy," the audience is told, 'but the enemy's were far heavier. . . . Who can tell the number of German torpe-does that will not be fired, the number of convoys that will get through now, the battles that will be won instead of lost . . . because of what these bombers and flyers did today?"

When Wyler first showed his completed film to his commanding officers, they didn't know what to make of it. That *The Memphis Belle* was impressive was beyond dispute; no film about air combat had come anywhere close to its immediacy and verisimilitude—even the static-muffled monotone of the re-created soundtrack felt unlike anything from a Hollywood movie. "This is a superb picture," wrote Brigadier General L. S. Kuter, who recommended that Wyler be awarded the Legion of Merit for his work after screening the forty-one-minute documentary.[*] "It is real." Perhaps too real. The army felt that a scene in which the young flyers were blessed by a chaplain after receiving their flight instructions would have to be omitted—it "suggests a resigned finality," Kuter wrote, rather than the can-do spirit that the army wanted to serve as the public image of the air force. Kuter also worried about a line of narration spoken during combat—"You try not to be where the next flak hits"—which he feared would imply that American pilots were in the busi-ness of "running away from anti-aircraft fire."

The War Activities Committee, the Hollywood board that vetted all Sig-

---

[*] Wyler received the honor, but not until early 1946.

nal Corps pictures intended for theatrical release, also had its concerns, and relayed them directly to the secretary of war. The line, "For Christ's sake, get out of that plane" was blasphemous and would have to be deleted. "Damn it, don't yell on that intercom" was also unacceptable. And even though Wyler had overdubbed the last word of the line "Come on, you son of a bitch" with machine-gun fire, the mere implication that the word was being spoken was taboo. In 1942, the committee's vice chairman reminded Secretary Stimson, Noel Coward and David Lean had collaborated on a drama about a British warship in combat called *In Which We Serve* in which sailors were heard to use the words "hell," "damn," and "bastard." The Breen Office refused to approve the British film for release in the United States, and when Breen was widely attacked, including by American servicemen, for suppressing a patriotic movie made by an ally, the office sniffily responded, "The function of the Production Code is not to be patriotic, it is to be moral." The resulting outrage was so great that Breen was forced to back down and issue a tortured one-time exemption for language used by "persons in active duty under pressure of great dramatic force apparent on screen whose pictures are produced . . . under sponsorship of government where words are not offensive per se." The War Activities Committee feared that the exemption for Coward and Lean had created a slippery slope, and it urged Stimson to see "the wisdom of making these suggested minor deletions."

Stimson wouldn't do it. He stood by the movie, knowing that he had the backing of Roosevelt, who had watched *The Memphis Belle* with Wyler in the White House screening room and then told the director, "This has to be shown right away, everywhere." In early February, the army approved it for general release. Wyler politely ignored a final request from the brass that the title be changed to something more exciting—for instance, "Big League Air War."

Memphis Belle was scheduled to open around the country on April 15, 1944, a date that Wyler came close to spending in an army jail cell awaiting court-martial. He was outside the Statler Hotel in Washington, D.C., days away from receiving orders for his next assignment, when he witnessed an argument between a hotel doorman and a guest over who was next in line for a taxicab. As the guest grabbed the taxi and slammed the door, the doorman turned to Wyler and, gesturing back at the departing cab, muttered, "Goddamn Jew."

"Look, you're saying that to the wrong fellow," Wyler responded.

"I didn't mean you, I meant him," said the doorman.

Wyler punched him in the face, and thought little of it when, in the ensuing commotion, an army officer who happened to be standing nearby asked him for his name. Wyler left the capital for New York the next day only to receive an army telegram ordering him to return to Washington immediately. He reported to the air force base at Bolling Field where he was told he would face charges of "conduct unbecoming an officer and a gentleman." He had hit a civilian without "legal provocation." Wyler explained that the language the doorman had used was the kind of provocation that had inspired him to leave Hollywood and put on a uniform in the first place. The investigating officer was unmoved. Wyler was arrested and told he could either defend himself in a court-martial proceeding, which would take months, or accept an official reprimand. He reluctantly took the reprimand.

When *Memphis Belle* opened, it became the first movie in history to be reviewed on the front page of the *New York Times*, which called it "one of the finest fact films of the war . . . a perfect example of what can be properly done by competent film reporters to visualize the war for people back home." Wyler had succeeded in making a war picture in the spirit of *With the Marines at Tarawa*—darker, tougher, more unflinching about the realities of injury and death faced by American men and boys than its onscreen predecessors. This was a picture designed to jolt moviegoers out of the apathy that overexposure to the war had bred, not simply to whip them into a patriotic frenzy. *Cue* magazine wrote that the movie "ought to go a long way toward [investing] the newspaper phrase 'Our Losses Slight' with a significance to shatter any complacency."

Some reviews noted that the aerial footage in *The Memphis Belle* was actually a composite of several different missions flown over or near Wilhelmshaven—a fact that Wyler had made no attempt to conceal in interviews—but most who saw the picture were tremendously impressed by its realism, even if they weren't quite certain how real it was. The critic for the *New Yorker* said its "best feature" was "the conversation of the boys while over the target," not realizing that their dialogue had all been recorded months after the fact, and Agee, who had roundly derided the falsification in Capra's *Tunisian Victory*, admitted in *The Nation* that while watching Wyler's film, he "could not guess which shots were reenacted and which were straight records." Critics seemed especially surprised that such a strong and unsentimental film had come from the director of what one of them called the "shrewd but somewhat plushy war poster" *Mrs. Miniver*, and Agee remarked that "postwar planners should work out a better fate for him than going back to Hollywood."

Wyler seemed to agree. He told reporters that *Memphis Belle* "says everything I've got to say—it is a kind of communiqué from the Army Air Force," but he also said he wasn't finished with his work for the Signal Corps. Hollywood wanted him back badly; Goldwyn still had him under contract, and Zanuck was hoping to persuade him to make a film version of Moss Hart's theatrical revue *Winged Victory*, a morale show cast largely with servicemen that was used to raise money for Army Emergency Relief; Wyler could have done the job while remaining on active duty, since the show had actually been produced on Broadway by the air force itself. But he declined, telling Hart, "I want to make more documentary films. I strongly feel this is where I can do the most good." A month after *The Memphis Belle* opened, Wyler flew to Italy and checked into Allied headquarters in Caserta to begin preparations for his next documentary, a short about the P-47 fighter planes known as Thunderbolts. He looked forward to getting back in the air with a camera as soon as possible. It was a decision, made almost casually, that would permanently alter the course of his life and career.

TWENTY

"A Sporadic Raid of
Sorts on the Continent"

*HOLLYWOOD, WASHINGTON, AND NEW YORK,
MARCH–MAY 1944*

John Bulkeley was a hero made for the movies at a time when the navy desperately needed one. In 1942, the young man, a lieutenant in the Pacific fleet who commanded the six boats in Motor Torpedo Boat Squadron Three, had navigated hundreds of miles of dangerous waters in order to pick up General MacArthur, his family, and his staff and lead them to safety as Bataan fell to the Japanese. "You have taken me out of the jaws of death," MacArthur is said to have told him when they reached port. "I shall never forget it." Bulkeley's daring became the subject of William White's *They Were Expendable,* the best seller that MGM had been urging John Ford to turn into a movie for a year.

But a picture based on the book hardly seemed possible. Although the story of the operation to protect MacArthur was in some ways perfect for Hollywood, the majority of White's account was an unremittingly angry study of loss—an oral history of the undermanned navy's hopeless fight to hold the Philippines in the months after Pearl Harbor. Bulkeley and the men with whom he served had been determined to stave off an inevitable Japanese victory for long enough to allow the U.S. fleet to rebuild in Hawaii. The navy did not go down to defeat for three months, a strategic victory for the Allies

that came at the cost of ten thousand American lives; when the Japanese took
Bataan, an additional seventy-five thousand Allied troops were seized as
prisoners of war. White explicitly framed his story as a cautionary tale, writing, "We are a democracy, running a war. If our mistakes are concealed from
us, they can never be corrected. These . . . sad young men differ from
those . . . in Europe only in that they are Americans, and the tragedy they
bear witness to is our own failure, and the smugness they struggle against is
our own complacency."

White's overall narrative was not, to put it mildly, natural material for a
studio war movie in 1944. The point of his book is that, as one naval officer
puts it, "In a war, anything can be expendable—most usually men. They are
expending you and that machine gun to get time. They don't expect to see
either one again. They expect you to stay there and spray that road with steel
until you're killed or captured, holding up the enemy for a few minutes or
even a precious quarter of an hour. You know . . . that those few minutes
gained are worth the life of a man to your army." Even Bulkeley himself was
not sure the story was worth telling to a public whose curiosity about the war
had lately given way to impatience and fatigue. He told White, "Look, never
mind about that. People don't like to hear about that. I've learned that in the
week I've been back."

If *They Were Expendable* hadn't been so popular, it's doubtful that MGM
would even have purchased the movie rights, and in 1943, after Donovan
refused to take Ford off active duty so that he could direct it, the project
seemed to languish. Frank Wead, a Navy pilot in the 1920s who had become
the successful screenwriter of movies like *Test Pilot* and *Dive Bomber*, had
taken a crack at adapting it; when Wead temporarily set aside the script to
move on to other work, the studio turned to Budd Schulberg, asking him to
flesh out Bulkeley's personal life by adding a wife and child so that the story
would appeal to women. Throughout 1943, Ford had kept the project at arm's
length, never quite giving MGM a definitive no, but always finding new reasons that it probably wouldn't work. "Every congressman in America would
be after my ass" if he quit the navy to make a movie, he told his friend James
McGuinness; besides, he had little faith that MGM would actually want to go
through with the picture. Louis B. Mayer was as spooked as every other stu-

dio head by the collapse of the war-movie market, and if the studio did produce *They Were Expendable,* surely it would insist on softening the story,
turning it into a melodrama, or tagging a victory in the Pacific onto the end
of the narrative in order to wrap up on a note of triumph. Whatever MGM
did, Ford told Wead, "the thing will probably be ske-rewed up."

Ford still couldn't let it go. He had spent time supervising Field Photo in
London and he had filmed a city under siege in North Africa, but for him the
war continued to be defined by his experience at Midway, by what he witnessed of the courage and sacrifice of men who knew they were risking their
lives, and by the devastating loss of young men in the aftermath of the battle.
A war picture that told the truth about the nobility of looking into the eye of
almost certain defeat would be a picture Ford wanted to make, but it seemed
impossible. On the other hand, he now had so little to do in the navy that
perhaps the time had come to return to the director's chair. Field Photo was
running smoothly under Ray Kellogg, and Ford's duties in Washington were
so inconsequential that in March 1944 the navy told him he could take a
couple of weeks and go home to Los Angeles. It seems to have been during
that time that he began to commit himself—creatively if not contractually—
to *They Were Expendable,* talking through script issues with Wead, who was
now working on the screenplay again.

But Ford was about to be called back to duty. Late in the month, orders
came through for him to report to London for preparations for the coming
Allied landing in Europe, and Ford told Wead he would not be available to
work on the movie for the time being. The studied casualness of his tone in
delivering the news—"I understand that there is to be a sporadic raid of
sorts on the Continent in the near future and I am leaving in the middle of
next week to take part in same"—could barely disguise his pride. The navy
still needed him after all.

Ford returned to Washington, where he received a promotion to captain
and prepared for his trip overseas. Over his months of idleness, his behavior
and demeanor had deteriorated considerably. He had never gotten around to
moving out of his hotel room and was now living in slovenly conditions and
drinking heavily, just as he had been used to doing between movie shoots.
His new assignment notwithstanding, he remained attracted to the idea of

directing *They Were Expendable*, and shortly before he left for Europe, he agreed to meet Bulkeley, now a lieutenant commander who was also about to go to London, where he would be in charge of a PT boat squadron. Bulkeley was summoned to Ford's dirty suite, where he found the director, who now outranked him, splayed in bed naked. He had clearly spent the night, and perhaps the morning, drunk. In Bulkeley's recollection, men and women, "hangers-on," were wandering casually in and out of the room. When Ford saw him, he threw off the sheets and jumped to his feet, announcing that he wanted to salute the man who had saved General MacArthur's life. The show of respect did not last long; Ford, still naked, then crawled back into bed and told his new visitor to open the closet door so that he could admire the new captain's stripes on his uniform. Bulkeley, disgusted, shot back at him, "What are you captain *of*?" Ford threw a plate of half-eaten food at him just as he turned to walk out of the room. The next time he and Bulkeley saw each other, it would be in a PT boat in the English Channel.

In May, Frank Capra learned that he would be staying in Washington, D.C., during the invasion. Rather than returning to London to coordinate the Signal Corps efforts to film the landing, he was to take charge of receiving their film and make sure the strongest material was apportioned to newsreel producers with all deliberate speed. His job as a kind of managing editor was several steps removed from the action, but at least it would involve events so urgent that there would be almost no opportunity for the War Department, the OWI, or any other interested government agency to interfere. Capra was now facing the real possibility that the ambitious program of war documentaries he had conceived two years earlier would end up taking longer to complete than the war itself. The *Know Your Ally/Know Your Enemy* series that he had originally hoped would include almost a dozen documentaries had become a case study in how diplomacy and red tape could join forces to prevent progress on almost any project. After years of planning, only one of the movies, *Know Your Ally—Britain*, was complete, and it felt so out of date that it was virtually useless as propaganda. After four years of watching movies from Hollywood and overseas alike about English valor, moviegoers would surely laugh at the forty-minute film's contention that out of all the Allies, Britain was the "hardest to understand." The frail metaphor on which the script relied—Russia, China, England, and the United States were treated as "four backs" on a "football team" in "a different kind of game—this one's for keeps!"—was patronizing, as was the picture's assertion that one of those players, John Britain, comes from "an old people, a stubborn people, and sometimes they have moved slowly. But in three years of blood, sweat and tears, Britain has found his soul." Capra's unit was now drastically under-funded, and since the importance of Russia and China in the war had largely been covered in the *Why We Fight* series, the rest of the *Know Your Ally* slate, which had at one time included plans for installments that would cover Australia, Canada, and France, was canceled.

One film close to Capra's heart had, however, been successfully com-pleted against steep odds and considerable resistance within the army itself. It had been two years since William Wyler, disheartened after his encounters with racism and segregation in the American Midwest and South, had bowed out of making *The Negro Soldier*, but Capra had not given up on the idea. He had brought in a director named Stuart Heisler who had in 1940 made a minor children's movie called *The Biscuit Eater*, about two little boys, one white and one black, who raised a dog together. Capra felt his handling of the material had been sensitive, and Heisler took his new assignment seriously; when he was told to start developing a script for *The Negro Soldier* in late 1942, his first request was to collaborate with Carlton Moss, the black writer Wyler had found. Moss had graduated from a black college in Baltimore and had aspirations to write screenplays. He came to Washington and worked on his script at a lunch table in the Library of Congress, one of the few research facilities that had an unsegregated cafeteria.

General Osborn had been Capra's closest ally in almost every one of his fights to get a movie made, but when Capra sent him Moss and Heisler's proposed screenplay with a letter strongly endorsing it, the general was discouragingly cool to the proposed film. "It is undoubtedly a powerful script," he wrote to Capra. "But the fact that it is, as you say in your letter, an emotional glorification of the Negro war effort puts it in a different class from the [movie] we had intended and makes us very doubtful about showing it to the troops without changes. . . . Who is going to see the Negro picture? Under what circumstances? What effect is it desired to [produce]?"

The army was at that moment caught in a bind created by its own hypocrisy: It wanted to make a movie that would convince skeptical African American men and their families that this was their war too, but only if it could avoid the subject of racism altogether and find a narrative of inclusion that would somehow manage not to unsettle any white GIs. There was little in the way of progress that a movie could showcase; the armed forces were still segregated by unit, and the Army Air Corps had not even allowed black pilots or mechanics in its ranks until 1940, when the Selective Service Act outlawed racial discrimination in the induction of soldiers. Many high-ranking officers still freely espoused the belief that the army's 875,000 black soldiers lacked the intelligence for overseas deployment, and racism among the rank and file was so endemic that when the OWI's Sam Spewack went to England in late 1942, he reported back to Capra that "apparently the big problem here is the fact [that] the British are nice to our Negro troops and the white soldiers resent it."

Hollywood wasn't much better. In 1943, black characters were depicted as inferior in 80 percent of the movies in which they appeared, and minstrel-show stereotypes were still the rule, especially in entertainment films that depicted African Americans in uniform. The year's highest-grossing picture, the musical revue *This Is the Army*, featured as its highlight Joe Louis and an all-black male chorus in a number called "What the Well-Dressed Man in Harlem Will Wear." The lyrics explained that "Mr. Dude has disappeared" and that black men were trading in their "Lenox Avenue . . . flashy ties" for "olive drab." The chorus danced in front of a painted backdrop of strutting, bug-eyed caricatures in gaudy coats and hats. The message that the exuberantly performed song intended to send was that the army offered black people a chance to straighten up and fly right, not that their contribution to the war effort would be meaningful enough to matter to white America. The determination to avoid any commentary on the unhappier aspects of race relations in the United States was only reinforced by the OWI's own guidelines, which as late as 1944 stated that "films in which there is reference to racial minorities should avoid showing segregation wherever possible, and not deal too lengthily with sharp contrasts between the conditions of majority and minority peoples."

Capra didn't back off from his insistence on making *The Negro Soldier,* nor did he reassign it. Over the following year, Heisler and Moss continued to work on the film. "I'll say this for him," Moss said many years later. "We had all the money we wanted, and he did leave us absolutely alone. . . . If Capra had been hostile, personally hostile in this area, the film would never have been made. He could have sabotaged it." By October 1943, they had a movie ready to show, and with Capra still working on *Tunisian Victory* in England, his replacement Anatole Litvak arranged a screening for senior army officers. He got back a number of requests, all of which were meant to soothe white sensitivities. Even though the film's primary intended audience was not white GIs but soldiers in all-black platoons, the role of black enlistees in combat was to be deemphasized lest it raise hopes among African Americans that they would be welcome on the front lines. A scene showing a white physical therapist administering aid to a black soldier would have to be eliminated since its inclusion might stoke fears that in the new army white men could be subservient in any way to black men. And for the same reason, the film's depiction of black officers would have to be, if not eliminated entirely, underplayed.

Heisler and Moss made the necessary revisions and held their breath when in February 1944 the movie was shown to the New York press and, soon after, to an invited audience of African Americans at a theater in Harlem. The lights went down, and the first image they saw on the screen after the War Department insignia was a large crowd of African Americans— played by actors who had been hired for $10.50 a day—as they entered a church. A black sergeant sings a solo, and then a minister—the most crisply spoken, uncaricatured black preacher ever seen in an American film up to that point—takes the pulpit and delivers his sermon. The preacher, played by Moss himself after he and Heisler failed to find an actor whom they thought was suitable for the role, invokes Joe Louis's fight against Max Schmeling, seen in newsreel footage, and then tells the congregation that now, "these two men . . . are matched again, this time in a far bigger arena and for far greater stakes." African Americans of all generations, conservatively dressed, hushed and attentive, are shown in the pews as Moss's preacher moves into a selective history lesson about how black people have helped safeguard the country's liberty from 1660 all the way through the 371st Negro Infantry in World War I. He follows with a quick, Capra-esque tour of great black Americans— Booker T. Washington, George Washington Carver, judges, a North Pole explorer, a surgeon, musicians, publishers, educators, curators, sculptors, singers (represented by a shot of Marian Anderson), an orchestra conductor, and Jesse Owens.

Then, halfway into the forty-minute movie, a question comes from the congregation: "What about the infantry?" The speaker is the mother of a soldier named Robert who's about to go to officer candidate school. As she reads a letter from her son recounting his experiences, the audience follows, in montage, a sterling and dapper young man from his induction and intake interview through training and service and all the way up through Pearl Harbor (depicted in staged footage that was borrowed from *December 7th*). It was Heisler and Moss's intention to introduce black moviegoers to the rigor and pride of army life, but what made a stronger impression on the crowd was that, for the first time, black men in military service were being portrayed straightforwardly and uncomedically; they're shown relaxing, playing ping-pong, using the base library (one reads from *An Anthology of American Negro Literature*), and even dancing with WAVES at an all-black club. The audience is then told that "black, brown, yellow and white men" are about to give the Nazis a big surprise: "The men we knew as caterers, printers, bricklayers, cooks, entertainers, carpenters, bellboys, schoolteachers, farmers are today soldiers in a modern army . . . every man schooled in the meaning of teamwork . . . every man ready to do his share." *The Negro Soldier*'s final image is the same V-for-victory sign that ended all of the movies produced by Capra's unit.

The Negro Soldier was received far more positively than Capra or its creators had anticipated. Richard Wright, whose novel *Native Son* had been published a few years earlier, attended the Harlem screening and told a reporter for the *Brooklyn Eagle* that before the picture started, he had written down thirteen offensive black stereotypes on the back of his program— Excessive Singing, Indolence, and Crap Shooting among them—and intended to make a mark next to each one as it appeared onscreen. He didn't check off a single box and told the reporter that he found the movie "a pleas-

Huston (*left*) with his *Juarez* cowriters Wolfgang Reinhardt and Aeneas Mackenzie and producer Henry Blanke. The movie was his first foray into political filmmaking. (*Everett Collection*)

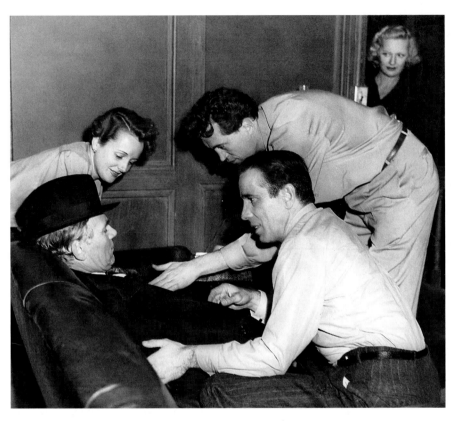

(*Clockwise from top right*): Lee Patrick (*in doorway*), John Huston, Humphrey Bogart, Walter Huston, and Mary Astor on the set of the director's 1941 breakthrough *The Maltese Falcon*. (*The Kobal Collection*)

Huston's affair with Olivia De Havilland, whom he directed in 1942's *In This Our Life*, was an open secret in Hollywood. (*Bettmann/CORBIS*)

Huston and the actor Edward G.
Robinson at a wartime party given in
honor of Madame Chiang Kai-Shek.
(*John Florea/Time & Life Pictures/Getty Images*)

Although *San Pietro* was presented to the moviegoing public as
a wartime documentary, all of the film's combat footage was staged.

A veteran institutionalized for combat-related psychological trauma is interviewed by a doctor in Huston's *Let There Be Light*, which was suppressed for thirty-five years.

Stevens with Katharine Hepburn on the set of *Woman of the Year* (1942). After the war, she urged him to return to directing comedy; he never did. (*Everett Collection*)

Stevens's military passport. He was the last of the five directors to enter the war, and the last to return home. (*Margaret Herrick Library/Academy of Motion Picture Arts and Sciences*)

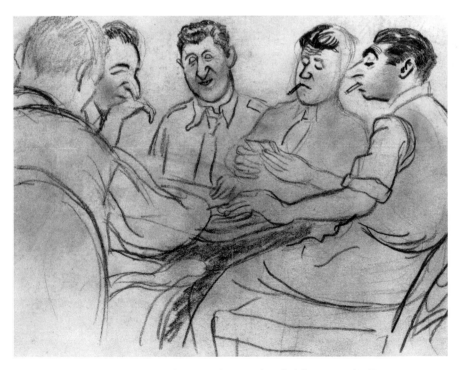

A sketch of the running poker game Stevens played while stationed in Europe.
From left: William Saroyan, Irwin Shaw, Stevens, Robert Capa.
(*Collection Capa/Magnum Photos*)

Stevens (*center, without helmet*) and Irwin Shaw (*right foreground*),
as American G.I.s and civilians celebrate the liberation of France.
(*Margaret Herrick Library/Academy of Motion Picture Arts and Sciences*)

Stevens's filming at Dachau included several segments of direct testimony to the camera
from freed prisoners. (*Margaret Herrick Library/Academy of Motion Picture Arts and Sciences*)

Italy, 1944: An Army Pictorial Service cameraman films a burning DUKW ("Duck"), an amphibious vehicle that was shelled by German planes. (*U.S. Army/Getty Images*)

Walt Disney (*right*) discusses the use of animation techniques for an instructional film about naval flight training. (*Mark Kauffman/Time & Life Pictures/Getty Images*)

A giant miniature of Tokyo Bay used in an army film that was intended to brief air force crews about Japanese targets. (*National Archives/Time & Life Pictures/Getty Images*)

1945: Jack Warner (*center*) cuts a welcome-home cake for returning contract players (*from left*) Wayne Morris, Ronald Reagan, Gig Young, and Harry Lewis as they bid farewell to the K-rations on the table. (*Bettmann/CORBIS*)

During the war, former newspaperman Lowell Mellett ran the OWI's Bureau
of Motion Pictures and clashed frequently with filmmakers.
(Thomas D. McAvoy/Time & Life Pictures/Getty Images)

Harry Truman on the cover of *Time*
magazine, shortly before his Senate
committee took aim at what they
perceived as the wastefulness of the
military's filmed propaganda effort.

20th Century Fox's Darryl F. Zanuck, who turned his brief time in Tunisia into both a book and a poorly received movie, left military service and returned to Hollywood soon after. (*Everett Collection*)

Frank Capra and Jimmy Stewart on the set of *It's a Wonderful Life*, the first venture of the director's ill-fated postwar company, Liberty. (*CinemaPhoto/CORBIS*)

Homer (Russell) shows his girl, Wilma (Cathy O'Donnell), his prosthetics in a moment that brought the personal cost of war home to audiences in *The Best Years of Our Lives*. (*Everett Collection*)

Wyler in the spring of 1943, photographed just after an army photographer told him he had won the Oscar for *Mrs. Miniver*. (*AP Photo*)

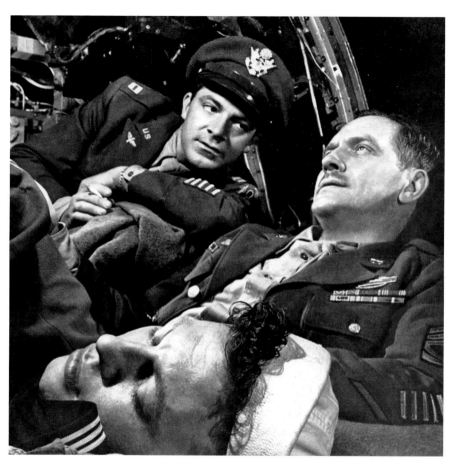

Dana Andrews, Fredric March, and (*foreground*) the untrained non-actor Harold Russell fly home in *The Best Years of Our Lives*. (*Everett Collection*)

Wyler receives a Best Director Academy Award for *The Best Years of Our Lives* from his admiring colleague Billy Wilder. (*Everett Collection*)

ant surprise." Langston Hughes called the picture "distinctly and thrillingly worthwhile," and New York's black paper the *Amsterdam News* marveled, "Who would have thought such a thing could be done so accurately . . . without sugar-coating and . . . jackass clowning?"

Moss knew that *The Negro Soldier* wasn't perfect; he told journalists that it was tailored to "ignore what's wrong with the Army and tell what's right with my people." *Time* magazine commented that "the makers of the film have not included any of the dynamite implicit in the subject" such as "friction between Negro soldiers and white soldiers." A columnist for the *New York Post* who liked the movie and respected its representation of "the dignity and expertness with which Negro men and women are serving in the Armed Forces" nonetheless warned that "what it does not show . . . is the fact that even in our own country, there is a difference between the way we treat the white man and the way we treat the colored man." But the overall reaction to the picture was strongly positive. After the Harlem screening, several members of the audience asked Moss, "Are you going to show this to white people?" When Moss asked why, they said, "Because it will change their attitude." Soon after that preview, the Signal Corps decided that *The Negro Soldier* would be shown not just to GIs but to the general public; it would be commercially marketed with the slogan "America's Joe Louis Vs. The Axis!"

The army made one hundred 35-millimeter prints available for theatrical distribution, but its original ideological intent remained unchanged: *The Negro Soldier* was meant to attract black men into the armed services, not to sell the rest of America on the value of their contribution. Accordingly, the picture was booked to play almost entirely in black movie houses in the South; its distribution was more widespread in the North and West, where its reach extended to some theaters in predominantly white towns and neighborhoods. By the middle of the year, it had become what one newspaper called "the real sleeper of the season," playing in more than three hundred different theaters in the New York area and another 250 in and around Detroit.

Moss hoped *The Negro Soldier* might open doors for him in Hollywood, and decades later he told Capra biographer Joseph McBride that it was not until after the movie became a success that he and Capra had their first conversation of any substance. "Why don't you go to some of those rich colored guys and start a company for yourself?" Capra asked him. When Moss replied that there weren't enough wealthy black men to finance any kind of competitive studio, Capra seemed disappointed, and suggested to Moss that if that were the case, maybe he would be better off leaving the country. (In later years, Capra took much more credit for a hands-on role in shaping the film than his actual participation merited. He claimed that Moss was a hothead who "wore his blackness as conspicuously as a bandage" and filled his script with an "angry fervor" that Capra had to eliminate with the explanation that "when something's red-hot, the blow torch of passion only louses up its glow.")

With the successful release of the movie, Capra could at least check off one project as having been completed to his satisfaction. *Know Your Enemy—Japan* was now on its fourth and most unlikely creative team, the husband-and-wife duo Albert Hackett and Frances Goodrich, best known in Hollywood for writing the *Thin Man* movies. *Know Your Enemy—Germany* also was stalled; Capra had recently pulled Theodor Geisel off the *Private SNAFU* cartoon series and asked him to try his hand at a new draft. Capra had to beg Osborn for the resources to complete the two films, arguing that "the lack of general information on Japan itself is so appalling that we would be derelict in not doing something. . . . *Know Your Enemy—Japan* and *Know Your Enemy—Germany* are on the list to be made and have been officially approved. What I am asking for now is that you insist they be completed." But as the War Department prepared to pour resources into Europe, it was less inclined than ever to allocate money or personnel to the Signal Corps. Even the final two installments of *Why We Fight*, *The Battle of China* and *War Comes to America*, were, Capra angrily told General Surles, "limping along under reduced staff due to the stealing of personnel away from them. The taking away of [Anthony] Veiller . . . and Litvak and other key personnel has certainly raised hell. . . . I must say again that all these pictures will suffer from now on."

Capra was still looking for new stories to tell, and according to some biographies, he chose that moment to commission a propaganda short about the $11 billion in American aid that had gone to Russia under the Lend-Lease Act, dispatching George Stevens to film supply lines at the border between Iran and Turkmenistan, which was then a Soviet republic. The timing of this assignment seems improbable, and accounts suggesting that Stevens made a quick trip to Tehran just before the Allied landing in Normandy almost certainly stem from a typographical error in government records.* Stevens was still in London, waiting to deploy his SPECOU unit in France—a mission that Capra would have been unlikely to interrupt for a nonurgent project. By May, Stevens was heading west to Bristol, a staging area for the army. He took an evening train out of the city to prepare for his journey east, and he noted the somber atmosphere in his diary. "It is the gloaming when the train pulls out," he wrote. "All the blackout [curtain]s have not [yet] been drawn when we leave the station. The interior lights are extinguished and we roll along for a while in the restful period of the long English springtime twilight. . . . From the train interior one could hardly distinguish the expressions on people's faces as they stood there saying goodbye. The naval officer standing in the coach door said goodbye to the woman wearing the tweed coat and felt hat—He stayed there . . . until the very last. The order to close the doors—and the shout from the woman guard, 'Draw the blackout.' Then the train pulled out—9.50 exactly. Wartime London stations at dusk. Desperate goodbyes."

A few weeks later, the orders every American soldier in England had been awaiting for months came through. Stevens, Ford, and their teams were to cross the Channel and prepare to start filming as 156,000 Allied troops landed on the north coast of France. D-Day was one week away.

---

* The timing of Capra's assignment to Stevens has been a subject of confusion and uncertainty for decades. In his 1971 autobiography, Capra wrote that he conceived the Lend-Lease short and sent Stevens to the Iran/USSR border in May 1942, a clear failure of memory since Stevens hadn't even joined the army yet. Twenty years later, biographer Joseph McBride caught the error, checked it against Capra's army file, and concluded that the assignment was actually made two years later. His basis for this was a letter dated May 27, 1944, in which Capra and Osborn asked the USSR for access "to photograph the activities of the Lend-Lease supply into the Soviet Union." But circumstantial evidence strongly suggests that the date in the army file is a typo and that the request was actually made a year earlier, on May 27, 1943. In his letter, General Osborn refers to the proposed film as covering "the full operation of the Persian Gulf Service Command"—the U.S. Army outpost in charge of coordinating the supply line. But the designation "Persian Gulf Service Command" was only in use from August 1942 to December 1943; after that, its name was changed. Moreover, a May 1943 assignment to Stevens would logically have led into the trip that he and one of the men in his unit, *Gunga Din* screenwriter Joel Sayre, took from Egypt to Iran one month later. On July 4, 1943, Stevens was in Tehran and wrote in his journal, "Photographed celebration here, commemorating American Independence Day and the delivery of TONS of material to U.S.S.R." In any case, the short was abandoned when the Soviet army refused to let Stevens and Sayre cross the border so that they could film American supplies arriving at their destination.

TWENTY-ONE

"If You See It, Shoot It"

FRANCE, JUNE–JULY 1944

John Ford, who loved to tell war stories, didn't talk about D-Day for twenty years. George Stevens, a prolific letter writer and journal keeper, fell uncharacteristically silent, leaving three weeks almost blank in his diary. At first, the events of June 6, 1944, were too overwhelming for them to re-count clearly to their loved ones—Ford made no mention at all of what he had seen and experienced on the beaches of France in a letter to his wife two days later—or even to themselves. The two men were there to supervise the creation of a filmed record of D-Day and its aftermath, but they found that simply describing what took place before their eyes was almost impossible. Ford later said that he perceived those first twenty-four hours "in discon-nected takes, like unassembled shots to be spliced together afterward in a film." What happened on Omaha Beach was war on a scale so large and at times so horrific that he felt he could not grasp it; he fought simply to concentrate on what was right in front of him. "My staff and I had the job of 'seeing' the whole invasion for the world," he said, "but all any one of us saw was his own little area. . . . As I think back on it now, I doubt if I saw—really saw—more than twelve of our men at one time."

The collective effort to photograph the Allied landing in France was, as an attempt to amass a comprehensive real-time document of a military campaign, without precedent in the history of warfare. Five hundred 35-millimeter cameras, each loaded with magazines that contained four minutes of film, were mounted on the fronts of ships and tanks and rigged to operate without manual supervision, and another fifty cameras were placed in the first wave of landing craft. Dozens of American cameramen and almost two hundred still photographers were assigned throughout the Allied platoons to capture material for newsreels, papers, and magazines, and Ford and Stevens were each in charge of dozens of soldiers who found themselves under enemy fire while they were manning cameras.

Ford and Stevens were not close friends—they were both introspective and hard to read, and in Hollywood they largely avoided the company of other filmmakers—but they did admire and respect each other. Ford thought Stevens was an "artist"—a word he rarely used about fellow directors—and Stevens felt a kind of kinship with Ford as well; they were men who often found themselves at a loss for words, and in Ford, Stevens saw someone who, like him, had discovered "in motion pictures the only medium in which he could express himself." Ford was running Field Photo under the supervision of the navy and Bill Donovan at the OSS. Stevens was working for Capra and the Army Pictorial Service, and, typically, they had not been asked by the armed forces to coordinate their efforts. Nonetheless, in the weeks leading up to D-Day, Ford reached out to ask his colleague for help. Ford had been working with other Allied film units, giving the British and the Canadians a crash course in war photography and telling them to concentrate on their own country's soldiers while filming, but the British army didn't have enough cameramen on its ships to do the job, and Ford's Field Photo Unit would already be stretched thin covering navy ships. Ford contacted Stevens and asked him if he could spare some camera operators from his SPECOU unit for the British. Stevens readily agreed, volunteering to serve on a British ship himself during the trip across the Channel and joking that Ford would owe him "two bottles of booze" from liberated France for his efforts.

Stevens arrived first, with his own 16-millimeter camera and magazines loaded with Kodachrome Safety Color Film for Daylight; the men with him included Irwin Shaw, William Saroyan, Bill Mellor, and Ivan Moffat. The work that SPECOU did was a team effort, and there are no labels on the surviving footage that indicate who was behind the camera for any given shot. But the film Stevens was able to preserve shows that the healthy men he photographed smoking and chatting at the train station as they prepared to leave London for the coast of England were grim and worn-looking by the time they were aboard HMS *Belfast*, a six-hundred-foot Royal Navy cruiser that was among the largest of the thousands of ships bound for one of the five designated Allied landing points. The seas were so rough that General Eisenhower had considered postponing the landing for another day; the soldiers all wore life jackets, and many of the men, full of tinned army rations and adrenaline and buffeted by the surf, were throwing up over the sides of the lurching boats. From the deck, Stevens's men tried their best to capture the immensity of the fleet with long shots of the serried rows of ships and the barrage balloons that protected them from bombers overhead. Before they landed, the *Belfast*'s captain called for attention and read the men the Saint Crispin's Day speech from *Henry V:*

And Crispin Crispian shall ne'er go by,
From this day to the ending of the world,
But we in it shall be remembered—
We few, we happy few, we band of brothers;
For he today that sheds his blood with me
Shall be my brother.

Within hours of the first landing, Stevens was making his way out of the ocean at Saint-Aubin-sur-Mer, the sector the Allies had named Juno Beach.

Ford was aboard USS *Plunkett*, a 350-foot destroyer bound for Omaha Beach that had already seen action in the North African and Italian campaigns and had survived a strike from a 500-pound bomb that had killed dozens of its crewmen. The ship had set out, along with the rest of the American fleet, on June 3, only to have to turn back because of reports of violent storms on the French coast. The next day, the skies and the water were even more punishing, tossing the jittery soldiers and sailors from side to side for hours. "What I'll never forget is how rough that sea was," Ford said in 1964.

"The destroyers rolled terribly. Practically everybody was stinking, rotten sick. How anyone on the smaller landing craft had enough guts to get out and fight I'll never understand, but somehow, they did."

The *Plunkett* was to be used to provide protection for the transport vessels that were running supplies from the ships to the beachfront. Shortly before 6 a.m., it dropped anchor just off Omaha Beach, where the resistance from Axis forces positioned in the hills and low cliffs overlooking the shoreline was most heavily concentrated. Within a few days, the British navy would construct a giant artificial harbor known as a "Mulberry" to protect the Allied fleet from the sea, but at the moment, they were exposed on all sides. "Things began to happen fast," said Ford. "It was extreme low tide and all the underwater obstacles put there by the Germans stuck out crazily like giant kids' jackstraws with mines and shells wired all over them. There were demolition teams on the first landing craft that were supposed to blow such things out of the way for the landings to follow. As the first landing craft started past the *Plunkett,* I could see the troops bailing with their helmets, stopping to heave their guts out every few throws. I could even hear them puking over the noise of motors and waves slapping flat bows all the way to the beach."

Although Ford later recalled the *Plunkett* as having abruptly moved during the Channel crossing from the rear of its huge convoy of vessels to the front, so that he ended up "leading the invasion with my cameras," it was not a landing ship, and in all probability Ford himself did not set foot on the beach until a few days later. Soon after the fleet had arrived, the $1 million of camera equipment the ship was carrying was unloaded and the Field Photo men were packed into DUKWs (amphibious landing craft that were known as "ducks") that took them up to hip-deep water at the edge of the shore. Ford, their commanding officer, told them their objective was "simple—just take movies of everything" that was happening on the beach. He recalled watching a black GI who worked for the Services of Supply division (even at Normandy, whites and blacks were segregated by duties) unloading materiel from a DUKW while Germans shot at him. "He . . . just kept going back and forth, back and forth, completely calm. I thought, by God, if anybody deserves a medal that man does. I wanted to photograph him, but I was in a relatively safe place at the time, so I figured, the hell with it. I was willing to admit he was braver than I was.'"*

Shortly thereafter, Ford was ferried over to USS *Augusta,* a 570-foot heavy cruiser from which Omar Bradley was running First Army operations. For the first couple of days, Ford would attempt to coordinate Field Photo operations from aboard ship, and hope for the best. "In all honesty," he said, "I was more or less a logistic officer. It was my job to see that everyone who should have a camera had one." Operation Overlord was now under way. "Not . . . I [nor] any other man who was there can give a panoramic wide-angle view of the first wave of Americans who hit the beach that morning," Ford said. "There was a tremendous sort of spiral of events. . . . and it seemed to narrow down to each man in his vortex on Omaha Beach."

With more than half a million American and British soldiers and naval personnel coming from five thousand ships along fifty miles of beach in the ten days following D-Day, creating a filmed overview of those first hours and of the week that followed would have been impossible, and neither Ford nor Stevens intended to try. Instead, they told their men not to put themselves in unnecessary danger and to focus on what was within their own field of vision as well as on their own safety. Ford's contention that he was on the beach that first day, which he repeated with less hesitation and more emphasis the older he got, was probably untrue, but initially, at least, he certainly didn't tell the story in order to suggest an amplified sense of his own courage. "Once I was on the beach I ran forward and started placing some of my men behind things so they'd have a chance to expose their film," he said. "I know it doesn't sound blazingly dramatic. . . . To tell the truth I was too busy doing what I had to do for a cohesive picture of what I did to register in my mind. We stayed on the job and worked that day and for several other days and nights too."

By the end of the first day of fighting, more than four thousand Allied

---

* Ford's more embellished claim in a 1966 interview with the French magazine *Positif* that he shed the last vestiges of racism when he saw "scores of black bodies lying in the sand" when he landed on Omaha Beach should probably be discounted as an overstatement at a moment when the somewhat enfeebled director was trying to defend the treatment of African Americans in his films.

soldiers were dead. Fourteen of the sixteen tanks that had tried to roll onto Omaha Beach that dawn had been destroyed. Some men, laden with equipment that included eighty-pound flamethrowers, sank and drowned when their landing craft foundered in shallow waters. Others were torn apart by machine-gun fire as they walked down the ramps into the water, or died because they became entangled in underwater obstructions placed just off the shore and panicked; others were killed by snipers or mortars as they took their first steps out of the surf and onto the beach; others were first injured, then killed along with the soldiers who tried to carry them on stretchers to the front lines where the medics were. Soldiers died because their map or their navigation was faulty and their boats landed at the wrong coordinates; they died because, weighed down by their water-saturated boots and uniforms, they couldn't move to shelter fast enough; they died because they took off their helmets so they could see through the smoke, rain, and mist, determine where the gunfire was coming from, and try to find any spot along the coast that looked safe; or they died because they were unlucky enough to be part of the first, expendable wave of sacrifice that cleared the way for the massive invasion force and material resources that were right behind them. Some soldiers who survived that first day later recalled that the constant, agonized screams of fear, pain, and confusion were the worst part of it. By nightfall, long stretches of the beaches were stained red-brown with blood and corpses lay in all directions, exposed and unretrievable.

"I saw very few dead and wounded men," Ford said. "I remember thinking, that's strange. Although later, I could see the dead floating in the sea." Miraculously, nobody in Field Photo was killed that day and only one member of the unit was injured. But most of the film for which Ford had planned so carefully was unusable: The stationary cameras that were mounted on ships were blown apart, or failed to function, or functioned only to have the film exposed and destroyed, or captured nothing but chaos. And all but three of the cameras in the first wave of landing craft were ruined.

In the days that followed, Ford's men moved inland with the troops, and miles away, so did Stevens and the British and American forces to which his SPECOU unit was attached. Eventually, the two men seem to have connected, if only briefly. Stevens was fond of telling a story about crouching behind a hedge in Normandy for shelter during a firefight only to look up and see Ford standing there above him, placidly surveying the action. The anecdote has more than a hint of mythmaking, but it speaks volumes about his admiration for the stoicism and unflappability that Ford projected under pressure. Stevens had suffered an especially rough few days as he tried to lead his team. "George had no right to be in the Army," recalled Irwin Shaw, "because he suffered from asthma, and he just hid [it] from the doctors. And in Normandy . . . the weather [was] awful. There was one period when he couldn't get [up]. . . . We had pup tents . . . under some trees in the side of a field, and he just lay there for three days. As a commanding officer, he was a little . . . softhearted. He couldn't stand the idea of the guys getting hurt, and he tried to keep a rein on all of us, to keep the casualties down."

Ford, according to an OSS report, would go ashore by day to check on the Field Photo men, but it seems likely that he mostly stayed on the *Augusta*, despite his claim decades later that "yes, I was one of the first men ashore . . . at the first hour." On June 8, he wrote a letter to Mary saying, "Dear Ma— My darling, I miss you terribly and our home and our family, but I guess that's what we're fighting for. Carry on, my sweet. I hope to be with you all again before many weeks. This thing here is going great. Jerry is bound to crack up any day. I love you. Daddy."

Less than seventy-two hours after D-Day, most of the retrievable film that Field Photo, the SPECOU team, the Coast Guard, the Canadian army, and the British had shot was sent to London. Some of it was in color; all of it was converted to black-and-white for use in newsreels. Working around the clock in four-hour shifts that alternated with four-hour respites, Americans and members of the British Army Film Unit sifted through every image and created a rough assemblage of footage, marking the scenes they thought were worth using. There were not many. Much of the footage was blurry, obscure, or jerky and frantic, and many of the clearest images were so explicit that they were immediately deemed inappropriate for any kind of general exhibition. There were shots of terrified wounded men, of open-eyed corpses floating face up in the shallows, of severed limbs, of waves clouded with blood lapping against the shore; the cameramen had followed Ford's dictum "If you see it, shoot it," but what they captured would not be shown in any major public venue for more than fifty years. "Very little was released to the public then," said Ford. "Apparently the government was afraid to show so many casualties on screen."

Reels of the footage—about one hour and forty minutes in all—were shown to Churchill, then flown to Washington and screened for Roosevelt. It was a week in which Americans flocked to theaters hungry for any news of the war, which was now coming at a dizzying pace. Monday had brought word of the Allied liberation of Rome, news that was broadcast by radio in thousands of theaters. D-Day was the next day, and for the second night in a row, movie houses across the country had turned off their projectors in the middle of their features so that their audiences could listen to Roosevelt's six-minute address to the nation, in which he asked Americans to join him in prayer. Theaters changed their newsreels weekly, usually as soon as they could thread the newest shipments into the projectors after they were delivered on Thursday or Friday afternoons. Capra, knowing that footage from Normandy could not possibly be prepared, processed, and shipped in time to be shown on the coming weekend, had had his unit prepare a twenty-minute documentary called *Eve of Battle*, about the run-up to the invasion, that would replace regular newsreels in many theaters on June 8 and also serve as a kind of preview of coming attractions for the D-Day footage that would finally become public on June 15.

By that evening, moviegoers were in a frenzy to see film from Omaha Beach, which had been touted all week with slogans trumpeting "First Invasion Pictures!" They were shown ten riveting army-approved minutes, all in black and white, that included the shooting of an American soldier but otherwise omitted the most brutal and explicit images that had been caught on film. The War Department's Bureau of Public Relations praised the collective work of the D-Day cinematographers as "the greatest pictorial team play" of the war.

Ford treated the completion of Field Photo's work documenting the first few days at Normandy as the wrap-up of the greatest film shoot of his career, and celebrated by going on an annihilating bender. Bill Clothier, who had shot much of the footage for Wyler's *Memphis Belle*, had become a friend of Ford's and would go on to film several movies for him; he was now overseeing his own small unit of Army Air Force photographers, and they were bunking at a house off the French coast in an area that had just come under Allied control. Sometime around June 12, Ford made his way to the house—he told Clothier he was looking for Stevens—and started drinking. For the next three days, he stayed in a sleeping bag, crawling out only when he needed more alcohol, even when he had to steal another officer's supply to obtain it. Occasionally he'd stagger outside and pick a fight with one of the French soldiers who were guarding the door. When Clothier looked in on him and saw that he was passed out in a sleeping bag that he had now soaked with urine and vomit, he lost his temper, called Mark Armistead, a buddy in Field Photo, and asked him to come collect the director immediately. By the time Field Photo showed up, Ford had wandered off to a tavern and was found out of uniform and barely coherent. "We just had to take care of him," Armistead said. "He [was] the type of person that one drink is too many and a thousand is not enough. . . . When he [drank], you would just have to stay with him day and night, let him get it out of his system."

Back on the *Augusta*, sober and worn out, Ford began to turn his thoughts toward his next movie. John Bulkeley was in the English Channel, leading a fleet of several dozen PT boats that were patrolling the area in order to fend off any attacks from *Schnellboote* (the fast, wood-hulled vessels that the Allies called E-boats, essentially the German counterparts of PTs). Ford radioed Bulkeley's boat and asked for permission to be lowered into it. He wanted to talk to Bulkeley about *They Were Expendable*, and he told him that he was now committed to directing it. Bulkeley, who had been hearing about the project for the last year, admitted that he wouldn't mind being played by Spencer Tracy; Ford scoffed at the idea. "He had not many nice words to say about Spencer Tracy, for whatever reason," Bulkeley recalled.

After their embarrassing encounter in Washington, Bulkeley was wary of Ford; he thought the director was a blowhard and a showboater and didn't particularly trust him. Over the next few days, Ford accompanied him on patrols, and Bulkeley got the impression that he had not witnessed much action on D-Day and wanted to get closer to where the war was really happening. When their PT boat came under fire from a distant German machine gun, Ford didn't flinch; "he loved the excitement of it," said Bulkeley. By the end of their time together, his distaste for Ford had mellowed into grudging appreciation, but he made it clear to the director that he wanted no part of Hollywood, declined his offer to serve as a technical adviser on the picture, and added that he wished the movie weren't being made at all. Ford told him that he had no intention of turning his life story into "some goddamned two-bit propaganda flick," and, to ensure that the movie wouldn't be misused, told Bulkeley that it wouldn't go into production until after the war.

A day or two later, Ford was in the Mulberry harbor off Omaha Beach when a gale tore across the English Channel and ripped apart the breakwaters and caissons that the U.S. and British navies had constructed; the artificial port had been the conduit for 1.6 million pounds of supplies for the Allies every day. Ford had some of his Field Photo men station themselves on the caissons and photograph the destruction, not realizing that it would be the last time he would supervise any filming as a naval officer. It is not clear why Ford's time in France ended so abruptly, but his drinking binge, which had tested the patience of an air force captain and required the intervention of more than one navy officer, had been so embarrassingly public that it could have resulted in a dishonorable discharge. No official report of the incident seems to have been made, but Ford may have been urged by his own men or Bill Donovan to take himself out of harm's way and keep a lower profile. On June 19, he sailed back to London and checked into Claridge's. "Sorta winding this thing up," he wrote to Mary, providing no details. He would remain in England—except for a brief mission to Yugoslavia with Bulkeley—for another six weeks. But there was nothing more for Ford to do in the battlefield. His war was over. He was going home.

The day after Ford left France, Stevens took out his pocket journal and, for the first time since D-Day, made an entry, which he labeled, "D+16." "Second morning in marshaling area," he wrote. "Clear and bright morning after a very cold nite. Used the little sleeping bag that we picked up for the Navy job (D-Day). Procured personal carbine."

Stevens and his men had spent many of the days right after the Allied landing in tents they pitched over foxholes that they dug behind an airfield. In close quarters of a kind he had never experienced before, he got to know the soldiers under his command—and they, in turn, tried to figure him out.

Ivan Moffat later remembered him as "a very volatile, moody man, capable of tremendous laughter and a good deal of anger, quite easily upset, change-able from hour to hour. . . . He [was] a man of a good deal of a curious kind of half-amused, wry jealousy or pseudo-jealousy, sometime pretended, some-times not." That may have been particular to his relationship with Moffat, an urbane, ambitious, and slightly show-offy young T/5 (a technician fifth grade, equal to a corporal) who was the only man under Stevens able to speak fluent French. At first, Stevens appreciated Moffat's skill; then it started to grate on him; then, unsure what Moffat was saying at any given moment, he banned the speaking of French in his presence altogether. Moffat responded by writing a few lines of doggerel in which he joked about the new restrictions, and he showed them to his fellow soldiers. When Stevens saw the verse, "he laughed," said Moffat, "and after that the rule was no longer enforced."

Stevens was "forgiving," said Irwin Shaw. "There was none of the spit-and-polish martinet about him. And the guys really liked him—the disci-pline in his unit was very high, very good." But his men didn't know what made him tick any more than the actors on his Hollywood sets had. Stevens, playing off a popular caricature, would tell them that his Native American heritage—often mentioned, never confirmed—was responsible for his un-readable expression. More likely, it was Stevens's way of using social discom-fort to his advantage. Keeping his men uncertain about how he might react to them was his awkward way of asserting control. "He was taciturn, always grave-looking," said Shaw, "even when he was cracking jokes."

The safety of his men was a constant concern, even though after the first few days they were out of the line of fire, though not out of proximate danger. The French coastline and some of the roads were still rigged with tripwires and booby traps; one of Stevens's diary entries from late June was a set of roughly jotted sketches of what disguised land mines might look like. But what was foremost in Stevens's mind was his assignment, and he surprised some of the men in his SPECOU unit when he made it clear that he believed their role was not only to document combat but to create a record of the entire campaign—what the Nazis had done to France, what the shelled villages and roads looked like, how the injured were treated. Stevens had never been to France, and if he occasionally had a tourist's interest in what he saw, so did many of the wide-eyed American GIs who were then marching into Europe; he intended to document the war through their eyes, and to follow his own instincts about what to shoot as well.

Early on, he wondered if he was straying too far from his original assignment. He was, after all, in the army in part as a propagandist; a year earlier, he had found himself in North Africa, staging a fake war in the spot where a real one had just been fought, in order to make Americans feel that they were winning. Now he was in the middle of a war being waged on a scale that would defy the ability of any filmmaker to tidy it up or turn it into a simple narrative of perseverance or bravery leading to inevitable victory. His only responsibility aside from protecting his men was, he believed, to shoot what he saw, and shoot it the way he saw it. As he stood with Moffat at a crossroads in the rustic cheesemaking town of Isigny-sur-Mer watching Allied supply convoys rumble along the cratered, bomb-blasted roads, he was struck by the juxtaposition of the machinery of war coming to save the day in an almost bucolic village that the machinery of war had all but destroyed just a few days earlier, and immediately thought of lifting up his camera as the trucks rolled through. "I'd love to take a few reels of that, just for future record," he told Moffat.

"Why don't you, Colonel?"

"And ship them back to the War Department?" said Stevens. "They'd think I'd gone nuts."

For the most part, though, Stevens gave himself license to film whenever he had the impulse, and the result was a kind of home-movie account of France after D-Day that remains the most detailed visual document of those critical weeks. He had his men photograph two French townsmen holding up their flag in front of a wrecked building; Stevens can be seen showing them how to do it and then giving them the "OK" hand sign. The SPECOU unit filmed a wounded American soldier on a stretcher inside a coffinlike crate being lifted onto the deck of a ship with a grappling hook. They shot Stevens and another soldier digging what appears to be a grave in a grassy field; they shot a young GI chatting with an old Frenchman in front of a torn wall poster, a little French boy chasing after Stevens and Bill Mellor as they walked down a road, the American flag being raised next to the French one in the open balcony window of a home in a newly freed town. They photographed the shell of a ruined cathedral at twilight and roofless schoolhouses silhouetted against the afternoon sky. They shot camouflaged tanks rolling out of the woods, and GIs opening their rations and digging through their gear looking for packs of Camel cigarettes. And whenever he saw them, Stevens would have his men film road signs to orient viewers as they passed through dozens of tiny hamlets and villages.

Stevens had his unit look for the funny, the incongruous, the idiosyncratic, and the unexpected. "He would never go about anything very directly," Moffat wrote. "If there was something to be seen that a crowd was looking at, he would always look at the crowd looking at the scene. His was always the sense of indirection."

By July 4, 1944, the SPECOU team had been entrenched for a couple of weeks at Allied army HQ in Carentan, a small town near Cherbourg a little less than a mile back from enemy lines. There, Stevens filmed medal ceremonies involving Patton, Bradley, and British general Bernard Montgomery, and color footage of GIs relaxing, sunbathing, reading old issues of *Life* magazine, and eagerly opening letters from home. They had put up a sign at the entrance to their campground that featured mileage markers and directional arrows pointing toward New York, Paris, London, and "Shirley (4500 miles)." The men in Stevens's unit are identifiable in the candid film by the yellow-on-black sleeve patches they wore, which read "Official US War Photographer." At Patton and Bradley's instructions, Stevens and his men would accompany the army for the next two months as it moved southwest from Carentan to Brittany and then west toward Paris. It was on this 450-mile journey along often dangerous roads that Stevens started to collect the images that would define for a nation of moviegoers the Allied push into Europe and the turning tide it represented. They were exactly the pictures that John Huston had hoped to find and instead ended up manufacturing in San Pietro—ecstatic villagers emerging from their shattered homes to greet the American liberators, young women throwing flowers, children scampering alongside the convoys hoping for a chocolate bar. His cameras also captured images of the dangers American soldiers faced—GIs can be seen jumping and scattering after a land mine in the middle of a road detonates unexpectedly.

Stevens filmed the dead as well, in footage so disturbing it never reached the screen. He photographed French civilians, the victims of bombings, lying along a country road, his cameras not lingering on the images but holding on them long enough so that the lifeless eyes and expressions of slight, open-mouthed surprise would haunt anyone who saw them. And no matter what his men encountered, if they were holding cameras, Stevens's orders to them were to do their job and never look away. Soon after the army began its push toward Brittany, the team came upon a pair of dead soldiers in Wehrmacht uniforms. "They were near a farmhouse," Shaw said. "They'd been abandoned on stretchers by their own medical corps guys. They were all mangled, and both very young, and . . . we took pictures." The SPECOU team had been told that the Germans would sometimes wire the corpses of their own soldiers with explosives or place them on top of land mines. "We all warned everybody, stay away, don't touch," said Shaw. "So George got a big stick and poked them. It [was] macabre. Just to make sure . . . so we could get closeups and all that. I think they were the first Germans we'd seen since the beach."

TWENTY-TWO

"If Hitler Can Hold Out, So Can I"

HOLLYWOOD AND WASHINGTON, JULY–DECEMBER 1944

I n July, John Ford got the *Araner* back. The navy had chartered his boat right after Pearl Harbor, painting it black for camouflage and then using it to lead a fleet that watched for submarines off the California coast. Ford had turned over the ketch for a promised fee of one dollar plus permission to fly the flag of the Naval Reserve permanently after it was returned to him. He never collected the dollar, but he did fly the flag.

Although he was still officially on active duty, Ford, back in the United States after D-Day, was removed with jolting swiftness from the role he had had in the navy until then. A return to the front was not in the offing; he was in his office in Washington, D.C., in early August, then in Los Angeles with his family for two weeks, then in the capital again with nothing much to do for Field Photo or the OSS. The war in Europe continued with escalating intensity, but he would not be a part of it. His service was over, and he was, in some ways, desperate to have something to show for it. Ford's relationship with honors for his work had always combined feigned indifference with intense need; he had not shown up to collect any of his three Academy Awards for Best Director, but they had mattered so much to him that he had taken to telling people he had actually won four, counting the Oscar for *December 7th* even though he didn't direct it. Awards were a validation, a benchmark of recognition, and a yardstick of comparative success; they were also, even in the 1940s, the object of unseemly obsession in Hollywood.

That may explain why, even before his time in the military had officially ended, Ford became what his daughter called a "ribbon freak." He wanted a Silver Star, which was given to members of the armed forces for "gallantry in action against an enemy of the United States," and he asked the secretary of the navy to approve one for him. He also wanted a Distinguished Service Medal, which Frank Capra was soon to receive, a Naval Reserve Ribbon, given to men who had spent ten years in the Reserve, and a second Purple Heart to go with the one he had gotten after Midway; he claimed he was eligible because he had received an injury during a London bombing and explained that unfortunately he could not remember the name of the doctor who had treated him. He even asked for a Croix de Guerre from Belgium. For Ford, such decorations were among the only indices of bravery and valor he could trust, in part because he believed that they would provide a kind of proof toward posterity. In the fall, he received word that Junius Stout, one of his young Field Photo cameramen, had been killed. Stout had been atop one of the huge floating rectangular artificial breakwaters that had been towed in to Omaha Beach as part of the Mulberry harbor; he had survived that only to be shot down while flying back to England to be commissioned as an officer. Twenty years later, when Ford spoke of Stout's death, medals were still foremost in his mind. He said, "He did a fine job riding that big box—he got a Silver Star for it."

Even members of his own family thought Ford's quest for military honors was "shameless," but it may have come from a desire to quell his own fear that he had not done enough. He had seen so many men risk—and sometimes lose—their lives in the line of duty that he needed some form of tangible evidence that his own work in the navy had meant something. And although he had now firmly decided to make *They Were Expendable* for MGM, he was terribly concerned that the movie be seen as an extension, not a termination, of his service. In his request to the War Department to be placed on inactive status, he wrote, "The picture would have a big Navy motif which at the present would be very timely," and promised that he would return to work for the OSS as soon as it was completed. At the same time, he needed to make his navy colleagues believe that his departure was happening involuntarily and against his better judgment. "I have been ordered to Hollywood to do a commercial picture . . . and I am leaving tonight," he wrote to Albert Wedemeyer, the general under whom he had served during his OSS trip to Burma and China. "While I will at least get a chance to spend Christmas with the folks and play with my grandson's electric train, still I'm a bit ashamed that a great warrior like me should be in mockie-land while the good people are fighting. . . . I am getting a big chunk of dough for the picture, which I am turning over into a trust fund. . . . That at least clears my conscience a bit."

Ford was telling the truth about the money—although the widely published reports that he would be paid $300,000, "the highest salary yet given a Hollywood film director for one picture," appear to have been hyperbolic; the somewhat lower six-figure salary he did receive was a sum that no director but Capra had yet been paid. And Ford did, as promised, place the money in trust, but he omitted from his public statements the fact that he had no choice: The memory of Zanuck's vilification by a congressional committee for failing to put his Fox holdings in trust while in the army was still fresh, and long as Ford was an officer, even one on inactive duty, the armed forces would not be happy if he pocketed an extravagant salary for a civilian job.

Ford decided to use the money he would be paid to fund a sustained act of charity; he spent $65,000 to buy an eight-acre plot of land in Reseda, California, from Sam Briskin, a Columbia Pictures executive and close associate of Frank Capra. On the property, Ford established what he called "the Farm," a large clubhouse and private resort that he created as a refuge for the veterans of his Field Photo Unit; it included a bar, a pool, tennis and badminton courts, and six bedrooms, including one that was permanently reserved for Bill Donovan. The Farm's multiple functions were a direct expression of Ford's competing instincts for veneration and sentiment, grandiosity and generosity. It was in part a memorial, with the names of a dozen men in Field Photo who had died inscribed on the wall of an adjoining chapel. It was also an attempt to recreate the all-male, alcohol-saturated camaraderie of the Emerald Bay Yacht Club, his Hollywood getaway between movies in the years before the war. And, like Emerald Bay, the Farm was operated under archly ceremonial bylaws devised by Ford that included an annual parade and a specification that women would be allowed to visit on only one day a year. Not incidentally, it was also a shrine to Ford himself, with pictures and records of his accomplishments prominently adorning the walls.*

The press gave extensive coverage to Ford's decision to fund the Farm—which was formally called the Field Photo Memorial Home—reporting, with excessive generosity, that he would forgo his salary from MGM in order to create a "rehabilitation and benefit fund" for "former Hollywood studio technicians . . . in various war theatres." (The rehabilitative function of the Farm was dubious, and in later years Ford angrily rebuffed a suggestion from Robert Parrish that he turn it from a luxe hideaway into low-cost veterans' housing.) The news stories also ended up burnishing "Commander Ford"'s already secure public reputation as a war hero by making it clear that he would be back on active duty in the navy as soon as his picture was finished.

His plan was met with considerably more skepticism by his old boss Zanuck. Ford had spent most of his career under contract to 20th Century Fox and still owed the studio one more picture; when Zanuck heard that his return to work would be at MGM instead, he was furious. Ford hadn't even called Zanuck himself to discuss his decision; he had simply sent word that since *They Were Expendable* was to be made while he was still on duty and the navy itself was cooperating with the picture, his contractual obligation to resume his work for Fox once his service was over did not yet apply. Pleading for sympathy, he also told a go-between at the studio to let Zanuck know that he had just returned from Europe in order to "recuperate from shock and wounds sustained in combat." Zanuck, who knew the director's propensity for self-aggrandizement better than anyone in Hollywood, replied, "I do not choose to believe all the facts as related by Ford, including the wounds." But he was unwilling to play the role of a studio overlord thwarting such a public act of patriotism and charity, so he gritted his teeth and told Ford he could make the movie.

---

* In the years to come, Ford put at least $200,000 into the Farm's maintenance; it closed permanently in 1969 after being destroyed by a fire.

In the fall of 1944, Capra was also looking toward Hollywood. "What are you going to do after the war?" had become a commonplace conversational opener among stateside officers who believed that victory was in the offing, and Harry Warner's barb about the dangers of being forgotten if he stayed away too long had clearly struck home. In late summer, he had signed to produce a movie called *The Flying Irishman* and asked Albert Hackett and Frances Goodrich, the couple that had recently taken a crack at *Know Your Enemy—Japan,* to write the script. Capra had conceived the project as a tribute of sorts to Eric Knight, whose death in 1943 remained the most personally painful loss he had suffered since the war began. Knight had published a series of fanciful, interconnected short stories called *The Flying Yorkshireman* about an English immigrant to America who could fly, and Capra thought it would make a good vehicle for the twinkly character actor Barry Fitzgerald, who had become a household name after the success of *Going My Way.* Capra had bought the rights a couple of years earlier, refusing to surrender them no matter how long the war continued—"if Hitler can hold out," he told his agent, "so can I." He hadn't decided yet whether he would direct the picture himself, but he felt more than ready to return to work. The idea of studio servitude, however, held no appeal for him; after so many years at Columbia, he had been without a contract since *Meet John Doe,* and he found that it suited him. The war had postponed but not altered his plans to become a completely independent producer-director, and in August he began discussions with Sam Briskin about forming a new company, to be called Liberty Films, that would allow him complete autonomy.

Capra immediately began pressing the army to release him from his duties. He crafted a three-pronged argument built out of equal parts financial self-interest, nonspecific pleading about his physical condition, and a murky case that it would actually be in the War Department's best interests to allow him to return to Hollywood. Soon, he wrote, "I will have been away from my civilian profession nearly three years. Motion pictures are highly competitive and in [a] constant state of flux. I feel . . . staying away longer will seriously curtail my standing, ability, and future earning capacity. My health is gradually deteriorating and I feel it will affect the efficiency of my work. Most important, I feel I have given all I can possibly give toward the education of the orientation of the soldier. From this point on I feel I can do a bigger job on civilians."

Money was a pressing, though unexpressed, concern. Although Warner Bros. finally opened *Arsenic and Old Lace* that fall, three years after Capra had shot it, an army salary and the diminished royalties that continued to trickle in from his older movies were insufficient to keep Lucille and his children in the comfort to which they had long been accustomed. And Capra had reason to assume that the army no longer needed him urgently. His assignments had become vague and minor. He was sent to Hawaii for a month on a mission to organize Signal Corps cameramen in the army's push to document what it believed would be the final phase of the war in the Pacific, but he wasn't asked to oversee a specific documentary. Much of his time was instead spent resolving petty jurisdictional disputes or trying to wheedle cooperation out of the entertainment world, which was not quite so blindly willing to ignore its bottom line to aid in the war effort as it had been two years earlier. Capra had little patience for resistance; when Arturo Toscanini refused to grant the Army Pictorial Service permission to use his recording of "The Star-Spangled Banner" in the final *Why We Fight* film, Capra wrote him a polite and distressed letter expressing "deep regret, and some surprise" at the loss of his "magnificent rendition" for a "most important project," then told Robert Riskin to "tell the sweet old Maestro he either lets us use his recording, or he can go to hell and we'll use it anyhow."

Capra also missed his family; he had spent so little time at home since the end of 1941 that he felt his children were growing up fatherless; they communicated with him almost as if he were a distant but friendly stranger, writing short letters at the urging of their mother. "Dear Daddy," his ten-year-old son Frank Jr. wrote him. "How are you? I hope you are fine and dandy. I had a good report card, isn't that fine! I bet I can write all the states and their capitals in ten mins. . . . How much do you want to bet? Everyone is fine here . . . the mother cat has babies on the trellis below mom's bedroom window. I am doing very good in school and I understand fractions and numerators and denominators. Love, Frank."

The army turned down Capra's request, telling him he was needed in Washington. Theodor Geisel had just turned in a new script for *Know Your*

Enemy—Germany, but it needed work, and General Osborn, still Capra's most reliable champion, had been unexpectedly blunt about his disappointment with the first cut of the sixth *Why We Fight* movie, *The Battle of China.* With war documentaries now relying more and more on actual (or at least cleverly feigned) combat footage, the bargain-basement principle on which the *Why We Fight* series had been created and budgeted now seemed out of date; audiences, even those composed entirely of GIs, were losing interest in movies that were patched together from foreign propaganda pictures, newsreels, and drawings of maps. *The Battle of China* relied heavily on narration, clips from old movies, clichés of Orientalism (the movie makes extensive use of gongs), and intense anti-Japanese rhetoric that emphasized the savagery of an entire people and the evil of the Tanaka plan, a document in which Emperor Hirohito was thought to have articulated his "mad dream," a sinister scheme for world domination, fifteen years before Pearl Harbor.[*]

The Battle of China was, Osborn told Capra, "the least satisfactory of the *Why We Fight* series"; he complained that "many of the sequences are not actually pictures of historical events, but scenes taken from entertainment or other film to produce the desired effect." Capra had padded out the movie with whatever was available to him, including several scenes that MGM had shot but not used in its 1937 China melodrama *The Good Earth.* Osborn thought the script talked down to its intended audience, and found the overall picture to be of such inferior quality that he told Capra he was recommending "that it be withdrawn from showing, pending consideration of its possible revision." Capra, chagrined, could offer only the weak defense that he had used exactly the same technique in the earlier movies in the series. "I'm not trying to alibi for the Chinese film," he added woundedly. "I know there are people in the War Department who claim we have put too much 'emotion' in these films. They may be right. A dry recitation of facts might have been a 'safer' way to present them. But my experiences with audiences . . . long ago taught me that if you want facts to stick, you must present them in an interesting manner.

---

[*] The Tanaka plan, widely accepted as factual during the war, is today considered to be a skillful anti-Japanese hoax that was created in China.

"I have a feeling that perhaps I've let you down," he concluded. "Knowing the full and generous confidence you have placed in me this is quite disturbing. . . . It is . . . not through lack of study or effort."

Capra still had one movie in the works that he believed could make a real impact. John Huston had spent the last few months before D-Day working on the script and editing of his movie *The Battle of San Pietro*, an assignment Capra had given him back when they were both in London but that had somehow never taken on the status of an official army picture for a particular department. Other than Capra, nobody in the army knew what, exactly, Huston was spending so much time and effort putting together. Capra told Huston that in order to get enough money to finish the film, he'd have to complete a rough cut, bring it from New York City to Washington, and show it to General Surles, who, he wrote, "always had some cockeyed idea Huston was making a picture for OWI" instead of for the army. Huston arrived in the capital and screened an early version of the picture. Surles liked what he saw enough to tell him to get it finished. "Now," Capra wrote, "we can spend money on it officially."

Huston was also beginning to worry about his financial security. The war had cut short his Hollywood career just as he had been about to start receiving his first large paychecks in the wake of *The Maltese Falcon,* and his army salary was not paying the bills. When his eighty-nine-year-old grandmother died in July, just as he was finishing *San Pietro,* Huston justified burying her in a plain pine box rather than an expensive casket by telling the mortuary director, apparently with a straight face, that he and she were both Orthodox Jews. With no end to his service in sight, he signed to write two screenplays that fall—an adaptation of Ernest Hemingway's *The Killers* for producer Mark Hellinger at Universal, and *The Stranger,* which Orson Welles would eventually direct at RKO. Huston skirted army regulations about drawing a civilian salary while on active duty by writing both scripts under pseudonyms—a decision that also allowed him to escape the scrutiny of Warner Bros., where he was under exclusive contract.

Before his work on those movies began, though, Huston devoted himself to the completion of *San Pietro.* (Capra, suddenly suffused with Catholic fervor, told him he strongly preferred the title *The Footsoldier and St. Peter*

but would "settle for" the name of the town where the battle had taken place
as a reasonable second choice.) In August, he returned to Washington to
show a more polished cut of the film, which ran between forty-five and fifty
minutes, to an assemblage of generals and senior military staff.

The reception was disastrous—and not because of Huston's extensive
use of reenactments. Still badly shaken by the loss of life he had seen in
Italy, he had chosen to make a documentary that was true to his own emotional experience, a film that emphasized the terrible cost of the Allied campaign in Italy rather than its strategic importance, tactics, or ultimate
success. He had included a shot taken near San Pietro, though not at the
battle, of dead Allied soldiers, their bodies covered with blankets, and instead of accompanying it with narration, he had used audio of interviews
with excited young GIs poignantly talking about their futures.

That moment, which Huston had placed about three-quarters of the way
through the film, was when the officers began to walk out—first a general,
and then, in descending order by rank, his subordinates. In Huston's account, the screening room had completely emptied by the time the picture
ended, "with the low man on the totem pole bringing up the rear." That was
undoubtedly an exaggeration, but Huston's initial reaction ("I shook my head
and thought, 'What a bunch of assholes! There goes *San Pietro!'* ") was confirmed when he was called into General Surles's office at the Bureau of Public Relations, where a number of officers were present.

"The War Department wanted no part of the film," Huston wrote. "I was
told by one of its spokesman that it was 'anti-war.' I pompously replied that if
I ever made a picture that was pro-war, I hoped someone would take me out
and shoot me. The guy looked at me as if he were considering just that."
Huston himself felt that perhaps he had gone too far in juxtaposing the dead
soldiers with the voice-overs, and he was troubled by a possibility he hadn't
considered, which was that the soldiers' families might find the scene too
much to bear; he felt that the brass was justified in telling him to remove it
from the picture. But he was infuriated by the generals' overall reaction, and
not inclined to back down. "My God, nobody ever wanted to kill Germans
more than I did," he said. "Or to see them killed. I thought it was 'anti-war'
to stop Hitler."

Huston had come to view *San Pietro* not just as an act of conscience, but as a tacit atonement for his earlier work. He thought back to *Report from the Aleutians* and felt angry at himself for the water carrying he had done as an army propagandist. ("In one of the missions [shown in the film], we said that everybody returned unscathed. Well, very rarely did [men] return unscathed.") And he had no interest in softening the facts he had presented in *San Pietro*, including its clear-eyed statement that some U.S. regiments in Italy had been so devastated that almost all of their soldiers would have to be replaced.

For the set of officers who saw the film, however, there was no question of cuts or emendations; *San Pietro* was unreleasable, and would have to be shelved permanently. The picture was saved only when General Marshall asked to see it weeks later. Marshall agreed with the others that it was completely unsuitable for general audiences, but he felt it might have value as a training documentary intended to introduce new GIs to some harsh truths about combat—if it could be shortened by as much as twenty minutes and completely reshaped.

Trying to save his movie, Huston went back to work. In the fall of 1944, he swallowed his pride and recut the film, taking every note that a senior officer had to offer. Colonel Curtis Mitchell of the Bureau of Public Relations at first insisted on the "deletion of certain footage in which the bodies of dead American soldiers are . . . pulled aboard a truck" as well as any "sequences which show recognizable human dead"; he then agreed to a bizarre compromise in which the shots could stay in the film as long as a voice-over clearly identified the corpses as Italian. Colonel Gillette, Huston's Signal Corps supervisor in Italy, quarreled with some explanatory narration about the goal of the campaign being to liberate Italian villages, writing to Huston that "most prefer to think that the objectives of the war are far greater than liberating towns of an enemy country." Huston even had to contend with a demand from Robert Patterson, the undersecretary of war, who was apparently slightly hard of hearing. "Alright, Huston, let's not have any more of this insubordination," Capra wrote to him, only half joking. He attached a request from Colonel Lyman Munson: "Patterson is irate that a rewrite has not taken care of what he views as a troublesome aural similarity between the words 'Italian' and 'battalion' which he fears will cause confusion. . . . [He insists that] synonyms for 'battalion,' such as 'units' or 'outfits' or similar words are used. I would not care to be in the projection room if it so happened that the Undersecretary ran into the pronounced similarity for the third time."

Huston did as he was told, but as 1944 came to a close, he believed that *San Pietro* would never be seen by civilian moviegoers. The only portion of his battle reenactments that he thought would make it to theaters would be a few scenes that the producers of *The Story of G.I. Joe*, the fictional film based on Ernie Pyle's columns, asked if they could use to make their movie more realistic. Huston gave his consent, since at that point there seemed to be no reason to withhold it.

With nothing more to do on *San Pietro* for the time being, he returned to Los Angeles, where Capra put him to work on another project, handing him all of the previous failed drafts of *Know Your Enemy—Japan* and telling him to take over and see what he could do with them. Doris Lilly, the magazine editor with whom Huston had had a fling in New York, was now pursuing him with more determination than ever, often showing up unannounced; she followed him to California and seems to have provided considerable distraction. One night while Huston was out, she climbed through his window at 3 a.m. and grabbed the first thing she could find to scribble a note on—a copy of the *Know Your Enemy—Japan* script that he had been revising by hand. On the back of one page, she wrote, "Dear John, 'tha Lilly' was bye to pay her umble respects—en route home—weeping bitter tears you were still out—but then you always are. Miss you madly—and will probably end up wiring my 'adios'—Sleep well ma love—of course! Ever loving. P.S. Stole some cigarettes."

Huston seemed bored by his latest assignment; his mind was clearly elsewhere. Many of the pages of the *Know Your Enemy—Japan* drafts on which he worked are filled with half-completed sketches of nude bodies, male and female, and his work on the scripts appears to have been sporadic. Earlier versions of the screenplay included extensive detail about the history of Japan designed to make the case that a centuries-long pattern of bizarre religious practices and blind fealty to royalty had led inevitably to Pearl Harbor. Huston deleted much of that and replaced it with cruder and more contemporary language, writing, "The Japanese are afflicted with a mission—to impose upon the world by force or otherwise their Emperor, their Shintoism, and their divine superiority. A nation so obsessed cannot stand still. It must go forward or be destroyed. There is no compromise possible with such fanaticism."

For more than two years, the army had wrestled with the vexing issue of just how anti-Japanese and anti-German the *Know Your Enemy* films should be: Would it be best to direct most of the blame for the war at political leaders, the military, or the people themselves, targeting some ineffable elements of their national character? After years of false starts, Capra had apparently decided the last option was best; under his direction, Huston wrote the most racist, unapologetically xenophobic version that had yet been drafted. To a previous writer's description of the typical Japanese soldier that read, "He is pigeon-toed and perhaps bow-legged," Huston added, "He is near-sighted and has buck teeth." He also sought to pad the movie with any footage that would establish the Japanese as being in the thrall of peculiar customs, going well past the by then customary use of foreign propaganda newsreels. He even contacted the producers of a British film version of *The Mikado* requesting permission to use scenes from their movie in the documentary (they approved on the condition that neither Gilbert and Sullivan nor the title of the operetta would ever be mentioned).

In the first eighteen months of the war, Lowell Mellett had used the OWI's Bureau of Motion Pictures as a bully pulpit from which to caution both Hollywood and Washington against the moral evil of incendiary race-baiting in movies. But with Mellett long gone and the BMP's power greatly diminished, his warnings were forgotten. War-related entertainment pictures in 1944 were unembarrassed about denouncing the Japanese people in the ugliest possible terms. In 20th Century Fox's *The Purple Heart*, the first Hollywood movie to depict Japan's treatment of American prisoners of war, a soldier suggested that the only path to peace was to defeat the Japanese by making sure to "wipe them off the face of the earth." The same phrase was used in director Raoul Walsh's *Objective, Burma!*, which he had shot for Warner Bros. over the summer and which featured not only GIs but an American newspaperman referring to the Japanese as "monkeys," "slopeheads," "degenerate moral idiots," and "stinking little savages." The outburst occurs when the GIs come upon the corpses of American soldiers who were tortured and mutilated by the Japanese army. In the original script, the picture's hero, a paratrooper played by Errol Flynn, had responded by saying, "There's nothing especially Japanese about this. . . . You'll find it wherever you find Fascists. There are even people who call themselves American who'd do it too." The movie's producer ordered the line cut over the heated objection of its two original screenwriters, letting the anti-Japanese language in the scene stand as the final word on the subject.

Huston's script for *Know Your Enemy—Japan* was almost as strident. He had cut some scare-tactic language from an earlier writer's introduction which posited that the Japanese would settle for nothing less than the conquest of North America and the growth of its population to "a billion people—[the] Japanese with their slaves." But he had replaced it with a recurring device that was almost as inflammatory, beginning a dozen sentences of the narration with the incantatory phrase, "If you are Japanese, you believe . . ." in lines intended to establish them as an alien and paranoiac race of animal-deity worshippers.

The script that Huston and Capra submitted to the War Department still retained some of the most overheated language from earlier versions, including narration suggesting that within Japan, the United States was characterized as "a fatuous booby with much money and much sentiment, but no cohesion . . . an immense melon, ripe for the cutting" and a voice-over adding that the average Japanese soldier "hates everybody who is not Japanese, particularly Americans. . . . Above all, he is a murderous fanatic" in the thrall of a religion that has "already brought suffering and death to untold millions."

Remarkably, the first response Huston received from the army was that he had not gone far enough. The Pentagon sent back a note attached to his draft in which it faulted the script for expressing "too much sympathy for the Jap people." In particular, a line that acknowledged the existence of some "free-thinking" Japanese citizens would have to go. Impatient to get the movie finished, Capra decided to pull Huston off the project. Almost three years after he conceived it, he would write the final draft of *Know Your Enemy—Japan* himself.

TWENTY-THREE

"Time and Us Marches On"

FRANCE, BELGIUM, LUXEMBOURG, GERMANY, AND ENGLAND, JULY 1944–JANUARY 1945

T he U.S. Army was getting closer to Paris every day, but not quickly enough for George Stevens. As he and his unit moved through France with the 4th Infantry Division in the summer of 1944, they were judicious about what they chose to photograph. With no opportunity to replenish their limited supply of film, they knew they had to conserve their resources for the liberation of the city that lay ahead. But during the advance, Stevens still wanted to document the ongoing capture of tens of thousands of German soldiers—some of them resigned, some relieved, only a few defiant—as they surrendered and were taken to the rear, where they were kept in makeshift roadside camps. By late July, the Allies were just two hundred miles from Paris; they had reached the bombed city of Coutances, where they drove the occupying German forces out after a siege of airstrikes. They were soon joined by Ernest Hemingway, who had been assigned by *Collier's* magazine to follow the army through France.

The mood of the Allies that summer was determined and, if not yet jubilant, extraordinarily optimistic. They knew that Paris would be retaken in a matter of weeks, and word had come to them that they would face little opposition. But the closer they got to the outskirts of the city, the more certain Stevens became that unless he took decisive action, he would miss everything that was worth filming. He had no ambition to make a stand-alone documentary the way that Wyler and Ford and Huston had, but the memory of traveling halfway around the world to record the North African campaign only to arrive after it had ended still stung. Stevens believed more than ever that his role was to document what happened as it happened, and knew that this time he would have to fight simply to make sure he had his SPECOU team's cameras in the right place at the right time.

The liberation of Paris and the arrest of various German and Vichy officials there would not in itself require a major military campaign; the Allies already knew that fiercer and more sustained fighting would likely come in their subsequent advance east to the French-German border at the Rhine. But the importance of retaking the capital more than four years after it had fallen to the Nazis was without parallel as an announcement to the world of Hitler's weakened position. When it became clear that Eisenhower was going to allow the Free French, led by General Philippe Leclerc's 2nd Armored Division, to enter the city first, with American troops to follow, Stevens asked for, and received, permission for his unit to jump armies. He would drive in with the French, not the Americans, and film liberation day as it happened.

On the road into the city, Stevens, as always, kept his cameras poised for the poignant, idiosyncratic, or surprising detail—a wide field covered in wooden posts that had been stuck into the earth to prevent enemy gliders from landing, a young GI giving an older soldier a quick haircut on the shoulder of the road, a dwarf in a jester's cap walking casually away from a jeep full of amused GIs. Alone among his colleagues, he also took a few moments to document the behind-the-scenes work of the Signal Corps crews themselves; he filmed his men loading, cleaning, and preparing their cameras, and they in turn filmed him giving them instructions, chatting with soldiers, and reading to and ruffling the hair of a little French boy not much younger than George Jr.

On the night of August 24, Stevens and the 2nd Armored were camped a few miles outside of Paris. They had halted their advance at about 2 a.m. and planned to take the city at dawn in order to avoid nighttime snipers. Once the army arrived at the edge of the city the next morning, Stevens and his men no longer had to look for surprising moments; they just filmed the history unfolding in front of their eyes, in what became some of the most well-remembered images captured by American filmmakers during the war. When footage of the citizens of Paris pouring out of their homes and shops, filling the streets and weeping and shouting for joy, reached American movie screens, the shots served as a symbolic bookend to images of the broken and sobbing populace that Americans had seen when the city fell to Hitler in 1940. This time, the men and women threw bouquets of wildflowers and cheered; they held their babies up to be kissed and waved flags from their windows. They pulled shy, grinning soldiers off their cars and tanks to hug them, and some of the bolder GIs reciprocated by pulling the girls up onto the jeeps for a short ride alongside them. It was, Stevens told his son, the greatest day of his life.

"One knew at the time it was going to be the most exhilarating day," said Ivan Moffat. "I mean, it couldn't help but be, particularly as we thought that the war was pretty much over and that the Germans were in headlong retreat. . . . The atmosphere was . . . intoxicating, exhilarating, with these thousands and thousands of people embracing us, embracing each other under an absolutely brilliant sky, Paris looking absolutely marvelous, not at all shabby . . . an atmosphere almost like a bullfight."

Stevens's instincts as a director took over immediately. In Hollywood, his style had been internal and deliberative; here, it was intuitive, swiftly decisive, and all-encompassing. Every scene of military might and ceremony made it into the film he sent home—the tanks and trucks, along with an endless procession of soldiers on foot, coming down the Champs-Elysées past the Arc de Triomphe; de Gaulle, Bradley, and Montgomery standing on a small portable bridge that had been turned into a makeshift reviewing stand; flowers being placed at the memorial for the Unknown French Soldier of the First World War. But for posterity, he made sure that his men documented scenes of anger and retribution as well, even knowing that they would probably be too raw for use in newsreels. In one sequence, French civilians angrily shove and pull at German officers and Vichy officials as they're marched out of a truck. In another, a woman, her hair crudely chopped off and her face covered with dirt, is pushed around and taunted by a seething crowd; someone has drawn swastikas on her cheeks and forehead. Stevens's men were even able to shoot some unexpected action: A handful of Germans who refused to surrender were still firing from some rooftops, and their cameras caught it. "He didn't have to do it," Moffat recalled. "The whole situation was exposed to danger . . . and he wasn't frightened. . . . When there was sniper fire and so forth breaking out and one of the drivers tumbled out of the Jeep and went and hid behind a tree . . . George came out from under cover and drove the Jeep off the road himself."

Stevens left no doubt who was in charge, capping the day with an extraordinary act of brio. He had set up his equipment inside the Montparnasse railway station to photograph the official German surrender, in which General Dietrich von Choltitz, who had been the military governor of Paris for just two weeks, would turn over his power to General Leclerc and be taken into custody. Stevens wanted to be certain that the exact moment at which Paris became a free city again was recorded, and when the surrender was completed, he worried that the low indoor light in which it had taken place would render the film unusable. He told Choltitz, Leclerc, and de Gaulle that he needed them to do it again, this time in the bright daylight of the street just outside the station. Fortified by a few drinks, Stevens barked at Choltitz, "*C'est la guerre, General, c'est la guerre!*" All three men agreed to his request, and Stevens's "second take" of the handover was the one shown around the world.

After so many nights spent in tents, camps, and foxholes since June, Stevens was tired, but in Paris his spirits soared. For the first time in weeks, he could wash his clothes and sleep in a bed. Irwin Shaw bet him that the war would be over in two months; Ernest Hemingway poured champagne and announced that he had just "liberated" the bar of the Ritz hotel, which only weeks earlier had been Luftwaffe headquarters. On September 1, Stevens wrote to Yvonne for the first time in two weeks. "The days and nights all ran over themselves and became pretty much one thing: The struggle to get to Paris . . . with the responsibility of getting in first thing and photographing the activity," he explained. "That we did, but the doing and the two weeks before were the most exciting, the most unbelievable time of my life. Including some of the great moments with you my little angel. . . . The morning that we came into Paris was the wildest thing that I have ever seen. The civilians

lined the streets and went mad as the tanks and armored cars came in. They
stood in the streets and cheered as the shooting went on all around them.
Our jeeps brought in the first cameras and I believe the first American flag,
which we got from a Frenchman just outside the city. Then at the break of day
we were off and three hours later after a ride that [western movie stuntman]
Yakima Canutt would have wanted $500 to do, we stood under the Eiffel
Tower, but not for long. . . . More of a ride through town then we holed up in
a railroad station, stood off the last attack that Natzies [*sic*] made before they
surrendered. . . . There is much I could tell you and will in further letters but
I do hope you and Georgie have seen the newsreels that carried our film. We
have heard that the films of the liberation of Paris were the best ever taken
of anything like that. We are completely exhausted at the moment and hoping
to get a chance for a few days rest but time and us marches on."

Within a week the Allies were on the move again, and Stevens and his
team rejoined the American forces and traveled with them as they went east;
the plan was to cross over into Luxembourg, then Belgium, and then northern Germany. As the army rolled across liberated France, Stevens felt
inspired by every new destination. Arriving in Reims, he visited a champagne factory and started to think, for the first time since he had entered the
war, about returning to Hollywood filmmaking—perhaps even to romantic
comedy, something about the bottles of bubbly he saw that day. "For whom
was [each bottle] destined?" he wrote in his journal. "For a wedding? For a
romance? Would it excite some poor mortal into an act that would change the
whole course of his life? . . . When and where would they be opened in 1947
[or] perhaps 1967? What a story if one could just sit in that dark cave and
foresee. A delightful movie could be made . . . so provocative to the imagination. . . . Enough speculation for one day. We drove on in the evening. It was
very cold and we put on our Army greatcoats and stopped beside the road to
Verdun and had cheese from a K-ration and cut a loaf of 'du pain.' "

Stevens kept his cameras at the ready at all times. As they approached
the border and the weather got worse, beginning what was to be the coldest
European autumn and winter in twenty years, he grew somber. He filmed
fields of white crosses and, here and there, Stars of David, row upon row of
open graves that had been dug for Allied soldiers and civilians who had been

killed in airstrikes. He also photographed the returning refugees he saw, sometimes alone, sometimes in twos and threes, trudging along the road toward the soldiers, bundled in the few clothes they owned, carrying whatever they could hold in a suitcase as they walked back into France. His unit had acquired a dog that followed them from town to town, capering for the cameras and begging for scraps of rations. His health began to suffer again; sleeping outdoors after long and arduous days was taking its toll. He was smoking constantly, and as the air got colder his asthma worsened. In just a few months, he aged visibly.

In early October, the Allies crossed into Luxembourg, where Stevens filmed a group of Axis collaborators in the country's main prison. "It is a wet day," he wrote in his journal, "and a good one for the photography of such a cheap yarn. When they march these prisoners through the streets, a little boy about ten marches bravely in the front rank. Probably his father is the prisoner marching by his side."

What remained of the SPECOU team was exhausted. Shaw's bet was now a distant memory, a childishly exuberant prediction made in the elated aftermath of a single victory. The war was nowhere near over, and with every day that the troops dragged themselves through another few miles of ice and mud, the end seemed farther away, not closer. Supplies were scarce, but alcohol was plentiful, and there was always more to be had in the next village. The men in Stevens's unit drank constantly and often excessively. "My new Jeep driver . . . came in drunk at 2 o'clock," he wrote. "He wanted to talk to the Colonel. Tell me what he liked and what he did not like about the outfit. He is the third one of these old Army boys who has done the same thing. I generally try to have an enlisted man deal with a drunk enlisted man, because a drunk does not know how to take an order to do what he should do for his own good, and such an incident provokes serious countermeasures."

As the army moved into Belgium, Stevens had a strange and unexpected encounter with his former life. "I came upon a theater in this little town the Germans had just left," he said, "and they were showing *Gunga Din*! The kids were more interested in the film than they were in the Sherman tanks going through the damned town!" Hollywood beckoned, but distantly and faintly. Letters from colleagues in the industry would reach him weeks after they were written, and the news they shared felt remote. "Though you have been out of circulation," his agent Charles Feldman told him, "not a week goes by but that some producer calls me in, attempting to discuss with me a possible deal for you upon your being released from the service." Stevens wasn't interested; like Capra, he did not at that moment envision following years in the army and an eventual victory over Hitler with a return to the oppression of a studio contract. Feldman put out some feelers nonetheless. "Jack Warner says he will make you a most attractive proposition," he wrote. "Darryl feels you belong at his studio. . . . Naturally . . . I tell them that I feel quite sure that George Stevens Productions will have to be set up in a most independent manner and under the best possible percentage terms and guarantees ever dished out."

It was almost November when Stevens set foot on German soil for the first time, when the Allies crossed from Belgium into Aachen, the westernmost city in Germany. Eisenhower had thought it would be the site of an easy victory, but resistance was fierce and there were thousands of casualties on both sides in a three-week battle that virtually destroyed the all but evacuated town. The victory had been won by the time Stevens crossed the border, and he mailed home souvenirs—a piece of a silk parachute that had been used in the initial invasion, a German soldier's belt, and anything else he could grab that he thought might interest his son. "The big Nazi flag is of value since it was taken by us at the surrender of . . . the first big German city to fall," he wrote to George Jr. "The two flashlights are very good. . . . They belonged to German soldiers. Take your pick. . . . The three Hitler stamps were laying along side of the body of a dead German officer, who was killed fighting in the cemetery at Aachen."

Stevens's approach to his duties rankled some who served with him. The battle for Aachen had been a significant one—the first moment that the Allies were fighting the Nazis on their home turf—but his unit had not sent home any combat footage for the newsreels; Stevens, who was sometimes thought even by the soldiers who served under him to be overprotective of his men, had grown more worried about their safety since Paris. He had kept them in the rear, well away from the fighting lines. The extensive work he had done filming the drive forward through France into Europe did not impress some in the army who felt his only job was to photograph victories that could be spliced together into newsreel-ready packages. Stevens received little guidance from Washington until November, when a letter from Capra that was both self-flattering and undermining arrived. "I've been hoping against hope to get a letter from you," he wrote to Stevens, "but you seem to be as allergic to writing as I am. George, I want you to know that as always, I personally have the greatest confidence in, and admiration for your ability and devotion to your job. . . . There has been much criticism of your outfit by returning 'heroes.' I never believed a goddam word of it and said so plenty. But some of it stuck, particularly when I was away. . . . Unfortunately, I've been so swamped with top priority work that I haven't been able to pay much attention to what is going on in the [war] theatres. Stick to it George, and please know that you have guys here that are pulling and pitching for you, even though it must seem to you that at times you and your gang are forgotten men."

Capra had a personal reason for getting in touch with Stevens; he wanted him as an equity partner in his new company Liberty Films after the war ended. Capra was the wealthiest director in Hollywood, but his plans for Liberty were on such a large scale that he knew he would need another couple of directors to cofinance the venture, and he assumed that Stevens— who for years had worked in the same kind of restrictive atmosphere at RKO as Capra had at Columbia—would probably be just as eager to go independent as he was. Stevens wrote him back expressing "great joy in mudville" at his letter, telling him he was completely unconcerned about being the object of backbiting in Washington, and thanked him for "the kind and stimulating things you directed to me personally. . . . I at no time had any doubt that you felt I was carrying on here as expertly as it was possible to do." But he told Capra he wasn't ready to make a decision about his postwar future yet, and asked if they could talk more about Liberty when he got back to the United States.

"Whew! Christmas is approaching fast," Stevens wrote in his journal on December 5. He and his team were just inside Germany awaiting orders to advance further, and there was little to do but kill time. "Wrote 8 letters today, 3 to Yonnie, 2 to George . . . took me all day," he noted. "As I was writing to Mom tonight, many airplanes were overhead. For a while I thought it was the Luftwaffe but as they kept right on flying by I became aware that it was the RAF."

The limbo in which he found himself ended abruptly ten days later, when the German army launched a major counteroffensive that caught the Allies off guard. Stevens was writing a letter to his wife when the ground outside quaked; they were being shelled, and German paratroopers were landing all around them. The enemy was, he wrote, "raising hell all over the place" in a sector near the Germany-Belgium-Luxembourg border that had been securely in Allied hands for two months. The Americans began a hasty and chaotic retreat. "IMPOSSIBLE," Stevens wrote in his journal on December 18, the day he turned forty. "The stunned look on the faces and this remark was all one could hear from the civilians as the news started to get around that the Americans were going—'liberation in reverse.' That phrase kept running through my mind. The situation has been quite confused today." The Battle of the Bulge—the last major show of German strength during the war—had begun. Over the next six weeks, before the Allies crushed the Wehrmacht, nineteen thousand American soldiers would lose their lives and forty-seven thousand more would be wounded in the single deadliest engagement of U.S. forces in the war.

Stevens, suddenly in the thick of combat, filmed scenes of devastation that shook him badly—people running for shelter to escape German fire and barely able to find an intact roof to hide under or a doorway that bombs had not already blown apart. "He had never understood or been faced with the proportions of horror and cruelty he was suddenly witness to," said Moffat, "and he took it very, very hard. There was a great deal of homesickness—the feeling that this might drift on for months and months and months." On the front of his jeep, he painted the word TOLUCA—a reference to Toluca Lake, the San Fernando Valley neighborhood in Los Angeles where he and his family lived—and when he couldn't summon the energy to write letters, he sent movie footage home as a present instead. Just before the Germans had begun attacking, he received a package from Yvonne and George Jr. full of Christmas and birthday gifts. Ten days later, he finally had a chance to open them, and he had one of his men turn the moment into a small movie for his family. The filmed message he sent them starts with a close-up of a stack of crated howitzer shells—no doubt a shot that was designed to excite George Jr.—then the camera tilts up to take in Stevens, who is smoking a pipe and jauntily leaning against his snow-covered jeep. Someone tries to write MERRY CHRISTMAS in the snow on the hood just before the reel of film runs out. When the next one begins, Stevens and his men are standing by their vehicle in an abandoned, largely demolished square in the German coal-mining town of Eschweiler, about thirty miles west of Cologne. He opens a cardboard box and removes a wrapped gift inscribed "To Dad from Mama and George," bringing it close to the camera so that the inscription, which is written on a five-pointed star held by a cutout greeting-card angel, is visible. He opens it and holds the contents, a shaving kit filled with candy, up to the lens. He looks at the camera and beams. There's a card in an envelope labeled "To Dad," and he starts reading his son's letter. As he opens another present, the men look up to see a plane roaring overhead, and they pack up the boxes and quickly drive away.

In January 1945, Capra pulled Stevens out of the action temporarily. He needed the director to go to London and supervise the planning for a documentary about the Allies in Europe called *The True Glory,* which was to be the first joint British-American film venture since *Tunisian Victory.* Once he got to England, Stevens discovered there wasn't much for him to do; the movie's codirectors, Garson Kanin for America and Carol Reed for Britain, had it well in hand, and Paddy Chayefsky, a young GI who had been wounded at Aachen, was already drafting a screenplay. The reassignment seems to have been made in order to give Stevens, who had been traveling with Allied troops for seven months without a break, a chance to get some rest and regain his strength. In short order, he left London for Paris, where he and his unit received a commendation from Eisenhower for their work.

William Wyler arrived in Paris at about the same time. When the Allies landed at Normandy, he had been in Italy for the liberation of Rome; he had shot footage of Nazi insignias and posters of Mussolini being torn from the walls and thrown into the street. One day in Los Angeles, Talli Wyler picked

up a copy of the *New York Times* and saw her husband's face in a crowd shot
at the Vatican, where Pope Pius XII had granted public audiences to Allied
officers after their victory and invited the press to photograph them. "You
have a most holy and uplifted expression," she joked to him in a letter. "Positively saintly."

Wyler had not anticipated being in the middle of such momentous events
when he was sent to Italy; he had gone there to begin preparation for *Thunderbolt*, the documentary about P-47 fighter planes that he intended as his
followup to *The Memphis Belle*, and after the liberation, he had stayed on in
Caserta to start working on a screenplay treatment for it. Through the summer, he had struggled with the project; unlike the *Belle*, which was a B-17,
Thunderbolts could not accommodate cameramen while in the air, so he
would have to figure out a way to install cameras in fixed positions alongside
the machine guns, and also find a narrative for his film that didn't simply
repeat what he had done in his earlier documentary.

Within the space of just a few months, the army's priorities had changed
so rapidly that the assignment Wyler had been given already seemed irrelevant. An explanatory short like *Thunderbolt* now lacked urgency, and in
Italy, Wyler was treated less as an active-duty filmmaker than as a curiosity,
a celebrity whose company was sought by the top brass; at one point he
was summoned to Capri for a "high-level mission" that turned out to be a
weekend-long poker game with General Eaker of the air force and Bill Donovan. Wyler himself found it difficult to give *Thunderbolt* his full attention,
and spent much of the summer traveling around Italy, documenting the
devastation wrought by bombs from both sides in towns and cities north of
Rome. Later in the summer, he was reassigned to Saint-Tropez to film the
Allied landing there, a decision he later called "a joke," since "the Free
French [Army] and the Resistance [already] had everything under control."

In France, Wyler had become obsessed with trying to get to Mulhouse,
the Alsatian town in which he had spent most of his childhood. He stayed
with the Allies as they moved north through eastern France, through Lyons
to Besançon. He was just eighty-five miles short of his destination when he
was ordered back to Paris to finish his movie. He had been working on *Thunderbolt* with John Sturges, an aspiring director who would go on to a long

career in Hollywood,* but both men were unhappy with the quality of the footage they had. By late November, the veteran director William Keighley, who was now overseeing the Signal Corps' motion picture unit, had become impatient; Wyler had been tasked with making the movie more than six months earlier, and it was still nowhere near finished.

Wyler stalled, pleading for more time. "First, the subject matter is very difficult," he said. "It's not a simple story of one mission, from start to finish, like *The Memphis Belle*. . . . Second, I didn't have a crew of my own." He told Keighley how hard it had been to get effective high-altitude images on color film, and added that "the weather has been so bad we haven't shot a foot of film in almost two months."

Wyler signed off by saying, "Here's hoping we can both sit in a director's chair again soon," but Hollywood was far from his thoughts. He was still determined to get to Mulhouse, and he decided to enlist Stevens's help. The two men had not seen each other since they briefly crossed paths in Washington years earlier when Frank Capra was setting up his film unit. In Paris, they met for a meal, and Wyler, who was aware that Stevens had passed through Belgium and knew his way around the region, told him that he wanted to get to the Belgian city of Bastogne—which was near the French border and about half a day's drive from Mulhouse—and asked for the name of a driver who could get him there.

Stevens told Wyler he had just the man, Ernest Hemingway's twenty-nine-year-old brother, Leicester, a driver for the army and a daredevil who would not flinch at the idea of motoring into dangerous territory. Wyler started making plans to leave Paris right away. The next day, he and Hemingway were in a jeep filled with magazines of film and enough supplies to get them across the border to Bastogne two hundred miles away. From Bastogne, they drove to Luxembourg, where a general tried to persuade Wyler to make a *Memphis Belle*–style documentary about the men of the Ninth Air Force, whom he said had driven the Germans from Bastogne with a single day of bombardment. Mostly as a courtesy, Wyler shot some footage of the flyers

---

* Sturges directed almost fifty movies after the war, including *Bad Day at Black Rock*, *The Magnificent Seven*, and *The Great Escape*.

and their planes, but he didn't linger. Soon he and Hemingway moved on to Strasbourg, where the writer André Malraux was leading a ragtag platoon of local armed resistance fighters. "He ran his own war," Wyler recalled. "He took me to several of his posts. . . . There was a fierce loyalty to him wherever we went—all these fellows with old-fashioned rifles and . . . one tank. . . . Anyway, we talked about movies and he was very interested in making a documentary. . . . He said we must meet again after the war."

Wyler and Hemingway continued on. His quest to reach his boyhood home was all he could think about, even though he had no idea what, or who, he would find there. His parents had left the town almost twenty years earlier for California, where they had lived near him and his brother Robert; their father, Leopold, had died of a stroke just before the war began. Wyler didn't know if the relatives or friends he had tried to help emigrate years earlier had ever made it out of France, or whether the shops and homes so familiar from his youth would still be standing; Mulhouse had been a major staging center for German troops in the region, and thus an Allied target.

When they reached the town, Wyler had Hemingway drive him down the Rue du Sauvage. His father's haberdashery, the Magasin L. Wyler, was still there, unchanged, and Henriette Helm, the woman to whom the Wylers had turned over their business when they left for America, was standing in the doorway. She greeted Wyler effusively and handed him a set of folded bills—the money she had set aside representing his family's share of the store's profits for the last four years, about $4,000 in all. The store, she explained, had survived only because Wyler's father had been Swiss, not French, and because she followed the rules of occupation to the letter, including displaying a picture of Hitler in the shop window every year on his birthday. Collaboration had become a fact of daily life for almost every resident who was still there. But when Wyler, speaking Alsatian for the first time in years, told her that he was in the American air force, her face fell and she gestured sadly at the ruined buildings in the town's center. When the people of Mulhouse had heard that American planes were coming to free them, she told Wyler, they had run into the street waving white bedsheets to signal that they were friendly. The planes bombed them anyway. Children were killed.

"You know you've got big factories here working for the Germans, that this is a big railway depot," Wyler replied. "We're fighting a war, Madame Henriette." Wyler explained that the Allies had dropped leaflets warning residents to evacuate; she was not mollified.

Wyler's tour through Mulhouse was brief and heartbreaking. The local synagogue still stood, but the Jews were gone, and nobody could say where they were now. He could not find a single member of his mother's family or any of his childhood friends. He went to the town hall seeking help. The mayor of Mulhouse told him, "Take my advice, don't look for anybody. If you see people you know, be glad they're alive. But don't look for them. You won't find them."

Wyler returned to Paris, and walked into air force headquarters to find the office in an uproar. He had neglected to tell anyone he was leaving. The air force had reported him as missing in action, and the *Hollywood Reporter* had picked up the story. Wyler told HQ that he had been shooting additional footage for *Thunderbolt,* dashed off a letter to Talli reassuring her that he was fine, and got out of France as quickly as possible, returning to Italy, where he now knew he had to finish his movie.

TWENTY-FOUR

"Who You Working For—Yourself?"

HOLLYWOOD, FLORIDA, ITALY, AND NEW YORK, FEBRUARY–MAY 1945

O n February 21, 1945, after three weeks of fighting, American and Filipino forces retook Bataan. The victory, at the site of one of the most devastating losses for the Allies three years earlier, came just two days before John Ford started shooting *They Were Expendable,* a movie he said was intended to honor a group of American soldiers in the Philippines who had, in those first months after Pearl Harbor, been "glorious in defeat."

"I *like* that," he explained. "I despise these happy endings, with a kiss at the finish. I've never done that." Despite the recent good news for the Allies, Ford had no intention of appending a rah-rah epilogue to the script, or of rewriting the history of America's setbacks in the early days of the war in the Pacific. "What was in my mind was doing it exactly as it had happened," he said. "We are sticking to facts. Lieutenant Bulkeley did not go back to the Philippines." If that threatened to strike a discordant note at a moment when American moviegoers were celebrating a hard-won turnaround in the war against Japan, Ford, as he headed to Key Biscayne, Florida, for the start of location shooting right after the birth of his second grandson, betrayed no concern about being out of step with the times. He wanted to fulfill Secretary

Forrestal's wish that the film "would be helpful to the Navy"—which was the only reason the OSS had agreed to release Ford from his duties and let him make it—but not if it meant making an inaccurate film. *They Were Expendable* was to serve not only as a tribute to the valor of the men of the U.S. Navy, but as a memorial to those who were killed in action; Ford hoped his movie might, in General MacArthur's words, "speak for the thousands of silent lips, forever stilled among the jungles and in the deep waters of the Pacific which marked the way" for what he called the "great victory" that had just taken place.

There were some areas in which Ford's fidelity to the truth was less strict. When they had been together in a PT boat after D-Day, Bulkeley had said with embarrassment that he thought William White's book-length portrait of him, on which the movie was to be based, was wildly exaggerated. In 1942, Bulkeley had won the Medal of Honor for his "dynamic forcefulness and daring in offensive action against the Japanese . . . with a complete disregard for his own personal safety" in the fight to hold the Philippines, but he told Ford he didn't think he deserved the honor. "The whole thing happened at a time when the country was looking for heroes," he said. "Frankly, I've already had too much publicity." Ford wouldn't hear it; to him, Bulkeley was a hero—"the most decorated man of the war," he would frequently (and incorrectly) claim, "and a wonderful person." The navy had a regulation against active-duty officers being identified by name in motion pictures, so in Frank Wead's screenplay, Bulkeley was changed to "Brickley." The minor alteration was, in a way, the first permission Ford gave himself to take possession of the story told in *They Were Expendable* and to begin to turn it into the kind of war narrative he wanted to create.

Working closely with Wead, he developed a script about two men, Brickley and Rusty Ryan, a fictionalized version of his right-hand man,* each of whom represented a side of Ford's own personality. Ryan is a hothead, a good sailor hungry to command his own fleet of PT boats; he operates by his own rules and resents the know-nothings who outrank him. "From here on in," he

---

* Ryan's real-life counterpart was a sailor named Bob Kelly, who ended up disliking the way he was portrayed so much that he sued for defamation; he was awarded $3,000.

says at the beginning of the movie, "I'm a one-man band." Brickley is the levelheaded adult who understands the importance of discipline and structure and respects the chain of command; paradoxically, he achieves personal glory by insisting that personal glory doesn't matter. ("What are you aiming at, building a reputation or playing for the team?" he asks Ryan.) "Listen, son," Wead and Ford had him tell the younger man in what would become the movie's most famous line. "You and I are professionals. If the manager says sacrifice, we lay down a bunt, and let somebody else hit the home runs. . . . That's what we were trained for, and that's what we'll do."

Ford wanted *They Were Expendable* to offer a lesson about forgoing maverick impulses or dreams of heroism in favor of the greater good, and he also wanted it to serve as a tribute to underdogs—not just his two protagonists, but the PT boats themselves, which are dismissed by a senior navy officer in the opening scene as not "substantial" enough to do any good in the war and over the next two hours prove that verdict wrong. The story told by Ford and Wead—who shared a title card as director and screenwriter— isn't only Brickley's and Ryan's. It goes much further than the book—and much further than many in the navy, including Bulkeley, thought the facts merited—in making the case that small vessels were able to do the dirty work of the navy, darting in and out of tough spots while under fire in order to level torpedoes at Japanese ships, even though skeptics belittled the wood-hulled PTs in favor of destroyers, battleships, cruisers, and aircraft carriers and claimed that their only real value was as couriers and messenger boats. The "they" in the title refers to the navy's attitude toward both the PTs and the sailors who manned them, and the story, which covers the four months after Pearl Harbor, becomes an articulation of one of Ford's favorite themes— that the marginalized can prove indispensable.

The rhythm of *They Were Expendable,* in which brief and intense battle sequences alternate with long stretches of indolence or quietly tense anticipation, mirrored Ford's own experience of the war, as did the many scenes of all-male comradeship, the gentle maritime comedy that he asked James Mc-Guinness to thread through the screenplay in a rewrite, the testy rivalries navy men felt with other branches of the service (by the time his ships see action, Ryan complains that "the air force will have won the war"), and the

strong notes of elegy and sentiment throughout. Ford had his heroes learn of
the attack on Pearl Harbor while they sat down to a meal with their commander, just as he had; he even inserted a small implicit tribute to two Field
Photo men who had been killed while Wead was working on the script; they
are represented in the movie by a pair of modest crosses in a jungle graveyard. Ford's memories of Midway—particularly of the young men who were
there one day and gone the next—informed his approach to a movie that has
more moments of gloomy, uncertain parting than any other war picture of the
time. Wead wrote one scene after another in which men are seen saying
goodbye to each other. ("Like many fine artists," Ford's frequent screenwriter
Dudley Nichols said later, "his true feeling was for the man-man or man-men
relationship. I cannot recall one of his films in which the man-woman relationship came off with any feeling or profundity.") The idea of a combat unit
as a surrogate family in which every leave-taking could be final was underscored by Ford's casting of extremely young-looking men as navy enlistees,
and reaches its climax in a scene in which Brickley departs from his young
squadron and says, "You older men, with longer service records . . . take care
of the kids." The paternalism of the moment echoes the way Ford had long
seen himself as the caretaker of the men his son's age who filled the ranks of
Field Photo.

The screenplay for *They Were Expendable* had little time to spare for
patriotic speeches, calls for support from the home front, or exemplifications
of squad unity, nor did it have anything to say about the reasons the war was
being fought, all of which, by 1945, had become such overused staples of war
movies that even the Office of War Information was no longer pushing for
their inclusion in Hollywood pictures. Wead and Ford even revisited some
controversial terrain when they inserted into the script some of the questions
about the navy's preparedness before Pearl Harbor that Gregg Toland had
brought up in his first cut of *December 7th;* they included a chorus of voices
in a crowd asking, "How did [Japanese flyers] get in undetected? Where were
our search planes? What about our carriers? They're set to invade the West
Coast now! And they got away scot-free." Perhaps sensing that he had hurt
Toland's feelings by recutting his documentary two years earlier, Ford, at
one point, asked him to codirect *They Were Expendable,* telling him that

"it would be a great experience for you"; Toland was still out of the country on active duty, and was not available. When the OWI saw the script, it raised no initial objections; the office felt that *They Were Expendable* would serve as "an outstanding contribution to the government's War Information program," and requested the deletion of only one line, in which a black enlistee said that the loss of the Philippines would "be bad back there in the South— no hemp—what'll dey do for lynchin's?"

Ford cast a uniquely qualified actor to play Brickley. Robert Montgomery was a former president of the Screen Actors Guild and two-time Best Actor nominee who had left Hollywood three years earlier, at thirty-eight, to join the navy as an officer. In the summer of 1944, he was aboard USS *Barton,* one of the destroyers at Normandy. After the invasion, Montgomery was briefly reassigned to Bulkeley's PT fleet, possibly at the behest of Ford; he wanted to come up with an alternative to Spencer Tracy, MGM's choice for the role, and thought Montgomery could use the opportunity to study Bulkeley, who later remembered the actor "watching me carefully" as soon as he came aboard his boat. Montgomery bore a passing resemblance to Bulkeley, and Ford, who knew he would have no problem coming off as a believable navy man on screen, pulled strings to arrange for his transfer to inactive duty so he could take the part.

When Montgomery's casting was announced in November 1944, MGM told the press that the ensemble would "be comprised almost wholly of actors who have been in the military or naval service." Ford had originally hoped to stock much of the crew with Field Photo veterans; that proved impractical, but the movie's close ties to the navy were so important a part of the surrounding publicity that in the opening credits, Ford, Wead, cinematographer Joseph August, and second unit director James Havens were each listed with their military rank and branch of service. To play Rusty Ryan, the studio first wanted another member of the armed forces, Robert Taylor, a popular contract star whose stock had risen during the war. But Taylor was unavailable—he had joined the air force in 1943 as a flying instructor—and so in January, just a few weeks before production was scheduled to begin, MGM turned to its second choice, John Wayne.

Wayne had not worked with Ford since *The Long Voyage Home* five years earlier. Since then, he had become a major star, appearing in almost twenty movies and always managing to maintain the public fiction that he was just a couple of professional commitments away from joining the army. He and Ford, and their families, had remained friendly—Pat Ford had even thought of asking Wayne to be godfather to Ford's grandson—but Ford had long made clear to his wife that he found Wayne's behavior cowardly and dishonest. To compound what Ford felt was an insult, Wayne turned out to be especially popular whenever he played a war hero: He had starred as a pilot in *Flying Tigers* and again in *Reunion in France,* and as a lieutenant commander in the navy—Robert Montgomery's actual rank—in *The Fighting Seabees.* Just before signing for *They Were Expendable,* Wayne had completed *Back to Bataan,* another movie about the fight for the Philippines, but one which, unlike the one Ford was about to make, had no compunction about setting up a hasty reshoot with a new last scene that depicted the recent Allied victory.

When Wayne arrived to begin work, Ford was in a punitive mood. The director's prewar habit of picking a victim on each new production—someone to bully or humiliate—had not left him, and although Ford's movie *Stagecoach* had marked the beginning of Wayne's ascendancy, he had always been hard on the actor, berating him as lazy and slow. Now, however, there was real animus behind the jabs: He saw Wayne as an imposter, someone who had lined his pockets pretending to be a war hero while others did the real work and put themselves on the line. ("Well, Jesus, I [was] 40 years old and of fair standing and I didn't feel I could go in as a private," Wayne said. "I felt I could do more good going around on tours and things. Most of the ones who were doing the fighting were 18-year-old kids and I was America to them. They had taken their sweethearts to that Saturday matinee and held hands over a Wayne western. So I wore a big hat and I thought it was better.")

Ford was unconvinced by the argument. Working with dozens of men in uniform (even if the uniforms were costumes) and commanding the fleet of six PT boats that the navy had loaned MGM for the movie, he managed to convince himself that he was in the middle of a quasi-military operation. The film was being made with the cooperation of the navy and the Coast Guard, which provided both materiel and extras. He had little patience for someone he saw as a pampered movie star.

But before he could turn his attention to Wayne, Ford had to deal with an unexpected crisis caused by his costar. Montgomery had "said yes without reflection" when Ford had asked him to play Brickley, as he thought the role "seemed an ideal way to get back to acting. But when we were down in Miami to shoot the first scenes . . . we started out with the boats going through their maneuvers, out in Manila Bay, that's when it really hit me," he said. "I was seized with panic." He had not been in front of a camera for four years, and the jolt of going so suddenly from being a naval officer to playing one, from combat in the English Channel to tooling around in speedboats off a Florida beach, was too much for him.

"I'd forgotten everything," he recalled. "Forgotten acting, forgotten what the whole thing was about. I felt I couldn't do it anymore." At four o'clock in the morning, wild with anxiety, he called Ford to his hotel room.

"You in any trouble?" the director said calmly. Montgomery told him he was quitting, that he never should have agreed to make the film, and that Ford would have to find another actor.

Ford listened to him, then asked him how he would feel about just taking a PT out in the water by himself—no cameras, no film crew. Montgomery said he thought he could do it.

Good, said Ford. "Take the boats. Play with them. When you're ready to start, we'll start. It may be three days, it may be three weeks, or three months. We'll wait till you're ready."

Ford was as good as his word. The next day, Montgomery took off for a ride; the day after, he did the same thing, "and got used to command again" while Ford and his crew waited. "At lunchtime on the third day," he said, "I suddenly felt it. I walked over to Ford and I said 'Shoot!' And we started."

Ford had intense sympathy for Montgomery and his rough readjustment; as they began to work, he stripped down the actor's dialogue, often reducing long speeches to just a few lines and allowing Montgomery to draw on his military experience and shape a strong and convincing performance by playing Brickley as a terse, watchful, quiet commander. "Bob Montgomery was his pet on that picture," Wayne said. "He could do no wrong. I guess it was because he had been in the Navy. Jack picked on me all the way through it."

Wayne had virtually worshipped Ford, whom he called "Coach," since the director had first taken him under his wing a decade earlier. But the two men got off on the wrong foot almost immediately, when they were filming a shot in which an airplane strafes a PT boat being captained by Rusty Ryan. A prop man was throwing metal ball bearings meant to simulate bullets at the boat's windshield, but, Wayne recalled, he "had forgotten to replace the windshield with a non-breakable Plexiglas one." As the cameras rolled, "real glass went flying into my face. In a rage I grabbed a hammer and went after the guy. But Jack stepped in front of me and said, 'No you don't. They're my crew.'"

"Your crew?!" said Wayne. "Goddamnit, they're my eyes!"

Not long after that, Ford went too far. He was shooting one of the script's first scenes, in which an admiral disdainfully inspects the fleet of PT boats led by Brickley and Ryan and dismisses the idea that they could be of any use in the war, then walks off. The set was filled with dozens of extras playing navy men, but the shot didn't require much work from Wayne or Montgomery aside from their salutes to the actor playing the admiral. Ford filmed a first take, then, without any instruction to either of the two stars, asked for a second one. When he asked for a third, Wayne murmured to Montgomery, who was standing next to him, "What's wrong with it?"

"Duke!" Ford yelled to Wayne in front of the extras and crew. "Can't you manage a salute that at least *looks* like you've been in the service?"

That was it for Wayne. Without a word, he walked off the set and returned to his hotel room. Shooting was done for the day. Montgomery had already observed what he called a complicated "father and son" tension between his director and his costar, and now saw that it was out of control. After Wayne left, he walked over to Ford. "I put my hands on the arms of his chair and leaned over and said, 'Don't you ever speak like that to anyone again.'" Ford at first denied that he knew what Montgomery was talking about. "I know you're doing this for my benefit," said Montgomery quietly, "but it's not amusing and I don't like it." He told Ford he would have to apologize to Wayne.

Ford at first blustered, then said he never meant to hurt Wayne's feelings, and finally started to cry. He soon made up with Wayne, and, as a way of apologizing, even added a scene to the script that gave the actor one of his strongest moments in the movie, in which, after two of his men die, Rusty recites Robert Louis Stevenson's eight-line epitaph for himself, ending with "Home is the sailor, home from the sea / And the hunter home from the hill."

The rest of the filming of *They Were Expendable* proceeded smoothly; Ford and both of his stars had all now experienced low moments on the set, after which they were able to work together with a kind of sober focus that is evident onscreen. "Jack was awfully intense on that picture," said Wayne, "and working with more concentration than I had ever seen. I think he was really out to achieve something."

After several weeks of location shooting, Ford and his cast and crew returned to Los Angeles to finish *They Were Expendable* on the MGM lot. Shortly before production was scheduled to end, Montgomery and Wayne were on a soundstage to shoot close-ups that Ford intended to cut into battle sequences that he had already filmed. Ford was standing on a camera platform several feet above them adjusting the lighting when he stumbled backward, lost his footing, and fell into the darkness.

"Jesus Christ, you clumsy bastard!" Wayne yelled, not realizing how far he had fallen. When the two actors ran behind the platform to help him, Ford was lying on the ground. He had broken his right leg below the knee.

"He wouldn't let anyone else touch him," said Montgomery. "We lifted him onto a stretcher and took him to [the] hospital." As the two men rode up in the elevator with Ford, he locked eyes with a woman who wouldn't stop staring at him. Finally, he barked, "Alcoholic!" It is not clear whether he was referring to her or to himself.

Ford was told he would have to spend the next three weeks in traction. The next day, Wayne and Montgomery were visiting him when the telephone rang. It was MGM's general manager Eddie Mannix, wanting to know when Ford thought he'd be well enough to resume production.

"I'm not coming back," Ford told him. "I'm staying here and getting my leg right. Then I'm going back to the Navy. Montgomery'll finish the picture."

It was "the first I heard of it," Montgomery said, adding that "by that time I felt so in tune with the way Jack thought and felt that it didn't seem difficult. I just tried to imagine how he'd have done it." The actor spent the next two weeks shooting the close-ups and insert shots that had already been mapped out and scheduled, but Ford came back against his doctor's orders to film the movie's downbeat final scene himself.

The end of *They Were Expendable* sums up all of Ford's feelings about the conflict between a private code of ethics and a larger sense of responsibility. The scene portrays a hollow victory for Brickley and Ryan: Thanks to their heroism and the bravery of their men, many of whom have been killed, the brass now believes in the value of the PT boats. With the Philippines about to fall, the navy pulls the two men out of the Pacific and orders them to Washington to oversee the building of more PTs, putting them on the last plane out and forcing them to separate from their men, who look unlikely to get out unharmed. "That makes a fine pair of heels out of us," mutters Brickley. But when Ryan tries to bolt from the plane just before it takes off so he can stay with his men, Brickley sternly pulls him back. "Who you working for—*yourself*?" he snaps. "We're going home to do a job—and that job is to get ready to come back." The darker resonance of the scene is unmistakable: One of the costs of war is that both men—and the handful of other officers going home—will have to live with the nagging fear that they could have, or should have, done more. In the picture's last minutes, their commander tells Brickley and Ryan to bring a message to the War Department: "When you see the general, tell him the end here is near. If he should ask you what we want, tell him a navy task force, a tanker loaded with gasoline, and 100,000 men. Give me that and we can start taking the islands back." Brickley and Ryan salute him. This time, no additional takes were necessary. Ford took the film to the editing room. He had two months to complete it before he was due back in Washington.

Around the time that Ford started to shoot *They Were Expendable*, William Wyler returned to Italy to finish *Thunderbolt*. Before dropping the film and taking a long detour to Mulhouse, he had shot enough footage of P-47s so that John Sturges and writer Lester Koenig, who had been working with him on the movie, could pull together a preliminary narration script. But he couldn't shake the sense that he had failed to crack the material the way he had on *Memphis Belle*, and his suspicions were confirmed when he saw the draft Koenig and Sturges had roughed out.

When he started working on *Thunderbolt*, Wyler had been determined to avoid turning it into the start-to-finish story of a single bombing run. He hadn't wanted to repeat the idea he used in *Memphis Belle,* and he knew that since he wasn't up in the air in the P-47s himself, he wouldn't be able to create a story about the experience of flying a mission that was as personal and rich in detail as he had in the previous movie. But Koenig and Sturges had, he felt, gone too far in the other direction. "You minimize the mission," he complained to them in a long set of notes attached to their proposed draft. "A. You don't give it enough buildup. B. You don't give it enough in drama, i.e., you spread it. C. You follow it up with lots of unexciting anti-climax."

Wyler was now willing to forget his earlier reservations about reusing the structure of *Memphis Belle;* the army wanted the movie done quickly, and there was no time to find a fresh way to tell the story. "You've got to make the mission the Big Thing," he wrote. "This outline gives the impression that the Mission is merely one among many picayune little sorties. Pedestrian warfare. Maybe it is. But for the movie, it should be life-or-death crucial. For my money—give everything to the destruction of the enemy . . . and then finish quick."

Sturges, in response, told Wyler that what they really needed was the kind of aerial footage that they hadn't been able to obtain by screwing stationary unmanned cameras into position aboard the P-47s. They had placed Eyemos in cockpits, under wings, and in the tails of the Thunderbolts, and rigged them so that all it took to operate them were two buttons, one marked "Start" and one marked "Stop." But some of the men aboard the fighter-bombers didn't want to have to bother operating cameras while they were in the air, others thought their mere presence on a plane was bad luck, and others simply forgot to use them in the heat of the moment. Wyler and his team had compensated for the lack of good footage every way they knew how; they had even driven into the north of Italy, chasing the planes to the planned targets of their strikes so that they could get usable film of how effective the P-47s were from the ground, if not the air. But nothing they got was good enough to make the picture work.

When Wyler went back to Italy, Sturges asked him to try to get some aerial footage of the damage done by bombers to Rome and to Corsica, where the fleet of Thunderbolts in their movie was based. Although he couldn't do it from an actual Thunderbolt, he didn't need to, since this wasn't supposed to be the record of a particular bombing but just a chance to flesh out the movie with what Wyler called "atmosphere shots." The film could be shot by any cameraman who was willing to lie in the bottom—the "waist"—of a B-25, an American twin-engine bomber that was ideal for aerial photography, since it was low-flying and had plenty of openings through which to shoot with no obstruction.

On April 4, 1945, the afternoon of the first night of Passover, Wyler boarded a B-25 bound for Grosseto, the city about a hundred miles northwest of Rome where the Allied Italian headquarters were now located. The plan was to make several runs back and forth over Corsica and then along the bomb-scarred Italian coast in order to give him a chance to shoot all the film he needed, then to drop an army captain off in Rome, and then to land in Grosseto, where Wyler would get off. He decided not to risk the possibility that a cameraman would fail to get the images he wanted; at some point during the flight, he crawled into the belly of the plane himself with an Eyemo, lay down, and started to shoot. The roar of the engines and the high shriek of the wind in the open plane caused him to lose his hearing, but he wasn't worried; it wasn't the first time that had happened. He would do what he usually did—wait for his ears to open up when the plane descended.

Wyler didn't realize anything was wrong until, shortly before the sun went down, the B-25 landed at Grosseto. When he stepped out of the plane, his ears still hadn't popped, and he couldn't find his balance or walk a straight line. "I thought it was nothing," he said. "A lot of times, you step out of an airplane, and you can't hear for a while." He tried to smile when the airmen on the landing strip saw him and started imitating his drunken reel, but hours later, after he was indoors and far from the engine noise, his hearing had not returned.

A surgeon at Grosseto examined him. "This is serious," he said, and ordered that he be taken to a navy hospital as soon as possible. The next day, he was flown to Naples, where doctors examined him and wrote down their verdict so he could read it: His time in the army was over. And so was his time in the air; Wyler was told he could not risk another flight. Five days later, he was put aboard a ship bound from Naples to Boston. He was going home. And he was deaf.

On April 20, the telephone rang at the Wyler home in Los Angeles. When Talli picked it up, she heard her husband on the other end of the line, but if she had not known he was calling, she might not have recognized his voice. Wyler had cabled her that he was on his way home, but he hadn't told her the extent of the damage to his ears—something he didn't yet know himself. For more than a week, he had been on a ship, alone, waiting to see if he could discern any improvement. A few days into the crossing, a tiny bit of hearing had returned in his left ear, but by the time he disembarked in Boston, it was clear to him that he was not getting better, and he plunged into depression.

"Instead of a happy voice, I heard an absolutely dead voice, toneless, without emotions, totally depressed," Talli said. "I was stunned and shocked and couldn't imagine what had gone wrong. He sounded totally unlike himself, terribly disturbed. He talked as if his life was over, not only his career."

Wyler told his wife not to bother traveling east, and also said that he wasn't coming home yet. He hung up and took a train to New York, where he entered an air force hospital at Mitchell Field on Long Island. Doctors examined him and told him that he had irreparable nerve damage in his right ear. They suggested that he have his adenoids removed, but they were not encouraging about the likelihood that the operation would do much to improve his condition.

Wyler couldn't bear the idea of a visit from Talli or his young daughters, and the few old friends he allowed to come to Mitchell Field to see him found a shattered man. "I'd never seen anybody in such a real state of horror," said Lillian Hellman. "He was sure his career was over, he would never direct again." They were, said Wyler, the "worst weeks of my life."

When the army doctors told him that there was little more they could do for him and released him from the hospital, suggesting that he might do better to see specialists in Washington, D.C., or in California, Wyler tried to resume his life. He took a train to the capital, checked in with some old colleagues at the War Department, and looked into the progress of Koenig's new and improved draft of *Thunderbolt*. He still couldn't hear, but he had at least regained his balance. From the capital, he called Talli and told her he would be home soon; he was taking the train from Washington to Los Angeles.

Talli picked him up at Union Station. "He was terribly thin," she said. "He wasn't eating. His face was so drawn I almost didn't recognize him." Seeing her husband, she realized, for the first time, how serious his condition was. "You had to talk directly into his left ear," she told Wyler biographer Jan Herman. "And you had to speak with great clarity or he couldn't understand you. He felt very isolated."

Wyler was tormented by more than his physical problems. He was afraid that his loss of hearing "might affect the marriage," he later admitted. "I wasn't sure whether what worked before might work again." Increasingly desperate, he had Talli take him to a hearing rehabilitation center for returning veterans in Santa Barbara. Psychiatrists injected him with sodium pentothal to try to determine whether a mental block was responsible for his deafness. When Talli next saw him, he was pacing back and forth in a padded room, trying to shake off the drug's sedating effects. Psychiatrists told her that her husband's hearing was perfectly fine—that once the drug took hold, he could hear what was being said two rooms away. It was not until years later that she realized they had lied to her in order to give her some hope that in the future, his condition might reverse itself.

Wyler's years at war—what he later called "an escape into reality"—had come to an end he never could have anticipated: A release, this time final, from the medical care of the army, a disability check—"sixty dollars every month from Uncle Sam, tax free" for the rest of his life—and a future that seemed as uncertain personally as it did professionally. He still felt both a duty and a desire to finish *Thunderbolt*, although it was hard to imagine that the army would have any use for it. And he still owed Sam Goldwyn one more film on a contract that dated back to 1941. But how could he hope to make a movie when even background noise or music made it impossible for him to understand a sentence? That spring, as Wyler shuttled from one doctor to another, the war in Europe was ending. And nothing felt possible.

TWENTY-FIVE

"Where I Learned About Life"

GERMANY, MARCH–AUGUST 1945

G eorge Stevens was not supposed to be on his own, but with Wyler's injury and Ford's abrupt departure from active duty, he was by March 1945 the last major American filmmaker covering the war in Europe. There had been a time, months earlier, when Capra had reassured him that reinforcements were just around the corner, but now Stevens knew it wasn't true: The war filmmaking program was winding down, and he didn't expect any help or guidance from Washington. When he finally got his marching orders, they came from Eisenhower, and they were simple and direct: Stevens and his crew were to join sixteen thousand American and British paratroopers as they began a final push into Germany. The SPECOU team's job would be to document whatever they found there.

The mission was called Operation Varsity, a one-day, largely airborne initiative on March 24 that brought Stevens from Paris to the banks of the Rhine, where the Allies captured three bridges and secured several towns and villages on the western border of a now severely weakened Germany. Over the next three weeks, he and his unit stayed with the army as General Bradley's troops began their drive east toward Berlin.

Stevens did his first substantial filming inside Germany on April 11— the day before President Roosevelt's sudden death at Warm Springs—when

American forces took control of Nordhausen, a town in the center of the country that had been the site of a huge underground plant used to build V-2s, the long-range ballistic missiles that the Nazis had used against England. During the war, more than fifty thousand prisoners had been kept at Dora, a nearby concentration camp whose inmates were used as slave labor in the Nordhausen missile factory. A week earlier, the RAF had bombed the town, destroying most of it and killing thousands. When Stevens got there, one of the first people he saw was an emaciated man on a cot. The man turned his head, smiled at the arrival of his liberators, then rolled over quietly and died. It was the first time Stevens had seen a concentration camp prisoner.

Forty miles of tunnels had been dug into the side of a mountain at Nordhausen, and as Stevens began to film, he felt he was discovering, for the first time since he had entered the army, the dark heart of the war. It was almost impossible to shoot inside the murk of the winding factory passageways and dimly illuminated chambers, but he and Ivan Moffat wrote reports about what they saw, including a crematorium that had been used to incinerate those who had become too weak to work; it had been swept clean of ashes, and a pile of small human bones was mounded in a corner. As Stevens joined the army's inspection of the facility and the camp, he realized that he had come upon a scene of mass murder on a scale he had never imagined possible. "So completely without record of their past lives had these creatures been left," he wrote in the memo he sent back to Washington accompanying the Nordhausen footage, "that of two thousand odd men and women and children it was possible to identify but four men by name and nationality."

The War Department had long been aware of Nazi atrocities, but Stevens's account was among the first eyewitness reports to come from an American officer inside Germany. On April 15, he sent his superior officers a communiqué calling Nordhausen "as stark an example as could be found anywhere of the utter German indifference to human life reaching a very high peak of brutality side by side with a supreme example of technical perfection in the science of mass destruction." That day, the Allies liberated the camp at Bergen-Belsen, where they discovered fifty-three thousand famished, freezing prisoners living and dying in filth. Four days later, Capra received his first report from the army film unit at Belsen at the same time as Stevens's footage arrived in Washington. From that day forward, the primary mission of men in the Army Pictorial Service would change. They would no longer be combat photographers; they would be gatherers of evidence.

But before those orders came through, Stevens and his eighteen-man unit were sent from Nordhausen to Torgau, where, for the last time in the war, he was asked to serve as a chronicler of the ceremonial for newsreels. On April 25, the armies of the United States and the Soviet Union, which had fought throughout the war on separate fronts, finally came together at the Elbe. The joining of forces was more than just symbolic: The U.S. and the British armies had been advancing east from France and Belgium as the Russians moved west; their meeting at the river would mark the moment at which Germany had been taken from both sides, and serve as an affirmation of the intentions of the United States, Britain, and the Soviet Union to win the war and forge the peace jointly.

For a few days, Stevens could try to forget the nightmarish tunnels and vaults of Nordhausen. The first Russian soldier they saw at the Elbe was "a bald-headed private," Moffat recalled. "They had some quite old privates in the Russian army. . . . He had a big spool of wire on his back and he came up to me . . . and grinned. 'Capitaliste!' he said, to me, then pointed to himself and said, 'Communiste!' and grinned again." The footage Stevens's unit shot at Torgau is cheerful, almost manic in its desire to seek out comedy. The Americans imitated the Russians, the Russians imitated the Americans, the camera became an excuse for clowning. They filmed a drunken man in a top hat, staggering around the riverbank holding a freshly killed rabbit, then falling over. Stevens can be seen jovially trying to convince a young, grave-looking Russian soldier to shake his hand. He filmed the Russians dancing and the Americans laughing and clapping; he shot footage of the Russians teaching the Americans how to use a Soviet-made machine gun and of the Americans teaching the Russians how to use an Eyemo camera. A mood of celebratory cultural exchange prevailed; at the water's edge, someone had placed a large painted mural adorned with the slogan "East Meets West" in which an American GI, with the Stars and Stripes and the Statue of Liberty behind him, greets a Russian soldier for the first time as both men wipe their boots on a fallen Nazi flag.

After the war, some would criticize the Allies for lingering at Torgau and wallowing in triumphalism at a time when Berlin hadn't yet been taken and most of the camps were still under Nazi control. "People talk glibly of why we didn't push on to Berlin," Moffat wrote later, explaining that the feeling that the "war couldn't last long" overwhelmed all of them. At the Elbe, they felt they "could relax"; there was "no enemy . . . for the first time," a "nice feeling if you're driving around in a Jeep."

For Stevens, Torgau turned out to be a final interlude before unremitting horror. Less than a hundred miles to the north, thousands of Russian tanks were rolling into Berlin, and he assumed that he and his team would join the Allies there to film the defeat of Hitler and the Nazis in their last stronghold. Instead, they received orders to proceed south to Dachau. The 99th Infantry Division was about to liberate the camp. Stevens and a dozen of his men loaded their jeeps with Browning machine guns, confiscated German artillery, K-rations, and camera equipment and started to drive, with one member of the unit standing in the back of each car, his gun at the ready, scanning the horizon in all directions. They had three hundred miles to cover quickly, but no other unit in Germany at the time had sound cameras, and Stevens assumed that he and his team might be needed to record filmed testimony from both the prisoners and the guards.

They stopped only to down their rations quickly, or to film what felt like the step-by-step disintegration of Hitler's army that revealed itself to them with every new turn of the road. Fallen planes with swastikas on their tails dotted the countryside; the number of American and British flyers they had hit was hatchmarked in paint near the wings. They passed hundreds of German army POWs penned along a riverbank, waiting, with expressions of stunned devastation, to be loaded into the backs of empty trucks by impassive American soldiers who monitored them at riflepoint. When Stevens's unit reached Dachau, they dropped their gear in a house where they were to be billeted with another film unit that had just arrived from the south, and they drove to the camp.

It was almost May, but patches of snow and ice still covered much of the frozen ground behind the fences. Stevens and his men bundled themselves in greatcoats that had been taken from SS guards and drove through the gates. What Stevens saw there would change his life and work, and profoundly alter his understanding of his own nature. "It was," he said, "like wandering around in one of Dante's infernal visions."

At first, he was numb. Not knowing what else to do, he loaded his camera and started to film: A desiccated corpse by the train tracks. Another inside a boxcar, half covered in snow. Then, farther into the boxcar, another, naked, frozen, blue. A field full of skeletal dead men on their backs, their eyes open to the gray sky. A pile of striped pajamas. A second boxcar, this one full of dead bodies, some with bullet holes, many with the unmistakable marks of torture and privation, piled in a bloody tumble of limbs. Outside, row upon row of the dead, and then, row upon row of men and women who only looked dead. Their heads were shaved; the starvation they had endured made their ages hard to guess and their genders indistinguishable until the Americans started to strip off their clothes for delousing.

No rumor or report that Germany had long housed factories of death had prepared the first Allied soldiers into the camps for the cruelty, the desperation, the pestilential squalor, the waking nightmare of what they encountered. Some of the crematoria still had their flames lit. Typhus ran rampant through Dachau; the prisoners were sprayed with DDT, turning from side to side naked as the insecticide cloud enveloped them. Stevens aimed the lens of his camera skyward to film the smoke that was still drifting from some chimneys, then back down to eye level, where piles of naked bodies—hundreds of them—were mounded six and eight feet high. "We went to the woodpile," he said, "and the woodpile was people."

Some thirty thousand prisoners were found alive at Dachau, but many of them were barely holding on; help was slow in arriving, and there was no place they could be moved immediately and cared for in such numbers. For some of the men in Stevens's unit, simply bearing witness to so much suffering without taking action themselves was impossible. They abandoned their cameras and became nurses, comforters, ministers. One of them put down his equipment and started wandering from bed to bed in the camp's first makeshift infirmary, letting the dying dictate letters to their relatives while he wrote around the clock. He didn't stop or sleep for days. Stevens kept filming, his camera pushing into corners and shadows, his movements steady as he recorded the carnage that surrounded him. His eye was unwavering and unsentimental. He was not in search anymore of small, personalizing details but of images that would capture both the vastness and the specific sadism of crimes against humanity of a kind he had never imagined. Dachau, he said later, was "where I learned about life."

Stevens felt bound to use his camera to make the unspeakable manifest, even as he felt nothing but endless despair. After the war, he wondered, for the rest of his life, if he had filmed enough, if he had brought to the task before him the ruthlessness and skill it required. "Strange thing," he said. "When you find things are at their worst, and [it's] most necessary to film, you can't do it the way you should do it. You can't walk up to a man that think[s] of rescue, and . . . stick a camera in his face." But he pressed on, and he did much of the most painful work himself, allowing nobody to replace or relieve him. "You can send three or four guys out with some weapons to do something, but I couldn't send anybody into the goddamn boxcar," he recalled. "I had to do it. And I climbed up on this thing, and people [who were alive] a few days before, they're all piled up. . . . One just couldn't know . . . it just doesn't relate to *people*, how they should be all piled up on top of one another." While he was at Dachau, he would not speak of what he saw and filmed, even to the men in his unit. "Particularly with G.I.'s, you don't talk about those things," he said. "You don't say, 'I saw this . . .' You file it. So I'm here, and I'm looking at these people, who they are, and what—and I know this was never written—cannibalism. In the boxcar. Jesus Christ, how does one . . . I never heard anybody ever talk about it."

Ultimately, it was the living who haunted Stevens more than the dead. He would walk into a field with his camera and see what he thought were bodies racked by malnutrition and covered with sores; then some of them would begin to move. His stomach would turn; he would rear back. The dead were everywhere, intermingled with the living. Their smell hung in the air, but in the Allies' first days at the camp, as one young American soldier after another would double over heaving, the survivors themselves seemed not to react. They had lived and slept and eaten among corpses for so long that they continued to do so, almost as if they didn't notice them. The Allies had not anticipated the amount of humanitarian aid that would be needed. They quickly put the Germans they had taken prisoner to work carrying supplies and buckets of water, and young GIs taught the camp inmates who were well enough to stand how to make themselves meal-and-water mush in small out-door cauldrons while they waited for the first truckloads of bread to arrive. Some of the people at Dachau were so used to imprisonment and punishment that they could barely tell their liberators from their captors. "I would come around a block and there would be one of these poor devils, stricken, stand-ing there shaking and trembling," Stevens said. "I've got the uniform on, and he thinks I'm going to do some kind of outrage on him. We take off our tin hats and try to look as [un-]soldier-like as possible, but they'd just stand at attention and salute . . . in a paroxysm of terror . . . begging you not to be a beast. . . . Every time you turn a corner, because of your uniform, people think of you like that. . . . You want to escape them, push them aside. You don't want to catch their lice."

In his first days at Dachau, Stevens felt he was losing another piece of his own humanity every time he opened his eyes. The prisoners lived like animals, unembarrassed when they squatted to relieve themselves or when they were stripped to be disinfected or photographed as living proof of war crimes. Harry Truman had been president for just a few weeks when he re-ceived a devastating report of conditions in the liberated camps from the delegate he had appointed to inspect them. Help and food were not arriving quickly enough and the freed prisoners were still suffering terribly; "as mat-ters now stand," the report to Truman stated, "we appear to be treating the Jews as the Nazis treated them, except that we do not exterminate them."

It had been almost a year since Normandy, and Stevens had grown close to the men in his unit, but at Dachau, even as they did their jobs, the team seemed to come apart; every man was alone. "Almost everybody was in shock," Stevens said. "There wasn't anybody I could communicate with." When a freed inmate crawling with bugs would claw at his uniform and look at him with supplication, imploring him for something he didn't understand in Polish or German or begging in a few words of broken English, he would have to fight the instinct to pull away in revulsion. "Everything evil will be exposed in a day in a concentration camp," he said. "I hated the bastards [in the German army]. What they stood for was the worst, the worst possible thing that happened in centuries. And yet, when a poor man hungered and unseeing because his eyesight is failing grabs me and starts begging, I feel the Nazi in any human being . . . I feel a Nazi because I abhor him and I want him to keep his hands off me. And the reason I abhor him is because I see myself as being capable of arrogance and brutality to keep him off me. . . . That's a fierce thing to discover within yourself, that which you despise the most."

Even at moments when Stevens could push the images of need and hunger and fear out of his mind, the words of the German prisoners that the Allies had taken at Dachau would echo as a kind of mocking affirmation of his own worst fears. At one point, Stevens walked into a room in one of the camp buildings where American officers were interrogating an SS officer who had been hiding in the back of a wagon bound for Munich until a freed Polish prisoner had spotted him and somehow found the strength to drag him back. The German was on his knees, screaming, as a GI stood above him with a rifle butt, ready to strike. Other captured Germans were crowded into a corner of the room, waiting for their own interrogations. "Americans are supposed to be honorable people!" cried the man on the floor. "They're dirty torturers!"

In his movies, from the Laurel and Hardy shorts to *Alice Adams*, Stevens, who had been acutely sensitive to instances of embarrassment or personal mortification since he was a small boy, had often turned episodes of humiliation into the stuff of slapstick or light farce. Moffat, who was with him at Dachau, believed that during Stevens's time at the camp, he came to feel that his work in transforming moments of cruelty or hurt into popular comic entertainment made him somehow culpable. "He'd always been an observer of human frailty," he said, "[as] a sort of picaresque, minor thing. It was never enlarged onto the tragic scale that he suddenly saw [of] people behaving and being treated in fashions that he'd never dreamed that human nature [would allow]. He took it very very hard . . . it had a profound effect on him."

He kept filming, even when his instinct was to turn away. Only a small portion of what he photographed was deemed suitable for use in American newsreels, and even the limited amount of footage that was sent out by the army was rejected by many theater owners as inappropriate for their audiences. One of the few pieces of Dachau footage that many moviegoers at home saw at the time was an event that was then taking place all over Germany: Whenever a camp was liberated, the Allies would gather adult men and women from the surrounding German villages and towns, put them in army trucks, and take them on a nonoptional tour of the scene of Nazi crimes. Stevens filmed these visits with particular attention to the faces of the visitors, training his camera on them to see who would eventually break down and cry, and who would set his jaw and refuse to look at anything but the back of the head of the man in front of him. He seemed to know before it happened which middle-aged woman was likely to pull a handkerchief from her purse and hold it to her mouth in shock, and which would simply press her lips together and shake her head quickly as if to deny the reality of what was before her. He also filmed GIs escorting prisoners up and down a line of suspected camp guards, some of whom had thrown away their uniforms, shaved their heads, and dressed in striped pajamas, hoping to evade capture. As the prisoners, some of whom were virtually blind from the conditions in which they'd lived, moved closer to their former captors, peering at them, Stevens moved in with prosecutorial determination, bringing his camera so close that both faces filled the frame. Sometimes he would not move the camera or cut away; he would simply hold fast on a single image until his film ran out, as if all of the deep and essential proofs that anyone could possibly require resided in the faces, or the bodies, or the bones themselves.

After the first few days, signs of civilization—food, blankets, doctors, medicine—started to reach the camp, and the freed prisoners there, many of whom stayed because they had no families left and no place they could now call home, became more used to the presence of cameras. They understood why they were being photographed, and even the sickliest among them tried to summon the strength to cooperate. In the infirmaries, men with sunken eyes and hollow cheeks would, when they saw Stevens's cameras, move toward even frailer patients who were too weak to raise their heads, and cup the backs of their skulls, gently lifting them to face the lens so that they might be seen or remembered by someone, as unrecognizable as many of them had become. In the makeshift morgues, the prisoners would hold up dead men for Stevens to film; they too were evidence. And many of the men in the camp gave testimony on camera; Stevens himself interviewed former prisoners. He received no instructions from the military to elicit testimony from them or to film it; he believed it was part of the job he was there to do and was certain that it would eventually be needed.

Some of the Dachau inmates asked for a religious service, and on May 5, Captain David Eichorn, a Jewish army chaplain, and Rabbi Eli Bohnen conducted a Jewish service as part of a larger memorial ceremony that was attended by thousands of former prisoners (the next day, a delayed Easter mass was held). Stevens took sound film from the vantage points of both the pulpit and the crowd, which stood raptly beneath flags of more than a dozen Allied nations as they heard the words, "Europe has suffered with you." Stevens, who had been raised Protestant, shuddered at some of what was said; Dachau caused him, for a time, to turn away from any religious faith, particularly from the "wholesomely, exuberantly schmaltzy" Christianity practiced by the Germans that he saw. Twenty years later, he recalled that what he had felt then was, "The better the Christian, the better the anti-Semite. . . . It justified the whole goddamned terror, to have this kind of a [Christian] belief. They wanted to have it, and they had it."

Two nights later, the war in Europe ended. Still at Dachau, Stevens, along with the rest of the army, heard the news of V-E Day on the radio the same way they had learned of Roosevelt's death a month earlier and Hitler's suicide just as they entered the camp. There was no celebration that evening. They listened to Churchill tell the world that the German government had signed an agreement of unconditional surrender that was approved by the Supreme Headquarters Allied Expeditionary Force and the Soviet high command, and they heard President Truman mark the "solemn but glorious hour" of victory by saying, "Our rejoicing is sober and subdued by a supreme consciousness of the terrible price we have paid to rid the world of Hitler and his evil band." He reminded the world that "work, work, and more work" lay ahead. But the fighting in Europe was, at last, over.

Stevens stayed on at Dachau for several weeks, continuing to film and to send footage back to London and Washington. At the end of each week, he would sit alone and write a log to be sent to the War Department detailing what was on each reel of footage: "Closeups of the prisoners—very good of their faces," "More dead bodies—closeups of their heads," "Shot of naked prisoners shivering with the cold." He wasn't in any hurry to return to the United States; more than at any time since he had entered the war, he believed that his job was essential; everything else, including thoughts of his future, would have to wait. When he finally left the camp in July, it was to serve as an American delegate to the Potsdam Conference at which Truman, Churchill, and Stalin gathered to map out postwar policy. He and some of his men drove to Hitler's retreat at Berchtesgaden, in the Alps near the German-Austrian border, to take some of the spoils of war—silverware and dinner plates. (He eventually brought what he had pilfered to Paris and, he said, traded it for cognac.) They went into Goering's house and saw his underground screening room, where a list of motion pictures that had been projected there was posted; Stevens couldn't resist looking to see if any of his movies were on it. And in Berlin, he filmed the Olympiad stadium, where Leni Riefenstahl had shot her famous documentary for Hitler nine years earlier, and he saw the trench in which Hitler and Eva Braun had died. That footage was the last recorded work of his SPECOU unit, which had now fractured into small subgroups. After leaving Dachau, Stevens began drinking heavily; the remaining men in his unit found him "troublesome" and "difficult" when he wasn't sober and they started to steer clear of him. "As soon as we were off duty, as soon as night fell, we'd avoid him," said Moffat. "He'd come out looking for company, somebody for a chat, or to drink and open his rations with, and he couldn't find anybody. . . . He was lonely."

The unit broke up. The rest of the men wanted to go home. Stevens filmed young Allied soldiers leaving Germany, joyously boarding planes bound for half a dozen different countries, but he stayed on; there was too much still to do. On August 8, the London Charter defined the charges that would be brought against captured members of the European Axis powers who were to be tried that winter at Nuremberg—war crimes, crimes against peace, and crimes against humanity. Stevens and Budd Schulberg would remain in

Europe until then to assist Supreme Court associate justice Robert Jackson and his team of prosecutors. In the coming months, Stevens would devote himself to the creation of two feature-length documentaries about the war. The first would cover crimes and conditions at Dachau and other camps; the second, *The Nazi Plan,* would demonstrate that Germany's war crimes were the result of more than a decade of planning and premeditation. The films were intended to have only one showing, and only one audience: the judges at Nuremberg.

TWENTY-SIX

"What's This Picture For?"

WASHINGTON AND HOLLYWOOD, SUMMER 1945

A s the war ended in Europe, the Signal Corps sent a filmed message to American soldiers stationed there: "The German people are not our friends." In the spring, certain that Hitler's end was imminent, Frank Capra and Theodor Geisel had prepared a short movie called *Your Job in Germany* that was intended for the U.S. troops who would soon be charged with keeping the peace in a defeated nation. More than any other propaganda film that had been shown during the war, this one placed the blame squarely at the feet of the German citizenry. "Take no chances," the narrator warned. "You are up against German history. It isn't good." In a voice-over that sneered at the notion that Germans were "tender, repentant, *sorry*," Geisel made clear that he thought any show of contrition was a ruse. "It *can* happen again—the next war," his narrator said, because "Gestapo gangsters" are now "part of the mob. Still watching you, and hating you, and thinking . . . thinking about next time. . . . They're not sorry they caused the war. They're only sorry they lost it. . . . Trust none of them. Someday the German people might be cured of their disease—their super-race disease, their world conquest disease. But they must prove that they have been cured beyond a shadow of a doubt before they are allowed to take their place among respectable nations."

Geisel, who wrote and produced *Your Job in Germany*, hired the actor John Lund to deliver those lines in an aggressive, almost menacing style. (Ronald Reagan had auditioned but, according to Geisel, "didn't seem to have the understanding, that morning, of the vital issues.") He stood by the harsh, unsparing tone of the film he had created, with one exception. After Germany surrendered, Eisenhower mandated a strict nonfraternization policy between U.S. soldiers and German civilians. Geisel thought the rule was "impossible and ill-advised," but, "acting under orders," he inserted army language telling GIs and officers that while they were to respect German customs, religion, and property, they were also to remain aloof: "Don't visit their homes. . . . They cannot come back into the civilized fold just by sticking out their hand and saying they're sorry. . . . That is the hand that *heil*ed Adolf Hitler. . . . Don't clasp that hand."

Capra told Geisel to fly to Europe and show *Your Job in Germany* to the military leadership, who would then decide if it was appropriate viewing for the rank and file. Patton, who advocated an approach that would make the German people partners in peace, was disgusted by the film's combative tone and walked out of the screening, calling it "bullshit." But Eisenhower thought the general was too soft on denazification, and after Patton publicly referred to the National Socialists as just another political party, he warned him to "get off your bloody ass and [stop] mollycoddling the goddamn Nazis." Eisenhower approved the film, and as the postwar occupation of Germany began in May, ordered it to be shown to all U.S. soldiers in the country.*

That spring, Capra continued actively pursuing his separation from military service. Most of the projects that mattered to him were finished, or close to it. *Know Your Enemy—Germany*, which had gone through years of revisions, was finally completed but was virtually useless since Germany and the United States were no longer at war; in the coming months, it would be refashioned into an anti-German historical documentary called *Here Is Germany*. *War Comes to America*, the seventh and last film in the *Why We*

---

* Although *Your Job in Germany* was not originally made to be seen by American moviegoers, the War Activities Committee eventually gave the short to Warner Bros., which recut it and rewrote the narration, adding some cautions about the possible rise of Fascism in the United States. It was released theatrically in December 1945 under the title *Hitler Lives*. The following spring, that version, which was overseen by Don Siegel (later the director of *Invasion of the Body Snatchers* and *Dirty Harry*) won the Academy Award for Best Documentary Short Subject.

Fight series, was also ready for release; Darryl Zanuck generously told Capra that it was "the greatest documentary film I have ever seen" and said he would be glad to distribute it theatrically through 20th Century Fox. But the promise never materialized into a firm offer, probably because Zanuck was enough of a businessman to know that as the war in the Pacific continued, the last thing moviegoers wanted to see in mid-1945 was a history lesson that ended, as *War Comes to America* did, with Pearl Harbor. Capra was still working on a pair of short propaganda documentaries, *Two Down and One to Go!* (which was intended for home-front moviegoers and featured cartoon images of Hitler and Mussolini being obliterated, with Tojo to follow) and *On to Tokyo,* a film for GIs in which General Marshall explained to a group of soldiers why troop numbers in the Pacific would have to be increased and why even exhausted veterans of the war in Europe would now have to fight against Japan. But once those two shorts and *Know Your Enemy—Japan* were completed, Capra told Lyman Munson, "I will consider myself through with my Army work. . . . I am just afraid that if I don't return to my civilian occupation soon I will be so rusty, tired, and fagged out I'll never make any more pictures."

Capra had been begging the army to let him go for almost a year. He wasn't lying about being tired, but he was also motivated by the intense ambition that had propelled him to the top of the film business in the 1930s, and was now shading into panic as a new group of directors started to gain a foothold in Hollywood. "I want to remain active as long as I can be of service," he had told Munson back in January. "Beyond that, naturally, I'd rather not stick around. . . . I wish you could . . . give some thought to my position as well as the position of such men as Litvak, Veiller . . . Huston, etc. These men all gave up careers and perhaps some of their future to volunteer for service. They will have to go back and compete with those who weren't quite so patriotic . . . who stayed home and got the gravy during the greatest boom the industry ever had." Capra was still trying to find partners for Liberty, the production company that he and Sam Briskin were launching; he had recently invited Leo McCarey, the director of *Going My Way* and one of the loudest voices among Hollywood's increasingly assertive anti-Communists, to join him as a partner. He also put out a feeler to Robert

Riskin, the liberal screenwriter who had written five of his biggest hits, but both men declined.

Munson kept stalling Capra, telling him that "to be as frank as I can . . . I just don't know" when a discharge might be granted. But a week after V-E Day, Capra submitted a formal Application for Separation. At the time, such requests were considered using a mathematical formula: He was awarded one point for each of the forty months he had been in the army, an additional point for each of the four months he had spent overseas preparing *Tunisian Victory*, five points for receiving the Legion of Merit, and twelve points for each of his three dependent children. His total, eighty-five, was exactly enough to win him a discharge. On June 8, 1945, Capra left Fort Fox in Los Angeles for Washington, D.C., where he took his final army physical. Soon after that, he was summoned to Marshall's office, where he learned he had been awarded the Distinguished Service Medal, an honor that the general himself wanted to present to him. The citation read in part, "The films produced by Colonel Capra under the direction of the Chief of Staff had an important influence on the morale of the Army."

Capra was beside himself. "Surprise! Glorious surprise!" he wrote in his journal. "Gen. Marshall pinned on the DSM! I acted like an idiot, being completely speechless. I had to go out to the can and cry for 10 minutes. Nothing has ever made me so proud!"

That moment helped take the sting out of the tepid reception for *War Comes to America*, which was finally released in a few theaters; it was the third *Why We Fight* installment to be shown to civilians, but Capra had largely said what he wanted to say about the causes of World War II in the previous chapters and had turned this one into a protracted ode to American values. His first edit of the film had run over ninety minutes, and when General Osborn saw it, he gently suggested "substantial cuts," telling Capra that while he thought the movie had "superb possibilities," much of the material "describing what kind of people we are" could probably be eliminated, and so could some of the overwrought sentiment. "Don't you think we might cut out the rows of cots in the maternity hospital?" he wrote. "To me they were a little reminiscent of the mass production of babies." Capra got the movie down to just over an hour, but it still felt long; unlike the rest of *Why*

We Fight, which had moved briskly through the rise of Germany and Japan and the start of the war in Europe, this episode began with the American Revolution and took its time moving forward. Perhaps because he was almost at the end of his service, Capra even decided to include a pat on the back to Hollywood in the picture. *War Comes to America* cites the release of Warners' 1939 melodrama *Confessions of a Nazi Spy* as a prewar milestone, praising the film as a bold warning to a complacent nation with the commentary, "We sat in our theaters unbelieving as motion pictures exposed Nazi espionage in America. Could these things really be?"

But by 1945, no moviegoer needed to be chided for prewar complacency, let alone shaken out of it. *Confessions of a Nazi Spy* seemed like a movie from an infinitely more innocent era, and the *Why We Fight* series, which had been designed to explain to soldiers the reasons America was entering the war, held no appeal to moviegoers who were now desperate to put it behind them. Hollywood, which had saturated the public with war-themed movies in its first two years, had also gotten the message; from 1943 to 1945, production of war pictures by the studios dropped by more than 60 percent. Nonetheless, Capra was accorded a hero's welcome upon his heavily publicized return to Hollywood. The industry viewed *Why We Fight,* which had been seen by more than four million people, both in and out of uniform, as the signal filmmaking accomplishment of the war. William Wyler spoke for many at the time when he predicted that "Frank's series . . . will live longer than *Gone With The Wind* and will have a greater effect on the development of the medium." With such praise came widespread recognition of Capra as an industry leader whose status had only grown in his absence, and intense curiosity about what he would do next. He and Briskin had recently announced the formation of Liberty, but they still couldn't finance it without partners, and Capra hadn't yet picked a script for what would be his first movie in five years. (In the spring, he had gone to see the hit comedy *Harvey* on Broadway; he thought it had possibilities, but he couldn't secure the rights.) Now he would have plenty of time to plan his next move. On June 25, after a three-day cross-country train ride, Capra got back to Los Angeles and ended his war years with a two-word diary entry: "Arrived home!"

In July, John Huston's *San Pietro* was shown in theaters for the first time.

Army publicity materials explained that the thirty-two-minute film had been shot "over a period of five months," but otherwise did not disclose to a credulous press corps that it was composed almost entirely of reenactments. In fact, the Public Relations Bureau of the War Department went out of its way to tout *San Pietro*'s authenticity. Journalists and reviewers were sent a press release that read, "This was the first time a complete photographic crew stayed with any one outfit in the line. Major Huston was given complete freedom of action, and was able to [place] his cameramen advantageously throughout the filming of the picture. . . . As the battle progressed, Major Huston was able to start work on his script for the narration." A separate press release, titled "Facts and Fiction" but trafficking almost entirely in the latter, stated that "Huston's first task was to decide how to make his rather small unit spread out during the battle, so that he could have complete coverage from many sides, and at the same time be able to give directions to his men. . . . He knew beforehand what the tactics were to be. . . . Many times during the filming, he would lead several of his men ahead to the infantry, preceding an attack by several hours into no-man's-land, and wait for the attack to start, and then start the cameras grinding."

These were all outright lies about a battle at which Huston had not even been present, but the waves of celebration and memorialization that followed the end of the war in Europe seemed to dull critical acuity. A title card within the film contended that "all scenes in this picture were photographed within range of enemy small arms or artillery fire" but added that "for purposes of continuity a few of these scenes were shot before and after the actual battle." That qualifier, which was placed not at the beginning of *San Pietro* but in its last ten seconds, was ignored by most who wrote about the movie. Had it been released six months earlier, *San Pietro* might have been more closely scrutinized as news from the front. But in peacetime, it was treated with reverence, as an invaluable record of recent American history. James Agee, who had previously demonstrated an unerring eye for any war film that smacked of falsity, filled his review for *Time* with a rephrasing of much of the army's press release; he went on to call Huston's movie a work of "pure tragic grandeur" and "as good a war film as any that has been made . . . in some respects it is the best"; he predicted that "history is likely to recognize it as . . . great." He never questioned its authenticity, nor did the *New York Times*, which praised Huston's "daring" in shooting during combat.

Critics may have been taken in by the reenactments that filled *San Pietro*, but their praise was not limited to its purported realism; they also recognized that Huston had done something genuinely new, creating a fresh visual and emotional vocabulary for war films. The narration was delivered in a flat, almost bitter tone that could not have differed more from the sincere emotional throb of many earlier army-film voice-overs. And, largely because he had had the leisure and safety to stage battle sequences exactly as he wanted to, Huston had been able to refine an onscreen version of "realism" in which the shakiness of the camera, the fitfulness of the advance of troops, and the stoic inexpressiveness of the men all announced that while this was not a Hollywood version of war, it was perhaps a version of war that Hollywood could hope to emulate. The somberness of *San Pietro* also marked a departure from Signal Corps standards. Huston had deliberately lingered on images of death, loss, and destruction, redeemed only by the last scenes, in which, after a (staged) return to their village, peasant mothers are seen breastfeeding their babies. (The final minutes of *San Pietro* seem to anticipate the dawn of the Italian neorealist movement that would enthrall discerning moviegoers over the next few years.)

For critics, *San Pietro* was the perfect film for a moment in which, for the first time since before Pearl Harbor, it was no longer necessary for every war movie to make the case for war. None of them echoed the army's initial fear that Huston had subversively crafted an "antiwar" statement; they felt that *San Pietro*'s cold-eyed depiction of life on a battlefield was long overdue, and the movie confirmed their belief that Huston, who still had only three feature films to his credit, was Hollywood's most important new director. Writing in the *New Republic*, Manny Farber was stunned by how "absolutely unromantic" and "depressing" the film was; for the first time, he wrote, an American director was willing to show that battles were "confused, terrifying, surprising and tragic." And the *New Yorker* praised Huston's depiction of war as "a dirty, deadly business" that was free of "romantic gestures."

Huston did not do many interviews to promote the release of *San Pietro*. At the time, his own feelings about the movie were ambivalent; shortly before its release, he wrote to Zanuck after a screening and called it "a dolorous goddamn picture full of hacked up towns and tanks and bodies. . . . I succeeded in making [the audience] miserable which is the purpose of the picture."* The dark and angry mood that had plagued him since his return from Italy had only worsened. His wife, Lesley, had finally gone to Reno to fulfill the six-week residency requirement she needed in order to obtain a divorce (she spent most of her time there with Humphrey Bogart's soon-to-be-ex-wife, who was in Reno for the same reason). In Los Angeles, Huston was drinking heavily; he didn't have anything close to the number of points that would have entitled him to apply for a return to civilian life, and the army was in no hurry to get rid of him. At times, his uncontrolled belligerence became public and embarrassing; just before V-E Day, at a party at David O. Selznick's house, he and Errol Flynn got in a fistfight, apparently over Olivia de Havilland, that landed both of them in the hospital—Flynn with broken ribs and Huston with a broken nose—and in the headlines. "I remember that the language on both our parts . . . was about as vile as it could get," Huston wrote later. "Errol started it, but I went right along with it."

That summer, the army gave Huston orders to make a new documentary, and he was genuinely excited by the subject—the plight of returning veterans who were suffering from war-related psychological trauma. Huston had not been able to put a name to the depression and anger that he had felt since returning home, but his interest in the treatment of mentally ill soldiers was personal. Rey Scott, his cameraman in the Aleutians, had declined rapidly since he had been hospitalized after firing his gun one night at the army's film studio in Astoria; early in 1945, Scott's wife had told Huston that the care he was receiving in the psychiatric ward of an army hospital was "callous and inhumane." Huston decided he would try to intervene; he wrote a letter expressing his concern about the hospital's plan to use shock treatment on Scott and pleaded for his colleague to be discharged. "Scott has made as many and as great personal sacrifices as anyone I know who is alive and in

---

* Huston never publicly acknowledged that the film was a reenactment, including in his autobiography thirty-five years later.

possession of all of his arms and legs," Huston wrote to the hospital's administrator. "He should he out of the army. . . . He is a peculiar cuss, but certainly not crazy. Unless it is craziness that leads a man to volunteer to fly
time after time on bombing missions of an exceedingly fatal nature or to
sweat it out in foxholes in advance positions for weeks on end. That is hardly
the kind of craziness that requires electrical shock therapy. It is rather the
kind that has given [the Army Pictorial Service] its present splendid reputation in the field."

Two army psychiatrists wrote Huston patient and thorough replies, explaining that Scott had been diagnosed not as insane but as depressed and
suicidal, that he had exaggerated the conditions of his confinement to his
wife, and that his doctors were working hard not only to treat him but to keep
what one of them called "a lot of rather unpleasant incidents which I would
rather not write about" out of his army files so that he could continue to receive medical care. Huston came away from the exchange moved by the
knowledge, compassion, and persistence of the doctors, and he welcomed
the chance to explore their work in a documentary.

The army had a different purpose in mind. Huston was told that the prospective film was intended not to explore the workings of psychiatry or the
struggles of patients, but to convince business owners around the country
that they had nothing to fear in hiring war veterans. Taking no chances,
Huston's superiors gave him an itemized list of what the movie it was planning to call *The Returning Psychoneurotic* should do: "(1) Point out what a
small proportion fall into this category; (2) Eliminate the stigma now attached to the psychoneurotic through a thorough explanation of what it really
is—thus to offset the exaggerated picture that has already been given to the
public through the press, magazine, and radio stories; and (3) Explain that in
many cases the reason that makes a psychoneurotic unsatisfactory for the
Army is the very reason for which this same person could be a real success
in civilian life. (It has been stated by [veterans who have undergone treat-
ment] that those qualities which made them a success as a civilian were the
very things that made them crack up as a soldier.)"

Huston ignored the army's specifications, but he took to the assignment with enthusiasm. He had no intention of making a film about civilian employment; his documentary would be an intimate examination of psychiatric process—a chronological narrative of the six to eight weeks of treatment that a hospitalized GI typically received. By the end of the summer, he had settled on Mason General, the army hospital near Astoria where Scott had been treated, and he made plans to spend the rest of the year filming its doctors and patients.

Huston welcomed the chance to start something new—even if it was for the army—since the last piece of propaganda on which he had worked had come to nothing. In August, *Know Your Enemy—Japan,* which was largely based on his script, was finished after three years. Capra had taken Huston's rewrite and added a few flourishes of his own, disparaging Japanese soldiers as interchangeable "photographic prints off the same negative" and emphasizing his often-repeated belief that the citizenry of Japan was culpable for accepting "their fate in dumb, regimented silence" as "willing prisoners of a vicious, ironclad social structure." ("The one thing that Americans are against in principle is regimentation," he told the *Los Angeles Times.*) The hour-long documentary Capra submitted to the army was a patchy assemblage of racist rhetoric, faulty history, and indictment of the Japanese military, Shintoism, and the national character. With little actual film from wartime Japan available to him, Capra had relied so heavily on a hodgepodge of stock footage that he even included a shot from George Stevens's melodrama *Penny Serenade* that was meant to pass as the record of a 1923 earthquake in Tokyo.

Know Your Enemy—Japan was sent overseas, where it was to be shown to all U.S. troops in the Pacific. It arrived three days after the atom bomb was dropped on Hiroshima. At that point, the triumphant promise with which Capra had ended the movie—a vow to "concentrate the full fury of our total power" on Japan—was no longer a message the War Department wanted to send. General MacArthur had been overseeing plans for a massive Allied invasion of Japan and was shocked that the bomb had been used; after he watched the movie and listened to the narration that Huston and Capra had written, he cabled Washington that he would not allow soldiers to see it "due

388   MARK HARRIS

to change in policy governing occupation of Japan," and added, "Also recommend no press releases or showing to public in United States." The film was suppressed for more than thirty years.

Huston and Capra were hardly the only filmmakers whose late-arriving movies were suddenly rendered irrelevant; after V-J Day, Wyler found himself up against an army that was completely indifferent to his documentary *Thunderbolt*. Through the summer, Wyler had struggled to regain his footing and adjust to life both as a civilian and as a disabled veteran; he had been fitted with a hearing aid that maximized the little hearing he had in one ear, and he had tried to shake off his misery by returning to work. In July, he wrote to the War Department's Bureau of Public Relations that *Thunderbolt* was "nearly finished and I think it will be pretty good. It has a definite story to tell." Wyler then made a pitch that had been a constant refrain of filmmakers throughout the war: Twenty minutes wasn't enough time to tell the story well. Unless he received permission to make the movie longer, the result would be "nothing more than a glorified newsreel."

Wyler got his way, just as he had on *Memphis Belle*. He and John Sturges prepared a forty-three-minute cut and had it scored and processed. They completed the picture just as the Japanese army surrendered. When Wyler took the movie to Washington, D.C., to screen it for senior air force officers, after the lights came up, General H. H. Arnold looked around and said, "Is Willy here?" Wyler stood up.

"Willy," Arnold said, "what's this picture for?"

According to Sturges, "Willy was literally speechless. Maybe it was because of his hearing, but he didn't say a word. He could have given fifty reasons why we made the picture. He knew them all. . . . Willy finally mumbled something. He was fumbling around. Arnold needed positive answers. He just walked out, and that was the end of that."

Wyler wouldn't give up. He took *Thunderbolt* to the Hollywood trade press and tried to get them interested in covering it; a sympathetic journalist at the *New York Times* wrote, "Mr. Wyler doesn't feel that his own readjustment to civilian life is complete, or that it will be until his last Army assignment, the production of a documentary about the operations of fighter-bombers, is released to theatres." In Hollywood, he showed the film to colleagues and friends—James's brother William Cagney, Lloyd Bridges—to try to get them talking about it. After his official separation from the army after thirty-eight months of service on October 31, he kept writing letters to anyone he thought might be able to get the film onto the big screen. Even his closest colleagues brushed him off. Sam Goldwyn told him that it was the "government's problem" and claimed his hands were tied. The coordinator of the War Activities Committee, which was in the process of being dismantled, wrote Wyler to say, "It is too bad that this wonderful film could not have been made available closer to the date [on] which the events portrayed took place." Wyler wrote back to say that he regretted it too; "the war ended sooner than expected," he explained, "though I can't express any regret over that."

He then turned back to the air force, imploring General Eaker to pay for one hundred copies of the film in the belief that free prints would be an offer too good for the studios to resist. "If you personally contacted the heads of the major companies with this proposal," he told Eaker, "I don't see how they can refuse—or I'll be ashamed to be a member of the picture business." But every studio had a different reason for declining: The film's moment had passed; war documentaries were box-office poison; Wyler's work was, of course, wonderful but the company's marketing money was already committed to other pictures. Finally, he had to let it go. *Thunderbolt* would not be shown theatrically until late 1947, when the minor studio Monogram gave it a token release. By then, Wyler had to contextualize it for audiences by filming an introduction in which Jimmy Stewart referred to the events in the movie as "ancient history."

The polite but firm rejection of his work by all of the men he had known as colleagues rattled him. In 1942, *Mrs. Miniver* had made Wyler the toast of the American and British film industries; three years later, he was just another director returning from the war and discovering that the motion picture business had gone on without him and was in fact thriving. Wyler wasn't sure where he stood anymore, and didn't know how he was going to continue to direct unless his hearing improved, but he was eager to get back in the game. In July, he accepted an offer from Capra and Briskin to become a partner in Liberty, borrowing against his life insurance to put in the $150,000 that would purchase him a quarter of the company and the freedom to direct and produce movies of his own choosing for the next five years. Capra was still looking for a third director to join them, and he was also trying to make a studio distribution deal for the company's films, but the delay suited Wyler, since he still owed Goldwyn one final movie.

Goldwyn had a couple of projects in mind for him. One was a dramatized biography of Eisenhower, whose life rights the producer had been working to secure for months. Robert Sherwood, who had won the Pulitzer Prize for Drama three times before leaving the theater to become a speechwriter for Roosevelt and the overseas director of the Office of War Information, had agreed to write an outline for the screenplay, and Goldwyn, who idolized Eisenhower, was passionate about the project. Wyler wasn't; he declined an invitation to go and meet the general face-to-face. Nor was he interested when Goldwyn offered him *The Bishop's Wife*, a family fantasy about an angel and the building of an Episcopal cathedral. Goldwyn wanted something big, bright, and popular from his star director. "[His] point was, 'Come on now, the war's over, let's forget the war and do something funny or sexy,'" said Wyler. But the director longed for something else. "I wish that I could go back [to Hollywood] quietly and make a small picture," he said, "just to get the feel of things." And even if he were given the chance, he wasn't sure he could pull it off. "I've learned so much dealing with real people in very real roles of life," he said, "that I dread the day when I have to get back to telling actors how to get into a plane or put on a hat."

"I was still full of the war," said Wyler, "and although I was now out of it, I wanted to do something that had . . . to do with my experience." Finally, he found a "small picture" that suited him. It was a property that Goldwyn already owned; he had bought the rights to the source material a year earlier and registered the title so no other producer or studio could use it. *The Way Home* was a simple story about men returning from the war. Wyler thought it was perfect for him. "I spent four years being one of those characters," he said. It would be "the easiest picture I ever made."

TWENTY-SEVEN

"An Angry Past Commingled with the Future in a Storm"

HOLLYWOOD, NEW YORK, AND GERMANY, 1945

T he story of *The Best Years of Our Lives* began long before William Wyler had any inkling he was going to make it. In July 1944, while he was still flying missions over Italy, a *Time* magazine correspondent half a world away was accompanying 370 members of the 1st Marine Division, all of whom had just returned from fighting in the Pacific, as they boarded a train in San Diego that would over the next several days slowly make its way east. The men had been granted thirty-day furloughs, and they called the train the "Home Again Special," writing its name in chalk on the sides of the old Pullman cars. They talked enthusiastically about seeing their families and nervously about seeing their girls. They told war stories, and then they told stories about how everybody exaggerates when telling war stories. They bragged and they joked; at some stops they were given free beers, and at others townspeople assembled to cheer and wave flags. The closer the train got to its final destination, the more it emptied out, until the quiet moment when just a handful of marines were left, suddenly subdued, looking at the Manhattan skyline and nervously hoisting their duffel bags over their shoulders. After a week in their company, *Time*'s watchful reporter was able to capture some of the vulnerability beneath the bravado; the closer they got to home, the more the men seemed to turn back into boys—their average age was just twenty-one—and the more they began to wonder what they were coming back to and whether they would be accepted. "My stomach's tied in knots," admitted one GI. "I'm a little worried about how I'll look to them," said another. "About how much I've changed."

"The Way Home," which was published just two months after the invasion of Normandy and a year before the end of the war, may have been little more than a snapshot, but it was one of the first pieces of national journalism to anticipate the emotional uncertainties that returning veterans might face. When Sam Goldwyn read it, he knew that the subject, if not the story itself, had the makings of a great movie, albeit probably not one that could be produced until the war was over. To write the script, he turned to Mackinlay Kantor, a novelist and screenwriter who had recently served as a war correspondent in London and had acquired a good deal of experience interviewing young GIs. He had since come to Los Angeles, and Goldwyn paid him $12,500 to create an original treatment, telling him, "Returning soldiers! Every family in America is part of this story. When they come home, what do they find? They don't remember their wives, they've never seen their babies, some are wounded—they have to readjust."

Kantor began work that fall, keeping his pages to himself and holding off the inquiries of his eager producer. "The story is going along tolerably well," he wrote to Goldwyn. "I have to date about 70 manuscript pages, but I believe that is about one half of the eventual length. Because of the unusual form in which this story is couched, I cannot estimate accurately exactly how long the completed draft will run."

When that draft was finally handed in, Goldwyn learned exactly what Kantor had meant by "unusual." Instead of a treatment or a screenplay, he had written a 268-page novel in blank verse. Kantor's *Glory for Me* tells the story of three returning vets—Al, a middle-aged officer who feels, for the first time, alienated from his family, his familiar desk job at a bank, and his comfortably upper-middle-class life; Fred, a hardened soldier haunted by the savagery of his time on the battlefield; and Homer, the very young victim of a brain injury that had rendered him, in the widely used parlance of the time, a spastic.

Kantor's narrative, which followed the three men back into their lives as civilians, charting their rough adjustments and small victories, was very much the template for *The Best Years of Our Lives*. But from its first sentence—"Fred Derry, twenty-one, and killer of a hundred men / Walked on the width of Welburn Field"—it was darker, grimmer, sadder, and more explicitly brutal than any movie of the time could have been. Homer is introduced as

> . . . a death—one piece of death
> Alive on its right side, and dying, jerking on its left
> It walked with pain and twisted muscles
> It was so young . . . it had a face without a beard . . . He went
> In as a child, as many went
> He came out as a monster.

His homecoming is described as "an audience of horror on the porch"; "one thing about spasticity, you always seem to drool," Kantor adds later. The rest of *Glory for Me* is at least as harsh, particularly in its depiction of war as both a sexual playground—it's made clear that Fred slept with many women while in the service—and a sexual nightmare: Al is tormented by memories of child prostitutes.

Even if the unfilmable elements of Kantor's take on the material were to be eliminated, the hardbitten pessimism of *Glory for Me* was tonally closer to the budding genre of postwar noir than to the naturalistic, sympathetic drama that Goldwyn had in mind. At a low moment, Fred thinks about robbing the bank at which Al works; Fred's wife is portrayed as a faithless slut; Homer considers suicide; Al tosses away his secure job to sell flowers. The narrative is defined by the interiority of their misery and the unbridgeable distance between them and the peacetime world. Kantor ends with his three protagonists just barely holding on to sanity and facing the possibility that they will never be free of the spectre of their war years. He bids them farewell by describing them as

> . . . a lost battalion, huddled close—
> The three who'd known destroying flame,

And still perceived its blisters on their hide . . .

They looked, they saw an angry past

Commingled with the future in a storm.

Goldwyn didn't dislike Kantor's unorthodox treatment, which he thought contained the skeleton of a workable film story, but he knew that he needed someone else to write the screenplay. In the spring of 1945, just as his Eisenhower project was falling apart, he sent Miriam Howell, a story editor in his New York office, to woo Robert Sherwood for the job. After they met, Howell sent a telegram to her boss telling him that the playwright was "very discouraging"; she had persuaded him to read the treatment, but Sherwood warned her that it was "unlikely he will be available at all but if he should it would be for only six to eight weeks. . . . He is still under call to government although on inactive status at present and also is anxious [to] start working on play for fall production hence his unwillingness [to] make commitment."

By the end of May, Goldwyn had gotten Sherwood to read the first half of Kantor's poem. He gave his opinion of it to another of the company's story editors, Pat Duggan: "He thinks [it] is excellent but unfortunately exactly [the] type of assignment he does not wish to do at this time." Sherwood particularly disliked Kantor's use of spasticity, which he thought would be impossible for an actor to depict with any accuracy. Goldwyn told him he could simply get rid of the character, but for every concession the producer made, Sherwood found more reasons to say no. He was too busy with his play. He couldn't find the right approach to the story. He didn't want to let the Eisenhower project go, even though it seemed increasingly unlikely that it would be made.

His excuses masked a deeper objection: Sherwood was offended by *Glory for Me*'s assertion that an ugly divide had opened up between damaged soldiers and an uncaring home front. According to Duggan, he complained about the "criticisms of civilians in the book and disagreed with the idea that all returning soldiers were maladjusted." Furthermore, he felt the book—which was about to be published as a novel—"was going to be well established and successful, and he didn't want to be responsible for doing a typical Hollywood trick of softening a good property. . . . He said he would like to have written this story from the beginning because he would have written a story of these guys returning to a town and expecting the civilians to be cruel and unaware of what they had been through, only to discover that they had an agreement and an adjustment between them and a future together." Sherwood had spent the last several years in the Roosevelt administration trying to shape public opinion, and he couldn't imagine writing a movie that suggested that the country, having united for war, was now about to mishandle its aftermath.

Goldwyn thought that a top-tier director might induce Sherwood to try his hand at a draft, and he had one in mind: John Ford. In July, while Ford was still waiting for his broken leg to heal completely, Goldwyn sent him a copy of *Glory for Me*, with a note that read, "I'm very excited about it and I believe you will be too." Ford turned him down. Having finished his own war movie, *They Were Expendable*, he was about to return to active duty in Washington for two months; after that, he owed his next picture to Zanuck.

Goldwyn kept working on Sherwood, and told him he could change *Glory for Me* into anything he wanted it to be. On August 14, 1945, after months of wooing, Sherwood finally reluctantly signed a contract to write the screenplay. He lasted just two weeks before telling Goldwyn that taking the assignment had been a huge mistake and that they should abandon the whole project. "This is entirely due to the conviction that, by next spring or fall, this subject will be terribly out of date," he wrote. The film would be "doomed to miss the bus," and would probably succeed only in sparking resentment among veterans that the "small minority . . . afflicted with war neuroses" was getting so much attention.

Goldwyn reminded Sherwood that "there will be several million men coming home next year," and told him that "to release a picture at that time presenting their problems seems to me to be hitting it right on the nose." But by then, the project had a new and more persuasive champion. Wyler had told Goldwyn that he was eager to direct it, and it was his encouragement as much as Goldwyn's that kept the development of the script moving forward. Sherwood was moved by Wyler's argument that the film could potentially "prevent a lot of heartaches and even tragedies among servicemen who were confronting demobilization and return to civilian life." And Wyler was sympathetic to Sherwood's desire for the movie to carry a message that, in the wake of Hiroshima and Nagasaki, "the whole country and the whole world face the necessity of finding a way to live at peace with each other." He told the reluctant playwright to take a breath and start from scratch on a more optimistic version of Kantor's story.

Before long, Sherwood had completed a two-hundred-page draft. He flew from New York to Los Angeles to stay in a cottage on Goldwyn's estate while he and Wyler worked on revisions. As they collaborated, *The Best Years of Our Lives* gradually evolved into Wyler's own story. He openly identified with Al, the family man who gives up the comfort of success to go into the military and then comes back only to realize that, as Wyler put it, "no man can walk right into the house after two or three years and pick up his life as before." But Sherwood infused all three of his main characters with aspects of Wyler's own experiences: The anger that had almost gotten him court-martialed after he threw a punch at an anti-Semite was given life in the pugnacious, hard-bitten Fred, and Homer became a repository for all of the director's anguish about living with a disability. "I explained all my own fears and problems to Bob Sherwood," he said, "and he worked them in just the way I wanted them." At the end of their time at Goldwyn's house, Sherwood almost gave up again, saying, "I just can't get this story—something blocks me." But by the next morning, he had had a breakthrough: He had decided that the three men, as different as they were, should become comrades and weave in and out of one another's narratives as they collectively discover their paths to renewed hope. He sat down with Goldwyn at the breakfast table and, scene by scene, told him exactly what *The Best Years of Our Lives* was going to be.

The plight of the returning veteran was at that moment perhaps the most avidly discussed domestic issue in the country; the question of how to resume a normal life, and what exactly "normal" meant, opened up other subjects—from spousal abuse to mental illness—that finally had room to be aired now that the war was over. As Wyler and Sherwood worked on their script, John Huston began to explore the same issues in his documentary, immersing himself in life at Mason General Hospital, where he filmed for three months and eventually amassed more than seventy hours of footage. He would shoot all day, then at night start to sketch out a script for narration that would eventually be spoken by his father. "The guns are quiet now, the papers of peace have been signed, and the oceans of the earth are filled with ships coming home," Huston's screenplay began. "In faraway places, men dreamed of this moment—but for some men the moment is very different from the dream."

In the press, much of the coverage of veterans tended toward lurid examples of what the historian Joseph Goulden called "the War-Crazed Veteran theory . . . the following [headlines] were not atypical: 'Veteran Beheads Wife with Jungle Machete,' 'Ex-Marine Held in Rape Murder,' 'Sailor Son Shoots Father.'" Huston wanted to counteract the crime stories that seemed to be transfixing the public with a set of case studies that would be grounded in compassion. He had plenty of men from whom to choose. Even in the last months of 1945, Mason General was crowded to capacity. During the war, one out of every five U.S. soldiers who was listed as a casualty required psychiatric treatment, and at Mason alone, 150 new patients were still being admitted every week for a therapy regimen that would typically last two months. Huston's plans to shoot the documentary there had already made headlines, and the hospital accorded him and his crew VIP treatment, allowing them virtually unlimited access to doctors and patients. He filmed the soldiers—"human salvage," he wrote, "the final result of all that metal and fire could do to violate human flesh"—as they were wheeled into the hospital by nurses, and the tough but empathetic language he used to describe them was in some ways autobiographical. His characterization of the men who were hospitalized at Mason as "casualties of the spirit . . . born and bred in peace, educated to hate war, they were overnight plunged into sudden and terrible situations" was not far removed from his description of himself as "someone raised in conventional America—taught to abhor violence and believe that killing was a mortal sin" who, after what he had seen in Italy, felt he was "living in a dead man's world."

At Mason, each patient's course of treatment was determined by an intake interview conducted by a psychiatrist in a tiny room. The new arrivals were informed that they would be filmed and told not to be alarmed by the

presence of three cameras positioned at different angles (the space was too
small to accommodate cameramen, so the filming was done automatically).
Huston shot dozens of the interviews, then assembled them into a troubling
and intimate sequence that would form the first part of his film. A thin-
voiced soldier, playing with his hands and never making eye contact, talks
about a shot comrade "clawing at my feet . . . he was the last one of the
original boys with me." A soft-spoken black GI insists he's "doing well" but
then admits that he has been suffering from "crying spells" and breaks down,
unable to continue. A soldier who can barely speak above a whisper says that
after his brother was killed at Guadalcanal, he "just didn't feel like living,"
and would start shooting wildly into the night every time he was on sentry
duty. There are men with terrible twitches, men with nervous laughs, men so
lost they can barely form sentences. Hollywood had begun to explore psychiatric practice and mental illness, but dramatic films like Alfred Hitchcock's
Spellbound generally treated therapy with a combination of fascination, suspicion, and naiveté. What Huston was now cataloging was revelatory—the
devastation of healthy men turned into hopeless lost souls telling their stories
in voices that were virtually drained of feeling. No American soldiers like
them had been seen in any fact or fiction film about the war.

Some of the hospital staff feared that Huston's portrait of the toll the war
had taken on America's men would overshadow any positive message the film
contained about therapy and rehabilitation. They suspected that audiences
would remember only the stricken faces, not the successful cures, and that
the war would come to be viewed not as a victory but, in the words of one
reporter covering the movie, a "monstrous subnormal thing which can twist
good-looking high-school boys into shivering, frightened wrecks." Huston
wanted the patients "to act like cry-babies," insisted one indignant psychiatrist at Mason. "He wanted to sentimentalize how the poor boys suffered. I
didn't feel comfortable about the way he conveyed the feeling . . . that we had
a lot of weak-willed namby-pambies." Huston ignored their objections, and
he had the men he was filming on his side. As they became used to the cameras and started to get better, they would playfully drape the director's chair
with toilet paper; at one point, they hung a sign reading "Hollywood and
Vine" in their ward. The extra attention they were getting proved beneficial;

the recovery rate of the seventy-five men Huston and his crew followed was the highest in the hospital.

If Huston's filming of the intake interviews was raw and unvarnished, his depiction of psychiatric practice was so credulous as to be misleading; he focused almost exclusively on the rare phenomenon of the quick fix. Huston chose to highlight improvements in what was then known as "battle neurosis" that were so instant and drastic they could actually be captured in a minute or two of film. In the picture, one patient with apparently intractable amnesia suddenly recovers his memory while under hypnosis. Another needs just one injection to regain his power of speech ("Oh God, I can talk! Listen, I can talk!"). Another, suffering from hysterical paralysis, abruptly stands up and moves around the room in a sodium-amytal-induced dream state immediately after a psychiatrist tells him, "You're gonna get right up and walk." (More persuasive are the scenes of "group therapy"—really lectures—in which two dozen patients at a time are told by an army psychiatrist, "You have nothing to hide, nothing to be ashamed of. Your time in the service has not been entirely wasted.")

Huston admitted that he highlighted only the most dramatic cases. "Certainly you can't expect to reach an original trauma, the original cause of neurosis, in six weeks' time," he said, "but I think it is fairly true that these men were put back into as good shape as they were when they came in [to the war]." He insisted that, contrary to their appearance, the miracle-cure scenes were not fabricated, and no evidence has ever turned up to contradict him; in contrast to *San Pietro*, this film begins with an onscreen title asserting that no scenes were staged.

After shooting was completed, Huston holed up in Astoria, working on the first cut of the movie. He was not averse to using Hollywood techniques, from dramatic crosscutting to an ominous, thrumming musical score, to make his points, and he ended the picture with a contrivance that was likely arranged for his benefit: a baseball game played on the grounds of Mason General in which the men he followed, now at the end of their treatment, are shown to have been transformed back into energetic, cooperative team members. When he was making *San Pietro*, Huston had been forbidden by the army to juxtapose images of dead American soldiers with voice-overs of them talking hopefully about their futures. But for the last scene of what he was now calling *Let There Be Light,* he revived and reversed the technique: As the patients were throwing strikes, catching fly balls, and rounding the bases, he overdubbed their inconsolable, timid initial intake interviews to emphasize how far they had come.

To please the army, Huston ended his picture with an image of healthy men looking forward to productive employment as civilians. Nowhere in the film is there any suggestion of untreatable problems, or even of the reality of fitful rather than immediate progress. But whatever he overemphasized, omitted, or exaggerated for effect, Huston finished his time at Mason General feeling that he had made an honest movie about a private hardship afflicting tens of thousands of veterans. He knew that he had done his job without either sweeping the plight of the mentally ill under the rug or exploiting it for shock value. And in doing so, he had finally started to regain his own bearings. "For some reason, to see a psyche torn asunder is more frightening than to see people who have physical wounds," he later said. His months of filming were "an extraordinary experience—almost a religious experience." He left Astoria believing that his third and final documentary for the army would send him back to civilian life on a high note.

On September 29, 1945, John Ford's time in the navy officially ended. He had served for four years and three weeks, longer than anyone else in Hollywood, and his final Officer Fitness report praised the "superb accomplishments" of Field Photo and cited his "outstanding ability, his devotion to duty, and"—somewhat unusually—"his loyalty to and love for his subordinates." Ford had been as good as his word; as soon as his leg had mended, he returned to Washington, D.C., where he spent his final weeks of active duty in communication with George Stevens. Stevens was still in Europe, traveling between London and Berlin and working hard to compile footage for *Nazi Concentration and Prison Camps* and *The Nazi Plan,* the two documentaries that were to be entered into evidence that fall at Nuremberg. Ford assigned the few remaining staffers in Field Photo to help him from Washington in any way they could; his division had over the years come into possession of a wealth of filmed Nazi propaganda and newsreels, and he had Robert Parrish search the navy's archives for images that could be used to demonstrate a long-standing pattern of intentional abuse in the camps over the last decade. He had any footage that might be of value flown to Europe, where Stevens quickly culled fourteen hours of film down to one.

Ford planned to fulfill his contractual commitment to Fox by shooting the western *My Darling Clementine* in early 1946. But when Zanuck offered him the chance to extend their relationship with what would have been the richest deal for any director in Hollywood—$600,000 per year to make movies for Fox—Ford said no. Like many directors and actors returning from the war, he was through with studio servitude. Just as Capra was doing, Ford would now work independently, choosing and producing his own movies and then selling them to studios, a move he had been considering even before Pearl Harbor. With former studio executive Merian Cooper, a longtime friend who had just come out of the air force, Ford made plans to form his own company.

As the Nuremberg trials neared, Ford hesitated one last time before leaving the war behind, and considered traveling to Germany to make a feature-length documentary about the proceedings. The pursuit of war criminals was a subject of increasingly intense public interest and was already being processed into entertainment. *The Stranger,* the suspense script that Huston had written pseudonymously a year earlier in which he presciently anticipated what he called an "Allied War Crimes Commission" and toyed with the idea that fleeing Nazis might try to hide in plain sight in America, was about to start shooting with Orson Welles as both director and star. But Ford ultimately decided not to attend the trials, feeling that a documentary might impede the normalization of relations between the United States and what would, in a few years, be known as West Germany.

Besides, Ford knew that any filmmaker's attempt at a documentary might be preempted by the work that his colleague was doing. Months after the end of the war, Stevens was still on active duty, and virtually single-minded in his purpose. He no longer considered himself "retired" from movies; that fall, while in Germany, he started to read, for the first time in twenty years, Theodore Dreiser's *An American Tragedy* and to make some notes about how it might be adapted as a film. It had been two and a half years since he had completed his last feature, *The More the Merrier*, for Columbia, and when Harry Cohn came to Paris, he asked Stevens to sit down with him at the Ritz Bar and talk about his plans. Stevens showed up unshaven and in a rumpled uniform.

"You're coming back to the studio," he recalled Cohn saying in a tone that was poised halfway between a question and an answer. Stevens felt caught off guard; he hadn't even thought about it. "He was seducing me by saying, 'You want to come to work? You want a job when you get out of that suit?' What could I say, no?" he recalled. "I guess I said yes. . . . I didn't say 'Of course'—that's more definite than I would be in such a situation. I said yes." Stevens still wasn't sure when he would get home, but once that day came, he knew he was unlikely to return to Columbia; Capra had recently approached him to become the third directorial partner in Liberty Films, and Stevens, who greatly respected both Capra and Wyler, had all but decided to join them. Cohn went back to Hollywood, and when he learned of Stevens's decision, it created "undying enmity" between the two men. Cohn was "the only guy ever to tell me I broke a contract," said Stevens, who regretted having misled him, even briefly, for the rest of his life. The notoriously unlikable studio czar, a man for whom Stevens had made movies only on the condition that he could never visit one of his sets during production, "was just being sweet," said the director. As a matter of conscience, he felt, "I should have come back [to] Columbia."

The Nuremberg trials began on November 20 in that city's Palace of Justice. Eight of the twenty-one defendants who would eventually be tried sat in the dock under a spotlight. There were four judges, one from each of the major Allied powers, and four chief prosecutors, with a score of lawyers assisting them; a team of defense attorneys, most of them German; a large staff of simultaneous translators; and a packed crowd of reporters and observers from around the world. After what was widely described as an electrifying opening by the chief American prosecutor, Justice Jackson, the trial seemed to meander through the next week, bogging down in procedural motions and prosecutorial housekeeping. Then, on November 29, the hall was darkened and Stevens's *Nazi Concentration and Prison Camps* was shown.

The movie began with two sworn affidavits of authenticity, the first signed by Stevens and the second signed by Field Photo acting head Ray Kellogg and witnessed by Ford. Then the images took over. "The impression we get is an endless river of white bodies flowing across the screen, bodies with ribs sticking out through the chests, with pipe-stem legs and battered skulls and eyeless faces and grotesque thin arms reaching for the sky," wrote one correspondent who was present that day. "On the screen there is no end to the bodies, tumbling bodies and bodies being shoved over cliffs into common graves and bodies pushed like dirt by giant bulldozers, and bodies that are not bodies at all but charred bits of bone and flesh lying upon a crematory grave."

Stevens had omitted nothing—from the vermin-infested bunkhouses to the thumbscrews to the gas chambers and ovens to the harvesting of gold from the teeth of the murdered to the lampshades made of human skin for the amusement of an officer's wife. During the screening, the spotlight illuminating the defendants' box had not been dimmed, and the journalists recorded every one of their reactions. Ribbentrop, Hitler's minister of foreign affairs, covered his eyes but would then drop his hands, unable to prevent himself from looking. Wilhelm Keitel, the head of the Wehrmacht, turned bright red and started to wipe his eyes with a handkerchief. Julius Streicher, publisher of *Der Stürmer*, leaned forward and nodded as if in endorsement. And Goering remained expressionless, staring straight at the screen and betraying his nerves only by wiping his sweaty palms again and again. After the film ended, Rudolf Hess started to speak. "I don't believe it," he said, but Goering immediately hushed him. The defendants were "shattered," said Telford Taylor, an army lawyer who was assisting Jackson. "Even for those who, like me, had had an earlier viewing, these pictures were hard to bear . . . the effect was stunning. Dr. [Victor] von der Lippe [a defense lawyer] recorded that the film would rob its viewers of sleep and that he heard one of the defense counsel say it had become intolerable to sit in the same room" with the men they were there to represent.

Two weeks later, Stevens's second evidentiary film, *The Nazi Plan*, was shown at the trial with narration that Budd Schulberg had written. It offered a history of German politics and aggression in two sections, the first covering the years 1921 to 1933, the second tracing Hitler's rise and his war crimes.

This time, the defendants, again spotlighted, reacted differently, bouncing their knees to the marching songs and appearing enthralled anew by the Nazi rallies, including those that had taken place in the very building that was now being used for their trial. As they watched Hitler speak at Zeppelin Field, Albert Speer beamed and Ribbentrop wept: "Couldn't you just feel the force of the Führer's personality?" he said that night. When the movie was finished, Goering turned to Hess in the box and said, "Justice Jackson will want to join the Party now!" But as the trial's spectators stared at them, aghast, their jubilation dissipated. That night, an army psychiatrist who had been assigned to monitor the mental state of the defendants reported that most were "despondent." Stevens's films had done what weeks of testimony had not: It had made their crimes irrefutable, and their fates inevitable.

Stevens did not attend the trials. His work was finished. At the end of the year, he cabled Yvonne that he planned to sail for New York on RMS *Queen Mary* and would be home soon. It was a moment, John Huston said later, "when hopes ran higher for the world than I've ever known them to before or since. And I know George had that high sense of the fate of the world. He thought, with all the rest of us, that everything was going to be all right afterwards."

TWENTY-EIGHT

"A Straight Face and a Painfully Maturing Mind"

HOLLYWOOD, NEW YORK, AND WASHINGTON, DECEMBER 1945–MARCH 1946

The war in the Pacific had been over for only four months when *They Were Expendable* started to open across the country, but time had already done its damage to the movie's prospects. In December, critics greeted John Ford's return to Hollywood filmmaking with respect that was tinged with a kind of detachment, as if they had been presented with a hand-crafted curio from the past. War movies, as a genre, were now outmoded; a movie about the beginning of the war that stopped in 1942 felt arbitrary and mistimed; and a drama that took as its subject the nobility of American failure and the necessity of honoring the greater good by obeying shortsighted orders seemed almost defiantly out of step with the appetites of a battle-weary audience that was, after so many years, bored with the whole subject. The few war movies that did succeed in 1945 were either action-packed chronicles of victory or escapist larks; the most popular sailor onscreen that year was Gene Kelly, a navy man without a care in the world, on joyous shore leave and dancing with Tom and Jerry in *Anchors Aweigh*.

MGM knew the movie faced a hard road; a long picture that ended with its two protagonists flying back to the United States, leaving their troops to face what everyone knew would be either death or capture in the Philippines, would be virtually impossible to market honestly. Ford had insisted that *They Were Expendable* end where it did, but MGM did demand a final title card—"We Shall Return"—as "The Battle Hymn of the Republic" played. In later years, Ford all but disowned the picture, telling the director Lindsay Anderson in 1950, "I just can't believe that film's any good. . . . I was ordered to do it. I wouldn't have done it at all if they hadn't agreed to make over my salary to the men in my unit." He also claimed that MGM "cut the only bits I liked," and contended that he "was horrified to make it. . . . I didn't put a goddamned thing into that picture." But in truth, Ford had closely supervised the movie's postproduction, even bringing his twenty-two-year-old daughter into the editing room as an apprentice, and the finished product was in almost every particular the picture he wanted it to be. He lost a few small battles—the cacophony of voices that the script had included questioning whether Pearl Harbor had caught the navy napping was omitted from the final cut, as was his and Wead's original idea for the final scene, in which Robert Montgomery's Brickley was to read out an angry roll call of the names of the "expendable" men who were staying behind. But Ford won most of the big victories, including over the film's length—*They Were Expendable* was released at a deliberately paced 135 minutes, a running time that even he admitted was a half hour longer than he had imagined when he shot the picture.

The promotional materials MGM released to the press were unflaggingly upbeat. Trade ads featured big pictures of a beaming Montgomery, Wayne, and costar Donna Reed with the words, "Big Smile! (Because they just finished a big picture)," and emphasized the fact that the film had been made by war heroes: "Robert Montgomery (don't you feel like shaking his hand and saying: 'Welcome home, Bob!') plays 'Brick.' He's in love with a couple of tons of wood and steel, a PT boat." Local newspapers were sent human interest featurettes with headlines like "Montgomery Role Parallel to Own Navy Experience" and "Veterans Given Priority for Extra Roles"; MGM also provided what it called "prepared reviews" which claimed that "the picture owes much of its distinction to the brilliant direction of Capt. John Ford, himself a veteran of Navy action."

Actual critics, though not dismissive, were somewhat more subdued in their praise; they admired *They Were Expendable*'s low-key style and its attempt at a kind of near-documentary realism in depicting the small details of navy life, but few were moved to passionate endorsement. "If this film had been released last year—or the year before—it would have been a ringing smash," Bosley Crowther wrote in the *New York Times*. "Now, with the war concluded and the burning thirst for vengeance somewhat cooled, it comes as a cinematic postscript to the martial heat and passion of the last four years . . . a moving remembrance of things past." *Time* magazine was more blunt, calling it "long and late" but expressing admiration for the fact that Ford's actors "always seem to be more like themselves—or at least more like human beings—than they are in any other picture." And *Variety* predicted that "regardless of any actual or supposed reaction against war films, this one is virtually certain to go over big."

That proved to be too optimistic. While grosses around the world were enough to cover the movie's $3 million budget, its performance fell short of both the studio's and Ford's hopes. For many moviegoers, *They Were Expendable* faded from memory quickly; in his initial review, James Agee called it "so beautiful and so real that I could not feel one foot of the film was wasted," even though for much of its length "all you have to watch is men getting on or off PT boats, and other men watching them do so." But just two weeks later, revisiting his feelings, he admitted that his ardor had cooled; he now found Ford's movie "visually beautiful, otherwise not very interesting" and compared it unfavorably to Huston's *San Pietro* as well as to another treatment of the campaign in Italy, the tough and dynamic picture that *Wings* director William Wellman had made out of *The Story of G.I. Joe*. MGM had touted *Expendable* as its "picture of the year," but when the Academy Award nominations were announced in February, for the first time in six years none of the Best Picture nominees was war-related, and Ford's movie was recognized only for its visual effects and its sound recording.

For Ford, an honorable defeat was, in a way, the apt coda to a journey through the war that had begun with a prescient commitment to service more than a year before Pearl Harbor and had ended with a drunken collapse on the coast of France. Although he would shortly resume a robust and prolific career behind the camera as a civilian, there was no avoiding the

fact that the years in Field Photo had drained him of some of the vigor that
had allowed him to make seven films in three years before the war. When he
had left Hollywood in 1941, his children Barbara and Pat were still teenag-
ers; four years later, he had come back to his family and their home on Odin
Street with hair that was going white, a bad eye, and ten missing teeth, a
grandfather of two who had earned the nickname that many of his colleagues
would use for the rest of his career, the "Old Man."

After his discharge, Ford found a kind of relief in being home with Mary.
The Hollywood Canteen, which had filled her time and satisfied her hearty
appetite for gossip and political machinations during the years of her husband's absence, had closed in November, having fulfilled its wartime mission to serve and hearten the troops. For the first long stretch in memory, the
Fords had time on their hands, and time for each other. But his transition into
domestic life, which had never been an area in which he excelled, was not
easy. He mourned the young men in Field Photo who had been killed in action and devoted himself to writing long and emotional letters to their parents
and survivors. He grieved to learn that Jack Mackenzie, the cameraman who
had served alongside him at Midway and whom Ford had sent to the Oscars
to collect the award for *December 7th* in his place, had come home safely only
to die at twenty-seven in a jeep accident on a Hollywood road not far from the
Fords' home. At times, he seemed to find his own record of service wanting
in comparison to those who had risked more than he had. Robert Parrish,
who had admired Ford while serving under him in Field Photo, pulled away
after the war; he felt that his mentor couldn't let go of the navy, and that his
founding of the Farm was part of a desire "to extend his OSS–U.S. Navy unit
into civilian life," to build a kind of fantasy barracks that could serve as a
sanctuary from women, responsibility, and sobriety.

Ford still yearned for commemoration—for the medals and honors and
recognitions that would tell him his time away had meant something. But by
degrees, he let go of the war by finding other ways to preserve his own experience of it. In 1946, he rejoined the Screen Directors Guild, volunteering to
serve on its Veterans Committee alongside Capra and Wyler. And later in the
year, when he heard from the Office of the Bureau of Archives in Washington
that it was short on space and might have to destroy all unused footage from

propaganda films made during the war, he intervened with a plea to protect just one movie—not his own, but Gregg Toland's long version of *December 7th,* which had never been shown publicly. "As this is the picture which some of my men risked their lives to make," he wrote to the bureau, "it has great value to us. We would like to preserve it for sentimental reasons at the Field Photo Memorial Home. . . . I sincerely hope this picture can be turned over to us." It was.

In his final Qualifications Questionnaire, a form that naval officers had to fill out annually, Ford attempted to summarize his own service for the first of what would be countless times over the next twenty-five years. He had, he noted, commanded as few as fifty and (one last time, he could not resist exaggerating) as many as a thousand men. "I was instrumental in establishing the procedure of naval & military photography during late war as head of field photo branch O.S.S.," he wrote. "The first combat film 'Battle of Midway' personally shot by me set the pace for all similar films." And he made it clear that, at fifty-one, he didn't yet feel his service had to be over. "More than anxious to return to active duty in case of an emergency," he wrote. "I am sure I would be of value to the effort with my knowledge of Motion Pictures."

On February 13, 1946, John Huston went to the army base at Fort Monmouth, New Jersey, and received his official notice of separation after forty-five months of service. He then drove straight to his tailor in Manhattan, where he picked up three suits that had been waiting for him. No filmmaker was happier to get out of uniform. Unlike Ford, Huston had no affection whatsoever for military trappings or hunger for decoration; he had hated army clothes from the first weeks he spent sweating through them in a Washington office, and after that day, he never wanted to put on the uniform again. When he changed into his new suit, it was, he wrote, "like dressing for a costume party."

For Huston, the discharge was largely a formality. Since finishing *Let There Be Light* at the end of the year, he had been living like a civilian in New York City, making the rounds of parties and nightclubs and looking ahead to the resumption of his career at Warner Bros. But before returning to Hollywood, he intended to see his last work for the army through to its general release. In January, the Museum of Modern Art had selected his film for inclusion in a large-scale festival of documentaries that was to unfold over the following six months; Huston had attended the cocktail party at which the planned April showing of his picture was announced. *Let There Be Light* was to be one of the museum's spotlight attractions that spring; it was already getting a good deal of attention from journalists who were treating it not as yet another piece of army propaganda but as a major new film by a celebrated young director that promised to explore a previously verboten subject. In the fall, stills from the movie had appeared in *Life* magazine, which used them to illustrate an article by John Hersey about mentally ill veterans.

On his first day as a civilian, Huston left New York for Washington to take care of a final army formality; he brought a print of *Let There Be Light* to the leadership of the Army Pictorial Service and the Bureau of Public Relations, which needed to screen the picture before it could be cleared for general release. A week later, the APS issued its approval.

But in early March, with no warning, that order was reversed. Huston was told that the film could be shown only to men in army psychiatric hospitals, Veterans Administration and navy facilities, and army libraries. The problem seemed easy to rectify: The musical score, which he had stitched together from various Hollywood movies, had been licensed for army use only, not for theatrical release. Huston was slightly taken aback by the news; he had already begun to shift his attention to the preparation of a screenplay for his next film, *The Treasure of the Sierra Madre,* and he hadn't planned on being pulled back into the miasma of army memos, rulings, and technicalities, but altering the score would be only a brief disruption.

Huston did not even have a chance to return to the editing room before the army came back at him with the news that *Let There Be Light* had more serious problems. The Pictorial Service had decided to reexamine the waivers that had been signed by the patients of Mason General allowing their images to be used and concluded that the permissions they had granted were only "in furtherance of the war effort. . . . Since the [war] is terminated," an army memo stated, "it is difficult to see how distribution of this film to the public at large or to groups other than military would be permissible." Moreover, a theatrical release would constitute "an invasion of the right of privacy" of the men who appeared in it.

Huston had won his tangles with the army over *Report from the Aleutians* and *San Pietro,* but this was different: He knew that *Let There Be Light* was now in real trouble, and the succession of unrelated pretexts he had been given signaled to him that one way or another, the military was going to find a way to suppress the movie. The only leverage he had was that a print of the film remained in his possession, and he immediately started to show *Let There Be Light* to colleagues in Hollywood in order to rally their support, telling them that "the Army Bureau of Public Relations (those old obstructionists) have, for some reason, given it a 'secret' classification" and that the only hope of reversing it would be to make the movie "a cause celeb like the 'A' bomb, Colonel Roosevelt's dog,* and Winnie's next speech." He also lobbied officials in the Truman administration whom he thought would be sympathetic, but when he appealed to William C. Menninger, the surgeon general, the response he received was discouraging. "I still feel that it is the best picture of psychiatry that I have ever seen," Menninger told him. "There are, however, some very grave questions about it. . . . Anyone with legal experience knows that a patient in a psychiatric hospital who signed . . . a release is going through the motions. The paper he signs is really worthless and I think it would necessitate a statement from each of these men after they had recovered and left the hospital." In addition, Menninger told Huston that unless the men in *Let There Be Light* agreed to the film's release after they had been shown the movie, the ban would have to stand.

The army almost immediately appropriated Menninger's argument, adding that it had examined its own records and could not even find signed consent forms from four of the patients in the film. Huston went back to the army's editing facility in Astoria on a hunt for the missing documents that he suspected would be fruitless, since he believed that the army had already made sure they could not be found. He was furious but virtually powerless:

---

* Elliott Roosevelt, the president's second son, had been the subject of several days of critical newspaper stories in 1945 when he had displaced three servicemen from an army plane so that he could ship a pair of dogs from London to his wife in California.

If privacy and competency were issues for the subjects of the film, he asked, why had the army commissioned him to make *Let There Be Light* in the first place? Why had the Bureau of Public Relations granted permission to both *Life* and *Harper's Bazaar* to use images from the movie in which the soldiers' faces were clear? And why had the question of missing consent forms been raised only after the army had tried two other grounds for objection?

Huston wrote back to Menninger arguing that the movie could "dispel prejudice on the part of the public against service men with a psycho-neurotic history" and that, having spent $150,000 on *Let There Be Light* already, the Signal Corps would do well to offer up a few thousand dollars more in order to obtain all necessary clearances. Menninger forwarded his appeal to the assistant secretary of war, but to no avail. In late April, shortly before a showing of the movie that Huston had arranged for friends and a couple of sympathetic journalists, military policemen arrived at the Museum of Modern Art and seized the print. The museum had no choice but to announce that *Let There Be Light* had been withdrawn from the documentary festival; it would be replaced by a British short called *Psychiatry in Action!*

Only a couple of critics had seen the film at that point; one was Archer Winsten, the movie reviewer and columnist for the *New York Post*. Huston telegrammed him with a plea to "raise your voice . . . shoot the works if you so desire," and Winsten obliged, reporting on the dramatic seizure of the print and excoriating those who wanted to suppress it: "The Army," he wrote, "having shrunk to its unleavened core of pre-war top executives, is re-embarking upon a do-nothing, say-nothing, think-nothing policy" at the expense of "so great a picture, so inspiring medically and humanly . . . that they just don't know what to do with it. . . . Seeing it, I felt as if I had never before witnessed emotion on a screen so stripped of extraneous self-consciousness." From there, James Agee took up the cry in *The Nation*, writing, "I don't know what is necessary to reverse this disgraceful decision, but if dynamite is required, then dynamite is indicated. . . . The glaring obvious reason [for the movie's suppression] has not yet been mentioned: that any sane human being who saw the film would join the armed services, if at all, with a straight face and a painfully maturing mind."

During the war, the Bureau of Public Relations and the Pictorial Service had been acutely sensitive to bad press. When Huston had gone to journalists with his fight to release a longer version of *Report from the Aleutians,* his brinksmanship had worked. This time, it did not. The army held fast. By the summer, Huston had exhausted his last hope for an appeal; the independent distributor with whom he had hoped to work tossed in the towel, telling the director he was tired of "the whole gruesome story of setbacks, slight gains and slashing defeats. . . . I am beaten." *Let There Be Light* would not be shown publicly for thirty-five years.

The experience left Huston with a profound feeling of skepticism and dejection about his years in the army. "In the Second World War I had as high hopes as anybody," he said. "It looked to me as if we were on our way to some kind of understanding of life." What he came to feel instead was that he had colluded in a lie. The army "wanted to maintain the 'warrior' myth," he wrote, "which said that our American soldiers went to war and came back all the stronger for the experience, standing tall and proud. . . . Only a few weaklings fell by the wayside. Everyone was a hero, and had medals and ribbons to prove it.

"That," he said, "was my most interesting experience with the government. It seemed to me to be a wonderfully hopeful and even inspiring film. . . . And the War Department felt it was too strong medicine. This is only my opinion. But it's the only opinion that stands up under scrutiny."

As the new year began, George Stevens opened a 1946 desk calendar and decided to keep a diary. What he wrote down, in the three weeks before he tossed it aside, was the bare-bones record of a man struggling to rediscover the contours of his former life. He noted the names of the people with whom he had lunch, and the titles of the movies that he saw and the books that he read, and how long it took to drive from one place to another, and what the food and the weather were like. He was home, returned at last to his wife, his son, and his house in Toluca Lake, and he was determined to make a fresh start, although his heart hardly seemed to be in anything he did. The Stevenses attended the Rose Bowl game in Pasadena and watched the Trojans fall to the Crimson Tide; they had dinner out most evenings, dining at the Beachcombers with his old friend Gene Solow or his agent Charles Feldman. Stevens felt that his prewar existence was somewhere waiting to be reclaimed by him, but when he tried to resume his old habits, he felt ungainly and ill at ease. When he played poker, he would gamble too much and lose too quickly. When he and Yvonne attended a party, he would get drunk and sometimes need to be driven home. In Europe during the war, Stevens had poured his feelings for his wife and son into dozens of letters home, but now that they were all back together, his marriage began to fall apart. In the first months of 1946, all he really wanted was to be left alone. He would sequester himself in a room with a pile of novels and spend the day reading, or he would leave the house first thing in the morning, go to his country club, and play eighteen holes, day after day, always by himself.

His friends and colleagues were solicitous and patient. Capra was now ready to launch Liberty Films publicly; Huston had turned down his invitation to become a partner, but Stevens had said yes, and a press conference was scheduled for late February at which the two of them and Wyler would tout Liberty as a new business model, the dawn of a golden era of creative autonomy for movie directors. All Stevens needed to do, Capra told him, was to find a project that would rekindle his excitement about making movies. He just had to roll up his sleeves and concentrate on something. In those first weeks, Capra would invite him over to his house and try to tempt him, first with lists of novels and then with scripts. He told Stevens about the movie with which he was planning to inaugurate Liberty, a Christmas-themed comedy-drama called *It's a Wonderful Life*, and showed him the screenplay, hoping to spark some enthusiasm. Stevens took the script home and a week later let Capra know apologetically that he just hadn't gotten around to reading it. He hadn't, in fact, gotten around to much of anything.

Yvonne Stevens began to worry. Before Stevens entered the war, they had bought a Lincoln Continental Cabriolet, "the small one, with the tire in the back," she recalled. "There were only three of them in town at the time." One day, she watched him sit behind the wheel "and he just started shaking," she said. "He couldn't get a hold of himself. Well, it was a long time away."

Capra knew that his friend was, for the time being, unreachable, held hostage by memories he felt he might never be able to shake. "The whole [war] became, for him, a kind of nightmare," he said, "a nightmare of the stupidity of man. He became hard to talk with because I don't think he wanted to express his real—or maybe he just couldn't—express the horror that he'd been through. It just grew on him. . . . He was not the same George Stevens."

Everyone seemed certain that he would eventually bounce back except for Stevens himself. They all imagined that work was the answer, that if he could just get back in the swing of things with the kind of charming adult comedy that had helped make his reputation, the images of Dachau and the boxcars that plagued him would recede and he could resume a career that had been on a steady upward trajectory until the war interrupted it. But Stevens felt hobbled, both literally—a taxicab had run over his foot in London and he was having some difficulty walking—and emotionally. He forced himself to get out of the house for social and professional engagements, but rather than draw him back into the industry, his encounters with colleagues only increased his sense of dislocation and alienation. Walter Wanger invited him out to his office at Universal, and David O. Selznick brought him and Capra to his lot in Culver City to show them scenes from the new picture he was producing, an epic Technicolor showcase for Jennifer Jones and Gregory Peck called *Duel in the Sun*. Stevens politely told Selznick how magnificent the picture looked, but he went home that night unsettled by the realization that three years away from the movie business had been an eternity. It had gone on without him. He had no idea who Gregory Peck and Jennifer Jones were; they certainly hadn't been stars when he left. And the new Hollywood movies he was seeing all felt to him, he later said, "not made from life, but made from old films . . . guided by what [the director] had *seen* in films, rather than what was going on at that time."

On occasion, Stevens sought out his old army life, looking for comfort. He went to an Academy screening of Wyler's air force short *Thunderbolt;* he arranged to have lunch with a couple of his old SPECOU buddies who were now out of the army and hoping that he could use his Hollywood clout to get them jobs; he went to a party for General Eaker that turned into an impromptu reunion of many of his former comrades in arms. When he dined at Romanoff's in Beverly Hills with Ivan Moffat, he put on his army uniform for the occasion. Walking into the restaurant was tantamount to making a major public appearance, since what seemed like half of Hollywood showed up there routinely for lunch. Alfred Hitchcock was at the next table and, seeing Stevens, gave him what Moffat described as "a ceremonious but at the same time negligent little bow" that stopped just short of an ironic salute. Jean Arthur, who had starred in Stevens's last two movies before the war, spotted him and embraced him with real warmth and affection. And an old colleague who had sat out the war strolled by their table and said, "Well, George, welcome home! When are you going to take that suit off?" Stevens glowered up at him and replied, "When are you going to put yours on?" He was "very bitter about the people who stayed home and made all the movies," said Yvonne. But whereas in Capra that very resentment fueled an intense desire to get back in the director's chair and prove his worth once again, Stevens withdrew further into himself with every prickly encounter. "He didn't look for a job at all," his wife said. "He just went out and played golf every day. I just couldn't understand it."

He refused to talk about the war, except obliquely. "He [was] so quiet," said Yvonne. "He couldn't express himself, really. He just kept it in and thought about it." On more than one occasion, he suggested that the only subject that could lure him back to a soundstage was World War II itself, claiming that "when I think I have the skill, I'm going to make a film about the war." But even that idea would quickly give way to a sense of futility. He was surprised and hurt that no offers to make a war picture came his way; the studios didn't see him as that sort of director, and they certainly weren't interested in the kind of story he might want to tell. "They tell me you can't make a film about the war. . . . Nobody wants to see it," he said. "Nobody wants to be disillusioned about the fun and games."

Stevens knew that soon he would have to at least feign a public gesture of returning to work as part of the announcement of Liberty Films. He didn't want to disappoint Capra or Wyler, who had invested their professional and financial futures in the fledgling company, and he also had a stake in its success, having paid a first installment of $100,000 to buy in as a partner who, like Wyler, would control 25 percent of the stock. (Capra, as the founder, controlled 32 percent; the remaining 18 percent belonged to Sam Briskin.) Capra was already hard at work on preproduction for *It's a Wonderful Life* and Wyler was amassing a list of projects that might serve as his inaugural feature for Liberty after he finished *The Best Years of Our Lives* for Goldwyn. Stevens was nowhere near as far along. "I wasn't ready," he said, "but because it was Frank and Willy, I went into it. And when I did go into it, that meant I went to the studio, [even though] I hadn't been home long enough to go to a studio."

Stevens leased office space for himself and moved tentatively toward making a movie with Ingrid Bergman, who, between *Casablanca* and *Gaslight*, had become the most important new Hollywood actress to emerge in the last few years. After the war ended, she told her friend Irene Selznick that she didn't care about money anymore; all she wanted was to work with the best directors in the world. Stevens was one of the five names on her list.* The director started developing a comedy script called *One Big Happy Family* for her, and took a train to New York City, intending to watch her perform in *Joan of Lorraine* on Broadway and then take her out to dinner to talk about their collaboration. But by the time he got to New York, he had decided that the project was awful. He brought her to a late supper at "21," told her that his work on the screenplay had been worthless, that the material was beneath an actress of her talent, and that he was dropping out. Bergman was crestfallen and confused; Stevens couldn't find the words to explain his change of heart to her. "I didn't quite know what had brought this reversal about," he said. "I had done my pictures before on the basis that the principal thing needed was just film, unexposed film, and the rest would follow." He wondered, not for the first time, if he would ever have the self-confidence to direct again. "There were many people who had come back from a long period away in the war and couldn't get going," he said. "Had circumstances changed and shut them out, or had they themselves become different? . . . Obviously something had changed." Stevens went back to Los Angeles and told Wyler and Capra that he had no idea when, or if, he would find a movie he wanted to make. "Being the men they were," he said, "they understood." And they still wanted him to be part of Liberty.

Stevens hoped, more than anything, to find a project that reflected his

* The others were Huston, Wyler, Billy Wilder, and Roberto Rossellini.

changed understanding of the world. "Our films should tell the truth and not pat us on the back," he said that year. Otherwise, he asked, "isn't there the slight chance that we might be revealing America as it is not? Would that be encouraging us in our own delusions about ourselves?"

Those who knew him begged him to forget the idea of making a statement and to simply try doing what he did best. Katharine Hepburn, a good friend and one of his greatest champions, told him he needed to return to comedy, a genre in which she believed his talents were unrivaled by any other director in Hollywood. But Stevens would never, for the rest of his career, direct anything but drama. "After the war," he said, "I don't think I was ever too hilarious again."

"I hated to see him leave comedy for the other stuff that came later on, the more serious stuff," said Capra. "None of us were the same after the war, but for him . . . The films that he took of Dachau, the ovens, and the big, big piles of bones that nobody could believe existed . . . He had seen too much."

"You can never be right after you've seen things like that," said Yvonne Stevens. "He was just shocked. He never got over it."

TWENTY-NINE

"Closer to What Is Going On in the World"

HOLLYWOOD, MAY 1946–FEBRUARY 1947

A change is in the making in Hollywood," Frank Capra announced in 1946, shortly after he started to shoot *It's a Wonderful Life*. "It might be termed a revolution. . . . Perhaps you'll leave your neighborhood theatre one evening and remark to your companion, 'Haven't we been seeing an unusual number of good pictures lately, different from the typical Hollywood product?' The reason behind this is [that] experienced filmmakers with records of achievement [are] willing to gamble their hard-earned savings to gain independence."

When Capra wrote those words in a *New York Times Magazine* article called "Breaking Hollywood's 'Pattern of Sameness,'" Liberty Films was not yet three months old. But as he returned to the director's chair after five years away, he wasted no time in appointing himself the spokesman for what he saw as an industry on the cusp of a historic metamorphosis. The war, he wrote, had caused American filmmakers to see the movies that studios had been turning out "through new eyes" and to recoil from the "machine-like treatment" that, he contended, made most pictures look and sound the same. "Many of the men who had been . . . producers, directors, scriptwriters returned from service with a firm resolve to remedy this," he said; the production companies they were now forming would give each of them the "freedom and liberty" to pursue "his own individual ideas on subject matter and material."

Capra was evangelizing for Liberty with an impresario's noisy flair; he even had the company issue a manifesto that included proclamations that "story value will have foremost precedence in production," "quality of product both from an artistic and an entertainment standpoint is to come first," and big budgets "will in no way be highlighted or exploited as an indication of . . . entertainment value." But self-promotion notwithstanding, Capra genuinely believed that, as filmmakers like Preston Sturges, Leo McCarey, and Robert Riskin joined the ranks of established independent producers like Goldwyn, Selznick, and Wanger, the balance of power would soon shift permanently away from studios and toward producers and directors. His taste for bold pronouncements, already in evidence before the war, expanded into high-flying pontification with the launch of his new venture. But when he was asked what, specifically, more independence would mean for his own movies, Capra retreated into aesthetic timidity. At a time when many of his fellow filmmakers, including his two new partners, were becoming outspoken advocates for increased candor and frankness in Hollywood movies and a more adult approach to storytelling, he flinched at anything that smacked of controversy. Over the past several years he had become so enthralled by the use of film as propaganda that in peacetime he was finding it hard to think of movies any other way. "There are just two things that are important," he told the *Los Angeles Times* in March. "One is to strengthen the individual's belief in himself, and the other, even more important right now, is to combat a modern trend toward atheism."

As he tried to recapture his position as an industry leader, Capra was, in his way, as shaky and unsure of himself as Stevens. Wyler recalled a get-together at which he had chatted with Capra, Ford, and Huston about their decision to leave their careers behind and go off to war; they all predicted anxiously that "if the war lasted more than a couple of years we'd be the gone-and-forgotten boys when we came back." But while Ford and Wyler seemed to be returning to their places in the movie business without worrying too much about where they stood, Capra had a difficult time ridding himself of his anxiety. He had been certain that his work during the war would only elevate his stature in Hollywood, and his reception when he returned had seemed to confirm that. He even planned to capitalize on the esteem in which his army work was held by using the image of the ringing Liberty Bell—with which he had ended all of his documentaries and *Why We Fight* episodes—as the logo for his new company.

But Hollywood's consciousness of what Capra had contributed to the war effort, and even its collective memory of who had served and who hadn't, now seemed to be receding with a rapidity that alarmed him and inflamed his sense of injustice. There were no more grand welcome-home parties to honor his achievements; the only real nod his colleagues gave to the completion of *Why We Fight* came in a letter from Academy president Jean Hersholt, reminding Capra that the plaque and trophy he had been awarded for *Prelude to War* was actually, because of wartime shortages, made of plaster, and explaining that "the Academy will replace your ersatz plaque with a gold statuette if you will bring the plaque to the Academy office." He felt underappreciated, and he began to bridle at every perceived slight. A handful of encounters with people in the industry whom he felt took a moment longer than they should have to recognize his face or register his name gnawed at him, and he couldn't quite manage to separate injuries to his ego from doubts about his ability. "It's frightening to go back to Hollywood after four years, wondering whether you've gone rusty or lost touch," he said.

His colleagues, including Wyler, had no hesitation about tackling social issues in their new movies. When Wyler talked about his reason for joining Capra and Stevens in Liberty, he said that he and his partners had all "participated in the major experience of our time, and . . . I believe it will have a healthy effect on our work. . . . I know George Stevens is not the same man for having seen the corpses of Dachau." Wyler argued that Liberty could serve as the corrective to an industry whose movies were "divorced from the main currents of our time" and did "not reflect the world in which we live." And he expressed his hope that he and other American directors would meet the challenge of the exciting new films that were now coming out of Britain and Europe, the work of David Lean, Vittorio De Sica, Roberto Rossellini, and other directors who had lived "through the war in a very real sense and . . . are closer to what is going on in the world than we are."

Capra took that creative boldness almost as an affront; he was dismissive of any emphasis on what he derided as "message films" or "think films." Without a war to focus his always scattershot politics, his quasi-populist ideology had become as muddled as it had been in the 1930s. Having served in Washington for four years, he was no longer inclined to turn congressmen or government officials into bad guys, but he had difficulty conceiving new movie villains, and he struggled to grasp the national mood. "How could you make a message picture with universal appeal?" he asked. "People are disillusioned. Statesmen's words are not worth much. Whom are the people going to believe?" In one breath, he would talk about the advent of a new freedom in Hollywood; in the next, he would directly contradict Wyler by arguing that the average American was less inclined to go to the movies to think, to be challenged, or to engage with the world than ever before. "People are numb after the catastrophic events of the past ten to fifteen years," he insisted. "I would not attempt to reach them mentally through a picture. . . . I would not know how to make a picture that would illuminate the bigger problems of today." Besides, he said, "no independent producer is big enough to lick" the system, and "even if he had ideals and ideas, he has to compromise them if he wants to stay in business."

His first instinct had been to retreat into the past. To inaugurate Liberty, he wanted to remake a horse-racing comedy he had shot for Columbia in 1934 called *Broadway Bill*. It was only when the studio wouldn't sell him the rights that he settled on *It's a Wonderful Life*. He defined the choice as a "compromise," one that came to him at a moment when his anger and fear were at their peak. He would make a movie "about a small town guy who thinks he is a failure and wishes he had never been born." When he pitched *It's a Wonderful Life* to Jimmy Stewart, he told the story so poorly that the actor's agent, Lew Wasserman, sat in the office "dying" until Capra finally spluttered, "This story doesn't tell very well, does it?" "Frank," Stewart replied, "if you want to do a movie about me committing suicide, with an angel with no wings named Clarence, I'm your boy."

He had found the bare bones of *It's a Wonderful Life* in a short story reminiscent of *A Christmas Carol* called "The Greatest Gift," which was

written in 1939, sold to the movies in 1944 after its author, Philip Van Doren
Stern, had had it printed as a gift booklet, and finally published by *Good
Housekeeping* in early 1945 under the title "The Man Who Was Never Born."
Capra saw the brief parable as a means to explore the idea that faith in a
benevolent guiding hand could encourage someone to look at his life from a
different perspective, and thus help to combat a kind of plunging depression
that he called "discouragement" about one's value in the world. But in developing the script, he chewed through one writer after another trying to achieve
the alternately light and melodramatic tone he had always found most appealing. Clifford Odets came and went; so did Dalton Trumbo (who turned
the film's main character, George Bailey, into a failed politician in an adaptation that felt too close to *Mr. Smith Goes to Washington* and *Meet John
Doe*), Jo Swerling, and *Green Pastures* author Marc Connelly. Finally, Capra
brought in Frances Goodrich and her husband, Albert Hackett, and told
them to discard all previous drafts and start from scratch. The Hacketts,
both veteran screenwriters, had willingly worked on propaganda films for
Capra during the war, but they counted their time on *It's a Wonderful Life* as
the unhappiest of their long careers. After a while, the director, whom they
called a "horrid man" and "an arrogant son of a bitch," dropped them and
decided to rewrite the picture himself.

It's a Wonderful Life was the only major film on which Capra ever received a screenplay credit (alongside Goodrich and Hackett), and the final
version of the movie is a remarkably naked rendering of its director's state of
mind at the time. His conviction that after the war moviegoers were yearning
to retreat into nostalgia and fantasy is evident in the Currier-and-Ives-style
sketches that begin the movie. His still fresh experience as a propagandist
echoes faintly in his unusually heavy use of narration and, despite his de-
murrals, in the explicit, repeated articulation of a message. And his reliance
on the work of the men who had written his most successful movies in the
1930s is evident in what he cribs from his earlier hits—the pious veneration
of small-town life, the distrust of a set of friends and neighbors who can easily turn into a hateful mob, and the depiction of the nervous hysteria to which
hopelessness can drive a man. Capra stayed true to his desire to make a

movie about "the individual's belief in himself," but he connected it to the issue that was then troubling him the most—his intense need to be appreciated by others. In an earlier draft by Connolly, the "alternate" life that George and the angel Clarence visit is one that includes a second George who is alive and well but lacks the real George's good character. In the version that Capra chose to pursue, George instead watches what would happen in his world if he had never existed at all, and sees it quickly fall to ruin. For Capra, who was returning to an industry that he felt had recently erased him from its history, a what-if story about a man's feelings of inconsequentiality and his dark fears of nonexistence felt autobiographical. *It's a Wonderful Life* was a project driven by fears, desires, and wounds that he could no longer keep private.

It was also a considerably larger gamble than he had ever meant it to be. The ever-changing roster of writers, the three cinematographers Capra went through, and the long shooting schedule drove the picture's costs skyward. By June 30, 1946, Liberty had already spent almost $2 million on *It's a Wonderful Life*—including a hefty $163,000 salary for its director—and it was still weeks away from the end of production. The expenditure put considerable pressure on the new company, and on Capra's partners. In late 1945, Capra and Sam Briskin had completed a deal with RKO in which the studio agreed to distribute Liberty's first nine pictures—three apiece from Capra, Wyler, and Stevens—over the next six years. The company had been structured so that, as Wyler explained it, "majority rules for story ideas and budgets. After that each of us is autonomous. We'll each have the advantage of the other's advice all through the making and assembling of the pictures. But the man in charge won't have to take that advice. It will be his picture." Neither Wyler nor Stevens felt any particular kinship with the material Capra had chosen, but they were supportive, even when they had to swallow hard. "Jesus Christ, I never signed so many goddamn checks in my life!" Stevens complained as Capra's production became more and more elaborate. "I was getting to realize, you know, why Harry Cohn is Harry Cohn, because I hate to see all this money . . . he's putting snow scenes in! Why the hell couldn't it be springtime?"

Wyler kept more of a distance from *It's a Wonderful Life*. By the beginning of 1946, he was fully immersed in what would become the most personal film he ever made. As the screenplay of *The Best Years of Our Lives* continued to take shape, he and Sherwood reached an important decision: The character of Homer would no longer suffer from spasticity. Goldwyn had earmarked the role for the promising young actor Farley Granger, but Wyler believed that the facial contortions, impaired speech, and uncontrolled movements the part would require were unplayable and perhaps undirectable. Instead, he had Sherwood rewrite the character as a young man who had lost his arms during the war—and he decided that they would find an actual amputee to play him. Their wary producer was sure that casting the role wouldn't be possible; Goldwyn had once famously told Wyler, "You can't have a Jew playing a Jew, it wouldn't work on screen," and he urged them to abandon their search and simply drop the idea of depicting a disabled character or using a disabled actor. And when Wyler began visiting veterans' hospitals, the patients he met were just as skeptical. "So you're gonna make a movie about fellows like us," one GI sneered. "You're gonna make a lot of money."

Wyler finally found his Homer not in a hospital but at the movies. One of the last films the Army Pictorial Service had produced during the war was a twenty-two-minute short called *Diary of a Sergeant,* a documentary about a thirty-year-old soldier from Cambridge, Massachusetts, named Harold Russell whose hands had been blown off in a training accident on June 6, 1944. "I got [my injury] on D-Day, all right, but it was in North Carolina when a half a pound of TNT exploded ahead of schedule," he said. "I didn't have a German scalp hanging from my belt, I didn't have a Purple Heart. I didn't even have an overseas ribbon. All I had was no hands." *Diary of a Sergeant* begins with a reenactment of Russell being wheeled into surgery, then recreates the two months of rehabilitation that followed, during which he was trained in the use of the prosthetic hooks that replaced his lower arms, and was eventually discharged. The film had been intended to spotlight the quality of care received by injured veterans and the pension and educational allowance they were given upon their release. Russell was never even identified by name, and, probably because he had a distinctive, high-pitched New England accent that didn't sound quite all-American enough for army propagandists, he was never heard in the movie either; his first-person narration was spoken by the deep-voiced actor Alfred Drake. But his sweet demeanor, and his understated recreation of his own nervousness for a scene in which he prepares to go out on a date, convinced Wyler to fly the young man from Cambridge, where he was studying at Boston University and working in a YMCA, to Los Angeles. Over lunch at the Brown Derby, Wyler told Russell the part was his.

It would not be easy. Russell had no acting experience at all, and Wyler, who had long preferred to cast smart, flinty stars like Bette Davis with whom he could speak in a kind of abrupt, impatient shorthand, said candidly that it was "difficult" and "painful" to extract a performance from him. "I didn't try to teach him to act," he said. "I concentrated on guiding his thinking more than his actions, because I reasoned that if he was thinking along the right lines, he just couldn't do anything wrong. . . ." "It was more work. . . . I had to treat him a little better than I do professional actors . . . but this boy had this one thing: He understood the character because he'd gone through it himself. I didn't have to explain to him how it felt to lose your hands."

For the first time in his career, Wyler became obsessed with realism, considering every creative decision he made on *The Best Years of Our Lives* not simply in terms of its narrative effect but also its accuracy and truthfulness. He was still embarrassed by his own, belated realization that he had gotten some of the details wrong in *Mrs. Miniver*, and as he prepared to shoot his new movie, he imagined an audience of millions of returning veterans and tried to see any potential Hollywood-style evasion or falseness through their eyes. Two years earlier, Selznick's popular *Since You Went Away* had attempted to dramatize the long separation of husbands and wives and the uneasy prospect of a return to civilian life for what one character cynically called "all these irresponsible forty-year-old fathers dashing off into uniform." But back then the war was still on, and Selznick had avoided any unhappy realities, turning the picture into a tribute to what he called "that unconquerable fortress, the American home." His film was full of exactly the kind of bromides and easy answers that Wyler was determined to avoid. "We had to be honest in . . . the three stories," he said. "We could not indicate any solution to a problem which would work only for a character in a movie." He and Sherwood had cleverly positioned their three protagonists to appeal to the widest possible range of servicemen. Al was a regular army sergeant, Fred was an officer in the Air Corps, and Homer was a sailor; Al was well-to-do, Homer was middle-class, and Fred was from the wrong side of the tracks. But across that range, Wyler felt that everything had to be true to his own experience or to the lives of the men he had known in the service.

Wyler had not made a movie about contemporary American life since *Dead End* a decade earlier, and his desire for verisimilitude extended even to the look of the sets—he told his production designer he didn't want his characters to live in the high-ceilinged, gorgeously appointed homes that were often a default choice in studio movies. He also broke with studio tradition when it came to costumes: Before he began production, he gave Myrna Loy and Teresa Wright, who were playing Al's wife and daughter, modest stipends and told them to go to a local department store and buy their characters' wardrobes off the rack, an unusual decision in an era in which leading ladies almost always had a series of gowns designed for them. Loy and Wright didn't hesitate, nor did they flinch when Wyler told them that because he wanted them to look ordinary, they would be wearing far less makeup and powder than they had in other movies.

Unlike Ford, Wyler didn't attempt to stock the cast and crew of his first postwar picture with actual veterans. But he did tell Dana Andrews, who was cast as Fred, and Fredric March, who was to play Al, that they needed to look the parts. In particular, March, who was nearing fifty and had acquired the bloat of a prosperous and well-fed middle age, got a gentle talking-to before filming began. "It's very important that your figure suggest a K-ration diet rather than the '21' Club," Wyler warned him. "You should make every effort to be as trim and wiry as possible. . . . I know it's not easy for fellows our age. I've gained twenty pounds since coming back. . . . But the entire approach to this picture will be along realistic lines. . . . I would hate to have something like the proverbial little 'pouch' spoil the illusion."

Wyler was just as tough on himself. "I have always tried to direct my pictures out of my own feelings," he wrote in an essay about the making of *Best Years*. "I have tried to make them 'by hand,' and it has been hard work." As production neared, he struggled to be faithful both to his own instincts about psychological and pictorial accuracy and to a statement made by the American Veterans Committee that "the veteran could not be isolated from the main body of the nation, for his problems were also national problems." Wyler intended *Best Years* to be both a personal drama and exactly the kind of "message film" that Capra found so distasteful; even the most casual scene between husband and wife would need to reach for a kind of recognizability that he felt other movies had too long avoided. So he was not surprised when, as soon as Joseph Breen saw the script, the Production Code office announced its trepidation. In March, Wyler received a list of requests for changes that ran to eight single-spaced pages. Among them, Breen insisted that Al and his wife would have to sleep in twin beds, that moments depicting "the sacred intimacies of married life" would need to be toned down, and that a comic scene in which a puppy urinates on the floor from excitement was an unacceptable gateway to further vulgarity. ("You pass stuff like that," said Breen, "and the next thing you know, you have a scene of a dapper young fellow in Paris standing at a pissoir, leaking away with a smile on his face.")

Most significantly, Breen took issue with the scene that had grown out of Wyler's own intemperate encounter with an anti-Semitic doorman, in which Fred throws a punch after he hears a man at a drugstore lunch counter complain that the Roosevelt administration had duped Americans into supporting the war. As written by Sherwood, the scene was a pungent condemnation of the last vestiges of American isolationism. "The Japs and the Germans had nothing against us," the man at the counter insisted. "They just wanted to fight the limeys and the Reds—and they'd have whipped them too, if we hadn't got deceived into it by a bunch of radicals and Jew-lovers in Washington." Breen, whose own anti-Semitism was hardly a secret within the industry, insisted that the words "Jew-lover" be taken out. Wyler knew he had to comply, but before the movie opened he became the most prominent director in Hollywood to attack Breen publicly, telling the *New York Times* that his experience dealing with Code restrictions on *Best Years* "convince[d] me that those people have no real judgment."

Days before the start of shooting in April, Wyler had received a lovely and unexpected note of reconciliation from Bette Davis, with whom he had not spoken since their falling-out after *The Little Foxes* five years earlier. "The war should be over between us," Davis wrote to him. "It is so long ago, and so much has happened in the meantime. It seems sort of unimportant, the only important thing being, we should be friends. We should work together again. . . . It will always be for me the only right direction—yours." The vote of confidence arrived at the right moment. He and Capra started shooting their movies at almost the same time, and Wyler was tightly wound; there was a genuine sense of competition beneath the surface of the jesting telegrams they exchanged, with Wyler cabling Capra, "Last one in is a rotten egg," and Capra writing back, "My first day was easy but do you know they're using sound today?"

Wyler still wasn't sure he could direct at all; he remained almost completely deaf, and didn't know if he would be able to hear the actors or pick up on the subtleties that differentiated each take from the last. In a rare show of anger, he lost his temper with Russell when the anxious novice confessed that in preparation for his role he had secretly been taking acting lessons. "I didn't hire an actor!" Wyler told him. "I hired a guy to play a role." He also had to contend with Dana Andrews's alcoholism—one morning, realizing that the actor was hungover, he exacted his punishment by making him do twenty-five takes of a scene in which he banged his head on the frame of a taxicab door. And early on it was clear that Fredric March's insecurity and vanity would cause its share of problems as well: "When I say my lines, keep those goddamn hooks down!" the older actor snapped at Russell during the filming of a comradely scene set in a local bar. "Don't lift that bottle. I want people listening to what I'm saying, not watching you drink beer."

To make matters more difficult, Sherwood, who had struggled with his self-doubt at every stage of the writing process, had fled to New York before the cameras rolled. On April 9, just six days before the scheduled first day of filming, he told Wyler that the final 220-page script he had submitted was nowhere near ready and that the project would have to be postponed. The exhausted director, whose third child, a boy named William Jr., had been born just a week earlier, did not at that moment have the time or the patience to calm his collaborator, and so Sherwood hunkered down on the East Coast, unwilling to come to California and watch the production of a movie he had suddenly decided he didn't want made.

Goldwyn responded to the writer's absence by showing up on the set in a meddlesome mood and insisting that Wyler treat the script as finished and inviolable. "When I come to a set, I've studied the scene and I have a vague idea of how I want to play it," Wyler said. "But I haven't mapped it out exactly. . . . Before I can make up my mind definitely, I've got to see the actors doing it." Goldwyn would have none of it. "I am writing you in order that there will be no mistake or misunderstanding," he scolded his director on what would be their final collaboration. "Before you started shooting . . . I told you that there were to be no changes made in the script without discussing them in advance . . . even dialogue which may have been in one of the earlier versions. . . . I do not want something that Bob Sherwood had once discarded to be revived and used in this picture without our first carefully considering and discussing it."

Wyler badly wanted Sherwood to make the trip to Los Angeles and at least watch the dailies, in part because he thought the footage he was shooting was good and might soothe the nervous writer for long enough to get some essential final revisions out of him. One crucial scene remained unwritten—neither Sherwood nor Wyler had been able to figure out how to stage the moment that was to serve as the emotional conclusion of Fred's storyline, in which the despondent former pilot, while wandering through an airfield of now useless fighter planes, has a kind of emotional collapse while flashing back to the trauma of aerial combat. It was a moment close to Wyler's heart, one that he had wanted to dramatize since his time in the *Memphis Belle*, and the resolution of a kind of cliffhanger—an answer to the question of why Fred was so troubled that by then would have been consuming the audience for more than two hours. "I want to make one last effort to sell you the idea of coming here for a few days," he wrote to Sherwood. "Naturally I will do everything I can with the scene in the B-17 but frankly I am terribly worried that the last part of the picture may be a let down. A third act means the same to a picture as it does to a play. Sorry to sound a little desperate," he concluded, "but perhaps we are not completely clear on your ideas and you know that telegrams and telephones are no substitute for talking things over."

Wyler's most essential and trusted collaborator during the making of *The Best Years of Our Lives* turned out to be his cinematographer. For the fifth time, he was working with Gregg Toland, whose own military service had ended and who understood the stripped-down, unshowy style that Wyler wanted to use to tell his story. It was Toland who helped Wyler come with up a kind of jerry-rigged hearing aid that allowed him to make the movie in the first place; the director discovered that by sitting beneath the camera with a large set of headphones that were connected to an amplifier, he could hear the actors well enough to judge their performances. As they began their first working partnership since *The Little Foxes,* Wyler found himself grateful for Toland's stated willingness to "sacrifice photography any time if it means a better scene." And as Toland watched Wyler work, he felt he was witnessing a new level of creativity and integrity in the director. "He used to go overboard on camera movement," Toland said, "but he came back [from the war] with, I think, a better perspective on what wasn't important. . . . I think *Best Years* was well photographed because the photography helped to tell the story. It wasn't breathtaking. It would have been wrong to strive for effects. We were after simple reproduction of the scenes played without any chi-chi. . . . If I had to label the photographic style of the picture, I'd call it 'honest.'"

Toland created that style by making extensive use of deep focus, which he had brought into the cinematic mainstream when shooting *Citizen Kane;* the technique allowed moviegoers to take in different expressions, gestures, and moods within different planes of a single frame. He encouraged Wyler to film unbroken shots that sometimes lasted more than two minutes, and to eschew gratuitous camera movements and fast cross-cutting. And although Wyler still indulged his penchant for filming twenty or thirty takes of a scene, uncharacteristically he would allow his cast to play out the entire sequence without interruption several times. "I shot most of the scenes through from beginning to end," he said, "and by letting the camera turn with the actors, it caught their actions and reactions. In that way, the players did their own cutting." Wyler also kept close-ups to a minimum, using them only when he wanted "to make a point by excluding everything else from the audience's view."

As production continued, his confidence grew. When he arrived on the set every morning, he said, "I knew these [characters], had shared a good many of their experiences. . . . It was no problem to imagine what they would do in a situation because I already knew it in my heart." That assurance made him more patient with his actors, who rose to meet his perfectionism and admired his insistence that "whatever extra trouble was necessary to make a scene right, or better, was worth it. Often, toward the end of a day, when people wanted to get home to their wives and children, I could sense a resentment. . . . I knew I was not making myself popular. . . . But I also knew that if I kept working on the scene, it would be a better scene."

He was demanding with the cast, but rarely brusque. When he asked for multiple takes, Loy came to feel that it was because he "suspects some wonderful new thing is going to happen, and it usually does." He made Russell endlessly redo a scene, early in the film, in which he looks through the window of a transport plane that is carrying the three men back to their hometown. Wyler watched him become uncomfortable and actorish around take ten, then begin to improve in takes thirteen and fourteen, and finally allow a natural, believable set of mixed emotions to flicker across his features in take twenty. "I hated that—we all liked him so much and acting wasn't his business," Wyler said. But, he added, "I think there's a lot in that shot. . . . Often a slight movement or the way a word is said makes the difference whether the audience will cry."

It had been almost a year since the war had ended, but as Wyler shot the movie, his own emotions about his time away and return home remained raw, even as he was weaving them into the lives of his characters. He told Toland about when he had come back to New York on leave and gotten his first glimpse of Talli from a distance, down the long hallway of the Plaza Hotel, and Toland turned it into one of the picture's most famous shots, in which Al steps through his front door for the first time in years and sees Milly at the other end of their apartment as she emerges from the kitchen. He took his fear that his hearing loss might destroy his marriage and translated it into the achingly intimate sequence in which Homer, sure that his young fiancée will flee, invites her into his bedroom to watch him remove his hooks and harness for the night as he changes into his pajamas. "This is when I know I'm helpless," he tells his girl as he shows her the stumps of his arms, a scene that was so utterly without precedent that Wyler worried the Production Code would seek to prevent the movie's release. Aware that many of his colleagues had struggled with alcoholism and emotional problems both during and after their military service, he showed Homer giving in to sudden flashes of anger, and Al and Fred trying to anesthetize themselves by drinking too much. Even the wounded pride that he and his fellow directors had felt upon their return to a Hollywood that had thrived without them became fodder for the film, in a scene in which Fred is rudely rebuffed by the drugstore that used to employ him and has to accept a demotion and salary cut, a sequence that directly indicts healthy American businesses for their indifference to veterans. And he was perfectly attuned to the national mood when he worked to capture something that he had felt since losing his hearing and coming home—a sense of disorientation at the speed with which the world had changed. "Last year it was kill Japs, and this year it's make money," says Al. "Why don't they give a fella time to adjust?"

With just a few weeks of filming left, the question of what to do in Fred's final scene remained unsolved. At the end of *The Best Years of Our Lives,* Wyler wanted his main characters to have overcome their difficulties with enough success so that they could move forward in postwar America. Al would go back to his bank job, but he would channel his frustration at the mistreatment of returning servicemen into a new position in which he could provide small-business loans to veterans. Homer would draw strength from the support of his parents and understanding girlfriend, and his wedding ceremony would be the scene of joy and reconciliation that would end the movie. But Fred's story remained a problem. His marriage had disintegrated; his parents were indifferent; he had been a high-flying hero in the air force, but at home he lacked a direction or any professional prospects. The story Wyler and Sherwood wanted to tell in *The Best Years of Our Lives* was not about the end of the war, but about the end of its aftermath—the moment at which, sometimes with resignation, sometimes with renewed hope, and often with uncertainty, the men of World War II would begin to live in a world that was no longer defined by their military service. They would have to write their own futures.

And Wyler would have to write Fred's. Although Sherwood was supportive, he told the director that he could not finish the scene in which Fred comes upon a B-17 bomber and begins to purge himself of the tormenting memory of his years at war before realizing that he has to start from scratch and build a new life. "I know just what we want to say," he told Wyler, "but it isn't to be said in words—it must be said with the camera, and that's your business." Sherwood had come up with the idea of placing Fred in a field full of discarded planes that were destined to become scrap metal, which Wyler understood as "an outer manifestation of [Fred's] feelings about himself." But beyond that, Wyler would need to find a way to demonstrate that "in order to win his personal battles as a civilian, it was necessary to apply the same courage and strength of character that he and twelve million others applied to win the war."

Wyler thought back to his own time in the air, flying over Germany in the *Memphis Belle,* and also about his time in a Hollywood studio, recreating the buzz of the bomber intercom and the growl of the engines for his documentary; he also thought about his time shooting aerial images over Italy, the last moment of his life in which he could hear. What came back to him were not images, but sounds. He never wrote out the climactic scene he ended up shooting; instead, he, Toland, Andrews, and the crew drove out to the airfield they had rented in Ontario, California, and began to film. Wyler had Andrews wander through what felt like an otherworldly graveyard of planes from which the engines had been removed and then clamber into the bombardier's nest of one of them. He wanted to have Fred "lose himself in the dream, or rather in hallucination." Toland shot Fred appearing to sweat himself into sickness as he sat in the plane and mimicked the motions of dropping a bomb. The camera became increasingly frantic, pushing toward Andrews until it was up against the scratched, smeary Plexiglas of the windshield, then swooping under the grounded bomber as if to capture it in flight, then coming up on the actor again from the back as he crouched in the B-17's nose. But it was not until the movie wrapped that Wyler would "write" the rest of the scene. In the editing room, he layered the soundtrack first with an urgent and almost menacing musical score, then with the hum of a single plane's motor starting—a noise that George Bailey, in a line from Capra's *It's a Wonderful Life* script, calls "one of the three most exciting sounds in the world." Wyler added another motor, and another, creating a nightmarish vibrating roar of planes readying for their bombing runs, and building it to a crescendo that was not only maddening but, intentionally, deafening.

And then he switched it off. For Wyler, the excitement, the adrenaline, and the emotional and physical trauma of the war years would end with a brief exchange between a panic-stricken Fred and a calm airfield mechanic who comes upon him and tells him to get out of the plane.

"Reviving old memories?" he asks.

"Maybe getting some of them out of my system," says Fred.

It was an accident of scheduling that at the end of 1946, Capra and Wyler's diametrically opposed visions of what a postwar Hollywood movie should look like ended up in a head-to-head competition for audiences, acclaim, and prizes. *The Best Years of Our Lives* was originally scheduled for release in mid-1947; Wyler's first cut of the movie was 172 minutes, and Goldwyn worried that audiences wouldn't sit still for it. After a wildly successful test screening in Long Beach, Wyler persuaded him to open the film before December 31 in order to qualify for that year's Academy Awards. Goldwyn booked the picture for an exclusive reserved-ticket run in New York City at Thanksgiving, and began to sell the film as a story "with something important to say . . . that reflect[s] these disturbing times in which we live."

Goldwyn thought he had the field to himself; RKO had always planned to open *It's a Wonderful Life* in January, just after the Oscar deadline. But when one of its big Christmas movies was delayed, the studio decided to release Capra's film in December instead. Moviegoers had an unusually clear choice: Wyler's new realism or Capra's old-fashioned sentiment; a vision of a world in which the war could finally be left behind, or a dream of a world in which war might have been nothing more than a terrible waking nightmare. More than they ever had, or ever would again, both men had put their lives onscreen.

For reviewers, it wasn't much of a contest. Praise for *The Best Years of Our Lives* was fervent and unanimous, with many critics heralding the arrival of a maturity and seriousness in Wyler's work that they believed signaled exactly the new era for American movies that Capra had promised. "William Wyler has always seemed to me an exceedingly sincere and good director; he now seems one of the few great ones," James Agee wrote. "He has come back from the war with a style of great purity, directness, and warmth, about as cleanly devoid of mannerism, haste, superfluous motion, aesthetic or emotional overreaching, as any I know." The *New York Times* called it the year's best movie, "not only . . . superlative entertainment but . . . food for quiet and humanizing thought" that "catches the drama of veterans returning home . . . as no film, or play or novel we've yet heard of has managed to do." Praise rang out from congressmen and generals, on editorial pages, and from Wyler's fellow filmmakers, with Billy Wilder, the most recent winner of the Academy Award for Best Director, calling it "the best-directed film I've ever seen in my life."

The response to *It's a Wonderful Life* was more muted. While some critics were delighted and moved—the *Hollywood Reporter* called it "the greatest of all Capra pictures, and in saying that, one must mean one of the greatest pictures of this or any other year"—just as many were left cold. The *New Republic* derided the film for the "hysterical pitch" of its "moralizing," the *New York Times* called it quaint and sentimental, and *Variety* noted that, despite its "oldtime craft," Capra had not "taken the stride forward in filmmaking technique" that many of his colleagues had.

When the Academy Award nominations were announced, both movies were in contention: *The Best Years of Our Lives* was up for eight Oscars and *It's a Wonderful Life* for five. But there was little suspense about the outcome. In a ceremony at the Shrine Auditorium on March 13, 1947, Wyler's film swept the board, beating Capra's for Best Picture, Director, and Actor. Robert Sherwood's screenplay also won, and Russell took home Best Supporting Actor, as well as an honorary Oscar.

It's A Wonderful Life went home empty-handed, a disappointment that was only underscored by the swift and stark verdict of the moviegoing public. As *Best Years* continued around the country, theaters were packed; the film became essential viewing and the occasion for an extended national examination of America's obligations to the men who had served in World War II. By the end of its run, it was the second-highest-grossing movie in history. But postwar audiences had little fondness for *It's a Wonderful Life*. "Frank, I'm worried," Capra's partner Briskin wrote in a cable. "Just our luck if the gravy train slows down now."

The movie's failure at the box office proved to be fatal for Liberty Films. Capra had gone almost 50 percent over his $2 million budget, and staked far too much of his fledgling company's capital on *It's a Wonderful Life*'s success. By Oscar night, he, Stevens and Wyler were already struggling to refinance their company by agreeing to cut their weekly salaries by two-thirds and committing to make five pictures each for Liberty instead of three. Their gambit failed; within a year, Capra would reluctantly sell Liberty to Paramount Pictures, where all three directors would henceforth be tied to the kind of long-term studio contracts they had hoped never to sign again. Liberty, said Capra, had turned out to be "the most gentlemanly way of going broke, and the fastest way, anybody ever thought of."

Capra was devastated by the collapse of Liberty and, with it, a dream of independence he had had since before the war. But Stevens, who was still not ready to make a picture, was glad to be relieved of what was becoming considerable financial pressure, and Wyler's disappointment was only mild. "It was a good idea," he said. "It didn't work out." Wyler spent little time mourning its demise; instead, for the first time in many years, he looked to the future. With the success of *The Best Years of Our Lives*, his war, and his homecoming, were over. He never complained about what his years in combat had cost him; he spoke only of how enriched he felt. He had gone into the war as a respected technical perfectionist; he had come out, he said, interested only in making movies that reflected his deeper understanding of human yearning and vulnerability. "This is the kind of picture I couldn't possibly have done with conviction if I had not been in the war myself," he had said just before *Best Years* opened. He was frank about how much of an effort the production had been, but he explained with great passion a belief that he would hold to for the rest of his career—that without serious struggle, filmmaking was pointless.

"Somebody should be on fire about any picture made, or it shouldn't be made. If somebody doesn't feel that certain thing, the miracle never happens," he said. "The trouble with Hollywood is that too many of the top people are too comfortable and don't give a damn about what goes up on the screen so long as it gets by at the box office. How can you expect people with that kind of attitude to make the pictures the world will want to see?"

Epilogue

F rank Capra never forgave himself for his decision to sell Liberty Films, and he believed that he never recovered from it. "I got cold feet," he said, "and I think that probably affected my picture-making forever after. Once your daring stops . . . you're not going to make the proper films anymore. That is, I couldn't. When I sold out for money . . . I think my conscience told me that I had had it. All we had to do was hang on, to accept much less money and make nothing but quality films. That's what my partners wanted to do and what we should have done. . . . As the cowardly reigning apostle of the crusade, I went back on my own idea, having lost my guts and courage. It was the beginning of my end as a social force in films."

The poor reception of *It's a Wonderful Life* cut Capra to his heart. The public's indifference to his film felt to him like evidence that during the war years he had lost his greatest gift, the ability to anticipate what average Americans might want to see and give it to them. Capra had given up four years of his life to serve his country, but he had not been engaged in the same fight as his colleagues. They had gone to war; he had gone to Washington. They had sought truth with their cameras, though they had sometimes failed to convey it; Capra's task had been to package and sell it. The difference in their duties had not seemed significant during his time in the capital when, for all of his complaining, he had delighted in being in charge. Every decision had been high-stakes, and every propaganda picture had seemed like a make-or-break act of patriotism. But in the war's aftermath, Capra was lost. As alienated, uncertain, and confused as Wyler had been upon his return home, his instinct to follow his own path helped him rediscover his place in a new America. Capra couldn't find that place; he had barely left the country, but he could no longer recognize it.

Stevens, Huston, and Ford went their own ways and seemed not to worry about whether or not the public would follow them. Their experiences during the war had strengthened their resolve to let nothing compromise their work, not even popular taste. As Wyler had done, over the next few years they would infuse their movies with their own personalities—Huston gave vent to his sardonic cynicism in *The Treasure of the Sierra Madre,* Stevens peered into the ugliest recesses of human nature and personal ambition in *A Place in the Sun,* and Ford, ever iconoclastic, chose to eschew the prestige of films like *The Grapes of Wrath* and instead embrace the degraded genre he loved best, shaping his own vision of America through the majestic, elegiac, morally complex westerns that, though they would win him no awards, would eventually form his most enduring legacy. If Capra could not follow them—if he could not even find a way to follow his own heart—it was in part because, alone among his colleagues, he never imagined that the war would change him, or the world. He had always assumed it would be an interruption—a long, ghastly pause after which everything would return to a normality that he instead discovered had vanished.

The social realism that audiences craved after World War II—the dramas about alcoholism and mental illness and anti-Semitism and racism that would catapult a new generation of directors like Billy Wilder and Elia Kazan to the forefront of Hollywood picturemaking—was not a road that Capra could have taken even if he had wanted to. He had spent too many years trying to convince Americans and himself that there were no problems that could not be solved by hard work, good cheer, and a burst of spirited rhetoric. Eventually, his belief that movies should be uplifting calcified into didacticism. He never turned sour or nasty about his fellow filmmakers, but he didn't know how to do what they were doing, which seemed to be all that people wanted to see. So he stopped. After *It's a Wonderful Life,* he barely worked at all. He directed only five more movies. None of them were particularly successful. In 1961, after remaking his own 1933 comedy-drama *Lady for a Day* as *Pocketful of Miracles,* he decided to retire.

In the postwar years, Wyler, Huston, and Stevens were emboldened not just in their professional lives but as private citizens who had the power to galvanize public attention; although they were now out of uniform, none of them had lost their taste for a good fight. In the late 1940s, they became active in the industry's central political cause of the postwar years, the fight against the resurgent House Un-American Activities Committee, and they united in public opposition to the blacklisting of suspected Communists that had begun in Hollywood. Just months after the release of *The Best Years of Our Lives,* Wyler gave a nationally broadcast radio address in which he said that in the current climate of paranoia and mistrust, he never could have made the picture that had just won him the Academy Award. HUAC, he said, was "making decent people afraid to express their opinions. They are creating fear in Hollywood. Fear will result in self-censorship. Self-censorship will paralyze the screen. In the last analysis, you will suffer. You will be deprived of entertainment which stimulates you, and you will be given a diet of pictures which conform to some people's arbitrary standards of Americanism." Soon after his speech, he and Huston, who also believed that a "sickness [had] permeated the country," joined forces to spearhead Hollywood's Committee for the First Amendment, a group that lobbied for free expression and an end to red-baiting. Capra did not join them; he could never shed his fear of being labeled a Communist sympathizer, and his infrequent public political comments had been mostly restricted to nervous declarations that he was stoutly against Communism and had never even voted for Roosevelt.

Like Capra, Ford declined to put himself at the center of political controversy or activism in the years following the war. Except for one memorable showdown in 1950, when all five men joined forces to thwart Cecil B. De-Mille's attempt to institute an anti-Communist loyalty oath for the members of the Directors Guild, Ford kept his own counsel, largely continuing to avoid the company of fellow filmmakers. In 1952, he won a fourth directing Oscar—a record that still stands—for *The Quiet Man.* Military life figured in more than half of the movies he made in the twenty years after his navy service, but except for the light comedy *Mister Roberts*, he avoided returning to the rigors of combat in World War II as a subject.

Capra and Ford had never been particularly close. Both men were Catholics, and when they saw each other, it was most often on Sundays, when their wives would convince them to come to mass. But ten years after Capra retired, when he decided to write his autobiography, it was Ford to whom he turned with a request that he write the introduction. By then, Ford was in his seventies, himself retired, enfeebled and largely bedridden. He surprised and touched Capra by providing a foreword in which he called his colleague "a great man and a great American . . . an inspiration to those who believe in the American dream," and "the greatest motion picture director in the world." After a series of strokes that left him incapacitated in his final years, Capra died at ninety-four, in 1991.

Ford had made his last movie in 1966, but until the end of his life, he talked enthusiastically of trying to direct one more picture—either a dramatic feature about the war in the Pacific, or a movie about the OSS that he had promised Bill Donovan he would make just before Donovan's death in 1959. Ford died in 1973; he was seventy-nine years old. A threadbare flag from the Battle of Midway was draped over his coffin and then presented to his wife.

Huston and Wyler remained close friends for the rest of their lives, and when Wyler died in 1981 at the age of seventy-nine, Huston delivered one of the eulogies, leaving the lectern early when he was overcome by grief. After *The Best Years of Our Lives*, Wyler directed a dozen more movies, including *The Heiress, Detective Story, Ben-Hur*, for which he won a third Academy Award, and *Funny Girl*. He retired in 1970 after illness forced him to withdraw from directing the "unusual war story, different from most that have been made" that he had developed and long hoped to film, *Patton*. His memorial service was held in the theater of the Directors Guild of America, where hundreds of his colleagues came to pay their respects. Bette Davis and Roddy McDowall sat side by side. "This entire town should be at half-mast," Davis told McDowall. "When the king dies, all the flags are at half-mast." Until his final years, Wyler kept in touch with the crew of the *Memphis*

Belle, always answering their letters and inquiring about their lives and families.

Huston won Academy Awards for both directing and writing *The Treasure of the Sierra Madre,* his first postwar picture, which was released in 1947. He went on to direct three dozen more films, making him one of the most prolific filmmakers to come out of World War II. Unlike many of his colleagues in the Signal Corps, he expressed no desire to make a combat film, but over the next forty years, he frequently explored the subject of bravery and cowardice under pressure in movies ranging from *The Red Badge of Courage* to *The African Queen* to *The Man Who Would Be King.* Huston worked steadily until his death at eighty-one in 1987. He never stopped petitioning the government to allow the release of *Let There Be Light.* The Pentagon rejected the formal request he submitted in 1952, reiterating that the documentary was a violation of the privacy of its subjects, and rebuffed him again in 1971. Finally, after intervention from Vice President Walter Mondale, the army agreed not to stand in the way of an unauthorized showing of an old print of the movie in 1980. It opened the following year in New York City and is now preserved, along with Huston's other wartime film work, in the National Archives and at the Library of Congress.

In 1948, George Stevens finally returned to directing with the gentle and well-received comedy *I Remember Mama.* Two years later, he won his first of two Academy Awards for his direction of *A Place in the Sun,* his long-planned adaptation of *An American Tragedy.* "As time went on," he said, "I kept feeling I should do a picture about the war. All the other guys had done or were doing pictures about their experiences—Ford, Wyler, and so on. And here I was avoiding the experience." As the years passed, Stevens became troubled by the growing popularity of violent westerns among children, something he had first noticed in Germany immediately after the war, when he watched little boys in cowboy hats play with cap pistols. In 1953, as a response, he made *Shane,* the somber drama about the effect of a roving gunslinger on the lives of an isolated frontier family. He called the movie "a Western, but really my war picture. . . . In *Shane,* a gun shot, for our purposes, is a holocaust. And when a living being is shot, a life is over."

In 1975, Stevens, who was seventy, helped to plan a gathering of the

surviving members of his SPECOU unit, who had come from around the
country to celebrate with him. Just before the reunion, he died suddenly of a
heart attack. Many of the veterans who had traveled to California to see him
attended his funeral, as did dozens of his colleagues. "I just loved the man
and I'm sure he loved me," said Capra soon after his death. "And when I
die . . . I'm certainly going to look George up. . . . I think we'll start another
Liberty Films up there. We can make pictures in heaven and send them
down. And maybe we can get out of heaven once in a while and go to some of
those other places, just like George went to hell in the Army when he went to
Europe."

Shortly after the war, Stevens packed up all of the color footage he had
shot overseas, from North Africa to D-Day to Dachau, and drove it to a
Bekins storage facility in North Hollywood. The footage had never been
shown publicly. He carefully labeled each canister with titles like "Eyewitness at Dachau" or simply "Atrocity." He retrieved the reels only once, in
1959, when he was preparing to direct *The Diary of Anne Frank*. Alone in a
screening room, he started to watch what he had shot, but turned the projec-
tor off after the first minute, returned the canisters to North Hollywood, and
locked them away once again. Only his son and a few close colleagues knew
of the existence of the film. It remained in storage until his death.

NOTE ON SOURCES AND ACKNOWLEDGMENTS

This is a work of history and of collective biography. In attempting to recreate the lives of Frank Capra, John Ford, John Huston, George Stevens, and William Wyler during the World War II years, I have turned as often as possible to archival source materials, including letters, diaries, memos, cables, contracts, scripts, handwritten notes, travel logs, financial records, budgets, receipts, and U.S. Army and Navy documentation, as well as to contemporaneous accounts and interviews from newspapers, magazines, and trade journals. I have drawn in particular from the George Stevens Collection and the Filmmaker's Journey Collection, the John Huston Collection, the William Wyler Archives, and the Samuel Goldwyn Collection, all of which are housed at the Margaret Herrick Library of the Academy of Motion Picture Arts and Sciences at the Fairbanks Center for Motion Picture Study in Los Angeles; from an additional collection of William Wyler's papers in the Charles E. Young Research Library at UCLA; from the Frank Capra Collection in the Wesleyan Cinema Archives at the Center for Film Study, Wesleyan University; and from the John Ford Collection at the Lilly Library, Indiana University at Bloomington. Access to the Goldwyn and Ford collections required special permission from their heirs; my grateful acknowledgment goes to the estate of Samuel Goldwyn and to John Ford's grandson Dan Ford, himself the author of a lively Ford biography, for granting those permissions. Catherine Wyler and George Stevens Jr. both produced documentaries about their fathers' lives; in the Wyler, Stevens, and Filmmaker's Journey collections, they have generously included their own research materials, including unedited interview and oral history transcripts. This book would not have been possible without their scrupulous preservation of the words and work of their fathers.

Special thanks go to Barbara Hall, for allowing me access to uncatalogued material in the Stevens Collection, including correspondence between Stevens and his wife and son during the war. I am also grateful to Jenny Romero, Kristine Krueger, and the staff of the Margaret Herrick Library, to Amy Wong at UCLA, to Jeanine Basinger and Joan Miller at Wesleyan, and to the staffs of the New York Public Library, the New York Public Library for the Performing Arts, the Lilly Library at Indiana University, Bloomington, the Butler Library at Columbia University, the Beinecke Rare Book & Manuscript Library at Yale University, the Naval Historical Center, and the Mémorial de la Shoah, Musée, Centre de Documentation Juive Contemporaine in Paris. For access to all of the documentary footage George Stevens shot during and after World War II, thanks to Rosemary C. Hanes and the staff of the Motion Picture & Television Reading Room at the Library of Congress, and for access to the unedited reels of John Huston's restaged footage of the battle of San Pietro as well as to a wealth of material archived by the War Department, the Office of War Information, and many other government agencies and entities, thanks to the staff of the National Archives in College Park, Maryland.

A complete list of the books I used in my research is in the bibliography. But I want to express particular appreciation for the work of several writers whose scholarship about these five men informed and challenged my writing and thinking. They are Scott Eyman, whose Ford biography *Print the Legend* is as rich and thoughtful as one could hope; Joseph McBride, whose remarkable biographies *Searching for John Ford* and *Frank Capra: The Catastrophe of Success* are essential for anyone seeking to understand the lives of these men; Jan Herman and the late Axel Madsen, whose books are the deepest, most thoroughly researched biographies of William Wyler; Lawrence Grobel, author of the fascinating family biography *The Hustons;* and Marilyn Ann Moss, whose *Giant* is as of this writing the only full-length biography of George Stevens. The University Press of Mississippi's Conversations with

Filmmakers series, which includes separate volumes of interviews with each of the five directors in this book, was also of great value. Of the many studies of Hollywood films and Hollywood politics during World War II, I returned again and again to Thomas Doherty's *Projections of War,* Bernard F. Dick's *The Star-Spangled Screen, Hollywood Goes to War,* by Clayton R. Koppes and Gregory D. Black, and the reference guide *Hollywood War Films, 1937–1945,* by Michael S. Shull and David Edward Wilt. And any writer seeking to understand the culture and politics of this period in the movie industry owes debts to Otto Friedrich's *City of Nets* and Larry Ceplair and Steven Englund's *The Inquisition in Hollywood.* The autobiographies *The Name Above the Title,* by Frank Capra, and *An Open Book,* by John Huston, are, like all autobiographies, both vital and unreliable, and I have tried to quote only those passages from them that shed more light than heat.

I am very fortunate to have Andrew Wylie as my agent, adviser, and remarkably thoughtful and patient guiding hand. My thanks also to Jess Cagle, Dan Fierman, Jeff Giles, Henry Goldblatt, Adam Moss, and David Wallace-Wells, the great editors who helped me keep one foot planted in the twenty-first century during the years I worked on this book with encouraging words and gainful employment; to Michele Romero for the photo supplement and much more; and to Scott Brown, Kate Clinton, Elly Eisenberg, Linda Emond, Oskar and Laurie Eustis, Betsy Gleick, Michael Mayer, Jeremy McCarter, Eric Price, Lisa Schwarzbaum, Mary Kaye Schilling, Brian Siberell, Alisa Solomon, Urvashi Vaid, and Roger Waltzman for all their reserves of comradeship and support.

I'm immensely grateful to Scott Moyers, who played an extraordinary number of crucial roles in the evolution of this book, all of them with characteristic grace, generosity, and wisdom. It's a privilege to work with him, with Ann Godoff, and with the wonderful people at Penguin Press, especially Mally Anderson and Yamil Anglada.

To my steadfast family—those who are here and who are gone—my thanks and my love. They are too many to name, but as I worked on *Five*

Came Back, the wartime service of my late father Lewis Harris and of my uncles Edward, Chet, and Ray Wisniewski was never far from my mind.

Finally, to Tony: Yes, I do know how lucky I am. Thank you for a million things, including the fact that you'd never ask that question. My love for you and gratitude for your love would fill a book; I hope you know that it fills this one.

NOTES

List of Abbreviations Used

EKP—Eric Knight papers, Beinecke Rare Book and Manuscript
Library, Yale University

FCA—Frank Capra Archives, Wesleyan University

FJC—Filmmaker's Journey Collection, Margaret Herrick Library,
Beverly Hills

GSC—George Stevens Collection, Margaret Herrick Library

JFC—John Ford Collection, Lilly Library, Indiana University,
Bloomington

JHC—John Huston Collection, Margaret Herrick Library

NA—National Archives, College Park, MD

SGC—Samuel Goldwyn Collection, Margaret Herrick Library

WWA—William Wyler Archives, Margaret Herrick Library

WWUCLA—William Wyler Collection, Charles E. Young Research
Library, UCLA

Prologue: Pearl Harbor

1   **When news of the bombing came:** Joseph McBride, *Searching for John Ford: A Life* (New York: St.
Martin's, 2001), 347.

1   **She showed the Fords a bullet hole:** Tag Gallagher, *John Ford: The Man and His Films* (Berkeley and
Los Angeles: University of California Press, 1986), 202–3. Gallagher credits an unpublished interview with
Mary Ford conducted by Anthony Slide and June Banker for this story.

1   **"I never let them plaster over that":** Dan Ford, *Pappy: The Life of John Ford* (Englewood Cliffs, NJ:
Prentice Hall, 1979), 165.

1   **"everybody at that table":** Gallagher, *John Ford*, 202–3.

2   **just three weeks after completing production:** Scott Eyman, *Print the Legend: The Life and Times of John Ford* (New York: Simon & Schuster, 1999), 245.

2   **failed the entrance exam:** McBride, *Searching for John Ford*, 67.

3   **"I think it's the thing to do":** Frank Farrell, "John Ford Dons Naval Uniform Because 'It's the Thing to Do,'" *New York World-Telegram*, November 1, 1941.

3   **"They don't count":** Letter from John Ford to Mary Ford, October 2, 1941, JFC.

3   **He checked into the Carlton Hotel:** McBride, *Searching for John Ford*, 346.

3   **"of a man who might set out to sea":** Farrell, "John Ford Dons Naval Uniform."

3   **"It would take volumes":** Letter from John Ford to Mary Ford, September 30, 1941, JFC.

3   **a proper Catholic wedding ceremony:** McBride, *Searching for John Ford*, 347.

3   **Ford and his men welcomed America into the war:** Andrew Sinclair, "John Ford's War," *Sight and Sound*, Spring 1979.

4   **"Willy and I wanted":** Jan Herman, *A Talent for Trouble: The Life of Hollywood's Most Acclaimed Director, William Wyler* (New York: Da Capo, 1997), 232–33.

4   **the aftereffects of a childhood defined by frail health:** Lawrence Grobel, *The Hustons: The Life and Times of a Hollywood Dynasty*, updated ed. (New York: Cooper Square, 2000), 101.

4   **Wyler was a Jewish immigrant:** Herman, *A Talent for Trouble*, 16–17.

4   **He had relatives trapped in Europe:** Sarah Kozloff, "Wyler's Wars," *Film History* 20, no. 4 (2008).

5   **"I was only a kid":** "A Man of Unsartorial Splendor," *New York Times*, January 25, 1942.

5   **It "seemed dated":** John Huston, *An Open Book* (New York: Alfred A. Knopf, 1980), 85.

6   **"the worst bunch of shit":** Kenneth L. Geist, *Pictures Will Talk: The Life and Films of Joseph L. Mankiewicz* (New York: Da Capo, 1978), 106–7.

6   **"all film," including his own:** Marilyn Ann Moss, *Giant: George Stevens, a Life on Film* (Madison: University of Wisconsin Press, 2004), 83.

7   **caught the eye of General George Marshall:** Joseph McBride, *Frank Capra: The Catastrophe of Success* (New York: Simon & Schuster, 1992; revised 2000), 455.

7   **"To fight the war":** Stewart Alsop, "Wanted: A Faith to Fight For," *Atlantic Monthly*, May 1941.

8   **Not until the army tried to process him:** McBride, *Frank Capra*, 88–89.

8   **"That was his politics":** Ibid., 261.

8   **"I thought, 'Well, if I go'":** Richard Schickel, *The Men Who Made the Movies: Interviews with Frank Capra, George Cukor, Howard Hawks, Alfred Hitchcock, Vincente Minnelli, King Vidor, Raoul Walsh, and William E. Wellman* (New York: Atheneum, 1975), 81.

8   **"Patriotism? Possibly":** Frank Capra, *The Name Above the Title: An Autobiography* (New York: Da Capo, 1997; originally published 1971), 316.

8   **Fully one-third of the studios' male workforce:** Thomas Doherty, *Projections of War: Hollywood, American Culture, and World War II* (New York: Columbia University Press, 1993), 60.

10   **more than three hundred movies:** An exhaustive list of American movies with World War II–related content made during the war appears in Michael S. Shull and David Edward Wilt's invaluable reference guide *Hollywood War Films, 1937–1945* (Jefferson, NC: McFarland, 1996).

Chapter 1: "The Only Way I Could Survive"

15   **Jack Warner hosted an industry dinner:** Michael E. Birdwell, *Celluloid Soldiers: Warner Bros.'s Campaign Against Nazism* (New York: New York University Press, 1999), 27–28.

17   **"militant anti-Hitler campaign in Hollywood":** "Jack Warner's Dinner to Exiled Thom. Mann May Touch Off a Militant Anti-Hitler Campaign in Hollywood," *Variety*, March 23, 1938.

17   **"the leader of the fight":** Birdwell, *Celluloid Soldiers*, 30–31.

19   **But when he tried early in 1938 to get Zanuck:** Memo from John Ford to Darryl Zanuck, March 1, 1938, and reply, March 2, 1938, JFC.

19   **"If you're thinking of a general run of social pictures":** Joseph McBride, *Searching for John Ford: A Life* (New York: St. Martin's, 2001), 228.

19   **"May I express my wholehearted desire":** "Hollywood Anti-Nazi League," Spartacus Educational, http://www.spartacus.schoolnet.co.uk/USAdies.htm.

20   **"a definite socialist democrat—always left":** Scott Eyman, *Print the Legend: The Life and Times of John Ford* (New York: Simon & Schuster, 1999), 186.

20   **"the picture racket is controlled from Wall Street":** McBride, *Searching for John Ford*, 193.

20   **Ford helped found organizations:** Larry Ceplair and Steven Englund, *The Inquisition in Hollywood: Politics in the Film Community, 1930–1960* (Berkeley: University of California Press, 1979), 115.

20   **he also served as vice chairman:** Ibid., 118.

20   "America is not free from . . . Nazi activity": "Anti-Nazis Hear Warning: Audience of 4000 Cheers
       Assaults on German Propaganda," *Los Angeles Times*, January 30, 1938.
20   "War itself is so ugly": "War Films Round Out Long Cycle," *New York Times*, November 11, 1938.
23   "I said, 'What better time for an anti-war picture?'": Stevens's account of his disagreement with
       Berman comes from the unedited transcript of his 1967 interview by Robert Hughes, file
       3677, GSC.
23   "Imperialist propaganda": Marilyn Ann Moss, *Giant: George Stevens, a Life on Film* (Madison:
       University of Wisconsin Press, 2004), 61.
23   "The film is delightfully evil": George Stevens Jr., *Conversations with the Great Moviemakers of
       Hollywood's Golden Age at the American Film Institute* (New York: Alfred A. Knopf, 2006), 228.
24   he had not hesitated to pay $200,000: "Columbia's Gem," *Time*, August 8, 1938.
24   "worship at the shrine of an inspiring figure": Brooks Atkinson, "The Play: Philip Merivale in 'Valley
       Forge,'" *New York Times*, December 11, 1934.
25   Cohn said he couldn't bring himself to finance a movie: Joseph McBride, *Frank Capra: The
       Catastrophe of Success* (New York: Simon & Schuster, 1992; revised 2000), 327.
25   "After all, I'm a Jew": Ibid., 242.
25   "little wop": John Stuart, "Fine Italian Hand," *Collier's*, August 17, 1935.
25   Capra was a "bitter Roosevelt hater": McBride, *Frank Capra*, 256–57.
26   "Salesmen, politicians, moochers": Except as noted, this and all subsequent quotations of dialogue are
       transcribed from the movies themselves.
26   his growing interest in the fight for directors' rights: McBride, *Frank Capra*, 375–76.
26   "I can't stand the sight of so much war paraphernalia": "Stenographic Notes from the Cinema Section
       of the U.S.S.R. Society for Cultural Relations with Foreign Countries," FCA.
27   "throw everything up and play the harmonica": Review originally published in *Spectator*, November 11,
       1938. Reprinted in John Russell Taylor, ed., *Graham Greene on Film: Collected Film Criticism, 1935–1940*
       (New York: Simon & Schuster, 1972), 203–4.
27   his severely disabled three-year-old son John had died: Frank Capra, *The Name Above the Title: An
       Autobiography* (New York: Da Capo, 1997; originally published 1971), 250–52. Capra wrote that his son had
       a massive blood clot in his brain; McBride writes that an autopsy performed on the boy revealed an
       undiagnosed brain tumor.
28   "with a political theme. He wants to show one": Interview originally published in *Christian Science
       Monitor*, November 9, 1938. Reprinted in Leland Poague, ed., *Frank Capra Interviews* (Jackson: University
       Press of Mississippi, 2004), 20–21.
28   "Capra likes American institutions": Alva Johnston, "Capra Shoots as He Pleases," *Saturday Evening
       Post*, May 14, 1938.
28   the president's "awesome aura" made his "heart skip": Capra, *The Name Above the Title*, 259.
28   "capitulation to Hitler": Thomas Doherty, *Hollywood's Censor: Joseph I. Breen and the Production Code
       Administration* (New York: Columbia University Press, 2007), 210.
29   an unusual summit meeting the day of the rally: Thomas Doherty, *Hollywood and Hitler, 1933–1939*
       (New York: Columbia University Press, 2013), 289–90.
29   "the most interesting and most pathetic city": Jan Herman, *A Talent for Trouble: The Life of Hollywood's
       Most Acclaimed Director, William Wyler* (New York: Da Capo, 1997), 96–98.
29   he would write a hundred-dollar check to the Hollywood Anti-Nazi League: Letter from William
       Wyler's secretary to Jack Warner's secretary, March 15, 1938, file 743, WWA.
30   he would donate two hundred dollars to a relief fund: Herman, *A Talent for Trouble*, 186.
30   "because of all the terrible things happening in Europe": Ibid., 200.
30   the only guests Wyler invited to the wedding: Axel Madsen, *William Wyler: The Authorized Biography*
       (New York: Thomas Y. Crowell, 1973), 174.
31   "an iron gray man in a gray flannel suit": "Snapshots of a Movie Maker," syndicated column by Dorothy
       Kilgallen, undated but ca. 1946, file 38, WWA.
31   the *New York Times* called him "The Great Unpressed": "A Man of Unsartorial Splendor," *New York
       Times*, January 25, 1942.
31   "Famed Nepotist Carl Laemmle": "New Picture," *Time*, June 29, 1942.
31   It was Laemmle who had paid for Wyler's emigration: Herman, *A Talent for Trouble*, 25–27, 32–33.
32   "Willy was certainly my best friend": Ibid., 103–4.
32   "long-legged, lobster-nosed": Ibid., 125.
32   Wyler and Huston cemented their comradeship: Lawrence Grobel, *The Hustons: The Life and Times of
       a Hollywood Dynasty*, updated ed. (New York: Cooper Square, 2000), 147. The film Wyler and Huston were
       researching, *Wild Boys of the Road*, was made by William Wellman for Warner Bros. in 1933.
32   he was branded a spoiled, irresponsible wreck: Ibid., 155–61.

32   **"The experience seemed to bring my whole miserable existence":** John Huston, *An Open Book* (New York: Alfred A. Knopf, 1980), 63–64.

32   **"Whatever I turned my hand to":** John Huston interviewed by Bill Moyers for the TV series *Creativity with Bill Moyers*, 1982, available on the Criterion Collection DVD of *Wise Blood*.

32   **"never amount to more than an awfully nice guy":** James Agee, "Undirectable Director," *Life*, September 18, 1950.

33   **"He was a good writer":** William Wyler interviewed by Ronald L. Davis, Southern Methodist University oral history project, 1979, reprinted in Gabriel Miller, ed., *William Wyler: Interviews* (Jackson: University Press of Mississippi, 2009), 82.

33   **"apparently knows Huston personally":** Rudy Behlmer, *Inside Warner Bros. (1935–1951)* (New York: Viking, 1985), 41.

33   **"the dialogue, as far as it is political and ideological":** Paul J. Vanderwood, ed., *Juárez* (Madison: University of Wisconsin Press, 1983), 20.

34   **"by way of being dialectic"** to **"those of Benito Juárez":** Huston, *An Open Book*, 73.

34   **"Our task is to fight the tyrant":** Script with handwritten annotations, JHC.

34   **"The first thing Muni wanted":** Bernard Drew, "John Huston: At 74 No Formulas," *American Film*, September 1980.

35   **"Hecht and MacArthur had written a beautiful screenplay":** Grobel, *The Hustons*, 201.

35   **"*I* made *Wuthering Heights*":** Ethan Mordden, *The Hollywood Studios: House Style in the Golden Age of the Movies* (New York: Alfred A. Knopf, 1988), 191.

35   **Warner Bros. immediately cut twenty-five minutes:** Bernard F. Dick, *Hal Wallis: Producer to the Stars* (Lexington: University Press of Kentucky, 2004), 51.

35   **"in the contest between dictator and democrat":** Frank S. Nugent, "The Screen in Review: The Warners Look Through the Past to the Present in 'Juarez,' Screened Last Night at the Hollywood," *New York Times*, April 26, 1939.

35   **"I knew that if I'd been the director":** Drew, "John Huston: At 74 No Formulas."

36   **"The Picture That Calls A Swastika A Swastika!":** Bernard F. Dick, *The Star-Spangled Screen: The American World War II Film* (Lexington: University Press of Kentucky, 1993), 51–60.

Chapter 2: "The Dictates of My Heart and Blood"

37   **"unchallenged political"** . . . **"one of the most lamentable mistakes":** Clayton R. Koppes and Gregory D. Black, *Hollywood Goes to War: How Politics, Profits, and Propaganda Shaped World War II Movies* (New York: Free Press, 1987), 27–30.

38   **"I want to do that for my people":** Rudy Behlmer, *Inside Warner Bros. (1935–1951)* (New York: Viking, 1985), 82.

38   **"The world is faced with the menace of gangsters":** "Little Caesar Waits His Chance," *New York Times*, January 22, 1939.

38   **"Hitler's pledge of non-aggression":** Frank S. Nugent, "The Screen in Review: The Warners Make Faces at Hitler in 'Confessions of a Nazi Spy,'" *New York Times*, April 29, 1939.

38   *Variety* **wondered about its "bearing on":** *Variety* review, signed by "Land.," May 5, 1939.

38   *Time* **called it:** "Cinema: Totem and Taboo," *Time*, May 15, 1939.

39   **When Stevens urged Schaeffer's lieutenant Pandro Berman:** Marilyn Ann Moss, *Giant: George Stevens, a Life on Film* (Madison: University of Wisconsin Press, 2004), 62–63.

40   **"do first-rate pictures" that were "comparable in quality":** Ibid., 63–64.

40   **In February, when the Academy presented him:** Mason Wiley and Damien Bona, *Inside Oscar: The Unofficial History of the Academy Awards*, 10th anniversary ed. (New York: Ballantine, 1996), 88–90.

41   **"it is probable that the industry has never faced blacker days":** Douglas W. Churchill, "Hollywood Jitters: The War Jeopardizes $6,000,000 Worth of New Films," *New York Times*, May 26, 1940.

41   **Buchman . . . said that Capra was:** Joseph McBride, *Frank Capra: The Catastrophe of Success* (New York: Simon & Schuster, 1992; revised 2000), 412.

42   **"He was a very simplistic man":** Ibid., 414.

42   **"Are you a Fascist?":** Ibid., 415.

42   **"the mob is so lazy":** Ibid., 256.

43   **"graft could rear its ugly head":** Frank Capra, *The Name Above the Title: An Autobiography* (New York: Da Capo, 1997; originally published 1971), 281–83.

44   **"silly and stupid":** *New York Times*, October 24, 1939.

44   Republican senator Henry Cabot Lodge Jr.: "Mr. Smith Riles Washington," *Time*, October 30, 1939.

44   anti–block booking legislation: Ibid.

44   "one of the most disgraceful things": David Nasaw, *The Patriarch: The Remarkable Life and Turbulent Times of Joseph P. Kennedy* (New York: Penguin Press, 2012), 421.

44   "to show this film in foreign countries": Capra, *The Name Above the Title*, 292.

44   "With all those things they've got to do": McBride, *Frank Capra*, 422.

44   "that unwritten clause in the Bill of Rights": Frank S. Nugent, "The Screen in Review: Frank Capra's 'Mr. Smith Goes to Washington' at the Music Hall Sets a Seasonal High in Comedy," *New York Times*, October 20, 1939.

45   "the Senate and the machinery of how it may be used": Otis Ferguson, "Mr. Capra Goes Someplace," *New Republic*, November 1, 1939. Reprinted in *The Film Criticism of Otis Ferguson* (Philadelphia: Temple University Press, 1971), 273–74.

45   in the words of the *New Yorker*: Geoffrey T. Hellman, "Thinker in Hollywood," *New Yorker*, February 20, 1940.

45   "My dear Frank": Letters from Lionel Robinson to Frank Capra, October 2, 1939, and October 31, 1939, FCA.

45   "I am glad your wife and children": Letter from Frank Capra to Lionel Robinson, November 21, 1939, FCA.

46   "I never cease to thrill": Hellman, "Thinker in Hollywood."

46   he and the Academy's Research Council met: McBride, *Frank Capra*, 439.

47   street scenes were dressed with army recruiting posters: Michael S. Shull and David Edward Wilt, *Hollywood War Films, 1937–1945* (Jefferson, NC: McFarland, 1996), 120.

48   "In the film": Unedited transcript of George Stevens interviewed by Robert Hughes, 1967, file 3677, GSC.

48   "heavy and stolid": *Variety*, February 7, 1940.

48   "The world's most famous doctor": Marilyn Ann Moss, *Giant: George Stevens, a Life on Film* (Madison: University of Wisconsin Press, 2004), 67.

49   "after several weeks of friction": *New York Times*, March 5, 1940.

49   "You make a picture here": Hughes interview with George Stevens, 1967, file 3677, GSC.

49   If a war or national emergency: Letter from William B. Dover to George Stevens, file 3550, GSC.

49   While in Tijuana, they ran into Franz Planer: Jan Herman, *A Talent for Trouble: The Life of Hollywood's Most Acclaimed Director, William Wyler* (New York: Da Capo, 1997), 204.

50   "I don't know of anything that will breed": Letter from Harry Warner to William Wyler, January 19, 1940, file 743, WWA.

50   "swarming with refugees": Senator Gerald Nye, speech reprinted in *Vital Speeches of the Day* 8, no. 23 (September 15, 1941).

50   he had already planted an item: Jimmie Fidler, "Fidler in Hollywood: Hollywood's Community Chest Drive Has Caused Trouble," *St. Petersburg Times*, January 15, 1940.

50   acknowledging that it wasn't the "real generous contribution": Letter from Willam Wyler to Harry Warner, January 26, 1940, file 743, WWA.

51   "I know your heart has been disturbed": Letter from Harry Warner to William Wyler, January 29, 1940, file 743, WWA.

51   at a salary of $6,250 a week: Production file on *The Letter*, Warner Bros. Archives, University of Southern California.

51   "Mein Lieber Willy": Sarah Kozloff, "Wyler's Wars," *Film History* 20, no. 4 (2008).

51   "We were stunned": Herman, *A Talent for Trouble*, 208.

51   After a few days at a smaller resort: Ibid., 209.

52   most of them were ultra-low-budget: "Cinema: New Westerns," *Time*, March 13, 1939.

52   tested the limits of the Production Code: Letters from Joseph I. Breen to Walter Wanger, October 28, 1939 and November 8, 1938, JFC.

52   "Why are you moving your mouth": Scott Eyman, *Print the Legend: The Life and Times of John Ford* (New York: Simon & Schuster, 1999), 200.

53   proclaiming at a press conference that: Matthew Bernstein, *Walter Wanger: Hollywood Independent* (Minneapolis: University of Minnesota Press, 2000), 140.

53   "one of the best directors of the day": John Russell Taylor, ed., *Graham Greene on Film: Collected Film Criticism, 1935–1940* (New York: Simon & Schuster, 1972), 241–32.

53   "leap at the chance": Letter from John Ford to Darryl Zanuck, July 17, 1939, JFC.

54   "the best cussed pitcher I ever seen": Joseph McBride, *Searching for John Ford: A Life* (New York: St. Martin's, 2001), 313.

54   "If the conditions which the picture tends": Eyman, *Print the Legend*, 224.

54   "Pinkos who did not bat an eye": "The New Pictures," *Time*, February 12, 1940.

54 **"resoluteness of approach":** Frank S. Nugent, "The Screen in Review: Twentieth Century-Fox Shows a Flawless Film Edition of John Steinbeck's 'The Grapes of Wrath,' with Henry Fonda and Jane Darwell, at the Rivoli," *New York Times,* January 25, 1940.

54 **"a shocking visualization":** *Variety,* January 31, 1940.

55 **"There is no country":** *The Film Criticism of Otis Ferguson* (Philadelphia: Temple University Press, 1971), 282–85.

55 **"*The Grapes of Wrath* is possibly":** "The New Pictures," *Time,* February 12, 1940.

55 **"when they threw the people off":** Peter Bogdanovich, *John Ford,* revised and enlarged ed. (Berkeley and Los Angeles: University of California Press, 1978), 23.

55 **he named the *Araner,* as a tribute:** McBride, *Searching for John Ford,* 200–201.

55 **"Drinking," said John Wayne:** Dan Ford, *Pappy: The Life of John Ford* (Englewood Cliffs, NJ: Prentice Hall, 1979), 112–19.

56 **"The Japanese shrimp fleet":** Report from John Ford to Captain Elias Zacharias, December 30, 1939, and reply from J. R. Defrees, January 16, 1940, JFC.

56 **"green with envy":** Ford, *Pappy,* 151.

56 **letters from friends in England:** Letter from Lord Killanin to John Ford, January 12, 1940, JFC.

56 **"over-age and rich":** Eyman, *Print the Legend,* 251.

57 **"show that a Democracy can":** McBride, *Searching for John Ford,* 320–22.

57 **told to recruit up to two hundred volunteers:** Memo from the chief of the Bureau of Navigation to the 11th Naval District commandant, September 7, 1940, JFC.

57 **They combed lists of employees:** Field Photo application file, box 10, folder 30, JFC.

57 **The men would meet on Tuesday:** Ibid.

57 **"all the officers were going to wear swords":** Ford, *Pappy,* 151–52.

Chapter 3: "You Must Not Realize That There Is a War Going On"

59 **Capra, who was there to represent the Directors Guild:** Thomas Brady, "Films for Defense," *New York Times,* December 1, 1940.

60 **Warner promptly had his speech printed:** Warner Bros. Archives, University of Southern California, and WWA.

60 **mailed not just to his colleagues and rivals:** Michael E. Birdwell, *Celluloid Soldiers: The Warner Bros. Campaign Against Nazism* (New York: New York University Press, 1999), 83.

60 **a year later Jack Warner would loan Davis:** A. Scott Berg, *Goldwyn* (New York: Alfred A. Knopf, 1989), 357–58.

60 **she kept it a secret and had an abortion:** Ed Sikov, *Dark Victory: The Life of Bette Davis* (New York: Henry Holt, 2007), 167.

60 **"I should have married Willy":** Whitney Stine, *"I'd Love to Kiss You . . .": Conversations with Bette Davis* (New York: Pocket, 1991), 126.

61 **"I did it his way":** Bette Davis, *The Lonely Life* (New York: G. P. Putnam's Sons, 1962), 204.

61 **"You are a very good director":** Warner Bros. daily progress report, June 26, 1940, and letter from Jack Warner to William Wyler, June 27, 1940, file 252, WWA.

61 **he had started to send packets of cash:** Sarah Kozloff, "Wyler's Wars," *Film History* 20, no. 4 (2008).

61 **"Please be assured that I have no intention":** Handwritten drafts of William Wyler's response to Jack Warner, file 252, WWA.

62 **Martin Dies had rarely missed an opportunity:** "Reply of Dies to President," *New York Times,* October 27, 1938, and "Ex-Rep. Martin Dies Is Dead," *New York Times,* November 15, 1927.

62 **Among the biggest names on his list:** "Film Stars Named in 'Red' Inquiry," *New York Times,* July 18, 1940.

62 **Dies announced that he intended to hold hearings:** A. M. Sperber and Eric Lax, *Bogart* (New York: William Morrow, 1997), 131–33.

63 **Ford, whose real name was Sean Aloysius O'Feeney:** Last Will and Testament of John Ford, October 30, 1940, JFC.

63 **make a statement against Fascism:** Matthew Bernstein, *Walter Wanger: Hollywood Independent* (Minneapolis: University of Minnesota Press, 2000), 167.

64 **"You're a thorny guy":** Letter from Dudley Nichols to John Ford, ca. April 1940, JFC.

65 **"With their foreign market already lost":** "Cinema: Unpulled Punches," *Time,* October 28, 1940.

65 **"the highest pitch of realism":** *Variety,* October 9, 1940.

65 **he borrowed $750,000:** Joseph McBride, *Frank Capra: The Catastrophe of Success* (New York: Simon & Schuster, 1992; revised 2000), 430.

65   **"The 'Capra-corn' barbs had pierced":** This and all subsequent quotations from Capra in this chapter are from Frank Capra, *The Name Above the Title: An Autobiography* (New York: Da Capo, 1997; originally published 1971), 297–303.

67   **"a barefoot fascist":** Andrew Sarris, *The American Cinema: Directors and Directions, 1929–1968* (New York: Dutton, 1968), 87.

68   **"the most effective film expose to date":** *Variety*, June 12, 1940.

68   **"that can be considered of any major consequence":** John Mosher, "The Current Cinema: A German Story," *New Yorker*, June 22, 1940.

68   **Paramount had cautiously insisted on shooting "protection takes":** Kevin Lally, *Wilder Times: The Life of Billy Wilder* (New York: Henry Holt, 1996), 94.

68   **"Films are fast assuming the role":** Bosley Crowther, "Propaganda—Be Prepared: 'The Ramparts We Watch,' 'Pastor Hall,' and Other Current Films Provoke Thought upon an Inevitable Trend," *New York Times*, September 22, 1940.

Chapter 4: "What's the Good of a Message?"

70   **"for as long as the fish are biting":** Mason Wiley and Damien Bona, *Inside Oscar: The Unofficial History of the Academy Awards*, 10th anniversary ed. (New York: Ballantine, 1996), 109–11.

70   **"all had to slink back to their tables":** Jan Herman, *A Talent for Trouble: The Life of Hollywood's Most Acclaimed Director, William Wyler* (New York: Da Capo, 1997), 216.

70   **"Awards are a trivial thing":** Wiley and Bona, *Inside Oscar*, 111.

70   **many small-circulation papers:** *Brooklyn Citizen*, March 22, 1941.

70   **Ford himself had little use for the movie:** Ford interviewed by Claudine Tavernier, 1966, reprinted in Gerald Peary and Jenny Lefcourt, eds., *John Ford Interviews* (Jackson: University Press of Mississippi, 2001), 101.

71   **"Darryl F. Panic":** Dan Ford, *Pappy: The Life of John Ford* (Englewood Cliffs, NJ: Prentice Hall, 1979), 97.

72   **"Zanuck . . . said to me":** Peter Bogdanovich, *John Ford*, revised and enlarged ed. (Berkeley and Los Angeles: University of California Press, 1978).

72   **In January, he drew up a budget proposal:** Letter from John Ford to Merian C. Cooper, January 24, 1941, JFC.

72   **quasi-spy mission for the *Araner*:** Joseph McBride, *Searching for John Ford: A Life* (New York: St. Martin's, 2001), 274.

72   **Wyler had written to him:** A. Scott Berg, *Goldwyn* (New York: Alfred A. Knopf, 1989), 289.

73   **"the only . . . people in the Goldwyn asylum":** Ibid., 269.

73   **Zanuck offered Wyler $85,000:** Contract memo from 20th Century Fox to William Wyler, September 26, 1940, file 221, WWA.

74   **"into a labor story":** Story conference memo by Zanuck, May 22, 1940, reprinted in Rudy Behlmer, ed., *Memo from Darryl F. Zanuck: The Golden Years at Twentieth Century–Fox* (New York: Grove, 1993), 40.

74   **Wyler went through a hardcover copy:** Wyler's personal, hand-annotated copy of the novel *How Green Was My Valley*, file 202, WWA.

74   **"The little English refugee":** 20th Century Fox memo from Lew Schreiber to William Wyler and Wyler's handwritten notes, file 217, WWA.

74   **was horrified when Dunne turned in a 260-page first draft:** Drafts of Philip Dunne screenplays, August 23, 1940, and November 11, 1940, file 207, WWA.

74   **"Willy couldn't write a line":** Philip Dunne, *Take Two: A Life in Movies and Politics* (New York: McGraw-Hill, 1980), 93.

75   **"It is going to be a very simple job":** Memo from Darryl Zanuck to William Wyler, November 14, 1940, file 222, WWA.

75   **"smooth—even—and dull":** Memo from Freda Rosenblatt to William Wyler, November 18, 1940, file 210, WWA.

75   **"The lack of suspense is still felt:** Memo from Freda Rosenblatt to William Wyler, December 28, 1940, file 214, WWA.

75   **"so far failed to achieve":** Letter from Darryl Zanuck to Philip Dunne and William Wyler, December 6, 1940, file 222, WWA.

75   **"I must ask that in matters of taste":** Handwritten draft of letter from William Wyler to Darryl Zanuck, December 1940 (undated), file 221, WWA.

75   **he ran into an executive:** Memo from William Wyler to Darryl Zanuck, December 20, 1940, file 222, WWA.

76   **Philip Dunne was called into a meeting:** Dunne, *Take Two*, 97.

76 A special Oscar was awarded: Wiley and Bona, *Inside Oscar*, 109–11.

76 Its young star, John Justin: Andrew Moor, "'Arabian' Fantasies," supplement to Criterion DVD release of *The Thief of Bagdad*.

76 "The Great American Letdown": Frank Capra, *The Name Above the Title: An Autobiography* (New York: Da Capo, 1997; originally published 1971), 304.

77 "You just don't kill Gary Cooper": Capra interviewed by Richard Glatzer, 1973, reprinted in Leland Poague, ed., *Frank Capra Interviews* (Jackson: University Press of Mississippi, 2004), 119.

77 he was nearly broke because the government: Capra, *The Name Above the Title*, 299.

77 "the director is more zealot than showman": *Variety*, March 19, 1941.

77 "Capra's familiar and favorite American type": *New Republic*, March 24, 1941.

78 "overwritten": Bosley Crowther, "'Meet John Doe,' an Inspiring Lesson in Americanism, Opens at the Rivoli and Hollywood Theatres," *New York Times*, March 13, 1941.

78 "topple artistically": "Cinema: Coop," *Time*, March 3, 1941.

78 "Do you know why today is so refreshing?": Capra, *The Name Above the Title*, 304.

78 "give a defense of Hollywood": Joseph McBride, *Frank Capra: The Catastrophe of Success* (New York: Simon & Schuster, 1992; revised 2000), 437.

78 "like any youngish, likable Italian": Margaret Case Harriman, "Mr. and Mrs. Frank Capra," *Ladies' Home Journal*, April 1941.

78 "Personally, I refuse to believe": McBride, *Frank Capra*, 438.

79 "Can you make a million people sit still": Ibid., 444.

79 "because my way had produced five home runs": Capra, *The Name Above the Title*, 202.

80 "I guess I was in a mood": Marilyn Ann Moss, *Giant: George Stevens, a Life on Film* (Madison: University of Wisconsin Press, 2004), 71.

80 "taciturn, always grave-looking": Irwin Shaw interviewed by Susan Winslow, October 14, 1981, FJC.

80 "he looked very much like an Indian chief": Joseph L. Mankiewicz interviewed in the documentary "George Stevens: Filmmakers Who Knew Him," available as a supplement on the Warner Home Video DVD of *Giant*.

80 "I just [realized] what that pacing": "The New Pictures," *Time*, February 16, 1942.

80 "I have often humbled actors": Unedited transcript of George Stevens interviewed by Robert Hughes, 1967, file 3677, GSC.

81 When he learned of the deaths: Marc Eliot, *Cary Grant: A Biography* (New York: Harmony, 2004), 222.

81 "employs not one but six or seven": Bosley Crowther, "Cary Grant and Irene Dunne Play a 'Penny Serenade' at the Music Hall," *New York Times*, May 23, 1941.

82 "proved to be a costly mistake": Douglas W. Churchill, "The Hollywood Round-Up," *New York Times*, May 18, 1941.

Chapter 5: "The Most Dangerous Fifth Column in Our Country"

83 "the one-man army.": "Cinema: Sergeant York Surrenders," *Time*, April 1, 1940.

84 "fat little Jew": Michael E. Birdwell, *Celluloid Soldiers: Warner Bros.'s Campaign Against Nazism* (New York: New York University Press, 1999), 105.

84 "I don't like war pictures": "Sergeant York Surrenders."

84 "I don't think I can do justice": Todd McCarthy, *Howard Hawks: The Grey Fox of Hollywood* (New York: Grove, 1997), 303.

85 "Hitler can, will, and must be beaten": "Sergeant York: Of God and Country," documentary supplement to Warner Home Video DVD of *Sergeant York*.

85 won a bitter arbitration battle: Lawrence Grobel, *The Hustons: The Life and Times of a Hollywood Dynasty*, updated ed. (New York: Cooper Square, 2000), 206.

85 "the strange sense of inevitability": Memo from John Huston to Hal Wallis, March 21, 1940, Warner Bros. Archives, University of Southern California.

86 "I want you to give the utmost attention": Memo from S. Charles Einfeld to Martin Weiser, July 17, 1940, Warner Bros. Archives, University of Southern California.

86 "I took that picture over": Grobel, *The Hustons*, 213.

86 "not a success story": Thomas Brady, "Mr. Goldwyn Bows Out," *New York Times*, February 16, 1941.

86 "blundering stupidities": McCarthy, *Howard Hawks*, 305.

87 "I don't believe that the film delivers": Ibid., 307.

87 "a result of World War II's menacing threat to democracy": Michael S. Shull and David Edward Wilt, *Hollywood War Films, 1937–1945* (Jefferson, NC: McFarland, 1996), 134.

87 The list of opening-night attendees: Clayton R. Koppes and Gregory D. Black, *Hollywood Goes to War: How Politics, Profits, and Propaganda Shaped World War II Movies* (New York: Free Press, 1987), 39.

88   greeted personally by Mayor Fiorello La Guardia: Hal Wallis and Charles Higham, *Starmaker: The Autobiography of Hal Wallis* (New York: MacMillan, 1980).

88   "Distinguished Citizenship Medal": Mason Wiley and Damien Bona, *Inside Oscar: The Unofficial History of the Academy Awards*, 10th anniversary ed. (New York: Ballantine, 1996), 114.

88   "The suggestion of deliberate propaganda": Bosley Crowther, "'Sergeant York,' a Sincere Biography of the World War Hero, Makes Its Appearance at the Astor," *New York Times*, July 3, 1941.

88   "stunt picture . . . about the army": *New Republic*, September 29, 1941.

88   "Hollywood's first solid contribution": "New Picture," *Time*, August 4, 1941.

88   "a clarion film": *Variety*, July 2, 1941.

88   Burton K. Wheeler: Koppes and Black, *Hollywood Goes to War*, 17–20.

88   "conducted and financed almost entirely by Jews": Thomas Doherty, *Hollywood's Censor: Joseph I. Breen and the Production Code Administration* (New York: Columbia University Press, 2007), 198, 206–7.

89   William Wyler was among those who attended: Telegram to William Wyler, April 1, 1941, file 743, WWA.

89   Gerald P. Nye, a Republican senator to "and Joseph Schenck?": *Vital Speeches of the Day* 7, no. 23 (September 15, 1941).

90   "in the best storm trooper fashion": Wayne S. Cole, *Senator Gerald P. Nye and American Foreign Relations* (Minneapolis: University of Minnesota Press, 1962), 190–91.

90   "propaganda [that] reaches weekly": *Propaganda in Motion Pictures: Hearings Before a Subcommittee of the Committee on Interstate Commerce, United States Senate, Seventy-Seventh Congress, First Session on S. Res. 152, a Resolution Authorizing an Investigation of War Propaganda Disseminated by the Motion-Picture Industry and of Any Monopoly in the Production, Distribution, or Exhibition of Motion Pictures, September 9 to 26, 1941* (Washington, DC: Government Printing Office, 1942). All subsequent quotes from the hearings in this chapter are from this transcript.

91   Willkie, who received $100,000: Koppes and Black, *Hollywood Goes to War*, 42.

91   after publicly debating Charles Lindbergh: Steve Neal, *Dark Horse: A Biography of Wendell Willkie* (New York: Doubleday, 1984), 210–12.

91   "the best men in the industry": Neal Gabler, *An Empire of Their Own: How the Jews Invented Hollywood* (New York: Crown, 1988), 346.

91   "the essential service of motion pictures is entertainment": Koppes and Black, *Hollywood Goes to War*, 20–22.

91   he encouraged them to speak forthrightly: Joseph Barnes, *Willkie: The Events He Was Part Of—The Ideas He Fought For* (New York: Simon & Schuster, 1952), 269–70.

91   the Screen Writers Guild fired off a telegram: Larry Ceplair and Steven Englund, *The Inquisition in Hollywood: Politics in the Film Community, 1930–1960* (Berkeley: University of California Press, 1979), 160–61.

92   the reality was closer to 140: Michael S. Shull and David Edward Wilt, *Hollywood War Films, 1937–1945* (Jefferson, NC: McFarland, 1996), 17.

95   Roosevelt publicly compared him to a Civil War "copperhead": A. Scott Berg, *Lindbergh* (New York: Putnam, 1998), 420–22.

95   "black gloom": Anne Morrow Lindbergh, *War Within and Without: Diaries and Letters of Anne Morrow Lindbergh, 1939–1944*. (New York: Harcourt Brace Jovanovich, 1980), entries dated September 11, 1941, and September 14, 1941.

95   "un-American" and "unpatriotic": Berg, *Lindbergh*, 401–2.

95   "the symbol of anti-Semitism in this country": Lindbergh, *War Within and Without*, entry dated September 15, 1941.

96   "I'm anti-Nazi and proud of it": Birdwell, *Celluloid Soldiers*, 145–46.

Chapter 6: "Do I Have to Wait for Orders?"

101   December 7, 1941, Catholic churches: W. R. Wilkerson, "Trade Views," *Hollywood Reporter*, December 8, 1941.

102   Sunday's gloomy revenue reports: "War Wallops Boxoffice," *Hollywood Reporter*, December 8, 1941.

102   ready to go to the movies again: "Nation's Boxoffice Booming," *Hollywood Reporter*, December 30, 1941.

102   "Stir yourself out of your depression": "War's Effect on Hollywood," *Hollywood Reporter*, December 9, 1941.

103   kids revealed that their favorite picture: "Annual Poll of Nation's Kids Puts 'York' on Top as Best Pix," *Hollywood Reporter*, December 15, 1941.

103   "It's just as much the duty": Michael E. Birdwell, *Celluloid Soldiers: Warner Bros.'s Campaign Against Nazism* (New York: New York University Press, 1999), 145–46.

103   "about the only places that were lit up": "Hollywood Works 8 to 5 Daily," *Hollywood Reporter*, December
       12, 1941, and "The Rambling Reporter," *Hollywood Reporter*, December 11, 1941.

104   "Hollywood wants to know" . . . President Roosevelt would ask Lowell Mellett: "Mellett Likely
       H'Wood Boss," *Hollywood Reporter*, December 11, 1941, and "Mellett Boss for Hollywood," *Hollywood
       Reporter*, December 23, 1941.

104   "I want no censorship of the motion picture": "President Says No Censorship," *Hollywood Reporter*,
       December 24, 1941.

104   *Variety* suggested that someone who already commanded respect: Clayton R. Koppes and Gregory D.
       Black, *Hollywood Goes to War: How Politics, Profits, and Propaganda Shaped World War II Movies* (New
       York: Free Press, 1987), 57.

104   made a formal request to Navy Secretary Frank Knox: Scott Eyman, *Print the Legend: The Life and
       Times of John Ford* (New York: Simon & Schuster, 1999), 245.

104   "Congratulations": Cable from Darryl Zanuck to John Ford, October 11, 1941, JFC.

105   Ford's initial fitness report: Joseph McBride, *Searching for John Ford: A Life* (New York: St. Martin's,
       2001), 336–39.

105   "Inopportune to make this film now": Eyman, *Print the Legend*, 235.

105   "looked like my mother": John Ford to Dan Ford, JFC.

105   "Picture went over marvelously": Dan Ford, *Pappy: The Life of John Ford* (Englewood Cliffs, NJ: Prentice
       Hall, 1979), 162.

105   "If this is not one of the best pictures": Memo from Darryl Zanuck to John Ford, June 13, 1941, JFC.

105   On his official entrance report: Entrance application completed by John Ford, ca. August 1941, JFC.

106   a guest of the first family: Letter from Mrs. J. M. Helm, secretary to the First Lady, to John Ford, October
       27, 1941, JFC.

106   new Field Photo Unit: Special Photographic Unit V-6 roster, July 24, 1941, JFC.

106   "It is beyond my comprehension": Letter from A. Jack Bolton to Commander Calvin T. Durgin, August
       13, 1941, JFC.

106   interviewed in November 1941: Frank Farrell, "John Ford Dons Naval Uniform Because 'It's the Thing to
       Do,'" *New York World-Telegram*, November 1, 1941.

107   "respect, awe, and a little bit": Kathleen Parrish interviewed in *John Ford Goes to War* (originally aired
       2002 on Starz), produced and directed by Tom Thurman, written by Tom Marksbury.

107   "I don't know that [I'd] like very much": McBride, *Searching for John Ford*, 339–43.

107   "I'm very courteous to my equals": Ford interviewed by Philip Jenkinson, 1968, BBC.

107   Donovan sent him to Reykjavik: Memo from the chief of the Bureau of Navigation to John Ford, December
       12, 1941, JFC.

107   then to Panama: Memo from the chief of the Bureau of Navigation to John Ford, December 20, 1941, JFC.

107   *The Story of Pearl Harbor: An Epic in American History*: McBride, *Searching for John Ford*, 353.

108   Donovan told him to go to Hawaii: Memo from Frank Knox to the secretary of the navy, ca. January 1942,
       JFC, and (for reference to Engel), Robert Parrish, *Hollywood Doesn't Live Here Anymore* (Boston: Little,
       Brown, 1988), 18–21; letter from Henry Stimson to William J. Donovan, February 3, 1942, JFC.

108   "all in good shape, everything taken care of": John Ford oral history, Naval Historical Center.

108   Ford said little, but he was unsettled: Parrish, *Hollywood Doesn't Live Here Anymore*, 16.

109   He didn't tell Toland and Engel: McBride, *Searching for John Ford*, 356.

109   "doing a great job of our assignment": Letter from Gregg Toland to Samuel Goldwyn, March 22, 1942,
       file 3902, SGC.

109   in Honolulu, all cars had to be off the streets: Ibid.

109   "Naturally one can't write a great deal": Letter from John Ford to Mary Ford, February 24, 1942, JFC.

109   "I love that request for Frank Borzage": Letter from John Ford to Mary Ford, ca. March 1942, JFC.

109   "Ah well—such heroism": McBride, *Searching for John Ford*, 343.

109   Ford finally lost his temper: Parrish, *Hollywood Doesn't Live Here Anymore*, 18–21.

109   Parrish assumed it was as punishment: Ibid.

110   "Americans badly needed a morale boost": General James H. "Jimmy" Doolittle with Carroll V. Glines,
       I Could Never Be So Lucky Again (New York: Bantam, 1991), 2.

110   "enemy alien": Joseph McBride, *Frank Capra: The Catastrophe of Success* (New York: Simon & Schuster,
       1992; revised 2000), 450.

111   In an unusual arrangement: *Arsenic and Old Lace* files, FCA and Warner Bros. Archives, University of
       Southern California.

111   Capra seemed to be planning: McBride, *Frank Capra*, 448, 451.

111   "I know only too well the standards": Letter from Captain S. S. Bartlett, War Dept., to Frank Capra,
       December 20, 1941, FCA.

112   the army's Morale Branch: David Culbert, "Why We Fight: Social Engineering for a Democratic Society

at War," in *Film and Radio Propaganda in World War II*, ed. K. R. M. Short (Kent, UK: Croom Helm Ltd., 1983).

112 **"Since General Osborn is reputed to be":** Letter from Bartlett to Frank Capra, December 20, 1941, FCA.

112 **"you will at all times have free access":** Cable from General Frederick Osborn to Frank Capra, January 8, 1942, FCA.

112 **"I suppose it was in my blood":** Frank Capra, *The Name Above the Title: An Autobiography* (New York: Da Capo, 1997; originally published 1971), 315–16.

112 **"Do I have to wait for orders":** Telegram from Frank Capra to Richard Schlossberg, February 4, 1942, FCA.

112 **"You Hollywood big shots are all alike":** Capra's account of Schlossberg's statement appears with slight variations in *The Name Above the Title*, 318, and Jan Herman, *A Talent for Trouble: The Life of Hollywood's Most Acclaimed Director, William Wyler* (New York: Da Capo, 1997), 239–41.

113 **Marshall had projected movies:** Culbert, "Why We Fight."

113 **frequently greeted with hooting and Bronx cheers:** Michael Birdwell, "Technical Fairy First Class," *Historical Journal of Film, Radio and Television* 25, no. 2 (June 2005).

113 **"a gross abuse of the principle of a training film":** Ibid.

114 **"didn't like them. He didn't think":** Leland Poague, ed., *Frank Capra Interviews* (Jackson: University Press of Mississippi, 2004), 127.

114 **"wanted a series of films made":** Ibid., 57–61.

114 **"I come to you with no salute":** Frank Capra, "A Proposed Address by the President," December 24, 1942, Mellett files, Records of the Office of War Information, box 1432, NA.

115 **"one of our greatest movie directors":** Memorandum from Mellett to President Roosevelt, February 25, 1942, Mellett files, Records of the Office of War Information, box 1432, NA.

115 **calling it "a good idea":** Letter from Roosevelt to Mellett, February 26, 1942, Mellett files, Records of the Office of War Information, box 1432, NA.

115 **"This is beginning to look like"** to **"nothing but us":** Several letters from Frank Capra to Lucille Capra, undated but all February 1942, FCA.

Chapter 7: *"I've Only Got One German"*

117 **there would be no dancing:** Mason Wiley and Damien Bona, *Inside Oscar: The Unofficial History of the Academy Awards*, 10th anniversary ed. (New York: Ballantine, 1996), 115–16.

118 **"the vicious character of Nazi plotting and violence":** Ibid., 119.

118 **"was playing Regina with no shading":** Ed Sikov, *Dark Victory: The Life of Bette Davis* (New York: Henry Holt, 2007), 180.

119 **"Miss Davis seemed intent":** Thomas Brady, "Peace Comes to 'The Little Foxes,'" *New York Times*, June 22, 1941.

119 **one of her worst performances:** Bette Davis, *The Lonely Life* (New York: G. P. Putnam's Sons, 1962), 207.

119 **"Are you thinking what the character":** Wyler in *New York World-Telegram*, September 9, 1941, cited in Barbara Leaming, *Bette Davis* (New York: Cooper Square, 1992), 181.

119 **"You will give the great performance":** Michael Troyan, *A Rose for Mrs. Miniver: The Life of Greer Garson* (Lexington: University Press of Kentucky, 1999), 129.

120 **"I jumped at it because":** William Wyler interviewed by Catherine Wyler, 1981, reprinted in Gabriel Miller, ed., *William Wyler Interviews* (Jackson: University Press of Mississippi, 2009), 112.

121 **"I've been thinking about that scene":** Versions of this story, with slight variations, appear in Jan Herman, *A Talent for Trouble: The Life of Hollywood's Most Acclaimed Director, William Wyler* (New York: Da Capo, 1997); Michael Anderegg, *William Wyler* (Boston: Twayne, 1979); and Wyler's 1979 interview with Ron Davis in Miller, ed., *William Wyler Interviews*, 96–97.

122 **In the shooting script that Wyler had approved:** Script of *Mrs. Miniver*, October 18, 1941, box 7, folder 13, WWUCLA.

122 **Wilcoxon was already on active duty:** Troyan, *A Rose for Mrs. Miniver*, 134.

123 **"wild to get involved":** Talli Wyler interviewed in *Directed by William Wyler* (episode of *American Masters*, originally aired 1986 on PBS), produced by Catherine Wyler, narration and interviews by A. Scott Berg, directed by Aviva Slesin.

123 **"about my status and what action has been taken":** Telegram from William Wyler to Richard Schlossberg, February 12, 1942, NA.

123 **"if he had qualms":** John Huston interviewed in *Directed by William Wyler*.

123 **"uncomfortably obvious":** Lawrence Grobel, *The Hustons: The Life and Times of a Hollywood Dynasty*, updated ed. (New York: Cooper Square, 2000), 229.

123 **his salary for *The Maltese Falcon*:** Ibid., 217.

124 **"We had an odd, childlike territorial imperative":** Ibid., 212, 221.

124 "The Monster is stimulating" and "a First Class Character": Stuart Kaminsky, *John Huston: Maker of Magic* (Boston: Houghton Mifflin, 1978), 26, 48.

124 "shrinking all the pauses" . . . "with the whole picture in mind": Rudy Behlmer, *Inside Warner Bros. (1935–1951)* (New York: Viking, 1985), 151–52.

124 "The Warners have been strangely bashful": Bosley Crowther, "'The Maltese Falcon,' a Fast Mystery-Thriller with Quality and Charm, at the Strand," *New York Times*, October 4, 1941.

125 "frighteningly good evidence": "The New Pictures," *Time*, October 20, 1941.

125 "a classic in its field": *New York Herald Tribune*, October 4, 1941.

125 "I felt rather ashamed of the way": Grobel, *The Hustons*, 223.

125 "Anyone could see that": Jack L. Warner with Dean Jennings, *My First Hundred Years in Hollywood* (New York: Random House, 1964), 255.

125 "There is something elemental about Bette": John Huston, *An Open Book* (New York: Alfred A. Knopf, 1980), 81.

125 "one of the worst films made": Davis on *The Dick Cavett Show*, 1971, cited in Sikov, *Dark Victory*, 188.

125 home movies from the time: Footage from Richard Schickel, *The Men Who Made the Movies*, documentary series (1973).

126 "Have you put your new Oscar": Letter from John Ford to Mary Ford, April 4, 1942, JFC.

126 "pain in the ass": Axel Madsen, *William Wyler: The Authorized Biography* (New York: Thomas Y. Crowell, 1973), 223.

126 an idea to make a documentary: Herman, *A Talent for Trouble*, 239.

126 "You say you love America" to "to risk their lives for you!": A. Scott Berg, *Goldwyn* (New York: Alfred A. Knopf, 1989), 369.

127 the rights to B. Traven's novel: Behlmer, *Inside Warner Bros.*, 276.

128 When his orders to report for duty arrived: File 1719, JHC.

129 "I can't believe the Army would not allow him": Vincent Sherman, *Studio Affairs: My Life as a Film Director* (Lexington: University Press of Kentucky, 1996), 189–91.

129 Huston listed his father, not his wife: Military records for John Huston, April 29, 1942, file 1719, JHC.

Chapter 8: *"It's Going to Be a Problem and a Battle"*

130 "was quite mad at us": A. M. Sperber and Eric Lax, *Bogart* (New York: William Morrow, 1997), 187.

130 their only compensation for the next four weeks: Otto Friedrich, *City of Nets: A Portrait of Hollywood in the 1940's* (New York: Harper & Row, 1986), 136.

131 "That," he said, "is the kind of thing": John Sanford, *A Very Good Fall to Land With: Scenes from the Life of an American Jew*, vol. 3 (Santa Rosa, CA: Black Sparrow, 1987), 210–16.

131 "So we're necessary evils?": Ibid.

131 He would require twenty-page scripts: Frank Capra, *The Name Above the Title: An Autobiography* (New York: Da Capo, 1997; originally published 1971), 335.

131 "the only way you could reach that guy": Frank Capra interviewed by George Bailey, 1975, collected in Leland Poague, ed., *Frank Capra Interviews* (Jackson: University Press of Mississippi, 2004), 127.

131 "Is there anything": Sanford, *A Very Good Fall to Land With*, 210–216.

131 "He was a big Francoite": Joseph McBride, *Frank Capra: The Catastrophe of Success* (New York: Simon & Schuster, 1992; revised 2000), 458–60.

132 Capra commandeered a few small unoccupied warrens: Letter from Frank Capra to Ralph Block, Screen Writers Guild, March 4, 1942, FCA.

132 "start thinking seriously about whether you should come": Letter from Frank Capra to Lucille Capra, March 1, 1942, FCA.

132 "I call them my seven little dwarfs": Letter from Frank Capra to Lucille Capra, early March 1942, FCA.

132 "I was aghast," he wrote: Capra, *The Name Above the Title*, 338.

132 "Frank thought *everything* was full": McBride, *Frank Capra*, 458–60.

133 telling them that while he personally didn't have a problem: Letter from Frank Capra to John Sanford, May 1942, FCA.

133 made a deal with the Department of the Interior: Memorandum by General Frederick Osborn, March 4, 1942, Mellett files, Records of the Office of War Information, box 1432, NA.

133 "I've got budget troubles": Letters from Frank Capra to Lucille Capra, February 22, 1942, and March 1, 1942, FCA.

134 "a 'Negro War Effort' film": Memorandum by General Frederick Osborn, March 4, 1942, Mellett files, Records of the Office of War Information, box 1432, NA.

134 **"that rare balance of humor and dignity":** Otis Ferguson, "The Man in the Movies," *New Republic,* September 1, 1941.

134 **In a survey conducted in Harlem:** Clayton R. Koppes and Gregory D. Black, *Hollywood Goes to War: How Politics, Profits, and Propaganda Shaped World War II Movies* (New York: Free Press, 1987), 86.

134 **in the South, paranoid chatter:** John W. Dower, *War Without Mercy: Race and Power in the Pacific War* (New York: Pantheon, 1986), 174.

135 **It was Hellman's notion:** Carl Rollyson, *Lillian Hellman: Her Legend and Her Legacy* (New York: St. Martin's, 1988), 192–93.

135 **research tour of army bases in the Midwest and South:** Jan Herman, a *Talent for Trouble: The Life of Hollywood's Most Acclaimed Director, William Wyler* (New York: Da Capo, 1997), 241–42.

136 *The Negro Soldier* **was still a "top priority":** Axel Madsen, *William Wyler: The Authorized Biography* (New York: Thomas Y. Crowell, 1973), 226.

136 **"Play down colored soldiers":** Thomas Cripps and David Culbert. "The Negro Soldier (1944): Film Propaganda in Black and White," *American Quarterly,* Winter 1979.

136 **"docile, tractable, light hearted":** Stephen E. Ambrose, *D-Day—June 6, 1944: The Climactic Battle of World War II* (New York: Simon & Schuster, 1994), 147.

137 **the Caravan was received at the White House:** Herb Golden, "Capital Gives Victory Caravan Rousing Welcome," *Daily Variety,* May 1, 1942; also *New York Times,* April 13, 1942; Theodore Strauss, "That Sandrich Man," *New York Times,* July 12, 1942.

137 **"I spent weeks and weeks doing nothing":** John Huston, *An Open Book* (New York: Alfred A. Knopf, 1980), 88.

137 **"self-centered" with an "odd personality":** Jeffrey Meyers, *John Huston: Courage and Art* (New York: Crown Archetype, 2011), 47.

137 **"a propaganda film":** Lawrence Grobel, *The Hustons: The Life and Times of a Hollywood Dynasty,* updated ed. (New York: Cooper Square, 2000), 234–35.

138 **"Because it's such a piece of junk":** Lillian Hellman interviewed in *Directed by William Wyler* (episode of *American Masters,* originally aired 1986 on PBS), produced by Catherine Wyler, narration and interviews by A. Scott Berg, directed by Aviva Slesin.

138 **"the finest film yet made about the war":** Bosley Crowther, review (headline unavailable), *New York Times,* June 5, 1942.

138 *Time* **called the film:** "New Picture," *Time,* June 29, 1942.

138 **"so rightly done that it glows":** *New York Post,* June 5, 1942.

138 **"one of the strongest pieces of propaganda against complacency":** *Variety,* May 13, 1942.

138 **Some critics complained:** *Nation,* December 26, 1942, and April 15, 1943.

138 **President Roosevelt asked the Voice of America:** Herman, *A Talent for Trouble,* 235.

138 **"give us a** *Mrs. Miniver* **of China or Russia":** Office of War Information collection, speech by Nelson Poynter dated June 13, 1942, file 1556, NA.

138 **"an exemplary propaganda film":** Herman, *A Talent for Trouble,* 250.

139 **one of the ten best films ever made:** MGM publicity material, August 1942, WWUCLA.

139 **"wondering whether he was French or German":** *Time,* June 29, 1942.

139 **"been some Catholic's privilege to have directed":** *Catholic World,* September 1942.

139 **"When I spoke to him," said Wyler:** William Wyler interviewed by Catherine Wyler, 1981, reprinted in Gabriel Miller, ed., *William Wyler Interviews* (Jackson: University Press of Mississippi, 2009), 130–31.

139 **"I was anxious to serve and give my talent":** Letter from Frank Capra to Lucille Capra, May 3, 1942, FCA.

140 **"It's almost a dime novel":** Ibid.

140 **"Frankly and sincerely":** Letter from S. Charles Einfeld to Frank Capra, April 24, 1942, FCA.

141 **"why they are fighting":** "First Capra Documentary Service Pic Due May 1," *Daily Variety,* March 15, 1942.

141 **Among those movies was** *Triumph of the Will*: Thomas Doherty, *Projections of War: Hollywood, American Culture, and World War II* (New York: Columbia University Press, 1993), 20, 23.

142 **"I could see where the kids of Germany":** Capra told the story of his viewing of *Triumph of the Will* many times; this quote is composited from remarks in Richard Schickel, *The Men Who Made the Movies: Interviews with Frank Capra, George Cukor, Howard Hawks, Alfred Hitchcock, Vincente Minnelli, King Vidor, Raoul Walsh, and William E. Wellman* (New York: Atheneum, 1975), 82; Dower, *War Without Mercy,* 16; and "WWII: the Propaganda Battle," in *A Walk Through the 20th Century with Bill Moyers,* documentary series.

142 **"Let our boys hear the Nazis":** Dower, *War Without Mercy,* 16.

142 **"gold mine":** Memorandum by General Frederick Osborn, March 4, 1942, Mellett files, Records of the Office of War Information, box 1432, NA.

142 **"Producing important series information films":** Cable from Frank Capra to Eric Knight, April 16, 1942, Eric Knight papers, EKP.

142 "love at first sight": Capra, *The Name Above the Title*, 331.

143 "to pull them all into a strong unity": Letter from Eric Knight to Frank Capra, April 15, 1942, FCA.

144 "making clear the enemies' ruthless objectives": Letter from Frank Capra to Lowell Mellett, May 1942, cited in Matthew C. Gunter, *The Capra Touch: A Study of the Director's Hollywood Classics and War Documentaries, 1934–1945* (Jefferson, NC: McFarland, 2011).

144 on June 6, 1942, a directive was issued: McBride, *Frank Capra*, 457.

Chapter 9: "All I Know Is That I'm Not Courageous"

145 send John Ford to Midway: John Ford oral history, Naval Historical Center.

145 "exercise full responsibility": Scott Eyman, *Print the Legend: The Life and Times of John Ford* (New York: Simon & Schuster, 1999), 257.

145 annual operating budget of $1 million: Joseph McBride, *Searching for John Ford: A Life* (New York: St. Martin's, 2001), 345–46.

145 Ford immediately volunteered himself for the mission: John Ford oral history, Naval Historical Center.

146 "Up here for a short visit": Letter from John Ford to Mary Ford, June 1, 1942, JFC.

146 "I think at the time there was some report": Ibid. Except where indicated, all subsequent quotes from Ford about Midway and accounts of his behavior in this section come from his Naval History Center oral history.

147 "the highest spot I could work from": Jack Mackenzie Jr., as told to Alvin Wyckoff, "Fighting Cameramen," *American Cinematographer*, February 1944.

149 their stories would soon be told in almost a dozen Hollywood movies: Among the most notable dramatic films to deal with the early war in the Pacific are *Wake Island*, *Bataan*, *Corregidor*, and *Cry Havoc*.

149 Midway brought America welcome news: David M. Kennedy, *Freedom from Fear: The American People in Depression and War, 1929–1945*, Oxford History of the United States (New York: Oxford University Press, 1999), 543.

149 "photographing records of the destruction": Mackenzie, "Fighting Cameramen."

150 George Gay, watched his comrades perish: George Gay oral history, Naval History Center.

150 "I am really a coward": John Ford interviewed by Philip Jenkinson, BBC, 1968 (transcribed by the author from video exhibit at Mémorial de la Shoah, Musée, Centre de documentation juive contemporaine, Paris).

150 the official medical report described: Medical History from H-8 report, June 4, 1942, JFC.

151 "OK. LOVE, JOHN FORD": Eyman, *Print the Legend*, 259.

151 his wound was categorized by the navy: Medical History from H-8 report, June 4, 1942, JFC.

151 "Mary is a wise Navy wife": McBride, *Searching for John Ford*, 366.

151 "We were thrilled at account of Midway action": Cable from George Stevens to John Ford, June 18, 1942, JFC.

151 "I did all of it": Peter Bogdanovich, *John Ford*, revised and enlarged ed. (Berkeley and Los Angeles: University of California Press, 1978).

151 one Japanese pilot had gotten so close: Dan Ford, *Pappy: The Life of John Ford* (Englewood Cliffs, NJ: Prentice Hall, 1979), 170.

151 "I had one boy with me": John Ford John Ford interviewed by Philip Jenkinson, BBC, 1968 (transcribed by the author from video exhibit at Mémorial de la Shoah, Musée, Centre de documentation juive contemporaine, Paris).

152 "had a lot to do with the success of the picture": Mackenzie, "Fighting Cameramen."

152 "Never mind the [travel] orders": Robert Parrish, *Growing Up in Hollywood* (New York: Little, Brown, 1976). Parrish, who died in 1995, was a skilled memoirist and raconteur who told the story of the editing and recording of *The Battle of Midway* many times, often with variants and embellishments. In this section, I have tried to err on the side of his least extreme versions, and while the conversations he recalled can sound suspiciously scripted, there is no reason to doubt the broad strokes of his account.

152 "associate producers and public relations officers": Ibid., 145.

153 "There'll be no problem": Ibid.

153 "This is a film for the mothers of America": I have chosen the account offered by Joseph McBride in *Searching for John Ford*, 362, since it seems the likeliest and most characteristic reply that Ford would have given. but it is worth noting that Parrish recounted highly variant versions of this exchange over the years, including one to an interview for TV's *Omnibus* in which Parrish paraphrased Ford's reply as, "This is a film for the mothers of America. The fathers know about the war. The mothers don't know their sons are dying."

153 Ford soon joined Parrish on the West Coast: Parrish, *Growing Up in Hollywood*, 146.

154 Ford handed him a small spool of film: Ibid.

155   **"wonderful":** Letter from A. Jack Bolton to John Ford, November 2, 1942, JFC.

155   **"Maybe he's right":** Robert Parrish, *Hollywood Doesn't Live Here Anymore* (Boston: Little, Brown, 1988), 19.

158   **"I want every mother in America to see this film":** Ibid.

Chapter 10: *"Can You Use Me?"*

161   **"Americans . . . will be better haters":** *Variety,* May 20, 1942, cited in John W. Dower, *War Without Mercy: Race and Power in the Pacific War* (New York: Pantheon, 1986), 322.

161   **he convinced General Osborn to let him move his unit:** Frank Capra, *The Name Above the Title: An Autobiography* (New York: Da Capo, 1997; originally published 1971), 339.

161   **"so far as it means we would see you less often":** Letter from Osborn to Frank Capra, July 16, 1942, FCA.

161   **"Some carping individuals will accuse you":** Joseph McBride, *Frank Capra: The Catastrophe of Success* (New York: Simon & Schuster, 1992; revised 2000), 474.

162   **"a secret base at Shangri-La":** "Screen News Here and in Hollywood," *New York Times,* June 25, 1942.

162   **The bureau called the movie:** Clayton R. Koppes and Gregory D. Black, *Hollywood Goes to War: How Politics, Profits, and Propaganda Shaped World War II Movies* (New York: Free Press, 1987), 75–76.

163   **"creating a false picture of America" . . . "misled by propaganda":** *Government Information Manual for the Motion Picture Industry* (Washington, DC: Office of War Information, 1942).

163   **"We didn't bother about your way of life":** William J. Blakefield, "A War Within: The Making of Know Your Enemy—Japan," *Sight and Sound,* Spring 1983.

163   **he was in touch with the National Film Board of Canada:** Letter from National Film Board of Canada to Frank Capra, August 21, 1942, FCA.

163   **Janet Flanner, the Paris correspondent:** Memo from Frank Capra, February 1943, FCA.

163   **"We have eliminated the Battle of the Atlantic":** Letter from Frank Capra to Colonel Herman Beukema, August 26, 1942, FCA.

164   **"as difficult to write as the Versailles Treaty":** Letter from Leonard Spigelgass to Frank Capra, September 22, 1942, FCA.

164   **"Can you use me?":** Capra, *The Name Above the Title,* 339.

165   **"getting over a bad spot":** "The New Pictures," *Time,* February 16, 1942.

165   **Louis B. Mayer had nervously forbidden him:** Scott Eyman, *Lion of Hollywood: The Life and Legend of Louis B. Mayer* (New York: Simon & Schuster, 2005), 342.

165   **The *New Yorker* suggested:** Russell Maloney, "The Current Cinema: A Good Movie," *New Yorker,* February 7, 1942.

165   **"the audience . . . accepting":** George Stevens interviewed in 1973, reprinted in Paul Cronin, ed., *George Stevens Interviews* (Jackson: University Press of Mississippi, 2004), 87.

165   **"*Woman* is a hell of a hit" to "All-Americans to pull us out of this one":** Letter from "Bill" to George Stevens, March 1, 1942, file 3196, GSC.

166   **He had no shortage of reasons:** Bruce Humleker Petri, "A Theory of American Film: The Films and Techniques of George Stevens" (doctoral thesis, Harvard University, May 1974; copyright 1987).

166   **he began preparing *The Talk of the Town*:** John Oller, *Jean Arthur: The Actress Nobody Knew* (New York: Limelight Editions, 1997), 136–44.

166   **"one of the basic things we are fighting for":** Marilyn Ann Moss, *Giant: George Stevens, a Life on Film* (Madison: University of Wisconsin Press, 2004), 95.

167   **"While there are men of draft age" to "stay true to life":** Ibid., 96.

167   **"You go in, this war will last seven years":** Unedited trasnscript of George Stevens interviewed by Robert Hughes, 1967, file 3677, GSC.

167   **"The war was on":** Cronin, ed., *George Stevens Interviews,* 112.

168   **"She doesn't like me anymore":** Letter from "Mimi" to John Ford, apparently December 5, 1938, JFC.

168   **"Dear Ma":** Letter from John Ford to Mary Ford, January 10, 1942, JFC.

168   **"The kid is really tops":** Letter from John Ford to Commander W. J. Morcott, July 29, 1942, JFC.

168   **feeling "like a failure":** Letter from Pat Ford to John Ford, July 20, 1943, JFC.

169   **"I have seldom been so busy":** Jan Herman, *A Talent for Trouble: The Life of Hollywood's Most Acclaimed Director, William Wyler* (New York: Da Capo, 1997), 245.

169   **suspend the deal he had recently renewed:** Letter from Samuel Goldwyn to William Wyler, August 25, 1943, in reference to suspension dated July 15, 1942, WWA.

169   **"After sober reflection":** Cable from Irwin Shaw to William Wyler (repunctuated here for clarity), July 10, 1942, WWA.

170   **John Huston's departure from Hollywood:** Lawrence Grobel, *The Hustons: The Life and Times of a Hollywood Dynasty*, updated ed. (New York: Cooper Square, 2000), 235.

170   **he left Hollywood for Alaska:** Memo, November 6, 1942, file 1719, JHC.

171   **"very difficult" and "painful":** Grobel, *The Hustons*, 235.

171   **"to determine the discretion":** Jeffrey Meyers, *John Huston: Courage and Art* (New York: Crown Archetype, 2011), 96–97.

Chapter 11: "A Good Partner to Have in Times of Trouble"

172   **"Commander John Ford" . . . "factual film record":** "Film of 'Midway' Released by Navy," *New York Times*, September 15, 1942.

172   **"corny" narration:** "The New Pictures," *Time*, September 28, 1942.

172   **"nothing . . . that a spy would waste":** "The Current Cinema: Epidemic," *New Yorker*, September 19, 1942.

173   **"many scenes where the concussion of bombs":** John T. McManus, "America Cheers Midway Battle," *PM*, September 15, 1942.

173   **"should be seen by all Americans":** "The New Pictures," *Time*, September 28, 1942.

173   **booked more than thirteen thousand times:** Thomas Doherty, *Projections of War: Hollywood, American Culture, and World War II* (New York: Columbia University Press, 1993), 253.

174   **Wanger politely replied that the war:** Robert Parrish, *Hollywood Doesn't Live Here Anymore* (Boston: Little, Brown, 1988), 19–20.

175   **"I had a 36 hour talk with John Ford":** Letter from Sam Spewack to Lowell Mellett, September 4, 1942, Mellett files, box 1446, Records of the Office of War Information, NA.

175   **"to prove that we were actually in the war with them":** Parrish, *Hollywood Doesn't Live Here Anymore*.

175   **the War Department had given them all pamphlets:** *Instructions for American Servicemen in Britain* (Washington, DC: War Department, 1942).

176   **The navy installed him in Claridge's:** Letter from John Ford to Mary Ford, ca. August 1942, JFC.

176   **Darryl Zanuck, who had just begun a leave:** Rudy Behlmer, *Memo from Darryl F. Zanuck: The Golden Years at Twentieth Century-Fox* (New York: Grove, 1993), 63.

176   **Two of his other ideas:** Jan Herman, *A Talent for Trouble: The Life of Hollywood's Most Acclaimed Director, William Wyler* (New York: Da Capo, 1997), 247.

177   **"it just drove Willy crazy":** Ibid., 248.

177   **"half of it had been sunk by the Germans":** Axel Madsen, *William Wyler: The Authorized Biography* (New York: Thomas Y. Crowell, 1973), 231.

177   **"[Ford] didn't like Willy Wyler":** Unpublished transcript of interview with William Clothier by Dan Ford, JFC.

177   **"The trouble with London":** Herman, *A Talent for Trouble*, 246.

177   **"The picture of England at war":** Michael Troyan, *A Rose for Mrs. Miniver: The Life of Greer Garson* (Lexington: University Press of Kentucky, 1999), 149–50.

177   **"defense of bourgeois privilege" . . . "unconsciously pro-Fascist propaganda":** Clayton R. Koppes and Gregory D. Black, *Hollywood Goes to War: How Politics, Profits, and Propaganda Shaped World War II Movies* (New York: Free Press, 1987), 230.

177   **"hogwash. . . . Oh, God, those Hollywood men":** Troyan, *A Rose for Mrs. Miniver*, 150.

178   **"propaganda worth many battleships":** John Douglas Eames, *The MGM Story*, 2nd revised ed. (New York: Crown, 1982), 176.

178   **"portrays the life that people live":** Telegram from Lord Halifax to William Wyler, July 3, 1942, WWUCLA.

178   **Olivier was granted a leave from service:** Donald Spoto, *Laurence Olivier: A Biography* (New York: HarperCollins, 1992), 165.

178   **"a propaganda picture doesn't have to be" and "Don't worry":** Herman, *A Talent for Trouble*, 237, 253.

178   **Olivier took Wyler's advice and went to Ford:** Spoto, *Laurence Olivier*, 165.

179   **"we might just as well" . . . "stripped down and getting tanned":** John Ford oral history, Naval Historical Center.

179   **"Can't I ever get away from you?":** Darryl F. Zanuck, *Tunis Expedition* (New York: Random House, 1943), 63–65.

179   **Zanuck had somehow managed to take possession:** Dan Ford, *Pappy: The Life of John Ford* (Englewood Cliffs, NJ: Prentice Hall, 1979), 177.

180   **getting to know the men of D Company:** John Ford oral history, Naval Historical Center.

180   **"the Germans were making sporadic [air] raids:** Ibid.

180   **"All along, I have inquired about Jack Ford":** Zanuck, *Tunis Expedition*, 125–26.

180   **"twenty-four hours a day for six weeks":** Letter from John Ford to James Roosevelt, March 20, 1943, JFC.

180   **before retreating, Ford had to turn over everything:** Ibid., 377.

181   **the *New York Times* called it:** Bosley Crowther, "'The World at War,' a Powerful Documentary Survey of the Past Decade, at Rialto," *New York Times*, September 4, 1942.

183   **"as tough and ferocious . . . as a super-bayonet":** Letter from Eric Knight to Frank Capra, April 15, 1942, FCA.

183   **"Superb!":** Forrest C. Pogue, *George C. Marshall: Organizer of Victory* (New York: Viking, 1973), 473.

183   **"Colonel Capra, how did you do it?":** Letter from Frederick Osborn to Lucille Capra, October 23, 1942, FCA.

183   **"Darling—Have so many things":** Letter from Frank Capra to Lucille Capra, October 25, 1942. FCA.

183   **"a bad picture in some respects":** Letter from Lowell Mellett to Franklin Delano Roosevelt, November 9, 1942, Mellett files, Records of the Office of War Information, NA.

184   **"Appreciate desire of Colonel Capra's Academy friends":** Wire from Lowell Mellett to Academy of Motion Picture Arts and Sciences, November 9, 1942, Mellett files, Records of the Office of War Information, NA.

184   **"This is the third instance":** Koppes and Black, *Hollywood Goes to War*, 122–23.

184   **General Osborn, who wrote to Mellett:** Joseph McBride, *Frank Capra: The Catastrophe of Success* (New York: Simon & Schuster, 1992; revised 2000), 476.

184   **"I don't know what got into Lowell Mellett":** Letter from Frederick Osborn to Frank Capra, November 26, 1942, FCA.

184   **"I have no particular objection":** Tony Aldgate, "Mr. Capra Goes to War: Frank Capra, the British Army Film Unit, and Anglo-American Travails in the Production of 'Tunisian Victory,'" *Historical Journal of Film, Radio and Television* 11, no. 1 (1991).

185   **"there is always one instant reaction":** Letter from Eric Knight to Frank Capra, November 21, 1942, FCA.

185   **when his plane crashed:** Charles Hurd, "Eric Knight Victim; Author Among Group of 26 Specialists and 9 in Crew to Die," *New York Times*, January 22, 1943.

Chapter 12: "You Might as Well Run into It as Away from It"

187   **thorough, imaginative lists:** Undated notebooks, sketches, notes, and memos from file 478, JHC.

187   **"nearer to the enemy":** Except as noted, all quotations and reminiscences from Huston about his experience on Adak in this section are from his autobiography *An Open Book* (New York: Alfred A. Knopf, 1980), 88–96.

188   **"Every day is Sunday":** War Department memo to John Huston, March 11, 1943, attached to script, file 477, JHC.

188   **the highly regarded cinematographer James Wong Howe:** Scott Eyman, *Print the Legend: The Life and Times of John Ford* (New York: Simon & Schuster, 1999), 252–53.

188   **"men who can serve as grips":** Memo from John Huston to General James Landrum, November 9, 1942, file 478, JHC.

189   **"a bloody, no-good rogue" and a "crazy son of a bitch":** John Huston interviewed by Peter S. Greenberg, *Rolling Stone*, February 9, 1981, reprinted in Robert Emmet Long, ed., *John Huston Interviews* (Jackson: University Press of Mississippi, 2001), 115–16.

189   **flying nine missions in six days:** Scott Hammen, "At War with the Army," *Film Comment*, March/April 1980.

189   **"Every time I went with them":** John Huston interviewed by Greenberg, in Long, ed., *John Huston Interviews*, 115–16.

189   **The first time Huston rode along on a mission:** Huston, *An Open Book*, 89–90, 92.

190   **Huston was awed by the indifference to danger:** Huston interviewed in *The Men Who Made the Movies*, documentary series (1973).

190   **"The thunder of engines makes the earth tremble":** Lawrence Grobel, *The Hustons: The Life and Times of a Hollywood Dynasty*, updated ed. (New York: Cooper Square, 2000), 236.

191   **"His loyalty and integrity":** Jeffrey Meyers, *John Huston: Courage and Art* (New York: Crown Archetype, 2011), 96–97.

191   **"access to confidential or secret information":** Ibid.

192   **"it was a very romantic period":** Grobel, *The Hustons*, 238.

192   "Having just returned from working": Huston, *An Open Book*, 96.

192   "most of the Hollywood professionals": Ibid., 102.

193   One night, he was at the entrance: Marilyn Ann Moss, *Giant: George Stevens, a Life on Film* (Madison: University of Wisconsin Press, 2004), 103.

193   "These were men who were way past military age": Interview with Irwin Shaw, file 67, Filmmaker's Journey Collection, Margaret Herrick Library.

194   McCrea, a minor star in westerns: Unedited transcript of George Stevens interviewed by Robert Hughes, 1967, file 3677, GSC.

194   Stevens had to reassure him: Memo from George Stevens to Harry Cohn, November 10, 1942, file 2723, GSC.

194   "We deem it very essential" . . . "some sort of bathrobe at all times": Letter from Joseph Breen to Harry Cohn, September 10, 1942, file 2723, GSC.

194   J. Edgar Hoover signed off on it personally: Letter from Hoover to Harry Cohn, September 18, 1942, file 2723, GSC.

195   among the names tested were: Memo from Duncan Cassell, October 16, 1942, and report from Audience Research Institute, November 30, 1942, file 2721, GSC.

195   he put together a cut of the film: Paul Cronin, ed., *George Stevens Interviews* (Jackson: University Press of Mississippi, 2004), 112.

195   "George Stevens is leaving" . . . "when Mr. Stevens returns": Moss, *Giant*, 100.

195   "One day he came home": George Stevens Jr. interviewed in the documentary "George Stevens in World War II," supplement to 20th Century Fox's 50th anniversary DVD of the *Diary of Anne Frank*.

195   "sent by the Special Service Division": Letter from Frank Capra to Local Board No. 179, North Hollywood, January 6, 1943, FCA.

195   "I certainly didn't know whether": George Stevens interviewed in 1964, in Cronin, ed., *George Stevens Interviews*, 39–40.

195   signing over his power of attorney: Power of attorney document, February 22, 1943, file 3806, GSC.

195   He then went to Washington: George Stevens notebook #15, February 22, 1943, GSC.

196   he became sick: Stevens's notebook from this time, numbered 15 in the George Stevens Collection, shows that he returned to New York City on February 25, 1943, became sick in early March, was hospitalized on March 11, 1943, was released from Fort Jay on March 28, 1943, and traveled to Washington, D.C., with his family on April 6, 1943.

196   "separation was really upon us" . . . "can come back to them": George Stevens notebook #15, entries dated April 7, 1943, April 20, 1943, and April 25, 1943, GSC.

196   "Almost everyone sick": George Stevens notebook #1, May 5, 1943, GSC.

197   "We flew along in the dark": Ibid., May 7, 1943.

197   "It was a film you would avoid seeing": Cronin, ed., *George Stevens Interviews*, 112–13.

197   the graffiti "Hitler is bastard": Loose page of one of Stevens's journals dated May 10, 1943, GSC.

197   "a smart, civilized [comedy]": "Current & Choice: New Picture," *Time*, May 17, 1943.

198   "Life's a journey": George Stevens journal entry, quoted in "George Stevens: A Filmmaker's Journey," unpublished transcript, file 13, FJC.

198   "THIS DAMN WAR": George Stevens notebook #1, May 12, 1943, GSC.

Chapter 13: "Just Enough to Make It Seem Less Than Real"

199   all they did was show up regularly: Axel Madsen, *William Wyler: The Authorized Biography* (New York: Thomas Y. Crowell, 1973), 232.

199   "organize and operate the activities": Memo from 8th Air Force HQ signed by Lieutenant Colonel Beirne Lay Jr., December 20, 1942, file 777, WWA.

199   Wyler had already requested flight training: Jan Herman, *A Talent for Trouble: The Life of Hollywood's Most Acclaimed Director, William Wyler* (New York: Da Capo, 1997), 249–50.

200   "Willy had this brand-new uniform": Madsen, *William Wyler*, 230.

200   Wyler still had only one piece of equipment: Thomas M. Pryor, "Filming Our Bombers over Germany," *New York Times*, March 26, 1944.

200   "Supply agencies have appeared to be mystified": Memo from Beirne Lay, December 20, 1942, file 777, WWA.

201   "We had to learn aircraft recognition": William Wyler interviewed by Catherine Wyler, 1981, reprinted in Gabriel Miller, ed., *William Wyler Interviews* (Jackson: University Press of Mississippi, 2009), 131–32.

201   "I was also glad to see I wasn't forgotten": Herman, *A Talent for Trouble*, 250.

201   The bomber's captain, Robert Morgan: Patrick Healy, "Robert Morgan, 85, World War II Pilot of Memphis Belle," *New York Times*, May 17, 2004.

202   The B-17s would typically fly: "Working for Uncle Sam," http://www.91stbombgroup.com/mary_ruth /Chapter_3.htm.

202   "All my thoughts are with you": Herman, *A Talent for Trouble*, 251.

202   "the flak was terrific": Madsen, *William Wyler*, 233.

202   "We could hear him cuss over the intercom": Ibid.

203   twenty-six-year-old Walter Cronkite: Walter Cronkite, "'Hell' Pictured as Flying Forts Raid Germany," *Los Angeles Times*, February 27, 1943.

203   Lay had arranged a showing of the film: Madsen, *William Wyler*, 232.

204   "As soon as I went to England": William Wyler interviewed in *Theatre Arts* 31, no. 2 (February 1947).

204   "I was handicapped by dealing with places": William Wyler interviewed in *Action!* 8, no. 5 (September/ October 1973).

204   the ceremony was filled with talk of the war: Mason Wiley and Damien Bona, *Inside Oscar: The Unofficial History of the Academy Awards*,10th anniversary ed. (New York: Ballantine, 1996), 128–29.

204   "It is a matter of deep satisfaction to me": Letter from Franklin Delano Roosevelt to Walter Wanger, reprinted in *Hollywood Reporter*, March 5, 1943.

204   "no one person could arrange anything this boring": Wiley and Bona, *Inside Oscar*, 131.

204   "I wish he could be here": Herman, *A Talent for Trouble*, 254.

205   "Have you got a photograph" to "Well, I'll be damned": William Wyler interviewed by Ronald L. Davis, Southern Methodist University oral history project, 1979, reprinted in Gabriel Miller, ed., *William Wyler Interviews* (Jackson: University Press of Mississippi, 2009), 98.

205   "a clean sweep": *Los Angeles Herald Express*, March 5, 1943.

205   Sam Goldwyn told him . . . "Only hope it won't take as long": Cables to William Wyler from Samuel Goldwyn, John Huston, and Talli Wyler; cables to Talli Wyler and Mack Millar from William Wyler, all in file 329, WWA.

208   the strongly anti-Japanese tone of Toland's cut: Gallagher raised this point in a controversial article titled "Two Big Missing John Ford Stories" that originally appeared in issue 12 of an online publication called *Film Journal* in 2005 but was later withdrawn by the editors after complaints from Joseph McBride that it mischaracterized his work. (The article appears on the IMDB.com chatboard for *December 7th*.) Gallagher's notion that Toland may have been trying to justify American internment policies was not challenged by McBride, and is thus included here.

208   "Crowd in every interesting foot": Letter from James Kevin McGuinness to John Ford, March 24, 1943, JFC.

210   "personal political propaganda": John Morton Blum, *V Was for Victory: Politics and Propaganda During World War II* (New York: Harcourt Brace Jovanovich, 1977), 39.

210   "I want our generals to put their time": Thomas Doherty, *Projections of War: Hollywood, American Culture, and World War II* (New York: Columbia University Press, 1993), 70.

211   Mellett aired his conviction that *Prelude to War*: "Mellett, War Dept. Clash over Prelude to War Film Release to Public," *Hollywood Reporter*, February 11, 1943.

211   The Roosevelt administration "should see to it": Leo Mishkin in *New York Morning Telegraph*, January 11, 1943.

Chapter 14: "Coming Along with Us Just for Pictures?"

213   "The goal of every man on the committee": "Billion-Dollar Watchdog," *Time*, March 8, 1943.

214   "All of Algeria reminds me of California": Darryl F. Zanuck, *Tunis Expedition* (New York: Random House, 1943).

214   "One would like . . . to have heard something": John K. Hutchens, "War Front Diary," *New York Times Book Review*, April 1, 1943.

214   His account of his conversation to racial annihilation: Zanuck, *Tunis Expedition*.

215   "I feel like a character" . . . fire off a tommy gun: Mel Gussow, *Darryl F. Zanuck: Don't Say Yes Until I Finish Talking* (New York: Doubleday, 1971), 105–10.

215   "arty shots of tank treads": "New Picture," *Time*, March 15, 1943.

215   When the Truman Committee decided to take aim: George F. Custen, *Twentieth Century's Fox: Darryl F. Zanuck and the Culture of Hollywood* (New York: Basic Books, 1997), 258–59.

215   Zanuck was furious and humiliated to "these fellows backing out": Ibid., citing an article by David Robb headlined "Zanuck Caught in D.C. Gunsights," *Variety*, date unavailable.

216   Ford had kept scrupulous records: Dan Ford, *Pappy: The Life of John Ford* (Englewood Cliffs, NJ: Prentice Hall, 1979), 178–80.

216   When the committee, casting a wide net: Scott Eyman, *Print the Legend: The Life and Times of John Ford* (New York: Simon & Schuster, 1999), 269.

216   **Capra was similarly called to account:** Letter from Frank Capra to Colonel K. B. Lawton, February 20, 1943, FCA.

217   **George Marshall had brushed off:** Joseph McBride, *Frank Capra: The Catastrophe of Success* (New York: Simon & Schuster, 1992; revised 2000), 477.

217   **"That goddamned Lowell Mellett!":** Clayton R. Koppes and Gregory D. Black, *Hollywood Goes to War: How Politics, Profits, and Propaganda Shaped World War II Movies* (New York: Free Press, 1987), 123–24.

217   **"Torrid conference today":** Letter from Stanley Grogan to Alexander Surles, April 22, 1943, FCA.

218   **he hoped Americans would find it "inspirational":** Bosley Crowther, "'Prelude to War' Shown to Public," *New York Times*, May 14, 1943.

218   **"respectably written":** *Nation*, June 12, 1943.

218   **"the broad contents of [which]":** "The New Pictures," *Time*, May 31, 1943.

218   **War Activities Committee had struck 250 prints:** Crowther, "'Prelude to War' Shown to Public."

218   **The sales pitch to theaters read:** Thomas Doherty, *Projections of War: Hollywood, American Culture, and World War II* (New York: Columbia University Press, 1993), 79.

218   **"the greatest gangster movie ever filmed":** John W. Dower, *War Without Mercy: Race and Power in the Pacific War* (New York: Pantheon, 1986), 17.

218   **General Surles, who was bitterly convinced:** Koppes and Black, *Hollywood Goes to War*, 124–25.

219   **"I knew he was this great Hollywood director":** Jan Herman, *A Talent for Trouble: The Life of Hollywood's Most Acclaimed Director, William Wyler* (New York: Da Capo, 1997), 255–56.

220   **"It was all done with these 16-millimeter cameras":** William Wyler interviewed at the American Film Institute in 1975, reprinted in George Stevens Jr., *Conversations with the Great Moviemakers of Hollywood's Golden Age at the American Film Institute* (New York: Alfred A. Knopf, 2006).

220   **"hanging out the window with a camera in [his] hand":** Herman, *A Talent for Trouble*, 256–57.

220   **"Talked with Queen about 5 minutes":** William Wyler in his journal, May 25, 1943, cited in Axel Madsen, *William Wyler: The Authorized Biography* (New York: Thomas Y. Crowell, 1973), 236.

221   **"Bad show" . . . "a 5-mile run":** William Wyler in his journal, May 19, 1943, cited in ibid., 235.

221   **on May 29—an extremely dangerous raid on Saint-Nazaire:** The dates and destinations of all of the sorties in which Wyler participated are from a 324th Bombardment Squadron memo, May 29, 1943, file 777, WWA.

221   **Wyler was awarded the Air Medal:** "Major Wyler Wins Medal," *New York Times*, June 12, 1943.

221   **"Suggest brushing up Cathy":** William Wyler to Talli Wyler, June 4, 1943, cited in Herman, *A Talent for Trouble*, 259.

222   **there had been some talk of plans:** Letter from Lowell Mellett to Sam Spewack, January 15, 1943, Lowell Mellett files, Records of the Office of War Information, box 1446, NA.

224   **Mellett then turned to his own deputy:** Memo from Lowell Mellett to Elmer Davis and Gardner Cowles Jr., May 18, 1943, Mellett files, Records of the Office of War Information, box 1431, NA.

224   **"it is certain to be more successful":** Memo from Lowell Mellett to Alexander Surles, June 22, 1943, Mellett files, Records of the Office of War Information, box 1431, NA.

224   **"universally favorable":** Memo from Alexander Surles to Lowell Mellett, June 23, 1943, Mellett files, Records of the Office of War Information, box 1431, NA.

225   **"The U.S. Army, which has consistently trailed":** *Variety*, July 14, 1943.

225   **called the delay "deplorable" . . . "wasteful argument back home":** Theodore Strauss, "A Delayed Report—The Signal Corps' Fine Film on Aleutians Was Held up by Lamentable Argument," *New York Times*, August 8, 1943.

225   **his suggestion that they conserve resources:** Thomas F. Brady, "Government Film Chief on Hollywood Tour; Lowell Mellett Finds Opposition to His Anti–Double Bill Stand—Other Matters," *New York Times*, November 29, 1942.

226   **the Bureau of Motion Pictures fell victim:** Allan M. Winkler, *The Politics of Propaganda: The Office of War Information, 1942–1945* (New Haven, CT: Yale University Press, 1978), 70–71.

226   **"unfinished business" . . . "a limited number":** Memo from Lowell Mellett to Elmer Davis, July 9, 1943, Mellett files, Records of the Office of War Information, box 1431, NA; also "Mellett Drops out as OWI Film Head," *New York Times*, July 10, 1943.

226   **Despite generous praise for Huston's work:** Doherty, *Projections of War*, 113–15.

Chapter 15: "How to Live in the Army"

231   **when Darryl Zanuck went to Algeria:** Journal kept by Darryl Zanuck, November 17, 1942, reprinted in Darryl F. Zanuck, *Tunis Expedition* (New York: Random House, 1943), 70.

232   **carefully coordinated effort to reenact the North African campaign:** John Huston tells this story in *An Open Book* (New York: Alfred A. Knopf, 1980), as does Brigadier General William H. Harrison in

Joseph McBride, *Frank Capra: The Catastrophe of Success* (New York: Simon & Schuster, 1992; revised 2000), 483.

232 **"the finest film of actual combat":** "The New Pictures," *Time,* April 12, 1943.

233 **"there is hardly a shot":** *Nation,* May 1, 1943.

233 **"The casualties they suffered in its production":** David Lardner, "The Current Cinema: Westward Ho!," *New Yorker,* April 17, 1943.

233 **"The captious will certainly find room":** *Variety,* March 31, 1943.

234 **Theodor S. Geisel:** Judith Morgan and Neil Morgan, *Dr. Seuss and Mr. Geisel: A Biography* (New York: Random House, 1995).

235 **"he has a remarkably good brain":** Letter from Leonard Spigelgass to Frank Capra, January 4, 1943, FCA.

235 **"He gave me the tour":** McBride, *Frank Capra,* 474–75.

235 **Capra teamed Geisel with a thirty-year-old animator:** Supplementary documentary on *Frank Capra's the War Years: Two Down and One to Go* video (RCA/Columbia Pictures Home Video, 1990).

235 **With Mel Blanc providing voices:** Phlip Nel, "Children's Literature Goes to War: Dr. Seuss, P. D. Eastman, Munro Leaf, and the *Private SNAFU* Films (1943–46)," *Journal of Popular Culture* 40, no. 3 (2007).

236 **they should "make it racy":** Michael Birdwell, "Technical Fairy First Class," *Historical Journal of Film, Radio and Television* 25, no. 2 (June 2005).

236 **"It's so cold it would freeze the nuts off a jeep!":** Morgan and Morgan, *Dr. Seuss and Mr. Geisel.*

236 **"I imagine you have seen *Desert Victory*":** Letter from Bob Heller to Frank Capra, April 1, 1943, FCA.

237 **"Our . . . uniforms look like outing clothes" to "for 'medicinal purposes'":** George Stevens journal entry, notebook #2, June 1, 1943, GSC.

237 **"We are going to use some infantry and five tanks":** George Stevens journal entry, notebook #2, June 4, 1943, GSC.

238 **"they didn't know whether to send him":** George Stevens interviewed in 1974, in Paul Cronin, ed., *George Stevens Interviews* (Jackson: University Press of Mississippi, 2004), 113.

238 **"would always scream when you went through" to "to live in the Army":** Unedited transcript of George Stevens interviewed by Robert Hughes, 1967, file 3677, GSC.

238 **His work is perfectly framed:** Unedited George Stevens World War II footage, reel 6, Library of Congress.

239 **"Although Gillette had agreed" . . . "too dumb to know its value":** George Stevens journal entry, notebook #15, June 14, 1943, GSC.

239 **for him to move on to Iran:** See the footnote on page 309 for a fuller explanation of Stevens's assignment in Iran.

239 **"25th Day—Escape From Algiers":** George Stevens journal entry, notebook #15, June 16, 1943, GSC.

239 **"a foul, filthy little village":** George Stevens journal entry, unnumbered, July 8, 1943, GSC.

240 **"The trucks have just been assembled":** Ibid.

240 **at night, the officers would drink:** George Stevens journal entry, notebook #15, July 5, 1943, GSC.

240 **"Alright":** George Stevens journal entry, unnumbered and undated but apparently July 1943, GSC.

240 **"Construct a celluloid monument":** Ibid.

240 **"a cameraman on the most formidable":** Draft of letter from George Stevens to General Osborn, unnumbered and undated journal, GSC.

241 **"We should have gone to [Pantelleria]":** Draft of letter from Geroge Stevens to Lyman Munson, unnumbered and undated journal, GSC.

241 **"'manufacture' a North African film":** Huston, *An Open Book,* 102–3.

241 **"We had troops moving up and down" . . . planes bombed the empty shells:** Ibid.

242 **"The work is getting more complicated":** Letter from Frank Capra to Lucille Capra, July 17, 1943, FCA.

242 **"I set it up so that the fighters":** Huston, *An Open Book,* 102–3.

242 **"Looking back on it":** McBride, *Frank Capra,* 484.

242 **Capra and Huston were called back to Washington:** Letter from Frank Capra to Lucille Capra, August 16, 1943, FCA.

243 **"The English were told that we had":** McBride, *Frank Capra,* 484.

Chapter 16: "I'm the Wrong Man for That Stuff"

244 **"With a new wing and a patched-up tail" to "the tail gunner, was wounded":** "Big Bomber Flies Home from Europe; Scarred Veteran Still Has Original Crew," Associated Press, June 16, 1943 (reprinted in *New York Times*).

244 **Captain Robert Morgan, the bomber's pilot:** "Greets Memphis Belle," *New York Times,* June 19, 1943.

245 **their relationship ended almost immediately:** "Major Morgan to Wed Texas Girl," *New York Times,* August 12, 1943.

245   **a six-week morale-building tour:** Memo headed "Corrected Schedule for Memphis Belle Tour," box 20, file 13, WWUCLA.

245   **"DEAD (tired)":** Wyler's daybook, May 20–23, 1943, cited in Axel Madsen, *William Wyler: The Authorized Biography* (New York: Thomas Y. Crowell, 1973), 237.

245   **"I was standing in the door":** Talli Wyler oral history, file 751, WWA.

245   **"I got the room number":** William Wyler interviewed by Catherine Wyler, 1981, reprinted in Gabriel Miller, ed., *William Wyler Interviews* (Jackson: University Press of Mississippi, 2009), 136.

245   **"Fear," he told the reporter:** Transcript of William Wyler interview with *Army Hour*, late June 1943, box 20, file 14, WWUCLA.

246   **"you're inclined to worship the skipper":** Ibid.

246   **where they themselves would record the comments:** Letter from Captain Richard G. Elliott to William Wyler, July 19, 1943, file 326, WWA.

246   **as he began to piece together:** Thomas M. Pryor, "Filming Our Bombers over Germany," *New York Times*, March 6, 1944.

247   **"complete authenticity and [the] fact that Morgan"** to **more substantial film:** Jan Herman, *A Talent for Trouble: The Life of Hollywood's Most Acclaimed Director, William Wyler* (New York: Da Capo, 1997), 261, 263.

247   **"very exciting air stuff":** Letter from Frank Capra to Lucille Capra, July 27, 1943, FCA.

247   **"Just a last-minute note":** Letter from Frank Capra to Lucille Capra, August 12, 1943, FCA.

247   **"is a tough job":** Letter from Frank Capra to Lucille Capra, August 16, 1943, FCA.

247   **"Politically, the war is going stale":** Undated journal entry, sometime between August 5 and August 16, 1943, GSC.

248   **"I didn't even have time":** Lawrence Grobel, *The Hustons: The Life and Times of a Hollywood Dynasty*, updated ed. (New York: Cooper Square, 2000), 241.

248   **"representation . . . of the part played":** Notes on a meeting by Jack Beddington, head of the film division, Ministry of Information, July 20, 1943, cited in Tony Aldgate, "Mr. Capra Goes to War: Frank Capra, the British Army Film Unit, and Anglo-American Travails in the production of 'Tunisian Victory,'" *Historical Journal of Film, Radio and Television* 11, no. 1 (1991).

248   **"inadequate impression of [the] joint operation":** Cable from Samuel Spewack to General Surles, August 2, 1943, War Department Public Relations files, NA.

248   **"said it was a swell picture":** This and all subsequent quotations in this chapter from the diaries of James Hodson are from Aldgate, "Mr. Capra Goes to War."

249   **"Something screwy here":** Diary labeled "Itinerary" kept by Capra, August 16, 1943, FCA.

249   **"Dialectics"** and **"[British] film boys heartbroken":** "Itinerary," August 17, 1943, and August 18, 1943, FCA.

249   **"good, authentic material":** Grobel, *The Hustons*, 241.

249   **"England was just wonderful during the war":** Ibid., 242–43.

250   **they moved out of Claridge's:** Joseph McBride, *Frank Capra: The Catastrophe of Success* (New York: Simon & Schuster, 1992; revised 2000), 485.

250   **"Party at John Mills' house":** "Itinerary," August 29, 1943, FCA.

250   **"Shock of my life":** "Itinerary," August 30, 1943, FCA.

250   **"Now convinced we're right":** "Itinerary," August 31, 1943, and September 1, 1943, FCA.

250   **a new and final deal was reached:** "Itinerary," September 3, 1943, FCA.

251   **"Tough people, these English":** Letter from Frank Capra to Lucille Capra, August 22, 1943, FCA.

251   **"[I] never cease marveling at British people":** "Itinerary," August 29, 1943, FCA.

251   **"doing a little fighting to prevent our picture":** James Hodson diary, September 21, 1943.

251   **"so long that" . . . "but we're 100% for that":** James Hodson diary, September 15, 1943.

251   **"Please":** Letter from Frank Capra to Lucille Capra, September 16, 1943, FCA.

252   **"This is the real thing":** "Itinerary," September 16, 1943, FCA.

252   **"war lost its glamour for me":** Frank Capra interviewed by Richard Glatzer, 1973, reprinted in Leland Poague, ed., *Frank Capra Interviews* (Jackson: University Press of Mississippi, 2004), 122.

252   **"unmoved and not very excited":** "Itinerary," September 26 and September 27, 1943, FCA.

252   **"really weary both physically and mentally":** Letter from Frank Capra to Lucille Capra, October 6, 1943, FCA.

252   **"a bright [moonlit] night, cold as hell":** "Itinerary," October 7, 1943, FCA.

252   **"British big wigs":** "Itinerary," October 8, 1943, FCA.

253   **"Between his genius and his social life":** Letter from Frank Capra to Lucille Capra, October 3, 1943, FCA.

253   **a high-level assistant in the British Army Film Service:** Letter from M. Carsans, War Office, October 27, 1943, JHC.

253   **"The idea, dreamed up . . . by Colonel Frank Capra":** Eric Ambler, *Here Lies: An Autobiography* (London: Weidenfeld & Nicolson, 1985), 190–91.

253   **preparation for two new training films:** Memo from General Osborn, September 27, 1943, FCA.
253   **"It was from one of the OWI people" to then for Naples:** Ambler, *Here Lies,* 190–91.
254   **throwing him a farewell party:** James Hodson diary, November 4, 1943.
254   **"Well the British have passed the opus"** . . . **"his particular little share":** Letter from Frank Capra to Lucille Capra, October 19, 1943.
255   **"I'm the hatchet man":** Letter from Frank Capra to Lucille Capra, January 17, 1944.
255   **"No war documentary can be made":** James Hodson diary, December 1943.

Chapter 17: *"I Have to Do a Good Job"*

257   **"You come back or I get a replacement":** Jan Herman, *A Talent for Trouble: The Life of Hollywood's Most Acclaimed Director, William Wyler* (New York: Da Capo, 1997), 263.
257   **"thousands of theaters all over the country":** "Report on CU-12 Activities," December 15, 1943, file 326, WWA.
258   **happily chatted and flirted:** Herman, *A Talent for Trouble,* 262.
258   **they met with Wyler:** "Daily Reports of Activities," August 17–August 22, 1943, file 326, WWA.
258   **punitive amendment to his contract:** Amendment to contract between Samuel Goldwyn and William Wyler, August 25, 1943, file 170, SGC.
258   **He got on a C-54 army transport plane:** Herman, *A Talent for Trouble,* 263.
258   **gave the director everything he wanted:** "Report on CU-12 Activities," October 6–December 15, 1943, file 326, WWA.
259   **"The recording crew":** Letter from Major George Groves, OIC Sound Dept., to Lieutenant Colonel Paul Mantz, CO, AAF First Motion Picture Unit, December 9, 1943, file 326, WWA.
259   **"recording sound to go over some of the scenes":** Written response from William Wyler, December 13, 1943, file 326, WWA.
259   **"The co-pilot asks the pilot"** . . . **"that last assignment":** Full script draft by Maxwell Anderson, box 20, file 14, WWUCLA.
260   **"How about my polishing up *Hamlet?*":** Ibid.
261   **he had spent the last two months:** GS notebook #15, entries from September 12 to October 23, 1943, GSC.
261   **"When I am put on the ground":** George Stevens journal entry, undated, late 1943, GSC.
262   **Eisenhower, "to keep me in my place":** Unedited transcript of Bruce Petri interview with George Stevens, 1973, GSC.
262   **the men who would become his squad mates:** George Stevens journal entry, November 5, 1943, GSC.
262   **"I didn't really know much about":** Ivan Moffat interviewed by Susan Winslow, 1982, file 52, FJC.
262   **"When I first met him":** Gavin Lambert, ed., *The Ivan Moffat File: Life Among the Beautiful and Damned in London, Paris, New York, and Hollywood* (New York: Pantheon, 2004), 217–19.
263   **"We have, as you might know, been anxious":** Letter from George Stevens to Frank Capra, February 18, 1944, GSC.
263   **"In some vague way":** Letter from Frank Capra to George Stevens, January 14, 1944, cited in Joseph McBride, *Frank Capra: The Catastrophe of Success* (New York: Simon & Schuster, 1992; revised 2000), 490.
263   **the year's best director for his comedy:** "'Watch on Rhine' Voted Best Film," *New York Times,* December 29, 1943.
263   **"special, unique, irreplaceable":** Transcript of Sidney Buchman's acceptance speech, January 21, 1944, file 2721, GSC.
263   **"Miss you and my boy more than you can know":** Cable from George Stevens to Yvonne Stevens, February 7, 1944, GSC.
264   **"sounds as if it were written":** Letter from Eric Knight to Frank Capra, April 15, 1942, FCA.
264   **"scissors and paste":** David Lardner, "The Current Cinema: Pro Bono Publico," *New Yorker,* Novmber 20, 1943.
265   **"for propaganda, always for the maximum":** "The New Pictures," *Time,* November 29, 1943.
265   **"the best and most important war film":** *Nation,* October 30, 1943.
265   **"a real super-powered celluloid bomb":** Memo of the Cinema Section of the U.S.S.R. Society for Cultural Relations with Foreign Countries, March 25, 1944, FCA.
265   **"the trustworthy old American movie magic":** Alfred Kazin, *New York Jew* (Syracuse, NY: Syracuse University Press, 1996; originally published in 1978), 85–86.
265   **"my one-man army throughout the war":** Lawrence Grobel, *The Hustons: The Life and Times of a Hollywood Dynasty,* updated ed. (New York: Cooper Square, 2000), 236.
266   **"like a whore suffering from the beating":** John Huston, *An Open Book* (New York: Alfred A. Knopf, 1980), 107.

266 he found a "bit pretentious": This and all subsequent quotations from Eric Ambler in this chapter, as well as the specifics of his and Huston's time in Naples, Venafro, and San Pietro, come from his autobiography *Here Lies*, 198–209, 211, and 249–51, except as noted; Ambler's is the most complete and detailed account of the first phase of Huston's work on *San Pietro*.

267 "except for his snoring": Huston, *An Open Book*, 113.

267 "one of the coolest men I've ever seen under fire": Ibid.

268 San Pietro felt like the center of the war: Lance Bertelsen, "San Pietro and the 'Art' of War," *Southwest Review*, Spring 1989.

270 "embarrassing": A. M. Sperber and Eric Lax, *Bogart* (New York: William Morrow, 1997), 232.

Chapter 18: "We Really Don't Know What Goes On Beneath the Surface"

271 "didn't take one successful photograph": John Huston interviewed by Peter S. Greenberg, *Rolling Stone*, February 19, 1981, reprinted in Robert Emmet Long, ed., *John Huston Interviews* (Jackson: University Press of Mississippi, 2001).

272 Louis B. Mayer had acquired the rights: "Screen News Here and in Hollywood," *New York Times*, May 20, 1943.

272 he wanted to make it his next film: Garry Wills, *John Wayne's America: The Politics of Celebrity* (New York: Simon & Schuster, 1997), 332.

272 when MGM asked Bill Donovan: Proposed telegram from Eddie Mannix to Captain L. P. Lovette, and letter from Frank Wead to John Ford, both March 9, 1943, JFC.

272 "I guess we might just as well": Letter from John Ford to Mary Ford, July 19, 1943, JFC.

272 "I pray to God it will soon be over": Letter from John Ford to Mary Ford, June 26, 1943, JFC.

272 He was earning just $4,000: Scott Eyman, *Print the Legend: The Life and Times of John Ford* (New York: Simon & Schuster, 1999), 270–71.

272 John Wayne had made and broken: Letters from John Wayne to John Ford, ca. May 1942, JFC.

273 At the end of 1943, Wayne: Randy Roberts and James S. Olson, *John Wayne, American* (New York: Free Press, 1995).

273 Ford and two Field Photo colleagues: Andrew Sinclair, *John Ford* (New York: Dial, 1979), 115.

273 make a visual case for the usefulness of Donovan's new intelligence agency: Tom Moon, *This Grim and Savage Game: The OSS and U.S. Covert Operations in World War II* (New York: Da Capo, 2000; originally published 1991), 165–66.

274 made his first and only parachute jump: Joseph McBride, *Searching for John Ford: A Life* (New York: St. Martin's, 2001), 389.

274 Intelligence Documentary Photographic Project: Dan Ford, *Pappy: The Life of John Ford* (Englewood Cliffs, NJ: Prentice Hall, 1979), 185.

274 complained to him that the organization: Letter from Mary Ford to John Ford, December 8, 1943, JFC.

274 the Fords' son Patrick expressed disgust that Jews: Letter from Patrick Ford to John Ford ("this Ghetto called Public Relations . . . is too full of Jew boys and sons of the rich"), February 12, 1944. JFC.

275 "we've got to win": McBride, *Searching for John Ford*, 374 ("The Yid"), 370–71 (Mary Ford), 369 (Patrick Ford); letter from John Ford to Harry Wurtzel, January 12, 1942, JFC.

275 "Dear Christ-Killer": Eyman, *Print the Legend*, 261.

275 soon turned from "a charming man": Larry Ceplair and Steven Englund, *The Inquisition in Hollywood: Politics in the Film Community, 1930–1960* (Berkeley: University of California Press, 1979), 209.

275 Motion Picture Alliance: Ibid., 210–11.

275 Ford wrote a forty-dollar check: McBride, *Searching for John Ford*, 371.

276 *Know Your Enemy—Japan*: William Blakefield, "A War Within: The Making of Know Your Enemy—Japan," *Sight and Sound*, Spring 1983.

277 "the real rulers of Japan": Hans Schoots, trans. David Colmer, *Living Dangerously: A Biography of Joris Ivens* (Amsterdam: Amsterdam University Press, 2000), 174–76.

277 when Capra submitted Ivens's completed film: Ibid.

277 "only . . . as a tool of Japanese militarists": Thomas Doherty, *Projections of War: Hollywood, American Culture, and World War II* (New York: Columbia University Press, 1993), 135–36.

277 "totally unsophisticated when it came to political thought": Joseph McBride, *Frank Capra: The Catastrophe of Success* (New York: Simon & Schuster, 1992; revised 2000), 498.

277 "From FDR to General Marshall" to "toward the Japanese": Blakefield, "A War Within."

278 "I nearly vomited": Letter from Frank Capra to Alexander Surles, December 14, 1943, FCA.

278   **Christmas Day promotion:** Frank Capra, *The Name Above the Title: An Autobiography* (New York: Da Capo, 1997; originally published 1971), 357–58.

278   **straitened financial circumstances:** Ibid., 353.

279   **"and I hope that will be soon":** Letter from Harry Warner to Frank Capra, January 11, 1944, FCA.

279   **Ernie Pyle's report:** Ernie Pyle, "This One Is Captain Waskow," Scripps Howard wire copy, January 19, 1944. Reprinted in *Reporting World War II, Part One: American Journalism, 1938–1944* (New York: Library of America, 1995), 735–37.

280   **"What a welcome the people":** John Huston, *An Open Book* (New York: Alfred A. Knopf, 1980), 110–13.

280   **"When I made *San Pietro*":** John Huston interviewed in "The Triumph of the Good Egg," by Ezra Goodman, undated and unidentified newspaper clipping ca. late 1940s, San Pietro clipping file, New York Public Library for the Performing Arts.

280   **an extensive and confidential written account:** "Operations in Italy December 1943, 143rd Infantry Regiment," compiled by William H. Martin, 143rd Infantry, Commanding, file 504, JHC.

281   **"Greater clarity needed"** to **"they are retreating":** "Notes on San Pietro," handwritten memo apparently by John Huston, undated, file 501, JHC.

281   **Fourteen unedited reels:** All notes on Huston's unused footage come from the author's viewing of his unedited film reels dated January 3–February 22, 1944, National Archives, College Park, Maryland.

282   **"I had never before seen dead":** Huston, *An Open Book*, 120.

283   **"The re-enactments in most cases are done so poorly"** to **"in Indio or Palm Springs":** Memo to Colonel Curtis Mitchell from Second Lieutenant James B. Faichney, "Subject: North African Re-enactments," January 28, 1944, file 1443, JHC.

283   **outrage from Huston:** Memos from John Huston to Colonel Kirke B. Lawson, chief, Army Pictorial Service, March 4 and March 26, 1944, file 1443, JHC.

283   **"far superior in over-all quality"** . . . **"easily recognizable":** Memo from Faichney to Mitchell, March 4, 1944, file 1443, JHC.

283   **Huston received a promotion:** John Huston army records, record of promotion dated April 14, 1944, file 1719, JHC.

284   **he "couldn't take":** Lawrence Grobel, *The Hustons: The Life and Times of a Hollywood Dynasty*, updated ed. (New York: Cooper Square, 2000), 258–59.

284   **"He was in a uniform":** Ibid., 254.

284   **"But Astoria," Huston wrote:** Huston, *An Open Book*, 187–88.

284   **"Dear John Welcome home":** Telegram from Frank Capra to John Huston, file 1443, JHC.

284   **He would work at Astoria all day:** Grobel, *The Hustons*, 255.

Chapter 19: *"If You Believe This, We Thank You"*

287   **"We suffer . . . a unique and constantly intensifying"** to **"the root of the disaster":** James Agee, "So Proudly We Fail," *Nation*, October 30, 1943.

287   **out of 545 feature films:** OWI memo, October 8, 1943, Ulric Bell/W. S. Cunningham correspondence files, Records of the Office of War Information, NA.

287   **"Hollywood has finally thrown up its hands":** Mildred Martin, "Hollywood Producers Have Jitters About War Films," *Philadelphia Inquirer*, April 30, 1944.

287   **Oscar ceremony held in the spring of 1944:** Mason Wiley and Damien Bona, *Inside Oscar: The Unofficial History of the Academy Awards*, 10th anniversary ed. (New York: Ballantine, 1996), 138.

288   **"deficient," "inaccurate":** Bosley Crowther, "'Tunisian Victory,' Picture of the Allies' Cooperation, at the Rialto," *New York Times*, March 24, 1944.

288   **"all a bit too much like other guns and planes":** "The Current Cinema: Chapter Two," *New Yorker*, March 25, 1944.

289   **including the "unfortunate":** "The New Pictures," *Time*, April 17, 1944.

289   **"the continuity has been chopped":** *New Republic*, April 3, 1944.

289   **"The film," he wrote in *The Nation*:** *Nation*, April 25, 1944.

289   **"This is the price we have to pay":** Bosley Crowther, "Element of Time: Observations on War Documentaries as Inspired by 'Tunisian Victory,'" *New York Times*, April 2, 1944.

290   **"I feel like a big loafer":** Letter from Geoge Stevens to Yvonne Stevens, March 21, 1944, GSC.

290   **"You are all a lot of big shots":** Letter from George Stevens to George Stevens Jr., April 6, 1944, GSC.

291   **While he and his team waited:** Letter from George Stevens to George Stevens Jr., April 14, 1944, GSC.

291   **"Hello my pal":** Letter from George Stevens to George Stevens Jr., February 14, 1944, GSC.

291   **"What's this D in Gym?":** Letter from George Stevens to George Stevens Jr., March 26, 1944, GSC.

291   "Third in his class of many boys": Letter from George Stevens to George Stevens Jr., April 3, 1044, GSC.
291   "For Jeep's sake be careful": Letter from George Stevens to George Stevens Jr., April 14, 1944, GSC.
292   "These have been dreary months": Marilyn Ann Moss, *Giant: George Stevens, a Life on Film* (Madison: University of Wisconsin Press, 2004), 108.
292   "You know that I find much": Ibid.
292   "The fellows in our work overseas": Letter from George Stevens to Yvonne Stevens, February 13, 1944, GSC.
292   "How the audience . . . enjoyed": George Stevens journal entry, January 6, 1944, GSC.
293   "[They] have been taboo in Hollywood": Letter from Charles Feldman to George Stevens, May 27, 1944, cited in Moss, *Giant*, 113.
293   "the lousiest crap imaginable": Ibid.
293   "We ran the first print": George Stevens journal entry, April 18, 1944, GSC.
293   "The makers of this film wish": Unused introduction to *Memphis Belle*, box 20, file 12, WWUCLA.
295   "This is a superb picture": Memo from Brigadier General L. S. Kuter for the chief of the Air Staff, February 2, 1944, file 326, WWA.
296   In 1942, the committee's vice chairman: Letter from Francis Harmon, vice chairman of the War Activities Committee, to Henry Stimson, February 18, 1944, file 326, WWA.
296   "persons in active duty": Thomas Doherty, *Hollywood's Censor: Joseph I. Breen and the Production Code Administration* (New York: Columbia University Press, 2007), 157–58.
296   "the wisdom of making these": Letter from Francis Harmon to Henry Stimson, February 18, 1944, file 326, WWA.
296   April 15, 1944, a date that Wyler came close to spending in an army jail: Wyler's account of this incident, with slight variations, appears in Axel Madsen, *William Wyler: The Authorized Biography* (New York: Thomas Y. Crowell, 1973), 240–42, and Jan Herman, *A Talent for Trouble: The Life of Hollywood's Most Acclaimed Director, William Wyler* (New York: Da Capo, 1997), 266–68.
297   "one of the finest fact films": Bosley Crowther, "Vivid Film of Daylight Bomb Raid Depicts Daring of Our Armed Forces," April 14, 1944, and Bosley Crowther, "The Real Thing," April 16, 1944, *New York Times*.
297   "ought to go a long way": "The Memphis Belle—A Life Story," *Cue*, April 1, 1944.
297   "best feature" was "the conversation": David Lardner, "The Current Cinema: More of the Same," *New Yorker*, April 15, 1944.
298   "could not guess which shots": *Nation*, April 15, 1944.
298   "shrewd but somewhat plushy war poster": "The New Pictures," *Time*, April 17, 1944.
298   "postwar planners should work out": *Nation*, April 15, 1944.
298   "says everything I've got to say": "The Memphis Belle—A Life Story," *Cue*, April 1, 1944.
298   "I want to make more documentary films": Cable from William Wyler to Moss Hart, February 20, 1944, cited in Herman, *A Talent for Trouble*, 265.

Chapter 20: "A Sporadic Raid of Sorts on the Continent"

300   "We are a democracy": W. L. White, *They Were Expendable* (New York: Harcourt, Brace & Company, 1942), vii.
300   "In a war" . . . "I've been back": Ibid., 3–4.
300   "Every congressman in America": Joseph McBride, *Searching for John Ford: A Life* (New York: St. Martin's, 2001), 381–82.
301   "the thing will probably be ske-rewed up": Ibid., 403–4.
301   in March 1944, the navy told him: OSS memorandum, April 6, 1944, JFC.
301   orders came through for him to report to London: OSS memorandum, March 24, 1944, JFC.
301   "I understand that there is to be": McBride, *Searching for John Ford*, 392.
302   Bulkeley was summoned: Scott Eyman, *Print the Legend: The Life and Times of John Ford* (New York: Simon & Schuster, 1999), 274.
302   Ford, still naked, then crawled back: McBride, *Searching for John Ford*, 393–94.
303   *The Negro Soldier*: Thomas Cripps and David Culbert, "The Negro Soldier (1944): Film Propaganda in Black and White," *American Quarterly*, Winter 1979.
303   "It is undoubtedly a powerful script": Letter from Frederick Osborn to Frank Capra, September 2, 1942, FCA.
303   Who is going to see the Negro picture?: Letter from Frederick Osborn to Frank Capra, September 23, 1942, FCA.
304   belief that the army's 875,000 black soldiers: Cripps and Culbert, "The Negro Soldier."
304   "apparently the big problem here": Letter from Sam Spewack to Lowell Mellett, September 4, 1942, Mellett files, box 1446, Records of the Office of War Information, NA.

304   **In 1943, black characters were depicted:** Clayton R. Koppes and Gregory D. Black, *Hollywood Goes to War: How Politics, Profits, and Propaganda Shaped World War II Movies* (New York: Free Press, 1987), 179.

304   **"films in which there is reference to racial minorities":** "Operational Guidance on OWI Documentary Film," November 21, 1944, reiteration of April 21, 1944, guideline, Ulric Bell/W. S. Cunningham Files, Records of the Office of War Information, NA.

305   **"I'll say this for him":** Joseph McBride, *Frank Capra: The Catastrophe of Success* (New York: Simon & Schuster, 1992; revised 2000), 492–93.

305   **A scene showing a white physical therapist:** Memo from Lyman T. Munson to Anatole Litvak, October 1943, cited in Cripps and Culbert, "The Negro Soldier."

305   **an invited audience of African Americans:** Invitation to press screening from Major General A. D. Surles, February 14, 1944, in Special Collections file on *The Negro Soldier,* New York Public Library for the Performing Arts.

305   **actors who had been hired for $10.50 a day:** Cripps and Culbert, "The Negro Soldier."

306   **Richard Wright:** "Negro Film Pleases Novelist," *Brooklyn Eagle,* March 1944 (exact date unavailable).

307   **"distinctly and thrillingly worthwhile" and "Who would have thought":** Frank Capra, *The Name Above the Title: An Autobiography* (New York: Da Capo, 1997; originally published 1971), 359 and 262.

307   **"ignore what's wrong with the Army":** McBride, *Frank Capra,* 492.

307   **"the dignity and expertness":** Dorothy Norman, "A World to Live In," *New York Post,* March 6, 1944.

307   **"Are you going to show this" . . . "will change their attitude":** *Time,* "The New Pictures," March 27, 1944.

307   **"America's Joe Louis Vs. The Axis!":** Promotional material, Special Collections file on *The Negro Soldier,* New York Public Library for the Performing Arts.

307   **"the real sleeper of the season":** John McManus, "McManus Speaking of Movies," *PM,* July 12, 1944.

307   **"Why don't you go to some" to leaving the country:** Carlton Moss interviewed by McBride, *Frank Capra,* 494.

308   **He claimed that Moss was a hothead:** Capra, *The Name Above the Title,* 358.

308   **fourth and most unlikely creative team:** William Blakefield, "A War Within: The Making of Know Your Enemy—Japan," *Sight and Sound,* Spring 1983.

308   **Capra had recently pulled Theodor Geisel off:** Judith Morgan and Neil Morgan, *Dr. Seuss and Mr. Geisel: A Biography* (New York: Random House, 1995).

308   **"the lack of general information":** Letter from Frank Capra to General Osborn, February 25, 1944, FCA.

308   **"limping along under reduced staff":** Memo from Frank Capra to Alexander Surles, June 9, 1944, FCA.

309   **"It is the gloaming when the train pulls out":** George Stevens journal entry, May 1, 1944, GSC.

Chapter 21: *"If You See It, Shoot It"*

310   **John Ford . . . didn't talk about D-Day for twenty years:** "This is the first time I've ever talked about it." John Ford in Pete Martin, "We Shot D-Day on Omaha Beach (an Interview with John Ford)," *American Legion Magazine,* June 1964. Except as noted, all direct quotes from Ford and descriptions of his D-Day experiences in this chapter are from this interview.

310   **George Stevens . . . leaving three weeks almost blank in his diary:** George Stevens notebook #12, GSC.

310   **Ford made no mention at all:** John Ford to Mary Ford, June 8, 1944, JFC.

311   **Five hundred 35-millimeter cameras:** OSS report cited in Joseph McBride, *Searching for John Ford: A Life* (New York: St. Martin's, 2001), 395.

311   **fifty cameras were placed in the first wave:** Thomas Doherty, *Projections of War: Hollywood, American Culture, and World War II* (New York: Columbia University Press, 1993), 242.

311   **American cameramen and almost two hundred still photographers:** Ibid.

311   **Stevens was an "artist":** John Ford to Walter Wanger, in Wanger, *You Must Remember This* (New York: Putnam, 1975).

311   **"in motion pictures the only medium":** McBride, *Searching for John Ford,* 179.

311   **Ford was running Field Photo:** Martin, "We Shot D-Day on Omaha Beach."

311   **Ford would owe him "two bottles of booze":** Andrew Sinclair, "John Ford's War," *Sight and Sound,* Spring 1979.

311   **with his own 16-millimeter camera:** George Stevens Jr., in *George Stevens: D-Day to Berlin* (1994), written and produced by George Stevens Jr.

312   **Before they landed, the *Belfast*'s captain:** George Stevens's unedited color and black-and-white World War II footage. Except where noted, all subsequent descriptions of what Stevens and his SPECOU unit shot derive from the author's viewing of this footage at the Library of Congress, Washington, D.C.

314 **With more than half a million American and British soldiers:** Stephen E. Ambrose, *D-Day: June 6, 1944; The Climactic Battle of World War II* (New York: Simon & Schuster, 1994).

314 **By the end of the first day of fighting** to **exposed and unretrievable:** Ibid.

315 **But most of the film for which Ford had planned:** Doherty, *Projections of War*, 242.

315 **Stevens was fond of telling a story:** Scott Eyman, *Print the Legend: The Life and Times of John Ford* (New York: Simon & Schuster, 1999), 274–75.

316 **"George had no right to be in the Army":** Irwin Shaw interviewed by Susan Winslow, October 14, 1981, file 66, FJC.

316 **"yes, I was one of the first men ashore":** John Ford to Axel Madsen, 1966, reprinted in Gerald Peary and Jenny Lefcourt, eds., *John Ford Interviews* (Jackson: University Press of Mississippi, 2001), 90.

316 **"Dear Ma—My darling, I miss you terribly":** *John Ford Goes to War* (originally aired 2002 on Starz), produced and directed by Tom Thurman, written by Tom Marksbury.

316 **Less than seventy-two hours after D-Day:** Martin, "We Shot D-Day on Omaha Beach."

316 **Much of the footage was blurry:** The footage is shown in the British documentary *D-Day in Colour* (2004), produced by Kim Hogg.

316 **what they captured would not be shown:** It was not until the fictional recreation of D-Day at the beginning of Steven Spielberg's *Saving Private Ryan* in 1998, some shots of which were virtual recreations of long-suppressed images, that the moviegoing public saw an approximation of what D-Day had looked like to some of the men who filmed it.

317 **Reels of the footage to finally become public on June 15:** Doherty, *Projections of War*, 242–44.

317 **"the greatest pictorial team play":** *Variety*, July 5, 1944.

318 **Sometime around June 12, Ford made his way:** Versions of this incident were recounted by William Clothier and Mark Armistead in unpublished interview transcripts with Dan Ford, JFC.

318 **Ford began to turn his thoughts** to **until after the war:** McBride, *Searching for John Ford*, 399–403.

319 **Ford was in the Mulberry harbor:** Martin, "We Shot D-Day on Omaha Beach."

319 **"Sorta winding this thing up":** Letter from John Ford to Mary Ford, June 23, 1944, JFC.

319 **He would remain in England:** OSS memorandum to John Ford, September 1, 1944, JFC.

319 **"Second morning in marshaling area":** George Stevens in notebook #12, June 22, 1944, GSC.

320 **"a very volatile, moody man":** Unpublished interview with Ivan Moffat, file 52, FJC.

320 **"he laughed":** Ibid.

320 **"He was taciturn, always grave-looking":** Irwin Shaw interviewed by Susan Winslow, October 14, 1981, file 66, FJC.

320 **one of Stevens's diary entries from late June:** George Stevens in notebook #12, June 23, 1944, GSC.

321 **As he stood with Moffat . . . "They'd think I'd gone nuts":** Gavin Lambert, ed., *The Ivan Moffat File: Life Among the Beautiful and Damned in London, Paris, New York, and Hollywood* (New York: Pantheon, 2004), 149–150.

321 **Stevens gave himself license to film** to **"the sense of indirection":** Ibid., 219–21.

322 **The men in Stevens's unit are identifiable:** *George Stevens: D-Day to Berlin.*

323 **"They were near a farmhouse":** Irwin Shaw interviewed by George Stevens Jr., November 3, 1982, file 67, FJC.

Chapter 22: "If Hitler Can Hold Out, So Can I"

324 **The navy had chartered his boat:** Letter from Commander W. J. Morcott to Mary Ford, January 15, 1942, and Declaration by John Ford, January 19, 1942, JFC, and Charter Party for the Auxiliary Ketch "Araner" between John Ford and the United States of America, August 29, 1942, legal file #15, JFC; also Mary Ford interviewed by Dan Ford, JFC.

325 **a "ribbon freak":** Andrew Sinclair, *John Ford* (New York: Dial, 1979).

325 **a Distinguished Service Medal:** Memo from John Ford to CO, Naval Command, OSS, September 12, 1944, JFC.

325 **even asked for a Croix de Guerre:** Dan Ford, *Pappy: The Life of John Ford* (Englewood Cliffs, NJ: Prentice Hall, 1979), 207.

325 **"He did a fine job":** Pete Martin, "We Shot D-Day on Omaha Beach (an Interview with John Ford)," *American Legion Magazine*, June 1964.

325 **"shameless":** Ford, *Pappy*, 207.

326 **"I have been ordered to Hollywood":** Letter from John Ford to Albert Wedemeyer, October 430, 1944, JFC.

326 **he spent $65,000 to buy:** Joseph McBride, *Searching for John Ford: A Life* (New York: St. Martin's, 2001), 405.

326   **Ford established what he called "the Farm":** Scott Eyman, *Print the Legend: The Life and Times of John Ford* (New York: Simon & Schuster, 1999), 283–84.

327   **"rehabilitation and benefit fund":** Fred Stanley, "The Hollywood Agenda," *New York Times,* February 4, 1945.

327   **Ford angrily rebuffed a suggestion:** Robert Parrish, *Growing Up in Hollywood* (New York: Little, Brown, 1976), 159.

327   **when Zanuck heard that his return to work . . . "including the wounds":** Letter from George Wasson to John Ford, October 4, 1944, JFC, and letters from Darryl Zanuck to George Wasson, October 11, 1944, and from Wasson to Zanuck, October 11, 1944, from 20th Century Fox archives, UCLA, cited in Garry Wills, *John Wayne's America: The Politics of Celebrity* (New York: Simon & Schuster, 1997), 332, and letter from executive manager of 20th Century Fox to John Ford, October 23, 1944, JFC.

328   **"if Hitler can hold out":** Letter from Frank Capra to Phil Berg, June 13, 1942, FCA.

328   **began discussions with Sam Briskin:** Joseph McBride, *Frank Capra: The Catastrophe of Success* (New York: Simon & Schuster, 1992; revised 2000), 506.

328   **"I will have been away from my civilian profession":** Letter from Frank Capra, September 2, 1944, FCA.

329   **"tell the sweet old Maestro":** Letter from Frank Capra to Robert Riskin with enclosure, July 15, 1944, FCA.

329   **"Dear Daddy":** Letter from Frank Capra Jr. to Frank Capra, June 2, 1944, FCA.

330   **"that it be withdrawn from showing":** Letter from Osborn to the army chief of staff, November 1, 1944, FCA.

330   **"I'm not trying to alibi" . . . "not through lack of study or effort":** Letter from Frank Capra to Frederick Osborn, November 21, 1944, FCA.

331   **"Now," Capra wrote, "we can spend money":** Memo by Frank Capra, June 9, 1944, FCA.

331   **When his eighty-nine-year-old grandmother died:** Lawrence Grobel, *The Hustons: The Life and Times of a Hollywood Dynasty,* updated ed. (New York: Cooper Square, 2000), 261.

331   **he signed to write two screenplays:** Ibid., 264.

331   **he strongly preferred the title *The Footsoldier and St. Peter*:** Memo from John Huston to Frank Capra, August 5, 1944, file 501, JHC.

332   **"The War Department wanted no part":** John Huston, *An Open Book* (New York: Alfred A. Knopf, 1980), 119.

332   **"My God, nobody ever wanted to kill Germans":** Kaminsky, *John Huston: Maker of Magic,* (Boston: Houghton Mifflin, 1978), 41.

333   **"In one of the missions":** Midge Mackenzie, "Film: An Antiwar Message from the Army's Messenger," *New York Times,* April 16, 2000.

333   **"deletion of certain footage" . . . identified the corpses as Italian:** Memo from Colonel Curtis Mitchell, November 3, 1944, file 495, JHC.

333   **"most prefer to think that the objectives":** Letter from Colonel Melvin E. Gillette to John Huston, October 28, 1944, file 499, JHC.

333   **"Alright, Huston, let's not have any more" . . . "similarity for the third time":** Memo from Lyman T. Munson to Frank Capra with note from Frank Capra attached and sent to John Huston, December 22, 1944, file 501, JHC.

334   **The only portion of his battle reenactments:** Memos to John Huston, May 31, 1944, files 665 and 666, JHC.

334   **'Dear John, 'tha Lilly' was bye":** Handwritten note from Doris Lilly to John Huston written on back of page 70 of draft of *Know Your Enemy—Japan* script, dated September 11, 1944, file 222, JHC.

335   **"The Japanese are afflicted with a mission":** Handwritten note by John Huston in margin of *Know Your Enemy—Japan* script, dated September 11, 1944, file 222, JHC.

335   **"He is pigeon-toed and perhaps bow-legged":** Ibid.

335   **they approved on the condition:** Army Service Forces memo from First Lieutenant Lehman Katz to John Huston, November 15, 1944, file 226, JHC.

336   **Raoul Walsh's *Objective, Burma!*:** *Objective, Burma!* production file, Warner Bros. Archives, University of Southern California, cited in Bernard F. Dick, *The Star-Spangled Screen: The American World War II Film* (Lexington: University Press of Kentucky, 1993), 228.

336   **"a billion people" . . . paranoiac race of animal-deity worshippers:** Draft of *Know Your Enemy—Japan* dated January 4, 1945, file 223, JHC.

336   **"a fatuous booby":** Draft of *Know Your Enemy—Japan* dated September 11, 1944, file 222, JHC.

336   **"too much sympathy for the Jap people":** John W. Dower, *War Without Mercy: Race and Power in the Pacific War* (New York: Pantheon, 1986), 19.

337   **a line that acknowledged the existence:** William Blakefield, "A War Within: The Making of Know Your Enemy—Japan," *Sight and Sound,* Spring 1983.

Chapter 23: "Time and Us Marches On"

338 **They were soon joined by Ernest Hemingway:** Gavin Lambert, ed., *The Ivan Moffat File: Life Among the Beautiful and Damned in London, Paris, New York, and Hollywood* (New York: Pantheon, 2004), 150.

339 **Stevens asked for, and received, permission:** *George Stevens: D-Day to Berlin* (1994), written and produced by George Stevens Jr.

339 **he filmed his men loading, cleaning:** This and all subsequent descriptions in this chapter of the film shot by Stevens and his unit come from the author's viewing of Stevens's unedited war footage at the Library of Congress, Washington, D.C.

339 **Stevens and the 2nd Armored:** Letter from George Stevens to Yvonne Stevens, September 1, 1944, GSC.

340 **"One knew at the time":** Lambert, ed., *The Ivan Moffat File*, 215.

341 **"He didn't have to do it":** Unedited interview with Ivan Moffat, file 52, FJC.

341 **He told Choltitz, Leclerc, and de Gaulle:** This incident was widely recounted, including in *George Stevens: D-Day to Berlin.*

341 **Stevens barked at Choltitz:** Lambert, ed., *The Ivan Moffat File*, 155.

341 **Irwin Shaw bet him that the war:** *George Stevens: D-Day to Berlin.*

341 **"The days and nights all ran over themselves"** . . . **"time and us marches on":** Letter from George Stevens to Yvonne Stevens, September 1, 1944, GSC.

342 **"For whom was [each bottle] destined?":** George Stevens journal entry, October 7, 1944, GSC.

343 **"It is a wet day":** George Stevens journal entry, October 12, 1944, GSC.

343 **"My new Jeep driver":** Ibid.

343 **"I came upon a theater":** Paul Cronin, ed., *George Stevens Interviews* (Jackson: University Press of Mississippi, 2004), 59.

344 **"Though you have been out of circulation"** . . . **"guarantees ever dished out":** Letter from Charles Feldman to George Stevens, October 1944, cited in Marilyn Ann Moss, *Giant: George Stevens, a Life on Film* (Madison: University of Wisconsin Press, 2004), 113–14.

344 **"The big Nazi flag is of value":** Letter from George Stevens to George Stevens Jr., late October 1944, GSC.

345 **"I've been hoping against hope":** Letter from Frank Capra to George Stevens, November 7, 1944, FCA.

345 **"the kind and stimulating things":** Letter from George Stevens to Frank Capra, December 17, 1944, GSC.

345 **told Capra he wasn't ready:** Joseph McBride, *Frank Capra: The Catastrophe of Success* (New York: Simon & Schuster, 1992; revised 2000), 508.

345 **"Whew! Christmas is approaching fast":** George Stevens journal entry, December 5, 1944, GSC.

346 **"IMPOSSIBLE":** George Stevens journal entry, December 18, 1944, GSC.

346 **"He had never understood":** Unedited interview with Ivan Moffat, file 52, FJC.

348 **"You have a most holy":** Jan Herman, *A Talent for Trouble: The Life of Hollywood's Most Acclaimed Director, William Wyler* (New York: Da Capo, 1997), 271.

348 **"a joke," since "the Free French":** Ibid., 273.

349 **"First, the subject matter is very difficult":** Letter from William Wyler to Colonel William Keighley, November 22, 1944, file 418, WWA.

350 **"He ran his own war":** Axel Madsen, *William Wyler: The Authorized Biography* (New York: Thomas Y. Crowell, 1973), 249–51. The subsequent account of Wyler's trip into Mulhouse is taken from his own version of events as told to Madsen.

350 **Wyler had Hemingway drive him:** Note in Herman, *A Talent for Trouble*, 490.

Chapter 24: "Who You Working For—Yourself?"

352 **"I *like* that".** . . **"as it had happened":** Peter Bogdanovich, *John Ford*, revised and enlarged ed. (Berkeley and Los Angeles: University of California Press, 1978).

352 **"We are sticking to facts":** Fred Stanley, "The Hollywood Agenda," *New York Times*, February 4, 1945.

353 **"would be helpful to the Navy":** James Forrestal to Charles Cheston (acting director of the OSS), September 12, 1944, JFC.

353 **"speak for the thousands of silent lips":** Speech by General Douglas MacArthur following the signing of the Japanese Instrument of Surrender, September 2, 1945.

353 **"dynamic forcefulness and daring":** Congressional Medal of Honor citation for John L. Bulkeley.

353 **"The whole thing happened at a time":** Dan Ford, *Pappy: The Life of John Ford* (Englewood Cliffs, NJ: Prentice Hall, 1979), 196–97.

353 **"the most decorated man"** . . . **"a wonderful person":** Bogdanovich, *John Ford.*

354 **he asked James McGuinness to thread through:** "Notes for Jim McGuinness on 'Expendable,'" undated, *They Were Expendable* production file, JFC.

355 **a pair of modest crosses:** Joseph McBride, *Searching for John Ford: A Life* (New York: St. Martin's, 2001), 410.

355 **"Like many fine artists":** Letter from Dudley Nichols to Lindsay Anderson, April 22, 1953, quoted in Lindsay Anderson, *About John Ford* (New York: McGraw-Hill, 1981).

355 **questions about the navy's preparedness:** Andrew Sinclair, *John Ford* (New York: Dial, 1979), 120.

356 **"it would be a great experience for you":** Letter from John Ford to Gregg Toland, September 16, 1944, and reply, September 29, 1944, JFC.

356 **"an outstanding contribution"** . . . **"what'll dey do for lynchin's?":** OWI script report by Peggy Gould, November 21, 1944, cited in Randy Roberts and James S. Olson, *John Wayne, American* (New York: Free Press, 1995), 270.

356 **Ford cast a uniquely qualified actor:** McBride, *Searching for John Ford*, 406.

356 **pulled strings to arrange for his transfer:** Ford, *Pappy*, 197.

356 **"be comprised almost wholly of actors":** "Screen News," *New York Times*, November 8, 1944.

356 **MGM turned to its second choice, John Wayne:** "Screen News," *New York Times*, January 31, 1945.

357 **Pat Ford had even thought:** Letter from Patrick Ford to John Ford, February 4, 1944, JFC.

357 **"Well, Jesus, I [was] 40 years old":** John Wayne interviewed by Dan Ford, JFC.

358 **"said yes without reflection"** . . . **"And we started":** Robert Montgomery to Lindsay Anderson, *About John Ford*. (New York: McGraw-Hill, 1981), 226–28. All subsequent quotes from Montgomery in this chapter are from this interview.

358 **"Bob Montgomery was his pet":** Ford, *Pappy*, 200–201.

359 **"had forgotten to replace the windshield"** to **"they're my eyes!":** Ibid.

359 **Wayne murmured to Montgomery** . . . **"home from the hill":** Montgomery in Anderson, *About John Ford*, 226–28.

360 **"Jack was awfully intense":** Ford, *Pappy*, 199.

360 **He had broken his right leg:** Memo to Cheston from James McGuinness, May 22, 1945, JFC.

360 **"He wouldn't let anyone else"** . . . **to her or to himself:** Montgomery in Anderson, *About John Ford*, 226–28.

360 **"I'm not coming back"** . . . **"he'd have done it":** Ibid.

362 **"You've got to make the mission":** Handwritten note attached to "revised rough draft" of *Thunderbolt*, February 14, 1945, file 414, WWA. the note appears to be in Wyler's handwriting, suggesting it was intended for Koenig and/or Sturges, but is unsigned.

362 **They had placed Eyemos in cockpits:** Axel Madsen, *William Wyler: The Authorized Biography* (New York: Thomas Y. Crowell, 1973), 244.

363 **what Wyler called "atmosphere shots":** Ibid., 254. Except as noted, the account that follows in this chapter comes from Wyler's version of events as told to Madsen in his authorized biography.

363 **"I thought it was nothing":** Jan Herman, *A Talent for Trouble: The Life of Hollywood's Most Acclaimed Director, William Wyler* (New York: Da Capo, 1997), 275.

363 **"This is serious":** Ibid.

364 **"Instead of a happy voice":** Madsen, *William Wyler*, 255.

364 **he entered an air force hospital at Mitchell Field:** Ibid.

364 **"I'd never seen anybody":** A. Scott Berg, *Goldwyn* (New York: Alfred A. Knopf, 1989), 405.

364 **"worst weeks of my life":** Mary Morris, "Stubborn Willy Wyler," *PM*, February 2, 1947.

364 **checked in with some old colleagues at the War Department:** Letter from Major Monroe W. Greenthal to John Huston, April 26, 1945, file 499, JHC.

364 **Koenig's new and improved draft of *Thunderbolt*:** Lester Koenig, *Draft* of *Thunderbolt*, May 15, 1945, file 415, WWA.

365 **"He was terribly thin":** Herman, *A Talent for Trouble*, 276.

365 **hearing rehabilitation center for returning veterans:** Madsen, *William Wyler*, 256.

365 **"sixty dollars every month":** Ibid.

Chapter 25: "Where I Learned About Life"

366 **Stevens and his crew were to join** to **a concentration camp prisoner:** *George Stevens: D-Day to Berlin* (1994), written and produced by George Stevens Jr.

367 **"So completely without record"** . . . **"by name and nationality":** Letter from George Stevens accompanying Nordhausen footage, April 15, 1945, GSC.

367 "as stark an example as could be found": Ibid.

367 Capra received his first report: Letter from commander of film unit at Belsen to Frank Capra, April 19, 1945, FCA.

368 "a bald-headed private": Gavin Lambert, ed., *The Ivan Moffat File: Life Among the Beautiful and Damned in London, Paris, New York, and Hollywood* (New York: Pantheon, 2004), 226.

368 footage Stevens's unit shot at Torgau: This and all subsequent descriptions of the war footage Stevens's unit shot in this chapter are based on the author's viewing of his unedited reels at the Library of Congress, Washington, D.C.

369 "People talk glibly" . . . "if you're driving around in a Jeep": Handwritten notes by Moffat accompanying the guide to Stevens's footage, Library of Congress.

369 they received orders to proceed south to Dachau: Interview with George Stevens by William Kirschner, *Jewish War Veterans Review*, August 1963, reprinted in Paul Cronin, ed., *George Stevens Interviews* (Jackson: University Press of Mississippi, 2004), 18–19.

369 Stevens assumed that he and his team . . . "one of Dante's infernal visions": Ibid.

370 Stevens aimed the lens of his camera skyward . . . "and the woodpile was people": Unedited transcript of George Stevens interviewed by Robert Hughes, 1967, file 3677, GSC.

370 For some of the men in Stevens's unit . . . stop or sleep for days: George Stevens in Kirschner, *Jewish War Veterans Review*.

371 "where I learned about life": Unedited transcript of George Stevens interviewed by Robert Hughes, 1967, file 3677, GSC.

371 "Strange thing" . . . "never heard anybody ever talk about it": Ibid.

371 He would walk into a field . . . "stand at attention and salute": Ibid.

372 "in a paroxysm of terror": George Stevens to Kevin Brownlow, unpublished full transcript of interview, April 22, 1969, file 3671, GSC.

372 "Every time you turn a corner": Unedited transcript of George Stevens interviewed by Robert Hughes, 1967, file 3677, GSC.

372 "as matters now stand": Dennis Hevesi, "Abraham Klausner, 92, Dies; Aided Holocaust Survivors," *New York Times*, June 30, 2007.

372 "Almost everybody was in shock" . . . "which you despise the most": George Stevens to Kevin Brownlow, unpublished full transcript of interview, April 22, 1969, file 3671, GSC.

373 Stevens walked into a room . . . "They're dirty torturers!": George Stevens in Kirschner, *Jewish War Veterans Review*.

373 "He'd always been an observer": Unpublished transcript of interview with Ivan Moffat, file 51, FJC.

373 Only a small portion of what he photographed: Thomas Doherty, *Projections of War: Hollywood, American Culture, and World War II* (New York: Columbia University Press, 1993), 59.

375 Stevens, who had been raised Protestant . . . "and they had it": Unedited transcript of George Stevens interviewed by Robert Hughes, file 3677, GSC.

376 "Closeups of the prisoners": Official SPECOU report by George Stevens, June 20, 1945, exhibited at Mémorial de la Shoah, Musée, Centre de documentation juive contemporaine, Paris.

376 When he finally left the camp . . . traded it for cognac: *George Stevens: D-Day to Berlin*.

376 They went into Goering's house: Lambert, ed., *The Ivan Moffat File*, 219.

376 he filmed the Olympiad stadium: *George Stevens: D-Day to Berlin*.

376 "troublesome" . . . "He was lonely": Unpublished transcript of interview with Ivan Moffat, file 52, FJC.

Chapter 26: "What's This Picture For?"

378 Theodor Geisel prepared a short movie . . . "of the vital issues": Judith Morgan and Neil Morgan, *Dr. Seuss and Mr. Geisel: A Biography* (New York: Random House, 1995).

379 "get off your bloody ass": Ibid., and James C. Humes, *Eisenhower and Churchill: The Partnership That Saved the World* (New York: Prima, 2001).

380 "the greatest documentary film I have ever seen": Letter from Darryl F. Zanuck to Frank Capra, April 21, 1945, FCA.

380 "I will consider myself through": Letter from Frank Capra to Colonel Lyman T. Munson, April 27, 1945, FCA.

380 "I want to remain active": Letter from Frank Capra to Colonel Lyman T. Munson, January 30, 1945, FCA.

381 both men declined: Joseph McBride, *Frank Capra: The Catastrophe of Success* (New York: Simon & Schuster, 1992; revised 2000), 506–7.

381 "to be as frank as I can": Letter from Colonel Lyman T. Munson to Frank Capra, February 8, 1945, FCA.

381 enough to win him a discharge: Application for Separation from AUS by Frank Capra, May 18, 1945, FCA.

381 **Capra left Fort Fox in Los Angeles:** "Itinerary" by Frank Caora, entries dated June 8–11, 1945, and June 12, 1945, FCA.

381 **Distinguished Service Medal:** Frank Capra, *The Name Above the Title: An Autobiography* (New York: Da Capo, 1997; originally published 1971), 367.

381 **"Surprise! Glorious surprise!":** "Itinerary" by Frank Capra, entry dated Jne 14, 1945, FCA.

381 **"substantial cuts" . . . "mass production of babies":** Letter from General Frederick Osborn to Frank Capra, October 21, 1944, FCA.

382 **from 1943 to 1945, production of war pictures:** According to Michael S. Shull and David Edward Wilt, *Hollywood War Films, 1937–1945* (Jefferson, NC: McFarland, 1996), 334–410, the eight major studios released 198 movies with at least some content related to the war in 1943; in 1945 they released just seventy-eight.

382 **"Frank's series . . . will live longer":** Thomas M. Pryor, "Back to Work," *New York Times*, September 15, 1945.

382 **the hit comedy *Harvey* on Broadway:** "Itinerary" by Frank Capra, March 25, 1945, FCA.

382 **Capra got back to Los Angeles:** Ibid.

383 **Journalists and reviewers were sent a press release:** United States Army press materials for *San Pietro*, undated, file 503, JHC.

383 **"pure tragic grandeur":** "The New Pictures" (unbylined but written by James Agee), *Time*, May 21, 1945.

384 **"daring" in shooting during combat:** Bosley Crowther, "Army Film at 55th Street 'San Pietro,'" *New York Times*, July 12, 1945.

384 **"absolutely unromantic":** Manny Farber, "War Without Glamour," *New Republic*, July 30, 1945.

384 **"a dirty, deadly business":** John McCarten, "The Current Cinema: Brief Masterwork," *New Yorker*, July 21, 1945.

385 **"a dolorous goddamn picture":** Letter from John Huston to Darryl F. Zanuck, March 14, 1945, file 499, JHC.

385 **His wife, Lesley, had finally gone to Reno:** A. M. Sperber and Eric Lax, *Bogart* (New York: William Morrow, 1997), 302–3. Lesley Black Huston's petition for divorce was filed on April 6, 1945.

385 **at a party at David O. Selznick's house:** Otto Friedrich, *City of Nets: A Portrait of Hollywood in the 1940s* (New York: Harper & Row, 1986), 177–78.

385 **"I remember that the language:** John Huston, *An Open Book* (New York: Alfred A. Knopf, 1980), 97–98. In his autobiography, Huston erroneously places the fistfight with Flynn in 1942.

385 **"Scott has made as many and as great":** Letter from John Huston to Colonal Roland Barrett, February 5, 1945, file 1443, JHC.

386 **Two army psychiatrists wrote Huston:** Letters from Colonal Roland Barrett and Colonel Emanuel Cohen to John Huston, February 1945, file 1443, JHC.

386 **The Returning Psychoneurotic should do:** Gary Edgerton, "Revisiting the Recording of Wars Past: Remembering the Documentary Trilogy of John Huston," *Journal of Popular Film and Television*, Spring 1987, reprinted in John Huston, Gaylyn Studlar, and David Desser, *Reflections in a Male Eye: John Huston and the American Experience*, Smithsonian Studies in the History of Film and Television (Washington, DC: Smithsonian Institution, 1993).

387 **"photographic prints off the same negative":** William Blakefield, "A War Within: The Making of Know Your Enemy—Japan," *Sight and Sound*, Spring 1983.

387 **It arrived three days after the atom bomb to "showing to public in United States":** McBride, *Frank Capra*, 499.

388 **"nothing more than a glorified newsreel":** Letter from William Wyler to Major Monroe W. Greenthal, July 11, 1945, box 23, file 3, WWUCLA.

388 **General H. H. Arnold . . . "that was the end of that":** Jan Herman, *A Talent for Trouble: The Life of Hollywood's Most Acclaimed Director, William Wyler* (New York: Da Capo, 1997), 276–77.

388 **"Mr. Wyler doesn't feel that his own readjustment":** Thomas M. Pryor, "Back to Work," *New York Times*, September 16, 1945.

388 **showed the film to colleagues and friends:** Screening invitation list for *Thunderbolt*, October 12, 1945, box 23, file 8, WWUCLA.

389 **After his official separation from the army:** Army Separation Qualification Record, October 31, 1945, file 777, WWA.

389 **he kept writing letters to anyone . . . "a member of the picture business":** Letters from Samuel Goldwyn and Francis Harmon and telegram from Ned E. Depinet of RKO to William Wyler, with handwritten annotations by Wyler; letters from William Wyler to Harmon and General Ira Eaker, all November and December 1945, box 23, file 3, WWUCLA.

389 **become a partner in Liberty:** *Collier's*, February 4, 1950, cited in Herman, *A Talent for Trouble*, 295.

390 **a dramatized biography of Eisenhower:** A. Scott Berg, *Goldwyn* (New York: Alfred A. Knopf, 1989), 393.

390 **Goldwyn offered him** *The Bishop's Wife*: Axel Madsen, *William Wyler: The Authorized Biography* (New York: Thomas Y. Crowell, 1973), 260–61.

390 **"[His] point was"**: William Wyler interviewed by Catherine Wyler, 1981, reprinted in Gabriel Miller, ed., *William Wyler Interviews* (Jackson: University Press of Mississippi, 2009), 119.

390 **"I wish that I could go back"**: William Wyler to Thomas M. Pryor, September 1945, first printed by Pryor in "William Wyler and His Screen Philosophy," *New York Times*, November 17, 1946.

390 **"I've learned so much dealing"**: Pryor, "Back to Work."

390 **"I was still full of the war"**: Miller, ed., *William Wyler Interviews*, 131.

390 **"I spent four years being"**: Bernard Kantor, Irwin Blacker, and Anne Kramer, eds., *Directors at Work* (New York: Funk & Wagnall's, 1970).

Chapter 27: "An Angry Past Commingled with the Future in a Storm"

391 **a** *Time* **magazine correspondent . . . "About how much I've changed"**: "The Way Home" (unsigned), *Time*, August 7, 1944.

392 **telling him, "Returning soldiers!"**: Harriet Hyman Alonso, *Robert E. Sherwood: The Playwright in Peace and War* (Amherst and Boston: University of Massachusetts Press, 2007), 281.

392 **"The story is going along tolerably well"**: Letter from Mackinlay Kantor to Samuel Goldwyn, October 6, 1944, file 177, SGC.

393 **But from its first sentence . . . "Commingled with the future in a storm"**: Mackinlay Kantor, *Glory for Me* (New York: Coward-McCann, 1945).

394 **Howell sent a telegram to her boss . . . "his unwillingness [to] make commitment"**: Telegram from Miriam Howell to Samuel Goldwyn, April 4, 1945, file 177, SGC.

394 **"He thinks [it] is excellent"**: Interoffice memo from Pat Duggan to Samuel Goldwyn, May 31, 1945, file 177, SGC.

394 **Goldwyn told him he could simply get rid**: Telegram from Samuel Goldwyn to Pat Duggan, June 13, 1945, file 177, SGC.

394 **"criticisms of civilians" . . . "and a future together."**: Interoffice memo from Pat Duggan to Samuel Goldwyn, June 15, 1945, file 177, SGC.

395 **"I'm very excited about it"**: Letter from Samuel Goldwyn to John Ford, July 14, 1945, file 177, SGC.

395 **"This is entirely due to the conviction" . . . was getting so much attention**: Letter from Robert E. Sherwood to Samuel Goldwyn, August 27, 1945, file 177, SGC.

395 **"there will be several million men" . . . "hitting it right on the nose"**: Telegram from Samuel Goldwyn to Robert E. Sherwood, September 4, 1945, file 177, SGC.

395 **"prevent a lot of heartaches"**: Robert E. Sherwood to Samuel Goldwyn, August 27, 1945, file 177, SGC.

396 **"the whole country and the whole world"**: Alonso, *Robert E. Sherwood*, 283.

396 **"no man can walk right into the house" . . . "the way I wanted them"**: Thomas M. Pryor, "William Wyler and His Screen Philosophy," *New York Times*, November 17, 1946.

396 **"I just can't get (this story"**: A. Scott Berg, *Goldwyn* (New York: Alfred A. Knopf, 1989), 409–10.

396 **Huston began to explore the same issues**: Gary Edgerton, "Revisiting the Recording of Wars Past: Remembering the Documentary Trilogy of John Huston," *Journal of Popular Film and Television*, Spring 1987, reprinted in John Huston, Gaylyn Studlar, and David Desser, *Reflections in a Male Eye: John Huston and the American Experience*, Smithsonian Studies in the History of Film and Television (Washington, DC: Smithsonian Institution, 1993).

397 **"the War-Crazed Veteran theory"**: Joseph C. Goulden, *The Best Years: 1945–1950* (New York: Atheneum, 1976), cited in Edgerton, "Revisited the Recording of Wars Past."

397 **"human salvage" . . . "living in a dead man's world"**: John Huston, *An Open Book* (New York: Alfred A. Knopf, 1980), 120.

398 **"monstrous subnormal thing"**: Frances McFadden, "Let There Be Light," *Harper's Bazaar*, May 1946.

398 **"to act like cry-babies" . . . "weak-willed namby-pambies"**: Dr. Herbert Spiegel, quoted in Ben Shephard, "Here Is Human Salvage," *London Times Literary Supplement*, November 6, 1998.

398 **a sign reading "Hollywood and Vine"**: McFadden, "Let There Be Light."

399 **the recovery rate of the seventy-five men**: John Huston interviewed by Peter S. Greenberg, *Rolling Stone*, February 19, 1981, reprinted in Robert Emmet Long, ed., *John Huston Interviews* (Jackson: University Press of Mississippi, 2001), 117.

399 **"Certainly you can't expect"**: Stuart Kaminsky, *John Huston: Maker of Magic* (Boston: Houghton Mifflin, 1978), 43–44.

400 **"For some reason, to see a psyche" . . . "almost a religious experience"**: Gene D. Phillips, "Talking with John Huston," *Film Comment*, May/June 1973.

400   **On September 29, 1945:** U.S. Naval Personnel Separation Center, Washington D.C., form, September 29, 1945, JFC.

400   **"superb accomplishments" . . . "love for his subordinates":** Endorsement attached to above, October 18, 1945, JFC.

400   *Nazi Concentration and Prison Camps* and *The Nazi Plan:* Robert Parrish, *Hollywood Doesn't Live Here Anymore* (Boston: Little, Brown, 1988), 66–68.

401   **when Zanuck offered him the chance:** Joseph McBride, *Searching for John Ford: A Life* (New York: St. Martin's, 2001), 421.

401   **a move he had been considering:** Letter from Harry Wurtzel to John Ford, November 10, 1941, JFC.

401   **Ford ultimately decided not to attend:** Andrew Sinclair, *John Ford* (New York: Dial, 1979), 124.

401   **no longer considered himself "retired":** Marilyn Ann Moss, *Giant: George Stevens, a Life on Film* (Madison: University of Wisconsin Press, 2004), 142.

402   **"You're coming back to the studio" . . . "I said yes":** Unedited transcript of George Stevens interview with Bruce Petri, file 3692, GSC.

402   **"the only guy ever to tell me" . . . "come back [to] Columbia":** George Stevens interviewed by Patrick McGilligan and Joseph McBride, in Paul Cronin, ed., *George Stevens Interviews* (Jackson: University Press of Mississippi, 2004), 115.

403   **"The impression we get is an endless river":** Victor H. Bernstein and Max Lerner, *Final Judgment: The Story of Nuremberg* (originally published in 1947; reprinted by Kessinger Publishing Inc., 2010), cited in Ann Tusa and John Tusa, *The Nuremberg Trial* (London: Macmillan, 1983), 160.

403   **During the screening, the spotlight illuminating the defendants' box:** Tusa and Tusa, *The Nuremberg Trial,* 160, based on contemporary eyewitness accounts as reported in the *Daily Mail,* the *Daily Telegraph,* and the *New York Times.*

403   **"Even for those who, like me":** Telford Taylor, *The Anatomy of the Nuremberg Trials: A Personal Memoir* (New York: Alfred A. Knopf, 1992), 186–87.

404   **As they watched Hitler speak:** Joseph E. Persico, *Nuremberg: Infamy on Trial* (New York: Viking, 1994), 158.

404   **he cabled Yvonne that he planned to sail:** Cable from George Stevens to Yvonne Stevens, October 6, 1945, GSC. Stevens was scheduled to sail on the *Queen Mary* from Southampton, England, on November 4 and arrive in New York City five days later, but he was still working on the film when he sent the cable and may have left Europe on the *Queen Mary*'s next crossing (November 22–27).

404   **"when hopes ran higher for the world":** John Huston interviewed in "George Stevens: A Filmmaker's Journey," unpublished transcript, file 13, FJC.

Chapter 28: "A Straight Face and a Painfully Maturing Mind"

406   **"I just can't believe that film's any good" . . . "goddamned thing into that picture":** Lindsay Anderson, *About John Ford* (New York: McGraw-Hill, 1981), 20–21.

406   **Ford had closely supervised:** Joseph McBride, *Searching for John Ford: A Life* (New York: St. Martin's, 2001), 444.

406   **the cacophony of voices:** Andrew Sinclair, *John Ford* (New York: Dial, 1979), 121.

406   **Brickley was to read out an angry roll call:** Ibid., 121–22.

406   **the film's length:** Anderson, *About John Ford,* 21.

406   **"Big Smile!" . . . "a PT boat":** Advertisement, December 1945, publication unknown, *They Were Expendable* file, New York Public Library for the Performing Arts.

406   **"Montgomery Role Parallel to Own Navy Experience" . . . "himself a veteran of Navy action":** Pressbook for *They Were Expendable,* New York Public Library for the Performing Arts.

407   **"If this film had been released" . . . "a moving remembrance of things past":** Bosley Crowther, "The Screen: 'They Were Expendable,' Seen [at] Capitol, Called Stirring Picture of Small but Vital Aspect of War Just Ended," *New York Times,* December 21, 1945.

407   **"long and late" . . . "in any other picture":** "The New Pictures," *Time,* December 24, 1945.

407   **"regardless of any actual":** *Variety,* November 21, 1945.

407   **"so beautiful and so real . . . "watching them do so" and "visually beautiful" to *The Story of G.I. Joe*:** James Agee, *Nation,* January 5, 1946, and in "Best of 1945," *Nation,* January 19, 1946, both reprinted in *Film Writing and Selected Journalism,* ed. Michael Sragow (New York: Library of America, 2005).

408   **Jack Mackenzie, the cameraman:** McBride, *Searching for John Ford,* 386.

408   **"to extend his OSS–U.S. Navy unit into civilian life":** Robert Parrish, *Growing Up in Hollywood* (New York: Little, Brown, 1976), 158.

409 **"As this is the picture"**: Letter from John Ford to the chief of the Office of the Bureau of Archives, December 6, 1946, JFC.

409 **"I was instrumental in establishing"** . . . **"my knowledge of Motion Pictures"**: Annual Qualifications Questionnaire filled out by John Ford, 1945, JFC.

409 **official notice of separation**: Separation Center memorandum and Military Record and Report of Separation, February 13, 1946, file 1719, JHC.

409 **"like dressing for a costume party"**: John Huston, *An Open Book* (New York: Alfred A. Knopf, 1980), 126.

410 **Museum of Modern Art had selected his film**: "Documentary Films on View at Museum," *New York Times*, January 3, 1946.

410 **stills from the movie had appeared in *Life* magazine**: Gary Edgerton, "Revisiting the Recording of Wars Past: Remembering the Documentary Trilogy of John Huston," *Journal of Popular Film and Television*, Spring 1987, reprinted in John Huston, Gaylyn Studlar, and David Desser, *Reflections in a Male Eye: John Huston and the American Experience*, Smithsonian Studies in the History of Film and Television (Washington, DC: Smithsonian Institution, 1993), 52.

410 **he brought a print of *Let There Be Light***: Ibid., 51.

410 **the film could be shown only to men**: Memo to the chief of the Army Pictorial Service from the post legal officer (name redacted), March 11, 1946, file 251, JHC.

410 **"in furtherance of the war effort"** . . . **"an invasion of the right of privacy"**: Memo to the chief of the Army Pictorial Service from the post legal officer (name redacted), March 22, 1946, file 251, JHC.

411 **"the Army Bureau of Public Relations"** . . . **"and Winnie's next speech"**: Letter from John Huston to Walter Karri-Davies, March 21, 1946, file 252, JHC.

411 **"I still feel that it is the best picture"** . . . **the ban would have to stand**: Letter from Brigadier General William C. Menninger to John Huston, March 28, 1946, file 252, JHC.

411 **it had examined its own records**: Letter from chief of the Army Pictorial Service to John Huston, April 2, 1946, JHC.

411 **Huston went back to the army's editing facility**: Edgerton, "Revisiting the Recording of Wars Past."

412 **"dispel prejudice on the part of the public"** . . . **obtain all necessary clearances**: Letter from John Huston to Menninger, April 15, 1946, file 252, JHC.

412 **Menninger forwarded his appeal**: Letter from Menninger to assistant secretary of war, April 24, 1946, file 252, JHC.

412 **a British short called *Psychiatry in Action!***: "Co-Featured Role for Ruth Warrick," *New York Times*, April 28, 1946, and Museum of Modern Art press release, JHC.

412 **"raise your voice"**: Telegram from John Huston to Archer Winsten, late April 1945, file 252, JHC.

412 **"The Army"** to **"what to do with it"**: Archer Winsten, "Movie Talk: Lest You Forget a Film Everyone Ought to View," *New York Post*, July 2, 1946.

412 **"Seeing it, I felt as if"**: Archer Winsten, "Movie Talk: Huston's 'Let There Be Light' Hidden Under Army Bushel," *New York Post*, May 6, 1946.

412 **"I don't know what is necessary"** . . . **"the glaring obvious reason"**: James Agee, *Nation*, May 11, 1946, and January 25, 1947.

413 **"the whole gruesome story"**: Letter from Arthur Mayer to John Huston, August 14, 1946, file 252, JHC.

413 **"In the Second World War"**: Lawrence Grobel, *The Hustons: The Life and Times of a Hollywood Dynasty*, updated ed. (New York: Cooper Square, 2000), 299.

413 **"wanted to maintain the 'warrior' myth"**: Huston, *An Open Book*, 125–26.

413 **"That," he said, "was my most"**: Stuart Kaminsky, *John Huston: Maker of Magic* (Boston: Houghton Mifflin, 1978), 43–44.

413 **George Stevens opened a 1946 desk calendar**: All details of Stevens's activity during his first weeks back are, unless otherwise noted, from his 1946 diary, entries dated January 1–23, file 3602, GSC.

414 **"the small one"** . . . **"it was a long time away"**: Yvonne Stevens interviewed by Irene Kahn Atkins, unpublished transcript, file 3696, GSC.

414 **"The whole [war] became"**: Frank Capra interviewed for "George Stevens: A Filmmaker's Journey," unpublished transcript, file 13, FJC.

415 **a taxicab had run over his foot**: Yvonne Stevens interviewed by Irene Kahn Atkins, unpublished transcript, file 3696, GSC. Stevens, in an interview with Bruce Petri (file 3692, GSC), claimed that his problems walking were the result of a case of frostbite he suffered while in Luxembourg, when his army boots froze and had to be cut off.

415 **"not made from life"**: Unedited transcript of George Stevens interviewed by Robert Hughes, 1967, file 3677, GSC.

415 **When he dined at Romanoff's** . . . **"going to put yours on?"**: Gavin Lambert, ed., *The Ivan Moffat File: Life Among the Beautiful and Damned in London, Paris, New York, and Hollywood* (New York: Pantheon, 2004), 175–76.

416 **"very bitter about the people":** Marilyn Ann Moss, *Giant: George Stevens, a Life on Film* (Madison: University of Wisconsin Press, 2004), 123.

416 **"He didn't look for a job":** Yvonne Stevens interviewinterviewed by Irene Kahn Atkins, unpublished transcript, file 3696, GSC.

416 **no offers to make a war picture:** George Stevens to Hal Boyle, 1953, reprinted in Paul Cronin, ed., *George Stevens Interviews* (Jackson: University Press of Mississippi, 2004), 14.

416 **"They tell me you can't make a film":** George Stevens, characterizing his postwar frame of mind in unedited transcript of interview by Robert Hughes, 1967, file 3677, GSC.

417 **"I wasn't ready":** George Stevens to James Silke, *Cinema*, December 1964/January 1965, reprinted in Cronin, ed., *George Stevens Interviews*, 40.

417 **a comedy script called *One Big Happy Family*:** Herbert G. Luft, "George Stevens: The War Gave the Academy's New President a Social Conscience," *Films in Review*, November 1958.

417 **"I didn't quite know what" . . . still wanted him to be part of Liberty:** George Stevens to James Silke, *Cinema*, December 1964/January 1965, reprinted in Cronin, ed., *George Stevens Interviews*.

418 **"Our films should tell the truth":** Moss, *Giant*, 27.

418 **"After the war":** George Stevens interviewed by Patrick McGilligan and Joseph McBride, in Cronin, ed., *George Stevens Interviews*.

418 **"I hated to see him leave comedy":** Frank Capra, interviewed for "George Stevens: A Filmmaker's Journey," unpublished transcript, file 13, FJC.

418 **"You can never be right":** Yvonne Stevens interviewed by Irene Kahn Atkins, unpublished transcript, file 3696, GSC.

Chapter 29: "Closer to What Is Going On in the World"

419 **"A change is in the making":** Frank Capra, "Breaking Hollywood's 'Pattern of Sameness,'" *New York Times Magazine*, May 5, 1946.

419 **"Many of the men":** Ibid.

420 **"story value will have foremost precedence":** "New Picture: It's a Wonderful Life," *Time*, December 23, 1946.

420 **"One is to strengthen the individual's belief":** *Los Angeles Times*, March 3, 1946.

420 **"if the war lasted more than a couple of years":** Mary Morris, "Stubborn Willy Wyler," *PM*, February 2, 1947.

421 **"the Academy will replace your ersatz plaque":** Letter from Jean Hersholt to Frank Capra, May 17, 1946, FCA.

421 **"It's frightening to go back":** Thomas M. Pryor, "Mr. Capra Comes to Town," *New York Times*, November 18, 1945.

421 **"through the war in a very real sense":** William Wyler, "No Magic Wand," *Screen Writer*, February 1947.

422 **"People are disillusioned":** Pryor, "Mr. Capra Comes to Town."

422 **"People are numb":** *Los Angeles Times*, March 3, 1946.

422 **"no independent producer is big enough":** Pryor, "Mr. Capra Comes to Town."

422 **To inaugurate Liberty, he wanted:** Joseph McBride, *Frank Capra: The Catastrophe of Success* (New York: Simon & Schuster, 1992; revised 200), 508–9.

422 **"about a small town guy":** Pryor, "Mr. Capra Comes to Town."

422 **"This story doesn't tell very well":** Jeanine Basinger, *The It's a Wonderful Life Book* (New York: Knopf, 1986), 77–78.

423 **he chewed through one writer after another:** Ibid.

423 **"horrid man" . . . "an arrogant son of a bitch":** Frances Goodrich and Albert Hackett interviewed by Mark Rowland in *Backstory: Interviews with Screenwriters of Hollywood's Golden Age*, ed. Pat McGilligan (Berkeley: University of California Press, 1986), 210.

424 **By June 30, 1946:** Liberty Films financial statement, June 30, 1946, file 3753, GSC.

424 **"Jesus Christ":** Unedited transcript of George Stevens interview with Bruce Petri, file 3692, GSC.

425 **Goldwyn had earmarked the role:** Cast list, file 4111, SGC.

425 **"You can't have a Jew":** Axel Madsen, *William Wyler: The Authorized Biography* (New York: Thomas Y. Crowell, 1973), 90.

425 **"So you're gonna make a movie":** Jan Herman, *A Talent for Trouble: The Life of Hollywood's Most Acclaimed Director, William Wyler* (New York: Da Capo, 1997), 282.

425 **"I got [my injury] on D-Day":** *Diary of a Sergeant* (1945).

426 **"I didn't try to teach him to act":** Thomas M. Pryor, "William Wyler and His Screen Philosophy—And They All Had Big Heads the Next Morning," *New York Times*, November 17, 1946.

426 **"It was more work"**: William Wyler to Kantor, Blacker, and Kramer, reprinted in Gabriel Miller, ed., *William Wyler Interviews* (Jackson: University Press of Mississippi, 2009), 41.

427 **He also broke with studio tradition**: William Wyler to Ronald L. Davis, reprinted in ibid.

427 **"It's very important"**: Herman, *A Talent for Trouble*, 283.

428 **"the veteran could not be isolated"**: Wyler, "No Magic Wand."

428 **"You pass stuff like that"**: Leonard J. Leff and Jerold L. Simmons, *The Dame in the Kimono: Hollywood, Censorship, and the Production Code* (Lexington: University Press of Kentucky, 2001), 140, 155.

429 **"The war should be over between us"**: Herman, *A Talent for Trouble*, 228–29.

429 **"I didn't hire an actor!"**: *Ibid.*, 288.

429 **"When I say my lines"**: A. Scott Berg, *Goldwyn* (New York: Alfred A. Knopf, 1989), 411.

429 **On April 9**: Ibid.

430 **"When I come to a set"**: William Wyler in George Stevens Jr., *Conversations with the Great Moviemakers of Hollywood's Golden Age at the American Film Institute* (New York: Alfred A. Knopf, 2006), 208.

430 **"I am writing you"**: Letter from Samuel Goldwyn to William Wyler, May 29, 1946, file 177, SGC.

430 **"I want to make one last effort"**: Telegram from William Wyler to Robert Sherwood, June 6, 1946, file 177, SGC.

431 **"He used to go overboard"**: Lester Koenig, "Gregg Toland, Film-Maker," *Screen Writer*, December 1947.

431 **"I shot most of the scenes"**: Pryor, "William Wyler and His Screen Philosophy."

432 **"I knew these [characters]"**: Hermine Rich Isaacs, "William Wyler: Director with a Passion and a Craft," *Theatre Arts*, February 1947.

432 **"whatever extra trouble was necessary"**: Wyler, "No Magic Wand."

432 **"I hated that"**: Joseph McBride, "AFI Salutes William Wyler Who Can Say 'Auteur' Like a Native," *Variety*, March 17, 1976.

434 **"in order to win his personal battles"**: Wyler, "No Magic Wand."

434 **"lose himself in the dream"**: William Wyler in *Conversations with the Great Moviemakers of Hollywood's Golden Age*.

435 **After a wildly successful test screening in Long Beach**: Berg, *Goldwyn*, 417.

435 **"with something important to say"**: Mason Wiley and Damien Bona, *Inside Oscar: The Unofficial History of the Academy Awards*, 10th anniversary ed. (New York: Ballantine, 1996), 160.

436 **"William Wyler has always seemed to me"**: James Agee, "What Hollywood Can Do, Parts 1 and 2," *Nation*, December 7, 1946 and December 14, 1946.

436 **"not only . . . superlative entertainment"**: Bosley Crowther, "The Screen in Review," *New York Times*, November 22, 1946.

436 **"the best-directed film I've ever seen"**: Mason and Bona, *Inside Oscar*, 167.

436 **"the greatest of all Capra pictures"**: *Hollywood Reporter*, December 11, 1946.

436 **"hysterical pitch" . . . "moralizing"**: Manny Farber, "Mugging Main Street," *New Republic*, January 6, 1947.

436 **The *New York Times* called it quaint and sentimental**: Bosley Crowther, "'It's a Wonderful Life,' with James Stewart, at Globe," *New York Times*, December 23, 1946.

436 **"oldtime craft" . . . "taken the stride forward"**: *Variety*, December 25, 1946.

437 **"Frank, I'm worried"**: Frank Capra, *The Name Above the Title: An Autobiography* (New York: Da Capo, 1997; originally published 1971), 384.

437 **Their gambit failed**: Liberty papers from GSC and WWA.

437 **"the most gentlemanly way of going broke"**: Richard Schickel, *The Men Who Made the Movies: Interviews with Frank Capra, George Cukor, Howard Hawks, Alfred Hitchcock, Vincente Minnelli, King Vidor, Raoul Walsh, and William E. Wellman* (New York: Atheneum, 1975), 85.

438 **"Somebody should be on fire"**: Dorothy Kilgallen, "Snapshots of a Movie Maker," undated, file 38, WWA.

438 **"The trouble with Hollywood"**: Pryor, "William Wyler and His Screen Philosophy."

Epilogue

439 **"I got cold feet"**: Richard Schickel, *The Men Who Made the Movies: Interviews with Frank Capra, George Cukor, Howard Hawks, Alfred Hitchcock, Vincente Minnelli, King Vidor, Raoul Walsh, and William E. Wellman* (New York: Atheneum, 1975), 85.

439 **"All we had to do was hang on"**: Frank Capra in George Stevens Jr., *Conversations with the Great Moviemakers of Hollywood's Golden Age at the American Film Institute* (New York: Alfred A. Knopf, 2006), 82–84.

439 **"It was the beginning of my end"**: Frank Capra, *The Name Above the Title: An Autobiography* (New York: Da Capo, 1997; originally published 1971), 402.

441		**"making decent people afraid"**: Transcript of radio address by William Wyler, October 26, 1947, file 596, WWA.

441		**"sickness [had] permeated the country"**: John Huston, *An Open Book* (New York: Alfred A. Knopf, 1980), 135.

441		**Capra did not join them**: Lee Mortimer, "Hollywood in Gotham," syndicated, April 26, 1948.

442		**"a great man and a great American" . . . "director in the world"**: Introduction to Capra, *The Name Above the Title*, xvii–xviii.

442		**A threadbare flag**: Joseph McBride, *Searching for John Ford: A Life* (New York: St. Martin's, 2001), 682, 719.

442		**His memorial service**: Jan Herman, *A Talent for Trouble: The Life of Hollywood's Most Acclaimed Director, William Wyler* (New York: Da Capo, 1997), 467.

443		**He never stopped petitioning the government**: Memos from John Huston, file 251, JHC.

443		**"As time went on"**: Marilyn Ann Moss, *Giant: George Stevens, a Life on Film* (Madison: University of Wisconsin Press, 2004), 180.

443		**"a Western, but really my war picture"**: Joe Hyams, "Making 'Shane,'" *New York Herald Tribune*, April 19, 1953, reprinted in Paul Cronin, ed., *George Stevens Interviews* (Jackson: University Press of Mississippi, 2004), 116.

444		**"I just loved the man"**: Unedited transcript of interview with Frank Capra, file 13, FJC.

444		**Stevens packed up all of the color footage**: Correspondence and memos from George Stevens Jr., March 10, 1961, and March 21, 1961, file 3629, GSC.

BIBLIOGRAPHY

Books

Agee, James. *Film Writing and Selected Journalism.* Edited by Michael Sragow. New York: Library of America, 2005.

Alonso, Harriet Hyman. *Robert E. Sherwood: The Playwright in Peace and War.* Amherst and Boston: University of Massachusetts Press, 2007.

Ambler, Eric. *Here Lies: An Autobiography.* London: Weidenfeld & Nicolson, 1985.

Ambrose, Stephen E. *D-Day: June 6, 1944; The Climactic Battle of World War II.* New York: Simon & Schuster, 1994.

Anderegg, Michael A. *William Wyler.* Boston: Twayne, 1979.

Anderson, Lindsay. *About John Ford.* New York: McGraw-Hill, 1981.

Armes, Roy. *A Critical History of the British Cinema.* New York: Oxford University Press, 1978.

Bach, Steven. *Marlene Dietrich: Life and Legend.* New York: William Morrow, 1992.

Baker, Nicholson. *Human Smoke: The Beginnings of World War II, the End of Civilization.* New York: Simon & Schuster, 2008.

Barnes, Joseph. *Willkie: The Events He Was Part Of—The Ideas He Fought For.* New York: Simon & Schuster, 1952.

Basinger, Jeanine. *The It's a Wonderful Life Book.* New York: Alfred A. Knopf, 1986.

———. *The Star Machine.* New York: Knopf, 2007.

Bazin, André. *Jean Renoir.* Translated by W. W. Halsey II and William H. Simon. Edited by François Truffaut. New York: Simon & Schuster, 1973.

Behlmer, Rudy. *Inside Warner Bros. (1935–1951).* New York: Viking, 1985.

———. *Memo from Darryl F. Zanuck: The Golden Years at Twentieth Century-Fox.* New York: Grove, 1993.

———, ed. *Memo from David O. Selznick.* New York: Modern Library, 2000.

Berg, A. Scott. *Goldwyn.* New York: Alfred A. Knopf, 1989.

———. *Lindbergh.* New York: Putnam, 1998.

Bergan, Ronald. *The United Artists Story.* New York: Crown, 1986.

Bernstein, Matthew. *Walter Wanger: Hollywood Independent.* Minneapolis: University of Minnesota Press, 2000.

Birdwell, Michael E. *Celluloid Soldiers: Warner Bros.'s Campaign Against Nazism.* New York: New York University Press, 1999.

Blotner, Joseph. *Faulkner: A Biography.* Revised one-volume edition of 1974 book. Jackson: University Press of Mississippi, 2005.

Bogdanovich, Peter. *John Ford.* Revised and enlarged edition. Berkeley and Los Angeles: University of California Press, 1978.

Breuer, William B. *The Air-Raid Warden Was a Spy: And Other Tales from Home-Front America in World War II.* Hoboken, NJ: John Wiley & Sons, 2003.

Brown, John Mason. *The Ordeal of a Playwright: Robert E. Sherwood and the Challenge of War.* New York: Harper & Row, 1970.

———. *The Worlds of Robert E. Sherwood: Mirror to His Times.* New York: Harper & Row, 1962.

Callow, Simon. *Orson Welles. Vol. 2, Hello Americans.* New York: Viking Penguin, 2006.

Capra, Frank. *The Name Above the Title: An Autobiography*. Cambridge, MA: Da Capo, 1997. Originally published 1971.

Ceplair, Larry, and Steven Englund. *The Inquisition in Hollywood: Politics in the Film Community, 1930–1960*. Berkeley: University of California Press, 1979.

Cole, Wayne S. *Senator Gerald P. Nye and American Foreign Relations*. Minneapolis: University of Minnesota Press, 1962.

Cornfield, Robert, ed. *Kazan on Directing*. New York: Alfred A. Knopf, 2009.

Cronin, Paul, ed. *George Stevens Interviews*. Jackson: University Press of Mississippi, 2004.

Custen, George F. *Twentieth Century's Fox: Darryl F. Zanuck and the Culture of Hollywood*. New York: Basic Books, 1997.

Davis, Bette. *The Lonely Life*. New York: G. P. Putnam's Sons, 1962.

Davis, Bette, with Michael Herskowitz. *This 'N That*. New York: Putnam, 1987.

Dick, Bernard F., ed. *Dark Victory*. Madison: University of Wisconsin Press, 1981.

———. *Hal Wallis: Producer to the Stars*. Lexington: University Press of Kentucky, 2004.

———. *The Merchant Prince of Poverty Row: Harry Cohn of Columbia Pictures*. Lexington: University Press of Kentucky, 1993.

———. *The Star-Spangled Screen: The American World War II Film*. Lexington: University Press of Kentucky, 1985.

———. *Hollywood's Censor: Joseph I. Breen and the Production Code Administration*. New York: Columbia University Press, 2007.

Doherty, Thomas. *Hollywood and Hitler, 1933–1939*. New York: Columbia University Press, 2013.

———. *Projections of War: Hollywood, American Culture, and World War II*. New York: Columbia University Press, 1993.

Dower, John W. *Embracing Defeat: Japan in the Wake of World War II*. New York: New Press/W. W. Norton, 1999.

———. *War Without Mercy: Race and Power in the Pacific War*. New York: Pantheon, 1986.

Dumont, Hervé. *Frank Borzage: The Life and Films of a Hollywood Romantic*. Translated by Jonathan Kaplansky. Jefferson, NC: McFarland, 2006. Originally published in French in 1993.

Eames, John Douglas. *The MGM Story*. 2nd revised edition. New York: Crown, 1982.

Eames, John Douglas, with additional text by Robert Abele. *The Paramount Story*. New York: Simon & Schuster, 2002.

Edwards, Anne. *A Remarkable Woman: A Biography of Katharine Hepburn*. New York: William Morrow, 1985.

Eliot, Marc. *Cary Grant: A Biography*. New York: Harmony, 2004.

———. *Jimmy Stewart: A Biography*. New York: Three Rivers, 2006.

Eyman, Scott. *Lion of Hollywood: The Life and Legend of Louis B. Mayer*. New York: Simon & Schuster, 2005.

———. *Print the Legend: The Life and Times of John Ford*. New York: Simon & Schuster, 1999.

Fitzgerald, Michael G. *The Universal Story: A Panoramic History in Words, Pictures and Filmographies*. New Rochelle, NY: Arlington House, 1977.

Fonda, Henry, as told to Howard Teichmann. *Fonda: My Life*. New York: New American Library, 1981.

Ford, Dan. *Pappy: The Life of John Ford*. Englewood Cliffs, NJ: Prentice Hall, 1979.

Friedrich, Otto. *City of Nets: A Portrait of Hollywood in the 1940s*. New York: Harper & Row, 1986.

Gabler, Neal. *An Empire of Their Own: How the Jews Invented Hollywood*. New York: Crown, 1988.

Gallagher, Tag. *John Ford: The Man and His Films*. Berkeley and Los Angeles: University of California Press, 1986.

Geist, Kenneth L. *Pictures Will Talk: The Life and Films of Joseph L. Mankiewicz*. New York: Da Capo, 1978.

Grobel, Lawrence. *The Hustons: The Life and Times of a Hollywood Dynasty*. Updated edition. New York: Cooper Square, 2000.

Gunter, Matthew C. *The Capra Touch: A Study of the Director's Hollywood Classics and War Documentaries, 1934–1945*. Jefferson, NC: McFarland, 2011.

Gussow, Mel. *Darryl F. Zanuck: Don't Say Yes Until I Finish Talking*. New York: Doubleday, 1971.

Hamilton, Ian. *Writers in Hollywood, 1915–1951*. New York: Carroll & Graf, 1991.

Harmetz, Aljean. *The Making of "The Wizard of Oz": Movie Magic and Studio Power in the Prime of MGM—and the Miracle of Production #1060*. New York: Alfred A. Knopf, 1977.

Harris, Warren G. *Clark Gable: A Biography*. New York: Harmony, 2002.

Harrison, Rex. *Rex: An Autobiography*. New York: William Morrow, 1975.

Herman, Jan. *A Talent for Trouble: The Life of Hollywood's Most Acclaimed Director, William Wyler*. New York: Da Capo, 1997.

Hirschhorn, Clive. *The Columbia Story*. London: Hamlyn, 1999.

———. *The Warner Bros. Story*. New York: Crown, 1979.

Huston, John. *An Open Book.* New York: Alfred A. Knopf, 1980.

Insdorf, Annette. *Indelible Shadows: Film and the Holocaust.* 3rd ed. Cambridge: Cambridge University Press, 2002.

Jacobs, Diane. *Christmas in July: The Life and Art of Preston Sturges.* Berkeley and Los Angeles: University of California Press, 1992.

Jewell, Richard B., with Vernon Harbin. *The RKO Story.* New York: Arlington House, 1982.

Kael, Pauline. *5001 Nights at the Movies.* New York: Holt, Rinehart and Winston, 1982.

———. *Kiss Kiss Bang Bang.* Boston: Atlantic Monthly Press, 1965.

Kaminsky, Stuart. *John Huston: Maker of Magic.* Boston: Houghton Mifflin, 1978.

Kantor, MacKinlay. *Glory for Me.* New York: Coward-McCann, 1945.

Karl, Frederick R. *William Faulkner: American Writer.* New York: Ballantine, 1989.

Kazin, Alfred. *New York Jew.* Syracuse, NY: Syracuse University Press, 1996. Originally published by Alfred A. Knopf in 1978.

Kelly, Andrew. *"All Quiet on the Western Front": The Story of a Film.* London: I. B. Tauris, 1998.

Kennedy, David M. *Freedom from Fear: The American People in Depression and War, 1929–1945.* The Oxford History of the United States, vol. 9. New York: Oxford University Press, 1999.

Koch, Howard. *As Time Goes By.* New York: Harcourt Brace Jovanovich, 1979.

Koppes, Clayton R., and Gregory D. Black. *Hollywood Goes to War: How Politics, Profits, and Propaganda Shaped World War II Movies.* New York: Free Press, 1987.

Kracauer, Siegfried. *From Caligari to Hitler: A Psychological History of the German Film.* Princeton, NJ: Princeton University Press, 1947.

Kulik, Karol. *Alexander Korda: The Man Who Could Work Miracles.* New Rochelle, NY: Arlington House, 1975.

Lally, Kevin. *Wilder Times: The Life of Billy Wilder.* New York: Henry Holt, 1996.

Lambert, Gavin, ed. *The Ivan Moffat File: Life Among the Beautiful and Damned in London, Paris, New York, and Hollywood.* New York: Pantheon, 2004.

Leamer, Laurence. *As Time Goes By: The Life of Ingrid Bergman.* New York: Harper & Row, 1986.

Leaming, Barbara. *Bette Davis: A Biography.* New York: Simon & Schuster, 1992.

———. *Katharine Hepburn.* New York: Crown, 1995.

Leff, Leonard J., and Jerold L. Simmons. *The Dame in the Kimono: Hollywood, Censorship, and the Production Code.* Lexington: University of Kentucky Press, 2001. Originally published 1989.

Lindbergh, Anne Morrow. *War Within and Without: Diaries and Letters of Anne Morrow Lindbergh, 1939–1944.* New York: Harcourt Brace Jovanovich, 1980.

Long, Robert Emmet, ed. *John Huston Interviews.* Jackson: University Press of Mississippi, 2001.

Louvish, Simon. *Chaplin: The Tramp's Odyssey.* New York: Thomas Dunne/St. Martin's, 2009.

McBride, Joseph. *Frank Capra: The Catastrophe of Success.* Revised version of 1992 edition. New York: St. Martin's Griffin, 2000.

———. *Searching for John Ford: A Life.* New York: St. Martin's, 2001.

McCarthy, Todd. *Howard Hawks: The Grey Fox of Hollywood.* New York: Grove, 1997.

McGilligan, Patrick. *Backstory: Interviews with Screenwriters of Hollywood's Golden Age.* Berkeley: University of California Press, 1986.

———. *Fritz Lang: The Nature of the Beast.* New York: St. Martin's, 1997.

Madsen, Axel. *William Wyler: The Authorized Biography.* New York: Thomas Y. Crowell, 1973.

Mann, William J. *Kate: The Woman Who Was Hepburn.* New York: Henry Holt, 2006.

Meserve, Walter J. *Robert E. Sherwood: Reluctant Moralist.* New York: Pegasus, 1970.

Meyers, Jeffrey. *John Huston: Courage and Art.* New York: Crown Archetype, 2011.

Miller, Gabriel, ed. *William Wyler Interviews.* Jackson: University Press of Mississippi, 2010.

Miller, Frank. *Censored Hollywood: Sex, Sin, and Violence on Screen.* Atlanta: Turner Publishing, 1994.

Millichap, Joseph R. *Lewis Milestone.* Boston: Twayne, 1981.

Milton, Joyce. *Tramp: The Life of Charlie Chaplin.* New York: HarperCollins, 1996.

Moon, Tom. *This Grim and Savage Game: OSS and the Beginning of U.S. Covert Operations in World War II.* New York: Da Capo, 2000.

Mordden, Ethan. *The Hollywood Studios: House Style in the Golden Age of the Movies.* New York: Simon & Schuster, 1988.

Morgan, Judith, and Neil Morgen. *Dr. Seuss and Mr. Geisel: A Biography.* New York: Random House, 1995.

Moss, Marilyn Ann. *Giant: George Stevens, a Life on Film.* Madison: Terrace Books/University of Wisconsin Press, 2004.

Neal, Steve. *Dark Horse: A Biography of Wendell Willkie.* New York: Doubleday, 1984.

Oller, John. *Jean Arthur: The Actress Nobody Knew.* New York: Limelight Editions, 1997.

Parrish, Robert. *Growing Up in Hollywood*. Boston: Little, Brown, 1976.

———. *Hollywood Doesn't Live Here Anymore*. New York: Little, Brown, 1988.

Peary, Gerald, ed. *John Ford Interviews*. Jackson: University Press of Mississippi, 2001.

Persico, Joseph E. *Nuremberg: Infamy on Trial*. New York: Viking, 1994.

Pizzitola, Louis. *Hearst over Hollywood: Power, Passion, and Propaganda in the Movies*. New York: Columbia University Press, 2002.

Poague, Leland, ed. *Frank Capra Interviews*. Jackson: University Press of Mississippi, 2004.

Pogue, Forrest C. *George C. Marshall*. Vol. 3, *Organizer of Victory*. New York: The Viking Press, 1973.

Polito, Robert, ed. *Farber on Film: The Complete Film Writings of Manny Farber*. New York: Library of America, 2009.

Reporting World War II, Part One: American Journalism, 1938–1944. New York: Library of America, 1995.

Richie, Donald. *George Stevens: An American Romantic*. New York: Museum of Modern Art, 1970.

Riding, Alan. *And the Show Went On: Cultural Life in Nazi-Occupied Paris*. New York: Alfred A. Knopf, 2010.

Roberts, Randy, and James S. Olson. *John Wayne, American*. New York: Free Press, 1995.

Robinson, David. *Chaplin: His Life and Art*. New York: McGraw-Hill, 1985.

Rogers, Ginger. *Ginger: My Story*. New York: HarperCollins, 1991.

Ross, Lillian. *Picture*. Cambridge, MA: Da Capo, 2002. Originally published 1952.

Rukeyser, Muriel. *Willkie: One Life*. New York: Simon & Schuster, 1957.

Sanford, John. *A Very Good Fall to Land With: Scenes from the Life of an American Jew*, vol. 3. Santa Rosa, CA: Black Sparrow, 1987.

Sarris, Andrew. *The John Ford Movie Mystery*. Bloomington: Indiana University Press, 1975.

Schatz, Thomas. *The Genius of the System: Hollywood Filmmaking in the Studio Era*. New York: Pantheon, 1988.

Schickel, Richard. *The Men Who Made the Movies*. New York: Atheneum, 1975.

Schoots, Hans. *Living Dangerously: A Biography of Joris Ivens*. Translated by David Colmer. Amsterdam: Amsterdam University Press, 2000.

Seebohm, Caroline. *No Regrets: The Life of Marietta Tree*. New York: Simon & Schuster, 1997.

Sherman, Vincent. *Studio Affairs: My Life as a Film Director*. Lexington: University Press of Kentucky, 1996.

Sherwood, Robert E. *Idiot's Delight*. Copyright 1935. Republished by Dramatists Play Service Inc.

Short, K. R. M., ed. *Film and Radio Propaganda in World War II*. Beckenham, Kent, UK: Croom Helm Ltd., 1983.

Shull, Michael S., and David Edward Wilt. *Hollywood War Films, 1937–1945: An Exhaustive Filmography of American Feature-Length Motion Pictures Relating to World War II*. Jefferson, NC: McFarland, 1996.

Sikov, Ed. *Dark Victory: The Life of Bette Davis*. New York: Henry Holt, 2007.

———. *On Sunset Boulevard: The Life and Times of Billy Wilder*. New York: Hyperion, 1998.

Sinclair, Andrew. *John Ford: A Biography*. New York: Dial, 1979.

Spada, James. *More Than a Woman: An Intimate Biography of Bette Davis*. New York: Bantam, 1993.

Sperber, A. M., and Eric Lax. *Bogart*. New York: William Morrow, 1997.

Spoto, Donald. *The Art of Alfred Hitchcock: Fifty Years of His Motion Pictures*. Garden City, NY: Doubleday, 1976.

———. *The Dark Side of Genius: The Life of Alfred Hitchcock*. Boston: Little, Brown, 1983.

———. *Laurence Olivier: A Biography*. New York: HarperCollins, 1992.

———. *Madcap: The Life of Preston Sturges*. Boston: Little, Brown, 1990.

Sragow, Michael. *Victor Fleming: An American Movie Master*. New York: Pantheon, 2008.

Steinberg, Cobbett. *Reel Facts: The Movie Book of Records*. Updated edition. New York: Vintage, 1982.

Stevens, George, Jr. *Conversations with the Great Moviemakers of Hollywood's Golden Age at the American Film Institute*. New York: Alfred A. Knopf, 2006.

Stine, Whitney. *"I'd Love to Kiss You . . .": Conversations with Bette Davis*. New York: Pocket, 1991.

Stine, Whitney, with Bette Davis. *Mother Goddam*. New York: Berkley Medallion, 1975.

Studlar, Gaylyn, and David Desser, eds. *Reflections in a Male Eye: John Huston and the American Experience*. Washington, DC, and London: Smithsonian Institution Press, 1993.

Sturges, Sandy, ed. *Preston Sturges by Preston Sturges: His Life in His Words*. New York: Simon & Schuster, 1990.

Taylor, John Russell, ed. *Graham Greene on Film: Collected Film Criticism, 1935–1940*. New York: Simon & Schuster, 1972.

Taylor, Telford. *The Anatomy of the Nuremberg Trials: A Personal Memoir*. New York: Alfred A. Knopf, 1992.

Thomas, Bob. *Clown Prince of Hollywood: The Antic Life and Times of Jack L. Warner*. New York: McGraw-Hill, 1990.

Thomas, Tony, and Aubrey Solomon. *The Films of 20th Century-Fox: A Pictorial History*. Secaucus, NJ: Citadel, 1979.

Thomson, David. *"Have You Seen . . . ?": A Personal Introduction to 1,000 Films*. New York: Alfred A. Knopf, 2008.

———. *The New Biographical Dictionary of Film*. 4th ed. New York: Alfred A. Knopf, 2002.

———. *Showman: The Life of David O. Selznick*. New York: Alfred A. Knopf, 1992.

Tornabene, Lyn. *Long Live the King: A Biography of Clark Gable*. New York: Putnam, 1976.

Troyan, Michael. *A Rose for Mrs. Miniver: The Life of Greer Garson*. Lexington: University Press of Kentucky, 1999.

Turrou, Leon G, as told to David G. Wittels. *Nazi Spies in America*. New York: Random House, 1938, 1939.

Tusa, Ann, and John Tusa. *The Nuremberg Trial*. London: Macmillan, 1983.

Vanderwood, Paul J., ed. *Juarez*. Madison: University of Wisconsin Press, 1983.

Variety Film Reviews. Vol. 6, *1938–1942*, and vol. 7, *1943–1948*. New York: R. R. Bowker, 1983.

Walker, Alexander. *Fatal Charm: The Life of Rex Harrison*. London: Weidenfeld & Nicolson, 1992.

Wallis, Hal, and Charles Higham. *Starmaker: The Autobiography of Hal Wallis*. New York: Macmillan, 1980.

Walters, Ben. *Orson Welles*. London: Haus Publishing, 2004.

White, W. L. *They Were Expendable*. New York: Harcourt, Brace and Company, 1942.

Wiley, Mason, and Damien Bona. *Inside Oscar: The Unofficial History of the Academy Awards*. 10th anniversary edition. New York: Ballantine, 1996.

Wills, Garry. *John Wayne's America: The Politics of Celebrity*. New York: Simon & Schuster, 1997.

Wilson, Robert. *The Film Criticism of Otis Ferguson*. Philadelphia: Temple University Press, 1971.

Winkler, Allan M. *The Politics of Propaganda: The Office of War Information, 1942–1945*. New Haven, CT: Yale University Press, 1978.

Zanuck, Darryl F. *Tunis Expedition*. New York: Random House, 1943.

Supplementary Video and Documentaries

(This list does not include the Hollywood features, war documentaries, or propaganda films discussed in the book.)

Becoming John Ford (2007), produced by Nick Redman and Jamie Willett, written by Julie Kirgo, directed by Nick Redman.

"John Ford: An American Vision" (episode of *Biography*, originally aired 1998 on A&E), produced and directed by Kerry Jensen-Iszak, written by Douglas Green and Lucy Chase Williams.

D-Day in Colour (2004), produced by Kim Hogg.

Directed by John Ford (2006 version, originally aired on Turner Classic Movies), produced by Frank Marshall, written and directed by Peter Bogdanovich.

Directed by William Wyler (episode of *American Masters*, originally aired 1986 on PBS), produced by Catherine Wyler, narration and interviews by A. Scott Berg, directed by Aviva Slesin.

Frank Capra's American Dream (originally aired 1997 on American Movie Classics), produced by Charles A. Duncombe Jr. and Kenneth Bowser, written and directed by Kenneth Bowser.

John Ford Goes to War (originally aired 2002 on Starz), produced and directed by Tom Thurman, coproduced by Joseph McBride, written by Tom Marksbury.

"John Ford/John Wayne: The Filmmaker and the Legend" (episode of *American Masters*, originally aired May 10, 2006, on PBS), written and produced by Kenneth Bowser, directed by Sam Pollard. (Available on the two-disc Warner Video edition of *Stagecoach*.)

"John Ford, Part 1" (episode of *Omnibus*, originally aired December 1, 1992, on BBC), produced and directed by Andrew Eaton, written by Lindsay Anderson. (Available on the two-disc Criterion edition of *Young Mr. Lincoln*.)

John Ford Goes to War (originally aired 2002 on Starz), produced and directed by Tom Thurman, written by Tom Marksbury.

John Huston: The Man, the Movies, the Maverick (1989), produced by Joni Levin, written by Frank Martin and Charles Degelman, directed by Frank Martin.

"Meet Henry Fonda" (episode of *Parkinson*, originally aired 1975 on BBC). (Available on the two-disc Criterion edition of *Young Mr. Lincoln*.)

Shooting War (1998), produced, written, and directed by Richard Schickel.

"WWII: The Propaganda Battle" (episode of *A Walk Through the 20th Century with Bill Moyers*, originally aired 1982), produced and directed by David Grubin, written by Ronald Blumer, Bill Moyers, and Bernard A. Weisberger.

Articles, Papers, and Speeches

Aldgate, Tony. "Mr. Capra Goes to War: Frank Capra, the British Army Film Unit, and Anglo-American Travails in the Production of 'Tunisian Victory.'" *Historical Journal of Film, Radio and Television* 11, no. 1 (1991).

Bertelsen, Lance. "San Pietro and the 'Art' of War." *Southwest Review*, Spring 1989.

Blakefield, William. "A War Within: The Making of Know Your Enemy—Japan." *Sight and Sound*, Spring 1983.

Cripps, Thomas, and David Culbert. "The Negro Soldier (1944): Film Propaganda in Black and White." *American Quarterly*, Winter 1979.

Culbert, David. "'Why We Fight': Social Engineering for a Democratic Society at War." In *Film and Radio Propaganda in World War II*, edited by K. R. M. Short. Beckenham, Kent, UK: Croom Helm Ltd., 1983.

Doherty, Thomas. "Cold Case from the Film Archives: Film Historian Thomas Doherty Does Some Detective Work on a Mystery from the 1930s, When the Hollywood Studios Had to Deal with the Upsurge of Racism in Hitler's Germany." *History Today*, January 2006.

Edgerton, Gary. "Revisiting the Recording of Wars Past: Remembering the Documentary Trilogy of John Huston." *Journal of Popular Film and Television*, Spring 1987. Reprinted in *Reflections in a Male Eye: John Huston and the American Experience*, edited by Gaylyn Studlar and David Esser. Washington, DC, and London: Smithsonian Institution Press, 1993.

Kozloff, Sarah. "Wyler's Wars." *Film History* 20, no. 4 (2008).

Ledes, Richard. "Let There Be Light: John Huston's Film and the Concept of Trauma in the United States After WWII." Paper delivered at the Après-Coup Psychoanalytic Association, November 13, 1998.

Marcus, Daniel. "William Wyler's World War II Films and the Bombing of Civilian Populations." *Historical Journal of Film, Radio and Television* 29, no. 1 (2009).

Petri, Bruce Humleker. "A Theory of American Film: The Films and Techniques of George Stevens." PhD diss., Harvard University, 1974, copyright 1987.

IMAGE CREDITS

First insert

Page 1: Photofest
Page 2: ABOVE AND BELOW: Photofest
Page 3: Everett Collection
Page 4: AP Photo
Page 6: ABOVE: Mary Evans/Ronald Grant/Everett Collection
    BELOW: By permission of ZumaPress.com
Page 7: © Bettmann/CORBIS
Page 8: AP Photo
Page 9: Ministry of Information Photo Division/IWM/Getty Images
Page 11: AP Photo
Page 12: Everett Collection
Page 13: Hulton Archives/Fox Photos/Getty Images
Page 14: ABOVE AND BELOW: Thomas D. McAvoy/Time & Life Pictures/Getty Images
Page 15: Archive Photos/Photoquest/Getty Images

Second insert

Page 1: Everett Collection
Page 2: The Kobal Collection at Art Resource, NY
Page 3: © Bettmann/CORBIS
Page 4: ABOVE: John Florea/Time & Life Pictures/Getty Images
Page 6: Everett Collection
Page 7: ABOVE: Margaret Herrick Library/Academy of Motion Pictures Arts and Sciences
    BELOW: Collection Capa/Magnum Photos
Page 8: ABOVE AND BELOW: Margaret Herrick Library/Academy of Motion Pictures Arts and Sciences
Page 9: Archive Photos/U.S. Army/Getty Images
Page 10: Mark Kauffman/Time & Life Pictures/Getty Images
Page 11: ABOVE: National Archives/Time & Life Pictures/Getty Images
    BELOW: © Bettmann/CORBIS
Page 12: ABOVE: Thomas D. McAvoy/Time & Life Pictures/Getty Images
Page 13: ABOVE: Everett Collection
    BELOW: © CinemaPhoto/CORBIS
Page 14: ABOVE: Everett Collection
    BELOW: AP Images
Page 15: Everett Collection
Page 16: Everett Collection

INDEX

Aachen, 344

Abbott, Bud, 103

Academy Awards, 24, 69–70, 76, 77, 81, 117–18,
179*n*, 189, 203–6, 211, 238, 286–88, 290, 379*n*
Capra and, 24, 40–41, 52, 69–70, 205, 288,
435–37
Ford and, 2, 18, 52, 70, 72, 126, 174, 205,
288, 324–25, 407, 408, 441
Huston and, 288, 443
Stevens and, 288, 290, 443
Wyler and, 33, 52, 69–70, 72, 118, 123,
125–26, 203–5, 435–36, 442

Academy of Motion Picture Arts and Sciences,
40, 174, 183–84, 264, 421
Capra and, 7, 40, 46, 110
Research Council of, 46, 71, 215, 216

Across the Pacific, 127–29, 186

Adak, 170, 186–91, 222–23, 241

Address Unknown (Taylor), 39, 40

Adventure for Two, 178

Africa, *see* North Africa

Africa Freed!, 243, 248–49

African Americans:
Ford and, 314*n*
as movie characters, 304
The Negro Soldier, 134–36, 234, 303–8
racism and, 134, 136, 304
soldiers, 304

African Queen, The, 443

Agee, James, 32, 125, 138, 173, 218, 232–33,
265, 287, 289, 298, 383–84, 407, 412, 436

Aherne, Brian, 34

Air Force, 129, 203, 294

Alaska, 170

Aleutian Islands, 223–24
Huston in, 170, 186–91, 265, 269
Report from the Aleutians, 191–92, 222–27, 241,
264, 265, 284, 288, 333, 411, 413

Alexander Nevsky, 264

Algeria, 173, 197–98, 214, 231, 232, 238, 242

Algiers, 179–80, 197–98, 215, 237–39

Alice Adams, 21, 81, 373

Allgood, Sara, 105

All Quiet on the Western Front, 21, 22,
64–65, 87, 259

"Aloha Means Goodbye" (Carson), 127

Alsop, Stewart, 7

Ambler, Eric, 170, 253–54, 265–70, 279, 280

America First, 89–90, 93–95

American Cinematographer, 151–52

American Revolution, 1, 24–25, 53, 382

American Tragedy, An (Dreiser), 401, 443

American Veterans Committee, 428

Amsterdam News, 307

Anchors Aweigh, 405

Anderson, Marian, 306

Anderson, Maxwell, 259–61, 293
Valley Forge, 24–25, 28

Andrews, Dana, 108, 209, 427, 429, 434

Angels with Dirty Faces, 163

Animeshk, 239

Annie Oakley, 21–22

Anschluss, 15

Anti-Nazi League, *see* Hollywood Anti-Nazi League

Araner, 55–56, 72, 168, 272, 324

Arise, My Love, 68, 76

Arizona, USS, 207

Armistead, Mark, 318

Army Emergency Relief, 214, 298

Army Hour, 245

Army-Navy Screen Magazine, 234

Army Photographic Center, 192

Army Pictorial Service (APS), 253, 255, 283, 311,
329, 368, 386, 410, 412–13, 425

Army Training Film program, 215

Arnim, Hans-Jürgen von, 262

Arnold, H. H., 244, 388
Arsenic and Old Lace, 8, 110–12, 216, 278–79, 329
Arthur, Jean, 41, 166, 167, 193–95, 416
Association of Motion Picture Producers, 40
Astor, Mary, 123, 124, 127
Atlantic Monthly, 7
At the Front in North Africa, 215, 232–34
Attu, 170, 187, 188, 190–91, 223–26
August, Joseph, 356
Augusta, USS, 314, 316, 318
Austria, 29, 164
    Anschluss, 15
Awful Truth, The, 79–80

B-17s (Flying Fortresses), 176, 188, 199, 201–2,
    219–21, 246, 266, 430, 434–35
    Jersey Bounce, 201–3, 219
    Memphis Belle, *see* Memphis Belle
B-24s, 188–90, 220
B-25s, 110, 137–38
Background to Danger, 170, 253
Back to Bataan, 357
Balaban, Barney, 90
Bankhead, Tallulah, 118
Baptism of Fire, 288
Barkley, Alben, 43–44
Bartlett, Sy, 111, 123, 127, 139
Barton, USS, 356
Bastogne, 349
Bataan, 141, 149, 299–300, 352
Battle of Britain, The, 164
Battle of China, The, 164, 308, 330
Battle of Midway, The, 144, 145–59, 160, 172–75,
    179, 180, 182, 184, 205, 206, 209, 222, 224,
    275, 282, 301
Battle of Russia, The, 164, 264–65, 278, 288
Battle of San Pietro, The, 279–83, 322, 331–34,
    382–85, 399–400, 407, 411
Battle of the Bulge, 346
Belfast, HMS, 312
Belgium, 343–44, 346, 349, 368
Ben-Hur, 442
Bergen-Belsen, 367–68
Bergman, Ingrid, 417
Berlin, 29, 369, 276
Berlin, Irving, 245
Berman, Pandro, 22, 39
Bernds, Edward, 25, 42
Best Years of Our Lives, The, 390, 391–96, 417,
    425–38, 441, 442
Biscuit Eater, The, 303
Bishop's Wife, The, 390
Blanc, Mel, 235
Blanke, Henry, 32
Blood on the Sun, 277
Bogart, Humphrey, 62, 86, 124, 127, 128,
    186, 270, 385
Bogdanovich, Peter, 72, 151
Bohnen, Eli, 375
Bolton, Jack, 155

Bomber's Moon, 226
Bond, Ward, 109
Bône, 179–80
Borzage, Frank, 48, 109
Boyer, Charles, 59, 137
Bradley, Omar, 254, 314, 322, 340
Braun, Eva, 376
Breen, Joseph I., 16, 88, 428–29
Breen Office, 194, 296
Bremen, 202
Bridges, Lloyd, 389
Briskin, Sam, 380, 382, 389, 416, 424, 437
Britain, 175–76
    Germany and, 45, 56, 68, 76, 81, 92, 97, 105,
        121, 247–48, 252
    Know Your Ally—Britain, 302–3
    London, *see* London
    Royal Air Force, 176, 220, 248, 346, 367
    Tunisian Victory and, 243, 247–52, 254, 255
British Army Film Unit, 243, 248, 262, 268, 316
British films:
    Africa Freed!, 243, 248–49
    Desert Victory, 232–33, 236, 268, 288, 289
British War Office, 250, 254
British War Relief, 81
Broadway Bill, 422
Brooklyn Eagle, 306
Buchman, Sidney, 41, 42, 166, 263
Buck, Jules, 265, 267–69, 279, 280
Bulkeley, John, 299, 302, 318–19, 352–54, 356
Bureau of Motion Pictures (BMP), 162–63, 166,
    175, 206, 211, 225, 226, 335
Bureau of Public Relations, 217, 243, 333,
    383, 388, 410–13
Burma, 222, 273–74, 326
Burnett, W. R., 85, 170*n*
Bury the Dead, 169

Cagney, James, 62, 137, 163, 277
Cagney, William, 389
Cairo, 197
Cairo Conference, 278
California, 241, 243, 288
Canutt, Yakima, 342
Capa, Robert, 266, 291
Capra, Ann, 110
Capra, Frank, 7–9, 11, 18, 23–28, 40–41, 45–46,
    55, 59, 65, 69–70, 77–79, 82, 110–16, 119,
    129, 130–34, 137, 139–44, 145, 158, 161, 163,
    166, 169, 181, 191–92, 205, 211, 218, 233–34,
    261–63, 276, 278–79, 284, 288, 311, 325, 326,
    328–31, 344, 349, 366–68, 379, 401, 402,
    414–16, 419–22, 428, 429, 439–41, 444
    Academy Awards and, 24, 40–41, 52, 69–70,
        205, 288, 435–37
    Academy of Motion Picture Arts and
        Sciences and, 7, 40, 46, 110
    Africa Freed! and, 248–49
    Allied landing in France and, 302
    at Anti-Nazi League rally, 28–29

Arsenic and Old Lace, 8, 110–12, 216,
    278–79, 329
B-25 bomber film and, 137–38
Columbia left by, 46, 49, 79, 166
Communism and, 275–76, 441
death of, 442
discharge from army service, 380, 381
Distinguished Service Medal awarded to, 381
entry into army, 8, 110–12
Eve of Battle, 317
financial difficulties of, 77, 111, 278, 329
The Flying Irishman and, 328
Ford and, 442
Frank Capra Productions, 46, 65
Here is Germany, 379
Hey, Soldier! and, 234
Huston's Italy assignment and, 252–53, 265, 266,
    269, 281, 282, 331–32
It Happened One Night, 24, 130–31
It's a Wonderful Life, 414, 416–17, 419, 422–25,
    435–37, 439, 441
Knight and, 142–44, 163, 164
Know Your Allies, see Know Your Allies
Know Your Enemies, see Know Your Enemies
Lend-Lease Act and, 308–9
Liberty Films, 345, 380–82, 389–90, 402, 414,
    416, 417, 419–22, 424, 444
Liberty Films sold by, 437, 439
in London, 247–54, 257, 263, 276, 292
Lost Horizon, 161–62
Marshall and, 113–14, 133, 381
Meet John Doe, 46, 65–68, 69, 76–79, 183, 211,
    216, 423
Mellett and, 114–15, 144, 184, 205, 210,
    218, 264
Moss and, 303, 307–8
Mr. Deeds Goes to Town, 24, 26, 28, 65
Mr. Smith Goes to Washington, 41–46, 52, 65, 77,
    94, 110, 132, 166, 183, 423
Mussolini and, 25, 67
The Negro Soldier, 134–36, 234, 303–8
On to Tokyo, 380
politics of, 8, 274, 277, 422
Private SNAFU cartoon series, 234–36, 308
Roosevelt and, 28, 441
Roosevelt speech drafted by, 114–15
Schlossberg and, 111–13, 133
Screen Directors Guild and, 26, 40, 79, 110, 408
Stevens and, 164–65, 167, 195, 345, 347, 418
Truman Committee and, 216
Tunisian Victory and, 236–43, 247–52, 254, 255,
    278, 283, 288, 298, 305, 381
Two Down and One to Go!, 380
Why We Fight, see Why We Fight
You Can't Take It With You, 24, 26–27, 40–41
Your Job in Germany, 378–79
Capra, Frank, Jr., 329
Capra, John, 27
Capra, Lucille, 24, 27, 112, 115–16, 132–34, 139,
    140, 183, 242, 247, 251–55, 329

Capra, Tommy, 247
Capri, 348
Carey, Harry, 44
Carlotta of Mexico, 33, 34
Carson, Robert, 127
Carver, George Washington, 306
Casablanca, 231–32, 236
Casablanca, 130, 286, 290, 417
Casablanca Conference, 185
Caserta, 266, 348
Catholic World, 139
Cerf, Bennett, 261
Chamberlain, Neville, 47, 48, 59
Chaplin, Charlie, 38, 67, 89, 93
Chayefsky, Paddy, 347
Chennault, Claire, 241*n*
Chennault, Jack, 241–42
Chiang Kai-Shek, 278
Children's Hour, The, 33
China, 182, 222, 273, 274, 326
    The Battle of China, 164, 308, 330
    Japan and, 162, 189
    Know Your Ally—China, 303
Chodorov, Jerome, 169, 200
Choltitz, Dietrich von, 341
Churchill, Winston, 59, 60, 122, 178, 185,
    254, 278, 317, 376
Citadel, The, 46
Citizen Kane, 77, 262, 431
Civilian Conservation Corps, 113
Clampett, Bob, 235
Claridge's, 176, 179, 199, 200, 248, 250, 319
Clark, Bennett, 90, 93, 94
Clark, D. Worth, 97, 98
Clothier, William, 169, 177, 199, 219, 221,
    246, 293, 317–18
Cobb, Humphrey, 22–23
Coburn, Charles, 194
Cohn, Harry, 24–25, 28, 44, 49, 79, 155, 161, 167,
    194, 195, 424
Colbert, Claudette, 59, 68, 131
Collier's, 25, 91, 338
Colman, Ronald, 166, 167
Columbia Pictures, 23–24, 40, 65, 81, 137, 161,
    194–95, 345, 402
    Capra's departure from, 46, 49, 79, 166
    Stevens' contract with, 49, 79, 166, 167, 193
Committee for the First Amendment, 441
Committee to Defend America by Aiding the
    Allies, 59
Communism, 16, 17, 19–20, 26, 27, 41, 42,
    50, 54, 61–63, 132–33, 169, 226, 265,
    275, 441
    Capra and, 275–76, 441
    Ford and, 274, 275
    House Un-American Activities Committee and, 16,
    41, 62, 276*n*, 441
    Huston and, 171, 191
    McCarthyism and, 275
Communist Party USA (CPUSA), 191

concentration camps, 374, 401
 Bergen-Belsen, 367–68
 Dachau, 23, 369–77, 415, 421, 444
 Dora, 367
 Nazi Concentration and Prison Camps, 400,
  402–3
 Stevens and, 23, 367, 369–77, 400, 402–3, 415,
  418, 421, 444
Confessions of a Nazi Spy, 36, 37–38, 82, 382
Connelly, Marc, 135, 423, 424
Cooper, Gary, 25, 28, 41, 60, 65, 66, 73, 76–77, 84,
 88, 275
Cooper, Merian C., 56, 401
Corregidor, 142, 149
Costello, Lou, 103
Coutances, 338
Coward, Noel, 296
Crisp, Donald, 154, 156, 157
Cronin, A. J., 46
Cronkite, Walter, 203
Crowther, Bosley, 88, 218, 407
Cue, 297
Cukor, George, 69–70
Curtiz, Michael, 290
Czechoslovakia, 34, 59, 164

Dachau, 23, 369–77, 415, 421, 444
Daily Telegraph, 189
Daily Worker, 54
Darwell, Jane, 154, 156, 157, 172
Davenport, Harry, 108, 206
Davis, Bette, 33, 34, 51, 60, 69, 73, 117–19,
 125, 168
 Wyler and, 31, 33, 51, 60–61, 118–19, 426,
  429, 442
Davis, Elmer, 207, 217, 226
D-Day, 310–19, 324, 444
Dead End, 33, 427
December 7th, 107–9, 126, 147, 155, 191,
 206–10, 216, 271, 288, 306, 324–25,
 355, 408, 409
de Gaulle, Charles, 185, 340, 341
de Havilland, Olivia, 125, 258, 385
 Huston and, 123, 125, 129, 137, 170–71, 192,
  284, 385
DeMille, Cecil B., 441
Desert Training Center, 241
Desert Victory, 232–33, 236, 268, 288, 289
De Sica, Vittorio, 421
Desire Under the Elms, 32
Detective Story, 442
Diary of Anne Frank, The, 444
Diary of a Sergeant, 425–26
Dies, Martin, 16, 62, 213
Dies Committee, 16, 19, 62–63, 133
Dieterle, William, 34, 35, 85
Directors Guild of America, 442
Disney, Walt, 275
Disney Studios, 164, 182, 235, 276
Dive Bomber, 300

Divide and Conquer, 164
Dodsworth, 33
Donovan, William "Wild Bill," 3, 104, 106–8, 145,
 152, 173, 174, 207, 216, 272, 273, 311, 319,
 326, 348, 442
Doolittle, James, 110
Doolittle raid, 110, 145, 146
Dora, 367
Downey, Sheridan, 96
Drake, Alfred, 426
Dr. Ehrlich's Magic Bullet, 85–86
 Dreiser, Theodore, *An American Tragedy*,
  401, 443
 Drums Along the Mohawk, 53, 152
 Duel in the Sun, 415
 Duff, Warren, 163
 Duggan, Pat, 394
 DUKWs, 313
 Dunne, Irene, 79–80
 Dunne, Philip, 59, 62, 74–76, 105, 107

Each Dawn I Die, 163
Eagle Squadron, 176
Eaker, Ira, 199–200, 220, 221, 257, 258, 260–61,
 348, 389, 415
Eareckson, William, 190
E-boats, 318
Egypt, 233, 237, 261
 Cairo Conference in, 278
Eichorn, David, 375
Eifler, Carl, 273
Eisenhower, Dwight D., 262, 312, 339, 344, 347,
 366, 379, 390
Eisenstein, Sergei, 264
El Alamein, 233
Elbe, 368, 369
Elizabeth, Queen, The Queen Mother, 220, 260
Emerald Bay Yacht Club, 326–27
Emergency Peace Campaign, 84
Engel, Samuel, 108–9, 155
England, *see* Britain
Epstein, Julius, 130
Epstein, Philip, 130
Escape, 120
Evans, Vincent, 202
Eve of Battle, 317

Faichney, James, 283, 284
Farber, Manny, 289, 384
Farm (Field Photo Memorial Home), 326–27, 409
Fascism, 17, 20, 23, 26, 27, 35, 39, 41, 42, 63, 66,
 67, 77, 177, 274, 276, 336
 Prelude to War and, 182, 218
Faulkner, William, 170n
FBI, 194, 276
Feldman, Charles, 167, 293, 344, 414
Ferguson, Otis, 44–45
Fetchit, Stepin, 214
Fidler, Jimmie, 50
Field Photo Memorial Home (the Farm), 326–27, 490

Field Photo Unit, 56–57, 72, 106–9, 179–81, 188, 206, 208, 215, 216, 222, 271, 273, 275, 288, 301, 311, 324, 325, 400–401, 403, 408
  at Allied landing in France, 313–19
  Battle of Midway and, 145, 151, 153, 155
  They Were Expendable and, 355, 356
Fighting Seabees, The, 273, 357
FilmIndia, 23
Finkel, Abem, 86
1st Marine Division, 391
Fitzgerald, Barry, 328
Fitzgerald, Geraldine, 74
Fitzgerald, Marietta, 192, 241, 284
Flaherty, Robert, 192
Flanner, Janet, 163
Fleming, Victor, 52, 275
Florida, 242, 243, 288
Flying Fortresses, *see* B-17s
Flying Irishman, The, 328
Flying Tigers, 56
Flying Tigers, 357
Flying Yorkshireman, The, 328
Flynn, Errol, 336, 385
Flynn, John C., 93–94
Fonda, Henry, 53, 54, 70, 74, 154, 156, 157
Ford, Barbara, 105, 168, 408
Ford, Dan, 56, 57
Ford, John, 1–4, 7–9, 11, 18–20, 21, 22, 28, 52–53, 63, 70–72, 76, 104–10, 119, 126, 137, 168, 170, 173–76, 205, 210, 211, 219, 238, 271–75, 278, 288, 293, 301, 324–25, 339, 366, 395, 407–9, 420, 440–43
  Academy Awards and, 2, 18, 52, 70, 72, 126, 174, 205, 288, 324–25, 407, 408, 441
  at Allied landing in France, 301, 309, 310–19
  at Anti-Nazi League rally, 19, 20
  The Battle of Midway, 144, 145–59, 160, 172–75, 179, 180, 182, 184, 205, 206, 209, 222, 224, 275, 282, 301
  boat of (*Araner*), 55–56, 72, 168, 272, 324
  Bulkeley and, 302, 318–19
  Capra and, 442
  Communism and, 274, 275
  death of, 442
  December 7th and, 107–9, 126, 147, 207–10, 216, 271, 288, 324–25, 355, 408, 409
  Doolittle raid filmed by, 110, 145, 146
  Farm (Field Photo Memorial Home) established by, 326–27, 409
  Field Photo Unit of, *see* Field Photo Unit
  The Grapes of Wrath, 53–55, 63, 70, 76, 78, 98, 153, 154, 440
  How Green Was My Valley, 2, 73–76, 105, 106, 126, 152–54
  Jews and, 274–75
  leg broken by, 360, 400
  in London, 174–77, 319, 325
  The Long Voyage Home, 56, 63–65, 174
  Mellett and, 174–75, 205

military honors desired by, 325, 408
  and Motion Picture Alliance for the Preservation of American Ideals, 275
  Naval Volunteer Photographic Unit and, 2, 3
  navy commission of, 55–56, 72
  navy induction of, 104–5
  in North Africa, 179–80, 216
  Olivier and, 178–79
  OSS assignment of, 273–74
  politics of, 274–75
  requests transfer from Naval Reserve to active duty, 1–3
  return from war, 400–401
  Sex Hygiene, 71–72
  Stagecoach, 18, 49, 52–53, 63, 153, 174, 272, 357
  Stevens and, 311
  They Were Expendable, 299–302, 318–19, 325–27, 352–61, 395, 405–7
  Truman Committee and, 216
  War Department and, 105, 107, 325–26
  Wayne and, 52, 55, 63, 109, 272–73, 356–60
  Wyler and, 177
  Zanuck and, 327
Ford, Mary, 1–3, 56, 105, 109, 126, 146, 151, 168, 272, 274, 316, 319
Ford, Michael Patrick "Pat," 105, 168, 274, 357, 408
Foreign Correspondent, 48
Foreman, Carl, 276–78
Forrestal, James, 207, 352–53
For Whom the Bell Tolls, 275
Four Sons, 21
Fox, *see* 20th Century Fox
France, 57, 58–59, 61, 164, 167, 368
  Allied landing and aftermath in, 261–64, 290–91, 301, 309, 310–23
  liberation of, 261
  Mulhouse, 348–51, 361
  Paris, *see* Paris
  Stevens in, 338–44
  Wyler in, 347–51
Franco, Francisco, 25, 131
Frank Capra Productions, 46, 65
Freleng, Friz, 235
Fudd, Elmer, 235
Funny Girl, 442
Furthman, Jules, 67

Gabin, Jean, 59
Gable, Clark, 131
Gallagher, Tag, 208
Garbo, Greta, 59, 101
Garfield, John, 168
Garson, Greer, 119, 123, 204
Gaslight, 417
Gay, George, 150
Geisel, Theodor S., 234–36, 277, 308, 329–30, 378–79
George VI, King, 220, 260

Germany, 29, 60, 67–68, 92, 97, 141, 161, 164,
181, 183
Aachen, 344
Austria and, 15, 29, 164
in Battle of the Bulge, 346
Berlin, 29, 369, 376
Britain and, 45, 56, 68, 76, 81, 92, 97, 105, 121,
247–48, 252
citizenry of, 378–79
concentration camps of, *see* concentration camps
Czechoslovakia and, 34, 59, 164
France and, 57, 58–59, 61, 164
Here is Germany, 379
Italy and, 267
Know Your Enemy—Germany, 308, 329–30,
335, 379
Kristallnacht and, 29, 30
The Nazi Plan, 377, 400, 403–4
The Nazis Strike, 164
Nordhausen, 367–68
North Africa and, 180
Norway and, 64
Nuremberg Trials and, 376–77, 400–404
Poland and, 37, 43, 59, 164
postwar occupation of, 379
Prelude to War and, 182
Russia and, 87, 265
Stevens in, 344–47, 366–77, 401–2
Torgau, 368–69
Wilhelmshaven, 202–3, 205, 219, 220, 297
Wyler in bombing mission over, 201–3, 219–21,
245–46, 430, 434
Your Job in Germany, 378–79
Gilbert, W. S., 335
Gillette, Melvin, 238–39, 266–67, 269, 333
Glazer, Benjamin, 76
Glory for Me (Kantor), 392–95
Goebbels, Joseph, 38, 138, 141
Goering, Hermann, 121, 292, 376, 404
Going My Way, 328, 380
Goldwyn, Samuel, 34–35, 41, 46, 49, 59, 60, 109,
126, 205, 420, 425
The Best Years of Our Lives and, 392–96, 425,
430, 435
Wyler and, 72–73, 169, 245, 258, 298, 365,
389, 390
Gone with the Wind, 33, 35, 52, 73, 205, 382
Goodbye, Mr. Chips, 275
Good Earth, The, 330
Good Housekeeping, 423
Goodrich, Frances, 308, 328, 423
Goulden, Joseph, 397
Grable, Betty, 197
Grand Illusion, 19
Granger, Farley, 425
Grant, Cary, 8, 23, 79–81, 166, 167, 193
Grant, USS, 191
Grapes of Wrath, The, 53–55, 63, 70, 76, 78, 98,
153, 154, 440
Great Dictator, The, 38, 67, 89, 93

"Greatest Gift, The" (Stern), 422–23
Greene, Graham, 27, 53
Green Pastures, The, 135, 423
Greenstreet, Sidney, 127, 128
Grobel, Lawrence, 192
Grogan, Stanley, 217
Grosseto, 363
Gunga Din, 23, 38, 39, 81, 262, 343
Guthrie, Woody, 54

Hackett, Albert, 308, 328, 423
Halifax, Lord, 178
Hammett, Dashiell, 124, 127
Hansen, Edmund, 57
Harper's Bazaar, 412
Hart, Moss, 27, 298
Harvey, 382
Havens, James, 356
Hawaii, 329
Hawks, Howard, 82
Air Force, 129, 203, 294
Sergeant York, 73, 83–89, 93–94, 97, 103, 123
Hays, Will, 44
Hays Office, 91
Hayward, Louis, 289
Hecht, Ben, 34–35
Heiress, The, 442
Heisler, Stuart, 303, 305, 306
Heller, Bob, 236
Hellinger, Mark, 331
Hellman, Lillian, 33, 73, 118, 126, 135, 138, 364
Helm, Henriette, 350–51
Hemingway, Ernest, 275, 331, 338, 341
Hemingway, Leicester, 349–51
Henry V (Shakespeare), 178–79, 312
Hepburn, Katharine, 5–6, 8, 21, 81, 165, 168, 418
Here is Germany, 379
Herman, Jan, 219, 365
Hersey, John, 410
Hersholt, Jean, 421
Hess, Rudolf, 403, 404
High Noon, 276n
High Sierra, 85–86, 124
Hirohito, Emperor, 131, 160, 276–78, 335
Prelude to War and, 182
Tanaka plan and, 330
Hiroshima, 387, 396
Hitchcock, Alfred, 48, 69–70, 125, 398, 416
Hitler, Adolf, 15, 16, 17, 20, 22, 23, 25, 28, 36, 37,
38, 46, 67–68, 79, 84, 85, 87n, 88, 89, 92, 93,
95, 97, 98, 103, 120, 123, 131, 141, 160, 176,
181, 215, 235, 328, 332, 344, 350, 369, 378,
379, 380
Juárez and, 34, 35
Nuremberg Trials and, 403, 404
Paris and, 339, 340
Prelude to War and, 182
Stevens at Berchtesgaden retreat of, 376
suicide of, 375, 376
Tunisian Victory and, 255

Hitler Lives, 379n
Hodson, James, 248, 251, 255–56
Hollywood Anti-Nazi League, 16, 19, 29, 88
  Capra and, 28–29
  Ford and, 19, 20
  "Quarantine Hitler" rally of, 28–29
Hollywood Canteen, 168, 274, 408
Hollywood Community Chest, 50–51
Hollywood Reporter, 91–92, 102, 206, 211, 351, 436
Hollywood Victory Caravan, 137
Holman, Rufus, 210–11, 217
Home Again Special, 391–92
Hoover, J. Edgar, 115, 194
Hope, Bob, 118, 204, 250
Hornet, USS, 110, 147–50
House Divided, A, 32
House Un-American Activities Committee (HUAC),
  16, 41, 62, 276n, 441
Howe, James Wong, 188, 222
Howell, Miriam, 394
How Green Was My Valley, 2, 73–76, 105, 106,
  126, 152–54
Hughes, Francis Massie, 147
Hughes, Langston, 307
Huston, John, 4, 5, 11, 18, 30–36, 37, 73, 82,
    85–86, 123, 124, 127, 170, 191–92, 271,
    283–85, 288, 293, 322, 339, 380, 404,
    409–10, 420, 440, 441, 443
  Academy Awards and, 288, 443
  Across the Pacific, 127–29
  in Aleutian Islands, 170, 186–91, 265, 269
  Ambler and, 253–54, 265–69, 280
  B-25 bomber film and, 137–38
  The Battle of San Pietro, 279–83, 322, 331–34,
    382–85, 399–400, 407, 411
  on bomber missions, 189–90
  Capra and, 252–53
  death of, 443
  de Havilland and, 123, 125, 129, 137, 170–71,
    192, 284, 385
  discharge from army service, 409
  divorce of, 385
  in driving accidents, 32
  financial difficulties of, 331
  Fitzgerald and, 192, 241, 284
  infidelities and romances of, 123, 192, 249, 284
  investigation into suspected Communist ties of,
    171, 191
  in Italy, 252–53, 265–70, 279–80, 282–83, 332
  Juárez, 33–36, 85
  Know Your Enemy—Japan and, 334–37, 387–88
  Let There Be Light (originally *The Returning
    Psychoneurotic*), 386–87, 396–400,
    409–13, 443
  Liberty Films and, 414
  Lilly and, 284, 334
  in London, 247–53, 257
  The Maltese Falcon, 4, 86, 123–25, 127, 331
  Report from the Aleutians, 191–92, 222–27, 241,
    264, 265, 284, 288, 333, 411, 413

  Scott's breakdown and hospitalization and,
    284, 385–86
  Sergeant York and, 86–87, 123
  Signal Corps joined by, 5, 127–29
  The Treasure of the Sierra Madre, 127, 170, 293,
    410, 440, 443
  Tunisian Victory and, 241–43, 248–51, 254,
    281, 288
  Wyler's friendship with, 30–34, 442
Huston, Lesley Black, 30, 123, 125, 129, 170,
    192, 284
  divorce of, 385
Huston, Walter, 31, 32, 33, 108, 182, 191–92, 206,
    209, 223, 288

Iceland, 107
I'm an American!, 78
India, 273
Informer, The, 18–19, 52, 63
Intelligence Documentary Photographic Project, 274
In This Our Life, 123, 125, 128
In Time to Come, 5
In Which We Serve, 296
IRA, 18
Iran, 261, 309
I Remember Mama, 443
Italy, 161, 164, 197, 284
  The Battle of San Pietro, 279–83, 322, 331–34,
    382–85, 399–400, 407, 411
  Germany and, 267
  Huston in, 252–53, 265–70, 279–80,
    282–83, 332
  Operation Avalanche and, 253
  Prelude to War and, 182
  Rome, 317
  San Pietro, 267–70, 279–83, 322
  Wyler in, 298, 348, 351, 361
It Happened One Night, 24, 130–31
It's a Wonderful Life, 414, 416–17, 419, 422–25,
    435–37, 439, 441
Ivens, Joris, 276–77
I Wake Up Screaming, 197
I Wanted Wings, 200

Jackson, Robert, 377
Jaffe, Sam, 23
Japan, 102, 134, 135, 164, 181, 183
  Aleutian Islands and, *see* Aleutian Islands
  anti-Asian racism and, 127–28, 160–61, 206–7,
    276, 277, 330, 335–37
  atom bombs dropped on, 387, 396
  Bataan and, 141, 149, 299–300, 352
  Battle of Midway, *see* Midway, Battle of
  China and, 162, 189
  Doolittle raid and, 110, 145, 146
  end of war in, 387–88
  Know Your Enemy—Japan, 163, 234, 276–78,
    308, 328, 334–37, 380, 387–88
  Objective, Burma! and, 336
  On to Tokyo, 380

Japan (*cont.*)
  Pearl Harbor attack by, *see* Pearl Harbor
  Prelude to War and, 182
  The Purple Heart and, 335
  Shintoism in, 160, 335, 387
Japanese Americans, 160
  December 7th and, 206–10, 271
  internment camps and, 127, 162, 208
  Little Tokyo, U.S.A. and, 162, 206
Jews:
  Ford and, 274–75
  in Germany, 37
  in Hollywood, 15–16, 37–38, 50, 88–89, 91
Jersey Bounce, 201–3, 219
Jezebel, 33, 60, 118
Joan of Lorraine, 417
Johnson, Nunnally, 54
Jones, Chuck, 235, 236
Jones, Jennifer, 415
Journey into Fear, 253
Juárez, 33–36, 85
Juárez, Benito, 33–34
Juno Beach, 312
Justice Department, 41, 78, 90
Justin, John, 76

Kachins, 274
Kanin, Garson, 347
Kantor, Mackinlay, 392
  Glory for Me, 392–95
Kaufman, George S., 27
Kazan, Elia, 440
Kazin, Alfred, 265
Keighley, William, 349
Keitel, Wilhelm, 403
Keep 'Em Flying, 210*n*
Kellogg, Ray, 273, 301, 403
Kelly, Bob, 353*n*
Kelly, Gene, 405
Kennedy, Joseph P., 44
Kiel, 221
Killers, The, 331
Kingsley, Sidney, 33, 192
Kipling, Rudyard, 23
Kiska, 170, 186, 187, 189–91, 223–26
Kitty Foyle, 69
Knight, Eric, 142–44, 163, 164, 177, 183, 185,
    218, 264, 328
Know Your Allies, 133, 163, 302–3
  Know Your Ally—Britain, 302–3
  Know Your Ally—China, 303
  Know Your Ally—Russia, 303
Know Your Enemies, 133, 161, 208, 276, 302
  Know Your Enemy—Germany, 308, 329–30,
      335, 379
  Know Your Enemy—Japan, 163, 234, 276–78,
      308, 328, 334–47, 380, 387–88
Knox, Frank, 104
Koch, Howard, 5, 86
Koenig, Lester, 260, 361–62, 364

Kohner, Lupita, 49
Kohner, Paul, 49
Korda, Alexander, 46, 76, 93, 176
Kristallnacht, 29, 30
"Kukan": The Battle Cry of China, 189
Kuter, L. S., 295

Ladd, Alan, 204
Ladies' Home Journal, 78
Lady for a Day, 441
Laemmle, Carl, 31, 49
La Guardia, Fiorello, 88, 140
Lahr, Bert, 137
Lake, Veronica, 258
Lamarr, Hedy, 258
Landon, Alf, 26
Langford, Frances, 250
Lardner, David, 233
Lasky, Jesse, 83–84
Laurel and Hardy, 137, 373
Lay, Beirne, 200–201, 203, 221, 247, 260
Leaf, Munro, 235–36
League of American Writers, 191
League of Nations, 5
Leahy, William, 158
Lean, David, 296, 421
Leclerc, Philippe, 339, 341
Leech, John, 62
Leighton, Charles, 219
Lend-Lease Act, 76, 91
  Russia and, 308–9
Let There Be Light (originally *The Returning
    Psychoneurotic*), 386–87, 396–400,
    409–13, 443
Letter, The, 51, 69, 118
Levinson, Nathan, 76
Liberty Films, 345, 380–82, 389–90, 402, 414,
    416, 417, 419–22, 424, 437, 444
  sold to Paramount, 437, 439
Libya, 233
Life, 266, 322, 410, 412
Lilly, Doris, 284, 334
Lindbergh, Anne, 95
Lindbergh, Charles, 91, 94–96, 104, 235
Lippmann, Walter, 245
Little Foxes, The, 60, 73, 75, 118–19, 125, 126,
    134, 429, 431
Little Tokyo, U.S.A., 162, 206
Litvak, Anatole, 4, 37, 137, 141, 231, 232, 243,
    264, 305, 308, 380
Llewellyn, Richard, 73–74
Lodge, Henry Cabot, Jr., 44
Lombard, Carole, 80, 118
London, 247–48
  Capra in, 247–54, 257, 263, 276, 292
  Ford in, 174–77, 319, 325
  Huston in, 247–53, 257
  Stevens in, 257, 261, 262, 290–92, 309, 347
  Wyler in, 176–78, 199–204, 257, 258
London Can Take It, 76

London Charter, 376
Long Voyage Home, The, 56, 63–65, 174
Look, 124
Los Angeles Herald Examiner, 32
Los Angeles Herald Express, 205
Los Angeles Times, 387, 420
Lost Horizon, 161–62
Louis, Joe, 135, 304, 305
Loy, Myrna, 427, 432
Lubitsch, Ernst, 118
Luce, Henry, 54
Lund, John, 379
Lupino, Ida, 74
Luxembourg, 343, 346, 349
Lynn, Leni, 249

MacArthur, Charles, 34–35, 299, 302, 353, 387–88
MacDonald, Jeanette, 204
MacKenzie, Aeneas, 33–34
Mackenzie, Jack, Jr., 109, 147–52, 408
MacLeish, Archibald, 140
Madame Curie, 286
Madsen, Axel, 200
Majae al Bab, 180
Malraux, André, 350
Maltese Falcon, The, 4, 86, 123–25, 127, 331
Manchuria, 164, 181
Mankiewicz, Joseph L., 6, 80
Mann, Thomas, 15, 16–17
Mannix, Eddie, 360
Man Who Would Be King, The, 443
March, Fredric, 62, 427, 429
March of Time, The, 58, 142
Marshall, George, 7, 9, 113–14, 131, 133, 182, 183, 217, 218, 277, 288, 333, 380, 381
Martin, Mildred, 287
Marx, Groucho, 137
Mason General Hospital, 387, 396–400, 410
Maugham, W. Somerset, 51
Maurois, André, 20–21
Maximilian I of Mexico, 33, 34
Maxwell, Elsa, 245
Mayer, Louis B., 16, 120–21, 165, 169, 178, 272, 300–301
McBride, Joseph, 105, 274, 307, 309*n*
McCall's, 79
McCarey, Leo, 380, 420
McCarthy, Todd, 86–87
McCarthyism, 275
McCrea, Joel, 48, 193–95
McDowall, Roddy, 74, 105, 442
McFarland, Ernest, 92, 94, 98
McGuinness, James Kevin, 153, 208, 275, 300, 354
Meet John Doe, 46, 65–68, 69, 76–79, 183, 211, 216, 423
Mellett, Lowell, 91, 104, 110, 134, 138–40, 158, 162–63, 174, 181–84, 205–7, 210, 211, 217, 224–27, 236, 265, 288, 335
    Capra and, 114–15, 144, 184, 205, 210, 218, 264
    Ford and, 174–75, 205

Report from the Aleutians and, 224–26
    The World at War, 181–83
Mellor, William, 238, 242, 262, 292, 311, 321
Memphis Belle, 201, 219–21, 244–46, 257–58, 260–61, 430, 434, 442–43
Memphis Belle, The: The Story of a Flying Fortress (originally *25 Missions*), 246–47, 257–61, 293–98, 317, 348, 349, 361, 362, 388
Mencken, H. L., 192
Menninger, William C., 411, 412
Meredith, Burgess, 192, 255
Merrie Melodies, 235
Methot, Mayo, 270
MGM, 5, 16, 23, 40, 48, 67–68, 81, 101, 119–23, 138, 139, 168–69, 178, 205, 271–72, 299–301, 327, 330, 356, 357, 360, 405–7
Midnight, 59
Midway, Battle of, 170, 172, 273, 325, 355, 408, 442
    The Battle of Midway, 144, 145–59, 160, 172–75, 179, 180, 182, 184, 205, 206, 209, 222, 224, 275, 282, 301
Midway Atoll, 146
Mikado, The, 335
Milestone, Lewis, 21, 126*n*
Milland, Ray, 68
Millar, Mack, 205
Mills, John, 250
Ministry of Information, 232, 249, 252, 254
Mishkin, Leo, 211
Mister Roberts, 442
Mitchell, Curtis, 333
Mitchell, Thomas, 63, 64
Moffat, Ivan, 262–63, 311, 320–22, 340, 341, 346, 367–69, 373, 376, 415–16
Mojave Desert, Calif., 241, 243, 288
Mondale, Walter, 443
Monogram, 389
Montgomery, Bernard, 322, 340
Montgomery, Robert, 356–60, 406
Morale Branch, 112, 113, 137, 140, 216–17
More the Merrier, The, 167, 193–95, 197, 263, 290, 401–2
Morgan, Robert, 201, 219, 244–45, 247, 259–61, 294
Morocco, 173, 231, 232
Mortal Storm, The, 39, 40, 46, 48, 67–68, 82, 120
Moss, Carlton, 135–36, 303, 305–8
Motion Picture Alliance for the Preservation of American Ideals (MPA), 275–76
Motion Picture Artists' Committee to Aid Spain, 20, 29–30
Motion Picture Committee Co-operating for Defense, 59
Motion Picture Daily, 54
Motion Picture Democratic Committee, 20
Motion Picture Producers and Distributors of America, 44, 91
Mr. Deeds Goes to Town, 24, 26, 28, 41, 65
Mrs. Miniver, 4, 5, 119–23, 126–27, 129, 134, 138–39, 169, 172, 177–78, 203–5, 211, 220, 298, 389, 426

Mr. Smith Goes to Washington, 41–46, 52, 65, 77,
    94, 110, 132, 166, 183, 423
    as sequel to *Mr. Deeds Goes to Town*, 28, 41
Mulberry harbor, 313, 319, 325
Mulhouse, 348–51, 361
Muni, Paul, 34, 85, 86
Munson, Lyman T., 114, 196, 240–41, 333–34,
    380, 381
Museum of Modern Art, 141, 222, 410, 412
Mussolini, Benito, 45, 98, 160, 347, 380
    Capra and, 25, 67
    Juárez and, 34, 35
    Prelude to War and, 182
My Darling Clementine, 401
My Favorite Wife, 80

Nagasaki, 396
Name Above the Title, The (Capra), 132
Naples, 266, 267
Napoleon III, 34, 35
Nash, Ogden, 31
Nation, 233, 289, 298, 412
National Film Board of Canada, 163, 276
National Fund Raising Campaign for Russian
    Relief, 191
National Labor Relations Board, 40
National Legion of Decency, 101
Native Son (Wright), 306
Naval Reserve Armory, 72
Naval Volunteer Photographic Unit, 2, 3
Navy Relief Society, 135
Nazi Concentration and Prison Camps, 400, 402–3
Nazi Plan, The, 377, 400, 403–4
Nazis Strike, The, 164
Negro Soldier, The, 134–36, 234, 303–8
Neutrality Act, 59
New Deal, 9, 26
Newman, Alfred, 154
New Republic, 44, 55, 77, 88, 134, 384, 436
newsreels, 5, 9, 10, 29, 36, 58, 88, 92, 142, 227, 287
Newsweek, 172
New Yorker, 45, 68, 79, 163, 165, 172–73, 233, 264,
    288–89, 297–98, 384
New York Film Critics Circle Award, 35, 263–64
New York Herald Tribune, 125
New York Morning Telegraph, 211
New York Post, 138, 307, 412
New York Times, 5, 24, 31, 35, 44, 49, 54, 68,
    77–78, 81–82, 87n, 88, 119, 124–25, 138,
    172, 181, 214, 218, 225, 288–90, 297, 348,
    384, 388, 407, 428–29, 436
New York Times Magazine, 419
New York World-Telegram, 119
Nichols, Dudley, 52, 63–64, 153, 355
Nigeria, 196
Nimitz, Chester, 145–47
Nine Lives, 176
91st Bomb Group, 201–3, 219, 246
Ninotchka, 59
Ninth Air Force, 349–50

Nordhausen, 367–68
Norris, George, 44
North Africa, 164, 167, 173, 237, 278, 279
    Africa Freed!, 243, 248–49
    At the Front in North Africa, 215, 232–34
    Desert Victory, 232–33, 236, 288
    Ford in, 179–80, 216
    Stevens in, 196–98, 237–41, 261, 266, 321,
        339, 444
    Tunisian Victory, see Tunisian Victory
    Zanuck in, 179–81, 184, 211, 214, 215, 231–32
North Star, The, 126n
Norway, 64
Nugent, Frank S., 35, 54
Nuremberg Trials, 376–77, 400–404
Nye, Gerald P., 89–90, 92–96, 213, 235
Nye Committee, 92–94, 96–98, 103, 120, 212

Oberon, Merle, 74
Objective, Burma!, 336
Odets, Clifford, 192, 423
Office for Emergency Management, 104
Office of Strategic Services (OSS), 104, 153, 174–76,
    180, 273–74, 288, 311, 316, 326, 353, 408,
    409, 442
Office of the Bureau of Archives, 408–9
Office of War Information (OWI), 134, 138, 140,
    174, 181, 184, 207, 211, 217, 224, 226,
    227, 253, 277, 287, 288, 302, 304, 331,
    355, 356, 390
    Bureau of Motion Pictures, 162–63, 166, 175,
        206, 211, 225, 226, 335
Olivier, Laurence, 74, 178–79
Omaha Beach, 312, 313, 315, 317
    Mulberry harbor off of, 313, 319, 325
One Big Happy Family, 417
O'Neill, Eugene, 32, 63, 64
On to Tokyo, 380
Open Book, An (Huston), 86
Operation Avalanche, 253
Operation Overlord, 262, 314
Operation Roundup, 261
Operation Sledgehammer, 261
Operation Torch, 167, 176, 231
Operation Varsity, 366
Orlando, Fla., 242, 243, 288
Osborn, Frederick, 111–14, 133, 134, 140, 142,
    161, 182, 184, 216, 239, 240, 253, 303,
    309n, 330, 381
Oscars, *see* Academy Awards
Our Gang, 221
Owens, Jesse, 306
Ox-Bow Incident, The, 154

P-47s (Thunderbolts), 298
    Thunderbolt, 298, 348–39, 351, 361–65,
        388–89, 415
Panama Canal, 107, 127
Paramount Pictures, 23, 29, 37, 68, 84, 129, 140
    Liberty Films sold to, 437, 439

Paris, 59, 322, 338–39, 376
  liberation of, 339–42
  Wyler in, 347–49, 351
Parker, Dorothy, 20
Parrish, Kathleen, 107
Parrish, Robert, 106–7, 109–10, 152–56, 175,
    208, 209, 327, 401, 408
Parsons, Louella, 151
Pascal, Ernest, 74
Pastor Hall, 68
Paths of Glory, 22–23, 38
Patterson, Robert, 217, 333–34
Patton, 442
Patton, George S., 231, 232, 322, 379
Pavlinchenko, Lieutenant, 164
Pearl Harbor, 1, 3–7, 9–11, 101–3, 107, 110, 111,
    113, 117, 119, 121, 127, 128, 139, 146, 149,
    193, 299, 330, 335, 352, 354, 355, 406
  December 7th, 107–9, 126, 147, 155, 191, 206–10,
    216, 271, 288, 306, 324–25, 355, 408, 409
  War Comes to America, 164, 308, 379–82
Pearson, Drew, 115
Peck, Gregory, 415
Penny Serenade, 80–81, 387
Philadelphia Inquirer, 287
Philadelphia Story, The, 69
Philippines, 141, 299, 352, 353, 356, 357, 361, 405
Phyllis Was a Fortress, 176
Pichel, Irving, 154, 157
Pickens, Andrew, 1
Pickford, Mary, 204
Pidgeon, Walter, 121
Pier, Kenneth, 147–50, 152
Pinewood Studios, 249–52, 268
Pius XII, Pope, 348
Place in the Sun, A, 440, 443
Planer, Franz, 49–50
Plunkett, USS, 312, 313
Pocketful of Miracles, 441
Poland, 37, 43, 59, 164
Polk, Margaret, 244–45
Popular Front, 19
Positif, 314n
Potsdam Conference, 376
Power, Tyrone, 204
Poynter, Nelson, 138, 166
Prelude to War, 144, 164, 182–85, 205, 210, 211,
    217–19, 224, 234, 264, 421
Pride of the Yankees, The, 275
Private SNAFU cartoon series, 234–36, 308
Production Code, 16, 17, 37, 52–53, 88, 89, 194,
    236, 296, 428–29, 433
propaganda, Nazi, 141, 142
  Triumph of the Will, 6, 141, 142, 376
propaganda, U.S., 6–7, 9–10, 35–36, 59, 82, 87, 88,
    102, 120, 153, 163, 175, 181, 184, 207, 210,
    211, 213–14, 216–17, 227, 231, 253, 255, 288
  anti-Japanese rhetoric in, 160–61, 206–10, 276,
    277, 330, 335–37
  Senate hearings on, 90–94, 96–98, 103, 120

Psychiatry in Action!, 412
PT boats, 146, 148, 318, 353, 354, 356, 357, 359,
    361, 407
Purple Heart, The, 335
Pyle, Ernie, 266, 279, 334

Quebec Conference, 261–62
Quiet Man, The, 441

Radio City Music Hall, 139, 172, 217
Raft, George, 85–86, 124
Rains, Claude, 35, 77
Ramparts We Watch, The, 142
Rat Islands, 170
Reagan, Ronald, 379
Rebecca, 69, 70, 76
Red Badge of Courage, The, 443
"Red River Valley," 154
Reed, Carol, 125, 176, 347
Reed, Donna, 406
Reims, 342
Reinhardt, Wolfgang, 33–34
Remarque, Erich Maria, 21
Renoir, Jean, 19
Report from the Aleutians, 191–92, 222–27,
    241, 264, 265, 284, 288, 333,
    411, 413
Returning Psychoneurotic, The, see Let
    There Be Light
Reunion in France, 357
Revolutionary War, 1, 24–25, 53, 382
Reykjavik, 107, 245
Ribbentrop, Joachim von, 403, 404
Riefenstahl, Leni, 6, 141, 142, 376
Riskin, Robert, 26, 27, 65–67, 76–77. 329,
    380–81, 420
RKO, 18, 21–23, 38–40, 56, 331, 345,
    424, 435
  Stevens' departure from, 49, 79
Roach, Hal, 200, 221
Robeson, Paul, 135
Robinson, Edward G., 38, 85, 125
Robinson, Lionel, 45
Rogers, Ginger, 22, 69
Rome, 317
Rommel, Erwin, 262, 278
Roosevelt, Eleanor, 68, 87
Roosevelt, Franklin D., 9, 16, 17, 20, 25, 46, 59,
    60, 62, 76, 79, 88, 90–92, 94–96, 104–6,
    110, 113, 122, 126, 140, 162, 175, 183, 185,
    204, 210, 211, 217, 226, 232, 254, 276–78,
    288, 317, 390
  The Battle of Midway and, 156, 158
  Capra and, 28, 441
  Capra's draft of speech for, 114–15
  death of, 366, 375
  December 7th and, 207–8
  Ford and, 274, 275
  The Memphis Belle and, 296
  Mrs. Miniver and, 138–39

Roosevelt, James, 41, 46, 180
  The Battle of Midway and, 155–56, 158
Rossellini, Roberto, 421
Royal Air Force (RAF), 176, 220, 248,
  346, 367
Runyon, Damon, 214
Russia, *see* Soviet Union
Russell, Harold, 425–26, 429, 432, 436

Saint-Nazaire, 221
Saint-Tropez, 348
Salerno, 253
Sandrich, Mark, 137
Sanford, John, 131
San Pietro, 267–70, 279–83, 322
  The Battle of San Pietro, 279–83, 322, 331–34,
    382–85, 399–400, 407, 411
Saroyan, William, 192, 291, 311
Sarris, Andrew, 67
Saturday Evening Post, 127
Sayre, Joel, 309n
Schaeffer, George, 39, 48
Schenck, Joseph, 90, 93
Schlossberg, Richard, 111–13, 123, 126, 127,
  129, 133, 191–92
Schmeling, Max, 135, 305
Schnellboote, 318
Schreiber, Lew, 74
Schulberg, B. P., 62
Schulberg, Budd, 300, 376–77, 403
Scott, Phil, 153
Scott, Rey, 188–90, 192, 225
  breakdown and hospitalization of, 284, 385–86
Screen Actors Guild, 356
Screen Directors Guild (SDG), 7, 20, 26, 40, 151,
  408, 441
  Capra and, 26, 40, 79, 110, 408
  Stevens and, 79, 81, 166
Screen Writers Guild, 59, 74, 91
Searching for John Ford (McBride), 274
Selznick, David O., 46, 73, 293, 385, 415, 420
  Since You Went Away, 426–27
Selznick, Irene, 417
Senate Committee Investigating National Defense,
  see Truman Committee
Senate hearings on propaganda, 90–94, 96–98,
  103, 120
Sergeant York, 73, 83–89, 93–94, 97, 103, 123
Sex Hygiene, 71–72
Shakespeare, William, 178–79
Shane, 443
Shaw, Irwin, 80, 169, 192–93, 262, 291, 292, 311,
  316, 320, 323, 341
Sherman, Vincent, 128–29
Sherwood, Robert, 390, 394–96, 425, 428–30, 433,
  434, 436
Shintoism, 160, 335, 387
Shirley, Ann, 261
Shore, Dinah, 258
Siegel, Don, 379n

Signal Corps, 9, 46, 71, 112–14, 129, 134, 140, 141,
  169, 179–81, 215–17, 222–24, 227, 232–36,
  240–41, 246, 247, 253, 262, 264, 275, 278,
  293, 295–96, 298, 308, 329, 339, 349, 378,
  384, 412, 443
  Allied landing in France and, 302
  Capra's joining of, 8, 112–13
  Huston's joining of, 5, 127–29
  Italy and, 265, 267, 268, 279, 280, 283
  The Negro Soldier and, 307
  Sex Hygiene, 71–72
  Tunisian Victory and, 236–37, 239,
    243, 283
  Wyler's joining of, 4–5, 123, 126, 127
Simard, Cyril, 146–47
Sinatra, Frank, 261
Since You Went Away, 426–27
Sino-Japanese War, 162
SNAFU cartoon series, 234–36, 308
Solow, Gene, 414
Song of Bernadette, The, 286
"So Proudly We Fail" (Agee), 287
Soviet Union, 26, 126, 131, 170, 182, 368, 375
  The Battle of Russia, 164, 264–65, 278, 288
  Germany and, 87, 265
  Know Your Ally—Russia, 303
  Lend-Lease and, 308–9
Spaatz, Carl, 139
Spain, 191
Spanish Civil War, 2, 20, 25, 131, 276
Spanish Earth, The, 276
Special Coverage Unit (SPECOU), 261, 263,
  290–91, 309, 311–12, 315, 316, 320–23,
  339, 343, 366, 376, 415, 443–44
Spectator, 177
Speer, Albert, 404
Spellbound, 398
Spewack, Sam, 174–75, 224, 248, 304
Spigelgass, Leonard, 132, 164, 235
Stagecoach, 18, 49, 52–53, 63, 153, 174, 272, 357
Stalin, Joseph, 376
Stanwyck, Barbara, 21–22, 66
Stars and Stripes, 205
State Department, 277
Stein, Jules, 168
Steinbeck, John, 53
Stern, Philip Van Doren, 422–23
Stevens, George, 5–6, 11, 12, 18, 21–23, 38–40,
  46, 79–81, 136–37, 151, 164–66, 193–98,
  247, 261, 288, 290–93, 309n, 338–47, 366,
  413–18, 420, 440, 441, 443–44
  Academy Awards and, 288, 290, 443
  Alice Adams, 21, 81, 373
  at Allied landing and aftermath in France,
    261–64, 290–91, 309, 310–12, 314–16,
    318–23
  army enlistment of, 164, 167, 195–96
  asthma of, 196, 343
  in Belgium, 343–44
  Capra and, 164–65, 167, 195, 345, 347, 418

Columbia's contract with, 49, 79, 166, 167, 193
concentration camps and, 23, 367, 369–77,
    400, 402–3, 415, 418, 421, 444
at Dachau, 23, 369–77, 415, 421, 444
death of, 444
at Dora, 367
Eisenhower and, 262
Ford and, 311
in France, 338–44
in Germany, 344–47, 366–77, 401–2
Gunga Din, 23, 38, 39, 81, 262, 343
Lend-Lease to Russia and, 308–9
Liberty Films and, 345, 402, 414, 416, 417,
    421, 424, 437
in London, 257, 261, 262, 290–92, 309, 347
in Luxembourg, 343
Moffat and, 262–63, 311, 320–22, 341, 346,
    367, 373, 376, 415–16
The More the Merrier, 167, 193–95, 197, 263,
    290, 401–2
Nazi Concentration and Prison Camps, 400, 402–3
The Nazi Plan, 377, 400, 403–4
in North Africa, 196–98, 237–41, 261, 266,
    321, 339
Penny Serenade, 80–81, 387
A Place in the Sun, 440, 443
pneumonia contracted by, 196
Russian soldiers and, 368–69
Screen Directors Guild and, 79, 81, 166
Shane, 443
SPECOU team of, 261, 263, 290–91, 309,
    311–12, 315, 316, 320–23, 339, 343, 366,
    376, 415, 443–44
The Talk of the Town, 166–67, 169, 172, 263
The True Glory and, 347
Tunisian Victory and, 237–41, 254, 261, 288
Vigil in the Night, 39, 40, 46–49, 80
Woman of the Year, 5–6, 81, 165, 166
Wyler and, 349
Stevens, George, Jr., 166, 195, 196, 261, 290–92,
    339, 342, 344–47
Stevens, Yvonne, 195, 196, 263–64, 290–92,
    341–42, 345, 346, 404, 414, 416, 418
Stevenson, Robert Louis, 360
Stewart, Jimmy, 41, 389, 422
Stimson, Henry L., 183, 208, 296
Story of G.I. Joe, The, 279, 334, 407
Stout, Junius, 325
Stranger, The, 331, 401
Streicher, Julius, 403
Sturges, John, 348–49, 361–62, 388
Sturges, Preston, 420
Stürmer, 403
Strauss, Theodore, 225
Sullavan, Margaret, 31
Sullivan, Arthur, 335
Supreme Headquarters Allied Expeditionary
    Force (SHAEF), 262
Surles, Alexander, 217, 218, 224, 243, 250, 278,
    308, 331, 332

Swerling, Jo, 423
Swing Time, 21
Szekely, Hans, 76

Talk of the Town, The, 166–67, 169, 172, 263
Tanaka plan, 330
Tannenbaum, Harold, 169, 199, 200, 220,
    246, 259
Target for Tonight, 181
Tashlin, Frank, 235
Taylor, Robert, 356
Taylor, Telford, 403
Tebourba, 180, 215
Technicolor, 76, 152, 173, 257, 415
Tehran, 309
Temple, Shirley, 62
Test Pilot, 300
They Were Expendable (film), 299–302, 318–19,
    325–27, 352–61, 395, 405–7
They Were Expendable (White), 272,
    299–300, 353
Thief of Bagdad, The, 76
Thin Man movies, 308
This Above All (Knight), 142
This Is the Army, 304
"This One is Captain Waskow" (Pyle), 279
This Thing Called Love, 79
Thunderbolt, 298, 348–49, 351, 361–65,
    388–89, 415
Time, 24, 31, 38, 43, 54, 55, 78, 88, 138, 139, 165,
    172, 173, 197, 213, 232–33, 289, 307, 383,
    391–92, 407
Times (London), 177
Tobacco Road, 70
To Be or Not to Be, 118
Tobey, Charles, 93–94
Tobruk, 233
Tojo, Hideki, 160–61, 278, 380
Toland, Gregg, 57, 63, 108–9, 147, 155, 191,
    206–10, 288, 355–56, 409, 431, 432, 434
Toldy, John, 76
Torgau, 368–69
Torpedo Squadron 8, 150, 158
Torpedo Squadron 8, 158–59
Toscanini, Arturo, 329
To the Shores of Tripoli, 129
Town & Country, 284
Tracy, Spencer, 5–6, 165, 272, 318, 356
Traven, B., 127
Treasure of the Sierra Madre, The, 127, 170, 293,
    410, 440, 443
Treaty of Versailles, 141
Tree, Marietta (Marietta Fitzgerald), 192, 241, 284
Triumph of the Will, 6, 141, 142, 376
True Glory, The, 347
Truman, Harry, 213, 216, 217, 372, 375, 376
Truman Committee (Senate Committee Investigating
    National Defense), 213–17
    Zanuck and, 215–16, 224, 326
Trumbo, Dalton, 423

Tunis, 179, 180

Tunis Expedition (Zanuck), 214, 232

Tunisia, 173, 198, 214, 231–33

Tunisian Victory, 236–43, 254–56, 261, 278, 281, 283, 288–90, 298, 305, 347, 381

  British and, 243, 247–52, 254, 255

Turkmenistan, 309

20th Century Fox, 18–19, 23, 29, 53, 70, 73, 74, 93, 105, 111, 129, 142, 155, 258, 161, 162, 197, 293, 327, 335, 380

  Zanuck and, 214–16, 326

25 Missions, 246–47

Two Down and One to Go!, 380

Two-Faced Woman, 101

unions, 20, 26, 40, 41, 91, 105

United Artists (UA), 46, 52, 68

Universal Pictures, 24, 29, 31, 103, 176, 331

USAAF, 293

U.S. Film Service, 276

USO, 273

U.S. Relocation Authority, 162

USSR Society for Cultural Relations with Foreign Countries, 265

Valley Forge, 24–25, 28

Variety, 16–17, 38, 54–55, 68, 77, 88, 104, 138, 225, 233, 407, 436

Vatican, 348

V-E Day, 375, 381, 385

Veiller, Anthony, 247, 250–52, 262, 264, 308, 380

Venafro, 267–70, 279

veterans, returning, 396–97

  The Best Years of Our Lives, 390, 391–96, 417, 425–38, 441, 442

  Let There Be Light (originally *The Returning Psychoneurotic*), 386–87, 396–400, 409–13

Veterans Administration, 410

Vigil in the Night, 39, 40, 46–49, 80

Vivacious Lady, 22

V-J Day, 388

Voice of America, 138

von der Lippe, Victor, 403

Wake Island, 102, 147, 149

Wake Island, 129

Wallace, Irving, 277–78

Wallis, Hal, 33, 38, 84, 85, 86, 124, 127

Walsh, Raoul, 85, 336

Walt Disney Studios, 164, 182, 235, 276

Wanger, Walter, 46, 48, 52–53, 59, 63, 174, 204, 288, 415, 420

"Wanted: A Faith to Fight For" (Alsop), 7

War Activities Committee (WAC), 158, 217, 218, 224, 225, 265, 295–96, 389

War Comes to America, 164, 308, 379–82

War Department, 112, 133, 137, 152, 153, 160, 175, 207, 208, 210, 211, 224–26, 233, 243, 249, 254, 302, 308, 317, 321, 328, 330–31, 332, 336, 361, 376, 387, 413

Bureau of Public Relations, 217, 243, 333, 383, 388, 410–13

  Ford and, 105, 107, 325–26

  liaison between movie industry and, 9–10, 91, 104, 216, 217

  newsreel producers and, 10

War Department Report, 288

war movies, pre–World War II, 20–21

Warner, Albert, 15

Warner, Harry, 15, 16, 17, 50–51, 61–62, 73, 96–97, 103, 279, 328

  speech of, 60, 62

Warner, Jack, 29, 60, 61, 73, 94, 102, 103, 124, 125, 127, 129, 130, 344

  Mann dinner hosted by, 15, 16–17

Warner, Sam, 15

Warner Bros., 5, 8, 15, 17, 23, 33, 34, 35, 36, 37–38, 46, 59, 60, 65, 73, 82, 85–88, 97, 111, 123–25, 127, 129, 140–41, 170, 191, 235, 253, 278, 293, 294, 329, 331, 336, 379n, 410

Washington, Booker T., 306

Washington, George, 24–25

Wasserman, Lew, 422

Wayne, John, 10, 52, 55, 63, 109, 272–73, 275

  in *They Were Expendable,* 356–60, 406

Wead, Frank "Spig," 56, 208, 300–301, 353–56, 406

Wedemeyer, Albert, 274, 326

Wehrmacht, 346

Weizmann, Chaim, 89

Welles, Orson, 77, 123, 253, 331, 401

Wellman, William, 154, 407

Westerner, The, 49, 51

What Price Glory?, 259

Wheeler, Burton K., 88, 261

White, William, *They Were Expendable,* 272, 299–300, 353

Whitty, May, 121

Why We Fight, 113, 114, 131–33, 141–44, 163–64, 169, 181–82, 185, 217, 218, 234, 236, 264, 276, 303, 329, 330, 381–82, 421

  The Battle of Britain, 164

  The Battle of China, 164, 308, 330

  The Battle of Russia, 164, 264–65, 278, 288

  Divide and Conquer, 164

  The Nazis Strike, 164

  Prelude to War, 144, 164, 182–85, 205, 210, 211, 217–19, 224, 234, 264, 421

  War Comes to America, 164, 308, 379–80

Wilcoxon, Henry, 121–22

Wilder, Billy, 68, 436, 440

Wilhelmshaven, 202–3, 205, 219, 220, 297

Willkie, Wendell, 87–88, 91–94, 118, 245, 288

Wilson, Woodrow, 5

Winchell, Clarence, 202

Winchell, Walter, 17

Wing and a Prayer, 150n

Winged Victory, 298

Wings, 169, 407

Winsten, Archer, 412

With the Marines at Tarawa, 289–90, 297
Woman of the Year, 5–6, 81, 165, 166
Wood, Sam, 69–70, 275
World at War, The, 181–83
World's Fair, 84
World War I, 2, 4, 5, 7–8, 19, 21, 22, 63, 64,
        83, 84, 87, 113, 183, 221, 340
    as movie subject, 21, 87
World War II:
    beginning of, 49, 53, 103
    in Europe, end of, 365, 375, 383
    in Japan, end of, 387–88
    loss of American optimism in outcome of,
        141–42
    Pearl Harbor in, *see* Pearl Harbor
    U.S. entry into, 1–2, 121
Wright, Richard, 306–7
Wright, Teresa, 427
Wurtzel, Harry, 275
Wuthering Heights, 30, 34–35, 52, 178
Wyler, Cathy, 30, 170, 205, 221–22, 247
Wyler, Judy, 170, 222, 247
Wyler, Leopold, 350
Wyler, Margaret Tallichet "Talli," 4, 30, 31, 49,
        51–52, 60, 69, 70, 123, 126, 129, 169–70, 177,
        201, 202, 204–5, 220–22, 245, 247, 257, 290,
        347–48, 351, 364, 365, 432
Wyler, Robert, 350
Wyler, William, 4–5, 11–12, 18, 29–35, 49–52,
        60, 69, 72–73, 79, 89, 124–26, 136, 144,
        168–70, 176–79, 193, 211, 219, 221–22,
        244–46, 262, 263, 339, 347–52, 382, 408,
        420, 421, 425–35, 440–43
    Academy Awards and, 33, 52, 69–70, 72, 118,
        123, 125–26, 203–5, 435–36, 442
    Air Medal awarded to, 221
    The Best Years of Our Lives, 390, 391–96, 417,
        425–38, 441, 442
    on bombing missions, 201–3, 219–21, 245–46,
        430, 434
    Davis and, 31, 33, 51, 60–61, 118–19, 426,
        429, 442
    death of, 442
    in doorman incident, 296–97, 428
    and family and friends in Europe, 4, 11, 29, 51,
        61, 348–51
    Ford and, 177
    in France, 347–51

    Goldwyn and, 72–73, 169, 245, 258, 298, 365,
        389, 390
    hearing loss of, 363–65, 366, 388, 389, 431,
        432–33
    How Green Was My Valley and, 73–76, 105
    Huston's friendship with, 30–34, 442
    in Italy, 298, 348, 351, 362–64
    The Letter, 60–61, 69, 118
    Liberty Films and, 389–90, 402, 416, 417, 421,
        424, 437
    The Little Foxes, 60, 73, 75, 118–19, 125, 126,
        134, 429, 431
    in London, 176–78, 199–204, 257, 258
    marriage of, 30, 31, 60
    The Memphis Belle: The Story of a Flying Fortress
        (originally *25 Missions*), 246–47, 257–61,
        293–98, 317, 348, 349, 361, 362, 388
    Mrs. Miniver, 4, 5, 119–23, 126–27, 129, 134,
        138–39, 169, 172, 177–78, 203–5, 211, 220,
        298, 389, 426
    in Mulhouse, 348–51, 361
    The Negro Soldier and, 134–36, 303
    Olivier and, 178
    P-47 fighter plane documentary of, 298
    Signal Corps joined by, 4–5, 123, 126, 127
    Stevens and, 349
    Thunderbolt, 298, 348–49, 351, 361–65,
        388–89, 415
    25 Missions, 246–47
    Wuthering Heights, 30, 34–35, 52, 178
Wyler, William, Jr., 430

York, Alvin C., 83–86, 88, 95–96, 103
You Can't Take It With You, 24, 26–27, 40–41
Young Mr. Lincoln, 53
Your Job in Germany, 378–79

Zanuck, Darryl F., 18, 19, 53, 59, 70–72, 74–76,
        93, 97–98, 104–5, 112, 126, 134, 161, 176,
        196, 214–15, 224, 279, 298, 344, 380, 385,
        395, 401
    At the Front in North Africa, 215, 232–34
    Ford and, 327
    in North Africa, 179–81, 184, 211, 214, 215,
        231–32
    Truman Committee and, 215–16, 224, 326
Zeroes, 146–49, 188, 190, 207
Zukor, Adolph, 90